Nutrition

Nutrition

A Lifecycle Approach

Edited by

Ravinder Chadha and Pulkit Mathur

Orient BlackSwan

NUTRITION: A LIFE CYCLE APPROACH

ORIENT BLACKSWAN PRIVATE LIMITED

Registered Office
3-6-752 Himayatnagar, Hyderabad 500 029, Telengana, India
e-mail: centraloffice@orientblackswan.com

Other Offices
Bengaluru, Chennai, Guwahati, Hyderabad, Kolkata,
Mumbai, New Delhi, Noida, Patna, Visakhapatnam

First published by Orient Blackswan Pvt. Ltd. 2015
Reprinted 2018, 2020, 2023

ISBN 978 81 250 5930 1

Typeset in
Electra LT Std 10.5/12
by PrePSol Enterprises Pvt. Ltd, Haryana

Printed in India at
B.B. Press, Noida 201 301

Published by
Orient Blackswan Private Limited
3-6-752 Himayatnagar, Hyderabad 500 029, Telangana, India
e-mail: info@orientblackswan.com

This book is dedicated to our students,
who are our greatest source of inspiration

Contents

Boxes

Tables

Figures

Colour Images

PREFACE

Good health for all its citizens is a goal for every country. Malnutrition has been plaguing the growth and development of our nation for several decades. Initially, all efforts and intervention programmes focused on young children to reduce the burden of malnutrition. However, it soon became clear that pregnant and nursing mothers' health was important to give the infant a good start in life. Focus then shifted to the adolescent girl as 'the mother-to-be', and to improving her nutritional and health status. As the demographic profile changed, nations became concerned with the health of the expanding elderly population. With the rapid increase in the burden of over-nutrition and non-communicable diseases, the poor eating and lifestyle habits of adults was highlighted. Then came the realisation that each and every stage of the lifecycle is equally important to break the vicious intergenerational cycle of malnutrition, as well as for a healthy, progressive nation.

Thus, our book adopts a lifecycle approach to the study of nutrition. The book is divided into two sections—Introduction to Human Nutrition and Lifecycle Nutrition. The first section comprises 14 chapters dealing with basic concepts in nutrition. It is important that young students comprehend the basics well in order to apply their knowledge to real life situations. Beginning with the concept of food for different cultures and the relationship of food with nutrition and the health of an individual, we progress to how much of each kind of nutrient is required by the human body. Each of the nutrients, energy, carbohydrates, lipids, proteins, water, major and trace minerals, fat and water soluble vitamins, their functions, food sources, digestion and absorption, and problems of deficiency and excess have been discussed in detail.

As the food we eat is mostly in cooked form, a separate chapter details the different cooking methods and the effect they have on the nutrient content. The next chapter goes on to describe how the nutritional quality of the diet can be enhanced. The last chapter in this section makes the reader aware of the importance of food labelling, and improves their understanding of health and nutrition claims. It also introduces the concept of nutrient profiling.

The section on Lifecycle Nutrition has 13 chapters. It begins with a chapter that explains the principles of meal planning. This is followed by a chapter on food-based dietary guidelines for Indians, as well as a look at the global scenario of the kind of guidelines given by different nations. The different life stages are covered in separate chapters—adults, pregnant women, nursing mothers, preschool children, school-age children, adolescents, and the elderly. At each stage of life, the physiological changes happening in the body and the influence they have on nutritional requirements are discussed. Nutritional concerns, and how to deal with each problem at different life stages, have also been elaborated. A separate chapter has been dedicated to feeding children with special needs, as this needs to be addressed, and very few books have dealt with the issue.

This section also has two other chapters, which deal with sports nutrition and the link between nutrition and immunity. Dietary recommendations for exercise and competitive sports are important to know today, as people become more health conscious and try to improve their fitness levels. The relationship between nutrition, infection and immunity is important to study, as it has several biological and operational implications.

In a true sense, this book has been inspired by our undergraduate students. Over the years, we have made several improvisations in our teaching style in order to better communicate basic scientific concepts in a simple yet engaging manner. This book has been written keeping in mind the diverse educational backgrounds the students of nutrition come from. To make it simpler for students who come from non-science backgrounds, all scientific terms have been explained in the text as well as at the end of the chapter. Interesting facts about each topic have been included to highlight a new research finding or provide additional information about the topic under discussion. Questions have been provided at the end of each chapter for students to check their progress and understanding of the topic. References and useful web links at the end of each chapter encourage students to study a topic in greater detail. The appendices provide useful reference data. How to use the food exchange list for meal planning has been explained step-wise in the appendices, with suitable menu options and portion sizes. Clear and simple illustrations and contextual examples suitable for the Indian scenario are the selling points of this book.

It has been our endeavour to bring together all the faculty members of the Department of Food and Nutrition, Lady Irwin College, in the preparation of this manuscript, drawing upon their strengths and expertise in the field of nutrition.

We strongly recommend the use of this book by all undergraduate students of nutrition, whether they are pursuing a Home Science degree or one in Nursing, Food Technology, Sports, Medicine, and other allied courses. It is also a useful book for the health conscious who seek authentic, updated facts about nutrition.

FOREWORD

We are what we eat.

From womb to tomb, our health, productivity, well-being, and longevity are determined largely by the food we eat. Each of us should be armed with the information and practical wisdom to make wise choices about our food intake, thereby optimising the quality of our lives.

This book is a fine balance of pertinent information and insights into the practical application of that information. It gives the reader the tools to make good lifestyle choices.

The lifecycle approach is appropriate—indeed, essential—when discussing the subject of human nutrition. Every stage of life is a crucial stage in this regard; the nutritional choices in childhood years throw a long shadow into adulthood, and the choices made in adulthood portend the quality of life in later years.

This book, *Nutrition: A Lifecycle Approach*, covers the whole gamut of issues in a clear, yet comprehensive style, designed to be accessible not only to students, but to all individuals who wish to equip themselves with vital information that will help them make wiser nutritional and lifestyle choices.

The Editors, Dr Pulkit Mathur and Dr Ravinder Chadha, faculty members of the prestigious Lady Irwin College, New Delhi, are themselves experts in nutrition training, with long experience in teaching the subject. They have done a commendable job in arranging and presenting the material, all written by members of the faculty of the same institution.

Having devoted my entire working life to nutrition research, I am convinced that the fight to improve the nutritional status of people cannot be won without the active co-operation, participation and commitment of the people themselves. This book is a valuable addition to the arsenal in that fight.

Dr C. Gopalan

President, Nutrition Foundation of India, New Delhi

ACKNOWLEDGEMENTS

We acknowledge the cooperation of our colleagues in the Department of Food and Nutrition in the preparation of this book. In spite of their busy schedules, they have put in a lot of hard work into their chapters. We are also grateful to the former faculty members who have been our mentors, and have enthusiastically supported this endeavour. We thank Dr Anupa Siddhu, Director, Lady Irwin College, for her constant support and encouragement.

Our students have been our major inspiration. Their challenging questions and eagerness to learn has made the teaching-learning process very rewarding, and given us ideas with respect to the presentation of the content.

We are grateful to National Institute of Nutrition, ICMR, Hyderabad, for giving us permission to reproduce the Recommended Dietary Allowances for Indians and the Food Pyramid from the Dietary Guidelines for Indians.

Our special thanks to Mr Nikhil Mathur, husband of Dr Pulkit Mathur, for his help in the preparation of some figures used in the textbook, and computer-related assistance in the preparation of the manuscript. We thank Ms Reena Sajith nee Unnikrishnan, Laboratory Attendant, for the typing assistance rendered for some of the chapters and appendices.

All tables, figures, boxes, and photographs, unless otherwise stated, have been created / taken by the authors themselves.

We are grateful to the publishers, Orient BlackSwan, for their patronage.

SECTION I

INTRODUCTION TO HUMAN NUTRITION

1

FOOD, NUTRITION AND HEALTH

HIGHLIGHTS

- Meaning of food
- Functions of food
- Commonly used terms in nutrition
- Relationship between food, nutrition and health
- New frontiers in the field of nutrition

Knowledge of how food, nutrition and health are interrelated has evolved with the development of the science of nutrition. With the discovery of several essential food substances, mainly in the nineteenth century, knowledge progressed from food for survival to that of nutrition for health. We now know that food provides nutrients that are essential to satisfy the body's needs for energy, growth, repair, and protection. Food also provides many physiologically active compounds which are not considered essential nutrients, but may provide several health benefits. In this chapter, we shall understand what constitutes food and its importance in our life.

FOOD AND ITS USES

Food comprises various products derived from plants or animals, which we eat or drink to live, grow, remain healthy, and support the body's needs for energy. It is the source of all the nutrients that we require to remain healthy during the different stages of our life. Food is basic to our survival as it satisfies hunger and nourishes our body. Although there is a rich array of foods available for consumption, foods vary widely in their nutritive value. Knowledge about the various nutrients present in different kinds of foods has evolved mainly during the twentieth century. No food contains all the nutrients needed to grow well and keep healthy. The type and amount of food to be included in the daily diet is guided by the science of nutrition. Nutrition is all about the food we eat, and how it is used by our body.

Nutrition is defined as 'the science of foods, the nutrients and other substances therein; their action, interaction and balance in relationship to health and disease' (Robinson 1966: 206). It can also be understood as 'the processes by which the organism ingests, digests, absorbs, transports and utilizes nutrients and disposes of their end products' (ibid.). Since nutrients are derived from the food people eat, nutrition has to be concerned with the social, economic, cultural, and psychological implications of food and eating.

People across communities and nations consume very different kinds of food, even in this globalised era. In our country, where diversity is the norm in most spheres of cultural life, food is no exception. The daily diet of the Kashmiris of north India is very different from the Assamese of the northeast, or the Gujaratis of the west, or the Tamilians of the south. This is not all; there are also special foods for special occasions, different food preparations for different seasons, and varied food combinations. It could be said that there is an infinite variety of foods which can meet our nutritional needs. However, the challenge is to make the right kind of food available in sufficient amounts to all the people to promote good health and well-being among them.

Box 1.1: Uncommon Foods

'What is food?' This is a very difficult question to answer. What one community thinks of as food may be repulsive to another. Here are some examples of bizarre foods from around the world. Some of these are considered delicacies, while others were originally consumed during periods of famine and leanness, but which gradually became a part of the normal diet. Dog meat, rat meat, offal (integral organs and entrails of any animal), fish eggs (caviar), half-developed bird eggs, etc., are some such examples. Man is perhaps the only animal who eats all other living things. Here are some examples of special foods from around the globe.

Kiviak is a traditional winter food consumed by the Inuits of Greenland, where food shortages are common during the long, dark winter months. It is a seal's carcass stuffed with whole, fermented birds called Auks. The birds are caught and stuffed whole into the hollowed-out body cavity of a seal. All the air is pressed out and the bag is sealed with seal grease to prevent spoilage. The meat bag is covered with a large rock pile for approximately 3–18 months. During this time, the Auks ferment within the seal until they can be eaten raw. The smell is so strong that the dish is eaten outside the house!	
Insects like cockroaches, scorpions, spiders, grasshoppers, silkworms, cocoons of some moths, worms, etc., are common street foods in Asian countries like Vietnam, China and Thailand. In India, the tribal population of Chhattisgarh consumes *chaprah*, a chutney made from red ants and their eggs. *Eri polu,* pupa of the Eri silkworm, which is consumed after removing the silk thread, is a popular food ingredient in Assam	
Frog Legs are a delicacy in French and Cantonese cuisine. In India, it is popular dish among the Lepchas of Sikkim, and in Kerala. The dish is also known to have medicinal qualities. Prepared in multiple ways, it is believed that frog legs can cure various stomach-related diseases.	

Source: http://en.wikipedia.org/wiki/File:Parakeetauklets2.jpg
https://commons.wikimedia.org/wiki/File:Giant_water_bugs_on_plate.png
http://en.wikipedia.org/wiki/Frog_legs#mediaviewer/File:Swikee_Kodok_Oh_with_Rice.jpg

The food that we eat performs several nutritional as well as non-nutritional functions (Figure 1.1). The primary use of food is to satisfy hunger and provide a sufficient amount of energy to support the various activities of the body, and supply all essential nutrients for growth, development and maintenance. As the rate of growth of the human body varies in the different stages of life, food needs also vary.

Figure 1.1: Nutritional and Non-nutritional Uses of Food

NUTRITIONAL (Physiological)

Food is needed for

- Body growth and development
- Repair or maintenance of body tissues
- Regulation of body processes
- Protection against infections
- Promotion of optimal health.

NON-NUTRITIONAL (Socio-cultural, Psychological and Political)

- Promotion of friendliness / hospitality.
- Giving of food as a gift, or as a gesture of warmth or demonstration of love and affection.
- Food preparation as a means of creative expression.
- Expression of happiness during festivals and celebrations.
- Food as a symbol of wealth or status.
- Expression of comfort, security and belongingness.
- As a visible offering of sympathy / to honour the dead.
- As a means to relieve tension / boredom.
- Food can be used as a reward/ a weapon of punishment by withholding eagerly sought food or forced eating of unwanted food.
- As a part of religious and social rites.
- Control of food supply and food prices as a means of exerting political control.
- Food type, preparation methods and dietary rules as a means of expressing cultural identity.

Source: Lowenberg et al. 1968.

Food provides the energy to perform various voluntary and involuntary, or regulatory activities of the body. Energy requirement is more among individuals who are physically active, as compared to those who are physically inactive or sedentary. The various regulatory activities, such as breathing, beating of the heart, digestion and absorption of food, etc., go on even when a person is at rest. Energy is required for all these important body functions.

Food is also essential for the growth and maintenance of body tissues. Food protein is converted into tissue protein by our body. Minerals like calcium provide strength and hardness to our bones. In addition, food contributes significantly towards protecting the body from various infections, as it contains several bioactive phytochemicals (present in plants) and zoochemicals (chemicals present in animals) that may decrease the risk of diseases or promote optimal health. Besides these physiological functions, food has several socio-cultural, psychological, and even political functions that vary from group to group.

- Food acts as a measure to promote social warmth and build friendly, interpersonal relationships. It is often given as gifts to relatives, friends or neighbours. During festivals or special family occasions such as marriage, sweetmeats, dry fruits, or chocolates are given as gifts to strengthen the social bonds between friends and relatives.
- Food has a special place in many religious rites. Specific food preparations such as *ladoo* or *halwa*, or certain fruits like banana or coconut are distributed as *prasad*.
- Food is also a source of enjoyment. We often treat our friends or loved ones to special food, which may be homemade or come from restaurants/special food outlets. Eating out with family and friends has become a way of enjoyment and celebration, especially in urban areas, where such food is becoming easily available in even small towns.
- Certain foods have high prestige value, such as milk and milk products, nuts such as almonds, pistachio and cashewnuts, and many fruits, as these are expensive and considered to promote health. On the other hand, millets and green leafy vegetables have low prestige value and are often neglected foods, generally given up in favour of less nutritious options as people climb up the socio-economic ladder.
- The staple food fosters a **sense of security** among people, especially during crises. During war, strife or drought situations, people accept familiar foods readily.
- Certain food items, such as sweets and chocolates, are often given as **rewards** to young children for doing well in studies or being well-mannered. Food can also be used as a means of **punishment**, by withholding the food that is liked the most, or forced feeding of food that is not preferred.

However, any other meaning of food is relevant only when there is enough food to satisfy hunger, which is the primary and the most immediate need.

- There are several **taboos/culturally imposed dietary restrictions**. The most important in the Indian context are 'hot' and 'cold' foods. Foods such as egg, liver, *ghee* (clarified butter), dry ginger, etc., are considered 'hot', and others such as radish, orange, green leafy vegetables, watermelon, etc., are considered 'cold'. Many food preparations have similar connotations, and are avoided during pregnancy and childhood. 'Hot' foods are avoided during fever, and 'cold' foods are avoided if a person is suffering from cough/cold.
- Food has been used as a **means of demonstrating protest** against an oppressive regime. Gandhiji's 'salt *Satyagrah*' was a means of protest against British rule. He would often undertake a fast, shunning food altogether, as a form of protest. Even today, political leaders consider fasts a popular means of protest.
- There are certain Indian **festivals** in which **special food preparations** have an important place. Certain foods are associated with certain festivals, for example, *gujiya* with Holi, *cake* with Christmas, *sewain* (sweet vermicelli) with Id-ul-Fitr, *jalebi* with Dussehra, *pedas* with Janamashtami. Special feasts are also organised to celebrate harvests such as *Baisakhi*, *Bihu*, etc.
- Certain **culture-specific** preparations, such as *amla murabba, chyawanprash* and *gond ladoos*, are consumed as **dietary supplements** to promote health and prevent diseases.

- Special food/meals are prepared for friends/ children to express love and care. Mothers prepare special foods to **demonstrate their love** for their children.
- **Special foods** are consumed during **fasting**, such as non-cereal preparations during Navratra. Even the salt used in food is not the common sea salt, but a rock salt called '*sendha namak*'.

> Because of its fundamental role in the struggle for existence, food has acquired significance in human society, beyond that of providing nourishment for the body, which is reflected in many patterns of human behaviour. Food may be closely associated with feelings of security and prestige. It has an important place in religious observances. It is linked with countless superstitious and prejudices. Thus, it can arouse many emotions—pleasure, envy, confidence, and even violent fanaticism.
>
> *Ritchie 1950: 4*

COMMON TERMS AND DEFINITIONS

Let us now look at some of the common terms that you shall come across in the study of nutrition. You have already been introduced to what the study of nutrition entails.

Nutrients are the constituents in food that must be supplied to the body in suitable amounts. These include carbohydrates, fats, proteins, minerals, vitamins, and water. Depending on the amount of the nutrient present in our bodies, and hence the amount required in the daily diet, nutrients have been classified as macro and micronutrients (Figure 1.2).

Figure 1.2: Classification of Nutrients and Other Bioactive Substances in Food

- NUTRIENTS
  - Macro-nutrients
    - Water
    - Carbohydrates
    - Proteins
    - Fats
  - Micro-nutrients
    - Vitamins
      - Water soluble: Thiamine, Riboflavin, Niacin, Pyridoxine, Folic acid, Vitamin B_{12}, Vitamin C, Pantothenic acid, Biotin
      - Fat soluble: Vitamin A, Vitamin D, Vitamin E, Vitamin K
    - Minerals
      - Major / macro minerals: Calcium, Phosphorus, Magnesium, Sodium, Potassium
      - Trace / minor minerals: Iron, Zinc, Iodide, Fluoride, Selenium, Chromium, Molybdenum, Copper, Manganese
- NON-NUTRIENT BIOACTIVE SUBSTANCES
  - Phyto-chemicals: Flavonoids, Indoles, Isothiocyanates, Isoflavones, Catechins, Glucosinolates, Allyl sulphides, Lignans
  - Zoochem-icals: Omega-3 fatty acids, Probiotics

Source: Byrd-Bredbenner et al. 2013.

Macronutrients are those nutrients that our body requires in relatively large amounts (many grams daily), like carbohydrates, proteins and fat.

Micronutrients are the nutrients required only in small amounts (in milligrams or micrograms daily), like vitamins and minerals.

Carbohydrates, fat and protein are the three energy-yielding nutrients of the body, although the primary function of protein is tissue building and repair. All three are organic compounds. Vitamins and minerals perform multiple functions in the regulation of various metabolic functions, and hence are also considered regulatory nutrients. These also improve our ability to fight infections and protect us from diseases. Vitamins are organic substances that may be fat-soluble or water-soluble. They are vulnerable to destruction from heat, light and chemical agents. Hence, food needs to be handled carefully so that these vitamins can be delivered to the body intact. Minerals, being inorganic are indestructible, need not be handled with the special care that vitamins require. Minerals can, however, be bound by substances that interfere with the body's ability to absorb them.

Major or macrominerals are those that our body requires in quantities greater than 100 mg per day, otherwise they are considered **Trace or microminerals**. Water is perhaps the most important nutrient, as without this we cannot survive beyond a few days. It is a major component of our body, and all metabolic reactions take place in a fluid medium. In the chapters that follow, you will learn about each of these nutrients in detail.

Nutritional status is the condition of health of the individual, as influenced by the utilisation of nutrients. It can be determined only by the correlation of information obtained through a careful medical and dietary history, a thorough physical examination, and appropriate laboratory investigations. Nutritional status is assessed by looking at the medical history of the individual, the diseases s/he is suffering from, and the kind and amounts of different foods s/he has been consuming habitually. A physical examination covers the various body measurements (anthropometric measurements) like height, weight, waist circumference, etc., which help to assess whether the individual is obese or underweight, as well as measurements like blood pressure, and a visual examination for symptoms of deficiency of various nutrients. The hair, eyes, skin, teeth, gums, nails, and thyroid gland are usually examined for clinical signs that indicate a problem.

Malnutrition is a pathological state resulting from a relative or absolute deficiency or excess of one or more essential nutrients. Absolute deficiency of a nutrient results primarily from a low intake of that nutrient in the diet. Relative deficiency may arise when the nutrient, while present in the diet, cannot be absorbed or utilised by the body due to any reason. Problems resulting from an excess of nutrients are also termed as malnutrition. Malnutrition comprises four forms:

Overnutrition is a pathological state resulting from the consumption of an excessive quantity of food over an extended period of time, for example, obesity resulting from an excessive consumption of energy.

Undernutrition is the condition that results when insufficient food is eaten over an extended period of time, for example, Protein Energy Malnutrition.

Imbalance of nutrients is the pathological state resulting from a disproportion among essential nutrients, with or without the absolute deficiency of any nutrient, for example, an imbalance of amino acids like leucine and isoleucine, which can lead to niacin deficiency.

Specific Nutrient Deficiency is a pathological state resulting from a relative or absolute lack of an individual nutrient, for example, anaemia resulting from iron deficiency.

A nutrient deficiency develops in stages (Figure 1.3). From a normal state, a person can slip into a state of deficiency or excess nutrition. If food or a specific nutrient intake is more, the person can develop problems related to it. For instance, an excessive intake of energy would result in obesity and its associated problems. A state of deficiency can result from primary or secondary causes. Primary causes include a basic lack of food, perhaps due to poverty, or due to a lack of knowledge about which foods to choose or how much to eat. Sometimes, psychological factors like depression and loneliness can lead to a refusal to eat.

Secondary causes include a defective metabolism, like increased destruction or excretion of a nutrient, or malabsorption syndrome, where the body fails to absorb the required nutrients. Either way, deficiency starts to set in by first depleting all the tissue stores of the nutrient. Some amount of the nutrient is stored in the tissues as a buffer to tide over periods of leanness. However, if the lack of the nutrient in the diet continues for some time, the levels of the nutrient in the body start to fall, and storage tissues like the liver are the first to be affected. Tissue analysis is perhaps the only way to confirm depletion; however, this kind of testing works out to be very invasive, as it may, for instance, require a biopsy of the liver or bone marrow. Research is now focusing on identifying biomarkers for sub-clinical nutrient deficiencies, which can be analysed in more accessible tissues and body fluids like blood and urine.

Figure 1.3: Stages of Development of Nutrient Deficiency and Methods of Assessment of Nutritional Status

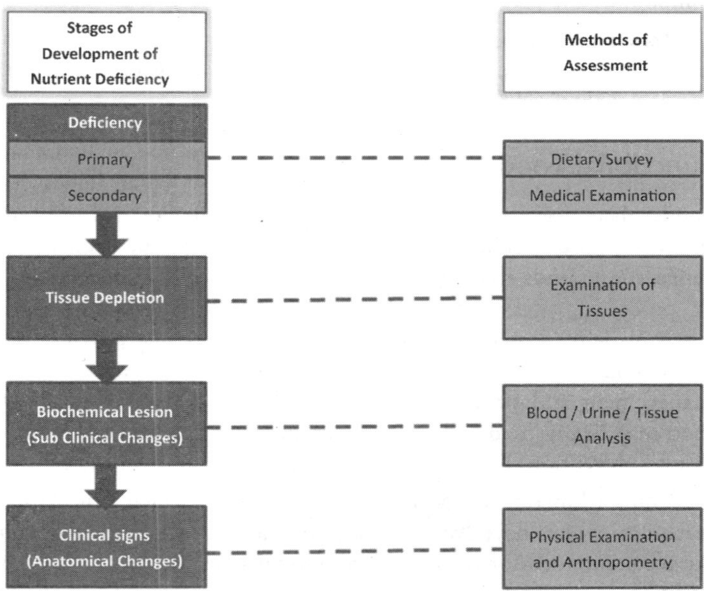

Source: Adapted from Robinson and Lawler 1982.

Sub-clinical deficiency is a covert condition which cannot be seen with the naked eye. However, some indication about its presence can be obtained from dietary data, obtained via an appropriate diet survey methodology. This is because a habitually low intake of a nutrient is known to lead to a state of deficiency. Tissue depletion ultimately leads to biochemical lesions, which can be estimated by analysing accessible body fluids like blood and urine for nutrients/ metabolites/ activity of enzymes that require the nutrient as a co-factor for better action. More overt deficiency signs that can be seen visually are referred to as clinical signs and symptoms, which can be seen during a physical examination, and by taking anthropometric measurements like weight, height and waist/hip/arm circumference.

A **balanced diet** is one that contains different types of food in such quantity and proportion that the need for energy, protein, vitamins, and minerals is adequately met, and a small provision made for extra nutrients to withstand short durations of leanness. Besides making an effort to ensure that the diet provides all essential nutrients and provides satiety, one must also consider psychological factors, and social, religious, cultural, and economic factors while planning balanced diets.

Nutritional care is the application of the science and art of human nutrition, and helping people select and obtain food to satisfy their nutritional needs in health and disease.

Phytochemicals literally mean the chemical substances present in plants (*phyto* means plant). Some of these chemical compounds are bioactive, that is, they have some effect in the body and provide health benefits. Hence, these are also referred to as **bioactive compounds**. Hundreds of such useful compounds have been identified to date, and their mechanism of action in the body worked out. There are several ways in which these chemicals exert their beneficial effect in the body. Some act as antioxidants and help to quench the damage-causing free radicals in the body. Others exert their influence by modulating the activity of enzymes that control metabolic processes. They may activate, deactivate, block, or suppress certain enzymes or hormones. Some others work by reducing the inflammation levels in the body. An inflammatory condition has been linked to an increased risk of cardiovascular diseases.

Some phytochemicals work by improving immunity. They may have antibacterial and antiviral properties. Certain others may help to maintain DNA stability and ensure repair. Several of these chemicals are also involved in detoxification mechanisms of the body, converting substances toxic to the body into harmless substances, or into substances that can be readily excreted from the body. Alteration of lipid and lipoprotein metabolism, regulation of blood sugar levels and blood pressure are some of the beneficial effects attributed to other phytochemicals. Table 1.1 gives some examples of foods with their bioactive compounds and health benefits.

Zoochemicals refers to physiologically active chemical substances obtained from animal sources, for example, omega-3 fatty acids obtained from fatty fish, and probiotics obtained from fermented dairy products.

According to the WHO, **Probiotics** are live micro-organisms (bacteria and yeasts) which, when administered in adequate amounts, confer a health benefit on the host. The introduction of this concept is generally attributed to Nobel Prize-winner Eli Metchnikoff, who in 1907 suggested that our intestinal flora can be altered by replacing the harmful microbes by useful microbes. **Prebiotics**, on the other hand, are non-digestible food ingredients that stimulate the growth and/or activity of bacteria in the digestive system in ways claimed to be beneficial to health. They were first identified and named by Marcel Roberfroid in 1995.

Functional Foods

Foods that provide benefits beyond their nutritional contributions are called **functional foods**. These benefits are usually due to the presence of physiologically active compounds that provide health benefits. Functional Food can be a natural or processed food that contains known biologically-active compounds, which, when in defined quantitative and qualitative amounts, provides a clinically proven and documented health benefit, and thus is an important source in the prevention, management and treatment of chronic diseases (Martirosyan 2011). A functional food may be given an additional function (often one related to health-promotion or disease prevention) by adding new ingredients, or more of the existing ingredients.

Thus, a functional food may be a whole food which is in its **natural form** (like tomatoes, which have lycopene, and oatmeal, which is rich in soluble fibre; both are recommended for reducing cardiovascular disease risk); it may be **fortified** with additional nutrients or phytochemicals (orange juice fortified with calcium for building strong bones); or it may be a **modified food** (for example, flavoured yoghurt with added soluble fibre inulin, as well as the live culture of microorganisms called probiotics, which have a number of health benefits).

Table 1.1: Health Benefits of Certain Foods and their Bioactive Compounds

Food	*Bioactive Compound*	*Health Benefit*
Green/yellow/orange coloured vegetables and fruits, like papaya, green leafy vegetables, mango, pumpkin, carrot, etc.	Carotenoids	Antioxidant activity, hence protective against cardiovascular diseases, cancer, cataract, and other degenerative diseases due to free radical damage
Cruciferous vegetables like cauliflower, cabbage, knol-khol, broccoli, mustard leaves, etc.	Glucosinolates, Indoles, Isothiocyanates	Decreases risk of cancer
Soya, soya products	Phytoestrogens, isoflavones	Lowered risk of osteoporosis, heart disease, breast cancer, and menopausal symptoms
Tomatoes, watermelon	Lycopene	Antioxidant, protects against cancer
Citrus fruits like lemon, orange, sweet lime, etc.	Limonene, monoterpenes	Protects against cancer, heart healthy
Allium vegetables like garlic, onion, etc.	Allicin, allyl sulphides, organosulphur compounds	Lower blood cholesterol, heart healthy, protects against cancer
Tea, especially green tea	Flavonoids, catechin	Antioxidant activity protects against cancer and cardiovascular diseases

Source: Byrd-Bredbenner et al. 2013, Polasa et al. 2009.

Functional foods are an emerging field in food science due to their increasing popularity among health-conscious consumers, and the ability of marketers to create a new interest in existing products. The term was first used in Japan in the 1980s. Japan has a government approval process for functional foods, called Foods for Specified Health Use (FOSHU). You will be learning more about these in Chapter 13.

RELATIONSHIP BETWEEN FOOD, NUTRITION, HEALTH, AND DISEASE

According to the WHO, **Health** is a state of complete physical, mental and social well-being, and not merely the absence of disease and infirmity. The essential pre-requisites (or dimensions) of 'health' include the following:

- Achievement of optimal growth and development, reflecting the full expression of one's genetic potential. Scientists now believe that all humans, irrespective of race and country of origin, have the same potential in their genes to grow tall and develop a certain stature (body-build). Adverse environmental influences, like the poor availability of food, poor sanitation—and hence a high rate of infection, especially during the growing years—result in poor health. Such children are then not able to achieve their genetic potential of height or body stature.
- Maintenance of structural integrity and functional efficiency of body tissues necessary for an active and productive life. If the body is to function properly, it is important that all tissues and organs function with full efficiency. An individual is able to lead an active and productive life if s/he is in good health.
- Mental well-being. This is as important as physical well-being. A person may be physically fit with no disease, but may not be mentally stable. A mentally well-adjusted person is considered healthy.
- Ability to withstand the inevitable process of ageing with minimal disability and functional impairment. Growing old is a reality that none of us can escape. A healthy individual is one in whom the age-related changes appear much later, and s/he is able to function normally for a longer period of time. Among your own families and acquaintances, you may have two 70-year-olds, one of whom still walks upright and does all the work her/himself, while the other is afflicted with aches and pains, walks with difficulty, and looks older than her/his age. It is clear that the former is healthier.
- Ability to fight disease by resisting infections and the effect of environmental toxins and pollutants. A person in good health is one who has good immunity and does not fall sick so often. Such a person is also able to tolerate the various toxic substances we are all exposed to in our environment—chemicals in the air that we breathe, the water we drink and the food we eat. Healthy people are also able to prevent, or at least delay, the onset of chronic degenerative diseases.

In addition, a healthy person is also socially well-adjusted. Social health pertains to the way a person socialises, interacts, has relationships, and gets along with other people in society.

An old saying goes: 'Prevention is better than cure'. Many of the health problems that people develop are related to the food they eat. Many diseases can be prevented with good nutrition (Figure 1.4). For those who have already developed a disease, diet can be modified to reduce the symptoms and manage the disease better.

Figure 1.4: Relationship of Nutrition with Health and Disease

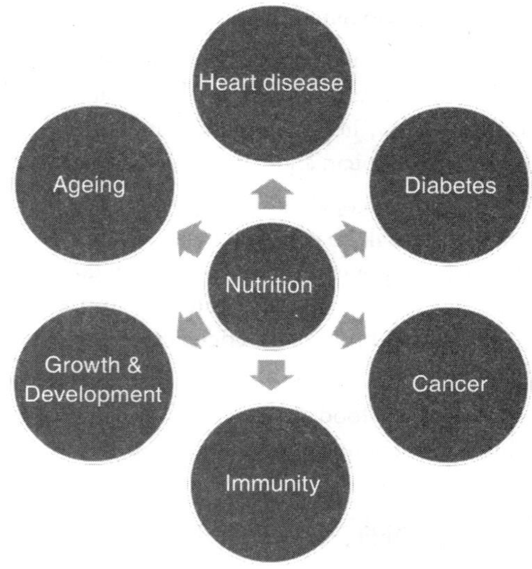

Source: Gopalan 1996.

Good nutrition is important for a child's **growth and development**. Those children who do not receive sufficient food, especially during the critical periods of growth, suffer from malnutrition. Good nutrition is important not only for children, but is also equally vital for adults as they age. Healthy eating habits **slow down the ageing process**. Nutrients and other phytochemicals, which act like antioxidants, help to neutralise and decrease the oxidative damage caused by free radicals. Good nutrition also improves mental function and increases immunity (the ability of the body to fight disease).

The **immunity** of a person is affected by her/his nutritional status. Under-nutrition can impair the response of the cells of the immune system. An undernourished individual will fall sick more often, suffer from the ailment for a longer duration, and the illness will take a more severe toll on the overall health of the individual. This may lead to the individual falling sick more often. Thus, it is a vicious cycle, which can be broken only by good nutrition. Nutrients like protein, lipids, zinc, iron, copper, vitamin A, vitamin C, etc., improve the immune response.

Undernourished children may also not respond as well to immunisation as normal healthy children. They may develop the disease later in life, despite having been given the vaccine to prevent the disease in childhood. This is probably because at the time of vaccination, the child may have been undernourished, and her/his immune system failed to respond to the vaccine in the appropriate manner.

Barker et al. (1993) proposed the hypothesis that children exposed to **undernourishment in intrauterine (foetal) life** are more likely to develop **chronic degenerative diseases**, like metabolic syndrome, diabetes, cardiovascular disease, etc., as adults. Metabolic syndrome, or Syndrome X, is characterised by abdominal obesity, disturbed blood lipid levels (high triglycerides and less amounts of good cholesterol), high blood pressure, and a decreased ability to control blood sugar levels. Hitherto, it was believed that only over-nutrition could cause these problems in adults. Under-nutrition in early life changes the way the body metabolises nutrients. Several studies are now showing that over-feeding an undernourished child can actually predispose her/him to chronic ailments. Balanced nutrition, on the other hand, can ensure that the child grows up to be a healthy adult. Thus, the ill-effects of under-nutrition are not just limited to the present, but may also extend to the distant future.

Nutritional factors have a role to play in the pathogenesis (manner of development of a disease) of **coronary heart disease** and **atherosclerosis** (hardening of arteries). Research has shown how changes in dietary behaviour can significantly reduce the prevalence of these diseases. An intake of high amounts of fat, saturated fat, trans fat, or cholesterol has been linked to heart disease. Similarly, a high intake of salt (sodium) is associated with high blood pressure (**hypertension**), and a high intake of simple sugars has been linked to **diabetes**.

Scientific evidence indicates that dietary factors could play a significant role in the initiation, promotion and progression of **cancer**. High intakes of fat, especially saturated fat, has been linked to rectal and breast cancers. High salt and nitrate / nitrite intake (present as preservatives in foods) favours the development of stomach and oesophageal cancers; high animal protein and red meat intake has been linked to prostate cancer; and a low intake of fibre to colon cancer.

Nutrients considered to protect against these chronic degenerative diseases are vitamins, minerals and phytochemicals that have an antioxidant role, like carotenoids, vitamins E and C, selenium, zinc, flavonoids, etc. Others, like potassium, magnesium, vitamin A, dietary fibre, and monounsaturated fatty acids and omega -3 fatty acids, are also considered protective nutrients. An increasing number of nutrients are now being linked to insulin secretion and function. Deficiency of zinc, chromium, manganese, copper, calcium, magnesium, and vanadium has been linked to insulin function, secretion and diabetes.

Thus, the food that we eat and the nutrients derived from it have a major impact on our health. Table 1.2 illustrates how nutrient deficiency and excess can have serious health consequences.

NEW FRONTIERS IN THE FIELD OF NUTRITION

Compared to other sciences, nutrition is a young science. Although we now know a considerable amount about different nutrients, newer research is throwing light on roles hitherto unrecognised, as well as substances that are now being given the status of essential nutrients.

With the sequencing of the human genome, a whole new discipline of study has opened up, called **nutritional genomics**. This is a field formed by the integration of the study of nutrition, molecular biology and genomics. It is the science of how nutrients affect the activities of genes (**nutrigenomics**), and how genes affect the interactions between diet and disease (**nutrigenetics**).

Observed differences in the individual response to diet have been attributed to differences in the genetic make-up. An exploration of nutrient-gene interactions in determining what will constitute a healthy combination is important. What we eat directly determines the genetic messages our body receives. This new science teaches us what specific foods tell our genes to do. Every protein synthesised by the cell is a product of gene expression.

Table 1.2: Consequences of Nutrient Deficiencies and Excesses

Nutrient Deficiencies		*Nutrient Excesses*	
Nutrient	*Consequences*	*Nutrient*	*Consequences*
Protein and energy	Retarded physical and mental growth, lowered immunity	Energy	Obesity and associated diseases
Iron, folic acid	Anaemia, decreased work capacity, effect on mental development birth defects	Sugars	Diabetes, dental caries (cavities)
Vitamin A	Irreversible blindness	Salt (sodium)	High blood pressure
Calcium, Vitamin D	Fragile bones, easy fractures, decreased quality of life	Fat (saturated fat, trans fat), Cholesterol	Cardiovascular diseases
Iodine	Thyroid hormone deficiency, swelling in neck, low IQ, mentally and physically retarded children born to iodine-deficient mothers	Fluoride	Weak bones, brownish stains on teeth, weakened tooth structure
Fibre	Constipation, colon cancer	Vitamins and minerals	Toxicity symptoms if consumed in large amounts. (You will learn more about them in later chapters.)

Nutrigenomics will ultimately help to tailor diets based on an individual's genetic make-up. Specific foods or constituents of food can be recommended, which can help modify the negative health effects of an individual's genetic profile. Nutrients and phytochemicals can interact with genomes, causing changes in their expression. At the same time, deficiency of a nutrient can hamper DNA repair, and hence normal function. A diet lacking in essential nutrients and leading to a state of deficiency has also been associated with an increased risk of diseases like cancer, diabetes and cardiovascular disease.

There is a growing awareness of the potential for modifications of food or diet to support health and reduce the risk of diet-related diseases. If we learn how our genes operate, and the instructions that the genes give to our body and its metabolism, we can radically change how food interacts with our body. This information can be used to lose weight and optimise health by preventing the development of diseases. Nutrigenomics can be used in the future for the development of customised neutraceuticals, based on specific genetic profiles. It can also be used to identify new mechanisms of action, as well as biomarkers that will more accurately depict the health status.

According to WHO (2002), **Genetics** is the study of heredity, while **Genomics** is defined as the study of genes and their functions, and related techniques. The **main difference** between genomics and genetics is that genetics scrutinises the functioning and composition of the single gene, whereas genomics addresses all genes and their interrelationships in order to identify their combined influence on the growth and development of the organism.

You have already seen how diet during early development can cause changes that last up to adulthood. Genetic variations in certain genes can alter an individual's sensitivity to developing ailments, like coronary heart disease. Several of these genes are susceptible to dietary intervention and may modulate the onset of the disease.

Nutraceutical

The word has been coined from 'nutrition' and 'pharmaceutical', and as the name suggests, refers to a product made from food, which contains nutrients that will provide some physiological benefit or protection against a chronic disease, improve health, delay the ageing process, increase life expectancy, or improve physical performance. Nutraceuticals are usually in a medicinal form like dietary supplements (tablet/capsule/powder/syrup), although the broad connotation of the term could also include functional foods and medical foods formulated for specific medical conditions. You will learn more about these in Chapter 13.

Nutraceuticals are now a big industry, with food and pharmaceutical companies racing to capture the market with products promising to cure ailments, enhance physical and /or mental performance, promote growth in children, protect bones, prevent cancer, and much more. It is a field in which constant research is going on, and the results show great potential.

SUMMARY

- Food provides nutrients that are essential to satisfy the body's need for energy, growth, repair, and protection. Food is basic to our survival, as it satisfies hunger and nourishes our body.
- Food also provides many physiologically active compounds that are not considered essential nutrients, but may confer several health benefits.
- The food that we eat performs nutritional as well as several non-nutritional functions.
- Food gives us energy for our body to function, it builds and maintains our body, and also protects it from diseases.
- Besides these physiological functions, food has several socio-cultural, psychological, and even political functions.
- From a normal state, a person can slip into a state of deficiency or excess nutrition.
- Diet surveys, anthropometric measurements, clinical examination, and biochemical investigations help us to assess the nutritional status of an individual.
- Phyto- (plant) and zoo- (animal) chemicals are bioactive compounds which provide health benefits.
- Foods that provide benefits beyond their nutritional contributions are called functional foods. These may be in their natural form, fortified, or modified to include the bioactive compounds in sufficient quantity, so as to confer a health benefit.
- Many of the health problems that people develop are related to the food they eat. Many diseases are preventable by good nutrition.
- Newer areas of research in nutrition are nutrigenomics and the development of nutraceuticals.
- There is a growing awareness of the potential for modifications of food or diet to support health and reduce the risk of diet-related diseases. If we learn how our genes operate, the instructions that the genes give to the body and its metabolism, we can radically change how food interacts with our body.
- Nutrigenomics can be used in the future for the development of customised neutraceuticals, based on the specific genetic profiles of individuals.

KEY WORDS

Anthropometry: Science of measuring the human body.

Chronic disease: A human health condition or disease that is persistent or otherwise long-lasting in its effects. The term 'chronic' is usually applied when the course of the disease lasts for more than three months.

Functional foods: Foods that contain physiologically active compounds that provide health benefits beyond their nutrient contributions.

Genome: The full set of genetic material (DNA) in the chromosomes of a cell. In humans, the genome consists of 46 chromosomes.

Nutraceutical (nutrition + pharmaceutical): Refers to a product made from food which has nutrients that will provide some physiological benefit or protection against a chronic disease.

Nutrigenomics: The science of how nutrients affect the activities of genes.

Nutrigenetics: How genes affect the interactions between diet and disease.

Phytochemicals: Biologically active non-nutrient compounds found in plant derived foods that have biological activity in the body.

Zoochemicals: Found in animal-derived foods that have biological activity in the body.

EXERCISES

1. What do you understand by the following terms:
   a. Nutrition
   b. Nutritional status
   c. Malnutrition
   d. Balanced diet
2. Explain the physiological functions of food.
3. Discuss the social, psychological and political functions performed by food, with suitable examples.
4. What are phytochemicals and how are they beneficial?
5. Describe the relationship between food, nutrition, health, and disease.
6. Define Health. Briefly explain the different dimensions of health.
7. Briefly describe how the study of nutrigenomics holds great potential for the future.

REFERENCES

Barker, D. J. P., C. N. Hales, C. H. D. Fall, C. Osmond, K. Phipps, and P. M. Clark, 'Type 2 (non-insulin dependent) diabetes mellitus, hypertension and hyperlipidaemia (Syndrome X): Relation to reduced foetal growth', *Diabetologia* 36, 1993, pp. 62–67.

Byrd-Bredbenner, C., G. Moe, D. Beshgetoor and J. Berning, *Wardlaw's Perspectives in Nutrition*, 9e, New York: McGraw-Hill International Edition, 2013.

FOSHU, Ministry of Health, Labor and Welfare, Government of Japan. http://www.mhlw.go.jp/english/topics/foodsafety/fhc/02.html (accessed 3 May 2014).

Gopalan, C., 'The Expanding Frontiers of Nutrition Science', in M. S. Bamji, N. Pralhad Rao and V. Reddy (eds), *Textbook of Human Nutrition*, New Delhi: Oxford & IBH Publishing Co. Pvt. Ltd, 1996.

Lawler, M. R., *Normal and therapeutic nutrition*, 16e, Macmillan Publishing Co., Inc.

Lowenberg, M. E., E. N. Todhunter, E. D. Wilson, M. C. Feeney, and J. R. Savage, *Food and Man*, New Delhi: Wiley Eastern Pvt. Ltd., 1968.

Martirosyan, D. M., *Functional Foods and Chronic Diseases: Science and Practice*, Texas: Food Science Publisher, 2011.

Polasa, K. and R. V. Sudershan, 'Functional Foods', in M. S. Bamji, K. Krishnaswamy and G. N. V. Brahmam (eds), *Textbook of Human Nutrition*, New Delhi: Oxford and IBH Publ Co., 2009, pp. 249–57.

Ritchie, J. A. S., F*ood Patterns and Nutrition. Teaching better nutrition—A study of Approaches and Techniques*, FAO nutritional Studies no. 6, Washington D.C.: FAO.

Robinson, W. D., 'Nutrition in medical education', Proceedings, Western Hemisphere Nutrition Congress 1965, American Medical Association, Chicago, 1966.

WHO, 'Genomics and World Health: Report of the Advisory Committee on Health Research', Geneva: WHO, 2002.

ONLINE SOURCE

www.healthypeople.gov

2

NUTRIENT REQUIREMENTS AND RECOMMENDATIONS

HIGHLIGHTS

- Human Nutrient Requirements
- Recommended Dietary Allowances
- Components of Dietary Reference Intakes
- Methods of Assessing Nutrient Requirements
- The Indian RDA
- Uses of RDA

The food that we consume each day contains several hundreds of specific chemicals. Some of these are well known as essential nutrients, required daily for a healthy and active life. In order to choose a well-balanced diet, it is important to know our daily requirements of each nutrient. Although all of us need the same nutrients, the required amounts vary with the stages of life.

During periods of growth, such as infancy, childhood and adolescence, nutrients are required for growth as well as maintenance of tissue integrity and proper body functions. Requirement for growth ceases in adults, and nutrients are needed mainly for maintenance. However, in physiological conditions such as pregnancy and lactation, nutrient requirements of adult women increase, as they have to meet all the nutritional needs of the growing foetus and the infant, in the early phase of life. During each stage of life, personal factors such as age, sex, genetic constitution, physiological status, as well as lifestyle habits such as physical activity, also affect nutrient needs.

THE CONCEPT

Nutrient requirement is the minimum amount of absorbed nutrient necessary to fulfil its physiological functions in the body. In other words, it is the amount of the nutrient that has to be consumed on a regular basis to prevent its deficiency in an individual and maintain health.

Individuals differ in their genetic make-up and also in their morphological and physiological aspects, which influence their metabolic efficiency and thereby their nutritional requirements. The range in individual nutritional requirements varies not only with individual biological variation, but also with nutrients. Therefore, to be practically useful, it is important to define nutrient requirement in terms of the specific amounts of essential nutrients that would cover the requirement of most individuals in a population group. This is referred to as **Recommended Dietary Allowance (RDA)**. In addition to individual variation in a group, diet quality and bio-availability of the nutrient from the habitual diet, that is, its digestion, absorption and availability for specific body functions, has to be taken into account while making recommendations for any population. Thus, RDAs represent the levels of the selected nutrients to be consumed daily to meet the nutrient needs of practically all healthy people in a population.

They are not minimum requirements or optimal intakes. They are adequate recommendations for the intake of nutrients, which include a liberal margin of safety. An individual's physiological requirements are invariably less than the recommended intake for the population.

The recommendations for appropriate nutrient intakes for a population are based on a review of the available scientific data by nutrition experts. These are revised periodically in the light of new scientific knowledge and social considerations about the quality of life to be supported. Therefore, they cannot be considered as final values. They are set by experts to guide people to meet their nutritional needs to remain healthy. Most countries have derived their own set of dietary standards, which are recommended intake values for nutrients.

Nutrient Requirement: The amount of nutrient an individual needs on a regular basis to remain healthy.

Recommended Dietary Allowance: The amount of nutrient a particular population group needs to remain healthy.

Minimum Nutrient Requirement: The least amount of nutrient that will prevent clinical symptoms of deficiency, support a well-defined biochemical or haematological response, or maintain specified level of a nutrient in blood or urine.

Safe Requirement Range: The range of intakes in which the risk of inadequacy or excess is zero for a population.

THE BACKGROUND

The evolution of dietary standards or reference values for nutrient intakes can be traced to the 1930s, when **Recommended Nutrient Intakes** (RNIs) were published by Health Canada and RDAs by the USA in the early 1940s. By this time, most nutrients in foods had been identified and measured by nutrition scientists. The goal of these standards was protection against nutrient deficiencies. These were revised from time to time as new scientific evidence became available. Since 1950, the Expert Committees of United Nations (UN) agencies such as the Food and Agriculture Organization (FAO) and World Health Organization (WHO) have defined human nutrient requirements periodically, with the purpose of providing population-based recommendations for nutrient intakes. Many other countries have formulated their own nutrient recommendations, and used terminologies like Recommended Dietary Allowances, Recommended Nutrient Intakes, Recommended Dietary Intakes, or Recommended Daily Amounts.

Figure 2.1: The Normal Curve

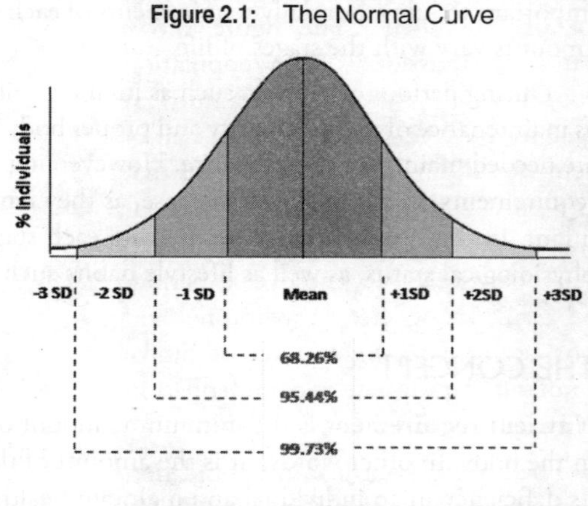

The normal distribution of individual nutrient requirements forms the basis for computing RDA. We must first understand what we mean by a normal curve (Figure 2.1).

In the case of energy, intake must equal expenditure to maintain a steady energy balance. Intakes above or below the actual requirements are not considered safe, as excess energy is stored in the body and results in obesity, while inadequate energy intake may cause under-nutrition. Thus, the energy requirement of a population group is set up at the average of the energy requirements of the individuals of the group. Figure 2.2 illustrates how the RDA for energy is set at the average daily requirement, while for protein and other nutrients, it is set at Mean + 2SD or the 'safe level'.

A major revision that replaced RDAs with **Dietary Reference Intakes** (DRIs) was first published in 1997 by the joint efforts of the USA and Canada. DRIs are a set of values for the dietary nutrient intakes of healthy people. These include levels of dietary intakes not only for adequacy, but also for optimal nutrition, as well as the prevention of chronic diseases.

These reference values, which are used for assessing and planning diets for healthy people, include five basic elements (Byrd-Bredbenner et al. 2013):

- Estimated Average Requirement (EAR)
- Recommended Dietary Allowance (RDA)
- Adequate Intake (AI)
- Tolerable Upper Intake level (UL)
- Estimated Energy Requirements (EER)

Box 2.1: The Normal Distribution

The Normal Distribution, also referred to as Gaussian distribution, is a probability distribution depicted by the Normal Curve. The curve is symmetrical about its mean (the average value). Its mean, median and mode are all equal. Its tail ends never meet the X-axis. It has one square unit area above the X-axis. It can be completely determined by its mean and standard deviation (the average deviation of all values from the mean). About 68.26 per cent of the total area lies between the Mean –1 SD and Mean + I SD; 95.44 per cent of the total area of the curve falls between the limits Mean –2SD and Mean + 2SD; and 99.73 per cent of the total area falls between M + 3SD and M –3SD.

The Normal Curve is a mathematical model used to understand the occurrence of various characteristics in real-life situations. It is very important in the field of statistics. Many human characteristics, such as stature, intelligence, nutrient requirements, etc., which vary due to inherent differences between individuals, are approximately normally distributed. Such characteristics, when assessed on a large random sample of a population, yield a frequency distribution graph, which approximates a normal curve. This implies that the mean nutrient requirements of all nutrients, except energy, of a population group plus 2 standard deviations would cover the nutrient needs of 97–98 per cent of that population for those nutrients.

Estimated Average Requirement, or average nutrient requirement, is the daily nutrient intake level that meets the requirements of half the healthy population during a particular life stage and gender group. The basis of this recommendation is the assumption that a nutrient requirement for a specific physiological or biochemical function in a population group (which could be children of a certain age group, pregnant women, adolescents of an age bracket or gender group) is normally distributed around the mean. The EAR is set at the midpoint of this distribution—a level that is sufficient to meet the estimated nutrient needs of 50 per cent of a given population group (Figure 2.3). EARs can be used to assess the nutritional adequacy of the diet of population groups, but not of individuals. The figure shows that if all individuals in a population group have the intake level of a nutrient equal to the average requirement, half of them would develop a deficiency of that nutrient. As the average daily nutrient intakes of people fall below the EARs, their body stores decline over a period, and result in deficiency symptoms and poor health. Thus, this level of intake is not an appropriate recommendation for everybody.

The EAR of a nutrient in a population group forms the basis of its **RDA**. As discussed earlier, the RDA is the daily nutrient intake level that meets the requirements of almost all healthy individuals in a population group. It is set at 2 standard deviations above the estimated average requirement of a nutrient. This implies that the RDA of a nutrient would cover the nutrient requirements of 97–98 per cent of the individuals in a population group. Only 2–3 per cent of the individuals

Figure 2.2: RDA for Energy and Protein

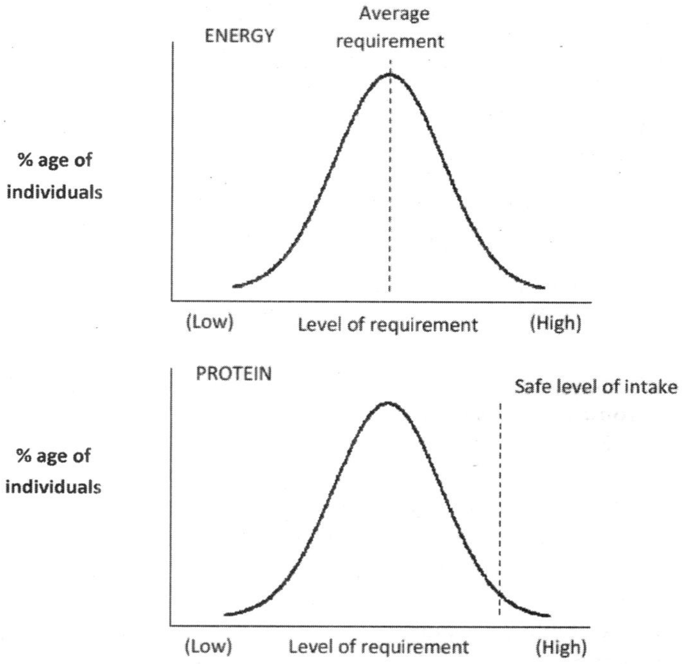

Source: WHO 1985.

in the group will require more than the recommended levels of intake. RDAs can be used as a guideline for planning and evaluating the diets of groups of people. At an individual level, RDAs can be considered a goal for the usual or average daily intake. However, it is not necessary to achieve this goal on a daily basis, as RDAs are much above the nutrient requirements of many people in a population group.

> Essentially, the RDAs were formulated to inform a particular group of people about the amount of nutrient that they need to consume on a regular basis to remain healthy.

In the case of nutrients for which sufficient scientific evidence is not available to establish EAR, AIs are determined on the basis of the observation of the habitual dietary intake of apparently healthy population groups. **Adequate Intake** is a recommended average daily intake level usually based on observed or experimentally determined estimates of the nutrient intakes of apparently healthy people. These intake levels are assumed to be adequate as they appear to sustain a defined indicator of health, which could be growth rate or bone health, in a specific population group. As there is inadequate evidence to set the RDA, the values set as AI usually exceed RDA. Therefore, AIs would meet the nutrient needs of more than 97–98 per cent of the population and, like RDAs, may be used as goals for usual intakes by individuals.

The upper level of intake of a nutrient is not a recommended intake, but the upper limit of the nutrient intake of most individuals in a healthy population. **Tolerable Upper Intake Level** is the highest daily nutrient intake level that is unlikely to pose adverse health risks in the long run. This level is above the recommended intake and is the maximum amount of a nutrient that is safe for most healthy people. Dietary intake of a nutrient above the upper limit is likely to lead to toxicity. This intake level for most nutrients is based on combined daily intake from food, fortified food and nutrient supplements. The purpose of this indicator is to caution against the overconsumption of nutrients.

Figure 2.3: Dietary Reference Intakes

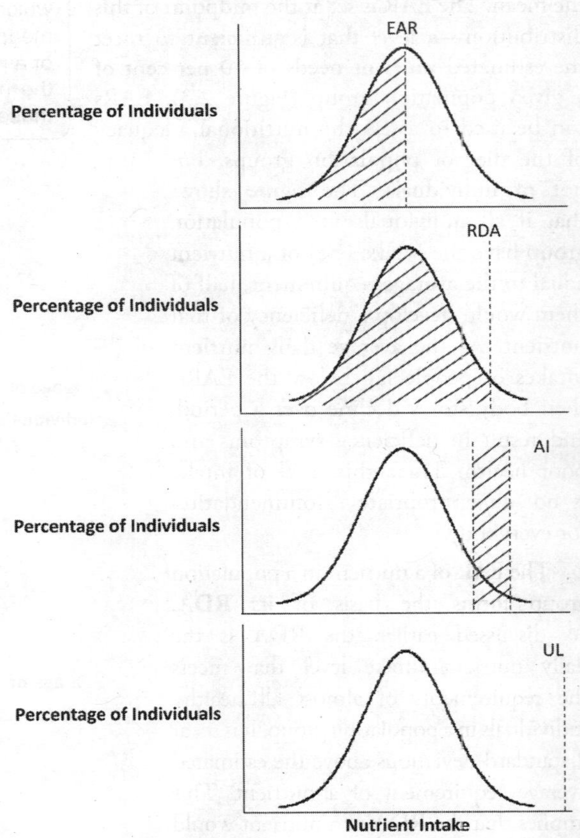

Source: IOM, FNB 2005.

Unlike the RDAs for nutrients, the estimated energy requirements are set at the average daily energy need of a population group. **Estimated Energy Requirement** is the level of energy intake that is estimated to maintain a balance between energy intake and expenditure in healthy individuals of a defined age, gender, weight, height, and physical activity. Excess intake of energy is stored in the body as fat, which increases the risk of chronic diseases. Therefore, no safe allowances are made for energy, and its requirement is set on an equivalent level as estimated average requirement for a population group.

Although not included as a DRI, **Acceptable Macronutrient Distribution Ranges** (AMDRs) indicate the recommended balance of energy sources (carbohydrates, proteins and fat) in diets for adults for the prevention of diet-related chronic diseases. AMDRs provide a suggested range of intake of each macronutrient as per cent of energy, which is associated with the reduced risk of chronic diseases (Table 2.1). Similar recommendations are also given by the WHO as population nutrient intake goals.

METHODS OF ASSESSING NUTRIENT REQUIREMENTS

The basic purpose behind determining nutrient needs is to ensure an adequate supply of food to an individual in order to maintain maximum efficiency in all bodily functions, and equip her/him for socially and economically desirable activities. Each tissue of the body has different requirements. The requirement of an individual is by and large an integration of the requirements of all the tissues of the body. Nutrient allowances should cover cellular requirements, unabsorbed nutrients and endogenous losses. There are a number of approaches that have been used to determine nutrient requirements in humans, in order to set RDAs for those nutrients. Some of the basic methods of assessment are given in Table 2.2.

In addition to the methods used for assessing nutrient requirements (explained in Table 2.2), some other approaches, such as the minimum intakes needed for normal functional tests or for tissue saturation, have also been used to assess the needs of various nutrients.

Table 2.1: AMDRs for Adults as Proportion of Total Energy (in %)

Dietary Component	*AMDRs* for North American Adults in %*	*WHO Goals **
Total Fat	20–25	15–30
Protein	10–35	10–15
Carbohydrate	45–64	55–75
n-6 PUFAs	5–10	6–10
α Linolenic acid	0.6–1.2	-

Notes: * Values expressed as percentage of energy intake
Saturated fat < 10%
Trans fatty acids < 1%
Sugar < 10%

Sources: IOM, FNB 2005; WHO 2003.

Table 2.2: Methods of Assessing Nutrient Requirements

Balance Studies	The minimum intake of a nutrient that can maintain equilibrium in adults over a long period, that is, a state in which intake is approximately equal to the output of the nutrient. This level of intake is used to arrive at the minimum nutrient requirement for adults. Requirement for growing children is a positive nutrient balance, which is consistent with their satisfactory growth.
Factorial Method	The requirements of the different functions of a nutrient are assessed separately, and added up to arrive at the total daily requirement. The minimum losses of a nutrient through urine (U), faeces (F) and skin (S) are determined on a diet devoid (or having a very low level) of that nutrient. These obligatory losses are added up to determine the maintenance requirement (R) of the nutrients in adults. In the case of growing children, the total daily requirement is a sum of the maintenance requirement and the requirement for growth (G). $R = U + F + S + G$
Nutrient Turnover	The radio-isotope or stable-isotope labelled nutrients are administered to a healthy person, and the daily nutrient turnover is determined at the rate of the loss of radioactivity, which reflects the total daily loss of nutrients from the body. This is utilised to estimate the nutrient requirements.
Depletion–Repletion Studies	This approach is relevant for nutrients that are not stored in any appreciable extent in the body, such as water-soluble vitamins. First, a deficiency of these vitamins is created by feeding a diet deficient in the nutrient. Then, graded doses of the nutrient are administered and the response monitored. The lowest corrective level of intake of the nutrient indicates the minimum requirement.
Dietary Intake Surveys	The habitual dietary intake of different nutrients of an apparently healthy population can provide information about nutrient intakes consistent with good health. This approach often overestimates the requirements, and provides only a rough assessment. Hence, diet surveys are generally not used independently, but in combination with other methods like balance studies, biochemical or clinical evaluation, etc.

Table 2.2 contd

Table 2.2 contd

Growth	The requirement of any particular nutrient for satisfactory growth has been utilised for defining needs during periods of rapid growth, like infancy. The intake of the nutrient via breast milk has been linked to growth performance; for instance, the volume of breast milk consumed and the energy content of breast milk is estimated to derive the energy intake of babies who are growing well. It is then assumed that the amount of energy they are consuming via breast milk is sufficient to support good growth in infants of that age. Zinc is a mineral that has been linked to growth performance.
Carcass Analysis	Autopsy data has also been used to get an idea of the nutrients retained by the body. It is not a routine method, but is used more in animal experiments. The carcass or the dead body of an animal can be analysed for its nitrogen content or trace mineral content (for example, level of calcium, copper, zinc, etc.)
Population Studies	This is an epidemiological approach in which the rates of mortality (death), morbidity (illness), and prevalence rates of nutrient-deficiency diseases (like iron-deficiency anaemia, vitamin A deficiency-related blindness, etc.) are estimated by surveys.

Source: ICMR 2010; Rao and Sivakumar 2009.

Energy

Energy requirement is currently assessed in terms of energy expenditure. Energy expenditure can be measured by several methods. The various components of energy expenditure, viz., Basal Metabolic Rate (BMR), Specific Dynamic Action (SDA) and physical activity are usually measured by direct or indirect calorimetry. You will learn about these methods in greater detail in Chapter 3. Total energy expenditure (TEE) can be calculated by the heart rate monitoring method, doubly-labelled water technique, and the factorial method.

- Factorial method: This method involves the calculation of the energy needs for each of the three categories of energy expenditure. BMR is estimated using calorimetry or using standard equations; 10 per cent of the energy intake is added for SDA; and then the cost of each physical activity is added.
- Heart rate monitoring method: Estimating total energy needs by constantly monitoring the heart rate is based on the strong positive correlation that exists between heart rate and oxygen consumption, and therefore energy release from food or energy stores. Since the oxygen needed to release energy from food is transported through the blood, increased oxygen consumption requires increased blood flow, powered by an increase in the heart rate. A mathematical equation is used to calculate the energy expenditure.
- Doubly-labelled water technique: This technique is based on the fact that the body loses hydrogen atoms of the body water via the usual routes of water loss—urine, sweat, saliva, and as evaporated water—while oxygen atoms are lost through these routes and also as carbon dioxide. Hence, some of the water in the body is labelled with two isotopes—2H, that is, Deuterium, and 18O—which are readily detectable. This is the best available method of assessing energy expenditure. However, it is expensive, and the measurement requires technical skills.
- Energy balance method: For this method, energy expenditure and energy intake have to be assessed. The energy value of food can be determined with the help of a bomb calorimeter. However, it is important that energy balance is maintained over a long period by people with a healthy body weight.

PROTEIN

- Factorial approach: The requirements for the different functions of protein are assessed separately, and added up to derive the total daily requirement of protein. This approach was employed earlier for assessing protein requirement.

- Balance studies: The minimum intake of protein for a state of equilibrium (intake = output) in adults, and nitrogen retention consistent with satisfactory growth in children, have been used widely to arrive at protein requirements. Growing children tend to be in a state of positive nitrogen balance, in which the intake is more than the loss or output. Nitrogen retained by the body is used to synthesise new tissues, and hence for growth. If the child is growing satisfactorily, then at that level of intake s/he must be in a desirable state of positive nitrogen balance.

Vitamins and Minerals

- Balance studies: These are used for stable nutrients like calcium, iron, and other minerals, where the intake and output routes are known and can be measured. If intake is equal to output, the person is in a state of equilibrium with respect to that nutrient. If intake is greater than output, the individual is in positive balance; for example, a growing child is usually in a state of positive calcium balance. If intake is less than output, the individual is in negative balance; for example, an elderly or bedridden person usually has negative calcium balance.
- Biochemical evaluation: Levels of nutrients and their metabolites in body fluids like blood, urine, and even faeces, and in tissues like the liver, provide us with vital information about the nutritional status of the individual. Sometimes, the levels or activity of enzymes, which require specific vitamins or minerals for their functioning, are measured. Load tests with water-soluble vitamins are conducted to estimate nutrient status. A mega dose of the vitamin is given to the individual, and per cent return of the test dose in urine is estimated between four to 24 hours. This gives an indication of the level of tissue saturation. If the body tissues are saturated with the vitamin, the percentage return (excretion) is high. If the tissues had very low levels of the vitamin, then the percentage return is less. This method is employed for vitamin C.
- Isotope tracers: These are also used for studying requirements. Labelled nutrients are injected or fed to the individual, and the turnover for nutrients is studied. Stable isotopes of vitamin A, vitamin C, iron, and vitamin B_{12} are used to determine the requirements of these nutrients.
- Clinical evaluation: The deficiency of minerals and vitamins can cause specific clinical signs and symptoms. The prevalence of these can be correlated with dietary intake and biochemical levels. For instance, at what level of vitamin A intake does an individual develop night blindness?
- Functional tests: Tests of mental and work performance, known as functional tests, also help in estimating vitamin and mineral requirements. For example, the ability to see in dim light (dark adaptation time) is studied with the help of photometers for the assessment of vitamin A requirements.
- Depletion and repletion studies: This approach is employed to calculate the requirement of water-soluble vitamins. The levels of vitamins or their coenzyme in serum or tissues (for example, white blood cells, red blood cells, etc.) are used as a biochemical marker of the vitamin status. The requirements of ascorbic acid, thiamine, riboflavin, niacin, and pyridoxine have been established using this approach. The subjects are first fed a diet that is very low in the nutrient under study, till the biochemical parameters reach a low level. The response to feeding graded doses of the nutrient is then determined. The level at which the response increases rapidly is an indication of minimum requirement.

THE INDIAN RDA

In India, such recommendations were first made by the Nutrition Advisory Committee of the India Research Fund Association in 1944. These were based on the recommendations on daily dietary allowances for each known nutrient, made in 1936 by an Expert Committee of the League of Nations. Since then, these recommendations have been revised by the Expert Group of the Indian Council of Medical Research (ICMR) from time to time, with the latest revisions taking place in 2010. Tables 2.3 and 2.4 present the RDAs for different age and gender groups.

Table 2.3: Recommended Dietary Allowances for Energy, Protein, Fat, and Minerals for Indians, 2010

Group	*Category / Age*	*Net Energy (kcal/d)*	*Protein (g/d)*	*Visible Fat (g/d)*	*Calcium (mg/d)*	*Iron (mg/d)*	*Zinc (mg/d)*	*Magnesium (mg/d)*
	Sedentary work	2,320		25				
Men	Moderate work	2,730	60.0	30	600	17	12	340
	Heavy work	3,490		40				
	Sedentary work	1,900		20				
	Moderate work	2,230	55.0	25	600	21	10	
	Heavy work	2,850		30				
Women	Pregnant	+350	78	30		35		310
	Lactating 0–6 m	+600	74	30	1,200		12	
	6–12 m	+520	68	30		21		
Infants	0–6 months	92 kcal/kg/d	1.16 kcal/kg/d	--	500	46 µg/kg/d	–	30
	6–12 months	80 kcal/kg/d	1.69 kcal/kg/d	19		5		45
	1–3 years	1,060	16.7	27		9	5	50
Children	4–6 years	1,350	20.1	25	600	13	7	70
	7–9 years	1,690	29.5	30		16	8	100
Boys	10–12 years	2,190	39.9	35		21	9	120
Girls	10–12 years	2,010	40.4	35		27	9	160
Boys	13–15 years	2,750	54.3	45	800	32	11	165
Girls	13–15 years	2,330	51.9	40		27	11	210
Boys	16–17 years	3,020	61.5	50		28	12	195
Girls	16–17 years	2,440	55.5	35		26	12	235

Source: Nutrient Requirements and Recommended Dietary Allowances for Indians, ICMR 2010.

Table 2.4: Recommended Dietary Allowances for Water-soluble and Fat-soluble Vitamins for Indians, 2010

Group	*Category / Age*	*Vitamin A (μg/d)*		*Thiamine (mg/d)*	*Riboflavin (mg/d)*	*Niacin equivalent (mg/d)*	*Vitamin B_6(mg/d)*	*Ascorbic Acid (mg/d)*	*Dietary Folate (μg/d)*	*Vitamin B_{12} (μg/d)*
		Retinol	*β-carotene*							
	Sedentary work			1.2	1.4	16				
Men	Moderate work	600	4,800	1.4	1.6	18	2.0	40	200	1.0
	Heavy work			1.7	2.1	21				
	Sedentary work			1.0	1.1	12				
	Moderate work	600	4,800	1.1	1.3	14	2.0	40	200	1.0
	Heavy work			1.4	1.7	16				
Women	Pregnant	800	6,400	+0.2	+0.3	+2		60	500	1.2
	Lactating 0–6 m	950	7,600	+0.3	+0.4	+4	2.5	80	300	1.5
	6–12 m			+0.2	+0.3	+3				
Infants	0–6 months	350	–	0.2	0.3	710 μg/kg	0.1	25	25	0.2
	6–12 months		2,800	0.3	0.4	650 μg/kg	0.4			
	1–3 years	400	3,200	0.5	0.6	8	0.9		80	
Children	4–6 years			0.7	0.8	11		40	100	0.2–1.0
	7–9 years	600	4,800	0.8	1.0	13	1.6		120	
Boys	10–12 years			1.1	1.3	15	1.6		140	
Girls	10–12 years			1.0	1.2	13				
Boys	13–15 years	600	4,800	1.4	1.6	16		40	150	0.2–1.0
Girls	13–15 years			1.2	1.4	14				
Boys	16–17 years			1.5	1.8	17	2.0		200	
Girls	16–17 years			1.0	1.2	14				

Source: Nutrient Requirements and Recommended Dietary Allowances for Indians, ICMR, 2010.

The nutrient requirement of an individual largely depends on age, gender and body weight. During childhood, nutrient requirements are in proportion to body weight and growth rate. During adulthood, nutrient requirements are primarily related to body weight and age. There are wide variations in the body weights and heights of apparently healthy children and adults belonging to different regions of the world.

In most developing nations, people face dietary constraints and lack of access to good healthcare, due to which their body measurements do not correspond to those belonging to developed nations. The reference body weight of Indians employed for computing RDA in 2010 (Table 2.5) are based on large population surveys conducted by the National Nutrition Monitoring Bureau (NNMB) and Department of Women and Child Development (DWCD), GOI, mainly in the rural areas of 16 states of India. In the case of children up to the age of three, body weight values from the WHO-MGRS (Multicentre Growth Reference Study) study (2006) were used.

Table 2.5: Reference Body Weights of Indians used for Computing RDAs

Group	*Age*	*Reference Body Weight (kg)*
Adult Men	18–29 years	60.0
Adult Women (Non-pregnant, non-lactating)	18–29 years	55.0
Infants	0–6 m	5.4
	6–12 m	8.4
Children	1–3 years	12.9
	4–6 years	18.0
	7–9 years	25.1
Boys	10–12 years	34.3
	13–15 years	47.6
	16–17 years	55.4
Girls	10–12 years	35.0
	13–15 years	46.6
	16–17 years	52.1

Source: Nutrient Requirements and Recommended Dietary Allowances for Indians, ICMR 2010.

In addition to age, gender and weight, the RDA is influenced by the bio-availability of a nutrient from habitual diets. Bio-availability depends on the nutrient and the quality of the diet. There is a low bio-availability of nutrients such as protein, iron, calcium, zinc, β-carotene (precursor of vitamin A), and vitamin B_{12} in the predominantly cereal-based vegetarian diets of Indians. Inhibitory factors, such as tannins, phytates and oxalates present in the usual diets consumed by Indians, result in poor absorption of nutrients, especially minerals like calcium, iron, zinc, etc., in the intestine. Typical Indian cooking methods also result in the destruction of heat-labile and water-soluble vitamins. These factors justify the need for formulating separate dietary allowances for Indians.

Changes in RDAs during Various Life Stages

Dietary recommendations vary with the stage of life, as nutrient needs differ with age, physical activity and gender (after the age of nine). There is a progressive increase in nutrient requirements with age, up to adolescence. However, in comparison to adults, the nutrient needs of children are much higher because of their additional needs for growth. Growth is very rapid during infancy and adolescence. Therefore, nutrient needs are also higher during these periods of life. As evident from Tables 2.6(a) and (b), the energy and protein recommendations computed per kg body weight are higher during childhood and adolescence, as compared with adult stage. Besides age, requirements vary with the individual's level of physical activity.

The physical activity level among adults is broadly categorised as sedentary, moderate and heavy, depending on the type of activities people indulge in while at work, and during their leisure time. The requirements of energy and certain nutrients that assist in the metabolism of energy in the body increase with the increase in the level of physical activity. As it is not possible to accurately measure the activity level of infants and children, their energy needs are based on the energy intakes of healthy infants, and children having normal growth.

Besides age and physical activity, physiological conditions such as pregnancy and lactation also increase the nutrient needs of women in the reproductive age group. During pregnancy, requirements increase to meet the needs of the growing foetus, and during lactation, for the production of milk for the infant. Requirements are higher during the period of exclusive breast-feeding, that is, from birth till six months. After six months, there is a reduction in the secretion of milk, and thereby a decrease in nutritional needs. Therefore, the nutrient recommendations for this stage are lower.

Table 2.6(a): Changes in RDAs of Energy and Protein with Age and Gender

	Infant		Preschooler		School-aged Child		Adolescent	
Age	**0–6 m**	**6–12 m**	**1–3 y**	**4–6 y**	**7–9 y**	**10–12 y**	**13–15 y**	**16–17 y**
Ref. Body weight (kg)	5.4	8.4	12.9	18.0	25.1	**Boy** 34.3 **Girl** 35.0	47.6 46.6	55.4 52.1
RDAs								
Energy (kcal/d)			1060	1350	1690	**Boy** 2,190 **Girl** 2,010	2,750 2,330	3,020 2,440
Protein (g/d)			16.7	20.1	29.5	**Boy** 39.9 **Girl** 40.4	54.3 51.9	61.5 55.5
RDAs per kg body weight								
Energy (kcal/kg/d)	92	80	82	75	67	**Boy** 64 **Girl** 57	58 50	54 47
Protein (g/kg/d)	1.16	1.69	1.29	1.12	1.16	**Boy** 1.16 **Girl** 1.15	1.14 1.11	1.11 1.06

USES OF RDAs

For the purpose of making nutrient recommendations for any population, the variability of the physiological requirement of nutrients between individuals in a population group, as well as the availability of nutrients from the habitual diets of that population group have to be considered. There are certain points that should be considered during practical applications of RDAs:

(i) The RDAs are formulated to maintain health in people who are already healthy. These are not applicable to people who are malnourished, ill, or recovering from illness. People with medical problems have special needs, and require additional or restricted intakes.

(ii) The RDAs are meant for groups of people. As the nutrient needs of individuals within a group vary widely, RDAs include a generous margin of safety to cater to those individuals whose needs are the highest. An individual's physiological requirements are invariably less than the RDAs for the population.

(iii) The RDA of a nutrient is valid when the needs of all other nutrients are met. For example, protein is the only energy-yielding nutrient for which RDA has been established. The underlying assumption is that protein is consumed along with sufficient amounts of carbohydrates and fats to provide adequate energy, and that the dietary intakes of other nutrients are also adequate. An adequate intake of carbohydrates and fats in the diet spares proteins from being used for energy, and permits them to be used for their important role in body growth and repair.

Table 2.6(b): Changes in RDAs of Energy and Protein with Physical Activity and Physiological State in Adults

	Adult (18–29 y) Sedentary		Adult (18–29 y) Moderate		Adult (18–29 y) Heavy		Adult Woman		
	Man	Woman (NPNL)	Man	Woman (NPNL)	Man	Woman (NPNL)	Pregnancy	Lactation 0–6 m	Lactation 7–12 m
Ref. Body weight (kg)	60.0	55.0	60.0	55.0	60.0	55.0			
RDAs									
Energy (kcal/d)	2,320	1,900	2,730	2,230	3,490	2,850	(1,900+350) 2,250	(1,900+600) 2,500	(1,900+520) 2,420
Protein (g/d)	60	55	60	55	60	55	78	74	68
RDAs per kg body weight									
Energy (kcal/kg/d)	39	34	45	40	58	52			
Protein (g/kg/d)	1.0	1.0	1.0	1.0	1.0	1.0			

Source: ICMR 2010.

The main use of RDAs is to evaluate the diets of groups of people and to identify groups at high risk of inadequate or excessive nutrient intake. The RDAs can be used to evaluate the diets of individuals only if their intakes are averaged over a period of time, which could range from a minimum of three days to seven days or more. As the intake deviates below or above the RDA, the risk of deficiencies or toxicities increases.

The RDAs can also serve as the basis for an early warning of a possible adverse trend in a population group. RDAs can also be used to set priorities for national food policies such as the export and import of food, for monitoring the food supply of a nation, for estimating the food needs of a population, educating consumers, and planning diets and food needs for supplementary feeding programmes for different vulnerable population groups. RDAs can also be used for taking decisions with respect to the fortification of foods with vitamins and minerals, especially those that are deficient in the usual diets of a population group.

They can be used to set dietary goals for individuals. Since these recommendations are applicable to the average daily intakes, it is not necessary to meet the RDAs of all nutrients on a daily basis. Nevertheless, they serve as yardsticks for planning healthy diets for individuals, and also for institutions such as childcare centres, hostels, hospitals, elderly homes, as well as households. The food needs of inmates of these institutions can be estimated on the basis of the RDAs, with the confidence that these estimates would adequately meet the nutritional needs of most of them.

RDAs are being used on food labels to provide information on the nutritional contribution of either 100g or one serving portion of any food item. The nutritional contribution is usually expressed as percentages of the RDAs. These help consumers to make wise selections of processed and packaged foodstuffs. Although useful, the percentages expressed this way are not really valid for everyone (across the lifespan), as only one reference point is selected for such computation.

It is also important to understand that the RDAs for most nutrients can be met by consuming a variety of foods in the daily diets. Different foods contain varying amounts of nutrients, as well as many health promoting non-nutrients. If selected judiciously, a variety of foods will provide more than the nutrient covered by recommendations.

At the international level, nutrient recommendations have become very versatile as these now include the lowest and highest nutrient intakes that are compatible with good health (for many nutrients). In India, the RDAs have undergone several revisions, and the latest revision (ICMR 2010) has given recommendations for many trace minerals such as Zinc, Selenium, Magnesium, Copper, Chromium, Manganese, Sodium, and Potassium, which were not included in detail earlier. Modifications have also been made in the RDAs of Energy, Protein, Fat, Calcium, Iron, Vitamin A and Carotenoids, and Folic Acid, based on new data on their requirements or bio-availability. Although RDAs are the only yardstick available for diet planning and evaluation for the Indian population, these are based on scientific data generated from different groups of Indians, and the nutrient content and bio-availability of their habitual diets. These population-specific recommendations have a useful role to play in the application of nutrition science.

SUMMARY

- During each stage of life, factors such as age, sex, genetic constitution, and physiological status, as well as lifestyle habits such as physical activity, affect nutrient needs.
- Nutrient requirement is the minimum amount of absorbed nutrient necessary to fulfil its physiological functions in the body, prevent its deficiency and maintain health.
- In addition to individual variation in a group, diet quality and bio-availability of the nutrient from the habitual diet, that is, its digestion, absorption and availability for specific body functions, has to be taken into account before making recommendations for any population.
- RDAs represent the levels of the selected nutrients to be consumed daily to meet the nutrient needs of practically all healthy people in a population.
- The DRIs are a set of values for the dietary nutrient intakes of healthy people. These include the levels of dietary intakes not only for dietary adequacy, but also for optimal nutrition as well as the prevention of chronic diseases. These include five basic elements—EAR, RDA, AI, UL, and EER.
- There are several methods used to assess nutrient requirements. These are balance studies, depletion–repletion studies, factorial approach, nutrient turnover studies, and obligatory loss of nutrients. Population studies, diet surveys, and the evaluation of clinical and biochemical signs of deficiency all help to work out the level of nutrients that people in a population should be consuming to maintain good health.

- Dietary recommendations vary with the stage of life, as nutrient needs differ with age, physical activity and gender (after nine years of age). There is a progressive increase in nutrient requirements with age, up to adolescence. However, in comparison to adults, the nutrient needs of children are much higher because of their additional needs for growth. Growth is very rapid during infancy and adolescence.
- In addition to age, gender and weight, the RDA is influenced by the bio-availability of a nutrient from habitual diets. Bio-availability depends on the nutrient and the quality of the diet. Indian diets tend to have a number of inhibitory substances which decrease the absorption of nutrients, especially minerals. Our cooking and processing techniques also lead to a loss of many nutrients.
- The RDAs are formulated to maintain health in people who are already healthy. People with medical problems have special needs, and require additional or restricted intakes.
- RDAs are meant for groups of people. The RDA of a nutrient is valid when the needs of all other nutrients are met.
- The main use of RDAs is to evaluate the diets of groups of people and to identify groups at high risk of inadequate or excessive nutrient intake. As the intakes deviate below or above the RDA, the risk of deficiencies or toxicities increases respectively.
- RDAs can also serve as the basis for the early warning of a possible adverse trend in a population group; can be used to set priorities for national food policies; for monitoring the food supply of a nation; for estimating the food needs of a population; educating consumers; and planning diets and food needs for supplementary feeding programmes, fortification of foods with vitamins and minerals, setting dietary goals for individuals, planning healthy diets for individuals, and also for institutions such as childcare centres, hostels, hospitals, elderly homes, as well as households.
- RDAs are being used on food labels to provide information on nutritional contribution of either 100g or one serving portion of any food item. These help consumers to make wise selections of processed and packaged foodstuffs.
- It is also important to understand that the RDAs for most nutrients can be met by consuming a variety of foods in the daily diets.

KEY WORDS

Acceptable Macronutrient Distribution Ranges (AMDRs): Provide the suggested range of intake of each macronutrient as per cent of energy, which is associated with a reduced risk of chronic diseases.

Adequate Intake: A recommended average daily intake level, usually based on observed or experimentally determined estimates of the nutrient intakes of apparently healthy people.

Balance studies: The minimum intake of a nutrient that can maintain equilibrium in adults over a long period, that is, a state in which intake is approximately equal to the output of the nutrient and nutrient retention consistent with satisfactory growth in children.

Depletion-repletion studies: The subjects are first fed a diet very low in the nutrient under study, till the biochemical parameters reach a low level. The response to feeding graded doses of the nutrient is then determined. The level at which the response increases rapidly is an indication of the minimum requirement.

Dietary Reference Intakes: A set of values for the dietary nutrient intakes of healthy people. These include levels of dietary intakes not only for dietary adequacy, but also for optimal nutrition, as well as the prevention of chronic diseases.

Estimated Average Requirement (EAR): The daily nutrient intake level that meets the requirements of half the healthy population in a particular life stage and gender group.

Estimated Energy Requirement (EER): The level of energy intake estimated to maintain a balance between energy intake and expenditure in healthy individuals of a defined age, gender, weight, height, and physical activity. Energy requirements are set at a level equivalent to the estimated average requirement of a population group.

Factorial Approach: Here, the nutrients required for different functions are assessed individually, and added to arrive at the total daily requirement.

Minimum nutrient requirement: The least amount of a nutrient that will prevent clinical symptoms of deficiency, or support a well-defined biochemical or haematological response, or maintain a specified level of a nutrient in blood or urine.

Nutrient requirement: The amount of the nutrient that has to be consumed on a regular basis to prevent its deficiency in an individual and maintain health.

Nutrient turnover studies: The radio-isotope or stable isotope labelled nutrients are administered to a healthy person, and the daily nutrient turnover is determined as the rate of loss of radioactivity, which reflects the total daily loss of nutrients from the body. This is utilised to estimate the nutrient requirements.

Obligatory losses: The minimum losses of a nutrient (through urine, faeces and skin) are determined on a diet devoid (or containing a very low level) of that nutrient.

Recommended Dietary Allowances (RDA): The daily nutrient intake level that meets the requirements of almost all healthy individuals in a population group.

Tolerable Upper Intake Level (UL): The highest daily nutrient intake level that is unlikely to pose adverse health risks in the long run. This level is above the recommended intake and is the maximum amount of a nutrient that is safe for most healthy people. Dietary intake of a nutrient above the upper limit is likely to lead to toxicity.

EXERCISES

1. What is the difference between nutrient requirements and Recommended Dietary Allowances?
2. Define DRIs. Explain the five basic elements of DRIs.
3. What do you understand by the term Acceptable Macronutrient Distribution Ranges? Why were these formulated?
4. Why is the energy requirement set at the EAR value rather than the safe level?
5. Explain how the following approaches are used to calculate nutrient requirements:
   a. Balance studies
   b. Nutrient turnover
   c. Factorial approach
   d. Depletion-repletion studies
   e. Obligatory loss of nutrients
6. Explain how individual variability and bio-availability are important criteria to keep in mind while calculating RDA.
7. Discuss the various uses of RDA.

REFERENCES

Byrd-Bredbenner, C., G. Moe, D. Beshgetoor, and J. Berning, *Wardlaw's Perspectives in Nutrition*, 9e, New York: McGraw- Hill International Edition, 2013.

ICMR, 'Nutrient Requirements and Recommended Dietary Allowances for Indians', A Report of the Expert Group of the Indian Council of Medical Research, 2010.

Institute of Medicine (IOM), *Dietary reference intakes for energy, carbohydrate, fiber, fat, fatty acids, cholesterol, protein and amino acids (macronutrients)*, Washington, D.C.: National Academies Press, 2005.

Rao, B. S. N. and B. Sivakumar, 'Nutrient requirements and Recommended dietary allowances', in M. S. Bamji, K. Krishnaswamy and G. N. V. Brahmam (eds), *Textbook of Human Nutrition*, 3e, New Delhi: Oxford and IBH Publ Co., 2009, pp. 154–78.

WHO, 'Energy and Protein Requirements', Report of a Joint FAO/WHO/UNU Expert Consultation, WHO Technical Report Series 724, Geneva: World Health Organization, 1985.

———, *WHO Child Growth Standards. Length/ Height for age, Weight for age, Weight for Length, weight for height and Body Mass Index for Age. Methods and devlopment*, Geneva: WHO, 2006.

WHO/FAO, 'Diet, Nutrition and Prevention of Chronic Diseases: Report of a Joint WHO/FAO Expert Consultation', Technical Report Series 916, Geneva, 2003.

3

ENERGY

HIGHLIGHTS

- Role of macronutrients in providing energy
- Units of heat and energy
- Energy requirements and its components
- Measurement of energy expenditure
- Concept of energy balance
- Health concerns related to energy imbalance

FUELS FOR THE BODY

The food we eat is fuel for the body. Like coal and other fuels, its end product is carbon dioxide, water and heat. The body needs this energy to carry out different metabolic activities, maintain the body temperature, and enable the body to perform physical activities. Antoine Lavoisier (1743–94) was the first to elucidate the importance of oxygen and explain the principle of combustion both within and outside the body. He also stated that carbon dioxide is exhaled during respiration, and that the intensity of metabolism depends on food intake, work and environmental temperature. He devised a calorimeter (calor = heat, metron = measure), which was quite accurate in measuring heat production.

In 1842, Justus von Liebig suggested that it is not carbon and hydrogen that burns in the body, but carbohydrates, fats and proteins. The energy content of fuels or food signifies potential chemical energy, which is released as heat on combustion and is measured as Calories (kcal). This measure of the gross energy of food is estimated in a bomb calorimeter. A **bomb calorimeter** is used to determine the heat evolved during the combustion of food (Figure 3.1). It is a steel container in which food is burnt in oxygen under pressure. A weighed amount of food (dried) is ignited. The rise in the temperature of the water surrounding the chamber holding the food gives a measure of the heat produced. This is still in use for estimating the potential energy content of new foods, aliquots of diets, processed foods, etc.

Figure 3.1: Bomb Calorimeter

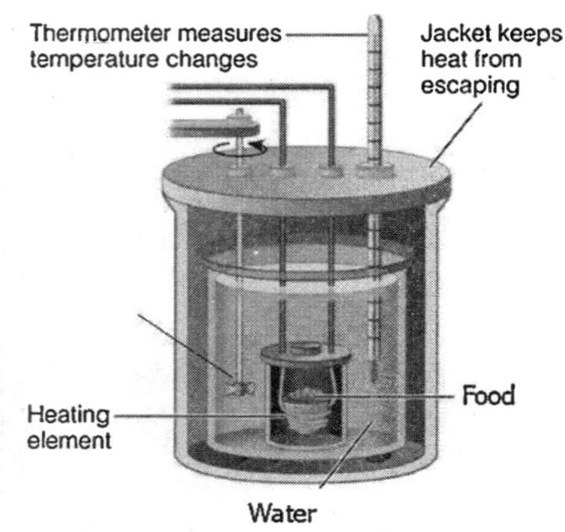

Source: http://www.techknow.org.uk/wiki/images/9/9a/Calorimeter.JPG

UNITS OF ENERGY

A **calorie** (cal) is a unit measure of heat. It is the amount of heat necessary to raise the temperature of 1 gram of water by 1 degree centigrade (specifically from 14.5°C to 15.5°C). This unit is too small to be used in the field of nutrition, and for the estimation of the heat produced by the fuel in the human body. The unit of heat in the field of nutrition is **Kilocalorie** (kcal), defined as the heat required to raise the temperature of 1 kilogram of water by 1°C, from 14.5°C to 15.5°C. This unit is still popularly used. However, the International System of Units recommends the use of joules, which is the physical unit of energy. **Joules** is *the energy required to move 1 kilogram of mass by 1 metre by a force of 1 Newton acting upon it.* The relationship between the two units is:

1 kcal = 4.184 kJ (kilojoules)
1kJ = 0.239 kcal
1000 kcal = 4184 kJ = 4.18 MJ
1 MJ = 239 kcal

Food contains macro and micronutrients. While macronutrients like carbohydrates, fats and proteins provide energy to the body, micronutrients like vitamins and minerals help the body to utilise this energy, as many of them function as coenzymes in energy metabolism. In the body, the major source of energy comes from carbohydrates, which have a protein-sparing action. That is, carbohydrates are preferentially used as a source of energy, thus sparing proteins for tissue synthesis. Carbohydrates ensure 45–65 per cent of calorie requirements, and Indian diets, on an average, derive 60 per cent of energy from carbohydrates.

Fat is a concentrated source of energy. It is also storable in the body as adipose tissue if the energy intake is in excess of need. This can raise body fat over a period of time, altering the body composition. In the interest of preventing obesity and its co-morbidities, like heart diseases, diabetes, hypertension, etc., the dietary fat should be less than 30 energy per cent (en %). Proteins are more for the synthesis and maintenance of body proteins, but they also contribute to meeting energy requirements. They contribute up to 15–20 en%.

Adenosine Triphosphate (ATP) is a high energy compound composed of a purine (adenine), a sugar (ribose), and three phosphate groups. ATP is the energy source used by your cells for different metabolic reactions.

Much of the energy released from carbohydrates, fats or proteins is captured in the bonds of adenosine triphosphate (ATP), also referred to as the energy currency of our bodies. The potential energy of fuels from food is given in Figure 3.2. Alcohol is not considered part of a food system; however, its contribution to total energy intake cannot be overlooked among populations that regularly consume alcoholic beverages. Ethanol provides 7 kcal per gram of metabolisable energy.

Figure 3.2: Potential Energy of Fuels from Food

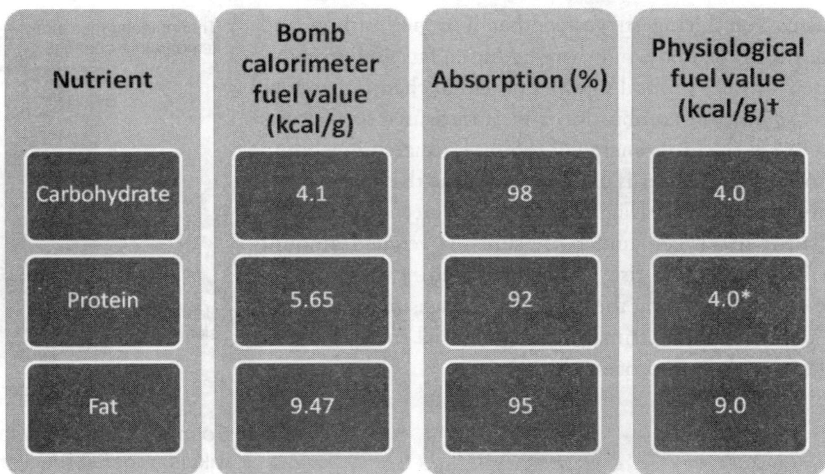

Nutrient	Bomb calorimeter fuel value (kcal/g)	Absorption (%)	Physiological fuel value (kcal/g)†
Carbohydrate	4.1	98	4.0
Protein	5.65	92	4.0*
Fat	9.47	95	9.0

Note: * The value is 1.65 kcal less due to the production of urea from proteins in the body, which is then excreted from the body.

† Also called **Rosa and Atwater factors** (or **physiological fuel values**), which refer to the actual metabolisable energy, obtained by multiplying coefficients of digestibility with respective calorimeter values.

Kinetic Energy

The energy utilised for physical activity and other energy expenditures are kinetic energy. Energy expenditure is estimated under two broad principles of calorimetry:

1. Measurement of the heat produced by the body, that is, Direct calorimetry.
2. Computation of the heat produced from gaseous exchange—oxygen used or carbon dioxide produced—that is, Indirect Calorimetry.

Equipments that use direct calorimetry are the metabolic chamber and suit calorimeter. Those using indirect calorimetry are the Douglas bag, Max Planck apparatus, KM meter, Oxylog, and metabolic chamber, where gaseous exchange was estimated. These methods could classically give the energy expenditure of the basal metabolic rate, resting metabolic rate, and the energy cost of various activities for different ages and sexes. This enabled the use of the factorial method for computing total 24-hour energy expenditure (TEE) by adding the energy costs of all activities. According to FAO/WHO/UNU (2004), the TEE now should be estimated by the heart-rate method or the doubly labelled water technique. The factorial method using individual costs as multiples of BMR is a good field method.

Direct Calorimetry

Although easy in theory, this is very difficult and expensive in practice. Measuring the heat evolved while placing the individual in a metabolic/respiration chamber (which is thermally insulated) demands a lot of cooperation on part of that individual. Atwater and Rosa (1892–97) had designed a respiration chamber which measured the heat produced and oxygen consumed. The change in the temperature of the circulating water in the chamber was used to measure the heat produced. Moisture was absorbed in the sulphuric acid and carbon dioxide produced in soda lime. Such metabolic chambers tended to be small, thus restricting movement and the type of activities that could be performed. Even though the chamber can be replaced by a suit calorimeter (an insulated suit that the individual can wear) devised in 1972, the method is cumbersome. It can be used in laboratory-based experiments, but it is not really suited for estimating energy expenditure in a community-based setting. Still, the direct calorimetric method is considered a gold standard and a yardstick for calibrating other methods. Direct calorimetric methods were, however, put to minimum use because of their limitations, and methods using indirect calorimetry were more widely used.

Indirect Calorimetry

This is a technically simpler procedure because, instead of heat produced, it is oxygen consumption that is measured. It is based on the fact that when an organic substance is completely combusted, either in a calorimeter or in the human body, oxygen is consumed in amounts directly related to the energy liberated as heat. The ratio of the carbon dioxide produced to the oxygen used is known as the **respiratory quotient (RQ)**. The RQ for the oxidation of glucose is 1.0, for lipids it is 0.7, and for proteins, it is 0.8.

Most measurements of oxygen consumption are undertaken when the subject is breathing into some form of apparatus (usually referred to as a respirometer), which can measure the total volume of gas expired and provide a sample of the expired air for analysis. The respirometer can have a closed or open circuit. In a **closed circuit system**, the person breathes in and out of a chamber, while in an **open circuit,** the person breathes in atmospheric oxygen and breathes out into a chamber or cylinder.

The **Benedict Roth spirometer** is a closed circuit system in which the subject breathes in oxygen from a metal cylinder, and the exhaled air passes through a soda-lime canister into the same cylinder, so that the carbon dioxide can get absorbed. The cylinder floats on water inside a second cylinder. As the oxygen is consumed, the inner cylinder falls, and the rate of fall is recorded by an ink writer on a rotating drum. This apparatus is bulky, and hence can only be used for measuring BMR or RMR. It is simple to use and gives a direct reading of the oxygen consumption, thereby avoiding the need for gas analysis. However, since carbon dioxide is not measured, RQ cannot be calculated.

To overcome the lack of portability, open circuit respirometers were designed, which could be carried along so that the energy cost of various activities could be measured. The **Douglas bag** was one such respirometer. The subject had to inhale room air and breathe out into the Douglas bag (made of rubber or plastic, and of 100 L capacity). The expired air, collected for a period of three to 10 minutes, was analysed through a gas meter for its oxygen and carbon dioxide content. The composition of inspired air could also be analysed, and thus it was possible to calculate the oxygen consumption and RQ. This equipment was also bulky and difficult to use in all field situations.

The **Max Planck respirometer** was a further improvement on the design of respirometers as it was lighter (weighing only 2.5 kg), and hence easily portable (could be worn like a backpack). The volume of expired air could be directly measured and simultaneously, a small fraction could be diverted into a plastic bladder for the analysis of gases later. It was used to measure the energy expenditure of industrial workers, miners, and even people doing different household chores.

Oxylog is used extensively for finding the energy cost of several activities in subjects of all ages. It was an improvement on Max Planck, as gases here are not collected in a bladder, but simultaneously estimated in the oxygen analyser built into the Oxylog apparatus. Figure 3.3 depicts the different equipment used for measuring energy expenditure.

Total Energy Expenditure

To compute the total energy requirements, we need to estimate 24-hours energy expenditure. Various methods have been used to compute 24-hours energy expenditure or Total Daily Energy Expenditure (TDEE), like the Factorial Approach/Diary Method, Minute-to-Minute Heart Rate Method and Doubly Labelled Water Technique. Let us read more about these methods.

Factorial Approach

Once the energy costs of various activities have been catalogued for various age and gender groups by any of the direct and indirect methods, they can be used in the Factorial Approach to compute the Total Daily Energy Expenditure (TDEE), and its components like Activity Energy Expenditure (AEE), Leisure Time Physical Activity (LTPA), etc.

Calculations of energy expenditure using the Factorial Approach involve identifying the different activities, like sleeping, resting, working, leisure activities, and other discretionary activities, in a day. By using the time spent and the energy cost of each activity, the total day's expenditure can be computed.

BMR has been computed from weight dependent, age-specific equations for the Indian man and woman by ICMR (1989). For international use, these equations have also been given by expert groups of FAO/WHO/UNU (1985, 2004; see Table 3.1).

Figure 3.3: Measurement of Energy Expenditure Using Different Equipment

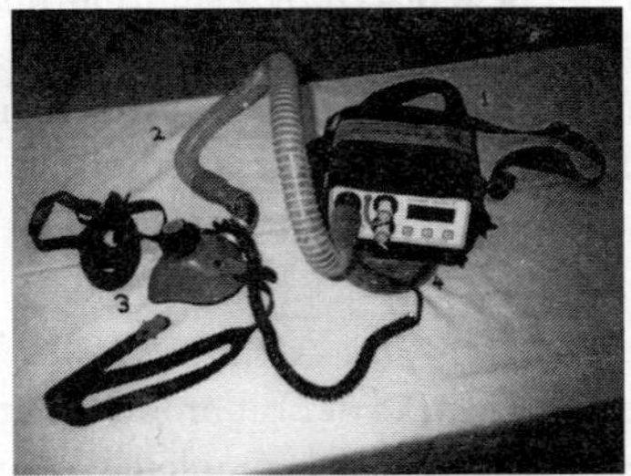

3.3(a): Oxylog

1= halter,
2 = tube connecting mask to instrument,
3 = mask or mouthpiece into which subject breathes,
4 = instrument which analyses and records data

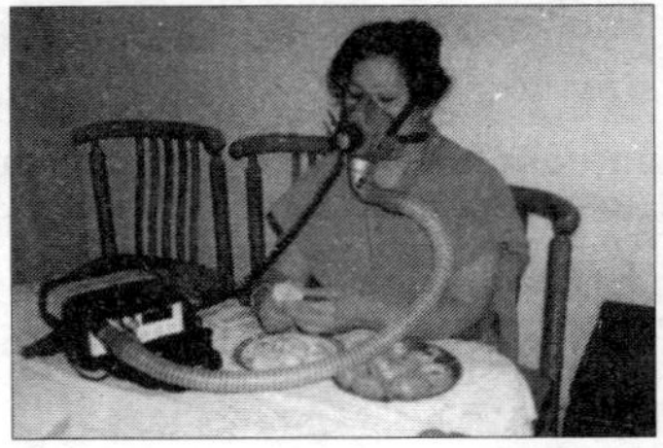

3.3(b) Measuring energy expenditure during housework using Oxylog in a study conducted by Lady Irwin College, University of Delhi

Source: Monika Gambhir Wasuja, 2002.

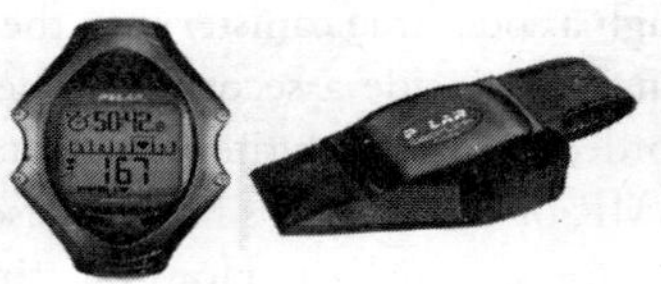

3.3(c) Heart Rate Monitor (POLAR RS 400), worn like a watch on the wrist with its wearlink transmitter worn across the chest above the heart.

Table 3.1: Equations for Predicting BMR (kcal/24 hours) for Adults

Sex	*Age*	*Prediction Equations Proposed for Indians by ICMR (1989)*	*Prediction Equations Proposed by FAO/WHO/UNU (1985)*
Males	18–30	14.5 x B.W.(kg) + 645	15.057 x B.W. (kg) + 692.2
	30-60	10.9 x B.W. (kg) + 833	11.472 x B.W. (kg) + 873.1
	>60	12.6 x B.W. (kg) + 463	11.711 x B.W. (kg) + 587.7
Females	18–30	14.0 x B.W. (kg) + 471	14.818 x B.W. (kg) + 486.6
	30–60	8.3 x B.W. (kg) + 788	8.126 x B.W. (kg) + 845.6
	>60	10.0 x B.W. (kg) + 565	9.082 x B.W. (kg) + 658.5

Note: B.W. = Body Weight
BMR of Indians is 5% lower than international values (FAO/WHO/UNU 1985).

Source: ICMR 2010; FAO/WHO/UNU 2004.

The **physical activity ratio** (PAR) is expressed as a ratio of the energy cost of an individual activity per minute to the cost of the basal metabolic rate per minute. PAR values for different activities of the day can then be added up to obtain the **physical activity level,** which is the ratio of energy expenditure for 24 hours and the BMR over 24 hours, as given below:

$$\text{Physical Activity Ratio (PAR)} = \frac{\text{Energy cost of an activity per minute}}{\text{Energy cost of basal metabolism per minute}}$$

$$\text{Physical Activity Level (PAL)} = \frac{\text{Energy expenditure for 24 hours}}{\text{BMR over 24 hours}}$$

According to ICMR (2010), a PAL value of 1.53 indicates that the person is sedentary, 1.8 indicates that s/he is a moderate worker, and 2.3 indicates a heavy worker. PAL> 2.4 is difficult to maintain over a prolonged period.

PAR values are similar in men and women, and in individuals of different ages and body weights. This is because PAR values are calculated as energy expenditure for specific tasks, expressed as a ratio of the BMR. PAR values for certain commonly performed activities, according to ICMR (2010), are sitting quietly—1.20, standing quietly—1.40, sitting at desk—1.30, standing and doing lab work—2.00, typing on a computer while sitting—1.58, and walking at 3 miles/hour speed—3.71. In fact, the Indian data for PAR values compares well with data from other population groups. The BMR of the Indian population is, however, lower than certain other groups. Compared to Western countries, the BMR of Indian adults is 5 per cent lower. Hence, energy requirements work out slightly lower than international values. There is no evidence to show that the BMR of Indian children is lower than their Western counterparts.

Thus, BMR can be calculated by putting the weight of the person in kilograms in the appropriate equation. If a 19-year-old girl weighs 55kg, for instance, then 14.0 x 55 + 471= 1241 kcal is her BMR. This is the BMR for 24 hours. This figure can be divided by 24 to give the BMR per hour, that is, 52 kcal/hour. If a person goes for a walk for an hour, then the amount of energy they spend is PAR value for walking x BMR (Kcal/hr) x time spent (hr), which in this case is 3.71 x 52 x 1 = 193 kcal. Similarly, the energy spent on each activity during the day can be calculated and then added up to give the total energy expenditure (TEE). This is known as the factorial approach for calculating energy expenditure/requirement.

Heart-rate Monitoring (HRM) Method

This method uses an array of small, non-invasive electronic devices to monitor and record the minute-to-minute heart rate in individuals. At variable heart rates, the volume of oxygen consumed (VO_2) is measured on the same individual. A relationship is then drawn between heart rate (HR) and VO_2 The VO_2 and its calorific value are derived for the whole day under free living conditions. It is a simple, cost-effective method of estimating TEE. The only limitation is its use in very sedentary individuals, as the heart rate does not register a significant change with most activities. It is an ideal method under free living conditions for moderately active persons, sports persons, school children, and army personnel. The individual costs of activity should not be calculated by this method, as it provides reliable data on long-term continuous measurements.

VO_2 (or oxygen consumption) is a measure of the volume of oxygen that is used by your body to convert the energy from the food you eat into the energy molecules ATP. **VO_2 max** (or maximal oxygen consumption) is simply the maximum possible VO_2 that a given person can achieve. VO_2 and VO_2 max are important in the context of exercise, because they are a measure of your body's ability to generate ATP and hence a measure of your cardiorespiratory fitness level.

Doubly Labelled Water (DLW) Technique

This technique uses water made from labelled hydrogen (^2H – deuterium) and oxygen (^{18}O). As both elements are labelled, the method is referred to as 'doubly labelled' water technique. A measured amount of this water is consumed by the individual whose energy expenditure is being measured. Over several days (usually 10–14 days), the rate of disappearance of the labelled elements is measured in blood, urine and saliva. Total carbon dioxide production, for instance, helps to calculate the respiratory quotient and total energy expenditure. This method is now considered the gold standard in determining energy requirements, as it is the most accurate technique available for free living individuals. This technique can be safely used for all age groups, including infants. The limitations are its high cost and availability of the doubly labelled water and the sophisticated equipment, along with the trained technicians required to conduct the analysis.

Energy Requirement

The energy requirement of an individual has been defined by FAO/WHO/UNU (2004) and ICMR (2010) as:

> The level of energy intake **from food** that **balances energy expenditure** when the individual has a body size and **composition** and **level of physical activity**, consistent with **long term good health**, also allowing for maintenance of economically essential and **socially desirable activity**. In children and pregnant and lactating women, it includes the energy needs associated with the **deposition** of **tissues** or secretion of milk at rates consistent with **good health**.

The definition encapsulates both the principle and the method of dealing with larger issues pertaining to energy requirements. The intake of energy comes from the food we eat. It is important to balance this with the energy we spend, so that the body is in a state of equilibrium. The basis for calculation of the energy requirement is the amount of energy that individuals spend in a day. Excess energy intake will result in weight gain and changes in body composition, because of the deposition of adipose tissue. Hence, any increase in intake needs to be matched with an increase in physical activity. Even for sedentary individuals, it is desirable to have moderate/ higher levels of physical activity, as physical activity is associated with good health.

In adults, the goal should be to prevent weight gain. The body size, composition and physical activity level should allow the individual to stay in good health for a long time. It should also enable the individual to indulge in activities that lead to economic gain, that is, the individual should be able to carry out work to earn a living. The person should also be socially active to meet her/his health goals. In the case of children, growth needs should be met by energy intake for optimal outcomes. In pregnant women, it should support energy needs for the growth of maternal tissues, and for foetal development. In lactating women, the additional needs for milk secretion should be met.

Estimating the Energy Requirements of a Population

The basic concept of estimating energy requirements is fundamentally different from that of other nutrients. Energy is the only nutrient for which a safety factor is not added to the estimated average requirement while deriving the recommended dietary allowance (RDA). Even a slight excess of energy is deposited in the body's reserve of adipose tissue as fat. Hence, the RDA for energy represents only the average daily requirement, which is in fact the average daily energy expenditure of an individual. The RDA value meets the need of only half of the age and gender category of that population. The descriptor is 'Average', and hence requirements are laid at EAR—Estimated Average Requirement—and not at the safe level. As per the definition, energy requirements should be calculated on the basis of energy expenditure, rather than in terms of intake.

Components of Energy Requirement

Energy is required by our body for primarily three functions—for all involuntary functions of the body like the beating of the heart, circulation of blood, respiration, function of the nervous system, and indeed, all the organs of our body (**basal metabolism**); for digestion, absorption and utilisation of food (**dietary induced thermogenesis),** and for all **physical activity,** which includes sitting, walking (with or without load), running, cooking, driving, office work, yoga, etc., that is, all the activities that we indulge in in a day (Figure 3.4).

Figure 3.4: Components of Energy Requirement

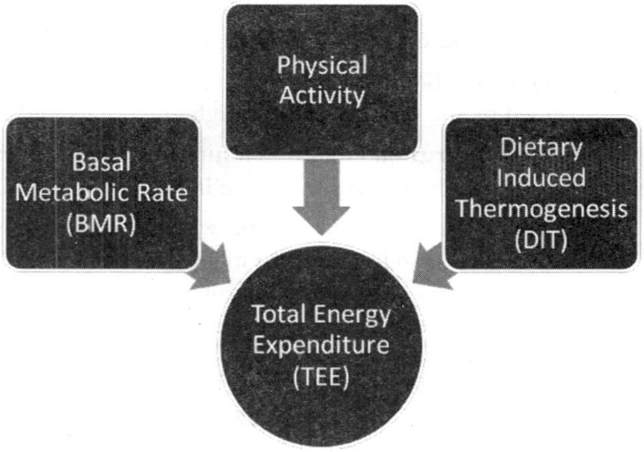

Basal metabolism includes a range of metabolic functions essential for life, such as cellular activity, synthesis and secretion of enzymes and hormones, maintenance of muscle tone and body temperature, work of the cardiac and respiratory muscles, and liver, kidney and brain function. Thus, **basal metabolic rate** is a measure of the energy used for the involuntary work of the body. It is measured under standard conditions that include being awake, in a supine position, after 10–12 hours of fasting and eight hours of physical rest (and hence the measurement is usually taken in the morning, after an overnight fast and rest in a metabolic laboratory). The individual has to be in a state of complete mental relaxation, without any fear or anxiety about the test itself. The ambient environment, temperature and humidity should be comfortable, so that it does not elicit heat-generating or heat-dissipating processes. In addition, the individual's body should also be at the normal temperature.

BMR is the largest component of energy expenditure, representing 45–70 per cent of the total daily energy expenditure.

Factors Affecting BMR

The rate of basal metabolism is affected by several factors.

- **Surface area.** Heat loss from the body is proportional to the skin surface area. A tall thin person has a greater surface area than an individual of the same weight who is short and fat. Thus, the tall thin person will have a greater basal metabolism.
- **Sex.** Women tend to have a lower BMR than men, probably as an influence of the sex hormones, and also because men have a greater proportion of lean tissue compared to more adipose tissue in women. Lean tissue is metabolically more active than adipose tissue.
- **Age.** BMR also changes with age. In the first two years of life, the BMR is the highest. It declines throughout childhood, accelerating slightly in adolescence, and then declining throughout life. It drops 1–2 per cent for each decade past the age of 30, as a result of the lean body mass lost with advancing age.

- **Physical activity** leads to an increase in BMR. Physical activity can help to preserve BMR throughout adulthood by helping to maintain the lean body mass.
- **Sleep**. During sleep, the BMR is lowered, although it depends on how soundly the person is sleeping. People who are restless in their sleep, constantly tossing and moving about, tend to spend a lot of energy even when they are sleeping.

Resting Metabolic Rate (RMR) is the energy expenditure at rest. It can be measured at any point in the day in a resting position, and thus may include the calorigenic effect of foods. The criterion for the measurement of RMR is also less stringent with respect to recent physical activity. Consequently, RMR is slightly higher than BMR.

- **Body temperature.** BMR is always measured at the normal body temperature, as any increase in body temperature above the normal 37 °C (98.6 °F) increases the basal metabolism by 13 per cent for each degree Celsius rise in temperature (7 per cent for each degree Farenheit).
- **Hormones** of the thyroid gland also regulate the rate of energy metabolism. Hyperthyroidism (overactive thyroid gland) can increase BMR by 75–100 per cent, resulting in rapid weight loss, while hypothyroidism (underactive thyroid gland) can decrease metabolism by 30–40 per cent, resulting in weight gain. Another hormone that increases the BMR is the growth hormone, which is partly responsible for the higher metabolic rate seen in growing children. Premenstrual hormones slightly raise the BMR.
- **Pregnancy**. BMR increases during the last trimester of pregnancy by 15–25 per cent as a result of the weight gained by the woman, and the high rate of metabolism of the foetus.
- **State of nutrition.** Prolonged fasting or chronic under-nutrition can lead to a decrease in the basal metabolic rate, probably due to a reduction in body weight and lean body mass.
- **Caffeine and Tobacco.** Caffeine, which we consume in tea and coffee, is known to increase basal metabolism. Tobacco use also increases the metabolic rate, which is why smokers tend to lose weight. A word of caution, however: using tobacco to control body weight is not recommended, because it increases too many health risks, like cardiovascular disease and cancer.

Dietary induced thermogenesis (DIT) is the metabolic response of our body to food. It accounts for about 10 per cent of the energy consumed each day. Eating requires energy for the ingestion, digestion, absorption, transport, interconversion, oxidation, and deposition of nutrients. These processes increase heat production and oxygen consumption. Other terms used to describe this are *specific dynamic action of food (SDA), specific dynamic effect (SDE), and thermic effect of food (TEF).* In individuals eating a mixed diet, the metabolic response to food increases the total energy expenditure by about 10 per cent over a 24-hour period. Protein, when eaten alone, has been shown to increase the metabolic rate by about 20–30 per cent, whereas carbohydrates (5–10 per cent) and fats (0–5 per cent) produce smaller increases. Heat production also increases when nutrients are given intravenously, due to a stimulation of cellular metabolism.

Physical activity is the second largest component of energy expenditure, and also the most variable. The types of physical activities usually performed can be classified as obligatory and discretionary. **Obligatory,** as the name suggests, refers to those activities that can be seldom avoided due to economic or socio-cultural demands, like going to school/office, tending to home and family, etc. Earlier, the classification of activities referred to these as 'occupational' activities, that is, related to a person's occupation in life (office worker, housewife, student, etc). **Discretionary activities,** although not socially and economically essential, are important for health, well-being, and a good quality of life. They include activities indulged in for personal enjoyment, social interaction, community development, family comfort, and well-being, fitness and health.

Physical activity not only ensures energy expenditure in the activity being performed, but also tends to raise BMR (probably because of an increase in lean body mass, and an increase in metabolism during the activity). This ensures that for every activity, the individual spends more energy (as the energy spent is a product of BMR and the PAR value of that activity). If BMR increases, the energy cost of each activity increases. Thus, the best way to lose/maintain weight is to increase the level of physical activity!

Leisure time physical activity (LTPA) has emerged to be of great significance in the prevention of obesity and its co-morbidities. Individuals need to be encouraged to indulge in outdoor games and sports activities during their free time, instead of sedentary activities like spending time in front of a screen (TV, computer, gaming device, or mobile phone).

The amount of energy needed for any activity depends on three factors—muscle mass, body weight and type of activity. The larger the muscle mass and the heavier the weight of the body part being moved, the more the energy expended. Duration, frequency and intensity of activity also influence energy expenditure; the longer, the more frequent, and the more intense the activity, the greater the energy spent.

Energy cost of growth (expressed as % of total energy requirement)

0–3 months – 35

12 months – 5

12–24 months – 3

Up to mid adolescence – 1–2

Late teens – negligible

Besides these major components, *growth, pregnancy and lactation* also add to the total energy requirements. The energy cost of growth has two components—the energy needed to synthesise growing tissues and the energy deposited in those tissues. During pregnancy, requirement increases due to the growth of the foetus, placenta and maternal tissues (uterus, breast and adipose tissues), as well as an increase in BMR. The energy cost of lactation again has two components—the energy content of milk secreted and the energy required to produce that milk. Fat stores during pregnancy partly help in meeting the increased energy cost of lactation.

Factors Influencing Energy Requirements

Energy needs are dependent on a number of factors, such as age, body size, physical activity, altered physiological status—such as pregnancy and lactation—and, to some extent, climate.

- **Adaptation.** This is perhaps one of the most important factors that need to be considered when the energy requirements of a population are being worked out. The body responds to the food and energy available by reaching a new steady state with respect to body mass. On a day-to-day basis, there is adaptation to increased or lowered intake levels due to feasting or fasting, respectively (known as short-term adaptation). On a long-term basis, like food shortages due to war or natural calamities that persist for a long period of time, adaptation to changes in energy intake can result in a reduction in body size (biological adaptation), lowering of BMR (metabolic adaptation), and decreased physical and socially desirable activities (behavioural adaptation) in order to conserve energy for vital body functions and enter a new state of energy balance. Energy requirements, or any nutrient requirement, should not be measured on adapted individuals.
- **Body size.** This is the major determinant of the absolute requirements for energy. Energy requirements are given in terms of defined body weights. Body size also determines body surface area, and we now know that the greater the body surface area, the greater the BMR, which is a major component of energy expenditure.
- **Body composition.** This is perhaps a better indicator of energy needs than just body weight, as it is sensitive to the true requirements of the body. The two-compartment model of body composition states that the body is composed of either fat mass (adipose tissue) or fat-free mass (bones, muscle, water, and other organs). Body fat is inversely related to energy needs, while lean body mass (muscle mass) is directly related to energy requirements. Although we now know that adipose tissue is not totally inert and that some metabolic activity takes place in it, lean body mass (LBM) is metabolically more active; hence, the greater the proportion of LBM, the greater the BMR and the energy cost of each activity. The quality of diet and physical activity influence body composition. It is also influenced by genetic factors.
- **Physical fitness and functional capacity.** During growth, there are marked changes in functional capacity. The natural peak in functional capacity coincides with high levels of spontaneous physical activity during adolescence. When requirements are estimated, the habitual physical activity levels of individuals, as well as their functional capacity to do work should be kept in mind. Estimated requirements should be enough to maintain health and sustain optimal bodily functions, including physical and mental fitness.

- **Age.** As people grow older, there is a reduction in LBM, and hence the resting metabolic rate declines. During the **growth** phases, there is a concomitant increase in energy requirements from the period of infancy to adolescence. The RDAs have been given for age categories that are selected to reflect the physiological characteristics of continual changes in the rate of growth. Changes are particularly rapid during three periods—infancy, adolescence (that is, the two periods of growth spurt) and old age (when rapid changes take place in physical activity, body composition and food intake patterns).
- **Gender.** Energy requirement per kg body weight is higher for men than for women. The BMR of men is 5–10 per cent higher at the same age, height and weight. This may be a result of differences in hormone levels, as well as the fact that men have a higher LBM and women a higher proportion of adipose tissue.
- **Climate.** Although earlier requirement estimates considered environmental temperature a factor that increased energy requirements, it is now believed that the body can acclimatise and adapt to these conditions. Moreover, with advancements in technology, there have been better clothing designs and air-conditioning of living and work environments. For people like soldiers, mountaineers, and others who work in extreme climatic conditions (like hot deserts, hot and humid coastal areas, or high-altitude cold areas), special requirements are worked out separately.

Energy Requirements for Different Groups through the Lifecycle

Energy requirements for different stages of the lifecycle have been discussed, along with each life stage, in Section II. Requirements for adults have been worked out based on the Factorial Approach, as well as the DLW and HRM methods. FAO/WHO/UNU (2004) have mostly adopted the HRM and DLW approach for all age groups. Their 1985 Committee had mostly used the factorial approach. The individual's BMR is calculated using prediction equations with body weight, as shown in Table 3.1. The requirements are given as PAL, which is 24-hours TEE divided by the predicted BMR.

Based on the concept of occupational activity pattern (that is, the kind of activity the individual indulges in to earn a living), three levels of activity have been defined—sedentary, moderate and heavy (Figure 3.5). In adults, PAL values have been calculated for each activity level, based on time spent in occupational activities and the intensity at which these are performed. PAL values greater than 2.4 are difficult to maintain over a prolonged period of time.

To prevent obesity, FAO/WHO/UNU (2004) recommends a PAL of 1.78 and above. Hence, all sedentary persons need to work towards becoming moderate workers! During pregnancy, energy requirements are calculated by adding the requirements for foetal growth and associated gain in the body weight of the woman, to the normal needs of an adult woman. BMR also increases during pregnancy, up to 5.3, 11.4 and 25.3 per cent during the first, second and third trimester

Figure 3.5: Levels of Activity

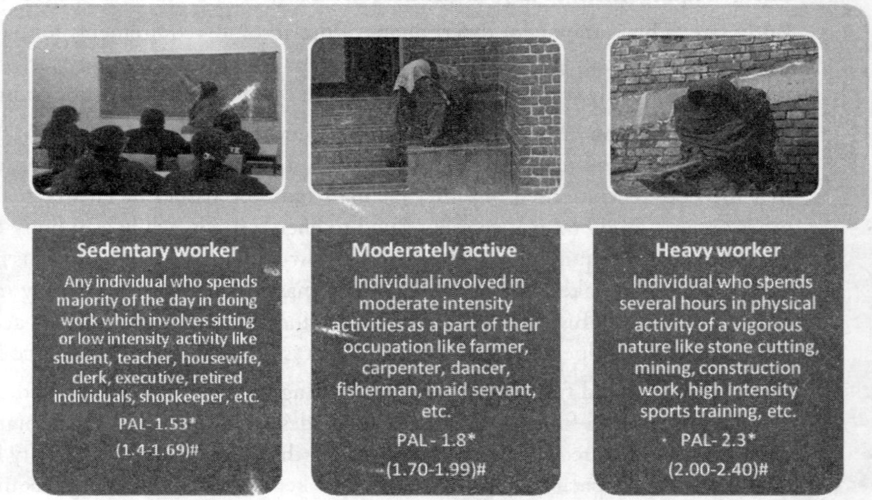

Sedentary worker
Any individual who spends majority of the day in doing work which involves sitting or low intensity activity like student, teacher, housewife, clerk, executive, retired individuals, shopkeeper, etc.
PAL-1.53*
(1.4-1.69)#

Moderately active
Individual involved in moderate intensity activities as a part of their occupation like farmer, carpenter, dancer, fisherman, maid servant, etc.
PAL-1.8*
(1.70-1.99)#

Heavy worker
Individual who spends several hours in physical activity of a vigorous nature like stone cutting, mining, construction work, high intensity sports training, etc.
PAL-2.3*
(2.00-2.40)#

Source: Gopalan et al. 1989, *ICMR 2010 and #FAO/WHO/UNU 2004.

of pregnancy, respectively (FAO/WHO/UNU 2004). Thus, the energy cost of pregnancy is calculated from the energy deposited in the body and the increase in TEE.

Energy cost of lactation is determined by the breast milk output and its energy content. Besides the energy content of breast milk and its efficiency of production, there is no additional requirement for a lactating woman, as compared to the non-pregnant non-lactating (NPNL) woman. Energy requirements during the first six months of lactation are higher than for the next 7–12 months as the milk output decreases; this is the period when the infant is no longer just dependant on the mother's milk for its nourishment, as the baby is weaned on to complementary feeds.

As we have no separate data on infant requirements available in India, we have adopted the requirements proposed by FAO/WHO/UNU (2004), which are based on the DLW method, to which energy deposition during growth have been added.

Similarly, the requirements for children and adolescents have been worked out by estimating TEE using DLW and HRM. Energy needed for growth (weight gain) is added to this estimate. The equations used to derive the TEE are given in Table 3.2.

The requirements given are based on ideal activity among children, and would be different for children who are physically highly active and those who primarily lead a sedentary lifestyle—use mechanised transport, do not participate in any organised sports, and spend their leisure time in front of a TV, computer or mobile phone/gaming device. Physical activity is vital for a child's normal physical growth and development. Teenagers should have a PAL of 1.8. To achieve this, they should participate daily in at least one hour of moderately intense sports activity like football, basketball, swimming, etc., in addition to spending at least one hour in a physical activity like walking/cycling, instead of taking motorised transport to school/market/tuition classes, etc. (if they are close to their homes). These activities need not be done at a stretch, and can be undertaken in bouts of 10–20 minutes, spread throughout the day.

Table 3.2: Calculating Total Energy Expenditure (TEE) of Infants and Children

Age Group	*TEE (MJ/day)*	*TEE (kcal/day)*
Infants (0–12 months)	−0.416 + 0.371 kg	−99.4 + 88.6 kg
Children and Adolescents		
Boys	1.298 + 0.265 kg – 0.0011 kg^2	310.2 + 63.3 kg – 0.263 kg^2
Girls	1.102 + 0.273 kg – 0.0019 kg^2	263.4 + 65.3 kg – 0.454 kg^2

Source: FAO/WHO/UNU 2004.

Equations taken from http://www.fao.org/3/a-y 5686e.pdf

The energy requirements for Indians of different age groups are given in Table 3.3.

Table 3.3: Recommended Dietary Allowances for Energy for Indians

Group	*Category / Age*	*Body Weight (kg)*	*Net Energy (kcal/d)*
	Sedentary work		2,320
Men	Moderate work	60	2,730
	Heavy work		3,490
	Sedentary work		1,900
	Moderate work	55	2,230
	Heavy work		2,850
Women	Pregnant	55+GWG*	+350
	Lactating 0–6 m		+600
	6–12 m	55+WG#	+520

Table 3.3 contd

Table 3.3 contd

Infants	0–6 months	5.4	92 kcal/kg/d
	6–12 months	8.4	80 kcal/kg/d
Children	1–3 years	12.9	1,060
	4–6 years	18.0	1,350
	7–9 years	25.1	1,690
Boys	10–12 years	34.3	2,190
Girls	10–12 years	35.0	2,010
Boys	13–15 years	47.6	2,750
Girls	13–15 years	46.6	2,330
Boys	16–17 years	55.4	3,020
Girls	16–17 years	52.1	2,440

Note: *GWG - gestational weight gain

WG – gestational weight gain remaining after delivery

The reference children for whom the requirement is given are assumed to have a moderate daily physical activity level.

Source: Nutrient Requirements and Recommended Dietary Allowances for Indians, ICMR 2010.

Energy Our Foods Provide

Typical Indian diets are based on plant foods. Carbohydrates in cereal grains contribute the most (50–80 per cent) to the energy intake of Indians. It is recommended that most of these be complex carbohydrates emanating from whole grains, vegetables and fruits, and less than 10 per cent of the energy be derived from simple carbohydrates like sugar and sugar-sweetened products. The amount of energy contributed by fats varies according to the economic status of the individual, being only about 5 per cent for a poor man and 30 per cent in the diet of an individual from an affluent family. Among the overweight and obese, the fat contribution is more than 30 en%. Calories from fat and fat-rich foods should not exceed 30 per cent of the total energy intake to prevent obesity and its co-morbidities.

High amounts of simple carbohydrates or fats in the diet are considered unhealthy because of their role in increasing the risk of chronic degenerative diseases like diabetes and cardiovascular disorders. Most Indian families derive nearly 10–12 per cent energy from proteins. Proteins should ideally not be used for providing energy, but should be used for tissue synthesis and growth.

Dietary fibre was earlier believed to be indigestible, and hence not a source of energy. However, we now know that dietary fibre undergoes fermentation in the colon due to the millions of bacteria residing there, resulting in the production of short chain fatty acids (butyric, propionic and acetic acids). These fatty acids can be utilised by the colonic cells, as well as be absorbed and used by the liver as a source of energy. So fibre that can be fermented produces 2 kcal/g. Thus, there is a need to recalculate the energy content of foods and diets.

Energy Balance and Health Consequences

You must have often heard friends or relatives expressing their fear of gaining weight after a lavish meal. It is difficult for individuals to maintain their energy balance on a day-to-day basis. On some days, one may eat more because of a celebration or a family outing; another day may pass without any significant physical activity. On yet another day, one may go for a marathon shopping trip, do some spring cleaning at home, or engage in outdoor games. These little bursts of increased physical activity or a few lazy Sundays will not really change our weight status. It is thus not essential to maintain energy balance on a daily basis. However, if the energy intake and expenditure is averaged out over a period of a week or a fortnight, there should be a **state of balance or equilibrium** among adults.

Adults who tend to maintain energy balance keep their body weights constant. Those who lose weight are spending more energy than they are consuming (**negative energy balance**). This means that their body reserves (fat stored in adipose tissue) are being used up to maintain the normal obligatory energy expenditure. This is often seen in the developing world, where food shortages lead to a low intake of calories, and consequent under-nutrition. Inadequate energy intake during childhood and adolescence results in a reduced body size (body weight and stature) and low body mass index (BMI). Both body fat and fat-free mass (muscles and bones) are decreased, as compared to a normally nourished individual.

Reduction in muscle mass leads to reduced skeletal muscle performance and a reduced work output. Adults with *chronic energy deficiency (CED)* have limited stamina—they tire easily and have decreased muscle strength. Low values of BMI in adults have been consistently associated with a decline in work output, productivity, and hence income-generating ability. Their ability to respond to stressful situations is also compromised, and thus these individuals (whether children or adults) usually have higher rates of mortality from infectious diseases (respiratory tract infections, diarrhoea and other gastrointestinal infections, etc.)

On the other hand, if the intake of energy is consistently higher than the expenditure over an extended period of time, it results in weight gain (**positive energy balance**). This is a major problem in people living in affluent countries, where food is available in plenty. India has a dual burden of under and overweight people. Weight gain is rapidly emerging as a public health problem in most developing countries as a result of better food security, but more because of increased mechanisation, and consequently less energy expenditure at work or while travelling. Weight gain leads to obesity, which is associated with a number of chronic disorders.

Abdominal obesity (excessive fat deposition in the abdominal area) in particular has been associated with increased insulin resistance (the body does not respond to the hormone insulin, which moves glucose into the cells for metabolism), and consequently an increase in blood glucose levels. This ultimately leads to diabetes mellitus. Obesity also increases the risk of hypertension, dyslipidemias (increased blood cholesterol and triglyceride levels), cardiovascular disease, gall bladder disease, some cancers, bone and joint diseases (as the joints, especially of the knees, of obese individuals have extra weight to bear), and sleep apnoea (inability to breathe normally during sleep, and thus suffering from a lack of oxygen). All of these are referred to as co-morbidities of obesity. Maintaining a moderate activity pattern (PAL =1.78) prevents obesity and its co-morbidities.

Weight, once gained, is very difficult to shed. Generally a dietician, in her/his clinical practice, would see that an intake of more than 1,500 kcal/day shows evidence of weight gain in some people. These probably are those people who land up in hospitals for weight maintenance after several cycles of weight loss and gain, usually very sedentary persons who are unable to lose weight permanently. This value is perhaps only 10–20 per cent above BMR. This level can be compared to the subsistence/ survival rations in natural disasters, which are supplied at 1,500 kcal for 15 days to a month. This is followed by a maintenance ration of 1,800 kcal. These rations do not include energy expenditure on income-generating activities.

Therefore, a knowledge of energy requirements is important. We need to spend energy well, if we want to eat well. What we eat needs to balance out with what we spend, to an extent that no weight gain is seen over a period of time. You will realise that this needs a dynamic and innovative approach towards life.

SUMMARY

- The body needs energy to carry out different metabolic activities, maintain the body temperature, and enable the body to perform physical activities.
- A bomb calorimeter is used to determine the heat evolved during combustion of food.
- Both Calories (measure of heat produced) and Joules (measure of work done) are used as the units for energy. 1 kcal = 4.184 kJ.
- Macronutrients like carbohydrates (4 kcal/g), fats (9 kcal/g) and proteins (4 kcal/g) provide energy to the body, while micronutrients like vitamins and minerals help the body to utilise this energy, as many of them function as coenzymes in energy metabolism.

- Carbohydrates are preferentially used as a source of energy, thus sparing proteins for tissue synthesis. Fat is a concentrated source of energy stored in the body in the form of adipose tissue.
- In the interest of preventing obesity and its co-morbidities like heart diseases, diabetes, hypertension, etc., the dietary fat should be less than 30 energy per cent (en %).
- Energy expenditure can be measured using the principles of calorimetry. Heat produced is measured in direct calorimetry using equipment like the metabolic chamber and suit calorimeter. Although easy in theory, this is very difficult and expensive in practice. Gaseous exchange during respiration is measured in indirect calorimetry using equipment like the Douglas bag, Max Planck apparatus, KM meter, Oxylog, and metabolic chamber.
- According to FAO/WHO/UNU (2004), the TEE should now be estimated by the heart-rate method or doubly labelled water technique. The factorial method, using individual costs as multiples of BMR, is a good field method.
- BMR has been computed from weight-dependent, age-specific equations. Calculations of energy expenditure using the factorial approach involve identifying the different activities like sleeping, resting, working, leisure activities, and other discretionary activities in a day. By using the time spent and energy cost of each activity, the total day's expenditure can be computed.
- The energy requirement of an individual is defined by FAO/WHO/UNU (2004) and ICMR (2010) as:

  > The level of energy intake from food that balances energy expenditure when the individual has a body size and composition and level of physical activity, consistent with long term good health, also allowing for maintenance of economically essential and socially desirable activity. In children and pregnant and lactating women, it includes the energy needs associated with the deposition of tissues or secretion of milk at rates consistent with good health.

- It is desirable to have moderate/ higher levels of physical activity, as physical activity is associated with good health. In adults, the goal should be to prevent weight gain.
- Energy is the only nutrient for which a safety factor is not added to the estimated average requirement while deriving the recommended dietary allowance (RDA).
- The three components of energy expenditure are BMR, SDA and physical activity. BMR is the largest component of energy expenditure, representing 45–70 per cent of the daily total energy expenditure.
- BMR is influenced by several factors like body surface area, age, gender, physiological states like growth and pregnancy, body temperature, physical activity, sleep, hormones, state of nutrition, and intake of caffeine and tobacco.
- Energy needs are dependent on a number of factors, such as age, gender, body size, adaptation, physical activity, altered physiological status such as pregnancy and lactation, and to some extent, climate.
- Based on the concept of occupational activity pattern (that is, the kind of activity the individual indulges in to earn a living), three levels of activity have been defined—sedentary, moderate and heavy.
- To prevent obesity, FAO/WHO/UNU (2004) recommends a PAL of 1.78 and above.
- Carbohydrates in cereal grains contribute the most (50–80 per cent) to the energy intake of Indians. It is recommended that most of these be complex carbohydrates emanating from whole grains, vegetables and fruits, and less than 10 per cent of the energy be derived from simple carbohydrates like sugar and sugar-sweetened products. Calories from fat and fat-rich foods should not exceed 30 per cent of the total energy intake to prevent obesity and its co-morbidities.
- Energy intake and expenditure needs to balance out in order for adults to maintain their body weights. During periods of growth, however, it is desirable to have a positive energy balance. Negative energy balance leads to weight loss and under-nutrition.
- If the intake of energy is consistently higher than expenditure over an extended period of time, it results in weight gain because of positive energy balance. Weight gain leads to the problem of being overweight and obesity. This has been associated with a number of chronic disorders, like increased insulin resistance, diabetes mellitus, hypertension, dyslipidemias, cardiovascular disease, gall bladder disease, some cancers, bone and joint diseases, and sleep apnoea.

KEY WORDS

Activity Energy Expenditure (AEE): The energy spent in performing various activities throughout the day. It is a component of the total energy expenditure (TEE).

Calorie (kcal): Heat required to raise the temperature of 1 kilogramme of water by 1°C from 14.5 °C to 15.5 °C.

Joule: The energy required to move 1 kilogramme of mass by 1 metre by a force of 1 Newton acting upon it.

Leisure Time Physical Activity (LTPA): The physical activity performed by individuals during their leisure or free time. It is an important contributor to the energy expended in a day.

Metabolism: The sum total of all chemical reactions that go on in living cells. Energy metabolism includes all reactions by which the body obtains and spends the energy derived from food.

Physical activity ratio (PAR): Expressed as a ratio of the energy cost of an individual activity per minute to the cost of the basal metabolic rate per minute.

Physical activity level (PAL): The ratio of energy expenditure for 24 hours and the BMR over 24 hours.

Total Daily Energy Expenditure (TDEE): Also called TEE (total energy expenditure), it is, as the term suggests, the total amount of energy spent in the entire day.

EXERCISES

1. Define energy requirement. What is meant by economically essential and socially desirable activities?
2. How is direct calorimetry different from indirect calorimetry?
3. What do you know about the 'doubly labelled water' technique? What is it used for?
4. What are the different components of energy expenditure?
5. Define BMR. What precautions would you take while measuring BMR?
6. Differentiate between BMR and RMR.
7. What is the difference between PAR and PAL? How is PAL calculated?
8. What are the principles of energy balance? Discuss the larger implications of energy balance.
9. 'Body composition changes with energy balance.' Comment on this statement.

REFERENCES

Byrd-Bredbenner, C., G. Moe, D. Beshgetoor, and J. Berning, *Wardlaw's Perspectives in Nutrition*, 9e, New York: McGraw-Hill International Edition, 2013.

FAO/WHO/UNU, 'Energy and Protein Requirements', Report of a Joint FAO/WHO/UNU Expert Consultation, Who Technical Report Series 724, Geneva, 1985.

————, 'Human Energy Requirements', Report of a Joint FAO/WHO/UNU Expert Consultation, Rome, 2001, Rome: FAO/WHO/UNU, 2004.

ICMR, 'Nutrient Requirements and Recommended Dietary Allowances for Indians', A report of the Expert Group of the Indian Council of Medical Research, 2010.

Rolfes, S. R., K. Pinna and E. Whitney, *Understanding Normal and Clinical Nutrition*, 8e, Wadsworth Cengage Learning, 2009.

Wasuja, M. G., 'Age related alterations in energy cost, energy requirement and energy status of affluent women (30-88 yrs) – A cross-sectional study', PhD Thesis, Lady Irwin College, University of Delhi, 2002.

WHO/FAO, 'Diet, Nutrition and Prevention of Chronic Diseases: Report of a Joint WHO/FAO Expert Consultation', Technical Report Series 916, Geneva, 2003.

4

CARBOHYDRATES

HIGHLIGHTS

- Types of carbohydrates
- Food sources
- Functions
- Dietary fibre
- Recommended allowances
- Problem of deficiency and excess

Carbohydrates contribute the most to the energy intake of individuals. This is because staple foods like cereals are rich in carbohydrates. In fact, all plant foods like legumes, fruits and vegetables provide ample carbohydrates. Chemically, carbohydrates are aldehyde or ketone derivatives of polyhydric alcohols. They occur as sugars or polymers of sugars such as starch, which can be hydrolysed to simple sugars by the action of digestive enzymes or by heating with dilute acids. Generally, but not as a rule, the hydrogen and oxygen in them are in the same proportion as in water (H_2O); hence the term 'carbo-hydrate' (that is, hydrates of carbon).

CLASSIFICATION OF CARBOHYDRATES

Carbohydrates can be classified based on the degree of structural complexity into mono-, di-, oligo-, and polysaccharides.

Monosaccharides, or simple sugars, consist of a single sugar unit (aldehyde or a ketone unit), which is not broken down further during digestion, for example ribose, glucose, fructose, mannose, and galactose. Monosaccharides are commonly found in foods like fruits and honey. Glucose, also known as dextrose, is found abundantly in fruits like grapes, strawberries, raspberries, and oranges, and in sweet corn and carrot. Fructose, also known as levulose or fruit sugar, is sweeter than cane sugar. It is found in honey, ripe fruits and some vegetables. Galactose is not found free in nature.

Disaccharides, or double sugars, consist of two sugar units (2 monosaccharides) bonded to each other. These include sugars like sucrose (table sugar), lactose (milk sugar) and maltose (malt sugar). Sucrose is made of two sugar units, glucose and fructose, and is found abundantly in sugarcane, beetroot and palm fruit. Sugar, commonly used as a sweetening agent, is nothing but sucrose. Lactose is present in milk and is made of one unit of glucose and one unit of galactose. Maltose is found in malted cereals and is made of two units of glucose.

Oligosaccharides are made of 3–9 sugar units. These are commonly found in pulses and legumes, for example raffinose, verbascose and stachyose. We cannot digest these, and consequently these reach the large intestine, where intestinal bacteria act on it and produce gas. That is why the consumption of whole pulses and legumes leads to flatulence.

Polysaccharides are long chains (more than nine units attached to each other) of sugar units. These are present in most foods in some form or the other. Polysaccharides are of two types—starch and non-starch polysaccharides. Starch polysaccharides are made of chains of glucose units attached to each other. Starch typically has two types of chains—amylose (straight chain) and amylopectin (branched chain)—and is present in plant foods like cereals, pulses, roots, and tubers. Glycogen, also known as animal starch, is made of highly branched chains of glucose. It is synthesised and stored in the liver and muscles of animals. Dextrins are breakdown products of starch, for instance, they are produced when flour is browned, bread is toasted, or during enzyme/ acid hydrolysis of starch.

Non-starch polysaccharides, also referred to as dietary fibre, include cellulose, hemicelluloses (found in stalks, leaves, seed covers), lignin (found in the woody part of plants, seeds), and pectins, gums and mucilages (found in fruits, vegetables and plant secretions).

In addition, there are sugar alcohols, which are derivatives of monosaccharides, like sorbitol, mannitol, xylitol, and inositol, and are used mainly as low calorie sweetening agents. Sugar alcohols do not lead to tooth decay, as they are not readily metabolised by bacteria in the mouth. They do not raise blood glucose levels significantly as they are absorbed and metabolised to glucose more slowly than sugars. However, as they cannot be completely absorbed, they tend to have a mildly laxative effect. They are fermented by the intestinal bacteria, and tend to draw water into the intestinal lumen. Hence, consumption in large quantities may lead to bloating and diarrhoea. Table 4.1 gives the food sources of different types of carbohydrates.

Table 4.1: Food Sources of Carbohydrates

Type of Carbohydrate	*Rich Sources*
Simple carbohydrates	
Fructose	Fruits, vegetables, honey, high fructose corn syrup (used to sweeten beverages and food products commercially)
Glucose	Fruits, vegetables, honey
Lactose	Milk and milk products
Sucrose	Table sugar, sugarcane, beetroot
Maltose	Malted/sprouted seeds, some alcoholic beverages
Sugar alcohols	Processed foods labelled as 'low calorie' or 'sugar free'
Complex carbohydrates	
Starch	Cereals grains, pulses, roots, and tubers
Resistant Starch	Whole legumes, beans, peas, oats, raw potato, unripe banana
Glycogen	Muscle tissues, liver
Soluble fibre	Oats, fruit pulp, legumes
Insoluble fibre	Whole grain cereals, seeds, beans, bran, stalks, peels and seeds of vegetables and fruits
Inulin	Wheat, onion, banana
β Glucan	Bran of grains like barley, oats, wheat
Oligosaccharides	
Raffinose	Beans, cabbage, brussels sprouts, broccoli, asparagus, other vegetables, whole grains
Fructooligosaccharides	Some fruits (banana), vegetables (onion, garlic, leek, asparagus), wheat, and barley
Stachyose	Green beans, soyabeans, some vegetables

Source: Byrd-Bredbenner et al. 2013; Rolfes et al. 2009.

Mono- and disaccharides are classified as simple carbohydrates, and oligo- and polysaccharides are classified as complex carbohydrates. Mono-, di- and starch polysaccharides are classified as digestible (available) carbohydrates, and oligo- and non-starch polysaccharides (fibre) are classified as indigestible (unavailable) carbohydrates.

FUNCTION OF CARBOHYDRATES

Foods rich in carbohydrates, like cereals, pulses, tubers, fruits, and vegetables, form an important part of our daily diet. Cooked carbohydrates are rapidly digested and absorbed. Hence, 97–98 per cent of the digestible carbohydrates are available to the body. The monosaccharides, glucose, fructose, and galactose, which are absorbed, are taken to the liver and converted into glycogen for storage. The blood circulates glucose all over the body, to be used as fuel for energy by the different tissues. Carbohydrates perform several important functions in our body.

> ***Resistant Starch***
>
> These starches escape digestion and absorption in the small intestine. They behave as dietary fibre, conferring similar health benefits. Consumption of foods containing natural resistant starch seems to positively affect weight management. Rich sources include whole legumes, beans, raw potato, and green banana.

1. The main function of carbohydrates is to **provide energy**. One gram of carbohydrate provides 4 kcal. Starch is digested and broken down into glucose. Glucose is then metabolised to release energy. Extra glucose is converted to glycogen and stored in the liver and muscle tissue.
   - The main source of energy for the **central nervous system** is glucose. Prolonged hypoglycaemia (low levels of sugar in the blood) has been known to lead to irreversible damage to the brain tissue.
   - Carbohydrates are also the main source of **energy for muscular work**. When muscles contract, they need energy, which is supplied by glycogen stored in them. Glycogen is broken down into lactic acid, and further oxidised to release energy if sufficient oxygen is available. If sufficient oxygen is not available, there is incomplete breakdown of glycogen, and lactic acid accumulates in muscles, leading to symptoms of soreness.
   - The **heart muscle** also uses glucose as a source of energy.
2. Several compounds in the body are carbohydrates or carbohydrate derivatives. Ribose, the pentose sugar (five carbon sugar), is a constituent of the cell's genetic material, RNA (ribonucleic acid) and DNA (deoxyribonucleic acid).
3. Carbohydrates have a protein-sparing action. Our body preferentially uses carbohydrate as a source of energy, sparing protein for tissue building. In weight-loss programmes, when adequate calories from carbohydrates are not consumed, protein gets oxidised as a source of energy.
4. Carbohydrates also help in the normal oxidation of fats. If carbohydrates are not eaten in sufficient quantity, fatty acids, instead of becoming completely oxidised to release energy, are converted to ketone bodies. If these ketone bodies accumulate in the blood and tissues, they produce a condition known as ketosis, which is commonly seen in diabetes. If not controlled, this can become a life-threatening condition.
5. Liver rich in glycogen is more resistant to certain poisons. Hence, glycogen protects the liver, as it has a **detoxifying action**. Glucuronic acid combines with toxins and facilitates their excretion from the body.
6. Dietary fibre helps in the **regulation of bowel movements**. It is beneficial in protecting the body from colorectal cancer, haemorrhoids, diverticulitis, and constipation. It also helps to **lower blood glucose and triglyceride levels** by decreasing their absorption, and helps the body to excrete more cholesterol, thereby lowering plasma cholesterol levels. For these reasons, indigestible carbohydrates are good for preventing and controlling diabetes and cardiovascular diseases.
7. Soluble fibre absorbs water and swells up. It delays the emptying of the stomach, thus making us feel sated. As it is indigestible, it lowers the energy density of the food it is present in. People who want to reduce their calorie intake for weight loss should hence eat high-fibre diets.

8. Some of the indigestible carbohydrates, like fructooligosaccharides and inulin, act as **prebiotics,** helping the growth of good bacteria in our gut.
9. Dietary fibre is fermented by the bacteria residing in our large intestine to **produce short chain fatty acids,** which can be absorbed and used as a source of energy. Soluble fibre undergoing fermentation in the colon would provide 2 kcal/ g of fibre. These fatty acids are good for the health of the intestinal mucosal cells.

DIETARY FIBRE

Dietary fibre is the portion of food derived from plant cells and analogous carbohydrates, which is resistant to hydrolysis/digestion by the enzymes produced by the human small intestine, but which may undergo complete or partial fermentation in the human large intestine. It consists of hemicellulose, cellulose, lignins, oligosaccharides, pectins, gums and waxes, and associated plant substances. Dietary fibre is of two types—soluble and insoluble . Both are indigestible, but soluble fibre dissolves in water, as opposed to the insoluble fibre, which does not. Table 4.2 compares the properties of soluble and insoluble fibres.

Table 4.2: Difference between Soluble and Insoluble Dietary Fibre

Parameter	*Soluble Fibre*	*Insoluble Fibre*
Solubility in water	Soluble	Insoluble
Types	Pectins, gums, mucilages	Cellulose, hemicelluloses, lignin
Action on gut motility	Increases transit time, delays gastric emptying, and hence gives a feeling of fullness	Decreases transit time in the colon and ensures regular frequency of emptying of bowel
Fermentability	More easily fermented	Fermented to a lesser degree
Health benefits	Lowers blood glucose, triglycerides and cholesterol	Prevents colorectal cancer, haemorrhoids, diverticulitis, irritable bowel syndrome, and constipation
Food sources	Fleshy part of fruits and vegetables, cereals like oats	Bran of cereals, seed coat of legumes, seeds and peels of fruits and vegetables, stalks of green leafy vegetables

Source: Byrd-Bredbenner et al. 2013; Rolfes et al. 2009.

Another term generally used, especially when estimating the fibre content of foods, is **Crude fibre,** which is the residue remaining after the treatment of food with sulphuric acid, alkali and alcohol. Its major component is cellulose. Figure 4.1 presents the fibre content of commonly eaten foods.

Figure 4.1: Fibre Content of Commonly Consumed Foods.

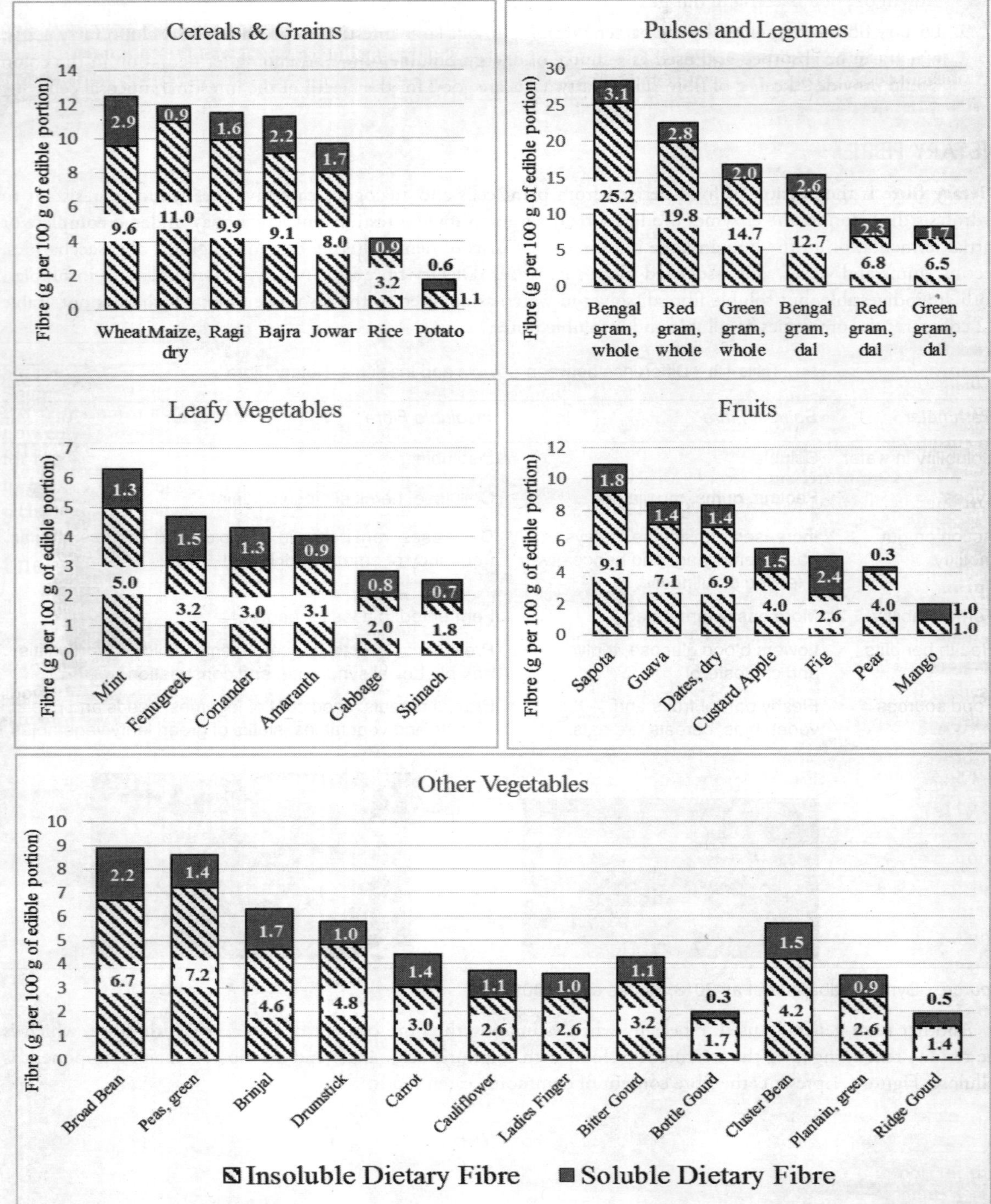

Source: Data taken from Gopalan et al. 1989.

RECOMMENDED DIETARY ALLOWANCES

It is usually recommended that 60–70 per cent of calories in a normal diet come from carbohydrates. One needs to consume 130 g of carbohydrates per day to supply glucose, which is the sole source of energy for the central nervous system, and to prevent the condition of ketosis. A minimal 50–100 g/day of carbohydrates is necessary for the complete breakdown of fats in the body, although about 300 g of carbohydrate is recommended for normal daily intake (Food and Nutrition Board 2002). Blood glucose levels also need to be maintained within a certain range (70–100 mg/dl). This control is brought about by two hormones—insulin and glucagon. Glucose that is not used by the body to provide energy is stored in the form of glycogen in the liver and muscles. When the storage capacity of both these tissues is exceeded, the extra glucose is converted to fat and deposited in the adipose tissues.

The amount of dietary fibre recommended for a normal healthy adult is 30–40 g/day. About half of this dietary fibre should come from cereals, and the other half from fruits and vegetables.

The ICMR (2010) does not give recommendations for different age groups. The type of carbohydrate to be included in the diet is more important than the quantity. We should include less of simple carbohydrates (sugars and products made from sugar, like soft drinks, jams, jelly, sweets, candy, etc.) and more of complex fibre-rich carbohydrates (whole grain cereals and pulses, fruits and vegetables). The WHO Committee on Chronic Degenerative Diseases (2003) has recommended a daily intake of 30 g of fibre. A level of 40 g / 2,000 kcal of dietary fibre is generally considered a safe level of intake.

Read Food Labels

When selecting processed foods, we must study the nutrition information on the label and avoid foods that have high total calories and carbohydrates or high sugars.

Choose products wisely. If there is a choice between juices, one with added sugar and one without, choose the latter. Similarly, select products with whole wheat flour and not refined. Fibre-rich foods are also healthy, so look for the amount of fibre.

HEALTH SIGNIFICANCE OF CARBOHYDRATES

We have seen how important carbohydrates are as a major supplier of energy, and for the normal metabolism of other macronutrients like fat and protein in our body. Dietary fibre, or the non-starch polysaccharides, play a special role, and have health promoting effects. In fact, fibre is considered a functional food. You may have come across psyllium husk, wheat bran, and several other products of fibre in the market. Let us learn a little more about the protective role of dietary fibre in our diet.

Dietary fibre has the ability to retain water and swell up. The swelling up of soluble fibre increases the viscosity of the intestinal contents, and slows down the passage of food through the stomach. As food stays longer in the stomach, there is a feeling of fullness or satiety when we eat a meal rich in soluble fibre. Hence, fibre is very good for people who want to control or lose weight, as it prevents them from overeating and, at the same time, does not contribute majorly to the calorie intake. Remember, it is indigestible and hence cannot be absorbed and metabolised to provide energy, even though it is technically a carbohydrate. Fermentation, especially of soluble fibres produces short chain fatty acids like acetate, propionate and butyrate. Acetate and propionate can actually be absorbed and metabolised by the liver to generate energy. Butyrate is the main substrate for the growth and metabolism of mucosal cells. Fermented soluble fibre can provide 2 kcal/g of fibre.

The insoluble fibre, and dietary fibre in general, increases faecal bulk and contributes to soft stools and ease of defecation. As the fibre intake increases, the transit time of intestinal contents decreases in the colon, and there is regular emptying of the bowel. People who eat a diet rich in dietary fibre do not suffer from constipation. Cereal bran is more effective than fruits and vegetables for relieving constipation. This is because fibre increases the faecal bulk, which helps in stimulating the intestinal mucosa by a mechanical effect (as the bulky faeces is touching the walls of the intestine, the nerves and muscles get stimulated, and encourage peristaltic movement). In the large intestine, millions of bacteria reside and feed on the undigested matter. The by-products of bacterial fermentation also help to stimulate the mucosa.

Decrease in the transit time of intestinal contents in the lower part of the intestine has other benefits besides the prevention of constipation. It decreases the time for which the mucosa is exposed to the harmful by-products formed/released during the process of digestion. It also decreases the time which the bacteria get to act on the faecal matter, producing harmful substances. This greatly decreases the risk of colon cancer in people consuming fibre-rich diets.

Dietary fibre also provides relief from disorders like irritable bowel syndrome, gall stones, haemorrhoids, and diverticulitis. In populations with a low-fibre intake, problems like haemorrhoids and diverticulosis are widely prevalent. This is because the faeces does not have sufficient bulk in a low-fibre diet to sufficiently stimulate the mucosal lining. This leads to constipation and straining to pass stool. Constant straining leads to the condition known as piles or haemorrhoids. Similarly, lack of stimulation decreases muscle tone, resulting in distortions in the colon wall. Little pouches called diverticuli develop, in which food gets stuck, and bacterial action leads to the production of harmful substances, which in turn lead to inflammation and symptoms of abdominal pain (diverticulitis).

A soluble fibre-rich diet helps in lowering blood glucose and triglyceride levels, simply because fibre acts as a physical barrier between food and enzymes, decreasing the digestion and absorption of carbohydrates and fats. Fibre binds faecal bile acids and increases the excretion of bile acid-derived cholesterol. It thus helps to throw out more of the bad cholesterol (Low density lipoprotein, LDL). As a consequence there is a lowering of the serum cholesterol levels. This is how it happens—if there is not enough fibre in the diet, the bile acids secreted as a part of bile juice into the small intestine during the process of digestion are reabsorbed, and taken back to the liver to formulate bile juice again. However, when there is sufficient fibre, the bile acids get bound to, and then excreted with, the fibre in the faeces, and do not return to the liver in sufficient quantity. The liver is then forced to make fresh bile acids, for which it needs cholesterol. The liver takes the cholesterol from the blood, lowering serum cholesterol levels in the process. This also prevents the formation of gall stones in the gall bladder.

Thus, dietary fibre is protective against and helpful in relieving symptoms of diabetes mellitus and cardiovascular diseases like hyperglycemia (high blood glucose levels), hypertriglyceridemia (high levels of triglycerides or fats in the blood) and hypercholesterolemia (high levels of cholesterol in the blood).

However, eating too much (> 60 g/day) of dietary fibre can also create problems. As fibre tends to absorb a lot of water, the fluid intake needs to be increased along with the fibre, as otherwise it results in hard, dry stools. Absorption of nutrients is delayed by fibre in the gut as it acts as a physical barrier between the enzymes and the nutrients, slowing down the process of digestion. Polysaccharides and lignins interact with metal ions like iron, calcium and zinc, and hence these cannot be absorbed. It may also cause irritation in the bowel and may lead to diarrhoea.

Energy Balance

The major concern regarding carbohydrate intake is whether we are able to maintain energy balance. The amount of energy consumed should be equal to the amount of energy spent by us. Only then will we neither gain nor lose weight. Adults should be in a state of energy balance. In fact, people of all ages have to be conscious about the kind of carbohydrates they are consuming. As mentioned earlier, eating foods rich in simple carbohydrates or 'junk foods', like sugar-sweetened beverages, candies, desserts, ice cream, biscuits, etc., whose major ingredient is a refined carbohydrate like *maida* (refined wheat flour) and sugar, would just give us 'empty calories', that is, only calories and no other nutrients in any significant quantity. Some of these foods are also rich in fat, which makes them even more energy-dense. If such foods replace the more nutritious foods in the diet, then the diet quality, and consequently health, suffers.

High intake of sugars and refined carbohydrates can increase the risk of weight gain and obesity. Obesity in turn increases the risk of diabetes and cardiovascular diseases. High intake of sugar, especially fructose, has also been associated with an increase in serum triglycerides. Similarly, a diet high in sugars has been linked to hyperactivity in children. Although the research evidence for this is not conclusive, it helps to reduce these carbohydrates in the diet of children, and replace junk foods with healthier alternatives. For adults who want to lose weight or simply control blood sugar levels, non-nutritive (not having any nutritional value) sweetening agents are available, which do not provide any calories (or very few calories). These sweeteners can replace sugar in the diet (Box 4.1). However, these sweeteners are not safe for consumption by children. Aspartame, an artificial sweetener which contains the amino acid phenylalanine, also cannot be consumed by people suffering from Phenylketonuria, a disorder in which individuals cannot metabolise phenylalanine.

Box 4.1: Low/Zero Calorie Sweeteners

To reduce the intake of calories from carbohydrates, people are generally advised to reduce the amount of simple carbohydrates in their diet. The first item to be struck off the list is sugar. However, for people used to sweet tea and other beverages and dishes, this restriction is difficult to comply with. Alternative sweeteners are, however, available, which do not raise blood glucose levels and do not provide any calories. Commonly used synthetic sweeteners include saccharin, Aspartame, Acesulfame-K, and Sucralose. Stevioside is a naturally occurring sweetener extracted from Stevia leaves. Although these sweeteners offer an alternative to diabetics and those who wish to reduce their calorie intake, one must be cautious and not consume too much of these sweeteners. Exceeding the Acceptable Daily Intakes (ADIs) can lead to toxicity. Saccharin, at one point, was linked to bladder cancer, while aspartame consumption in certain studies led to side effects like headache, nausea and dizziness.

ADI is the amount of the sweetener that an individual can safely consume daily over a lifetime. ADIs are generally expressed as mg of the sweetener per kg of body weight per day, for example, ADI of saccharin is only 5 mg/ kg body weight/ day, for sucralose it is 15 mg/kg/day, while for aspartame it is 40 mg/kg/day, according to the Joint Expert Committee on Food Additives (JECFA).

Dental Caries

High-sugar diets are known to increase the risk of dental caries (cavities). Our mouth is inhabited by bacteria, which feed on the food that remains stuck in our teeth. They produce acids, which slowly start dissolving the enamel of the teeth, causing decay. When the cavity reaches the nerve endings in our teeth, it produces pain and discomfort. Sticky and gummy foods high in sugar tend to stick to the teeth and are more likely to promote dental caries. Sipping juice, soft drinks and even milk (which has lactose) throughout the day bathes the teeth in sugar, and increases the risk of caries. That is why letting a child go to sleep after consuming milk from a milk bottle, without first rinsing his mouth, is discouraged. For the same reason, everyone should brush their teeth thoroughly before sleeping at night. Otherwise, throughout the night the bacteria will feed on the sugars and starch from refined foods, and produce acid which thins the enamel. Brushing teeth in the morning is important to throw out the bacteria, acid, and other waste products that have been formed by bacterial action overnight. Flossing is also important to remove food stuck in between teeth.

Lactose Intolerance

Lactase is an enzyme produced in the small intestine, which digests lactose (milk sugar). With age, the quantity of this enzyme generally tends to decrease. People who have low levels of this enzyme are not able to digest and absorb lactose. When the undigested lactose reaches the large intestine, the resident bacteria act on it, leading to symptoms of flatulence (gas), bloating and diarrhoea. This is known as lactose intolerance, and people suffering from this condition are unable to consume milk and products made from milk. Studies have, however, shown that these individuals may be able to tolerate curd, fermented milk products, and some kinds of cheese, because a major portion of the lactose in these foods has been converted to lactic acid by the bacteria or other microorganisms added during the processing of these foods.

SUMMARY

- Carbohydrates are organic compounds basically made of carbon, hydrogen and oxygen. Generally, the hydrogen and oxygen in them are in the same proportion as in water (H_2O); hence the term 'carbo-hydrate' (that is, hydrates of carbon).
- Carbohydrates can be classified based on the degree of complexity of structure into mono, di, oligo, and polysaccharides.
- **Monosaccharides** or simple sugars consist of a single sugar unit which is not broken down further during digestion, for example ribose, glucose, fructose, mannose, and galactose.
- **Disaccharides** or double sugars consist of two sugar units (2 monosaccharides) bonded to each other. These include sugars like sucrose (table sugar), lactose (milk sugar) and maltose (malt sugar).
- **Oligosaccharides** are made of 3–9 sugar units. These are commonly found in pulses and legumes, for example raffinose, verbascose and stachyose.
- **Polysaccharides** are long chains (more than nine units attached to each other) of sugar units. These are present in most foods in some form or the other. Polysaccharides are of two types—**starch and non-starch polysaccharides.** Starch polysaccharides include starch and glycogen, while non-starch polysaccharides include cellulose, hemicelluloses, pectins, gums, and mucilages (also known as dietary fibre).
- **Sugar alcohols**, like sorbitol, mannitol, xylitol, and inositol, are used mainly as low calorie-sweetening agents.
- The main function of carbohydrates is to provide energy. One gram of carbohydrate provides 4 kcal. It is the main source of energy for the brain, the central nervous system, heart, and other muscles.
- Ribose, the pentose sugar (5 carbon sugar), is a constituent of the cell's genetic material, RNA (ribonucleic acid) and DNA (deoxyribonucleic acid). Carbohydrates have a protein sparing action. Our body preferentially uses carbohydrate as a source of energy, sparing protein for tissue building. Carbohydrates are also important for the normal metabolism of fats. They protect our bodies from certain toxins.
- Dietary fibre also has several health benefits. Insoluble dietary fibre helps maintain normal bowel movements, prevents constipation, and decreases the risk of colon cancer, diverticulitis and painful haemorrhoids. Soluble fibre promotes satiety, helps in weight management, and decreases the risk of diabetes and cardiovascular diseases by lowering blood sugar, triglycerides and cholesterol levels.
- About 130 g/day of carbohydrates needs to be consumed to supply glucose, which is the sole source of energy for the central nervous system, and to prevent the condition of ketosis; although about 300 g of carbohydrate is recommended as the normal daily intake for adults. About 40 g of dietary fibre/2,000 kcal is generally considered a safe level of intake.
- The major concern regarding carbohydrate intake is whether we are able to maintain energy balance. A high intake of sugars and refined carbohydrates can increase the risk of weight gain and obesity. Obesity in turn increases the risk of diabetes and cardiovascular diseases. Synthetic sweeteners, which have no or very low amounts of calories, can be used by people trying to cut down on sugar intake.
- High-sugar diets are known to increase the risk of dental caries (cavities).
- People suffering from lactose intolerance are unable to consume milk and products made from milk as they lack the enzyme lactase, which is needed for digesting the milk sugar, lactose.

KEY WORDS

Acceptable Daily Intake (ADI): The amount of food additive (here, sweetener) that an individual can safely consume daily over a lifetime. ADIs are generally expressed as mg of the sweetener per kg of body weight per day.

Adipose tissue: A tissue containing masses of fat cells. Fat in our body is stored in this tissue.

Colorectal cancer: Cancer of the colon or rectum.

Constipation: Difficulty in passing stool, or passing infrequent stools which are unduly hard and dry.

Diverticulosis: A condition in which many small pouches or diverticula start extruding through the exterior wall of the large intestine.

Diverticulitis: Inflammation of the diverticula, caused by the growth of bacteria on food residues stuck on these pouches.

Flatulence: Excessive gas in the stomach and intestines.

Glycemic index: A method of classifying foods according to their potential for raising blood sugar.

Hemorrhoids: Or piles, are a mass of dilated veins in the anal area.

Ketosis: The accumulation of ketone bodies, which results as a consequence of incomplete metabolism of fatty acids. This condition is seen in starvation, carbohydrate deficiency, and high fat diets, but most commonly in diabetes.

Satiety: The feeling of fullness and satisfaction that one gets after eating food.

EXERCISES

1. What are simple sugars? Give examples of simple sugars, along with their food sources.
2. What are oligosaccharides? In which foods would you find them?
3. Differentiate between soluble and insoluble fibre.
4. What are the different types of alternate sweeteners that can be used in food products to cut back on calories in our meals?
5. Describe the functions of carbohydrates in our body.
6. What are dental caries and why are they caused?
7. Explain the health benefits of consuming soluble fibre.

REFERENCES

Byrd-Bredbenner, C., G. Moe, D. Beshgetoor, and J. Berning, *Wardlaw's Perspectives in Nutrition*, 9e, New York: McGraw-Hill International Edition, 2013.

FAO/WHO, 'Joint FAO/WHO Expert Consultation on Fats and Fatty Acids in Human Nutrition', Interim Summary of Conclusions and Dietary Recommendations on Total Fat and Fatty Acids, 10–14 November, Geneva: WHO, 2008.

Food and Nutrition Board, *Dietary reference intakes for energy, carbohydrate, fiber, fat, fatty acids, cholesterol, protein, and amino acids*, Washington, D. C.: National Academy Press, 2002.

Gopalan, C., B. V. Rama Sastri and S. C. Balasubramanian, *Nutritive value of Indian foods*, B. S. Narasinga Rao, Y. G. Deosthale and K. C. Pant (revised and updated), Hyderabad: National Institute of Nutrition, Indian Council of Medical Research.

ICMR, 'Nutrient Requirements and Recommended Dietary Allowances for Indians', A report of the Expert Group of the Indian Council of Medical Research, 2010.

Rolfes, S. R., K. Pinna and E. Whitney, *Understanding Normal and Clinical Nutrition*, 8e, Wadsworth Cengage Learning, 2009.

WHO/FAO, 'Diet, Nutrition and Prevention of Chronic Diseases: Report of a Joint WHO/FAO Expert Consultation', Technical Report Series 916, Geneva, 2003.

5

LIPIDS

HIGHLIGHTS

- Types of Lipids
- Functions
- Food Sources
- Recommended Allowances
- Health Significance

Lipids or fats are present in nearly all the food that we eat. They add a special flavour to food, which is why deep fried snacks are relished by most of us. Fats increase the energy density of foods so that even small portion sizes give us a feeling of satiety. Inside the body they have several functions to perform—they are a component of all cell membranes, help in the synthesis of hormones and other useful substances. Yet consuming fats in more than recommended amounts can have negative consequences on our health. Let us learn some interesting facts about this macronutrient in our diet.

Lipids are a heterogenous group of substances including fats, oils and fat-like substances that are greasy and insoluble in water but soluble in certain organic solvents such as ether, alcohol, chloroform and benzene. This property of being insoluble in water sets lipids apart from carbohydrates and proteins. Fats are basically organic compounds made of carbon, hydrogen and oxygen. The lipids present in our diet are mainly the triglycerides and some amounts of phospholipids and sterols.

Fatty acids are the main constituents of all lipids. They consist of chains of carbon atoms with a methyl (–CH3) group at one end and a carboxyl (–COOH) group at the other.

TYPES OF FATTY ACIDS

Fatty acids can be classified based on a number of features.

Classification Based on Carbon Chain Length

> ***Numbering Fatty Acids***
>
> Stearic acid, for instance, is written as (18:0). The numeral before the colon indicates the number of carbon atoms in the chain, and the numeral after the colon depicts the number of double bonds. Thus, 18:0 means that stearic acid has 18 carbon atoms in the chain with no double bonds.

Most fatty acids present in foods and in our body are straight, even numbered carbon chains between 4 to 24 carbon atoms long. Based on the length of the carbon chain, fatty acids can be classified as short, medium and long chain fatty acids. **Short chain fatty acids** are usually less than 6 carbon atoms in length. Examples include butyric acid, found in milk fat, ghee and butter. These are rapidly digested, and can be directly absorbed from the intestines into the blood circulation. **Medium chain fatty acids** contain between 6 and 10 carbon atoms, for example, caproic, caprylic and capric acids present in milk fat, coconut oil and palm kernel oil. These are also rapidly digested and directly absorbed from the intestines into the blood circulation. **Long chain fatty acids** have 12 or more carbon atoms. These include lauric (12:0), myristic (14:0), palmitic (16:0), stearic (18:0), oleic (18:1), linoleic (18:2), and linolenic (18:3) acids. These are found in all the vegetable oils we use for cooking. Most fatty acids present in animal tissues contain 16–26 carbon atoms. They take the longest to digest, and are absorbed and transported through the lymphatic system.

Classification Based on Degree of Saturation

Based on the degree of saturation in the carbon chain, the fatty acids can be classified as saturated or unsaturated. A **saturated fatty acid** is one in which each carbon atom in the chain has two hydrogen atoms and two carbon atoms attached to it. In other words, the valency of the carbon atom (that is, 4) is satisfied without the need for a double or triple bond. For instance, palmitic (16:0) and stearic acid (18:0) are fatty acids. Foods that are rich in saturated fatty acids include full fat milk and its products, butter, ghee, hydrogenated vegetable oil, coconut oil, palm kernel oil, and red meat and its products. Oils rich in saturated fatty acids tend to be solid at room temperature. That is why ghee, butter, *vanaspati* and coconut oil (especially in winters) are solid, as opposed to vegetable oils, which have more of unsaturated fatty acids. A hydrogen atom is missing from each of the two adjoining carbon atoms in an **unsaturated fatty acid,** thus necessitating a double bond between the carbon atoms. Unsaturated fatty acids are of two types—monounsaturated and polyunsaturated fatty acids.

Monounsaturated fatty acids (MUFA) are those which have only one double bond in the chain, for example oleic acid (18:1), which is found in food and body fats. MUFA-rich vegetable oils include red palm oil, palmolein, groundnut oil, sesame, olive, canola, ricebran, and cottonseed oil. **Polyunsaturated fatty acids (PUFA)** contain two or more double bonds in their carbon chain, for instance, linoleic (18:2) and linolenic (18:3) acids, with two and three double bonds, respectively, in an 18-carbon chain. All vegetable oils are rich in PUFA, except for coconut oil. Corn oil, safflower and sunflower oils are especially rich in PUFA.

Classification Based on Shape of the Carbon Chain

The shape of the carbon chain varies with saturation. Saturated and trans fatty acids have straight carbon chains, and unsaturated cis fatty acids have bent or carbon chains with kinks. The cis and trans forms are geometric isomers. Fatty acids normally exist in the **cis form** in food and in our body. The **trans form** is usually formed during the process of hydrogenation of vegetable oils to produce saturated fats. *Vanaspati*, margarine and bakery fats are examples of hydrogenated vegetable oils that have large amounts of trans fatty acids. Some trans fats may form naturally in meat and milk fat, as a result of microbial conversion. Structurally, the cis form of the fatty acid molecule is folded back upon itself at each double bond. The hydrogens attached to the double-bonded carbons are on the same side as the carbon chain. The trans form of the molecule, on the contrary, extends to its maximum length, is a straight chain, and resembles a saturated fatty acid. The hydrogens next to the double bonds are on the opposite sides of the carbon chain. The difference in the spatial arrangement of the molecules influences the melting point and other properties of the fats.

Classification Based on Nutritional Properties

Essential fatty acids are those that cannot be synthesised by the human body, but are very important for growth and development. The two essential fatty acids are linoleic (lin or n-6/omega 6) and linolenic (len or n-3/omega 3). The omega (ω or n) system of naming fatty acids indicates the position of the first double bond closest to the methyl (omega) end of the chain. These essential fatty acids in the body are converted to long chain fatty acids, for instance, arachidonic acid (AA) is formed from linoleic acid, while alpha-linolenic acid forms eicosapentaenoic acid (EPA) and docosahexaenoic acid (DHA). These long chain fatty acids are the precursors of eicosanoids, which are a group of hormone-like compounds (for example, prostaglandins, prostacyclins, thromboxanes, etc.). They play a role in the regulation of blood pressure, contraction of smooth muscles, transmission of nerve impulses, and many other functions.

Foods rich in essential fatty acids include fish liver oil, green leafy vegetables, seaweeds, algae, barley, oats and corn, cottonseed, safflower, and soyabean oils. Cereals and legumes in the Indian diet contribute to half the essential fatty acid requirement. All other fatty acids are considered non-essential, as they can be synthesised in the body.

> ***Fats versus Oils***
>
> The term 'Fat' is generally used for lipids which are solid at room temperature, whereas 'oil' is used for lipids which are liquid at room temperature. Fats typically have more of saturated fatty acids, while oils have greater proportions of unsaturated fatty acids. Saturated fatty acids are straight chained, and hence can be tightly packed together; hence, they are firm and do not melt at room temperature. Unsaturated carbon chains have kinks in their structure and cannot be tightly packed. This loose packing makes them soft or liquid at room temperature.

TYPES OF LIPIDS

A variety of lipids in our diet present themselves for digestion in the gut. Most of the lipid is in the form of **triglycerides,** also known as **triacylglycerols**. In addition, a small fraction of cholesterol esters, cholesterol, plant sterols, and fat-soluble vitamins are also present. The third type of lipid in the food is phospholipids, like lecithin.

> ***Cholesterol***
>
> Cholesterol is a sterol found in animal tissues. It is not found in plant food. Cholesterol is synthesised in our body and we also obtain it from our diet. It is an important component of cell membranes and used for the synthesis of hormones, Vitamin D, bile, and other important substances. However, high blood levels of cholesterol are undesirable, as they increase the risk of cardiovascular diseases.

Lipids can be classified into simple, compound and derived lipids. **Simple lipids** are esters of glycerol and fatty acids, and include glycerides and waxes. Glycerol is a three-carbon alcohol with three hydroxyl or alcoholic groups (–OH), each of which can combine with a fatty acid to form an ester. A monoglyceride is formed when one fatty acid combines with one –OH group of the glycerol molecule. If two fatty acids combine, it is called a diglyceride, and if three fatty acids combine, one to each of the OH groups, then it is known as a triglyceride. Triglycerides are the most common types of fats present in food and the body. They can be of two types—simple and mixed triacylglycerols. Simple triacylglycerols are those in which all three fatty acids attached to the glycerol molecule are the same. In mixed triacylglycerols, at least two out of three fatty acids are different. These account for 98 per cent of fat in foods, and more than 90 per cent of fat in the body.

Waxes, on the other hand, are esters of fatty acids and long chain or cyclic alcohols (as opposed to the glycerol present in glycerides). The most commonly known animal wax is beeswax, a major component of which is the ester myricylpalmitate, used in constructing honeycombs. Spermaceti occurs in large amounts in the head of the sperm whale. One of its main constituents is cetylpalmitate. Lanolin is a wax obtained from wool, consisting of esters of sterols.

Compound lipids are esters of glycerol and fatty acids, with substitution of other components such as carbohydrates, phosphate or nitrogenous groupings. For example, phospholipids like lecithin and cephalin, in which one of the fatty acids in the molecule is replaced by phosphate and nitrogen grouping; glycolipids like cerebrosides, which contain a carbohydrate component in their structure; and lipoproteins, which include a variety of lipid molecules bound to protein molecules, in order to facilitate transport in the aqueous medium of blood.

Derived lipids are substances liberated during the hydrolysis of simple and compound lipids, which still retain the properties of lipids. These include fatty acids, alcohols (glycerol and sterols), monoglycerides and diglycerides, steroids, terpenes, and carotenoids.

Fats are also classified based on the kind of fatty acids they contain. So if a fat contains large amounts of saturated fatty acids, then the fat is termed saturated fat. Fat in our diet can be **visible fat,** which we can see, for example, butter, cooking oil, ghee, etc. It is termed **invisible fat** if it is present inside a food and cannot be seen with the naked eye. Examples include the fat present in cereals, pulses, nuts, etc.

FUNCTIONS

Many of us believe that fat is not a good thing to eat, and the less we eat, the better for us. However, we must realise that fats perform many important functions in our body, and that all kinds of fats are not bad. It is the kind and total quantity of the fat we eat which we have to monitor.

1. The primary function of fat is to **provide energy**. One gram of fat gives us 9 kcal. It is the most concentrated source of energy, since carbohydrates and proteins just give us 4 kcal/g. This helps in reducing the bulk of diets, especially for children, who cannot eat a large quantity of food to meet their energy requirements. Adding a little amount of fat to a dish increases its energy density.
2. It is the **body's chief reserve of energy**. Fat is stored in the adipose tissue in our body, to be used when the need arises. Adipose tissue is present subcutaneously, in the abdominal cavity, surrounding the organs, and even laced throughout the muscle tissue. Excess glucose or amino acids in the body are also converted to fats and stored. Did you know that the human body can survive 30–40 days of starvation if it has sufficient stores of fat? Although it is important to have some body fat reserves, very small and large stores can pose numerous health risks.
3. All body cells contain some fat. Cell membranes have lipids that facilitate the transfer of nutrients. Phospholipids are in fact responsible for the integrity of cell membranes. Essential fatty acids and cholesterol are also important structural components of the cell membranes. Fat is very much a **part of the structure of our bodies**. In healthy, non-obese women, fat comprises about 18–25 per cent of body weight. In healthy, non-obese men, fat makes up 15–20 per cent of the body weight. As one ages, the proportion of fat tends to increase in the body.
4. Lipids are also required for the **synthesis of important substances** in our body, like cerebrosides (galactose-containing lipids), which are components of the myelin sheath of nerves and the white matter of brain; gangliosides (glucose and galactose containing lipids), which are constituents of brain tissue and synaptic membranes at nerve endings; cholesterol, which helps in the synthesis of provitamin D, bile salts, and hormones like adenocorticoids and sex hormones.
5. **Essential fatty acids** and long chain PUFA synthesised from them, like DHA, also play special roles in the body, as mentioned earlier. DHA is vital for the normal development and maturation of the nervous system and retina, in foetal life and infancy. In fact, throughout life, it helps to regulate nerve transmission and communication. Eicosanoids, which are made from essential fatty acids, act as hormones, and control more than 100 different functions, like blood pressure, blood clotting, immune responses, inflammatory responses, regulation of body temperature, etc.
6. The adipose tissue layer present under our skin provides **insulation** to the body, decreasing the loss of body heat in cold weather. This is because fat is a poor conductor of heat. This means that obese individuals would not feel so cold in winters; however, in summers, they would experience greater discomfort, as their body would not be able to lose heat easily.
7. Fat present as **padding** or packing around vital organs like kidneys keeps them from jostling around when we move, and hence from getting injured. It also protects bones against physical injury by providing a cushioning effect if we fall, or get hit.
8. Fat also acts as a **lubricant** for the gastrointestinal tract, allowing the easy passage of food.
9. Fat tends to decrease gastric motility, and the food remains in the stomach for a longer time. This delays the onset of hunger sensations and provides **satiety**.
10. The **palatability** or taste of the food improves with the addition of fat. Fat in meat, fish and poultry lends its own characteristic flavour. Fried food generally tastes better than food that has been cooked without fat.
11. Dietary fat is a **carrier of fat-soluble vitamins** (A, D, E, and K). Some amount of fat is necessary for their absorption, and hence a zero or very low-fat diet is not considered very healthy.

Box 5.1: Role of Fatty Acids in Early Growth and Development

There is mounting evidence in favour of the crucial role of certain fatty acids in early growth, and especially in brain development. During foetal and early infant development, there is rapid accretion of arachidonic acid and DHA in the infant brain and other rapidly growing tissues and organs. DHA is important for the function of rhodopsin (visual pigment) for vision and for neurotransmission. As the foetus and the young infant are completely dependent on the mother for their nutrition, it is crucial that the mothers' diet have significant amounts of essential fatty acids. Research studies have shown a close association between higher omega-3 fatty acid consumption during pregnancy, and beneficial effects on foetal and infant development.

FOOD SOURCES

About 50 per cent of our essential fatty acid requirement is met from the invisible fat present in cereals and pulses in a traditional Indian diet. Plant foods like cereals, pulses, fruits, and vegetables (with the exception of avocado or butter fruit) have a low content of fat and saturated fatty acids. However, nuts and oilseeds have considerable amounts of fat, although most of it is unsaturated. Most vegetable oils available for cooking purposes are obtained from these nuts and oilseeds, although rice bran oil and corn oil are extracted from cereals, and soyabean oil from a legume. Only coconut and palm oil among the vegetable oils have high amounts of saturated fatty acids.

Oil Derived from Palm trees

Palm oil is derived from the mesocarp (pulp) of the fruit of oil palms. It is naturally high in β-carotene. **Palm kernel oil** is derived from the kernel of the same fruit, but does not have β-carotene. Palm mesocarp oil is 41 per cent saturated, while palm kernel oil is 81 per cent saturated. **Palmolein** is a liquid fraction palm oil obtained after the process of refining and fractionation. It is about 39 per cent saturated, and has a high amount of MUFA, like palm oil.

Figure 5.1 gives the fatty acid profile of the commonly consumed fats and oils in India. Animal foods like whole milk, butter, *ghee,* cream, cheese, red meat, and egg yolk are sources of saturated fat, cholesterol, and naturally occurring trans fats. Animals and fish caught from the wild tend to have higher PUFA content than farm-raised animals, which are fed grain-based fattening diets. The diet of the animals determines the fatty acid profile of the meat, milk and eggs provided by them. In an effort to make these foods healthier, producers feed special diets to their animals, altering the fatty acid profile of these animal products. Now we can buy eggs with lower cholesterol and higher PUFA content.

Cholesterol is found in foods of animal origin, such as meat, fish, poultry, eggs, and dairy products (full cream milk and products made from it, like cheese, *paneer,* curd, etc.). It is important to know that foods of plant origin do not contain cholesterol. Very often, manufacturers mislead consumers by claiming that their vegetable oil is 'free from cholesterol'. Consumers should realise that the claim does not confer any special benefits on the particular brand of oil, as all vegetable oils are free from cholesterol. Plants, however, make other kinds of sterols and stanols, called phytosterols,, which are steroid compounds similar to cholesterol. The most commonly occurring phytosterols in the human diet are β-sitosterol, campesterol and stigmasterol, which account for about 65 per cent, 30 per cent and 3 per cent of content in diet, respectively. The most common plant *stanols* in the human diet are sitostanol and campestanol, which combined, make up about 5 per cent of dietary phytosterol. Another example is ergosterol, which is a form of vitamin D.

Good food sources of phytosterols include whole grains, unrefined plant oils, nuts, seeds, legumes, fruits and vegetables. It has been recognised for many years now that phytosterols reduce the total and LDL cholesterol levels in humans, which is why the National Cholesterol Education Program recommends that adults consume 2 gm of phytosterols daily to help protect against cardiovascular disease. Table 5.1 provides the rich sources of different types of fats and fatty acids.

Table 5.1: Food Sources Rich in Different Types of Fats or Fatty Acids

Type	*Examples*	*Rich Sources*
Short chain fatty acid	Butyric	Ghee, butter, cream (milk fat), cheese
Medium chain fatty acid	Capric, Caprylic	Ghee, butter, cream (milk fat), coconut oil, palm oil, palm kernel oil
Saturated fatty acid	Lauric, palmitic, myristic, stearic	Milk fat, butter, cream, ghee, coconut oil, palm kernel oil, hydrogenated fats (*vanaspati*, margarine, bakery fat), fat in meat (especially the red meat of cow, buffalo, lamb, goat, and swine), egg yolk, lard
MUFA	Oleic	Red palm oil, palmolein, groundnut oil, sesame, olive, ricebran and cottonseed oil
PUFA	Linoleic (LA), alpha linolenic (ALA), eicosapentaenoic acid (EPA), docosahexaenoic acid (DHA), arachidonic acid (AA)	All vegetable oils except for coconut oil, especially corn oil, safflower and sunflower oils, fish oil
Essential fatty acids	Linoleic, linolenic	Fish liver oil, green leafy vegetables, seaweeds, algae, barley, oats and corn, cottonseed, safflower and soyabean oils
Omega-3 fatty acids	Alpha-linolenic acid	Fatty cold water fish (salmon, tuna, sardines, mackerel) and fish oils, invisible fat of legumes like rajma, cowpea, soyabean, black gram, cereals like wheat and bajra, mustard and fenugreek leaves and seeds, green leafy vegetables, canola, mustard and soyabean oils, flaxseed, walnuts.
Trans fatty acids	–	Hydrogenated or partially hydrogenated vegetable oil, *vanaspati*, margarine, bakery shortening/fat
Cholesterol	–	Egg yolk, organ meats (liver, kidney, brain, etc), milk fat, red meat, shrimp, prawn
Phytosterols	β-sitosterol, campesterol, stigmasterol, sitostanol, campestanol	Whole grains, unrefined plant oils, nuts, seeds, legumes, fruits, vegetables
Phospholipids	lecithin	Egg yolks, wheat germ, peanuts, soyabean, liver

Source: Byrd-Bredbenner et al. 2013; ICMR 2010; Rolfes et al. 2009.

Concerns while Consuming Omega-3 Fatty Acids

Although fish are considered a rich source of omega-3 fatty acids, and their intake is considered healthy and desirable, we need to be careful about the source of the fish. Fish from polluted waters may do us more harm than good. Contaminants like heavy metals (for example methylmercury), pesticides (for example DDT), and others like PCBs, dioxin, etc., may be present in the water, and get concentrated in fish. The larger and more fatty the fish, the more toxins it is likely to have accumulated, especially if it is a predatory fish, eating other small fish. Hence, it is advisable to purchase fish from reliable sources. If it is not possible to check the source of the fish, choosing smaller, non-predatory fish would be a safer option, as these would not have accumulated significant amounts of toxin.

Vegetarians, and those who do not eat fish regularly, can get their supply of omega-3 fatty acids from other foods, like flaxseeds, walnuts, canola, and mustard and soyabean oils.

RECOMMENDED ALLOWANCES

Recommendations have been given for Indians (ICMR 2010), with regard to the **quantity and quality** of fat to be consumed in the daily diet. The minimum quantity of total and visible fat required according to age and activity level has been detailed in Table 5.2. This amount is recommended to support normal growth and development in children, and in pregnant and lactating women. It is also considered good for the normal physiological functions of adults. However, the level of total fat in the diet should not exceed 30 per cent of the total energy (about 60 g visible fat/day). Fat intake exceeding 35 per cent of total calories may increase the risk of diet-related non-communicable diseases, and should be avoided. Thus, a healthy amount of total fat in the diet ranges from 20–30 per cent of the total calories.

Table 5.2: Recommended Dietary Allowances for Lipids

Group	*Age*	*Minimum level of total fat (% Energy)*	*Visible fat*	
			% Energy	*(g/day)*
Adult Men	Sedentary	20	10	25
	Moderate			30
	Heavy			40
Adult Women	Sedentary	20	10	20
	Moderate			25
	Heavy			30
	Pregnant	20	10	30
	Lactating			30
Infants	0–6 months	40–60	Human milk	
	7–24 months	35	25	25
Children	3–6 years	25	15	25
	7–9 years			30
Boys	10–12 years			35
	13–15 years			45
	16–17 years			50
Girls	10–12 years			35
	13–15 years			40
	16–17 years			35

Source: Nutrient Requirements and Recommended Dietary Allowances for Indians, ICMR 2010.

The quality of fat is also important. Whether the fat in our diet comes from visible or invisible fat sources, the aim is to achieve intakes of individual fatty acids which are consistent with good health, and prevent us from developing chronic degenerative diseases.

The WHO/FAO Expert Group on Diet, Nutrition and Prevention of Chronic Diseases (2003) has recommended population nutrient goals, cited in Table 5.3.

Table 5.3: Recommendations for Dietary Fatty Acids

Fat/Fatty Acid	*% of Total Energy*
Total Fat	20–30
Saturated fatty acids (SFA)	< 10
PUFAs	6–10
n-6 fatty acids	5–8
n-3 fatty acids	1–2
Trans fatty acids	< 1
MUFAs	Calculated by difference (total-SFA-PUFA)
Cholesterol	< 300 mg/day

Source: WHO/FAO 2003.

Figure 5.1: Fatty Acid Profile of Commonly Used Fats and Oils

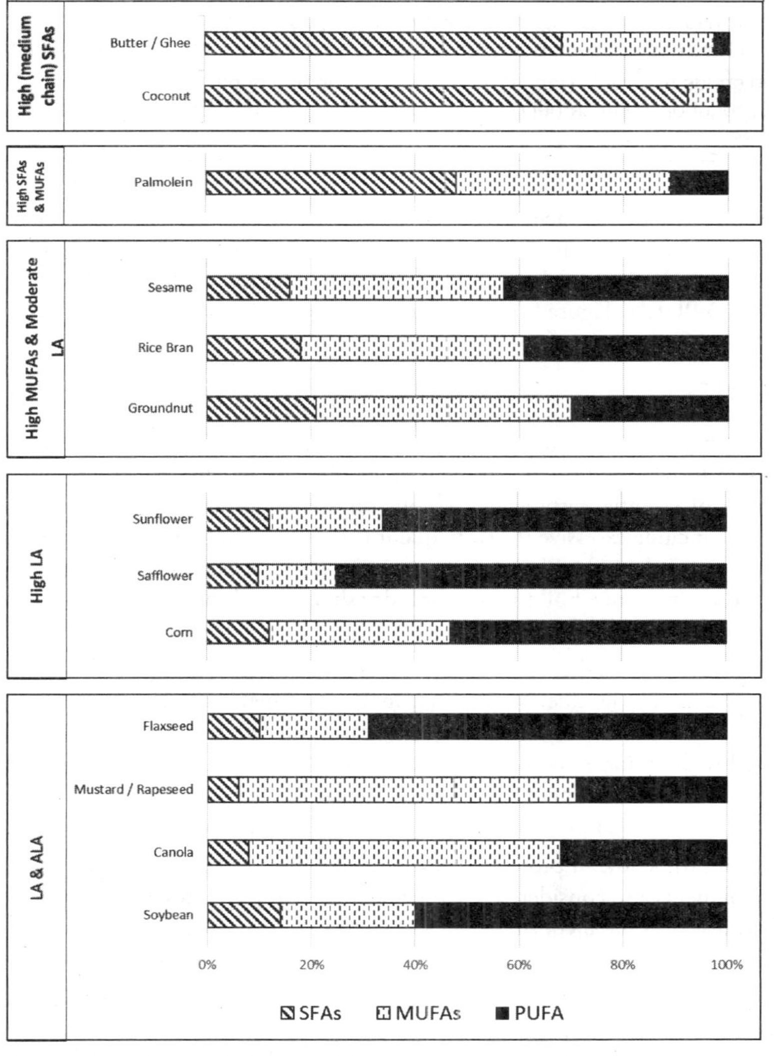

Source: Data from ICMR 2010.

Box 5.2: Choosing the Right Cooking Oil and Other Visible Fats

Here are some tips for selecting the right kind of visible fats, which will provide us with the appropriate types and amounts of fatty acids in our diet.

- No single cooking oil can fulfil the requirements of all kinds of fatty acids. Hence, one should use a combination of fats in our daily diet. This can be achieved by using blended oils (two or more oils premixed by the manufacturer), or by using different oils for preparing different types of dishes, for example, olive oil for salad dressings and pastas; mustard oil for some vegetable/pulse preparations; and sunflower/safflower oil for some others.
- The best oils for deep fat frying are palm oil, palmolein, sesame, cottonseed, canola, groundnut, or ricebran oil, as they have the perfect blend of fatty acids to make them stable at the high temperatures reached during frying. PUFA-rich oils should not be used for deep fat frying as they degrade easily, and form harmful breakdown products. Avoid reheating the same oil for frying again and again as the oxidation products formed are harmful. Instead, use the oil to make other preparations.
- Choose oils rich in omega-3 fatty acids and MUFAs, as these are protective fatty acids, for instance, soyabean, canola, mustard (omega 3 rich) and olive, canola, groundnut, ricebran, sesame, mustard (MUFA rich).
- Limit the use of butter, ghee and cream.
- Avoid using partially hydrogenated vegetable oils (*vanaspati*) as a medium of cooking. Even when you eat out, make sure that the food has not been prepared in this oil, as it is rich in the harmful trans fatty acids.
- To prepare baked goods or sweets (*mithai*), do not use shortening or bakery fat made of partially hydrogenated vegetable oils. Coconut oil, palm kernel oil, palmolein, or their blends can easily be used, as they have similar physical properties.

Linoleic acid (LA) and alpha linoleic acid (ALA), and their respective long chain PUFA, have distinct biological effects in the body, as their absolute levels and their ratio (n-6: n-3) modulate physiological functions. Although a dietary ratio in the range of 5:1 to 10:1 has been recommended, emphasis should be on increasing the absolute levels of ALA and long chain n-3 PUFAs. Figure 5.1 shows the fatty acid profile of commonly consumed fats and oils.

HEALTH SIGNIFICANCE

A deficiency of essential fatty acids leads to growth retardation. Skin lesions resembling eczema (a skin rash) have been known to develop in formula-fed infants in the past, or those on parental nutrition for a long period of time without supplementation of essential fatty acids. Various physical signs are associated with deficiencies of these essential fatty acids. These include excessive thirst, frequent urination, rough, dry or scaly skin, dry, dull or 'lifeless' hair, dandruff, and soft or brittle nails. Raised bumps on the skin are particularly characteristic. (This is called 'follicular keratosis', as it results from a build-up of hard, dry skin around the hair follicles). Liver degeneration has also been observed in essential fatty acid deficiency.

So while on the one hand a low fat diet can lead to problems of deficiency, a high fat diet can also adversely affect the health of a person. Excess calories due to a high fat intake in general can lead to weight gain, obesity, and its associated problems. It increases the risk of cardiovascular diseases and certain types of cancer. Diets high in saturated fats have been associated with an increased risk of colon, prostrate and breast cancer. This may be related to high fat diets, stimulating the liver to release more bile. Bile irritates colon cells and may lead to cancer. In addition, high fat diets raise blood lipid levels, which in turn raise oestrogen levels, which have been associated with breast cancer.

High fat diets also tend to be low in protective nutrients like fibre and protective phytochemicals that prevent cancer. A high cholesterol diet is also considered atherogenic, that is, it promotes fatty deposits in arteries. Trans fats increase the risk of heart disease, even if consumed in moderate amounts. But what will happen if we consume high amounts of the good fats? Box 5.3 details the health implications of consuming different types of fats.

Replacing saturated fatty acids in the diet with PUFAs has been shown to decrease LDL cholesterol, and thus reduce the risk of heart disease. Intakes of polyunsaturated fats greater than 10 per cent of total calories, however, seems to increase the cholesterol deposited in the arteries. High intakes may also impair the body's ability to fight disease.

Most people, including vegetarians, find it easier to simply consume supplements of omega-3 fatty acids to reap its benefits. Fish oil capsules would pose the same dangers as eating fish from contaminated waters. In addition, consuming high amounts of these fatty acids can lead to adverse effects, like reducing blood clotting abilities and resulting in uncontrolled bleeding. The functioning of the immune system is also impaired.

Box 5.3: Health Implications of Different Types of Fats

Saturated fats raise the levels of total and LDL cholesterol, and are therefore considered atherogenic. Some studies have also shown that they may contribute to insulin resistance, which ultimately leads to diabetes.

MUFA and PUFA decrease the total and LDL cholesterol, and are considered heart healthy or anti-atherogenic.

Omega-3 fatty acids (alpha-linolenic acid) are more beneficial for the prevention of inflammation and accumulation of fatty material in blood vessels, which lead to atherosclerosis (hardening of the arteries). They also prevent thrombosis or clotting of blood, thus protecting us against strokes. They are known to lower plasma triglyceride levels.

Trans fatty acids increase the risk of heart disease much more than saturated fats. Not only do they increase bad cholesterol (LDL), but they also decrease the good cholesterol (HDL) and increase inflammation in the body. Some studies have linked them to insulin resistance as well.

Low density lipoproteins (LDL), also termed as bad cholesterol, transports cholesterol from the liver to different tissues in the body. High levels of LDL in the blood result in the accumulation of these lipids along blood vessels walls, leading to plaques. If the LDL is oxidised, it becomes more atherogenic.

Very low density lipoproteins (VLDL) contains high amount of triglycerides. VLDL is considered a type of bad cholesterol, because it helps cholesterol build up on the walls of arteries.

High density lipoprotein (HDL), also termed as good cholesterol, removes the cholesterol that accumulates in peripheral tissues, and brings it to the liver for excretion into bile. HDL is thus considered anti-atherogenic. It also blocks the oxidation of LDL.

Phytosterols are steroid compounds present in plants, which help to reduce cholesterol levels by competing with cholesterol absorption in the gut. They are also known to lower blood triglyceride levels.

Lecithin is the major phospholipid present in our diets. Conflicting data are available from studies, which have linked lecithin with health benefits like weight loss, lowering of cholesterol and decreasing the risk of Alzheimer disease. High doses of lecithin supplements can cause gas, diarrhoea and weight gain.

Non-glyceride components of fats, like fat-soluble vitamins (carotenoids, A, D, E, K), plant sterols, oryzanols, and sesame lignans have their own nutritional and health promoting effects. They have antioxidant properties and a hypocholestrolemic effect. Increasing the intake of these non-glyceride components from natural plant foods and oils could help in increasing the antioxidant potential of human diets, as well as help in correcting dyslipidemia (an abnormal amount of lipids in the blood).

SUMMARY

- **Lipids** are a heterogenous group of substances that include fats, oils and fat-like substances that have a greasy feel and are insoluble in water, but soluble in certain organic solvents such as ether, alcohol, chloroform, and benzene.
- **Fatty acids** are the main constituents of all lipids. They consist of chains of carbon atoms with a methyl (-CH3) group at one end and a carboxyl (-COOH) group at the other.
- Based on the length of the carbon chain, fatty acids can be classified as short, medium and long chain fatty acids.
- Based on the degree of saturation in the carbon chain, fatty acids can be classified as saturated or unsaturated. Unsaturated fatty acids are again of two types, monounsaturated and polyunsaturated fatty acids.

- **Essential fatty acids** are those that cannot be synthesised by the human body, but are very important for growth and development. The two essential fatty acids are linoleic (lin or n-6/omega 6) and linolenic (len or n-3/omega3).
- The main lipids present in our diet are the triglycerides, although some amounts of phospholipids and sterols (cholesterol and plant sterols) may also be present.
- Lipids can be classified into simple, compound and derived lipids. **Simple lipids** are esters of glycerol and fatty acids, and include glycerides and waxes. **Compound lipids** are esters of glycerol and fatty acids with substitution of other components such as carbohydrates, phosphate or nitrogenous groupings. **Derived lipids** are substances liberated during the hydrolysis of simple and compound lipids, which still retain the properties of lipids.
- Fat in our diet can be **visible fat**, which we can see, for example, butter, cooking oil, ghee, etc. It is termed as **invisible fat** if it is present inside a food and cannot be seen with the naked eye. Examples include the fat present in cereals, pulses, nuts, etc.
- Fats perform important functions in our body. They provide us with energy and, in fact, are the chief reserves of energy in our body. They are a constituent of each and every cell of our body. Present in the cell membrane, they help in maintaining structural integrity, helping to transport substances in and out of the cell. It is also a structural component of brain and nerve tissues, plays a role in nerve transmission, and helps in the synthesis of various useful substances and in the absorption of fat-soluble vitamins. Adipose tissue provides insulation and padding, thus helping in the regulation of body temperature and protecting the body from injury.
- Fat also makes the food more palatable by improving taste and texture. It acts as a lubricant in the intestine and also increases the satiety value of meals.
- Plant foods like cereals, pulses, fruits, and vegetables (with the exception of avocado or butter fruit) have a low content of fat and saturated fatty acids. However, nuts and oilseeds have considerable amounts of fat, although most of it is unsaturated. Coconut oil and palm oil/palm kernel oil/palmolein are vegetable oils with a high content of saturated fatty acids.
- Animal foods like whole milk, butter, *ghee,* cream, cheese, red meat, and egg yolk are sources of saturated fat, cholesterol and naturally occurring trans fats. Fish and fish oils are a source of omega-3 fatty acids. Vegetarians, and those who do not eat fish regularly, can get their supply of omega-3 fatty acids from other foods like flaxseeds, walnuts, canola, mustard and soyabean oils.
- Fat intake exceeding 35 per cent of total calories may increase the risk of diet-related, non-communicable diseases, and should be avoided. Thus, a healthy amount of total fat in the diet ranges from 20–30 per cent of total calories.
- Kinds of fats/fatty acids which are good for us are PUFAs, MUFAs, omega-3 fatty acids, and essential fatty acids. Fats considered unhealthy are saturated fats, trans fats and cholesterol.
- **Non-glyceride components of fats,** like fat-soluble vitamins (carotenoids, A, D, E, K), plant sterols, oryzanols, and sesame lignans, have their own nutritional and health promoting effects.

KEY WORDS

Atherogenic: Refers to something that promotes fatty deposits and thickening of artery walls.

Atherosclerosis: Hardening and thickening of the walls of arteries. There is a build-up of fatty material (plaque) in the arteries, which ultimately blocks the arteries, preventing the flow of blood.

Chronic degenerative diseases: Diseases in which the function or structure of the affected tissues or organs will increasingly deteriorate over time, whether due to normal bodily wear, or lifestyle choices such as exercise or eating habits. The word chronic indicates that these diseases are of a long duration. The diseases being referred to here are diabetes, cardiovascular disorders, hypertension, and diet-related cancers.

Dyslipidemia are an abnormal amount of lipids (whether cholesterol or fat) present in the blood.

EXERCISES

1. How do you classify fatty acids on the basis of the degree of saturation in the carbon chain? Give examples.
2. What is the difference between cis and trans fats?
3. Which are the fatty acids that have to be essentially consumed in the diet?
4. What does a deficiency of essential fatty acids lead to?
5. List the functions of Lipids.
6. What are the recommendations regarding the intake of total fat and saturated fat?
7. List some food sources of MUFA and omega 3 fatty acids.
8. What would happen if you regularly consumed a lot of omega 3 fatty acids by way of supplements?

REFERENCES

Byrd-Bredbenner, C., G. Moe, D. Beshgetoor, and J. Berning, *Wardlaw's Perspectives in Nutrition*, 9e, New York: McGraw-Hill International Edition, 2013.

FAO/WHO, 'Joint FAO/WHO Expert Consultation on Fats and Fatty Acids in Human Nutrition', Interim Summary of Conclusions and Dietary Recommendations on Total Fat and Fatty Acids, 10–14 November, Geneva: WHO, 2008.

Gafoorunissa and A. Vajreswari, 'Lipids', in M. S. Bamji, K. Krishnaswamy and G. N. V. Brahmam (eds), *Textbook of Human Nutrition*, 3e, Oxford and IBH Publ Co., 2009, pp. 33–46.

ICMR, 'Nutrient Requirements and Recommended DietaryAllowances for Indians', A report of the Expert Group of the Indian Council of Medical Research, 2010.

Rolfes, S. R., K. Pinna and E. Whitney, *Understanding Normal and Clinical Nutrition*, 8e, Wadsworth Cengage Learning, 2009.

WHO/FAO, 'Diet, Nutrition and Prevention of Chronic Diseases: Report of a Joint WHO/FAO Expert Consultation', Technical Report Series 916, Geneva, 2003.

6

PROTEINS

HIGHLIGHTS

- Types of Proteins
- Functions
- Food Sources
- Recommended Allowances
- Health Significance
- Methods of assessment of protein quality
- Factors affecting protein quality
- Methods of improving the protein quality of human diets

The term 'protein' comes from the Greek word '*protos*', which means 'to take first place'. This name is appropriate, considering that each and every cell of our body is made up primarily of protein. Proteins are also crucial for the maintenance and regulation of essential body functions.

Proteins are nitrogen-containing constituents of food, which are needed by the body for growth, maintenance and repair of body tissues. Almost 50 per cent of the protein in our body is present in muscles, 20 per cent in bone, 10 per cent in skin, and the rest in other parts of the body.

All proteins are synthesised from amino acid molecules, and around 20 different amino acids are used in protein synthesis. All amino acids used in protein synthesis contain carbon, hydrogen and oxygen, just like carbohydrates and lipids, but what makes them different is the fact that they also contain nitrogen atoms. Proteins contain on an average 16 per cent nitrogen. Some amino acids, like cysteine and methionine, contain sulphur atoms in addition, while some others contain phosphorus atoms. Basically, all amino acids are organic compounds composed of a central carbon bonded to four groups—an amino group ($-NH_2$), a carboxyl group (-COOH), a hydrogen atom (-H), and a side chain represented by the letter-R (Figure 6.1). By varying the R group, many different amino acids are possible. The side chain makes the amino acid unique and also determines its structure and properties.

Figure 6.1: Basic Structure of an Amino Acid

```
       NH2
      /
R - C - COOH
     /
    H
```

STRUCTURE OF PROTEINS

Proteins consist of chains of amino acids joined to each other by a **peptide linkage**. An –OH group from the carboxyl end of one amino acid combines with one –H from the amino group of the other amino acid, and gets removed as water (H_2O). The linkage thus formed (-NH---OC-) is referred to as a peptide linkage. Two amino acids join to form a dipeptide, three form a tripeptide, and many amino acids in a chain are referred to as a polypeptide.

The basic or **primary structure** of a protein is determined by the chain of amino acids that it is made of. The chains can differ in:

- The number and kinds of amino acids present
- The number of times each amino acid appears in the chain
- Length of the chain

The **secondary structure** is determined by the kinds of bonds, such as hydrogen and sulphur, which are present between amino acids in the chain that are near, but not right next to each other. This means that amino acids that are adjacent/next to each other are connected with peptide linkages. However, bonds which connect amino acids present elsewhere on the chain, but near each other spatially, will determine the secondary structure of a protein.

The **tertiary structure** refers to the manner in which amino acid chains are bound together to give shape and performance characteristics to the proteins.

In some cases, two or more separate polypeptides interact to form a large, new protein with a **quarternary structure**. Haemoglobin is an example of a protein with quarternary structure.

CLASSIFICATION OF AMINO ACIDS

Based on the nutritional properties of the amino acids, they are classified as **Essential** and **Non-essential amino acids.** Essential (or indispensible) amino acids cannot be synthesised by the body at a rate sufficient to meet the needs for growth and maintenance. Nine of the 20 amino acids needed by the body to function are essential amino acids. The non-essential amino acids can be made in adequate amounts by our body if nitrogen is available in the diet. These are synthesised through a process known as transamination, which involves the transfer of an amino group from one amino acid to a carbon skeleton to form a new amino acid. We need these amino acids, too, but they are not essential components of the diet.

Table 6.1: Classification of Amino Acids based on Nutritional Properties

Essential Amino Acids	*Non-essential Amino Acids*
Histidine	Alanine
Isoleucine	Arginine
Leucine	Asparagine
Lysine	Aspartic acid
Methionine	Cysteine
Phenylalanine	Glutamic acid
Threonine	Glutamine
Tryptophan	Glycine
Valine	Proline
	Serine
	Tyrosine

Some amino acids are 'semi-essential'. These can be synthesised, provided certain essential amino acids are available in adequate amounts. For example, methionine, an essential amino acid, is converted to cystine in our body, and phenylalanine, another essential amino acid, is converted to tyrosine. Table 6.1 gives examples of different classes of amino acids. Some amino acids may become conditionally essential; for instance, tyrosine becomes 'conditionally essential' in disease conditions like Phenylketonuria, as the individual is unable to convert phenylalanine to tyrosine, making it important for the individual to consume this amino acid in the diet.

CLASSIFICATION OF PROTEINS

Proteins can be classified **based on their physico-chemical properties** into simple, conjugated and derived proteins. **Simple proteins,** upon hydrolysis or breakdown initiated by enzymes, acids or alkalies, yield only amino acids or their derivatives. Albumin and globulin in the body cells and blood, keratin in the hair and nails, collagen in the supportive tissues of our body, globin of haemoglobin, zein of corn, and gliadin and glutenin in wheat are all simple proteins.

Conjugated proteins are composed of simple proteins combined with a non-protein substance. For example, *lipoproteins*, which transport fat in the blood, are made of lipids attached to proteins. Similarly, *phosphoproteins*, for example, casein in milk and ovovitellin in eggs, has phosphorus attached to proteins; *metalloproteins* have a metal attached to proteins, for example, haemoglobin and indeed several enzymes, which contain mineral elements; *mucoproteins* like mucin found in saliva, and some gonadotropic hormones have a mucopolysaccharide group (a type of carbohydrate) attached to proteins; *chromoproteins* have a coloured component attached to the protein, for example, haemoglobin and visual purple or rhodopsin, which is responsible for dim light vision; and flavoproteins, which are enzymes that contain the vitamin riboflavin.

Derived proteins are substances resulting from the decomposition of simple and conjugated proteins. This can happen by a simple rearrangement within the molecule without breaking the peptide bond, for example, coagulation of casein in milk when curd is set, of the egg albumin when the egg is boiled, or the fibrinogen, when it is converted to fibrin during the clotting of blood. Derived proteins may also be formed during hydrolysis of proteins into smaller fragments, such as proteoses and peptones.

Based on physical shape, proteins can be classified as **Fibrous proteins,** which are long polypeptide chains bound together in more or less parallel fashion to form a linear shape. These are generally insoluble in body fluids. They are designed to give strength to the tissues. Examples of fibrous proteins are keratin in hair and nails, collagen in tendons and bone matrices, and elastin in blood vessel walls. **Globular proteins** are made of chains of amino acids that are coiled and tightly packed together in a round or ellipsoidal shape. These are generally soluble in body fluids. Examples of globular proteins include haemoglobin, insulin, albumin, and different enzymes of our body.

Based on nutritional properties, proteins can be classified into three categories—complete, partially complete and incomplete proteins. This depends on the essential amino acid content of the proteins. **Complete proteins** contain enough of all nine essential amino acids to maintain body tissues and to promote a normal rate of growth. These are referred to as proteins of 'high biologic value', which means that a large part of them can be converted from food protein into tissue protein. These proteins are found in meat, fish, poultry, milk, eggs, and dried yeast. **Partially complete proteins** are capable of maintaining life, but lack sufficient amounts of some amino acids necessary for growth, for example, cereal and pulse proteins. Adults under no physiologic stress (like pregnancy, lactation, etc.) can maintain a satisfactory nutritional status for indefinite periods on partially complete proteins. This is the situation among the poor in developing countries, who mostly consume a cereal-based diet. **Incomplete proteins** are incapable of replacing or building new tissues, and hence cannot support life, let alone promote growth. Zein, one of the proteins found in corn, and gelatin obtained from the collagen of animals (present in skin, bones and connective tissues) are examples of incomplete proteins, incapable of even permitting life to continue.

> Cells require a pool of all the essential amino acids for the synthesis of body proteins. Thus plant proteins like wheat or rice proteins, which are deficient in lysine, cannot support protein synthesis if they are the sole source of dietary protein. If proteins cannot be synthesized the remaining amino acids are used to provide energy or may be converted to carbohydrate or fat.

However, single foods like cereal grains are consumed alone in only very poor households. A mixed diet generally provides good quality protein, because proteins from different sources tend to supplement and make up for each others' deficiency. This is known as *mutual supplementation.* Cereal, if eaten with a pulse or with milk, meat or egg, will provide good quality protein. This will be further discussed in this chapter under methods to improve protein quality.

FUNCTIONS OF PROTEINS

Proteins perform several functions in metabolism and in the formation of essential compounds and structures in our body.

1. The main function of proteins is tissue building for **growth and maintenance**. Protein constitutes the chief solid matter of muscles, organs and endocrine glands. Proteins are the major constituents of bones, teeth, skin, nails, and hair. *Structural proteins* like collagen, actin and myosin provide a matrix for bone, connective tissue and muscle. In fact, every living cell and all body fluids (except bile and urine) contain proteins.
2. Body proteins have highly specialised functions to perform in the **regulation of body processes**. *Catalytic proteins,* like enzymes, facilitate anabolic (which result in the synthesis of substances) and catabolic (which result

in the breakdown of substances) reactions, and the process of digestion in the body. Pepsin, lipase and amylase are the names of certain enzymes involved in the digestion of proteins, lipids and carbohydrates, respectively. Amino acids are required for the synthesis of most hormones in the body. *Hormonal proteins* regulate the pace or control metabolic processes, for example, pituitary hormones, insulin and thyroid hormones. Many neurotransmitters, released by nerve endings, are also derived from amino acids. Dopamine and norepinephrine are synthesised from tyrosine, and serotonin is synthesised from the amino acid tryptophan.

3. Proteins play an important role in **regulating acid-base balance** and body pH. They act as buffers (compounds that help to maintain pH within a narrow range). Proteins are especially good buffers for the body because they have a negative charge, which attracts positively charged hydrogen ions. Hydrogen ions are accepted and released as needed, to prevent detrimental changes in pH.
4. *Nucleoproteins* are present in the nuclei of cells, and these contain the blueprint for the **synthesis of all body proteins.**
5. *Immune proteins* help to fight against germs invading our body, and thus help in **building the body's resistance to disease.** The different antibodies present in our blood are an example of immune proteins. Antibodies bind to foreign proteins (antigens) that invade our body, and prevent their attack on our cells and tissues.
6. *Contractile proteins* like actin and myosin present in muscles help to **regulate muscle contraction and relaxation**.
7. *Transport proteins* are usually present in the blood, and they help in **transporting nutrients**. Nutrients are taken to tissues and cells where they are needed, for example, transferrin helps in the transport of iron, lipoproteins ferry lipids, retinol-binding protein transports retinol (Vitamin A), and haemoglobin transports oxygen from the lungs to different cells in the body.
8. Proteins present in the serum or blood, for example, serum albumin and globulin, are very important in the **regulation of osmotic pressure and maintenance of fluid balance** between blood and the surrounding tissue space. In protein energy malnutrition, when the levels of blood protein fall, children tend to develop oedema (due to fluid retention in the interstitial spaces) as the protein in the blood is inadequate to pull fluid back into the blood vessels from the spaces between cells surrounding capillary beds.
9. Although carbohydrates and fats are the preferential **sources of energy**, proteins can potentially provide 4 kcal/g. If the diet does not furnish sufficient calories from carbohydrates and fat, the protein in the diet, and later, even tissue protein, is catabolised (broken down) to give energy. This is not a desirable state.
10. Amino acids can also be used to form glucose. This process is known as **gluconeogenesis**. The body must maintain blood glucose levels within a normal range as some tissues like the brain, other nervous tissue cells, and red blood cells rely almost exclusively on glucose for energy. If carbohydrate intake is inadequate to maintain blood glucose, the liver is forced to make glucose from the amino acids present in body tissues. In chronic starvation, this may lead to wasting or breakdown of muscles in the body.
11. **Individual amino acids** also **have specialised functions** to perform in metabolism. Tryptophan, an essential amino acid, is converted to niacin, a vitamin. It also helps to synthesise serotonin (a neurotransmitter). Methionine, another essential amino acid, is used to make the vitamin choline in our bodies. Choline helps to prevent the storage of fat in the liver. Glycine helps in the formation of the porphyrin ring in haemoglobin.

FOOD SOURCES

Protein can be obtained in our diet from both plant foods and animal foods. Generally, the proteins from animal sources are complete proteins, and hence of better quality. Rich sources of protein include meat, fish, poultry, eggs, milk and milk products (cheese, curd, *paneer,* etc.). Plant sources like legumes or pulses (rajma, soyabean, and indeed all *dals*), nuts and oilseeds contain a good quantity of proteins; however, these are partially complete proteins, as they are lacking in some essential amino acids. Pulses and legumes are deficient in the essential amino acid methionine. We eat a lot of cereals, and so a substantial portion of the protein in the diet is contributed by foods like wheat, rice and millets in India. While rice has less quantity of protein as compared to wheat, its protein quality is better than wheat.

Cereals are generally deficient in the amino acid lysine. If, however, cereals and pulses are eaten together, they mutually supplement and make up for the deficit in each other. Such combinations are then considered complete proteins.

Box 6.1: Choosing the Right Kind of Protein-rich Foods

The outer layer of cereals is richer in protein. During the process of dehusking and polishing grains, a lot of protein is lost from the outer layers, as well as due to the separation of the germ from the endosperm. Hence, polished rice has less protein than brown rice. Choosing whole grains over refined grain products makes better sense. So, whole wheat flour is better than refined wheat flour.

When choosing animal foods as sources of protein in our diet, we must be careful and select low fat products. Thus toned, double-toned, or skim milk is better than whole milk; and lean cuts of meat, poultry without skin, and fish should get preference over red meat (beef, pork, goat or sheep meat with marbling of fat). This is because the latter foods are rich sources of bad fats like saturated fat and cholesterol, an excessive intake of which is linked to cardiovascular diseases.

Protein supplements in the form of protein powders (whey protein/soya protein) or protein drinks are generally not recommended for normal healthy people. According to the recommendations made by ICMR (2010), good quality protein food sources should be included in the diet whenever the requirement increases, for example, during the growing years for children, and during pregnancy and lactation.

RECOMMENDED ALLOWANCES

An adequate intake of protein in diets is essential for adults to replace the proteins being broken down in the body. Children need proteins to synthesise new tissues for growth. During pregnancy, there is a need for additional protein to synthesise new tissues in the mother's body, as well as support the growth of the foetus and placenta. Lactating women need additional protein for the synthesis of breast milk. The requirement of protein for normal healthy adults is calculated as 1 gm/kg body weight. The protein requirement of different age groups is given in Table 6.2.

Table 6.2: Recommended Dietary Allowances for Protein

Group	*Age*	*Protein (g/day)*
Men	Adult	60
Women	Adult	55
Pregnant women	Adult	78
Lactating women	Adult (0–6 months of lactation)	74
	Adult (6–12 months of lactation)	68
Infants	0–6 months	1.16 g/kg/day
	6–12 months	1.69 g/kg/day
Children	1–3 years	16.7
	4–6 years	20.1
	7–9 years	29.5
Boys	10–12 years	39.9
Girls	10–12 years	40.4
Boys	13–15 years	54.3
Girls	13–15 years	51.9
Boys	16–17 years	61.5
Girls	16–17 years	55.5

Source: Nutrient Requirements and Recommended Dietary Allowances for Indians, ICMR 2010.

Nitrogen or protein balance (equilibrium) is seen in healthy individuals who are not growing, or recovering from illness or injury (Figure 6.2). Their protein intake equals the amount lost in urine, faeces, sweat, skin cells, hair, and nails. This balance is maintained as long as the energy intake is adequate, to prevent the use of protein for providing energy. When protein intake is less than the losses, an individual is considered to be in **negative nitrogen balance**. This is usually seen in individuals suffering from some disease or severe injury, especially if they have been bedridden for a prolonged period. Individuals with poor diets containing inadequate amounts of protein also exhibit negative nitrogen balance. When protein intake is more than the losses, a state of **positive nitrogen balance** is achieved. This is seen when a lot of new tissue synthesis occurs in the body, for instance, during childhood (growing) years, pregnancy, and during recovery from illness or injury.

Figure 6.2: Nitrogen Balance

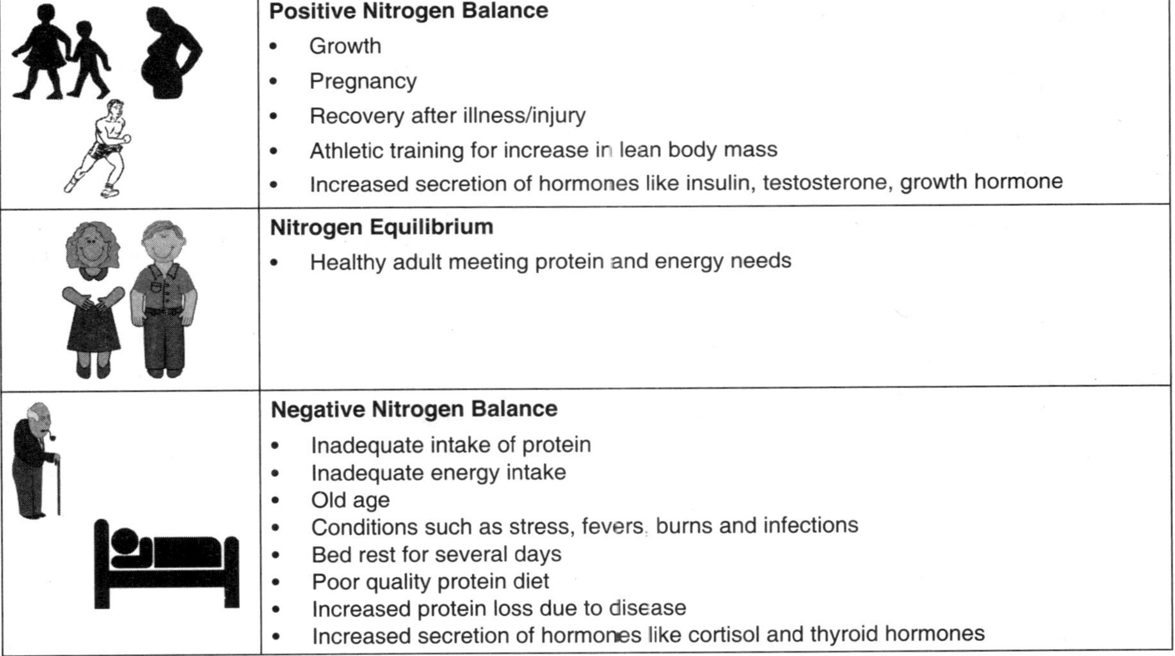

	Positive Nitrogen Balance • Growth • Pregnancy • Recovery after illness/injury • Athletic training for increase in lean body mass • Increased secretion of hormones like insulin, testosterone, growth hormone
	Nitrogen Equilibrium • Healthy adult meeting protein and energy needs
	Negative Nitrogen Balance • Inadequate intake of protein • Inadequate energy intake • Old age • Conditions such as stress, fevers, burns and infections • Bed rest for several days • Poor quality protein diet • Increased protein loss due to disease • Increased secretion of hormones like cortisol and thyroid hormones

Source: Adapted from Byrd-Bredbenner et al. 2013.

Images: https://openclipart.org
https://openclipart.org/detail/474/children
https://openclipart.org/detail/46819/pregnant-woman-silhouette
https://openclipart.org/detail/3043/runner
https://openclipart.org/detail/168269/mommy-2
https://openclipart.org/detail/31495/daddy-standing-01
https://openclipart.org/detail/202727/grandpa
https://openclipart.org/detail/181941/only-bed

HEALTH SIGNIFICANCE

Eating sufficient amounts of protein is required for good health. Getting too much or too little can have serious health consequences. Protein energy malnutrition (PEM) continues to be a major public health problem in many developing countries, including our own. Although PEM can affect people of all ages, it mostly affects children, and has the most devastating effect on those below the age of five, belonging to poor communities. Most of them are malnourished because they do not get enough food to eat. Protein deficiency rarely develops as an isolated condition. It most often occurs in combination with a deficiency of energy. The term PEM covers a wide range of clinical stages, ranging from severe forms like kwashiorkor and marasmus to milder forms, in which the most obviously seen effect is retardation or slowing down of the child's growth.

You might have seen severe cases of PEM during television news coverage of countries ravaged by long-term war, or of places where natural calamities like drought and famine have seriously affected the food supply, for example, some African countries like Ethiopia and Somalia. In India, according to NFHS 3 data, nearly 42 per cent of children under the age of five are underweight (having low weight for their age), 48 per cent are stunted (having a lower than normal height for their age), and 19.8 per cent are wasted (that is, they have a lower weight than normal for their height).

Aetiology

The study of aetiology, or the science of the causes of disease, is important for us to identify the people most likely to contract the disease, and also to find ways and means of preventing the disease. The primary reason behind small children developing PEM is their consumption of inadequate amounts of food. Surveys carried out in different parts of India have shown that the main problem in the diets of preschool children is a deficiency of calories, and not so much of protein. Although protein intake is relatively adequate, some of it is used to provide energy, leading to conditioned protein deficiency. Low intakes of food for a long period of time make the body weak and unable to fight infections. Unhygienic surroundings further increase the risk of children contracting serious infections and diseases. It is a vicious cycle. Weak, undernourished children fall ill easily, and the illness further weakens them, making them even more undernourished.

It has been seen that due to poverty, the child may be fed diluted formula milk or diluted gruels of staple food like wheat, rice, *ragi* or maize, etc., which do not fulfil the calorie requirement of the child. In poor communities, where both parents are working and young children are looked after by older siblings, the children may be deprived of appropriate care and attention. Faulty feeding habits arising from ignorance and prejudices also contribute significantly to making matters worse for an already malnourished child. Some families withdraw milk from the child's diet when s/he falls ill. Others simply restrict the diet and give less or nutritionally inadequate food to the child. All this can make the child even more malnourished.

Severe forms of malnutrition are mainly of two types—kwashiorkor and marasmus. The term 'kwashiorkor' was first introduced by Dr Cicely Williams in 1935. In a local language spoken in Ghana, Africa, it literally means 'disease of the displaced child', or 'the disease the first child gets when the new child comes'. In families where the age gap between children is less, it has been seen that the birth of the second child puts a lot of strain on the mother. The older child is possibly neglected, both in terms of the food offered and general care and affection. Such children were mostly seen to develop kwashiorkor.

The younger children (usually less than a year old), on the other hand, were more likely to develop marasmus as their mothers weaned them off breast milk onto foods that did not provide them with adequate nourishment. The word 'marasmus' means 'to waste away.' Over time, the severe lack of energy and protein results in a 'skin and bones' appearance, with little or no subcutaneous fat. The child may be given milk feeds excessively diluted with water, or a part of the adult diet based on cereals, which an infant cannot consume in sufficient quantities because s/he cannot chew properly.

Causes of PEM

- Poverty
- Ignorance
- Diluted feeds
- Delayed weaning
- Improper weaning
- Faulty feeding habits
- Repeated illness
- Food fads and taboos
- Poor child caring practices

Symptoms

The symptoms of different forms of PEM differ. The severity of the overall energy and protein deficit, and the related clinical characteristics, determines the difference between the two forms of PEM—Marasmus and Kwashiorkor. In children suffering from **kwashiorkor,** the main clinical sign is oedema (swelling) of the face and lower limbs. The child may also give the false impression of being chubby because of the facial swelling. These children, however, are far from healthy. The swelling is often so severe that the child develops a large pot belly due to ascites (accumulation of fluid in the abdominal cavity) or an enlarged liver. The swelling also masks the fact that severe wasting of the muscles has occurred. There is also moderate to severe failure of growth. The child may also develop diarrhoea and loss of appetite, which further worsens the situation. The skin, especially in the pelvic region and the thighs, often becomes dry and flaky and starts peeling off. The hair is easily plucked out, and is thin and a dull light brown colour, in contrast to the dark black hair of most Indian children. One of the more striking features of this deficiency is the apathy and general misery of the child. S/he whimpers, but does not cry or scream. S/he is not interested in or curious about her/his surroundings, but remains seated wherever s/he is put down. When s/he once again begins to smile, s/he is said to be on the road to recovery.

Table 6.3: Difference between Symptoms of Kwashiorkor and Marasmus

Characteristic/Symptom	*Kwashiorkor*	*Marasmus*
Nutrient deficiency	Severe protein with moderate energy deficit	Severe energy and protein deficit
Age of child	Usually 1–4 years of age	Usually seen in small children less than a year old, but also up to two years
Speed of onset	Rapid	Gradual
Growth failure	Present (60–80% of normal weight for age)	Severe growth impairment (less than 60% of normal weight for age)
Overall look on the face	Moon face	Old man's face
Wasting of muscles and body fat	Maintains some muscle and subcutaneous fat	Severe wasting of muscles and body fat, looks as if bones are covered only with skin
Weight loss	Mild to moderate	Severe
Fatty liver	Present	Absent
Hair changes	Sparse hair, brownish orange	Absent
Oedema	Present	Absent
Skin changes	Present. Flaky paint or crazy pavement dermatosis	Usually absent
Underlying infection and other diseases	Often present	Usually not present

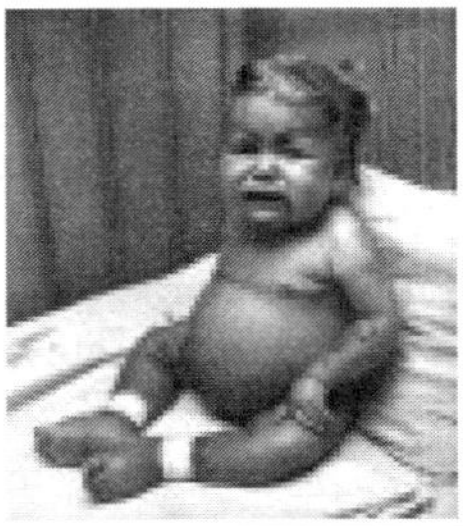

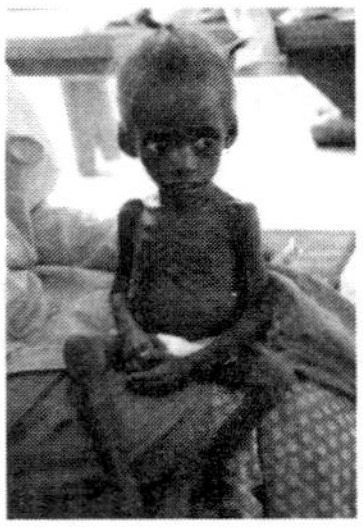

Source: Rolfes et al. 2009.

Images: http://pixshark.com/kwashiorkor-symptoms.htm
http://pixgood.com/marasmus.html

In children with **marasmus,** there is generally severe growth failure. The child's muscles are wasted, and there is absolutely no fat under the skin. The child thus looks like a mass of bones covered with skin. Such children are very irritable and fretful, and also apathetic, like the children with kwashiorkor. Diarrhoea is a frequent problem that these children suffer from. The differences between Kwashiorkor and Marasmus have been highlighted in Table 6.3.

Marasmic kwashiorkor is a condition in between the two extremes, and children suffering from this condition show symptoms of both kwashiorkor and marasmus.

Most children in India now show only milder forms of under-nutrition. The prevalence of severe forms of PEM is very low. These children are growing up smaller than their genetic potential. They are thin, weigh less and are shorter than children of their age who have access to a nutritionally adequate diet and healthcare, or those residing in developed countries of the world. These children are also at greater risk of developing respiratory or intestinal infections, which can precipitate the more severe symptoms of malnutrition.

Functional Consequences

Why should we be concerned about malnutrition? The answer lies in the fact that height and weight are only some of the outer and more visible effects of malnutrition. Underweight and stunted children may not achieve their full growth potential, and as thin short adults, their physical work capacity would also be impaired. However, the most serious effect is on mental development and learning. If brain development is irreversibly retarded, this could mean that nations with large numbers of malnourished children might be unable to achieve economic and social equality with the rest of the world. Malnutrition thus has serious consequences for human development and the productivity of a nation.

The marasmic infant is in great danger of retarded mental development. Retardation is less frequent and less severe in kwashiorkor. Malnutrition can have two effects on the child's potential mental development: first, if the nutrients required for the multiplication and growth of the brain cells are lacking during the period of most rapid development of the brain, it appears highly unlikely that the deficiency can be corrected by improved nutrition once the time cycle for brain development has gone by. It can be expected that the effects would be most profound in severe malnutrition during the first year of life. If nutrition is satisfactory during infancy and subsequently deteriorates, the effects are less devastating.

The second effect of malnutrition in the preschool years may be on the interference of learning that normally occurs in healthy preschool children at a truly fantastic rate. The apathy, lack of curiosity and reduced activity of the malnourished child over a long period of time will greatly reduce the amount of learning. Thus, the development of behavioural characteristics expected of the normal child at any given age may be delayed for months or years, and may sometimes never be fully corrected.

Hence, it is vital that children are given proper nutrition during these crucial years of growth and development. The consequences are far too serious and irreparable to ignore.

Prevention

PEM is a consequence not only of inadequate food intake, but also of poor living conditions, unhygienic environment, and lack of healthcare. Thus, its control and prevention requires a variety of intervention measures. The government runs the Integrated Child Development Services (ICDS) programme, under which food supplements are provided to children up to the age of five, and to pregnant and lactating women. Other health activities are also included under this programme, namely immunisation, treatment of minor illnesses, growth monitoring, and health education. Timely healthcare interventions are of great importance, as frequent and untreated diseases further deteriorate the nutritional status of children. Better sanitation and hygiene, provision of safe drinking water, and clean, wholesome food are also critical in preventing infection and illness.

Education programmes to improve child nutrition should stress:

- The importance of exclusive breast-feeding during the first six months.
- Avoiding infant formulae which, apart from being expensive, are often diluted with unclean water. Hygienic bottle feeding is almost impossible in a poor environment, and puts the children at greater risk of developing diarrhoea and malnutrition.

- Timely introduction of complementary feeds at the age of six months. These should be based on household foods, like cereals and pulses.
- Addition of oil and sugar to these complementary foods will increase the calorie density.
- In addition, mashed vegetables and fruits should also be included in the diet, as a source of vitamins and minerals.
- The health/*anganwadi* worker should check the growth chart of the child to assess the adequacy of feeding. Growth monitoring is an important tool to detect malnutrition in its early stages.
- Measures to maintain good personal hygiene and environmental sanitation should also be explained to mothers.

Problem of Excess

Intake of large amounts of protein does not provide us with any extra benefits. In fact, it is recommended that protein intake should not exceed 35 per cent of the energy intake. Most of the excess protein is simply broken down to release energy. This results in an increased production of nitrogenous waste products like urea, which need to be excreted by the kidney. This also increases the need for more water to excrete the waste products. In infants, especially those who were premature (and hence did not have fully developed kidneys), feeding concentrated formula feeds can have serious consequences, with the kidney being unable to tolerate heavy loads or the baby becoming dehydrated due to a loss of water in the form of urine. This is also of concern in individuals with impaired kidney function.

> Nitrogen makes up approximately 16% the weight of an amino acid. Therefore as,
>
> 16/100 = 6.25,
>
> An estimate of protein intake can be obtained from nitrogen intake by multiplying with this factor of 6.25
>
> **Nitrogen (g) x 6.25 = Protein(g)**

Very high protein diets may also increase the urinary loss of calcium, leading to a loss of bone mass and eventually increasing the risk of osteoporosis. If the protein is being derived mostly from animal sources, chances are that the person is consuming too much of saturated fat and cholesterol, which is bad for cardiovascular health. If the diet consists primarily of animal proteins (as most Western diets), it is likely to be low in plant-based foods. Consequently, it will be lower in protective phytochemicals, fibre, and some vitamins like vitamins C, E and folate, as well as minerals like magnesium and potassium.

Individual amino acid supplementation and excess protein supplementation is a concern with sportspersons. Whole proteins in our diets provide us with amino acids in a proportion needed for body functions. When individual amino acids are taken as supplements, chemically similar amino acids compete for absorption, resulting in amino acid imbalances, and sometimes toxicity. Methionine, cysteine and histidine are considered the most toxic amino acids.

PROTEIN QUALITY

The primary function of dietary proteins is to provide amino acids in appropriate patterns for the synthesis of tissue proteins during growth and reproduction, for the replacement of the endogenous losses of tissue proteins, and for other metabolic needs. The nutritive value of a dietary protein is an expression indicating its ability to meet the protein needs of the body. The first step in the evaluation of a protein is the determination of the content of essential amino acids (EAA). The efficacy of a food to provide the essential amino acids is defined as the **protein quality** of that food. The quality of a protein is dependent on its amino acid profile, and the availability of the amino acids relative to the requirement for EAA and non-specific nitrogen by the target species. The purpose of measuring protein quality is essentially to determine the usefulness of a protein for supporting life. It is also important for setting the protein requirements of a population. The protein quality of new foods is used to rank the foods. In addition, the effect of breeding, processing and storage on the proteins can be studied by assessing the change in protein quality.

The protein content of a food is estimated by measuring the nitrogen content of the food. This is usually done by *Kjeldahl's method*, which involves sulphuric acid oxidation of the organic matter to release nitrogen in the form of ammonia. The estimated nitrogen is then multiplied by a factor of 6.25 to get the protein content (as most proteins have 16 per cent nitrogen). The methods used for determining the contents of individual essential amino acids in proteins are chemical, microbiological and chromatographic. The protein needs to be hydrolysed to give amino acids. The chromatographic methods include paper, column, HPLC, and GLC.

Automated amino acid analysers are now available, which have greatly reduced the time and effort required for analysis. Microbiological methods depend on the assumption that the response of an organism is specific for the given amino acid. For instance, the bacteria *Streptococcus fecalis* is used for the assay of threonine. There are bio assay methods, too, which mostly use mammals like rats.

METHODS FOR ASSESSING PROTEIN QUALITY

Methods for assessing protein quality are either biological or chemical. In **Biological methods,** the protein food is introduced into a living system (for example, mammals, chicks, microbes, humans, etc.). These methods have an advantage—we come to know how a food will be handled inside the body with respect to digestibility and availability of amino acids. The food can also be checked for its efficacy for growth. Examples of these methods include growth studies (PER, NPR) and balance studies (NPU, BV).

Chemical methods are based on aminograms (which tell us how much of each type of amino acid is present in the food). Although these are rough estimates, the results correlate well with biologic methods. These methods are also less time-consuming. Foods with unknown toxicology and digestibility can be easily checked by the chemical methods first. The disadvantage of these methods is that we do not come to know about the digestibility of the protein food, or the availability of the amino acids. An example of chemical method is chemical score.

Chemical Score

The nutritive value of a protein depends on the quantity of EAA present in it. If one or more EAA are not present in adequate amounts, the nutritive value of the protein will be low, depending on the degree of the deficiency. This is because all amino acids must be present at the site of protein synthesis in adequate amounts for protein synthesis to proceed in the body. The first or the most limiting amino acid, that is, the one which is in the greatest deficit, would presumably determine the protein quality. Egg proteins contain all EAA in adequate amounts and possess the highest nutritive value among dietary proteins. Block and Mitchell (1946) assigned a chemical score of 100 to egg proteins, and evolved a system of chemical scores for rating the nutritive value of other dietary proteins by expressing the quantity of the most limiting amino acid in different food proteins as a percentage of the same amino acid present in egg proteins.

Reference protein is a standard protein against which we measure the quality of other proteins. It is a high biological value protein containing a specified pattern of essential amino acids, which is 100 per cent utilisable by the body. Earlier, in the 1990s, egg or milk protein were used as a standard. Now an amino acid pattern that represents all essential amino acids in the right quantities (per g of protein) as required by the body is used as a reference amino acid pattern (WHO 2007 scoring pattern). Usually, the four EAAs most likely to be limiting in our diets are lysine, sulphur-containing amino acids (methionine + cystine), threonine, and tryptophan.

$$\text{AMINO ACID SCORE} = \frac{\text{mg of amino acid in 1g test protein}}{\text{mg of amino acid in 1g reference protein}} \times 100$$

Advantages

The main advantage of the amino acid scoring method is that it can easily be determined, provided the data on the amino acid content of the food is available.

Limitations

1. It is calculated on the basis of the apparent quantity of amino acids. The influence of commercial and household processing on the availability of amino acids needs to be taken into account. Processing may alter the availability of the amino acids without changing the total quantity, for example, lysine may be bound by the maillard reaction and become biologically inactive.
2. Amino acid imbalance, for instance the excess of leucine in sorghum and maize, apparently increases the need for isoleucine, which is not indicated by the chemical score method.
3. It does not consider digestibility.
4. It does not take into account inhibitors and other toxic substances present in the protein source.

The effect of digestibility can be considered by using the **Protein Digestibility Corrected Amino Acid Score (PDCAAS)**. To calculate this for a protein, the chemical score is multiplied by the digestibility of the protein. Chemical score varies from 0 to 1. For example, the Chemical score of wheat is 0.47 and digestibility 0.90; the PDCAAS is thus 0.47 x 0.90 = 0.42 approximately. The maximum value is 1.0, which is the value of most animal proteins. A protein missing any of the nine EAA has a PDCAAS of 0, as the chemical score is 0. The protein quality values of individual foods are important, but the protein quality of a total meal is more important.

PDCAAS Values for Common Foods

Egg white	–	1.0
Soya protein	–	0.92 to 0.99
Meat	–	0.92
Wheat	–	0.40
Gelatin	–	0

Net Dietary Protein as Per cent of Calories (NDpCal%)

This method relates protein quality to energy intake. It is useful in the evaluation of human diets, in which the relation of protein to total calories may vary markedly. It is a proportion of the dietary calories supplied by the protein, corrected for the efficiency of protein utilisation or protein quality, and expressed as a percentage. It is useful for the evaluation of human diets to examine or predict if the protein needs of an individual would be met for the total energy consumed in the diet. Diets that provide less than 5 per cent of calories in the form of available protein will not meet the protein needs of human adults. For children, an NDpCal% of at least 8 per cent is needed to meet the requirements for growth.

$$\text{NDpCal\%} = \frac{\text{Protein calories} \times \text{Chemical score}}{\text{Total calories}}$$

Net Dietary Protein (NDp) is utilisable protein, determined as:

protein (g) × NPU (by biological method) or,

protein (g) × chemical score (by chemical method)

If it is expressed as utilisable protein calories as percentage of total calories, it is called NDpCal%. It is most useful when applied to groups, because the individual's protein and calorie needs are difficult to assess.

Biological Methods: Protein Efficiency Ratio (PER)

The method was proposed in 1917 by Osborn et al. (1919). It assesses how well a given protein supports weight gain in growing laboratory animals like rats. It is defined as the gain in body weight per gram of protein consumed.

$$\text{PER} = \frac{\text{Weight gain (g)}}{\text{Total protein intake (g)}}.$$

The procedure involves feeding a 10 per cent protein diet to weanling (21-day-old) rats *ad libitum* for a period of four weeks, and comparing the results with casein-based control diets. The PER of casein is 2.5. If the PER value of the casein control group is different in the experiment, a correction factor needs to be applied:

$$\text{Correction factor} = \frac{\text{PER of test protein}}{\text{PER of standard casein}} \times 2.5$$

Advantages

- Simplest biological technique to determine protein quality.
- Fairly reliable technique.
- Simple and quick.
- Can rank and order different foods according to protein quality.
- Regulatory authorities use PER to set standards for the labelling of foods intended for infants.
- Can compare difference in protein quality, that is, the effect of processing and breeding.

Limitations

- Acceptance of the test diet is important, otherwise the PER values are affected.
- No allowance is made for protein used for maintenance.
- Weight gain is neither constant nor dependent on the composition of diet alone. Also, weight gain may be a result of fat or water accumulation. The composition of weight gain may vary with the test proteins.
- Results vary with the duration of the study, the age and sex of rats, and the level of protein in the diet.
- High degree of variability seen in the results, especially with the level of protein fed.

Net Protein Ratio (NPR)

This method is a modification of the PER method, and was suggested by Bender and Doell (1957). The method involves feeding a 10 per cent protein diet to a group of weanling rats. The control group of animals is fed a non-protein diet, or a 4 per cent egg protein diet. The experimental period is 10 days.

$$\text{NPR} = \frac{\text{Wt gain on test diet} - \text{Wt. gain on basal (non-protein diet)}}{\text{Protein consumed (g)}}$$

Advantages

- Takes into account maintenance requirements.
- Sensitive method, which gives reliable results.
- Duration of the study is only 10 days.
- Can be used to rank protein sources.

Limitations

- Weight monitoring is the main variable, for which a 10-day period may be too short.
- One extra group has to be studied.

Biological Value (BV)

This is a measure of how efficiently absorbed protein or nitrogen is converted into body tissue protein for growth and maintenance. To determine BV, nitrogen retention in the body is compared with the nitrogen absorbed from food protein. More nitrogen is retained when a food's amino acid pattern closely matches the amino acid pattern of the body protein.

$$\text{BV} = \frac{\text{N retained}}{\text{N absorbed}} \times 100$$

BV is determined by nitrogen balance studies and is applicable to both humans and laboratory animals. Control animals are fed protein-free diets to get the values of endogenous losses. The test group is fed a 10 per cent protein diet. Rats (28 days old) are commonly used for the determination of BV. Chicks are also sometimes used. Records of food intake are maintained. Urine and faeces are collected by keeping the animals in metabolic cages. The diet, urine and faeces are analysed for nitrogen content. A protein of BV > 70 per cent is capable of supporting growth, provided that sufficient calories are also ingested. The BV of some commonly eaten foods is: Egg white – 100 per cent; milk – 93 per cent; rice – 86 per cent; corn – 72 per cent; and wheat gluten – 44 per cent. The BV of plant proteins is usually much lower than that of animal proteins, as plant amino acid patterns differ greatly from those of humans.

$$\text{BV} = \frac{I - (F - F_0) - (U - U_0)}{I - (F - F_0)} \times 100$$

where, I = Nitrogen intake

U = Urinary nitrogen

F = Faecal nitrogen

U_0& F_0 = Nitrogen excreted in urine and faeces, respectively, when subjects are maintained on a protein-free diet

Advantages

- BV aids in determining the amount of protein required for positive nitrogen balance.
- Useful for designing diets for sick people, especially in kidney and liver diseases, where it is desirable to have as much dietary protein, which will be used for tissue synthesis, with very few amino acids left over to burden the already elevated blood urea or ammonia levels.
- Aids in assessing the difference in protein quality due to processing.
- Can be conducted in animals in different physiological states like pregnancy, lactation and growth, in order to examine the effectiveness of a protein to meet demands during altered conditions.

Limitations

- Animals on a protein-free diet often do not consume sufficient feed to maintain their body weight. Endogenous losses may thus be overestimated due to the catabolism of tissue protein. The error is corrected by feeding a 4 per cent protein diet from a source that is totally utilised by the animals.
- The method does not take into account the digestibility of the protein.

Net Protein Utilisation (NPU)

The proportion of nitrogen consumed, which is retained by the body under standard conditions, is known as the NPU (Bender and Miller 1953). It is a measure both of the digestibility of the food protein and the biological value of the amino acid mixture absorbed from food. When food proteins are completely digested, the NPU and BV will be the same. When foods contain a lot of fibre and have a lower digestibility, the NPU will be lower than the BV.

$$\text{NPU} = \frac{\text{N retained}}{\text{N intake}} \times 100$$

The NPU represents the proportion of food nitrogen retained, whereas BV represents the proportion of absorbed nitrogen retained. NPU is therefore directly related to the dietary intake of nitrogen. Nitrogen retention can be measured by nitrogen balance studies, or by direct analysis of the animal body (**carcass analysis**). The method requires two groups of experimental animals matched for weight and age. One group is fed a test protein at 10 per cent level, while the control group is fed a protein-free diet. At the end of the feeding period (usually 10 days), the carcasses are analysed for the amount of nitrogen retained.

$$\text{NPU} = \frac{\text{Body N test group} - \text{Body N in zero N intake group}}{\text{Nitrogen intake}} \times 100$$

Using the N Balance technique, the protein (nitrogen) intake and N output in faeces and urine is measured. Skin and sweat losses are difficult to measure. One group is fed the test protein and the other group a protein-free diet.

$$\text{NPU} = \frac{I - (F - F_0) - (U - U_0)}{I} \times 100$$

where, I = Nitrogen intake

U = Urinary nitrogen

F = Faecal nitrogen

U_0 & F_0 = Nitrogen excreted in urine and faeces, respectively, when subjects are maintained on a protein-free diet

Advantages

- It helps in calculating the net available protein in the diet.
- The method has good correlation with PER and Chemical Score values.

Limitations

- Considerable care is required as a number of factors can influence the outcome of the procedure, viz., animals suffering from infections, or under stress; and the overall composition of the diet.
- Food alone gives a lower value than a mixed diet, for example, the NPU of mixed diet is about 65, whereas it is 50–55 for a rice diet.
- It is a tedious method.

FACTORS AFFECTING PROTEIN QUALITY

The most important among the factors affecting protein quality are:

1. **Amino acid content and availability of amino acids**

   All essential amino acids must be present in adequate quantities for a protein to be rated as a 'good quality protein'. These amino acids must be readily available, and not in a bound form that cannot be utilised.

2. **Amino acid imbalance**

   Certain amino acids, when present in excessive amounts, increase the requirements of one or more amino acids, and adversely affect the growth of experimental animals. A well-known example is the imbalance between leucine and isoleucine in maize, *jowar* and sorghum. These foods contain an excess of leucine, which interferes with the absorption of isoleucine and valine. All three have similar structures, and hence compete for the same carrier molecules during absorption. A relative deficiency of isoleucine and valine is created.

3. **Interference of dietary fibre in digestion and absorption**

   Present mostly in the cell walls, the non-available carbohydrates prevent the access of digestive juices to the proteins in the cells. Consequently, in whole cereals, millets, legumes, nuts, and oilseeds containing fair amounts of these carbohydrates (cellulose, hemi cellulose, gums, and pectin), the digestibility of the proteins is low.

4. **Interference by trypsin and growth inhibitors in absorption and utilisation**

   Trypsin and growth inhibitors such as haemagglutinins present in various legumes exert a deleterious effect on the utilisation of protein for promoting the growth of animals. Optimal heat treatment has been found to inactivate the inhibitors and haemagglutinins, and improve the quality of proteins for promoting growth.

5. **Influence of heat processing on protein utilisation**

   Heat processing produces both beneficial and deleterious effects on the nutritive value of proteins. The beneficial effects are due to the inactivation of toxic factors, while the adverse effects are due to the decrease in the availability of certain essential amino acids—such as lysine and methionine—as a result of a reaction with the reducing sugars and carbonyl compounds present in the food (Maillard reaction). The loss of amino acids depends on the severity of the heat treatment and the moisture content of the food. Severe heat processing of cereals, for instance, through toasting, puffing and gun explosion techniques, have been reported to cause a drastic reduction in the nutritive value of proteins (specially of oilseeds and nut proteins).

6. **Level of protein in the diet**

   As the level of protein in the diet is increased beyond the optimal level, there is a steady decline in the percentage of utilisation of the protein. Evaluation of protein quality is generally carried out at 10 per cent protein level, with foods containing 11 per cent or more of proteins.

7. **Effect of calorie intake on protein utilisation**

   Restriction in calorie intake adversely affects the utilisation of dietary proteins. Restriction of calorie intake to 66 per cent and 50 per cent, respectively, brings about a marked decrease in the NPU and NPR of casein.

8. **Effect of vitamin and mineral deficiencies in the evaluation of protein quality**

   Studies have shown that if diets deficient in certain vitamins and minerals are supplemented with an addition of salt mixture and vitamin premix, the PER is increased to a marked extent.

9. **Effect of stress on protein utilisation**

   Different types of stresses, such as infection, fever, injury, climatic extremes, and psychological stress, have been found to affect protein utilisation and requirements. They act either by interfering with the digestion and absorption of protein, or by increasing the endogenous metabolism of tissue proteins.

10. **Experimental conditions**

    In addition, protein quality estimations are also affected by factors like the length of the assay period, inability to study all routes of excretion in balance studies, the water intake, and meal frequency and timing. Thus, the limitations of balance and growth studies will also become factors that affect the evaluation of protein quality.

Methods of Improving the Protein Quality of Human Diets

Most people around the world consume diets in which the protein is derived mainly from plant foods. Plant proteins are generally deficient in one or more EAA. Foods need to be combined in order to supply sufficient amounts of all EAA. When appreciable amounts of plant proteins are fed with a small amount of animal protein foods, the quality of the mixture is as effective as if only animal proteins had been fed. For example, small amounts of milk, cheese, or egg will supply the lysine that is limiting in cereal foods. Legumes, whole grains, nuts, and vegetables provide a satisfactory combination of amino acids for pure vegetarians. In order for plant foods to supply all essential amino acids simultaneously, food combinations must be consumed preferably at the same meal. Legumes are low in methionine and cystine, but are good sources of lysine, whereas cereal grains and nuts are low in lysine but good sources of methionine and cystine. The two, eaten together, can provide good quality protein. This is known as **mutual supplementation,** and the proteins are known as **Complementary proteins** (Table 6.4).

Table 6.4: Use of Complementary Proteins to Improve Protein Quality of Diets

Food		*Limiting Amino Acid*	*Foods to Combine with*	*Combinations with mutual supplementation*
Cereal grains and millets (wheat, rice, corn, *bajra, ragi, jowar* etc.)		Lysine	Legumes	*Chapati with dal Rice with dal Khicheri (rice+ dal), idli, dosa, Besan toast*
Legumes (all *dals, rajmah, chole, lobia,* etc.)	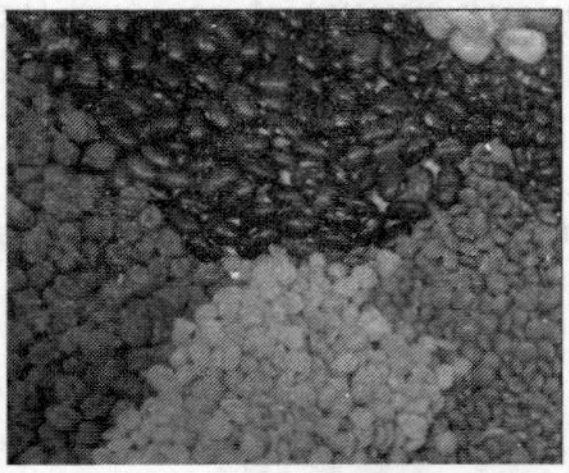	Methionine Tryptophan	Cereal grains Nuts Oilseeds	In addition to the above, *Besan ladoo/burfi* with nuts or til (sesame seeds), *dal halwa* with chopped nuts
Nuts and oilseeds (cashew nut, almonds, walnuts, sesame seeds, sunflower seeds)		Lysine	Legumes	In addition to the above *ladoo, burfi, halwa* preparations, Soya bread with sunflower seeds, *Besan pakora*/toast with sesame seeds

Source: Adapted from Byrd-Bredbenner et al. 2013.

Amino acid supplementation of foods has also been proposed as a way of improving protein quality. Thus, the addition of lysine to bread improves the biologic value of the bread. However, there is a possibility of creating an imbalance of amino acids in low-protein diets by such supplementation, which would actually retard growth.

Plant food mixtures using locally available plant foods have been developed, which are comparable to milk in their biologic value. In many developing countries, animal protein sources are scarce and expensive. For children, a protein supply of satisfactory quality is critical. *Incaparina*, a mixture of cottonseed and corn flours, torula yeast, vitamins, and minerals, has been used in Central America. Corn Soya Blend (CSB) was developed in the USA, and is a blend of pre-cooked maize, defatted soyabean flour, skim milk powder, sugar, vitamins, and calcium. In India, *BalAhar*, made of wheat and groundnut; *BalAmul*, a commercial product based on wheat, soyabean and green gram; and *Lac*-Tone, which was composed of groundnut flour, skim milk powder, wheat and barley flour, vitamins and calcium, have been extensively used in feeding programmes. Feeding programmes have now changed to freshly cooked food for the most part, although for infants, the food is usually in the form of a mix that can be made into porridge or *laddoo*, etc., at home.

Germination and Fermentation also improve protein quality by breaking down complex protein substances, and improving the digestibility of the food by removing inhibitory substances like trypsin inhibitors, haemagglutinins, etc. **Heat processing** also destroys the inhibitors and anti-nutritional factors.

Genetic engineering is being used to increase the protein content of cereals like wheat and maize, and also for increasing the amount of lysine so that it is no longer limiting.

In addition, care must be taken to include sufficient amounts of energy in the diet from carbohydrates and fats, so that proteins can be spared to perform the function of tissue building and growth. This is especially crucial during growth phases in childhood.

SUMMARY

- Amino acids are the building blocks of proteins. Out of the 20 amino acids needed by the body, nine must be provided in the diet, and hence are called essential amino acids. The other 11 can be synthesised in the human body.
- Proteins derived from animal foods are considered to be of high quality or 'complete proteins'. Plant proteins like cereal proteins and pulse proteins are 'partially complete', as they are deficient in amino acids like lysine and methionine, respectively.
- Proteins have an important role to play in providing structural support to body cells and tissues. They are also required for maintaining fluid balance, acid-base balance, helping in the synthesis of hormones, enzymes and neurotransmitters, contributing to immune functions, transporting nutrients, and also for providing energy or synthesising glucose if the need arises.
- Deficiency of protein in isolation is not common. It mainly occurs with energy deficiency. The condition is referred to as Protein Energy Malnutrition (PEM). There are two forms of PEM seen in children, Kwashiokor and Marasmus.
- A child with Kwashiorkor has oedema, hair and skin changes, fatty liver, moderate growth failure, and wasting. A Marasmic child, on the other hand, has much more severe wasting of muscles and loss of body fat, 'skin and bone' appearance, and severe growth impairment.
- Growth monitoring of young children, prevention of infectious diseases, food supplementation to improve diets, nutrition education to mothers, and information about correct weaning practices may help to tackle the problem of PEM.
- Protein quality is a measure of the food protein's ability to support body growth and maintenance. It is determined by the food's digestibility and amino acid composition. Digestibility of animal proteins is quite high, while in comparison, the digestibility of most plant proteins is lower.
- Chemical score, PDCAAS, PER, Biological Value, and NPU are some of the common methods of protein quality estimation.
- Protein quality of foods is affected by a number of factors like amino acid composition, imbalance, presence of fibre, and inhibitory compounds like enzyme inhibitors, the heat processing the food protein is subjected to, and the level of carbohydrates, proteins, vitamins, and minerals in the diet, which are important for the proper utilisation of the protein. Stress and other conditions during experiments for protein quality estimation can also affect the values obtained.

- The protein quality of diets can be improved by mutual supplementation, blending different types of protein foods to arrive at an ideal amino acid composition, fortification with individual amino acids, germination, fermentation, and genetic modification of foods.

KEY WORDS

Biological Value: A measure of how efficiently absorbed protein or nitrogen is converted into body tissue protein for growth and maintenance.

Chemical Score: Of a protein is calculated by dividing the amount of each essential amino acid present in a gram of test protein by the amount in a gram of reference protein. The lowest (limiting) amino acid ratio obtained is the chemical score of that protein.

Complementary proteins: Proteins which, when eaten together, make up for any deficiency in the amount of essential amino acids contained in individual proteins, thus making the combination a complete or good quality protein.

Essential Amino Acids: Cannot be synthesised by the body at a rate sufficient to meet the needs for growth and maintenance. Hence, these need to be consumed in the diet.

Mutual Supplementation: Achieved when a protein deficient in a certain amino acid (for example, cereal protein is lacking in lysine, but has sufficient amounts of other essential amino acids) is consumed with another protein (say, pulse protein, which has sufficient lysine but may be deficient in methionine). In such a food combination, each food makes up for the deficiency in the other.

Protein Digestibility Corrected Amino Acid Score (PDCAAS): Is a measure of protein quality. It is calculated by multiplying the chemical score of the protein by the digestibility of the protein.

Protein Efficiency Ratio (PER): Assesses how well a given protein supports weight gain in growing animals or humans. It is defined as the gain in body weight per gram of protein consumed.

Reference protein: A standard protein against which we measure the quality of other proteins. It is a high biological value protein, containing a specified pattern of essential amino acids, which is 100 per cent utilisable by the body.

EXERCISES

1. What is meant by 'complete' and 'partially complete proteins'? Explain, giving examples of food sources.
2. Describe the functions of proteins.
3. What happens if the diet is deficient in protein?
4. What situations increase the risk of being in negative nitrogen balance?
5. What can go wrong if you consume very high quantities of protein in your diet?
6. What is meant by 'protein quality'? Describe any two methods of assessing the protein quality of a food.
7. What are the factors that affect protein quality?
8. Discuss some ways of improving the protein quality of diets.

REFERENCES

Bender, A. E. and B. H. Doell, 'Biological evaluation of proteins. A new aspect', *Brit J Nutr.* 11, 1957, p. 140.

Bender, A. E. and D. S. Miller, 'A new brief method of estimating net protein value', *Biochem J.* 53, 1953, p. vii.

Byrd-Bredbenner, C., G. Moe, D. Beshgetoor, and J. Berning, *Wardlaw's Perspectives in Nutrition*, 9e, New York: McGraw-Hill International Edition, 2013.

ICMR, 'Nutrient Requirements and Recommended Dietary Allowances for Indians', A report of the Expert Group of the Indian Council of Medical Research, 2010.

Kalyansundaram, S., 'Proteins', in M. S. Bamji, K. Krishnaswamy and G. N. V. Brahmam (eds), *Textbook of Human Nutrition*, 3e, Oxford and IBH Publ Co., 2009, pp. 18–31.

Osborne, T. B., L. B. Mendel and E. L. Ferry, 'A method of expressing numerically a growth promoting value of proteins', *J Biol. Chem.* 37, 1919, p. 223.

Mitchell, H. H. and E. J. Block, 'Some Relationships between the Amino Acid Contents of Proteins and their Nutritive Value', *Rat. J. Biol. Chem.* 163, 1946, pp. 599–620.

WHO/FAO/UNU, 'Protein and Amino Acid Requirements in Human Nutrition', Report of a Joint WHO/FAO/UNU Expert Consultation, 2007.

7

WATER AND THE MAJOR MINERALS

HIGHLIGHTS

- The need for water
- Factors affecting water balance and its maintenance
- Dehydration and water intoxication
- Dietary sources of water and major minerals
- Functions of major minerals
- Problems of deficiency and excess of major minerals

Water is the largest component of the human body, making up 50 to 70 per cent of the body weight, depending on age and body composition. Water content is highest in infants and young children, gradually declining with age. It makes up about 75 per cent of the weight of lean tissue and less than 25 per cent of the weight of fat. Hence, a person's body composition influences the proportion of body weight present as water. For example, lean individuals have a greater percentage of body water than obese individuals. Typically, an adult male has 60 per cent of his body weight as water, compared to 55 per cent in an adult female. The difference is related to the fact that women have a higher body fat per cent than men.

Minerals are essential inorganic elements, which are needed by our body for its normal functioning. Our body is unable to synthesise these minerals as these are basic elements, and hence they are an essential part of our diet. Minerals are divided into two categories—major and trace minerals. Major or macrominerals are those that our body requires in quantities greater than 100 mg per day, otherwise they are considered trace or microminerals. Major minerals are also found in larger quantities in our body, as compared to trace minerals. In this chapter, we will learn about the major minerals, such as calcium, phosphorus, magnesium, sodium, and potassium.

Water in our bodies is basically present in two compartments—the intracellular compartment, inside each and every cell of our body, where about two-thirds of the body water is present; and the extracellular compartment, outside the cells, where one-third of the total body water is present. The extracellular fluid is present in the form of interstitial fluid (the fluid present in between cells) and intravascular fluid (the fluid present inside vessels, that is, blood and lymph). The amount of interstitial fluid is much greater than the amount of fluid in our blood vessels.

The fluid in these compartments is not pure water, but contains dissolved solids. Most of these solids are electrolytes. The intracellular fluids have potassium as the major cation (positively charged ion), along with magnesium. Sodium is the major cation in the extracellular fluid, followed by calcium. The major anions (negatively charged ions) present in intracellular fluid are phosphate and sulphate, while the major anions in extracellular fluid are chloride and bicarbonate.

FUNCTIONS

Water is perhaps the most essential nutrient for our body. It is needed in the largest quantity, and without it life is not possible. One cannot survive without water beyond a few days, whereas deficiency of any other nutrient would only prove fatal after many weeks, months, or years. Let us learn about the various functions of water.

1. Water as a Medium and Solvent: Water is the medium in which all metabolic processes of our body take place. Water itself participates in several metabolic reactions. It serves as a solvent for vitamins, minerals, amino acids, glucose, and many other substances, so they can participate in reactions. It is the medium of all cell fluids, digestive juices, lymph, blood, urine, and perspiration, and hence important for the process of digestion, absorption, transport, and excretion of nutrients and waste products.
2. Constituent of Structure: Water maintains the structure of large molecules such as proteins and glycogen. Many substances present in our body are in their hydrated forms.
3. Lubricant and Cushioning Effect: Water acts as a lubricant in joints (synovial fluid), making movement easier and minimising wear and tear of cartilage and bone. The lubricant action of saliva in the mouth helps in the easy movement of food down the oesophagus. Water also acts as a cushion around the joints, inside the eyes, and around the brain and spinal cord (cerebrospinal fluid). During pregnancy, the amniotic fluid in the amniotic sac surrounding the developing foetus acts as a shock absorber and protects the baby.
4. Temperature Regulation: Water helps in the regulation of normal body temperature. Blood takes away the heat produced during metabolic activities in the cells, distributing it throughout the body. Water has high specific heat, which means that a relatively large amount of heat is required to raise its temperature. Excess heat of the body is lost by the evaporation of sweat.
5. Maintenance of Blood Volume: Water, being the main constituent of plasma in blood, helps in the maintenance of blood volume.
6. Source of Dietary Minerals: The water consumed by us is a source of dietary minerals, like calcium, magnesium, zinc, copper, and fluoride. The amount of minerals present is dependent on the source of water. Hard water is a source of magnesium and calcium, while soft water may contain sodium.

REGULATION OF WATER BALANCE

When we talk of water balance, we have to consider both water intake and water output (losses). The hypothalamus is a part of the brain which acts as a centre for controlling the maintenance of water balance. It regulates the thirst sensation. When water intake is inadequate, the blood becomes concentrated, the mouth feels dry, and the message is sent to the hypothalamus. Thirst sensation makes us realise that we need to drink water. Unfortunately, this sensation comes only after the body has already started becoming dehydrated. We also tend to ignore the first thirst signals that our body gives us, due to preoccupation with work or unavailability of water in our immediate environment.

The best way to determine whether your water intake is normal is to observe the colour of your urine. If you are dehydrated, your urine will be dark yellow, whereas if you are adequately hydrated, the urine is clear or pale yellow. Concentrated urine increases the risk of kidney stones, as minerals and other substances precipitate out of the urine and get accumulated in kidney tissues. Drinking sufficient water also protects us against constipation.

In addition to the water we consume in foods and beverages, water is also produced as a result of several metabolic processes (up to 250–350 ml in a day). These constitute water input when looking at balance in the body. Water output is in the form of urine and heavy perspiration (sensible losses), and also in the form of normal perspiration, water vapour in breath, and moisture in faeces (insensible losses).

Kidneys are the main organs regulating fluid balance by controlling urine production (Figure 7.1). If the level of water in the body is low, less urine is produced. The kidney reabsorbs some amount from the water filtered in the kidney tubules. The intestine (especially the large intestine) also absorbs water from the intestinal contents. The hypothalamus plays a key role in maintaining water balance. It stimulates the posterior pituitary gland to produce the antidiuretic hormone (ADH) when water intake is low. ADH sends a message to the kidney to retain water by reducing urine output. Other hormones like renin, angiotensin and aldosterone also act in a sequence to retain more water in the body.

When water intake is more than that required by the body, the kidneys decrease the reabsorption of water, thus increasing the volume of urine produced. If, for any reason, the kidney is unable to excrete the extra water, it may lead to water intoxication.

Figure 7.1: Regulation of Blood Volume

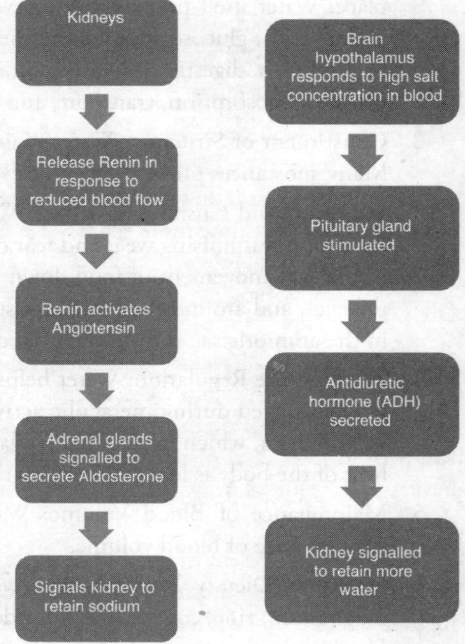

Source: Byrd-Bredbrenner et al. 2013.

PROBLEM OF FLUID IMBALANCE

Dehydration results if water output is more than the intake. This can happen due to a variety of reasons. Vomiting and diarrhoea are perhaps the most common causes of dehydration. Heavy physical activity or exercising in very hot, humid or dry environments increases the risk of dehydration, as people sweat excessively without matching the water loss by consuming sufficient fluids. Sweat loss can range from 750 ml to even 2 litres per hour. Dehydrated individuals are unable to perform well and can suffer from heat exhaustion and cramps. Special attention needs to be paid to the fluid intake of sick children and the elderly, as they are vulnerable to dehydration during illness, especially if they have diarrhoea and vomiting.

In mild to moderate dehydration, the person experiences dryness in the mouth, fatigue, muscle weakness, decreased urine output, deep yellow urine, dizziness, and headache (Figure 7.2). Dehydration can become a life-threatening situation as the blood pressure and blood volume decrease, but the heart rate increases, and there is laboured breathing and mental confusion. Ultimately the kidneys fail, and the person may experience seizures (fits) and delirium (disordered state of mind), and slip into a coma. If untreated, dehydration can result in death. Most of the deaths due to diarrhoea among children in developing countries are due to severe dehydration. Children have a high percentage of their weight in the form of body water, and so they tend to get dehydrated faster.

> ***Obligatory Water Loss***
>
> This is the amount of water the body has to lose daily in order to be able to excrete the waste products. In adults, this is a minimum loss of 500 ml each day (roughly about two cups).

Figure 7.2: Severity of Dehydration

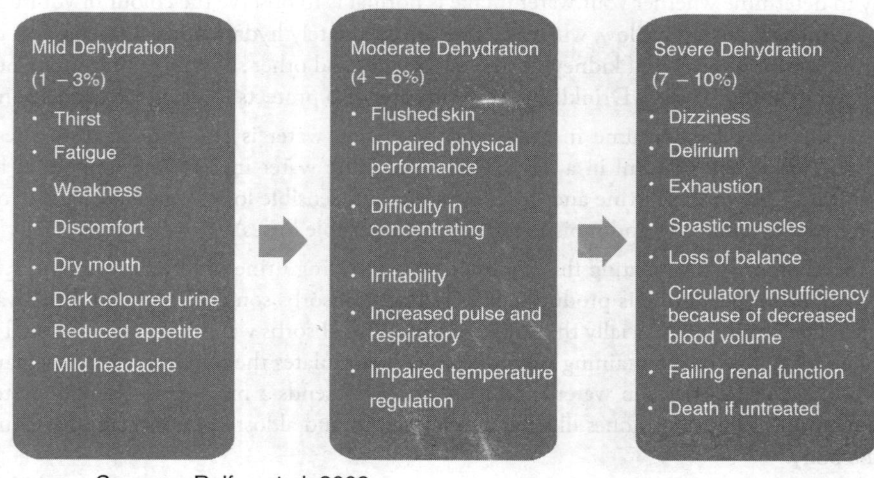

Source: Rolfes et al. 2009.

Water Toxicity can result from drinking too much water. This is also known as 'water intoxication'. Too much water dilutes the blood, disturbing the concentration of the substances dissolved in blood, which were otherwise supposed to be maintained within certain limits. The biggest problem arises when blood sodium levels decrease (hyponatraemia), and fluids start moving out of the blood vessels and into the cells by osmosis. If fluids collect in the interstitial spaces and tissues, there is swelling of tissues, known as oedema. Headache, blurred vision, muscle cramps, and convulsions result, especially if water accumulates in the brain cells. This condition is rare, but known to develop in people who over-consume water in an effort to prevent dehydration! It may also be seen in individuals with certain diseases, and where the kidneys are not functioning efficiently. It is generally recommended that individuals not consume more than 1–1.5 litre per hour of fluids, even when sweating heavily.

DIETARY SOURCES

Besides plain water, beverages like fruit and vegetable juices, milk, soft drinks, and soups also contribute to the total water intake. To satisfy our water needs, the best beverage to have is of course plain water. Milk is a healthy beverage as it also supplies protein, calcium, and a host of other nutrients. Sugar-sweetened beverages will, in addition to providing water, also increase the energy intake, which may be undesirable. Although tea and coffee are also beverages consumed daily, the caffeine in them can have a dehydrating effect, as caffeine is a mild diuretic (increases the production of urine). Similarly, alcoholic beverages also increase urine output.

Water is also present in fruits and vegetables, making up most of their weight. Fruits that are juicy have a higher water content, like watermelon, muskmelon, oranges, etc. Vegetables with a high percentage of water by weight include cucumber, bottle gourd (*ghia*), green leafy vegetables, etc. One can notice that they release a lot of water when they are heated while cooking.

Recommended Intakes

Water needs vary with factors such as body size, physical activity and environmental conditions. Adults need at least 2–3 litres (8–12 glasses) per day of fluids to replace daily losses. This amount includes pure water as well as the water present in foods and beverages.

MAJOR MINERALS

Minerals perform many important functions in our body. They are classified as nutrients, as their deficiency leads to certain clinical symptoms and disease conditions which disappear or decrease in severity if the person is supplemented with the mineral before severe damage has been done. For instance, calcium supplementation will help only if the intervention is started before serious bone loss takes place. Table 7.1 illustrates the role played by minerals in our body.

Table 7.1: Functions of Minerals in our Body

Function		*Minerals Required*
Water and electrolyte balance		Sodium, Potassium, Chloride

Table 7.1 contd

Table 7.1 contd

Blood pressure regulation		Sodium, Potassium, Magnesium, Calcium
Cell metabolism		Calcium, Phosphorus, Magnesium, Zinc, Chromium, Iodide
Growth and development		Calcium, Phosphorus, Zinc
Bone health		Calcium, Phosphorus, Magnesium, Iron, Zinc, Copper, Fluoride, Manganese
Blood cell formation and clotting		Iron, Copper, Calcium
Muscle contraction and relaxation		Sodium, Chloride, Potassium, Calcium, Magnesium

Table 7.1 contd

Table 7.1 contd

Nerve impulse transmission		Sodium, Potassium, Chloride, Calcium, Magnesium
Antioxidant defence		Selenium, Zinc, Copper, Manganese

Source: Images: Pixabay.com
Steven Fruitsmaak, wikipedia.org
commons.wikipedia.org
Bruce Wetzel, Harry Schafer, National Cancer Institute, USA, wikipedia.org
Byrd-Bredbenner et al. 2013, ICMR 2010, WHO/FAO 2004.

CALCIUM

Calcium is the most abundant mineral in our body. More than 99 per cent of calcium in the body is present in the bones and teeth. This represents 40 per cent of all minerals in the body. In an adult human body, this amounts to about 1,000–1,200g of calcium.

Functions

All cells need calcium. It is required for a number of metabolic reactions. But more importantly, it is an integral part of bone structure, imparting it strength. Studies have shown that calcium may play a role in maintaining healthy body weight by stimulating the breakdown of stored fat (Parikh and Yanovski 2003; Zemel 2003). The other important functions of calcium are:

1. Growth and bone development. Calcium is important for forming and maintaining bones. It lends strength to the bones. The bone matrix is made of the protein collagen. Calcium salts, in the form of crystals called hydroxyapatite, deposit in the matrix, giving rigidity to the bones. It is also important for the mineralisation of teeth.
2. Role in body fluids. Although there is very little calcium in the blood and other body fluids, it has an important role to play, and blood calcium levels are stringently maintained within a narrow range (around 9–11 mg/dl). Calcium is involved in maintaining normal blood pressure. Calcium may also protect against hypertension.
3. Blood clotting. Calcium participates in several reactions (like the conversion of prothrombin to thrombin) that lead to the formation of fibrin, the main protein in a blood clot. A clot will not form without sufficient calcium being present.
4. Transmission of nerve impulses to target cells.
5. Muscle contraction. Contractile proteins actin and myosin interact when calcium concentration in a muscle cell increases. This leads to contraction. During muscle relaxation, the calcium is returned to the intracellular stores, and actin and myosin disconnect.

6. Cell metabolism. Calcium present inside cells binds to proteins within the cells and activates them. Calmodulin is a cell protein that binds calcium. A calcium-calmodulin complex activates enzymes, including the ones involved in breaking down the glycogen present in muscles.

Maintaining Calcium Balance

We have just learnt that it is important to maintain blood calcium within certain limits as it has important functions to perform. If the level of calcium is not maintained, it can lead to serious consequences. Blood calcium above normal can lead to calcium rigor—muscles contract and cannot relax, resulting in hardness or stiffness. Similarly, blood calcium below normal causes calcium tetany, which is also characterised by uncontrolled muscle contraction. The person experiences intermittent spasms of the extremities (arms and legs) due to nervous and muscular excitability, caused by low blood calcium concentrations. Calcium deficiency does not lead to low blood calcium levels. It is usually due to abnormal secretion of regulatory hormones or due to vitamin D deficiency.

Blood calcium is regulated by the parathyroid hormone (PTH), which is produced by the parathyroid gland, and the hormone calcitonin, which is secreted by the thyroid gland. When blood calcium falls, it stimulates the parathyroid gland to secrete PTH, which helps to increase blood calcium by stimulating the activation of Vitamin D (Figure 7.3). Calcitriol and PTH then help to

- Increase the reabsorption of calcium in kidneys
- Increase the absorption of calcium in the intestine (primarily due to the increase in calcitriol)
- Increase the release of calcium from bones (by stimulating the activity of osteoclasts, that is, bone breakdown cells)

When blood calcium is high, the secretion of PTH is decreased. In order to decrease the blood calcium, the thyroid gland secretes the hormone calcitonin, which

- Inhibits the activation of vitamin D
- Increases the loss of calcium from the kidney
- Decreases the absorption of calcium in the intestine
- Decreases calcium loss from bones by inhibiting the osteoclast cells from breaking down the bone

Figure 7.3: Regulation of Blood Calcium

Low blood calcium
Production of parathyroid hormone (PTH)
Lower calcium excretion by kidneys
Production of 25-hydroxy vitamin D_3
Calcium absorption increased in small intestine
Calcium released from bones
Normal blood calcium
High blood calcium
Thyroid gland releases calcitonin
Increase calcium excretion in kidneys
Decreases calcium release from bones

Food Sources

Calcium is present in its most bio-available (readily absorbable and usable) form in milk and milk products. People who do not like to drink milk can get their calcium from an array of milk products like curd, cheese and *paneer* (cottage cheese), and dishes prepared from these. Calcium levels in cottage cheese are, however, lower than other dairy products, as a substantial amount of calcium is lost in the whey water when cottage cheese is prepared. However, people with lactose intolerance may not be able to consume sufficient quantities of milk to fulfil their requirements. Still others, like vegans, might actually avoid milk and its products.

Calcium can be obtained from other foods like cereals and millets, *ragi* being the richest source. Pulses, especially soyabean, are rich sources of calcium. Nuts like almonds, seeds like sesame (*til*), green leafy vegetables like mustard greens and broccoli, seafood like oysters, and fish eaten with their bones (like sardines) are considered rich sources of calcium. However, most plant foods may also contain inhibitors of calcium absorption. Calcium-fortified foods like breakfast cereal, juices, wheat flour, biscuits, etc., may also contribute to the calcium intake.

Absorption of calcium is generally about 25–30 per cent from the diet. However, when the body needs more calcium—for instance, during phases of growth in children or during pregnancy—absorption levels may increase to 60–75 per cent. Vitamin D helps by increasing the production of the calcium-binding protein, which is needed for calcium absorption. Certain factors increase calcium absorption, while others inhibit absorption.

Factors that increase calcium absorption include:

- Stomach acid, as it keeps the calcium soluble
- Vitamin D, as it synthesises the calcium-binding protein needed for absorption
- Presence of lactose
- Presence of protein or amino acids

Besides the fact that absorption enhancers like stomach acid and vitamin D are less or missing, other factors that decrease calcium absorption are:

- High fibre in diet, which binds the calcium and does not let it get absorbed
- Excess of phosphorus in the diet, which leads to an imbalance
- The presence of high amounts of phytates (present in whole grains, seeds and nuts), oxalates (present in large quantities in vegetables, especially green leafy vegetables), and polyphenols like tannins (present in tea, tamarind, etc.).

Why is milk the best food to fortify with vitamin D?

Vitamin D helps to make the calcium-binding protein needed for calcium absorption. Milk is a rich source of calcium. Fortifying it with vitamin D will ensure that the calcium in the milk is better absorbed. Vitamin D is capable of regulating gene expression, and affects the metabolism of calcium at the intestinal and bone cell level.

Low levels of oestrogen in blood, which are usually seen after menopause in women, result in decreased calcium retention in bones and increased excretion. In addition, the body may excrete excessive amounts of calcium when there is excess protein (especially animal protein) in the diet, when a person is bedridden (as physical activity is protective for bone health), or if there is excess consumption of sodium or caffeine.

Recommended Dietary Allowances

Calcium recommendations are based on the amount needed to retain the most calcium in bones. The highest attainable bone density for an individual is called peak bone mass. The RDA for calcium is high among growing children to ensure that the developing skeleton becomes strong and dense. It is high during pregnancy to take care of foetal needs, and during lactation to compensate for the amount secreted in milk. Table 7.2 gives the ICMR (2010) RDA for major minerals.

Table 7.2: Recommended Dietary Allowances for Major Minerals

Group	*Category / Age*	*Calcium (mg/d)*	*Phosphorus (mg/d)*	*Magnesium (mg/d)*	*Sodium (mg/d)*	*Potassium (mg/d)*
Men	Sedentary work	600	600	340	2100	3750
	Moderate work					
	Heavy work					
Women	Sedentary work	600	600	310	1900	3225
	Moderate work					
	Heavy work					
	Pregnant	1200	1200	310	–	–
	Lactating 0-6 m				–	–
	6–12 m				–	–
	Post-menopausal	800	600–800		–	–

Table 7.2 contd

Table 7.2 contd

Infants	0–6 months	500	750	30	410	630
	6–12 months			45	–	–
Children	1–3 years	600	600	50	590	1100
	4–6 years			70	1010	1550
	7–9 years			100	–	–
Boys	10–12 years	800	800	120	–	–
Girls	10–12 years			160	–	–
Boys	13–15 years			165	–	–
Girls	13–15 years			210	–	–
Boys	16–17 years			195	–	–
Girls	16–17 years			235	–	–

Source: Nutrient Requirements and Recommended Dietary Allowances for Indians, ICMR 2010.

Problem of Deficiency and Excess

Adequate consumption of calcium throughout life optimises the peak bone mass. Most people achieve their peak bone mass by the late 20s. A low calcium intake during the growing years will have adverse consequences on bone mass and density. This will lead to weak bones and an increased risk of osteoporosis. Osteoporosis refers to fragile, porous bones, with an increased risk of fracture. People suffering from osteoporosis also have a distorted body shape, decreased height and loss of teeth. It is considered a 'silent' disease, as the affected person does not realise s/he has the problem unless s/he undergoes testing for bone mineral density, or suffers a fracture (Box 7.1).

Box 7.1: Osteoporosis—Risk Factors and Prevention

What is osteoporosis?

Bone is living tissue, which consists of a network of protein fibres, primarily collagen, and minerals. Bone is continually built, broken down and reshaped. Osteoporosis occurs when the creation of new bone does not keep up with the removal of old bone. There are typically no symptoms in the early stages of bone loss. However, when the bones are weakened severely, signs and symptoms like back pain (caused by a fractured or collapsed vertebra), loss of height over time, stooped posture, and very easily fractured bones become a big problem.

What causes osteoporosis?

There are several risk factors for osteoporosis. Caucasian and Asian races seem to be more at risk. Women are much more likely to develop osteoporosis. The reduction of oestrogen levels at menopause is one of the strongest risk factors for developing osteoporosis. In fact, the older one gets, the greater is the risk of osteoporosis. Hormonal imbalance and prolonged intake of certain medications have also been linked to an increased risk.

Among dietary and lifestyle factors, low calcium intake, vitamin D deficiency, and a poor diet in general increase the risk of osteoporosis. Smokers, sedentary individuals, and those consuming excessive amounts of alcohol are at greater risk.

What can be done to prevent osteoporosis?

Adequate intake of calcium, vitamin D, phosphorus, magnesium, potassium, protein, and numerous other nutrients is required to build strong and healthy bones. In addition, an active lifestyle is important, with regular exercise. Strength training exercises can be combined with weight-bearing exercises. Strength training helps strengthen muscles and bones in the arms and upper spine, and weight-bearing exercises (such as walking, jogging, running, stair climbing, skipping rope, skiing) mainly affect the bones in the legs, hips and lower spine.

Source: Blausen.com staff. "Blausen gallery 2014". Wikiversity Journal of Medicine. DOI:10.15347/wjm/2014.010. ISSN 20018762. - Own work. Licensed under CC BY 3.0 via Wikimedia Commons - http://commons.wikimedia.org/wiki/File:Blausen_0686_Osteoporosis_01.png#/media/File:Blausen_0686_Osteoporosis_01.png.

Low blood levels of calcium, most commonly due to inadequate PTH, may lead to a condition called tetany. In this condition, the person suffers from muscle spasms as the muscles receive continual nerve stimulation. There is a forceful contraction of muscles without relaxation.

Excess intake of calcium, especially in the form of supplements, may have adverse effects, such as an increased risk of kidney stone formation. It may also affect the absorption of other minerals, like iron and zinc. Calcium supplements may increase calcium deposits in coronary arteries and increase the risk of heart attacks (Bollard et al. 2010).

PHOSPHORUS

Phosphorus is the second most abundant mineral in our body. About 85 per cent of the phosphorus is in combination with calcium in the hydroxyapatite crystals of bones and teeth. Soft tissues contain a much higher proportion of phosphorus in organic combinations. About 70 per cent of the dietary phosphorus is absorbed. Active vitamin D hormone enhances absorption. Kidney excretion primarily regulates blood phosphorus.

Functions

It has many widely differing functions.

1. It is a constituent of the sugar-phosphate linkage in the structure of DNA and RNA, and is hence necessary for growth.
2. Phospholipids are constituents of cell membranes, thus regulating the transport of solutes into and out of the cell.
3. The phosphorus-containing lipoproteins facilitate the transport of fats in the circulation.
4. Phosphorylation (addition of phosphate group to molecule) is a key reaction in many metabolic processes of energy metabolism.
5. Phosphorus compounds are essential for the storage and controlled release of energy—the ADP-ATP system.
6. It is also a component of several enzymes and coenzymes, for example, TPP, NADP.
7. Inorganic phosphates in the body fluids constitute an important buffer system in the regulation of body pH.
8. It is an important constituent of bones and teeth.

Food Sources

Phosphorus is widely distributed in foods, the milk and meat groups being the important contributors. A diet that furnishes enough protein and calcium will normally provide sufficient phosphorus. Whole grain cereals have more phosphorus than refined cereals. Much of this occurs in the form of phytic acid. Other good sources are eggs, nuts and fish. Vegetables and fruits contain only small amounts. Processed foods may have phosphorus-containing additives (for example, phosphoric acid in soft drinks).

Recommended Dietary Allowances

The ICMR recommendations (2010) for phosphorus intake are presented in Table 7.1. The requirements have been given based on an elemental Calcium : Phosphorus ratio of 1:1 for most age groups, except for infants, where the suggested ratio is 1:1.5.

Problem of Deficiency and Excess

Deficiency is unlikely in healthy adults, as phosphorus is found in a number of foods which we include in our daily diet. Marginal phosphorus status may be found in premature infants, vegans, alcoholics, the elderly on nutrient-poor diets, and chronic diarrhoea patients. Deficiency leads to bone loss and resultant weakness and pain.

High amounts can be a problem for people with certain kidney diseases. A chronic imbalance in the diet, resulting from a diet high in phosphorus (excessive amounts of meat, soft drinks and processed foods) and low in calcium, can contribute to bone loss.

MAGNESIUM

Magnesium is an intracellular cation. Over half the body's magnesium is found in the bones, and the rest in muscles and soft tissues. Only 1 per cent is present in extracellular fluid. Normal blood concentrations are maintained by bone magnesium. The kidney regulates how much of magnesium is excreted.

Functions

The major function of magnesium may be to stabilise the structure of ATP in ATP-dependent enzyme reactions. It is known to accelerate recovery from protein energy malnutrition. It is critical to heart function, and seems to protect against hypertension and heart disease (Jee et al. 2002). Magnesium has many other important roles to play in the body:

1. Magnesium supports bone mineralisation and maintenance of bone health.
2. Magnesium is a cofactor for more than 300 enzymes involved in several reactions, including the metabolism of glucose and the synthesis of many products like nucleic acids, fatty acids and proteins.
3. It has a role to play in blood clotting.
4. It has a role to play in neuromuscular transmission and activity. In normal muscle contractions, calcium acts as a stimulator and magnesium as a relaxer.
5. Magnesium supports the normal functioning of the immune system.

Food Sources

Magnesium is a constituent of chlorophyll, and hence dark green vegetables are a good source. Seeds, nuts, legumes, and unmilled cereal grains are also rich sources. Milk is a moderately good source if consumed in sufficient amounts. Hard water contributes both calcium and magnesium to the daily intake. The average absorption of magnesium from food ranges between 13–50 per cent.

> ***Interesting Fact***
>
> The word 'salary' is derived from the word salt, as in ancient times, Roman soldiers were paid their salaries in the form of salt. It was considered a precious commodity. In those times, salt was also used in the form of currency in trade.

Problems of Deficiency and Excess

Symptoms of abnormal neuromuscular function are seen in magnesium deficiency. Deficiency of magnesium is known to affect the homeostatic control of calcium, potassium and sodium ions. Severe deficiency is rare, but can lead to symptoms of tetany, convulsions, tremor, muscle spasm, anorexia, and vomiting. Deficiency, too, is rare, but can develop in a number of diseases like renal disease, diuretic therapy, alcohol abuse, protein malnutrition, prolonged vomiting and diarrhoea, and in malabsorption syndromes.

Moderate depletion of magnesium can occur in the elderly, especially those whose diets are habitually low in magnesium (avoiding dark green leafy vegetables, milk, and other good sources of magnesium). A low magnesium status has been suggested as a factor contributing to the development of chronic diseases like dysrhythmia (abnormal heart rhythm) and myocardial ischemia (inadequate flow of blood to the heart).

Toxicity has only been reported in cases where industrial workers have inhaled or ingested magnesium dust. Large doses may result in central nervous system depression, and even paralysis. Patients whose kidneys are not functioning optimally are especially at risk, and should not be given magnesium supplements. Excess magnesium can also inhibit bone calcification.

SODIUM

The principal contributor to the sodium intake in our diet is salt, or sodium chloride. Salt is obtained from sea water or from mines. About 50 per cent of the body's sodium is present in the extracellular fluid. It is the major cation (positive ion) in extracellular fluid. The body absorbs almost all the sodium that is eaten.

Functions

Sodium is the principal regulator of extracellular fluid volume. It also performs the following functions:

1. It is a key factor for retaining body water.
2. Fluid balance throughout the body depends partly on varied sodium and other electrolyte concentrations among the water-containing compartments in the body.
3. It also regulates acid-base balance and osmotic pressure. One of the ways that kidneys regulate the acid-base balance is by excreting hydrogen ions in exchange for sodium ions.
4. It participates in the absorption of other nutrients, like the active transport of glucose and some amino acids in the small intestine.
5. It participates in the conduction of nerve impulses and in muscle contraction.

Food Sources

About one-third to half the sodium in the diet comes from salt used during cooking, or sprinkled later. One teaspoon of salt is about 6g, in which there is about 2,300 mg of sodium (as sodium chloride has 40 per cent sodium and 60 per cent chloride). It is also added during food manufacture in the form of food additives, that is, baking powder (sodium bicarbonate), preservative (sodium benzoate), etc. Most natural foods also contain a little sodium. Foods can be classified as low, moderate and high sodium foods, depending on their sodium content. Foods with a considerable amount of sodium include milk, cheese, bacon, ham, pickles, relishes (preserved in brine), potato chips, and other salted snack foods, sauces, gravies, biscuits, etc. Softened tap water and certain medicines may also add to sodium intake.

> Have you ever wondered why you feel thirsty after consuming very salty food, like a bag of potato chips? This is because blood sodium levels rise upon consuming salty foods, and the thirst signal is activated so that the person drinks water, and the sodium to water ratio is restored in the blood. The extra sodium and water are then excreted by the kidneys.

Recommended Dietary Intake

The minimum requirement for a healthy adult is 500mg of sodium/day. If we use no salt in our cooking and eat only unprocessed foods, we will meet our minimum requirement. Salt intakes in Indian adults are in the range of <5 to 30 g/day in different states (NNMB 1987). More than 40 per cent of the families in India consume around 10g of salt per day. An intake of less than one teaspoon, that is, 5g of salt/day, is recommended for adults to reduce the risk of hypertension and stroke. The sodium requirements are given in Table 7.2. Those working in extremely hot environments, and hence sweating excessively, may need higher amounts, as sodium is lost from the body in sweat. Nutrition labels are important as they tell us the sodium content of foods, especially for those consuming sodium-restricted diets. Sometimes the sodium values may be mentioned in the mmol unit, which can be converted to milligrams by multiplying with 23 (the molecular weight of sodium).

Problem of Deficiency and Excess

Excessive perspiration, persistent vomiting and diarrhoea, coupled with a low sodium intake, deplete the body of sodium. This can lead to muscle cramps, nausea, vomiting, and dizziness, and later to shock and coma. Endurance athletes need to consume special beverages during competitions to replenish sodium and other electrolytes lost in sweat. People suffering from diarrhoea are given electrolyte beverages—and not just plain water—to make up for the electrolytes lost.

High sodium intakes have been correlated with high blood pressure. Most humans can adapt to various dietary salt intake levels. Approximately 10–15 per cent of adults are sodium sensitive. For them, high sodium intakes contribute to hypertension. Lowering the sodium in the diet often helps to correct the problem. A high intake of sodium may also lead to fluid retention in healthy adults. A sodium intake greater than 2 g/day also increases the urinary calcium loss. This may increase the risk of kidney stones. Tips to decrease the sodium content in our daily diets have been given in Box 7.2.

Box 7.2: Ways to Lower your Salt Intake

The taste for salt is acquired. If you slowly begin to lower the salt added to your cooking, you may not notice the change in taste, or may adjust to it really fast. In addition, you may also try the following strategies:

- Avoid putting salt in certain dishes, like salads
- Do not sprinkle additional salt on your food at the dining table
- To improve the taste of dishes, use low-sodium herbs and condiments like basil, garlic, ginger, mint, oregano, pepper, lemon juice, etc.
- Cut down on the intake of processed foods, as they may contain sodium in the form of additives
- Read labels carefully to see the amount of sodium in one serving before you select processed foods
- Consume pickles, *papads*, cured and salted meat, sausages, salami, cheeses, instant soups, and salty snacks like potato chips, *namkeens*, popcorn, etc., sparingly.

POTASSIUM

This mineral gets its name from the word 'potash', which means 'extracted in a pot from the ash of burnt trees'. Plant-based foods are rich sources of this mineral. Potassium is the principal cation of the intracellular fluid in our bodies. It performs many of the same functions as sodium; however, it operates inside rather than outside the cells. Intracellular fluids contain 95 per cent of the potassium in the body. The body absorbs about 90 per cent of the potassium consumed.

Sodium, potassium and chloride are electrolytes in our body. The impermeability of proteins and cations across cell membranes leads to the development of electrical potential across membranes. This potential difference is important for muscle contraction and nerve impulse conduction.

Functions

Potassium plays a role in maintaining cell integrity. The total body potassium corresponds closely to lean body mass and to the total body nitrogen. Controlling potassium distribution is very important for the body as it affects homeostasis (stability or equilibrium), and is important for maintaining a steady heartbeat. Potassium plays a key role in:

1. Maintaining osmotic pressure, water balance and acid-base balance.
2. Helping enzymes to function
3. Nerve impulse transmission
4. Muscle contraction and regular heart rhythm

Potassium is believed to help keep the blood pressure normal. High dietary potassium intake promotes the excretion of excess sodium and water from the body.

Food Sources

It is widely distributed in foods, especially plant foods. Fruits and vegetables are nutrient dense sources, for example, spinach, potato, tomato, lettuce, banana, pears, peaches, oranges, and *mausambi*. Milk, whole grains, dried beans, nuts, and meats are also good sources. Processed foods in general have low amounts of potassium.

Recommended Dietary Allowances

The recommended intakes according to the ICMR are given in Table 7.2. The molar ratio of sodium : potassium requirements has been kept as 1:1. The potassium present in vegetarian Indian diets is usually adequate to meet the daily requirements.

Problem of Deficiency and Excess

Diets low in potassium seem to play a role in the development of high blood pressure. Some diuretics used to treat hypertension deplete the body's potassium. High potassium foods need to be added to the diets of such patients. Diarrhoea can also lead to excessive loss of potassium from the body. Alcoholics, people suffering from anorexia nervosa or bulimia (eating disorders), people on very low calorie diets, and athletes who exercise very heavily are at risk of developing potassium deficiency. Low blood potassium is a life-threatening problem. Symptoms include loss of appetite, muscle weakness, mental confusion, glucose intolerance, irregular heartbeats, and decreased capacity of the heart to pump blood.

If the kidneys do not function properly, potassium builds up in the blood. This condition is called hyperkalemia (high blood potassium levels). It inhibits heart function, causing slowed heart beats and even death due to cardiac arrest. So in kidney disease, the potassium in the diet is also controlled.

SUMMARY

- Water in our bodies is present in two compartments—the intracellular compartment, inside each and every cell of our body, and the extracellular compartment, outside the cells. This is present in the form of interstitial fluid, the fluid bathing the cells, and intravascular fluid, present inside the blood and lymph vessels.
- Water is vital for survival. It is important for maintaining blood volume, as a medium or solvent for various metabolic reactions and transporting substances, for temperature regulation, as a lubricant, as a structural feature of certain substances, and also as a dietary source of minerals.
- Maintaining water balance is very important. If intake is less than the loss from the body, it results in dehydration. Water can also prove toxic if consumed in excessive quantities within a short span of time, as it leads to blood dilution and hyponatraemia.
- Water needs vary with factors such as body size, physical activity and environmental conditions. Adults need at least 2–3 litres (8–12 glasses) per day of fluids to replace daily losses. This amount includes pure water and the water present in foods and beverages.
- Calcium is the most abundant mineral in our body. More than 99 per cent of the calcium in the body is present in the bones and teeth.
- All cells need calcium. It is required for a number of metabolic reactions, and is an integral part of bone structure, imparting it strength. Calcium is also important for blood clotting, nerve impulse transmission, cell metabolism, and muscle contraction.
- Rich sources of calcium include milk and milk products, cereals and millets like *ragi,* pulses like soyabean, nuts like almonds, seeds like sesame (*til*), green leafy vegetables like mustard greens and broccoli, seafood like oysters, and fish eaten with their bones.
- Absorption of calcium is generally about 25–30 per cent from the diet. Stomach acid, vitamin D, lactose, and proteins improve absorption, while phytates, oxalates, tannins and excessive amounts of other divalent metals decrease absorption. High phosphorus, protein, caffeine, and sodium tend to increase excretion.
- Blood levels of calcium are maintained by two hormones—parathyroid hormone and calcitonin.
- Phosphorus is the second most abundant mineral. It is present in the bones and teeth, in DNA, RNA, phospholipids, lipoproteins, and coenzymes, and is actively involved in energy metabolism.

- It is present in several foods and deficiency is uncommon. A diet furnishing enough protein and calcium will normally provide sufficient phosphorus.
- Magnesium performs many functions, as it is a cofactor for several enzymes. It is important for bone health, nerve impulse transmission, and the normal functioning of the immune system.
- Dark green vegetables, seeds, nuts, legumes, and un-milled cereal grains are rich sources of magnesium. Symptoms of abnormal neuromuscular function are seen in magnesium deficiency.
- Sodium and potassium are electrolytes which maintain the fluid balance, acid-base balance, and participate in the conduction of nerve impulses and in muscle contraction.
- Sodium is the chief extracellular cation, while potassium is the chief cation inside cells.
- Sodium intake on the higher side increases the risk of hypertension. Potassium, on the other hand, is protective, and lowers blood pressure.
- Sodium is mostly obtained from salt, the intake of which should be kept at less than 5g (one teaspoon) a day. Potassium is present in plant foods. Eating plenty of fresh fruits and vegetables will give us the potassium we need.

KEY WORDS

Bioavailable: The degree to which the amount of an ingested nutrient is absorbed and is available to the body.

Diuretic: A substance that increases the production of urine.

Electrolytes: Compounds that form ions in water, and are able to conduct an electrical current, for example, sodium, potassium and chloride.

Extracellular compartment: Water present outside the cells in our body.

Hyperkalemia: High blood potassium levels.

Hyponatremia: Low levels of sodium in the blood.

Hypothalamus: The part of the brain responsible for many important functions, like maintaining water balance, regulating body temperature and controlling appetite.

Interstitial fluid: The fluid present in between cells.

Intracellular compartment: Water present inside each and every cell of our body.

Intravascular fluid: The fluid present inside vessels, that is, blood and lymph.

Muscle spasm: Painful, involuntary muscle contraction

Oedema: Water retention.

Osmosis: The movement of water across a membrane towards the side that has a greater solute concentration. This is what makes raisins soaked in water swell up.

Osmotic pressure: The amount of force needed to prevent water from entering the compartment containing higher particle concentration. Osmotic pressure develops when two solutions of different concentrations are separated by a semi-permeable membrane.

Peak bone mass: The highest attainable bone density.

Tetany: Continuous and forceful muscle contraction without relaxation.

Vegan: A vegetarian who does not consume any product of animal origin, including milk and milk products.

EXERCISES

1. What is the function of water in our body?
2. Name the major intracellular and extracellular cations and anions present in our body.
3. Discuss the importance of maintaining fluid balance. What would happen if your body loses a lot of water?
4. What is the role of calcium in our body?
5. What is osteoporosis? How is it caused?
6. Why is milk the best food to fortify with vitamin D?
7. What are the factors that affect the bioavailability of calcium?
8. What is the role of sodium and potassium in our body?
9. What is the recommendation for salt intake? Why do we need to limit salt intake?
10. Why is magnesium important for our body?

REFERENCES

Bolland, M. J. et al., 'Effect of calcium supplements on risk of myocardial infarction and cardiovascular events: Meta analysis', *BMJ* 341, 2010, c3691.

Byrd-Bredbenner, C., G. Moe, D. Beshgetoor, and J. Berning, *Wardlaw's Perspectives in Nutrition*, 9e, New York: McGraw-Hill International Edition, 2013.

ICMR, 'Nutrient Requirements and Recommended Dietary Allowances for Indians', A report of the Expert Group of the Indian Council of Medical Research, 2010.

Jee, S. H., et al., 'The effect of magnesium supplementation on blood pressure: A meta analysis of randomized clinical trials', *American Journal of Hypertension* 15, 2002, pp. 691–96.

Nair, K. M. and S. Kalyanasundaram, 'Electrolytes and Minerals', in M. S. Bamji, K. Krishnaswamy and G. N. V. Brahmam (eds), *Textbook of Human Nutrition*, 3e, New Delhi: Oxford and IBH Publ Co., 2009, pp. 33–46.

National Nutrition Monitoring Bureau (NNMB), *Achievements and Constraints*, Hyderabad: National Institute of Nutrition, 1987.

Parikh, S. J. and J. A. Yanovski, 'Calcium and adiposity', *Am J Clin Nutr* 77, 2003, pp. 281–87.

Rolfes, S. R., K. Pinna and E. Whitney, *Understanding Normal and Clinical Nutrition*, 8e, Wadsworth Cengage Learning, 2009.

WHO/FAO, 'Vitamin and Mineral Requirements in Human Nutrition', Joint FAO/WHO Expert Consultation on Human Vitamin and Mineral Requirements, Bangkok, Thailand, 1998 (2e, 2004).

Zemel, M. B., 'Mechanisms of dairy modulation of adiposity', *Journal of Nutrition* 133, 2003, pp. 252S–256S.

8

TRACE MINERALS

HIGHLIGHTS

- Types of trace minerals present in food
- Function of each mineral in the human body
- Dietary sources and RDA
- Problems of deficiency and excess

The different minerals you will study about are:

- Iron
- Zinc
- Iodine
- Fluorine
- Selenium
- Chromium
- Molybdenum
- Copper
- Manganese

IRON

Iron is found in every living cell. The total body content is only about 5g. Still, iron deficiency or anaemia is common worldwide, affecting more than 1.2 billion people. In most developing countries, about two-thirds of all children and women of childbearing age suffer from iron deficiency, and many of them have anaemia.

Functions

Iron plays several vital functions in the body.

1. Most of the iron in the body is present in erythrocytes (red blood cells) as haemoglobin. **Haemoglobin** helps in the transport of oxygen from the lungs to the tissues, and some carbon dioxide back to the lungs.
2. **Myoglobin** in muscle cells is the iron-containing oxygen storage protein.
3. **Cytochromes**, iron-containing enzymes of the electron transport chain in mitochondria, act as electron carriers within the cell. In this pathway, ATP (adenosine triphosphate) is made for the cell's energy use.
4. It functions as a co-factor for other enzymes, like those involved in the **synthesis** of steroid hormones, bile acids, collagen, etc.

5. It also participates in synthesis of some **neurotransmitters** like dopamine and serotonin in the brain.
6. It has an important role to play in **immune** function.
7. It plays a key role in the **drug detoxification pathway** in the liver, helping to break down toxic substances into harmless molecules that can be easily excreted.

Food Sources

The most bio-available form is non-vegetarian foods like meats (beef, organ meat like liver, fish, and seafoods, especially oysters). Other high nutrient density sources include peas, legumes, green leafy vegetables, whole grains—especially *bajra* and *ragi*—enriched flour, fortified breakfast cereals, etc. Using iron utensils for cooking helps increase the iron content of foods, although the absorption of contaminant iron is not very efficient.

Controlling absorption is important, because the body cannot easily eliminate excess iron once absorbed. Iron absorption is 5–10 per cent in healthy people, and 10–20 per cent in iron-deficient people.

Factors that increase iron absorption are:

1. Acid in stomach
2. High body demand for RBCs (for instance, in blood loss, high altitude, physical training, and pregnancy)
3. Low body stores of iron
4. Meat protein factor, a peptide that promotes the absorption of non-heme iron. (It appears to contain amino acids such as cysteine, which bind iron and enhance absorption. It facilitates in improving the absorption of non-heme iron as well.)
5. Vitamin C (it converts ferric ions to ferrous ions, which are absorbed better as vitamin C forms a chelate with it. At the cell membrane of the brush border, the ferrous is converted back to ferric ions, which bind to a receptor protein called membrane iron-binding protein, which transfers iron into the absorptive cell.). If a meal contains many inhibitors of iron, almost 25 mg of vitamin C would be needed to increase absorption from the meal.
6. Organic acids—such as citric acid—have also been shown to increase non-heme iron absorption.
7. Heme iron, present in haemoglobin (blood) and myoglobin (muscle), is absorbed more than twice as efficiently as simple elemental iron (non-heme). Consuming heme and non-heme iron together increases non-heme iron absorption.

The process of germination and fermentation also increases iron availability from foods as the bound iron is released. These processes activate enzymes like phytases, which decrease phytates in foods like cereals and pulses. Sauerkraut and other fermented vegetables and fermented soya sauces enhance iron absorption, although the mechanism is not clear.

Factors that decrease iron absorption:

1. Less stomach acid (with age, acid secretion decreases and so does iron absorption. Acid converts ferric ions to ferrous ions, and helps in solubilising non-heme iron). Regular consumption of antacids, which reduce stomach acid, will also reduce iron absorption.
2. High phytic acid in diet (diet high in dietary fibre, especially whole grains, will have high phytate content).
3. High oxalic acid in diet (present in vegetables, especially green leafy vegetables).
4. High polyphenol content in diet (for example, tannins present in tea, coffee, cocoa, tamarind). Thus, a cup of tea with the meal may greatly reduce iron absorption.
5. Full body stores of iron.
6. Excess of minerals such as zinc, manganese and calcium in the diet, as they compete for absorption.

What are Phytates?

Phytates are found in all kinds of grains, seeds, nuts, vegetables, roots (like potatoes), and fruits. Chemically, phytates are inositol hexaphosphate salts, a storage form of phosphate and minerals.

Certain green leafy vegetables (like spinach), herbs, spices, and betel leaves, which are commonly eaten in India and other Asian countries, have polyphenols containing galloyl groups, which decrease iron absorption.

Heme iron absorption is different from non-heme. It is absorbed directly into absorptive cells after the globin (protein) fraction has been removed. Once inside the absorptive cell, the iron is released from the heme portion. Iron is transported in blood bound to protein transferrin. The rest binds to apoferritin in intestinal cells to form ferritin. Seventy per cent of the iron in the body is in the form of haemoglobin and myoglobin. Some iron is stored in bone marrow. A small portion goes to other body cells, or to the spleen and liver for storage. Hemosiderin is an insoluble iron-protein compound in the liver. It stores iron when the amount of iron in the body exceeds the storage capacity of ferritin.

Problems of Deficiency and Excess

Anaemia is a major global problem affecting between 20–70 per cent of the population in various countries. In India, it is an important public health problem, affecting people from all walks of life, whether rich or poor. The disease is of particular significance in preschool and school children and pregnant women, because of the high prevalence (50–70 per cent). After the age of 15, females seem to be more susceptible to anaemia. In fact, 79 per cent of children below the age of three, 73 per cent of 5–11-year-olds, and 75 per cent of pregnant women have anaemia (NNMB 2005–06; NFHS-3). Anaemia is definitely a widespread problem, more among females than males, and higher among infants and children than adults.

> ***Types of Anaemia***
>
> Anaemia may be classified on the basis of the changes in shape and colour of the red blood cells. **Hypochromic and microcytic** anaemia occurs if there is an insufficiency of iron or pyridoxine. The red blood cells in this case are pale and smaller in size than normal.
>
> The anaemia is said to be **Megaloblastic** in case of either vitamin B_{12} or folic acid deficiency, as the RBCs are larger in size than normal, but are not pale in colour. If both iron and folic acid or vitamin B_{12} are deficient, it gives rise to **Dimorphic anaemia,** in which RBCs are large (macrocytic) or even normocytic (normal size), but immature and pale (hypochromic).

Haemoglobin, present in the red blood cells, contains iron, which is needed to carry oxygen to all parts of the body. For the formation and normal growth of red blood cells, iron and vitamins like folic acid and vitamin B_{12} are essential. Deficiency of any of these nutrients in the body can lead to nutritional anaemia.

Anaemia is basically defined as a reduction in the haemoglobin (Hb) level in circulation in our blood. The World Health Organization (WHO) gives the minimum levels (the cut-off points) of haemoglobin that should be present in our blood. Haemoglobin below these levels is diagnosed as anaemia (Table 8.1).

Aetiology

Among the different types of anaemia, the one resulting from a deficiency of iron is the most common. Deficiency in iron may occur as a result of the following:

- Blood losses may occur in accidental haemorrhage, in chronic diseases such as tuberculosis, ulcers or intestinal disorders, or excessive blood loss due to hookworm infestation. Excessive loss of blood during menstruation and childbirth can also lead to anaemia.
- Deficiency of iron in the diet during periods of accelerated demand, like pregnancy (rapidly expanding blood volume and growth of the foetus) and in infancy, early childhood (rapid growth) and adolescence (rapid growth and onset of menses in girls), can result in anaemia.
- Inadequate absorption of iron can occur in diarrhoea, or when there is a lack of acid secretion by the stomach, or in chronic renal diseases, and when antacid therapy is given (as the antacid neutralises stomach acid, which is important for solubilising and helping in the absorption of iron). Excessive amounts of phytates and phosphates in the diet and excessive consumption of tea (which has tannins) can decrease the absorption of iron.

The average cereal and legume-based diets consumed by most of us would appear adequate in iron content for an adult. But the availability of iron from such diets is very poor. Besides the various factors that inhibit absorption, deficiencies of ascorbic acid, protein commonly encountered in these diets, tend to lower iron absorption. Iron is better absorbed from non-vegetarian foods like meat, liver, etc. Only 5 per cent of dietary iron is absorbed in a normal, apparently healthy individual. In women, the absorption is higher (8–10 per cent).

Table 8.1: Cut-Off Points for Haemoglobin Values for Diagnosis of Anaemia

	Haemoglobin (g/dl)
Adult men	< 13
Adult women	< 12
Pregnant women	< 11
Lactating women	< 12
Children below 5 years	< 11
Children aged 5-11 years	< 11.5
Older children	< 12

Source: WHO/UNICEF/UNU 2001.

Symptoms

Anaemias give rise to the same general symptoms, whatever the cause. Symptoms arise when the transport of oxygen by the blood is not sufficient to meet the needs of the body.

The haematocrit (per cent of total volume occupied by RBCs) is decreased to less than 34–37 per cent. The blood haemoglobin concentration is less than 12 g/dl for adult women and less than 13 g/dl for adult men (according to WHO criteria). The type of anaemia seen is **microcytic** (reduced volume of each RBC) and **hypochromic** (less colour because of less haemoglobin in RBCs). Other symptoms are:

- Loss of appetite
- Apathy (lack of interest, enthusiasm or concern)
- Pallor (pale skin, conjunctiva, nails)
- Brittle fingernails
- Concave, spoon-shaped fingernails, called koilonychia
- Breathlessness on exertion
- Fatigue, tiredness
- Irritability and depression
- Weakness (all because of insufficient RBC and cytochromes)

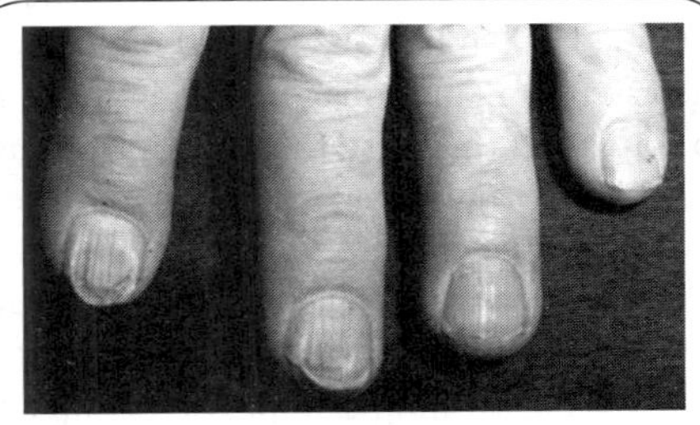

Koilonychia

Brittleness and dryness develops in iron deficiency anaemia in the nails, and they might flatten out and become concave in shape like a spoon.

Source: Standardizer, wikimedia commons.

Consequences of Anaemia

During pregnancy, anaemia increases the risk of maternal and infant death, and also preterm delivery. Some women who are severely anaemic die of heart failure during labour, while some others do not survive the blood loss during delivery. Anaemic mothers also have lower resistance to infections. It is estimated that nutritional anaemia contributes to about 24 per cent of maternal deaths every year (Health Information of India 2004), and is one of the important causes of low birth weight. During pregnancy, iron deficiency can result in poor foetal growth, premature deliveries, and even death of the baby due to severe anaemia. The baby is born with poor stores of iron at birth, and suffers from anaemia from early infancy due to the low levels of iron in breast milk.

During early childhood, anaemia interferes with longitudinal growth, weight gain and behaviour development. Anaemia has been associated with:

- Decreased mental and motor development in infants
- Decreased learning ability
- Decreased work performance
- Decreased immune status

Research has shown that even a mild iron deficiency is strongly associated with impaired brain development. What is worse, functional defects affecting learning and behaviour cannot be reversed by giving iron at a later date. Iron-deficient young adolescents perform poorly in school. They have been shown to score relatively lower in tests of academic performance. The fatigue, dullness, lack of concentration, reduced activity, all lead to poor performance. Also, they have been found to be more disruptive, irritable and restless in the classroom.

Iron deficiency results in a reduction in immunity, that is, a decreased ability of the body to fight infections. Anaemic children hence tend to fall ill more frequently.

In the **adult man or woman**, anaemia results in poor work output, since work capacity is reduced considerably due to muscle fatigue. Also, lack of concentration in the workplace results in mistakes, sometimes even fatal ones when people are operating heavy machinery. All these have a great effect on productivity, especially in the industrial and agricultural sectors.

Prevention

To prevent anaemia, low dosage iron is adequate. This is the basis of the **National Nutritional Anaemia Prophylaxis Programme (NNAPP),** launched in 1970, wherein pregnant women receive 60 mg elemental iron plus 500 µg folic acid daily for at least 100 days during pregnancy, and also during lactation. Women availing of the family planning scheme are also included in this programme. The dosage is now being increased to 100 mg in view of the poor response and high incidence of anaemia in the community.

Preschool children receive 20 mg iron plus 100 µg folic acid daily. The School Health Programme aims to cover school-going children (10–19 years) by giving them a weekly iron-folic acid supplement (WIFS) containing 100 mg elemental iron and 500 µg folic acid. The children would also be de-wormed biannually. In addition to increased iron and folate intake, improvement in environmental sanitation and personal hygiene are also needed to control worm infestations and infections. Regular de-worming would help in reducing the incidence of anaemia and improve the efficacy of iron supplements. Iron from the supplement is best absorbed if consumed in between meals or on an empty stomach, so that other diet ingredients do not affect absorption. Supplements should not be taken with tea/coffee (as they contain tannins) or milk (rich in calcium), as these inhibit the absorption. Vitamin C will not improve the absorption of iron from supplements as the iron is already in ferrous form.

The dietary approach for combating iron-deficiency anaemia is:

- To promote the consumption of green, leafy vegetables, pulses (which are rich in iron), liver, and meat.
- To regularly consume foods rich in vitamin C (orange, guava, *amla*, lemon, etc.), especially along with iron-rich dishes, to promote iron absorption. A molar ratio of 1:2 of iron to ascorbic acid is ideal to ensure 5 per cent iron absorption. This works out to about 20 mg of vitamin C /1,000 kcal when the iron intake is 7–9 mg/1,000 kcal.
- To discourage the consumption of tannin-containing foods like tea and tamarind along with iron-rich foods, as these inhibit iron absorption.
- To promote home gardening to increase the availability of common iron-rich foods such as green leafy vegetables.
- Fortification of food items with iron would also act as a long-term measure to control and prevent anaemia in the population.

Cooking in iron pots and pans increases the amount of iron in the food. Although this is mostly contaminant iron and not well absorbed, it adds to the total iron intake.

Some companies have voluntarily started fortifying their products—like wheat flour, biscuits, etc.—with iron. Salt has been found to be a suitable vehicle for this purpose, as it is cheap and universally consumed. Double fortified salt, containing both iodine and iron, is currently being used in food supplementation programmes like ICDS, and in the Mid-Day Meal programme.

Toxicity

Hemachromatosis is a disorder of iron metabolism characterised by increased absorption, saturation of the iron-binding protein, and deposition of hemosiderin in liver tissue. This leads to cirrhosis (degeneration) of liver and liver cancer. In adults, iron overload can also result from excess supplementation and frequent blood transfusions, as by the transfusion route, the protective *intestinal mucosal block* is bypassed. Normally, certain proteins prevent the absorption of more iron by the intestinal epithelium, when the rate of absorption passes a certain limit. This control mechanism at the absorption level prevents the body from accumulating too much iron.

Excess iron in blood may accelerate atherosclerosis in people with elevated LDL. This is because free iron acts as an antioxidant and can generate more free radicals. Thus, iron is also linked to certain types of cancer, where free radical activity has led to DNA damage. Large doses of iron supplements cause gastrointestinal distress, including constipation, nausea, vomiting, and diarrhoea. Relief can be obtained from the side-effect of constipation if a person drinks plenty of water.

Recommended Dietary Allowances

The body conserves and reuses iron. Adult men lose about 0.86 mg of iron per day via the gastrointestinal tract, urine and skin. In addition, women lose iron during menstruation (an average of 0.45 mg/day). This is the only nutrient for which women have a greater requirement than men. Adult women need 21 mg, while men need 17 mg. In pregnancy, the requirement increases to 35 mg, but for lactating women, it remains 21 mg (Table 8.2). This is because lactational amenorrhoea decreases the requirement for iron, even though the production of milk increases the need. It is very difficult to meet the RDA for iron as absorption is poor from many foods, and a vast majority of the population is vegetarian. Supplements are given as part of a national programme to pregnant, lactating women, preschoolers and adolescents who are very vulnerable to anaemia.

Table 8.2: Recommended Dietary Allowances for Trace Minerals

Group	*Category / Age*	*Iron (mg/d)*	*Zinc (mg/d)*	*Iodine (µg/d)*	*Copper (mg/d)**	*Chromium (µg/d)**	*Manganese (mg/d)**
Men		17	12	150	1.7	50	4.0
Women	NPNL	21	10	150	1.7	50	4.0
	Pregnant	35	12	250	–	–	–
	Lactating	21	12	250	–	–	–
Infants	0-6 mths—	46 µg/kg/d	–				
	6–12 months	5	–	90	–	–	–
Children	1-3 years	9	5	90	–	–	–
	4-6 years	13	7	90	–	–	–
	7-9 years	16	8	120	–	–	–
Boys	10-12 years	21	9	120	–	–	–
Girls	10-12 years	27	9	120	–	–	–
Boys	13-15 years	32	11	150	–	–	–
Girls	13-15 years	27	11	150	–	–	–
Boys	16-17 years	28	12	150	–	–	–
Girls	16-17 years	26	12	150	–	–	–

Notes: NPNL: Non-pregnant, non-lactating woman.

* Intakes recommended as 'adequate intake'.

Source: Nutrient Requirements and Recommended Dietary Allowances for Indians, ICMR 2010.

ZINC

Zinc deficiency in humans was first recognised in the early 1960s in Egypt and Iran. The deficiency was determined to be the cause of growth retardation and inadequate sexual development. It is estimated that globally, about half the population may be at risk of zinc deficiency due to inadequate dietary intake (Brown et al. 2001).

Functions

More than 300 enzymes require zinc for optimal activity. These enzymes participate in the synthesis and degradation of carbohydrates, lipids, proteins, and nucleic acids, as well as in the metabolism of other micronutrients. Carbonic anhydrase (required for the production of gastric acid), alcohol dehydrogenase (for facilitating interconversion between alcohol, aldehyde and ketones), and carboxypeptidase (for protein digestion) are some examples. Zinc is required by our bodies for:

1. **Nucleic acid synthesis** and function, and thus for the process of **genetic expression** (gene transcription fingers are also known as zinc fingers).
2. **Protein metabolism**, wound healing, and **cellular growth and differentiation.**
3. **Immune function.** Supplementation with zinc was found to lower the frequency and severity of infections like diarrhoea and pneumonia, and reduce mortality.
4. **Antioxidant** defence network as a part of the superoxide dismutase enzyme that aids in the prevention of oxidative damage to cells.
5. **Development of sexual organs** and bone.
6. Synthesis, storage and release of the **hormone insulin** in the pancreas.
7. Cell membrane structure and function, and maintenance of **cell integrity.**
8. Synthesis of the active form of vitamin A (retinal) in **visual pigments** and the retinol binding protein that transports vitamin A.

Zinc is important for growth and for behavioural development in infants. Catch-up growth is better with zinc supplementation. The frequency of stools and the severity and duration of diarrhoea has been shown to decrease with zinc supplementation. Some beneficial effects have also been shown in decreasing the duration of common colds and acute lower respiratory tract infections.

Food Sources

Protein-rich sources are also rich in zinc, for example, flesh foods like lean meats and shellfish (oysters are the richest source). Other nutrient-dense sources are liver, legumes and wheat germ. Nuts, beans and whole grains are good plant sources. However, the zinc content decreases on the milling and processing of grains. Beef and other red meats (high fat meats) are moderate sources. Roots and tubers, fish, green leafy vegetables, and fruits are modest sources of zinc.

The absorption of zinc is influenced by the overall composition of the diet and the body's need for the mineral. About 10–35 per cent of dietary zinc is absorbed from foods. When zinc is absorbed into intestinal cells, it induces the synthesis of metallothionein, a protein that binds zinc. This then enters the blood. Zinc binds to blood proteins such as albumin and to amino acids. One-third of the zinc enters the liver and the remainder goes to the rest of the body.

Factors which decrease the absorption of zinc are: high intake of phytate (present in whole grain cereals and legumes) and fibre, high intake of calcium, and the presence of copper and iron through supplements (as they compete for absorption). The high phytate content of typical Indian diets (basically vegetarian diets with mixed cereal and pulse) results in a low absorption of zinc. The effect of phytate is, however, modified by the source and amount of dietary protein consumed. Absorption is better from animal foods.

For the purpose of calculating requirements, an absorption figure of 20–25 per cent was used at habitual levels of intake in the Indian population, especially when the diet included animal foods like milk as well. The availability of zinc from the diet can be improved by reducing the phytate content by common household processes like germination and fermentation of cereals and pulses. It can also be improved by including sources of animal protein.

> ***Are nutrient supplements necessary for us?***
>
> There is a lot of research data now to show that people should use nutrient supplements conservatively, if at all. Supplementation, especially at doses higher than the RDA, can easily create imbalances. It can also cause more harm than good.

Recommended Dietary Allowances

The RDAs are based on the average amount needed to replace the daily losses in faeces, urine and sweat. The ICMR gives 12 mg/day for men and 10 mg/day for women as the RDA for adults. For pregnant and lactating women, the RDA increases to 12 mg/day.

Problems of Deficiency and Excess

Marginal zinc deficiency is likely to go undetected, as it does not result in specific physical symptoms. Children have especially high zinc needs because they are growing rapidly. If their diets do not meet their requirement, they exhibit signs of deficiency. The following signs and symptoms are seen in mild to moderate zinc deficiency:

- Growth retardation
- Acne-like rash or persistent rash
- Diarrhoea
- Impairment of immune function
- Impaired appetite or anorexia
- Alopecia (hair loss)
- Poor motor development, and cognitive performance and behavioural changes
- Low birth weight infants
- Delayed sexual maturation in children and adolescents
- Delayed bone maturation
- Decreased sense of taste and smell is also sometimes observed
- Impaired wound healing
- Impaired vitamin A function (visual adaptation to the dark)

Severe zinc deficiency can result from a rare genetic condition called **acrodermatitis enteropathica**. This condition results in impaired intestinal zinc absorption. The symptoms include dermatitis (skin inflammation) on the limbs and face, diarrhoea and hair loss. The condition is treated by giving zinc supplements.

Long-term high zinc intakes, that is, more than five times the RDA, can inhibit copper absorption. More than 100 mg/day may result in diarrhoea, cramps, nausea, vomiting, and decreased immune system function. Hence, the upper level of intake is set at 45 mg/day for an adult man, according to FAO/WHO (2004). Zinc in water from contaminated wells or in food cooked in galvanised cooking utensils could also lead to high zinc intakes and some of these symptoms.

IODINE

About one billion people worldwide are at risk of iodine deficiency-related disorders. The healthy human body contains about 20 mg of iodine, 70–80 per cent of which is concentrated in the thyroid gland. In food, it is present in the form of iodides.

Function

Iodine is stored in the thyroid gland in the form of thyroglobulin. Iodine has only one function, and that is that it is a constituent of **thyroid hormones**—thyroxine (T_4) and triiodothyronine (T_3). These hormones are synthesised from amino acid tyrosine and iodide. The thyroid gland actively accumulates and traps iodide from the blood stream to support the hormone synthesis. These hormones regulate the metabolic rate and promote physical and mental growth and development. They regulate the rate of oxidation within cells, functioning of the brain, nervous and muscle tissue, circulatory activity, and the metabolism of all nutrients. This makes iodine a very important nutrient to include in our diet.

Food Sources

Seafood, salt-water fish, seaweed, and iodised salt are rich sources of iodine. Soil levels determine the levels in plants. Some food additives, like dough conditioners, food colourants and sterilising agents in dairies and restaurants also contribute to iodine intake. Goitre is associated with the consumption of certain substances known as **goitrogens**. These are found in vegetables like raw turnips, cabbage, cauliflower, broccoli, and cassava. They are known to inhibit iodide metabolism by the thyroid gland, and in turn inhibit thyroid hormone synthesis. These are destroyed by cooking.

Problem of Deficiency and Excess

If a person's iodine intake is insufficient, the thyroid gland enlarges as it attempts to take up more iodine from the blood (see Figure 8.1). There is increased secretion of the Thyroid Stimulating Hormone (TSH) by the pituitary gland. This condition is known as **simple or endemic goitre**. It is a painless condition which, if uncorrected, can lead to pressure on the trachea and difficulty in breathing. If, however, a woman consumes an iodine-deficient diet during the early months of pregnancy, the infant is born with short stature and mental retardation. This condition is known as **Cretinism** It is characterised by a low basal metabolism, muscular flabbiness, weakness and spasticity, dry skin, enlarged tongue, thick lips, arrested physical development and severe mental retardation, and loss of hearing and speech abilities.

Figure 8.1: Location of Thyroid Gland

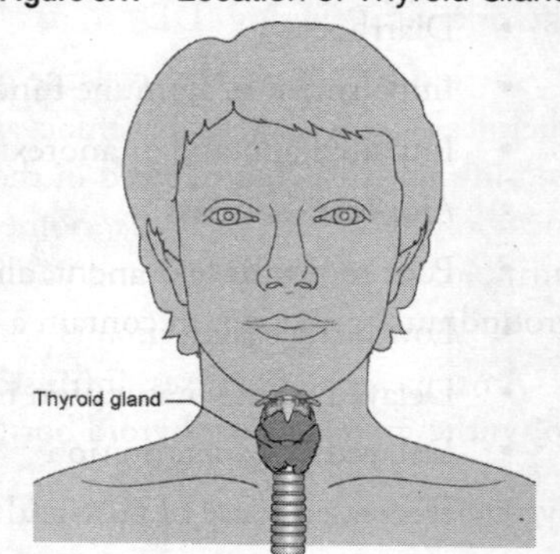

Source: http://upload.wikimedia.org/wikipedia/commons/b/b1/Diagram_showing_the_position_of_the_thyroid_gland_CRUK_363.svg

Iodine deficiency disorders (IDD) is a global problem. It is estimated that about one-third of the people around the world are exposed to the risk of IDD, that is, about two billion people have an insufficient intake of iodine. In developed countries, the problem of goitre and IDD has been virtually eliminated through the implementation of effective control measures such as iodine fortification of bread, salt, etc., but it continues to be a major nutritional problem in Latin America, Africa and Asia (de Benoist et al. 2008).

In India, there is an endemic belt of goitre and cretinism mainly along the slopes, foothills and plains adjacent to the Himalayas, extending over 2,400 km. The word 'endemic' means that the disease is found regularly or only among a particular group of people or in a geographical region. This sub-Himalayan belt of endemic goitre runs from Jammu and Kashmir in the west to the eastern states of Tripura and Arunachal Pradesh. In addition, several pockets of endemic goitre are being identified in other parts of the country, especially in hilly areas of Rajasthan, Madhya Pradesh, Gujarat, Orissa, Maharashtra, Andhra Pradesh, Karnataka, and Kerala—practically the whole country. In fact, it is estimated that about 167 million people are exposed to the risk of IDD in the country. Out of this, 54 million have goitre and 2.2 million suffer from cretinism. Another 6.6 million people are affected by milder neurological defects with psycho-motor handicaps due to IDD (NIN 2003).

Figure 8.2: Clinical Manifestations of Iodine Deficiency Disorders

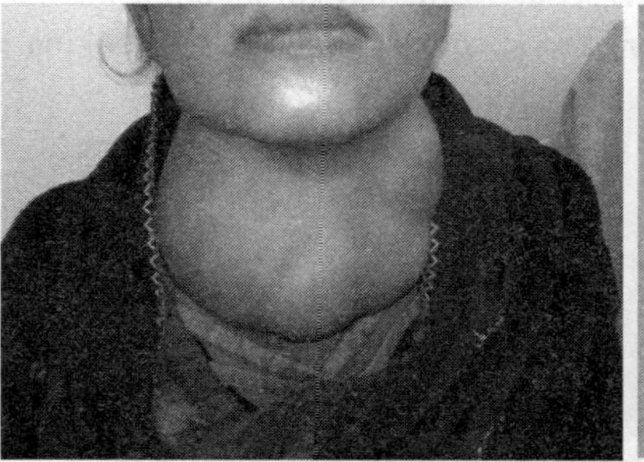

Goitre

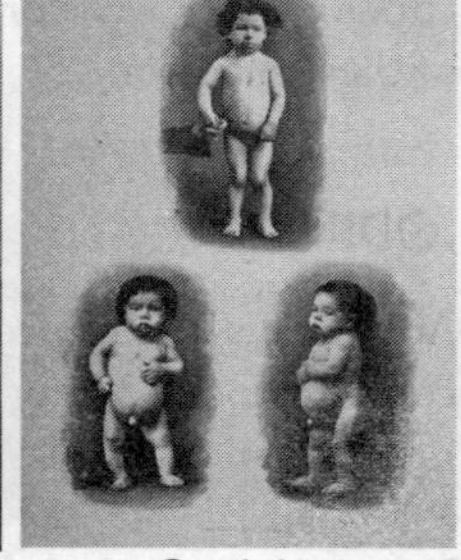

Cretinism

Source: http://commons.wikimedia.org/wiki/File:Goitre.jpg
http://commons.wikimedia.org/wiki/File:Sporadic_Cretinism_Wellcome_L0033881.jpg

Aetiology

As you can see, IDD is a public health problem in our country. Let us now examine why our food becomes deficient in iodine and how one gets this disorder, especially when all that we require is a few micrograms of this element.

The average daily requirement of iodine is 150 μg per person. Most of this is met from food and part of it through drinking water. Iodine exists in nature in large quantities in seawater. Seawater, along with iodine, evaporates to form clouds. These clouds, when condensed, reach the earth in the form of rain or snow, and enrich the top layers of the soil with iodine. The food crops grown on the soil and the animals grazing on the plants take in the iodine. The river water carries some of the iodine back into the sea.

However, in hilly slopes, especially when a lot of trees are cut and the thick vegetation cover removed, rain water either leaches out the iodine from the soil or erodes the top soil, leaving an iodine-deficient soil. Similarly, glaciers, floods, and changes in the course of rivers contribute to the removal of iodine from the soil. The food crops grown on iodine-deficient soils will naturally be deficient in iodine, and people subsisting solely on these foods will run the risk of developing IDD.

In addition, an intake of large quantities of goitrogens can lead to iodine deficiency in an individual. Certain chemical substances, such as thiocyanates, thio-oxazolidone, flavonoids, disulphides, phenols, phthalates, biphenyls, and lithium, which are found in the environment, are called '**goitrogens**', and are known to interfere with iodine metabolism at various levels. Some of these substances are found in certain tubers and vegetables, like tapioca, turnip, broccoli, cabbage, and cauliflower. Even common food items like sorghum, finger millets, mustard, and groundnuts are known to contain a fair amount of goitrogens.

In some sporadic cases, intrinsic factors like congenital or inherited defects may be responsible for the failure to synthesise or secrete thyroid hormones. The body may also develop a peripheral resistance to thyroid hormones.

Symptoms

Goitre

The prevalence of goitre can generally be seen among adolescents, young adults and school-age children. More females are affected than males. Goitre is simply defined as the enlargement of the thyroid gland. The normal thyroid gland is not palpable, or is barely palpable (that is, it cannot be touched or felt if we examine the neck of the patient). The moment one can feel the thyroid gland distinctly, the person is diagnosed with goitre. In severe cases, one can visually see the swelling in the neck (see Figure 8.1).

Box 8.1: Stages of Goitre

Stage 0: No palpable (that which can be touched or felt) or visible goitre

Stage 1: Goitre that is palpable but not visible when neck is in normal position

Stage 2: Swelling in the neck is clearly visible when neck is in normal position

If in an area, the **Total Goitre Rate** (TGR) = $\frac{\text{Number of Grade 1+2 goitres}}{\text{Total number examined}} \times 100 = \text{or} > 5\%$,

among children aged between 6–12 years, that area is said to be endemic for goitre.

Cretinism

Endemic cretinism is associated with severe iodine deficiency while the baby is still in the womb. Its prevalence is seen in areas with a very high prevalence of goitre. A wide range of defects, such as mental deficiency, deaf-mutism, and spastic paralysis of the legs in varying degrees are associated with this condition. Clinically, two types of cretinism are known: (*i*) Neurological cretinism, and (*ii*) Myxoedematous cretinism.

Neurological cretinism is seen predominantly in areas with environmental iodine deficiency. The symptoms include mental retardation, deaf-mutism, squint, and spastic rigidity affecting the lower limbs, leading to a characteristic style of walking. **Myxoedematous (Hypothyroid) cretinism,** on the other hand, is seen predominantly in areas where consumption of foods containing goitrogens is common. The children have coarse, dry skin, swollen tongue, deep hoarse voice, and mental deficiency. There is also growth retardation. This type of cretinism is seen in Zaire, among the population which consumes a lot of tapioca.

Table 8.3: Comparison between Neurological and Myxoedematous Cretinism

Features	*Neurological Cretinism*	*Myxoedematous Cretinism*
Mental retardation	Present, often severe	Present, less severe
Deaf-mutism	Usually present	Absent
Cerebral diplegia (paralysis)	Often present	Absent
Squint	Often present	Absent
Stature	Usually normal	Severe growth retardation
Physical signs of hypothyroidism	Not present	Coarse dry skin and husky voice
Reflexes	Excessively brisk	Delayed relaxation

Source: Chen and Hetzel 2010.

Functional Consequences

Iodine deficiency during pregnancy can lead to abortions, stillbirths, and increased perinatal and infant mortality. From the symptoms, especially those of cretinism, you can make out the serious effects of iodine deficiency. Those suffering from cretinism can never hope to recover as their development is permanently retarded. On the other hand, even mild iodine deficiency can have serious effects. Studies have shown that the child population from iodine-deficient areas show poor scores on IQ tests and impaired school performance. They also exhibit poor motor coordination. The population residing in iodine-deficient areas usually exhibit a reduced mental function, low intelligence levels and a high degree of apathy, reflected in a lack of initiative and decision-making capacity. In an iodine-deficient environment, school children can have about 10–15 IQ points lower than children in an iodine-sufficient environment, and as a result exhibit poor scholastic performance.

A wide variety of physical and neurological disorders are associated with iodine deficiency. Goitre and cretinism are two important clinical forms of IDD. Once the disease sets in, there is very little that can be done to reverse the process. The only way to combat the problem of IDD is to provide iodine to the community. This can be achieved by fortification of food items with iodine or by direct iodine supplementation, and, if necessary, by discouraging people from consuming foods known to contain high levels of goitrogens.

Prevention

Fortification of food items such as wheat flour, bread, milk, sugar, drinking water, and common salt is in practice in different parts of the world. Fortification of common salt is the most common method of iodine fortification.

Salt can be fortified with potassium iodate or potassium iodide. Salt fortified with potassium iodate is relatively more stable than that with potassium iodide. Hence, potassium iodate is commonly used for the fortification of salt in India. A daily consumption of 10 g of iodised salt provides about 150 μg of iodine. Goitre of mild to moderate degree can be effectively controlled by using iodised salt.

As soil levels are generally low in iodine, the main source of iodine in the Indian diet, especially in areas that are not coastal, is iodised salt. Thus, it is important to select and consume only iodised salt. In addition, we need to be careful to prevent iodine loss from salt. Salt sold only in sealed packets should be purchased. The label should be checked to ensure that the salt is iodised. After opening the packet, the salt should be stored in air-tight containers. To lower losses of iodine during cooking, salt should be added only towards the end.

> **Did you know...** that during cooking, a substantial amount of iodine (20–70 per cent) may be lost from food. It is best to add the fortified salt towards the end of cooking to retain more iodine.

Iodised Oil Supplementation

Oil fortified with iodine is available for oral or intra-muscular injections. Supplementation with iodised oil is the best method of immediate prevention of new cases of cretinism and mental retardation in communities living in severely iodine-deficient areas. However, once the iodised salt distribution programme is well-established, the iodised oil programme can slowly be phased out.

In India, the **National Iodine Deficiency Disorders Control Programme (NIDDCP)** has been in operation since 1962, working towards the control and prevention of IDD. Regular screening of communities is done by measuring urinary iodine levels to study the prevalence of this disorder, and accordingly preventive measures have been put into place. There is a ban on the sale of non-iodised salt in India. The mandatory fortification level is 30 ppm at the manufacturer's level, and 15 ppm at the retailer or consumer level.

Toxicity

Toxic goitre has been reported in people consuming 60–130 times the RDA. Here, the thyroid hormone synthesis is inhibited by an excess of iodine. This iodine-induced hypothyroidism is known as the '**Wolff-Chaikoff**' effect. The symptoms the person suffers from will depend on how much iodine the person was consuming before exposure to excess iodine. Toxicities have been reported in Japan, due to a high intake of iodine-rich seaweed, and in Chile due to high levels of environmental iodine and increased use in water purification. Excess iodine intake may also increase the risk of hyperthyroidism, autoimmune thyroid disease and thyroid cancer.

The **Jod-Basedow syndrome** is hyperthyroidism following the administration of iodine or iodide. This phenomenon is thus iodine-induced hyperthyroidism, typically presenting in a patient with endemic goitre (due to iodine deficiency). However, unlike the Wolff-Chaikoff effect, the Jod-Basedow effect does not occur in persons with normal thyroid glands, as thyroid hormone synthesis and release in normal persons is controlled by pituitary TSH secretion, which does not allow hyperthyroidism when extra iodine is ingested.

Recommended Dietary Allowances

The RDA for adults is 150 μg/day, which can be obtained by consuming 10g of iodised salt/day (as salt is iodised at the 15 ppm level). However, because of an increase in the prevalence of hypertension, the recommendation is not to have more than 5g of salt. Hence, fortification levels will have to be re-evaluated.

FLUORIDE

Fluoride occurs normally in the body, primarily as a calcium salt in our bones and teeth. It is required in very small quantities by our body. This small amount makes the crystalline deposits in our bones and teeth larger and more perfectly formed. A slight excess of fluorine, however, leads to problems.

Function

It aids in the synthesis of fluorapatite during bone and teeth development. The hydroxyl (OH) groups of hydroxyapatite (calcium and phosphorus crystals) in the bones and teeth are replaced by fluoride to form fluorapatite. This makes the tooth enamel more resistant to the action of acids produced in the mouth by bacteria. Fluoride also inhibits metabolism and the growth of bacterium that causes dental caries. Fluoride present in saliva directly inhibits tooth demineralisation and enhances tooth remineralisation.

Food Sources

Tea, seafood, seaweed, and water are considered to be significant sources. Toothpastes and other topical applications may also contribute to fluoride intake. Fluoride containing pesticides, fertilisers and emissions from industries also add to the fluoride content of soil and water.

Recommended Dietary Allowances

Concentrations of about 1 ppm (parts per million) in water are considered to be protective against dental caries in children. Endemic fluorosis is a serious problem in areas where the drinking water has fluoride greater than the 1 ppm level.

Toxicity

High fluoride intake can mottle teeth during the developmental stage. Children from infancy to 16 years are susceptible. Both boys and girls are equally affected. Children consuming fluoridated toothpastes are at risk. The tooth structure is weakened and can crumble. In mild cases, white specks develop on the teeth, and in severe cases, the enamel gets pitted and becomes permanently stained (dental mottling). These changes, known as **dental fluorosis** are irreversible and hence must be prevented. Excess fluoride also leads to skeletal changes, known as **skeletal fluorosis**. This is seen in areas where the fluoride level in the water is more than 1.5–2 ppm. Joint pains, arthritis, stiffness of spine, sometimes paralysis, kyphosis (excessive curvature of spine), abnormal hardening of bones, and calcification of ligaments, tendons and muscle attachments are seen in skeletal fluorosis. Fluorosis is endemic in India in parts of Andhra Pradesh (Nalgonda district) and Punjab.

Genu Valgum, or knock-knee syndrome, can also develop due to fluoride toxicity, along with other environmental factors like high levels of molybdenum, low levels of copper and a low intake of calcium. This was first seen in areas where huge dams and reservoirs were under construction; however, the causal association between the two has not been established. The symptoms included bone deformities like knock-knees, typical signs of dental and skeletal fluorosis, and in addition, extensive osteoporosis of the limb bones.

Prevention

Supplying surface water from nearby rivers, canals and dams to endemic areas will solve the problem to a great extent. However, where this is not possible, excess fluoride in locally available water will need to be removed through defluoridation. Several techniques to do this are available at the household level, as well as on a large scale. The simplest techniques involve precipitating out the fluoride. The Nalgonda Technology developed by the National Environmental Engineering Research Institute (NEERI) in Nagpur involves adding lime and alum to the water to precipitate out the fluoride.

Besides defluoridation, the general nutritional status (particularly that of protein, calcium and vitamin C) of people needs to be improved. In countries like the USA, levels of 8 ppm in drinking water have not caused skeletal fluorosis. The theory is that it is related to the nutritional status of people. The undernourished population of developing countries may be more susceptible to fluoride toxicity. The use of tamarind in daily diet increases fluoride excretion. People living in endemic areas should also avoid cooking and storing food in aluminium vessels and using foods that have high fluoride content, as this increases the risk of fluoride toxicity. Children in endemic areas should avoid using fluoridated toothpastes.

SELENIUM

Selenium as an important nutrient was discovered by Schwarz and Foltz during their study of liver necrosis. Selenium in food is present mainly in two forms—as selenomethionine in plant foods and selenocysteine in animal foods. About 30 per cent of the selenium in our body is present in the liver, another 30 per cent in the muscles, 15 per cent in the kidneys, and about 10 per cent in blood plasma.

Functions

Selenium is present as a part of proteins called selenoproteins, which play important roles in the body. Selenomethionine and selenocysteine exist in several proteins of the body. It plays an important role in the protection of body tissues against oxidative stress, and also in growth and development.

1. Selenium is a part of the enzyme glutathione peroxidase, which has been found in almost all cells as well as outside the cells in serum and milk. During stress, injury or infection, selenoenzymes may protect the body from the damaging effects of free radicals. Cellular peroxides and free radicals are reduced to water and other harmless molecules. The antioxidant effects of selenium and vitamin E may reinforce each other.
2. It protects the body against infections by helping in the development of immunity.
3. Selenium is seen in the protein matrix of teeth.
4. An enzyme which converts thyroxine (T_4) to triiodothyronine (T_3) is a selenoprotein, and in selenium deficiency, T_3 levels are known to decrease, creating a thyroid hormone imbalance.
5. Selenium also protects against the toxicity of heavy metals like mercury, cadmium and silver.

Food Sources

The selenium content of crops, and hence human tissue concentrations, are dependent on the selenium content of soil. Major food sources include seafoods, organ meats like kidney and liver, other meats and poultry, nuts like Brazil nut, etc. Cereals and grains may contribute significantly to selenium in the Indian dietaries, although they are not exactly rich sources (selenium content depends on soil levels). Fruits and vegetables are generally low in selenium; however, plants like mustard, garlic and broccoli are able to accumulate selenium from the soil, provided that the soil is rich in selenium.

Recommended Dietary Allowances

Selenium compounds are generally very efficiently absorbed. Dietary intake of about 40 µg/ day of selenium appears to be necessary to maintain glutathione peroxidise levels, and has been recommended as the acceptable intake for Indians. The FAO/WHO Committee (2004) recommended a selenium intake of 34 µg/ day for adult men and 26 µg/ day for adult women.

Requirements may increase with increased consumption of unsaturated fatty acids in the diet, because of the need for the antioxidant activity of selenium. The Upper Tolerable Nutrient intake level (UL) for adults has been proposed as 400 µg/ day.

Problem of Deficiency and Excess

Selenium deficiency is rare, except in China. The lowest selenium content of soil exists in a few regions of China, from the northeast to the southwest, especially in Keshan, where severe selenium deficiency was first reported in a human population in 1979. Although the clinical manifestations of the deficiency were described in literature more than 100 years ago, the association between selenium deficiency and the symptoms was established much later. The disease is known as **Keshan Disease** after the region, and is a kind of cardiomyopathy (heart muscle disease) that mainly affects children (2–10 years old) and women of childbearing age. The person experiences fatigue after mild exercise, has palpitations, cardiac arrhythmias (irregular heart beats), heart enlargement, and congestive heart failure. This disease may have a viral component, in which the virus flourishes, resulting in the development of myocarditis (inflammation of the heart muscle) in the absence of or low levels of selenium in the diet. Supplementation programmes have completely eradicated the disease. Other areas with low selenium soil levels are in Finland and New Zealand.

Kaschin-Beck disease was first identified in Russia. In China, it has been detected in children between the ages of 5–13. Southeast Siberia and North Korea are the other areas affected. The disease is characterised by joint necrosis, resulting in structural shortening of fingers and long bones with consequent growth retardation and stunting. The other symptoms include stiffness, swelling and pain in the joints of fingers, followed by generalised osteoarthritis. Among causative factors, mycotoxins (fungal toxins) or iodine deficiency have also been implicated along with simultaneous selenium deficiency.

Deficiency of selenium has also been linked to sperm abnormalities. This is related to the fact that selenoprotein is a component of the mitochondrial capsule of sperm cells, which may get damaged due to selenium deficiency. If there is a deficiency of iodine along with selenium, then the thyroid weight increases much more than if there is just iodine deficiency.

Mild deficiency can result in an increased susceptibility to certain infections due to viruses. Other clinical manifestations include muscular weakness and myalgia (pain in muscles). Deficiency may be seen in children receiving long-term total parenteral nutrition (feeding through the intravenous route), children suffering from protein energy malnutrition, and patients with certain types of cancer. A poor intake of selenium has been associated with an increased risk of cancer and heart disease. However, whether selenium supplementation protects against cancer is still debatable. The protective effect against heart disease may be related to its action as an antioxidant, or its influence on platelet aggregation.

Toxicity has again been reported mostly in China, in areas where the soil and water levels of selenium are high, or when people have been occupationally exposed to high levels of selenium. Indian studies from Punjab indicate that an intake of more than 600 μg /day was associated with symptoms of selenosis (Hira et al. 2004). **Selenosis** results in skin and nail changes (brittle nails), decay of teeth, and neurologic abnormalities (depression). A high protein diet is protective against selenosis.

CHROMIUM

The importance of chromium as an essential nutrient is slowly being recognised, as its role in important metabolic functions is emerging. Concentrations of chromium in human tissues are low, as most of it is excreted in faeces. It is mostly found in the bones, liver, kidneys, and spleen.

Functions

Chromium helps to maintain normal glucose levels by enhancing the activity of the hormone insulin. Although research evidence is lacking, many athletes are known to take chromium supplements to enhance muscle mass and strength, while some others take these supplements to reduce body fat.

Food Sources

Chromium is widely distributed in a number of foods. Seafoods (especially oysters), brewer's yeast, meat, liver, fish, broccoli, mushrooms, dried beans, nuts, dark chocolate, and whole grain products are good sources of chromium. Cheese is a concentrated source, while butter, eggs, potatoes, and other tubers also contribute significantly to intake. As chromium is one of the metals used to make steel, small amounts can leach into food (especially food containing acidic ingredients) through utensils and processing equipment.

Recommended Dietary Allowances

Normally, the absorption of chromium from foods is very low. Vitamin C seems to enhance the absorption. Phytates in whole grains seem to decrease absorption, although only limited data is available. ICMR (2010) recommends 50 μg/day for Indian adult men and women.

Problem of Deficiency and Excess

Impaired glucose tolerance (abnormally raised glucose levels in blood), peripheral neuropathy (nerve damage), and weight loss have been reported in chromium deficiency. Deficiency is usually seen in patients on total parenteral nutrition. Chromium supplementation reverses the symptoms of glucose intolerance to an extent. Research evidence highlighting the role of chromium in helping insulin to function effectively is accumulating.

MOLYBDENUM

Molybdenum is often classified as an 'ultra-trace mineral', as it is required in extremely small quantities.

Functions

It is a part of several metalloenzymes, especially several oxidase enzymes.

Food Sources

Molybdenum-rich foods include mostly plant-based foods like grains, legumes, nuts, green leafy vegetables, and also milk and liver. The concentration of the mineral in these foods varies with the soil content of the mineral.

Recommended Dietary Allowances

The ICMR does not give any recommendation due to a lack of available data on this mineral. The US Food and Nutrition Board has given the RDA for adults as 45 μg/day.

Problem of Deficiency and Excess

Molybdenum deficiency and toxicity is very rare in the community. Some studies have, however, reported toxicity symptoms of gout-like joint inflammation, growth retardation, and reproductive abnormalities in laboratory animals.

COPPER

The use of copper in traditional medicine systems dates back to 400 BC. However, its role as an essential mineral in our diet was recognised as late as 1964. The adult body contains only about 80 mg of copper, stored mainly in the liver, followed by the brain and muscle. Like zinc, it is absorbed through simple diffusion and by active transport. It competes with zinc for the same carrier proteins. High phytate intake decreases copper absorption. Copper is transported in the form of ceruloplasmin in blood. It is excreted through bile. Ceruloplasmin is the major copper-carrying protein in the blood, and in addition, plays a role in iron metabolism. Ceruloplasmin is an enzyme synthesised in the liver, containing 6 atoms of copper in its structure, and carries more than 95 per cent of the total copper in healthy human plasma.

Functions

Copper is an important component of many enzymes that participate in several metabolic reactions:

1. As a part of Cytochrome C oxidase, it participates in energy metabolism.
2. Along with zinc, it is a part of superoxide dismutase, which prevents oxidative damage to cells.
3. As a component of lysyl oxidase, which is involved in the cross-linking of collagen and elastin for connective tissue formation and strength.
4. Copper is involved with monoamine oxidase enzymes in the regulation of neurotransmitters like serotonin, dopamine and norepinephrine.
5. Enzyme Ceruloplasmin, also known as Ferroxidase I, is involved in oxidising ferrous to ferric iron for incorporation into transferrin, and subsequent transport from the liver to the body cells.

Food Sources

Copper is found in a variety of foods. Seafoods (shellfish), liver, pulses, soya products, dark chocolate, oilseeds like sesame, sunflower, and nuts are rich sources of copper. Fruits and vegetables are moderate sources. Meat is a marginal source, but it promotes copper absorption from other foods, just like it does for iron. Tap water may be an important source in areas where the water pipes are made of copper. High phytate content in the diet is known to decrease copper absorption.

Recommended Dietary Allowances

The recommendation for the intake of copper is about 2 mg/day for adults. The mean absorption of copper from Indian diets is around 18 per cent. As the data on the intake of this mineral is limited, the recommendation is given as 'acceptable intake'.

Problem of Deficiency and Excess

Severe copper deficiency is rare in humans. Deficiencies have been reported in milk-based formula-fed premature infants, infants recovering from malnutrition, patients on long-term parenteral nutrition, those consuming an excess of zinc, and those suffering from a genetic disorder called 'Menkes disease'. The symptoms of copper deficiency include:

- Anaemia, resulting from deranged iron metabolism (low transport of iron from storage, resulting in decreased haemoglobin synthesis).
- Decreased white blood cell count (leukopenia) and impaired immune function.
- Vascular complications, and cardiovascular changes.
- Osteoporosis and osteopenia. Decrease in lysyl oxidase leads to a decrease in collagen and elastin cross-linking. These two structural proteins give strength to connective tissues in the lungs, blood vessels, skin, teeth, and bones.
- Neurological manifestations (may increase the risk of Alzheimer's disease).

In Menkes disease, the hair becomes kinky, which is why it is also known as Menkes kinky hair syndrome.

Toxicity

Copper toxicity is not common. It has only been reported in children who accidently had an excess of supplements, in individuals consuming copper-contaminated food/water (copper leaching out of cooking or storage utensils), and in Wilson disease, a genetic disorder in which the body is unable to excrete copper. Excess copper gets stored in the body, resulting in symptoms of abdominal pain, nausea, vomiting, and diarrhoea. The upper limit of copper is set at 10 mg/day, because higher intakes increase the risk of liver damage (cirrhosis).

MANGANESE

The adult human body contains about 10–20 mg of manganese. The bone, liver, pancreas, and kidney are important tissues which contain manganese.

Functions

Manganese is generally found concentrated in tissues that are rich in mitochondria.

1. It is a component and activator of several enzymes like glutamine synthetase, pyruvate carboxylase, glycosyl transferase, and mitochondrial superoxide dismutase. It is involved in gluconeogenesis (formation of glucose from non-carbohydrate sources), and carbohydrate and lipid metabolism.
2. It is associated with the formation of connective and skeletal tissues, and hence growth and reproduction.
3. It is a part of the antioxidant defence system by being a cofactor for the enzyme superoxide dismutase.

Food Sources

The richest sources of manganese include plant foods like whole grain cereals (wheat, barley, rice bran), legumes, green leafy vegetables, nuts, and tea, while moderately rich sources, which might also contribute to daily intake, include fruits and vegetables. It is also present in relatively high amounts in instant coffee and tea.

Recommended Dietary Allowances

As with other trace minerals, the absorption from diet is relatively low. Absorption is decreased by phytates in the diet, and by a high intake of other minerals like iron and calcium. Although the data is insufficient to work out the requirement of this mineral for different age groups, studies have shown that the adult requirement is between 2–5 mg/day.

Problem of Deficiency and Excess

Deficiency in humans was first reported in 1972. Symptoms are non-specific, including weight loss, slow growth of hair, changes in hair colour, and transient dermatitis (inflammation of the skin). Animal studies have shown that manganese is essential for reproduction. Animals receiving diets deficient in manganese developed sterility and exhibited striking skeletal abnormalities. Abnormal insulin metabolism and glucose tolerance have also been reported in deficiency.

Signs of toxicity have been seen in miners who inhaled a lot of manganese dust. The mineral accumulated in the liver and the central nervous system and produced Parkinson-like symptoms (muscle stiffness and tremors). An Upper Level of 11 mg/day has been prescribed by the Food and Nutrition Board, USA.

Table 8.4: Summary of Functions, Rich Sources and Symptoms of Deficiency and Excess of Trace Minerals

Mineral	*Major Functions*	*Rich Sources*	*Symptoms of Deficiency*	*Symptoms of Excess (UL)**
Iron	Component of haemoglobin, myoglobin, cytochromes, energy metabolism, immunity, cognitive development	Meat, seafood, eggs, soyabean, legumes, green leafy vegetables	Anaemia, decreased immunity, poor cognitive development	Gastrointestinal upset (45 mg/day)
Zinc	Cofactor for enzymes, growth and sexual development, immunity, cell integrity	Seafoods, meats, whole grains, nuts, legumes	Poor growth, delayed sexual development, decreased appetite, infection	Diarrhoea, nausea, decreased copper absorption (45 mg/day)
Iodine	Production of thyroid hormones, which control several metabolic processes	Seafood, seaweed, iodised salt	Goitre, Cretinism	Inhibition of the functioning of thyroid gland (1.1 mg/day)
Fluorine	Provides strength to bones and teeth, improves resistance of tooth enamel to dental caries	Water, tea, seaweed, seafood	May increase risk of dental caries	Dental and skeletal fluorosis (10 mg/day)
Selenium	Part of antioxidant enzyme system, activates thyroid hormones, immunity	Meat, eggs, seafood, whole grains, nuts	Keshan disease, increased susceptibility to infection	Selenosis, hair and nail changes (400 µg/day)
Chromium	Improves insulin action	Liver, meat, seafood, eggs, whole grains, nuts, broccoli, mushroom	Glucose intolerance	Not reported
Molybdenum	Cofactor for several enzymes	Grains, nuts, legumes, green leafy vegetables	Not reported	Poor growth, joint inflammation and sterility in laboratory animals (2 mg/day)
Copper	Cofactor for antioxidant enzymes, connective tissue and iron metabolism	Liver, seafoods, nuts, cocoa, legumes, oilseeds	Anaemia, low WBC count, and poor development of connective tissues	Vomiting, diarrhoea, liver damage (10 mg/day)
Manganese	Cofactor for enzymes, carbohydrate and lipid metabolism, antioxidant	Nuts, tea, legumes, whole grains, green leafy vegetables	Poor growth, skeletal abnormalities and sterility in animals	Nervous system disorders (11 mg/day)

Note: *UL: Upper Tolerable Intake level given by the Food and Nutrition Board, USA.

SUMMARY

- The different trace minerals that you learnt about in this chapter are: Iron, Zinc, Iodine, Fluorine, Selenium, Chromium, Molybdenum, Copper, and Manganese. Trace minerals are needed by our bodies in very small amounts. Yet, they are very important for our body, playing vital roles as structural elements or as cofactors for enzymes controlling various metabolic reactions in our body. The importance of various trace minerals is slowly being realised as research studies unveil amazing facts about these nutrients. The summary of the main functions, rich food sources and problems arising from a deficiency/excess of these minerals are given in Table 8.4.

KEY WORDS

Aetiology: The study of the causes of disease

Apathy: Lack of interest, enthusiasm or concern

Co-factor: A substance that works with an enzyme to facilitate a chemical reaction

Cirrhosis: A chronic disease of the liver, marked by degeneration of cells, inflammation, and fibrous thickening of tissue

Deaf-mutism: When the person cannot hear or speak

Deteriorate: To worsen

Endemic: Habitual presence of a disease among a particular group of people or geographical region

Fatigue: Extreme tiredness after exertion

Koilonychia: Spoon-shaped nails (a sign of iron deficiency anaemia)

Hypochromic: Pale, having less than normal colour

Impaired glucose tolerance: A pre-diabetic state in which blood glucose levels remain high and the insulin is unable to decrease blood levels

Macrocyte: Large cell

Microcyte: Small cell

Necrosis: Death

Neurological: Related to the nervous system

Oedema: Swelling

Palpable: Can be touched or felt

Perinatal: From the 28th week of pregnancy to 28 days after birth

Peripheral neuropathy: A disorder in which the nerves, especially of the hands and feet, are damaged or destroyed, affecting movement and sensation

Retarded: Slowed down

Spastic paralysis: Rigidity of the muscles, accompanied by partial paralysis

Total parenteral nutrition: Receiving all nourishment intravenously

Wasting of muscles: Muscle tissues get destroyed

EXERCISES

1. Why is iron important for our body?
2. Describe the symptoms of anaemia. How would you alter the diet to improve the bioavailability of iron?
3. Define goitre. A deficiency of which element leads to this condition?
4. Can mild deficiency of iodine also have serious effects on our bodies?
5. How can fluorosis be prevented?
6. Why are the following minerals important for our body:
   a. Molybdenum
   b. Manganese
   c. Copper
7. Give the rich sources of the following minerals:
   a. Zinc
   b. Selenium
   c. Chromium
8. What does deficiency of zinc lead to?

REFERENCES

Brahmam, G. N. V., 'Iodine deficiency disorders', in M. S. Bamji, K. Krishnaswamy and G. N. V. Brahmam (eds), *Textbook of Human Nutrition*, 3e, New Delhi: Oxford and IBH Publishing Co., 2009.

Brown, K. H., S. E. Wuehler and J. M. Peerson, 'The importance of zinc in human nutrition and estimation of the global prevalence of zinc deficiency', *Food and Nutrition Bulletin* 22(2), 2001, pp. 113–25.

Byrd-Bredbenner C., G. Moe, D. Beshgetoor, and J. Berning, *Wardlaw's Perspectives in Nutrition*, 9e, New York: McGraw-Hill International Edition, 2013.

Chen, Z. P. and B. S. Hetzel,. 'Cretinism revisited. Best Practice and Research', *Clinical Endocrinology and Metabolism* 24, 2010, pp. 39–50.

Das, A. A., 'Fluorosis', in M. S. Bamji, K. Krishnaswamy and G. N. V. Brahmam (eds), *Textbook of Human Nutrition*, 3e, Oxford and IBH Publishing Co., 2009.

de Benoist, B., E. McLean, M. Andersson, and L. Rogers, 'Iodine deficiency in 2007: Global progress since 2003', *Food and Nutrition Bulletin* 29(3), 2008, pp. 195–202.

Food and Nutrition Board, Institute of Medicine, *Dietary Reference Intakes*, Washington, DC: National Academy Press, 2001.

Hira, C. K., K. Partal and K. S. Dhillon, 'Dietary selenium intake by men and women in high and low selenium areas of Punjab', *Pub Hlth Nutr* 7, 2004, pp. 39–43.

ICMR, 'Nutrient Requirements and Recommended Dietary Allowances for Indians', A report of the Expert Group of the Indian Council of Medical Research, 2010.

NFHS-3, *National Family and Health Survey 3 (2005–06)*, Mumbai: International Institute of Population Sciences, 2007.

NIN, 'Current status of IDD in selected districts of southern region of the country', Hyderabad: ICMR, 2003.

NNMB, 'Diet and nutritional status of population and prevalence of hypertension among adults in rural areas', National Nutrition Monitoring Bureau Technical Report No. 24, Hyderabad: National Institute of Nutrition, Indian Council of Medical Research, 2006.

Rolfes, S. R., K. Pinna and E. Whitney, *Understanding Normal and Clinical Nutrition*, 8e, Wadsworth Cengage Learning, 2009.

WHO/FAO, *Vitamin and Mineral Requirements in Human Nutrition*, 2e, Joint FAO/WHO Expert Consultation on Human Vitamin and Mineral Requirements, Bangkok, Thailand, 2004.

WHO/UNICEF/ICCIDD, *Assessment of Iodine Deficiency Disorders and Monitoring their Elimination. A Guide for Program Managers*, 3e, 2007. Available at http://www.unicef.org/ukraine/2_Guide_for_IDD_managers_eng.pdf (accessed 11 November 2014).

WHO/ UNICEF/ UNU, *Iron deficiency anemia: Assessment, prevention and control, a guide for programme managers*, Geneva: World Health Organization, 2001.

ONLINE SOURCES

http://www.who.int/vmnis/indicators/haemoglobin.pdf

http://www.who.int/nutrition/publications/micronutrients/anaemia_iron_deficiency/WHO_NHD_01.3/en/index.html

9

FAT-SOLUBLE VITAMINS

HIGHLIGHTS

- Discovery of vitamins
- Functions of different fat soluble vitamins
- Food sources of vitamins A, D, E, and K
- Recommended Dietary Allowances
- Problem of Deficiency and Excess

Vitamins are essential organic substances needed in small amounts in the diet for normal functioning, growth and maintenance of body tissues. These micronutrients are indispensable in human diets because most of them cannot be synthesised in sufficient quantities in the human body. Exceptions include vitamin D, which is synthesised by the skin in the presence of sunlight. Niacin can be formed in the body from the amino acid tryptophan. Vitamin K and biotin can be synthesised to some extent by the bacteria in the intestinal tract. For a substance to be classified as a vitamin, its absence from the diet for a definite period of time must produce deficiency signs and symptoms, which are quickly cured when the substance is resupplied.

DISCOVERY OF VITAMINS

Long before any of the vitamins were discovered, certain foods were known to have certain properties which would cure conditions that we now recognise as deficiencies of vitamins. The ancient Egyptians and Greeks treated night blindness with beef liver, which is a rich source of vitamin A. The fifteenth-century sailors who embarked on long sea voyages often suffered from spongy bleeding gums. The problem was traced to the lack of availability of fresh fruits and vegetables as ration on ships. Eating lemons and limes was found to keep sailors healthy and alive. Citrus fruit started being included in a sailor's ration. British sailors in fact earned the nickname 'limeys' because of this. We now understand that the condition they suffered from was scurvy, due to a deficiency of vitamin C.

The discoveries of different types of vitamins that are present in food, and the effects these vitamins had on human health, began around 1905 with the experiments of an English doctor, William Fletcher, in Kuala Lumpur. He showed that those who consumed polished rice developed **beriberi,** while those who ate unpolished rice were protected. This disease was common in countries of Asia, where polished rice was the staple, and the population hardly ate any other food. In 1906, English biochemist Sir Frederick Gowland Hopkins also discovered that 'accessory food factors' present in our diet were important to health.

Then, in 1912, while working at the famed Lister Institute in London, the Polish-born biochemist Casimir Funk took Fletcher's thinking a few steps further. He isolated the active substances in rice husks of the unpolished rice that were preventing beriberi. He named these missing dietary links *'vitamines'* (vital amines), in the belief that they were 'amines', compounds derived from 'ammonia'. (The 'e' at the end was dropped in 1920, when it became clear that not all vitamins were 'amines'.) Together, Hopkins and Funk formulated the vitamin hypothesis of deficiency disease—that a lack of vitamins could make you sick.

In 1913, attention turned to finding and isolating the vitamins themselves. Thomas Osborne and Lafayette Mendel showed in rat experiments conducted at Yale University that butter contained a growth-promoting factor necessary for development. Soon, this was identified as fat-soluble **Vitamin A.** Its chemical character was established in 1933, and it was synthesised in 1947.

Other vitamin discoveries came along in the early twentieth century. In 1922, while looking for a solution to the problem of rickets, Edward Mellanby dicovered **Vitamin D.** Experiments with rats in 1922 showed that rats reared exclusively on whole milk grew normally, but were sterile and could not reproduce. Herbert Evans and Katherine Bishop, at the University of California, showed that the missing factor was abundant in green leaves and wheat germ. This led to the discovery of fat-soluble **Vitamin E**.

The early sixteenth-century observation that citrus fruits could prevent **scurvy** on long sea voyages later led Harriet Chick of the Lister Institute to begin a series of painstaking investigations during the 1930s into the antiscorbutic qualities of various foods. Meanwhile, in 1932, Albert Szent-Gyorgyi isolated a substance from the adrenal glands. He called it *hexuronic acid.* At the same time in history, W. A. Waugh and Charles King isolated a vitamin from a lemon, and showed that it was identical to hexuronic acid. In 1932, this vitamin became the first to be synthesised in a laboratory. It was **Vitamin C.** Cow's milk was found to contain another growth-promoting factor, the water-soluble Vitamin B, which was isolated in pure form in 1936.

Thus, you can see that a lot of hard work by a number of scientists from across the world went into the discovery and isolation of vitamins. Vitamins can be classified as water or fat-soluble vitamins (Figure 9.1). In this chapter, you will be studying about fat-soluble vitamins A, D, E, and K.

Fat-soluble Vitamins are digested and absorbed in a similar manner. The digestion process in the stomach releases vitamins from food. The bile produced in the liver, and released into the lumen of the small intestine, aids in the absorption of fat-soluble vitamins. Fat-soluble vitamins are absorbed along with dietary fat in the small intestine. Small amounts of Vitamin K and biotin are made by bacteria in the terminal part of the small intestine and in the large intestine, and are absorbed there.

Figure 9.1: Classification of Vitamins

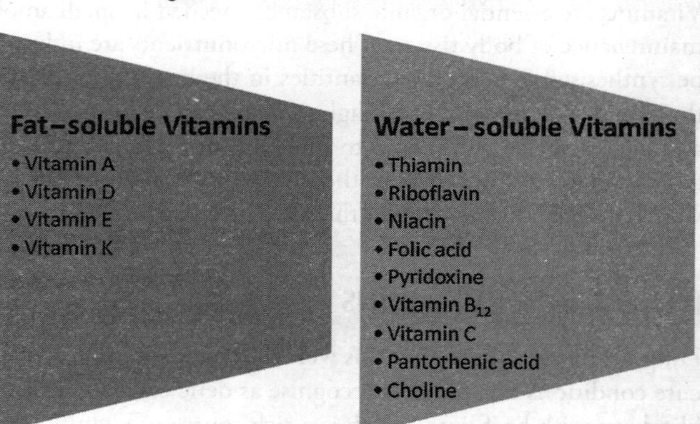

VITAMIN A

Elmer V. McCollum and M. Davis discovered vitamin A during 1912–14. In 1913, Yale researchers Thomas Osborne and Lafayette Mendel discovered that butter contained a fat-soluble nutrient, soon known as vitamin A. As early as in the 1930s, Moore provided the first evidence that a plant-derived carotenoid is the direct precursor for vitamin A in animals, describing a conversion of β-carotene to vitamin A. Thomas Moore demonstrated that the liver of rats given a diet deficient in vitamin A, but containing a high amount of carotene, for a few months, had high levels of vitamin A. Thus, it was established that there is a mechanism in the body by which dietary carotene is converted into vitamin A, and these were called the precursors of vitamin A. Vitamin A was first synthesised in 1947.

Carotenoids and Disease Prevention

Intake of carotenoid-rich fruits and vegetables may decrease the risk of certain eye diseases, cancers and cardiovascular disease. β-carotene may protect against cataract, while lutein and zeaxanthin protect against age-related macular degeneration of the eye. Carotenoid supplements have not shown the same beneficial effects. Hence, to reap these benefits, one needs to increase the consumption of carotenoid-rich fruits and vegetables.

Vitamin A is present in animal foods as a preformed vitamin, retinol or retinyl esters. Carotenoids are more than 600 or so yellow-orange pigments in plant foods. Some of them (alpha-carotene, beta-carotene and beta-cryptoxanthin) are precursors of vitamin A, which means that they can get converted in our body into retinol. They are also known as provitamin A. The form that shows maximum vitamin A activity is β-carotene. Some other carotenoids of physiological significance include lutein, lycopene and zeazanthin.

Retinoids is a term used for three biologically active forms of Vitamin A—retinol (alcohol form), retinal (aldehyde form), and retinoic acid (acid form). Up to 90 per cent of the retinoids can be absorbed from the diet, depending on the amount of fat in the diet.

Stability

Vitamin A is relatively stable to heat and alkali. It is, however, unstable to light and acid, and gets easily oxidised. Rapid destruction occurs with exposure to high temperature in the presence of air, with UV irradiation, or in the presence of rancid fats.

Measurement

The unit of measurement of vitamin A is micrograms. Values are also sometimes reported as International Units (IU).

1 IU vitamin A Activity = 0.3 μg retinol/ 3.6 μg β-carotene/ 7.2 μg β-carotene and β-cryptoxanthin

When a food is likely to contain both retinol and β-carotene, then the value of vitamin A is expressed as *retinol equivalents (RE) or retinol activity equivalents (RAE).*

According to the Food and Nutrition Board, Institute of Medicine, USA (2002),

1 RAE = 1 μg retinol
= 12 μg β-carotene
= 24 μg α-carotene and β-cryptoxanthin

According to ICMR (2010),
Retinol equivalents (μg) = Retinol (μg) + β-carotene (μg)/8

Functions

Retinyl esters, retinol and retinal (retinaldehyde) are readily converted from one form to the other in the human body. Retinoic acid, however, cannot be converted to other forms. It also cannot be stored in the body. It has a special role to play in some tissues, and does not function in the visual cycle or support reproduction in most species. vitamin A has several important roles to play in our body.

1. Vitamin A, in the form of retinal, has an important role to play in **vision**. The sensory elements of the retina consist of specialised cells known as Rods and Cones (names are symbolic of the shape of the cells). *Rods* are responsible for vision in dim light and black and white images. They have a photosensitive pigment called *Rhodopsin* or *visual purple*, made up of a protein called opsin and retinal. This pigment is critical to the night vision capability of rods. *Cones* are responsible for vision in bright light, or colour vision. They produce a photosensitive pigment called *Iodopsin* or *visual violet.* Cones are three different types of cells, in which retinal combines with three different types of proteins responsive to blue, green or red light (Figure 9.2).
2. Retinoic acid, as we know, is necessary for the **differentiation of cells**. It reacts with specific receptors in the DNA, triggering the process of differentiation. Differentiation is a process in which general precursor cells develop into specific cell types that produce characteristic proteins.
3. For the **health and maintenance of cells,** especially of the epithelium, vitamin A is very important. The epithelial layer covers the body externally in the form of our skin. It also lines the mucous membranes of the different passages in our body. Vitamin A, in the form of retinoic acid, influences the way in which epithelial cells differentiate into mature forms. This process is important for the maintenance of mucous-

forming cells. Retinoic acid is essential for the normal structure and function of epithelial cells. The mucous secretions maintain the integrity of the epithelium, especially the membranes that line the eyes, mouth, gastro-intestinal tract, and respiratory and genitor-urinary tracts. These membranes, maintained in their optimal condition, offer resistance to bacterial invasion.

4. Vitamin A is important for **Reproduction and Growth**. Retinoids play an important role in **embryonic development**. A lack of vitamin A during the early stages of pregnancy results in birth defects, and in extreme cases, death of the foetus. Animal studies have highlighted the involvement of vitamin A in the development of eyes, limbs, the cardiovascular system, and the nervous system. In men, vitamin A participates in sperm development. Children lacking this vitamin fail to grow well.

Figure 9.2: Diagram of the Eye showing a Section of the Retina

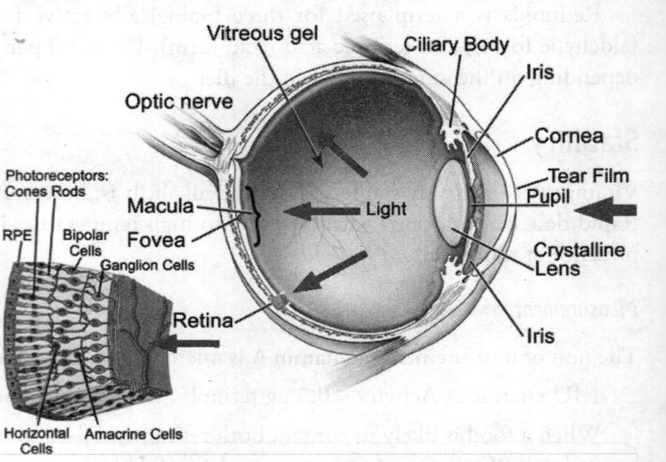

Source: http://www.intechopen.com/source/html/26714/media/image1.png

5. **Development and maintenance of bone** is especially dependent on adequate amounts of vitamin A. The synthesis of bone protein, and thus the enlargement of bone, is thought to require vitamins A and D. vitamin A is known to participate in bone re-modelling. Preliminary studies have also shown an association between carotene-rich foods and a decreased risk of rheumatoid arthritis.
6. Most forms of cancer arise from cells that are influenced by vitamin A, like the epithelial cells. Several studies on diets rich in fruits and vegetables containing carotenoids have shown a decreased risk of lung, reproductive and oral cancer. This is also linked to the fact that **carotenoids act as antioxidants**, preventing the free radical damage that has been linked to cancer.
7. Vitamin A helps to improve the **body's resistance to infection**. A deficiency of the vitamin results in insufficient mucous production, and deterioration of many types of cells. It thus weakens our first line of defence against microbes. The activity of some immune system cells, like T lymphocytes, also decreases. Night blindness in children is often accompanied by diarrhoea, and respiratory tract and other infections. In fact, the risk of a child dying from measles is increased if the child is vitamin A deficient.

The Visual Cycle

The role of Vitamin A in vision has been diagrammatically represented in Figure 9.3. When light strikes the rhodopsin, it splits into opsin and retinal. Retinal undergoes a structural change and the 11-cis-retinal is isomerised to all-trans-retinal. This stimulates the nerve fibres and an electrical signal is generated through the optic nerve, which sends a signal to the brain. This process, by which light depletes the rhodopsin concentration in the eye, is called the *bleaching process*. This fall in rhodopsin concentration allows the eye to become adapted to bright light. Regeneration of rhodopsin occurs in the dark. It is rebuilt after all-trans retinal is converted back to 11-cis retinal, which then combines with opsin. As the concentration of rhodopsin in the eye increases, the person is able to see better in the dark. This process is known as *dark adaptation*.

Figure 9.3: The Visual Cycle

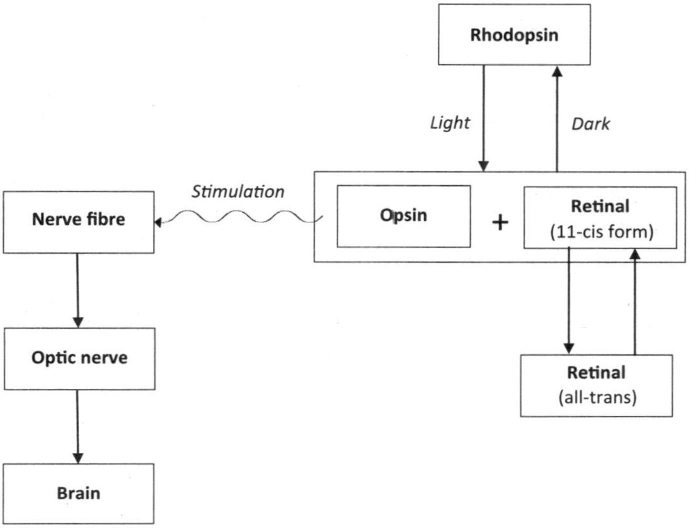

> ***Box 9.1: Significance of Dark Adaptation***
>
> When a person who has been in bright light enters a darkened room, his sensitivity to dim light is low and his vision is limited. Gradually, the ability to see improves because of the process of dark adaptation. This is linked to the increase in the amount of rhodopsin made in the rods, which occurs in dark conditions. When retinol in the blood is insufficient to replace retinal lost during the visual cycle, the cells in the eye recover from flashes of light more slowly. This condition is called night blindness, which decreases the ability of the eyes to quickly adapt to dim light following exposure to bright light. This can have serious consequences for people driving at night. Headlights of vehicles coming from the opposite direction can momentarily blind anyone, but vitamin A-deficient people may take too long to recover, resulting in often fatal accidents.

The amount of rhodopsin in rods gradually decreases as some retinal is lost from the cycle. This must be replaced by retinol from the blood stream. In the eye, retinol is converted to retinal.

Food Sources

Foods which are rich in retinol, the physiologically active form of the vitamin, come from animal sources. Liver, fish, fish oils, eggs, fortified milk, cheese, oil, etc., have the preformed vitamin. Provitamin A is present in dark green leafy vegetables, like spinach, fenugreek or *methi,* mustard greens or *sarson ka saag,* etc., and orange and yellow fruits and vegetables like carrots, pumpkin, papaya, sweet potato, mango, musk melon, peaches, apricots, etc.

Recommended Dietary Allowances

Vitamin A-rich sources in Indian diets are mostly plant foods containing β-carotene. Hence, Indian RDA are given in terms of both retinol and β-carotene. Table 9.1 gives the RDA according to ICMR (2010). Requirements increase during pregnancy and lactation. Children from the age of seven have the same requirements as adults. Infants in the first six months of life derive their requirements from breast milk, and hence the RDA is given in terms of retinol only.

Table 9.1: Recommended Dietary Allowances for Vitamin A for Indians—2010

Group	*Category / Age*	*Vitamin A (μg/d)*	
		Retinol	*β-carotene*
Men	Sedentary work Moderate work Heavy work	600	4800
Women	Sedentary work Moderate work Heavy work	600	4800
	Pregnant	800	6,400
	Lactating 0–6 m 6–12 m	950	7,600
Infants	0–6 months 6–12 months	350	– 2800
Children	1–3 years 4–6 years	400	3,200
	7–9 years	600	4,800
Boys Girls Boys Girls Boys Girls	10–12 years 10–12 years 13–15 years 13–15 years 16–17 years 16–17 years	600	4,800

Source: Nutrient Requirements and Recommended Dietary Allowances for Indians, ICMR 2010.

Deficiency of Vitamin A

Vitamin A deficiency (VAD) is a major problem among young children in India and several other developing countries, which may ultimately result in blindness. Globally, millions of children are estimated to have mild vitamin A deficiency at any point in time. VAD affects 190 million children under five, particularly in Africa and Southeast Asia, with India contributing to 85 per cent of cases in Southeast Asia. Both these regions are also home to the largest number of pregnant women affected by night blindness (WHO 2009). The prevalence of Bitot's spot, the objective sign of clinical VAD, is 0.8 per cent in India (NNMB Rural Survey 2005–06). The prevalence of subclinical vitamin A deficiency is 62 per cent in preschool children in India (Laxmaiah et al. 2012). Besides damage to the eyes, recent research also suggests that even mild vitamin A deficiency probably increases the incidence of illness and death in children.

Aetiology

Vitamin A deficiency is mostly seen in children. While it is rare during infancy, preschool age children are at a greater risk. There is a progressive increase in the prevalence up to the age of 12–13. The corneal lesions, however, are rarely seen in children above the age of six. A great majority of the cases of corneal xerophthalmia occur between one and three years, coinciding with the peak prevalence of severe protein energy malnutrition (PEM).

Inadequate dietary intake of vitamin A or its precursor, β-carotene, is the most important cause. In low-income group families, due to inadequate food intake, the intakes of vitamin A are also low in pregnant and lactating women. As a result, their children are born with poor liver stores of vitamin A. Although, during infancy, the mother's milk protects the child from vitamin A deficiency, the intake of vitamin A by children, either during the weaning period or at later ages, is woefully inadequate, and provides only 25–30 per cent of the recommended intakes. Due to female illiteracy and consequent ignorance, supplementing children's diet with vitamin A-rich foods is delayed, and certain rich sources of β-carotene, like green leafy vegetables and papaya, are avoided in the belief that these are deleterious to the health of the children.

Common childhood infections like measles, diarrhoea, respiratory tract infections, and worm infestations interfere with the absorption of vitamin A. It is estimated that an Indian preschool child spends at least a third of her/his childhood with one or more of these morbidities. As a result, the nutritional status of these marginally nourished children worsens. Even among these infections, the effect of measles is more significant, as it not only lowers the vitamin A status of children, but also leads to increased risk of nutritional blindness in children. Due to a lack of awareness, the community does not make use of the primary healthcare services for diarrhoea control, immunisation, vitamin A supplementation, and other basic health services.

Symptoms

In vitamin A deficiency, the mucous-forming cells deteriorate and no longer synthesise mucous. This loss of lubrication greatly affects the eye, especially the cornea. The term xerophthalmia means dryness of the eye, and is used to describe all the changes seen in the eyes of a person suffering from vitamin A deficiency. Some of the symptoms experienced in vitamin A deficiency are described here.

Night blindness (**Nyctalopia**) is an early symptom of vitamin A deficiency. You might ask: None of us can actually see in the dark. Does that mean we all have some vitamin A deficiency? The term 'night blindness' actually means the inability to see in dim light. Thus, in a dimly lit room or a street, a healthy individual can make out the shapes of objects lying around, which a person with vitamin A deficiency cannot. This symptom can be detected in young children by detailed questioning of the parents or the guardians. The children usually cannot see in dim light, either at dusk or at dawn. An observant mother can easily notice her child's hesitation to move around after dark, or notice that the child who does move around, frequently stumbles in dim light. In India, there is a specific term for night blindness in different languages; for example, in Hindi it is referred to as '*Rathaundi*'.

Conjunctival xerosis simply means dryness of the conjunctiva. When the eye is exposed for about 30 seconds and when the child ceases to cry, the tears appear like a sand bank in receding tide. It may be associated with various degrees of thickening, wrinkling and pigmentation (muddy colouring) of the conjunctiva.

Bitot's spot is commonly associated with the dryness of the conjunctiva. These spots are raised, muddy and dry triangular patches (Figure 9.3).

Corneal xerosis is diagnosed by the haziness or dryness of the cornea on examination. Generally, the changes start at the lower portion of the eye. The cornea takes the appearance of ground glass. Subsequently, *corneal ulcers* may occur. These ulcers are characteristically circular and sharply demarcated. If properly managed, these corneal changes usually heal, leaving vision intact.

Keratomalacia represents rapidly progressing necrosis and death of tissue, affecting the full thickness of the cornea. This, for the child, is the point of no return, and may end with irreversible blindness.

Vitamin A deficiency also produces skin changes referred to as **follicular hyperkeratosis**. In this condition, keratin, a protein, accumulates around the hair follicles which become plugged, giving a bumpy appearance and rough texture to the skin. Keratin is a normal component of the outer skin layers, helps to protect the inner layers and also decreases water loss through the skin.

Functional Consequences

Vitamin A deficiency can thus result in serious consequences, the worst-case scenario being total and permanent loss of vision. This is indeed sad, considering the fact that it is so easy and inexpensive to prevent the deficiency.

An inadequate supply of vitamin A may lead to definite changes in the epithelial tissues throughout the body. The tissues may further undergo hardening and shrinkage, resulting in increasing the risk of developing severe infections of the eye, the nasal passages, the sinuses, middle ear, lungs, skin, and the genitourinary tract.

Prevention

Nutritional blindness due to vitamin A deficiency is an important health problem, especially among young children in India. This is unfortunate, as vitamin A deficiency is one of the easily preventable nutrition disorders. Several strategies can control xerophthalmia and the consequent blindness:

- Dietary modification to promote the production and consumption of vitamin A-rich foods
- Fortification of commonly and widely consumed foods with vitamin A
- Periodic delivery of massive doses of vitamin A

Dietary modification is the most rational and sustainable long-term solution to control vitamin A deficiency. It ensures that the community regularly includes foods rich in vitamin A in their daily diets. The major inexpensive dietary sources of beta-carotene, the precursor of vitamin A, are dark green leafy vegetables, and deep yellow and orange fruits and vegetables. Pre-formed vitamin A is found only in costlier animal foods, such as egg yolk, fish liver, animal liver, and dairy products. Home gardening of vitamin A-rich fruits and vegetables has been suggested as one of the long-term strategies that can lead to higher intakes of vitamin A. Here, nutrition education plays a very important role.

Fortification of widely consumed foods with vitamin A is another strategy to prevent and control vitamin A deficiency. In some countries, food ingredients like sugar and monosodium glutamate (*ajinomoto*) have been used as vehicles for fortification. In India, foods like *vanaspati* (hydrogenated oil), vegetable oil, bread, and milk are fortified with vitamin A on a limited scale. However, these foods do not reach the most needy segments of our population. The inclusion of inexpensive, readily available vitamin A-rich foods like dark green leafy vegetables is perhaps the best way to prevent the deficiency. A lot of research is also being done to genetically modify staple crops to increase their β-carotene content. Golden rice is one such crop, in which β-carotene content is high because of genetic manipulation. Plant hybridisation techniques have also been developed to increase the β-carotene content of many fruits and vegetables.

Massive doses of vitamin A are delivered to preschool children in India as a preventive measure under the National Prophylaxis Programme for Prevention of Blindness Due To Vitamin A Deficiency (NPPVAD). The programme was started in 1971 in India, and was later revamped in 1988. It is mostly operational in rural areas, where one dose of 100,000 IU is given to the infant between 6–11 months of age (generally along with the measles vaccine at nine months), and then every six months, 200,000 IU of vitamin A is orally administered to preschool children up to the age of five. The coverage has now been reduced to children up to the age of three.

Problem of Excess

Fat-soluble vitamins are more difficult to excrete from the body, as compared to water-soluble vitamins. Hence, any excess amount gets stored in the body and can lead to toxicity. Symptoms of vitamin A toxicity have been observed in people who have consumed large amounts of foods like the liver of polar bears, oils from livers of fish and other marine mammals, and even in those who have consumed supplements of the vitamin in excess of the RDA. The Upper Level for retinol is set at 3,000 μg /day by the Food and Nutrition Board (2002) to prevent harmful effects.

Toxicity symptoms are referred to as **hypervitaminosis A.** Acute toxicity, resulting from the ingestion of one very large dose of vitamin A or several large doses over several days (around 100 times the RDA), can result in a gastrointestinal upset, headache, blurred vision, and muscular in-coordination. A 500 mg dose for children and a 10g dose for adults can be fatal. Chronic toxicity, due to consuming not so large a dose but for a prolonged period of time, can result in various skin disorders, like dry skin, hair loss, recurrent bone, joint and muscle pain, reduced bone minerals and hence an increase in the risk of fracture, loss of appetite, headache, vomiting, and an increase in liver size, with the possibility of permanent damage.

Hypercarotenemia (high levels of carotene in the blood) can result from an excess intake of carotenoids. The skin turns yellow-orange just like in jaundice, the difference being that in jaundice, the whites of the eyes also turn yellow and the liver gets enlarged. Hypercarotenemia is generally harmless.

Vitamin A is the only vitamin which can be **teratogenic**, leading to birth defects and spontaneous abortions. A pregnant woman should not consume oral supplements of vitamin A, as an excess of the vitamin has been linked to congenital malformations of the head of the foetus. Oral supplements are usually prescribed to reduce acne, wrinkling and skin problems.

VITAMIN D

In 1922, Edward Mellanby discovered vitamin D while researching a disease called rickets. Hess and Unger, during World War I, found that cod liver oil protected against rickets. In 1923, Harry Steenbock demonstrated that irradiation by ultraviolet light increased the vitamin D content of foods and other organic materials. Vitamin D has also been classified as a prohormone, that is, precursor of a hormone. The prohormone form of vitamin D is converted to the active hormone by the enzymes in the liver and kidney. About 80 per cent of the vitamin present in food is absorbed along with dietary fat. Bile is required for absorption. It is transported to the liver as a part of chylomicrons through the lymph circulation. It is stored in the liver and adipose tissue.

Figure 9.4: Synthesis of Vitamin D in the Human Body

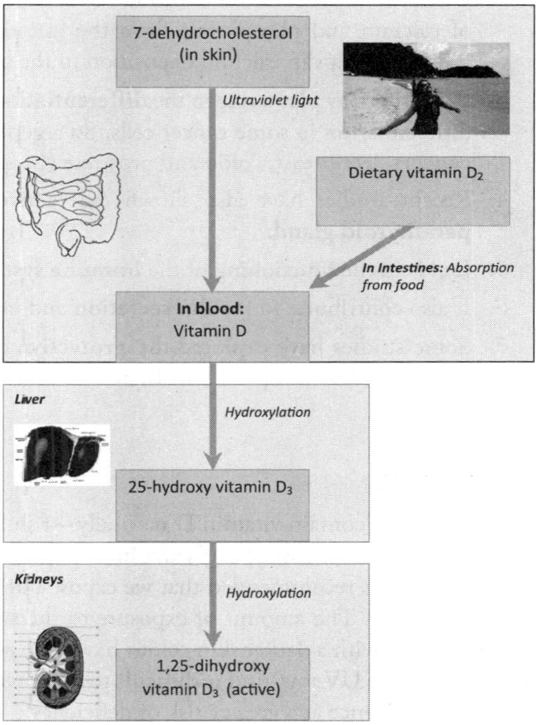

This is one vitamin whose requirements can be met by synthesising the vitamin in the body with the help of sunlight. In the skin, 7-dehydrocholesterol is converted by UV rays (290–315 nm wavelength) to vitamin D_3 or cholecalciferol. Similarly, ergosterol in plants is converted to vitamin D_2 by UV light. Vitamin D is bound to a carrier protein in the blood stream and transported to the liver. It is metabolised by the liver to 25-OH vitamin D. In the kidney, it is metabolised to 1,25 (OH)2 vitamin D (1,25 dihydroxy cholecalciferol or calcitriol), which is the active vitamin D hormone (Figure 9.4).

The vitamin D hormone works at multiple locations:

- In the kidney—it works with the parathyroid hormone to reabsorb calcium.
- In the bone—it stimulates the release of calcium and phosphorus if the serum calcium is low, and aids in bone mineralisation by helping to maintain high blood calcium and phosphorus levels.
- In the intestine—it helps in the absorption of calcium and phosphorus by stimulating the synthesis of the protein necessary for the transport of calcium across the intestinal mucosa.
- Other tissues like pancreas, brain, WBC, ovaries, uterus, and placenta also have some receptors for Vitamin D.

Stability

Pure vitamin D is stable to heat, alkali and oxidation.

Measurement

In International Units (IU) and in micrograms (µg)

1 IU = 0.025 µg, 400 IU = 10 µg

Functions

Although vitamin D is classified as a vitamin, it actually functions like a hormone (it is made in one part of the body, but its action is in other parts of the body).

1. It is required for **bone growth and maintenance**. It has an important role to play in the absorption of dietary calcium from the intestine and its deposition in bone.
2. It helps in the **regulation of blood calcium.** Calcitriol functions like a hormone and increases the absorption of calcium and phosphorus from the intestine, decreases the excretion of calcium by the kidneys, and indirectly helps in calcium deposition in the bones.
3. Calcitriol may play a role in the **differentiation of cells**. Recent studies show that it is capable of influencing differentiation in some cancer cells. So a good vitamin D status may be linked to **decreased risk of some cancers,** like breast, colon and prostrate (Lappe et al. 2007).
4. Recent studies have also shown that active vitamin D controls the growth and functioning of the **parathyroid gland.**
5. It aids in the functioning of the **immune system.**
6. It also contributes to **insulin secretion** and may offer protection against diabetes.
7. Some studies have explored the **protective role** of the vitamin in diseases like dementia, auto-immune disorders like multiple sclerosis, and certain types of infections like tuberculosis (Buell et al. 2010; Liu et al. 2006).

Food Sources

Only a few foods contain vitamin D naturally—fish liver oils, egg yolk, liver, fish, butter, and other fortified foods like milk and fat/oil. Most of our vitamin D requirement is met by the synthesis of the vitamin in our skin upon sun exposure. It is recommended that we expose our skin for 5–10 minutes to sunlight (hands, face and arms) on a clear sunny day. The amount of exposure to the sun depends on skin colour, age, time of the day, season, and location. People with a darker skin colour have to expose their skin for a longer period and take longer to synthesise vitamin D, as the UV rays find it difficult to penetrate. With age, the ability to synthesise the vitamin diminishes. The elderly are hence at a greater risk of deficiency.

During the day, synthesis will happen faster when direct rays of the sun are available. However, because of a fear of sunburn and skin cancer, it is recommended that you catch the early morning or the late afternoon sun, especially if you are going to be in the sunshine for a long period. It is much more difficult to synthesise vitamin D in winters as compared to summers. In winters, the rays of the sun are slanting; besides, people wear a lot of clothing as protection against the cold, in the bargain not exposing sufficient skin for vitamin D synthesis. Places located between latitudes 42° N and 42° S receive direct rays of the sun and ample sunshine throughout the year. People living in temperate zones and beyond find it difficult to get sufficient sunshine to fulfil their requirements of vitamin D . They may need to take regular supplements or ensure that they regularly eat fortified foods. UV rays are easily strained out by dust, smoke, fog, clothing, and ordinary window glass, even in regions with sufficient sunlight.

Recommended Dietary Allowances

According to WHO/FAO (2004), in most situations (between latitudes 42° N and 42° S), approximately 30 minutes of skin exposure (without sunscreen) of the arms and face to sunlight can provide all the daily vitamin D needs of the body. ICMR does not give any RDA as it considers sun exposure among Indians sufficient to meet the requirements for this vitamin. Only in cases of inadequate exposure to sunlight has a specific recommendation of a daily supplement of 400 IU been given for adults.

Problem of Deficiency and Excess

Deficiency is commonly seen in people living in dark overcrowded slums, women in *purdah/burqa* or traditional clothing that covers most of the skin, places where winters are prolonged and the sun is very mild, communities with a lot of poverty and ignorance, and in people who spend most of their time indoors (small children, the elderly, etc.). Deficiency leads to inadequate absorption of calcium and phosphorus from the intestine, and consequently to faulty mineralisation of the bones and teeth. Inability of the soft bones to withstand the stress of the weight results in skeletal malformations. Vitamin D deficiency in children leads to **Rickets** (Figure 9.5) and in adults to **Osteomalacia**.

Figure 9.5: Clinical Manifestations of Rickets in Children

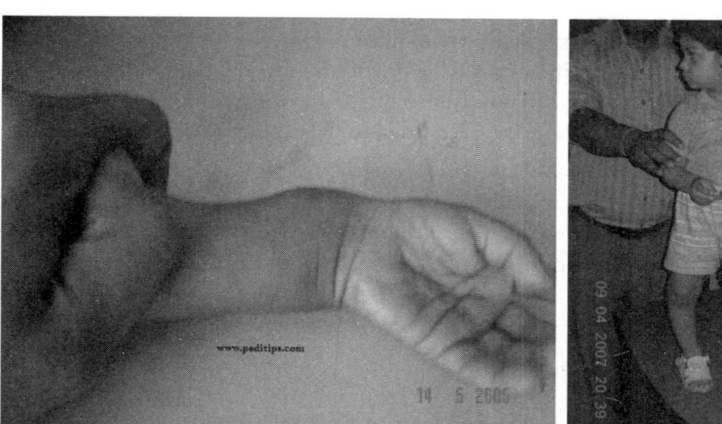

Source: http://upload.wikimedia.org/wikipedia/commons/1/1c/Rickets_wrist.jpg
http://upload.wikimedia.org/wikipedia/commons/4/4d/Rickets.jpg

Clinical Manifestations of Rickets

Figure 9.5 shows widening of the wrist and bow legs in children.

- Delayed closure of the fontanel (open spaces on top of the baby's skull), resulting in a rapid enlargement of the head
- Craniotabes—abnormal softening of the skull bones
- Bulging or bossing of the forehead
- Bowing of the legs
- Rachitic rosary—rows of knob or bead deformities on the ribs
- Pigeon breast—projection of the sternum
- Knock knees
- Restlessness, nervous irritability
- Poorly developed muscles, lack of muscle tone, pot belly
- Delayed dentition and malformation of teeth
- Permanent teeth more susceptible to tooth decay

Rachitic Rosary

In Vitamin D deficiency, there are poorly formed attachments of the bones to the cartilage in the ribs. This leads to the formation of beads, which resemble the beads of a rosary (prayer beads). Hence the name 'rachitic rosary' or the 'rosary of rickets' has been given to this manifestation.

Clinical Manifestations of Adult Rickets or Osteomalacia

- Bones soften (legs, spine, thorax, pelvis) and bend in deformities
- Pain of rheumatic type in the bones of legs and lower back
- General weakness
- Difficulty in walking, especially in climbing stairs
- Spontaneous multiple fractures as bones become brittle

A deficiency of vitamin D will ultimately result in a loss of calcium from bones, and the development of a condition called **Osteoporosis**. Osteoporosis leads to an increase in the porosity and fragility of bones, which tend to fracture easily.

Toxicity

Most people in the world depend on natural exposure to sunlight to meet their needs for this vitamin. There is no risk of toxicity, even if there is prolonged exposure to the sun. This is because the vitamin precursor in the skin is degraded on long exposure, and cannot be converted to the active vitamin form. However, prolonged exposure to sunlight on a regular basis can prematurely wrinkle the skin, and increase the risk of sunburn and cancer. Sunscreen lotions (especially those with an SPF > 8) help to decrease this risk, but unfortunately also prevent vitamin D synthesis. It is recommended that the sunscreen be applied after a sufficient time has been given to the exposed skin to manufacture vitamin D.

Since food sources contain very low amounts of vitamin D, toxicity results mostly from the intake of supplements. Irritability, nausea, vomiting, constipation, weight loss, and excessive thirst can result from prolonged daily intakes of as low as 1,000 IU. Excess vitamin D raises the concentration of blood calcium. Severe toxicity results in the calcification of soft tissues due to a precipitation of excess blood calcium in soft tissues such as the heart, blood vessels, bronchi, kidney tubules, etc.

VITAMIN E

In 1922, University of California researchers Herbert Evans and Katherine Bishop discovered vitamin E in green leafy vegetables and vegetable oil. Vitamin E was discovered by Evans and Bishop as an anti-sterility factor and called tocopherol, which means 'to bring forth offspring'. Vitamin E is the generic term for a group of lipid soluble compounds—tocopherols and tocotrienols. Each of them consists of four compounds—alpha, beta, gamma, and delta. Alpha tocopherol is the most active form of the vitamin. Vitamin E is most concentrated in body structures containing an abundance of fatty acids, especially in cell membranes rich in phospholipids, in adipose tissue, in muscle, testes, and the pituitary and adrenal glands.

Stability

High temperature and acids do not affect the stability of vitamin E. However, oxidation takes place readily in the presence of rancid fats, or lead and iron salts. Decomposition also occurs in UV light. The vitamin is lost from fried foods, foods that are frozen, and during the heating of oils and milling of grains (because the vitamin is present in the germ). If chlorine dioxide is used in the bleaching process of flour, the vitamin is further destroyed.

Measurement: 1 IU = 1 mg dl- α – tocopherol acetate

Functions

1. The principal role of vitamin E is as an **antioxidant**. It protects the body from the damage inflicted by free radicals. By accepting oxygen, vitamin E helps to prevent the oxidation of PUFA and phospholipids, thereby helping to maintain the integrity of cellular membranes.

2. Vitamin E has a **sparing effect** on vitamin A and ascorbic acid, by protecting them from oxidation.
3. It is considered an **anti-ageing** vitamin. It prevents ageing due to oxidative damage.
4. It **reduces the risk of cancer** by protecting the DNA and cells from oxidative damage (for example, from free radicals).
5. It **reduces the risk of heart disease** by protecting low density lipoprotein (LDL) against oxidation and reducing inflammation (Singh et al. 2005).
6. Vitamin E is required for iron metabolism in cells, for the maintenance of nervous tissue, and for immune function.

Food Sources

The principal source is vegetable oils—corn, soyabean, cottonseed, safflower oil, wheat germ oil, peanuts; in fact, it is found in whole grains, nuts and seeds. In milling whole grains, most of the vitamin E is lost. Animal fats have practically no vitamin E. One tablespoon of plant oil has an ample amount of vitamin E for the day. Human milk provides adequate vitamin E for the infant, but cow's milk is low in content.

> ***Free Radical Damage***
>
> A free radical is a molecule with one or more unpaired electrons. These molecules are unstable and highly reactive. To regain stability, the free radical looks for other stable compounds from which to 'steal' an electron, in the bargain setting off an electron-snatching chain reaction. Dietary antioxidants help to decrease the effect of these radicals.

Recommended Dietary Allowances

The need varies with the amount of PUFA in the diet, as vitamin E protects PUFA from oxidation. The suggested requirement of vitamin E (tocopherol) is 0.8 mg/g of dietary essential fatty acids. This roughly works out to 8–10 mg tocopherol/day, depending on the edible oil used.

Problem of Deficiency and Excess

Vitamin E deficiency leads to impaired neuromuscular function and the development of a form of muscular dystrophy.

Hemolytic anaemia is also seen, characterised by a breakdown of red blood cells (RBCs). The PUFA in the RBCs are very sensitive to attack by free radicals. Vitamin E can quench these agents, and thus help to prevent oxidative damage to RBC membranes. The deficiency is likely to develop in preterm infants who are born with limited stores, have inefficient absorption, and are growing rapidly. Deficiency is also seen in individuals with fat malabsorption syndromes. Patients exhibit increased RBC fragility and subtle neurological disorders affecting the spinal cord.

Toxicity

Daily supplements up to 800 IU are probably harmless for most people; however, some toxic effects have been reported at even lower levels of supplementation. These include impaired blood coagulation because of an inhibition of vitamin K metabolism, especially in people taking anti-coagulants. At very high doses (>1,000 mg/day) evidence of pro-oxidant damage has been seen (Brown et al. 1997).

VITAMIN K

Discovered in 1935 by Dr Dam of Copenhagen (Denmark), it was known as the Koagulation Vitamin ('coagulation' or clotting is spelt with a 'K' in Danish), which was necessary to prevent fatal haemorrhages in chicks by promoting normal blood clotting. It consists of a number of related compounds called quinones. vitamin K1 is known as Phylloquinone (found in plant sources, for example alfalfa) and vitamin K2 is known as Menaquinone (obtained from fish oils and meats, and synthesised by intestinal bacteria in humans). Half of our requirement of vitamin K is met by the vitamin K synthesised by gut bacteria. The remaining 50 per cent is met from plant sources. Menadione is the synthetic form of the vitamin.

Stability

Vitamin K is a fat-soluble vitamin which is resistant to heat. It is easily destroyed by acids, alkalies, light, and oxidising agents.

Measurement: It is measured in micrograms (μg).

Function

1. It is essential for the **formation of blood-clotting proteins** by the liver. It is a cofactor for enzymes in the liver, like the one that converts pre-prothrombin to prothrombin. It contributes to the synthesis of blood-clotting factors, which are produced in the liver from precursor proteins.
2. Vitamin K plays a **role in bone metabolism and formation**. It is associated with bone formation as it helps in the synthesis of osteocalcin, a protein in the bone which can bind calcium. Low circulating concentrations of vitamin K may be associated with low bone mineral density. Inadequate intake of vitamin K increases the risk of hip fractures in women.

Food Sources

Liver, pork, cauliflower, broccoli, peas, green beans, and green leafy vegetables like cabbage, spinach, turnip greens, etc., and some vegetable oils (soyabean and canola) are good sources of vitamin K. Vitamin K is abundant in the diet and deficiency is uncommon.

Recommended Dietary Allowance

FAO/WHO (2004) suggested an RDA of 55 μg of vitamin K/day for adults. The ICMR does not give an RDA, as limited data is available on the vitamin K content of foods in Indian diets. It, however, accepts the RDA suggested by the FAO/WHO. Vitamin K, given orally or by an intramuscular injection to a newborn at birth, is recommended, as the newborn infant has a very limited supply of vitamin K. Its intestinal tract is relatively sterile (it hardly has any microorganisms like bacteria, which can synthesise the vitamin), and human milk is a poor source of the vitamin.

About half of a person's needs are met by the vitamin synthesised by the bacteria living in the intestinal tract. Once synthesised, the vitamin is absorbed and stored in the liver. Vitamin K-rich foods, such as green vegetables and vegetable oils, can easily supply the rest.

Problem of Excess and Deficiency

The most reliable clinical evidence of vitamin K deficiency is an increase in clotting time. This is a measure of how quickly prothrombin in blood can form a clot. In vitamin K deficiency, there is an increased tendency to haemorrhage (bleed uncontrollably). Deficiency may be seen in premature infants born with a sterile intestinal tract, in which vitamin K-producing bacteria may take longer to establish themselves; those on strong antibiotic therapy (for instance, those who have undergone a major surgery), in whom the antibiotics have also killed the gut flora; those with liver disease (and hence with an inability to synthesise prothrombin); or those who fail to absorb this fat-soluble vitamin.

Toxicity

Vitamin K is more readily excreted from the body than other fat-soluble vitamins. Toxicity is not common. High doses of the vitamin have been shown to reduce the effectiveness of anticoagulant drugs used to prevent blood clotting. The medicinal form, Menadione, although water soluble, can lead to toxicity symptoms, like jaundice and haemolytic anaemia in newborns.

Table 9.2: Summary of Food Sources, Functions and Deficiency Symptoms of Fat-soluble Vitamins

Vitamin	*Rich Sources*	*Functions*	*Deficiency Signs and Symptoms*
Vitamin A	Liver, fish, fish oils, eggs, fortified milk, cheese, oil, etc. (retinol sources) Dark green leafy vegetables, orange and yellow fruits and vegetables like carrots, pumpkin, papaya, sweet potato, mango, musk melon, peaches, apricots, etc. (β-carotene sources)	Vision, health and maintenance of epithelial cells, bone health, growth and development, cell differentiation, immunity, reducing oxidative stress	Night blindness, Bitot's spot, conjunctival and corneal xerosis, corneal ulceration and loss of vision (eye changes) Follicular hyperkeratosis in the skin
Vitamin D	Sunshine Food sources—Fish liver oils, egg yolk, liver, fish, butter, and other fortified foods like milk, fat/oil	Bone growth and maintenance, regulation of blood calcium, cell differentiation, protection from diseases, cancer, diabetes	Rickets in children and osteomalacia in adults. Will ultimately lead to osteoporosis, as calcium absorption is affected.
Vitamin E	Vegetable oils—corn, soybean, cottonseed, safflower oil, wheat germ oil, peanuts, and in whole grains, nuts and seeds	Antioxidant, protects the body from diseases due to free radical damage, like cancer and cardiovascular diseases. It is an anti-ageing vitamin.	Haemolytic anaemia
Vitamin K	Liver, pork, cauliflower, broccoli, peas, green beans, and green leafy vegetables like cabbage, spinach, turnip greens, etc., and some vegetable oils (soyabean and canola)	Blood clotting and bone health	Delayed blood clotting, haemorrhages

SUMMARY

- The four fat-soluble vitamins—A, D, E, and K—play important roles in the growth and maintenance of the body.
- Vitamin A is present as the preformed vitamin in foods from animal sources, while provitamin A (β carotene) can be obtained from green leafy vegetables and orange-yellow fruits and vegetables.
- Vitamin A has a role to play in the vision, health and maintenance of epithelial cells, bone health, growth and development, cell differentiation and immunity. β-carotene is an antioxidant, and protects us against free radical damage and cancer.
- A deficiency of vitamin A causes night blindness, dryness, and other eye changes, which could eventually lead to total blindness.
- Vitamin D can be synthesised in our skin with the help of sunshine. We need to expose our face, hands and arms to sunshine for at least 30 minutes on most days to make vitamin D.
- Vitamin D is important for bone health and for maintaining blood calcium levels. It also has a role to play in cellular differentiation. It has several other protective benefits, like improving immunity, and preventing cancer and diabetes.
- A deficiency can lead to rickets in children and osteomalacia in adults. Lack of vitamin D leads to bone softening and consequent deformities.
- Vitamin E is a powerful antioxidant and thus helps to prevent diseases related to free radical damage.
- Deficiency of vitamin E is rare and causes haemolytic anaemia.
- Vitamin K is present abundantly in plant foods. Our gut bacteria also synthesise this vitamin and contribute to about 50 per cent of our requirement.
- Vitamin K is required for normal blood clotting and a deficiency, although rare, can lead to delayed blood clotting or haemorrhages.
- Vitamin K is also important for bone density and health.

KEY WORDS

Aetiology: The study of the causes of the disease

Bitot's spots: Raised, muddy and dry triangular patches on the white of the eye

Conjunctiva: The mucous membrane that covers the front of the eye and lines the inside of the eyelids

Conjunctival xerosis: Dryness of the conjunctiva

Cornea: The transparent circular part of the front of the eyeball

Corneal xerosis: Dryness of the cornea of the eye

Epithelium: The layer of cells covering internal and external surfaces of the body, such as skin, lungs, gastrointestinal tract, etc.

Fontanel: An open space between the flat bones on the top of a baby's skull. These openings close by the end of the first year when the bones fuse. In rickets, the closure is delayed.

Genitourinary: Refers to the genital and urinary organs

Haemolytic anaemia: An anaemia that results due to the breakdown of red blood cells. The fatty acids in the cell membrane of RBCs get oxidised, and the integrity of the membrane is lost. Consequently, the cells burst open, spilling out their contents.

Haemorrhage: Abnormal and severe bleeding, may be internal or external due to injury

Keratomalacia: Refers to necrosis and death of tissue, affecting the full thickness of cornea

Necrosis: Death

Night blindness: The inability to see in dim light

Osteomalacia: The adult form of rickets, in which the bones soften and bend into deformities

Osteoporosis: Reduction in the mass of bone per unit volume, increasing the fragility and porosity of the bone and consequently, the risk of fracture

Precursor: A compound that can be converted into an active vitamin

Rickets: Inadequate deposition of calcium leads to abnormalities in the shape and structure of the developing bones of children (bone softening)

Stem Cells: Unspecialised cells that can be transformed into specialised cells

Xerophthalmia: Literally, dryness of the eye

EXERCISES

1. In addition to poor dietary intake of vitamin A-rich foods, what can precipitate the deficiency disease in children?
2. How does the deficiency of vitamin A lead to blindness in a person?
3. What does the term night blindness actually mean? How can we make out if little children who have not yet started speaking are suffering from this?
4. Describe the clinical manifestations of vitamin D deficiency in children.
5. Which factors determine how much vitamin D can be synthesised in an individual's skin?
6. What does a deficiency of vitamin E cause?
7. What is the role of vitamin K in our body?
8. List some food sources of vitamins A, D, E, and K.

REFERENCES

Brown, K. M., P. C. Morice and G. G. Duthie, 'Erythrocyte vitamin E and plasma ascorbate concentrations in relation to erythrocyte peroxidation in smokers and non-smokers: Dose response of vitamin E supplementation', *Am J Clin Nutr* 65, 1997, pp. 496–502.

Buell, J. S. et al., '25-dihydroxyvitamin D, dementia and cerebrovascular pathology in elders receiving home services', *Neurol.* 55, 2010, A141.

Byrd-Bredbenner C., G. Moe, D. Beshgetoor, and J. Berning, *Wardlaw's Perspectives in Nutrition*, 9e, New York: McGraw- Hill International Edition, 2013.

Food and Nutrition Board, *Dietary reference intakes for vitamin A, vitamin K, arsenic, boron, chromium, copper, iodine, iron, manganese, molybdenum, nickel, silicon, vanadium and zinc*, Washington, DC: National Academy Press, 2002.

ICMR, 'Nutrient Requirements and Recommended Dietary Allowances for Indians', A report of the Expert Group of the Indian Council of Medical Research, 2010.

Lappe, J. M. et al., 'Vitamin D and calcium supplementation reduces cancer risk: Results of a randomized trial', *Am J Clin Nutr.* 85, 2007, p. 1586.

Laxmaiah, A., M. K. Nair, N. Arlappa, P. Raghu, N. Balakrishna, K. M. Rao, C. Galreddy, S. Kumar, M. Ravindranath, V. V. Rao, and G. N. Brahmam, 'Prevalence of ocular signs and subclinical vitamin A deficiency and its determinants among rural pre-school children in India', *Public Health Nutr.* 15(4), 2012, pp. 568–77.

National Nutrition Monitoring Bureau (NNMB), 'Prevalence of vitamin A deficiency among rural pre-schoolchildren', Report No. 23, Hyderabad: National Institute of Nutrition, 2006.

Liu, P. T., et al., 'Toll-like receptor triggering of a vitamin D mediated human anti-microbial response', *Science* 311, 2006, pp. 1770–73.

Rolfes, S. R., K. Pinna and E. Whitney, *Understanding Normal and Clinical Nutrition*, 8e, Wadsworth Cengage Learning, 2009.

Singh, U., S. Devaraj and I. Jialal, 'Vitamin E, oxidative stress, and inflammation', *Annual Review of Nutrition* 25, 2005, pp. 151–74.

WHO/FAO, 'Vitamin and Mineral Requirements in Human Nutrition', Joint FAO/WHO Expert Consultation on Human Vitamin and Mineral Requirements, Bangkok, Thailand, 2004.

WHO, 'Global prevalence of vitamin A deficiency in populations at risk 1995–2005', WHO Global Database on Vitamin A Deficiency, Geneva: World Health Organization, 2009.

ONLINE SOURCES

Kimpel, P., *Discovery of Vitamins*, Available at http://inventors.about.com/gi/dynamic/offsite.htm?site=http://iml.jou.ufl.edu/projects/Spring2000/Kimpel/vitamins.html.

http://www.sciencechannel.com/tv-shows/greatest-discoveries/videos/100-greatest-discoveries-the-discovery-of-vitamins.htm.

http://wcd.nic.in/research/nti1947/7.11.2%20Vitamin%20A%20Deficiency%20pr%20map.pdf.

10

WATER-SOLUBLE VITAMINS

HIGHLIGHTS

- Functions of different water-soluble vitamins
- Food sources of the vitamins
- Recommended Dietary Allowances
- Problem of Deficiency and Excess

Water-soluble vitamins include the B vitamins and vitamin C. Most B vitamins act as coenzymes and participate in energy metabolism. However, they have many other important functions to perform (Table 10.1). B vitamins are present in foods in their coenzyme forms, bound to special proteins. The bound vitamin coenzymes are released in the stomach and small intestine. The free vitamins are then absorbed in the small intestine. Typically, 50–90 per cent of the B vitamins in the diet are absorbed. Once inside the cells, the coenzyme form of the vitamins is re-synthesised. Most of these vitamins are easily destroyed during cooking due to the heat and alkalinity. They are all subject to leaching into the cooking water. Retention is best in foods prepared by steaming, stir frying, microwaving, and simmering in minimal moisture.

The water-soluble vitamins that you will be primarily studying are thiamine, riboflavin, niacin, pyridoxine, folate, vitamin B_{12} and vitamin C, along with some minor, less-known vitamins like biotin, choline and pantothenic acid.

Box 10.1: Bioavailability of Vitamins

The amount of vitamins available from a food, that is, the quantity that can be absorbed and used by the body, is a measure of the bioavailability of that vitamin. Bioavailability depends on many factors:

- *Efficiency of digestion*: How well the body is able to digest the food containing the vitamin, and release the vitamin from the food matrix for absorption. Nutrients are generally less bioavailable from foods rich in fibre, as fibre is indigestible.
- *Time of transit through the intestinal tract*: There should be sufficient time for the body to absorb the vitamin.
- *Other foods consumed at the same time*: Which either increase or decrease the absorption of the vitamin.
- *Method of food preparation*: Sometimes, vitamins are better absorbed from cooked foods rather than raw foods, for example β-carotene, while most of vitamin C is destroyed by cooking.
- *Source of vitamin*: Naturally occurring and synthetic forms may be differently absorbed and utilised.

Table 10.1: Overview of the Functions of Vitamins

Function	*Vitamin(s) involved*
Energy metabolism	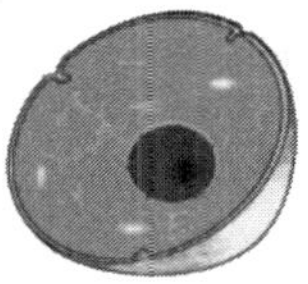 Thiamine, Riboflavin, Niacin, Vitamin B_6, Vitamin B_{12}, Folate, Pantothenic acid, Biotin
Protein metabolism	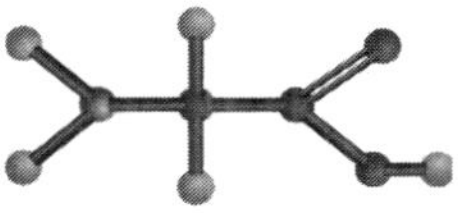 Vitamin B_6, Vitamin B_{12}, Folate, Vitamin C, Choline, Thiamine, Riboflavin
Expression of genes	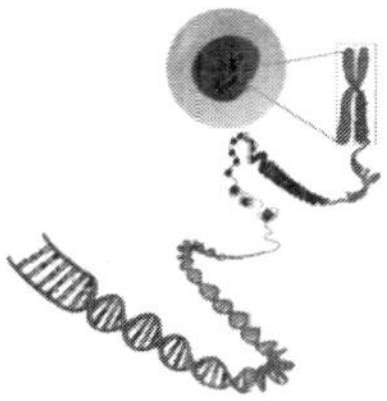 Vitamin A, Vitamin D
Immunity	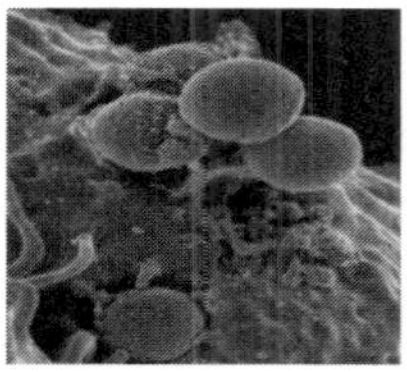 Vitamins A, D, C
Health and maintenance of bones	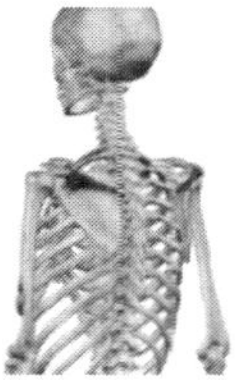 Vitamins A, D, K, C
Nerve function	 Thiamine, Niacin, Folate, Vitamin B_6, Vitamin B_{12}
Formation of blood cells and clotting factors	 Vitamin K, Folate, Vitamin B_6, Vitamin B_{12}
Protection against oxidative stress (antioxidants)	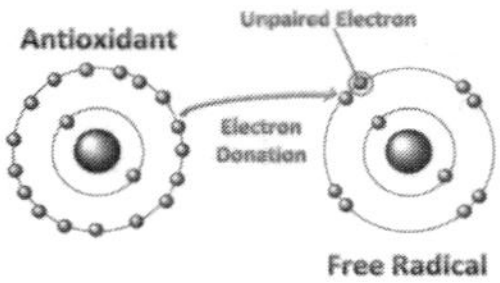 Vitamins E, C, Carotenoids, Riboflavin

Source: Adapted from Byrd-Bredbenner 2013.
Images taken from http://pixabay.com; http://commons.wikimedia.org; and http://en.wikipedia.org.

THIAMINE

Interest in accessory food factors developed in the latter half of the nineteenth century with the discovery of the first vitamin, thiamine. Thiamine was water-soluble, and was given the name vitamin B_1. For centuries, rice-eating populations had suffered from the ill-effects of deficiency of this vitamin. Polished rice lacks this vitamin as it is removed during the milling process (the bran and germ of the rice grain contain this vitamin). People whose diets consisted of polished rice and little else developed beriberi. Christiaan Ejikman was awarded a Nobel Prize in 1929 for his work on beriberi, and for helping to discover a cure. The name thiamine comes from two words—'thio' meaning sulphur, and 'amine', which refers to the nitrogen groups in the molecule.

Functions

1. **Thiamine pyrophosphate (TPP)** is the coenzyme form of thiamine. It participates in reactions where a carboxy group (-COOH) is removed from a compound and released as carbon dioxide (**decarboxylation reaction**) in **carbohydrate metabolism**.
2. TPP participates in other **decarboxylation reactions** in which carbon dioxide is removed from some **branched chain amino acids** (valine, leucine and isoleucine).
3. TPP also plays an active role in **nerve function.** It is believed that it aids in the synthesis of nerve transmitters, for example acetylcholine. It aids in the energy production needed by highly active nerve tissue. It also regulates nerve impulse transmission.
4. TPP takes part in the pathways for the synthesis of monosaccharides needed for **DNA and RNA synthesis**. It functions as a coenzyme for transketolase, an enzyme that converts glucose to pentose sugar, which is used to make DNA and RNA.

Food Sources

Thiamine is present in a wide variety of foods. The major contributors to our diet are whole cereal grains and cereal products, wheat germ, sunflower seeds, yeast, and legumes. Other good sources include pork, peanuts, mushrooms, liver, eggs, green beans, green peas, watermelon, etc. Some foods contain thiamine antagonists, which lower the bioavailability of the vitamin. Some species of fish and shellfish contain an enzyme called thiaminase, which destroys thiamine. The enzyme is inactivated by cooking. Ingestion of large amounts of tea and coffee, and chewing betel nut adversely affect the thiamine status because of the presence of tannins and caffeic acid. On an average, 40–50 per cent of the vitamin present in raw foods is lost during processing and the usual Indian cooking practices. It is destroyed not only by heat, but also if the cooking is done in an alkaline medium. Baking soda may sometimes be used to hasten the cooking of legumes. This practice should be discouraged.

Whole grains are an important source of B vitamins, minerals and fibre. However, when grains are dehusked and milled, most of these nutrients present in the husk, bran layers and germ are lost. What remains is just the starch-rich endosperm. That is why refined wheat flour (*maida*) and products made from it are considered less healthy as compared to whole wheat flour (*atta*).

Recommended Dietary Allowances

As thiamine facilitates energy utilisation, its requirements are expressed on the basis of energy intake, and will vary according to activity level. Hence, the rate of 0.5 mg of thiamine / 1,000 kcal has been worked out for adults, keeping in mind the cooking losses. However, a minimum daily allowance of 1 mg of thiamine is recommended even if the calorie intake is less than 2,000 kcal. The ICMR (2010) recommendations for adults are related to physical activity (Table 10.2). No Upper Level has been defined for the vitamin as it is water-soluble, and easily excreted in urine if excess amounts are consumed in foods or in supplement form.

Table 10.2: Recommended Dietary Allowances for Water-soluble Vitamins for Indians, 2010

Group	*Category / Age*	*Thiamine (mg/d)*	*Riboflavin (mg/d)*	*Niacin equivalent (mg/d)*	*Vitamin B_6 (mg/d)*	*Ascorbic Acid (mg/d)*	*Dietary Folate (μg/d)*	*Vitamin B_{12} (μg/d)*
	Sedentary work	1.2	1.4	16				
Men	Moderate work	1.4	1.6	18	2.0	40	200	1.0
	Heavy work	1.7	2.1	21				
	Sedentary work	1.0	1.1	12				
	Moderate work	1.1	1.3	14	2.0	40	200	1.0
	Heavy work	1.4	1.7	16				
Women	Pregnant	+0.2	+0.3	+2		60	500	1.2
	Lactating 0–6 m	+0.3	+0.4	+4	2.5	80	300	1.5
	6–12 m	+0.2	+0.3	+3				
Infants	0–6 months	0.2	0.3	710 μg/kg	0.1	25	25	0.2
	6–12 months	0.3	0.4	650 μg/kg	0.4			
	1-3 years	0.5	0.6	8	0.9		80	
Children	4-6 years	0.7	0.8	11	0.9	40	100	0.2–1.0
	7-9 years	0.8	1.0	13	1.6		120	
Boys	10–12 years	1.1	1.3	15	1.6		140	
Girls	10–12 years	1.0	1.2	13	1.6		140	
Boys	13–15 years	1.4	1.6	16	2.0	40	150	0.2–1.0
Girls	13–15 years	1.2	1.4	14	2.0		150	
Boys	16–17 years	1.5	1.8	17	2.0		200	
Girls	16–17 years	1.0	1.2	14	2.0		200	

Source: Nutrient Requirements and Recommended Dietary Allowances for Indians, ICMR 2010.

Problem of Deficiency and Excess

Deficiency of thiamine, as mentioned earlier, is known as **beriberi.** The deficiency is likely to develop if little is eaten besides polished rice for weeks at a time. In the Sinhalese language, beriberi means 'I can't, I can't', because thiamine deficiency affects all the major systems of the body—cardiovascular, muscular, nervous, and GI systems.

There are two forms of beriberi—dry and wet. In **dry beriberi,** the nervous and muscular systems are mainly affected, and it is characterised by symptoms of weakness, nerve degeneration, irritability, and loss of nerve transmission, resulting in tingling throughout the body, poor arm and leg coordination, and deep pain in the calf muscles. These symptoms are seen because the brain and nerve cells primarily use glucose for energy, and thiamine is important for glucose metabolism. There is no oedema (water retention). **Wet beriberi,** on the other hand, affects the neurological and the cardiovascular systems, and is characterised by oedema. The patient often develops an enlarged heart and related heart failure.

Frank symptoms of beriberi are a rarity. A mild deficiency of thiamine may result in neuropathies (nerve damage), which result in numbness or a tingling sensation in the extremities (legs and arms, especially the fingers and toes). Deficiency occurs in breast-fed infants whose mothers are deficient, and in adults with a high carbohydrate intake (mainly from milled polished rice), and/or intakes of anti-thiamine factors such as those present in certain raw fish.

Infantile beriberi appears in a breast-fed infant whose mother has thiamine deficiency. It is mainly the 'wet' form of beriberi, characterised by heart failure with marked peripheral oedema (swelling of the lower limbs). The infant exhibits difficulty in breathing, cyanosis (bluish discolouration of the skin due to inadequate oxygenation of blood), weight loss and wasting, vomiting, diarrhoea, rapid heart rate, hoarseness or aphonia (that is, when the child cries, there is no audible sound except for a weak moan). This condition is fatal in most cases.

Wernicke–Korsakoff Syndrome, also known as cerebral beriberi, is due to thiamine deficiency and is found mainly in people with alcoholism. Such people may have limited food intake; in addition, alcohol has the effect of increasing urinary excretion of thiamine and decreasing thiamine absorption. The disease is characterised by rapid involuntary movement of the eyeball, paralysis of the eye muscle, double vision or cross eyes, ataxia (in-coordination of muscle activity during movements), staggering, and mental confusion. It is a typical picture of uncontrollable drunken stupor.

RIBOFLAVIN

The first observation of a pigment in milk with yellow-green fluorescence can be traced to the English chemist Alexander Wynter Blyth in 1872, but it was not until the early 1930s that the substance was characterised as riboflavin. Riboflavin was the second vitamin to be isolated. The name comes from its yellow colour (*flavin* in Latin means the colour yellow). Riboflavin is a component of two coenzymes—**Flavin mononucleotide (FMN)** and **Flavin adenine dinucleotide (FAD)**. The coenzyme forms are present in many foods, and the free vitamin is found in milk and enriched grain products. Both forms are important.

Functions

1. FMN and FAD participate in many **oxidation-reduction reactions** in a variety of metabolic pathways, and in **energy production** from carbohydrates and fats via the respiratory chain.
2. Some **vitamin and mineral metabolism** also requires riboflavin, like vitamins K, folate, B_6 and niacin. Formation of niacin from tryptophan requires FAD. The formation of pyridoxal phosphate (the active vitamin B_6 coenzyme) requires FMN. As FAD is required for the synthesis of a folate metabolite (5-methyl-tetrahydrofolate), riboflavin indirectly participates in homocysteine metabolism.
3. Some riboflavin-dependent enzymes have an **antioxidant role** in the body. Enzyme Glutathione reductase in erythrocytes has riboflavin as a co-factor.

Food Sources

Milk and milk products like curd, cottage cheese, cheese, etc., are the major contributors of riboflavin to the diet. Other foods include eggs, meat, liver, legumes, nuts, mushroom, spinach and other green leafy vegetables, broccoli, and asparagus. Exposure to light (UV radiation) causes riboflavin to break down rapidly. Milk cartons and sachets are therefore opaque. Cooking losses of riboflavin in typical Indian preparations is about 20 per cent.

Recommended Dietary Allowances

The RDA of riboflavin for different age groups is presented in Table 10.2. The rate of 0.6 mg riboflavin / 1,000 kcal has been worked out for adults after allowing for cooking losses. However, a minimum intake of 1.2 mg/ day is recommended, even if the calorie intake is lower than 2,000 kcal. No Upper Level has been set as the absorption of the vitamin is limited, and it is easily excreted in urine.

Problem of Deficiency and Excess

Deficiency of riboflavin (**Ariboflavinosis**) is widespread in India. The NNMB (2006) surveys indicate that the average intake of riboflavin is only 43 per cent of the requirement. Respiratory infections increase the utilisation of riboflavin, and hence may precipitate deficiency. Several symptoms may be seen:

- **Glossitis**—inflammation of the tongue
- **Cheilosis**—a disorder of the lips, marked by scaling and fissures (cracks) at the corners of the mouth
- **Seborrheic dermatitis**—a common inflammatory disease of the skin, characterised by scaly lesions usually on the scalp, hairline, and face.
- **Stomatitis**—a general term for an inflamed and sore mouth
- Sore throat, oedema of the oral mucous membranes
- **Nasolabial dyssebacia**—a disorder of the sebaceous glands, marked by reddening and accumulation of greasy flaky scales on the nose and the upper lip
- **Scrotal dermatitis**—itching, redness and skin lesions on the scrotum
- Various eye and nervous system disorders
- Confusion

The less recognised consequences of riboflavin deficiency are impaired psychomotor performance, increased risk of normochromic, normocytic anaemia (RBCs are of normal colour and size), and reduced cross-linking of skin collagen. Some animal studies have also shown that deficiency may lead to impaired wound healing, reduced immunity, and interruption of pregnancy (abortion).

Riboflavin toxicity is not a problem because of limited intestinal absorption. It is also a water-soluble vitamin, and hence can be easily excreted from the body in case high amounts are consumed.

NIACIN

In 1914, Joseph Goldberger, an officer in the US Public Health Service, was put in charge of investigating the cause of cases of pellagra in the south of the country. People suffered from skin rashes which worsened on exposure to strong sunlight, diarrhoea, and mental changes, causing a high death rate. Pellagra was associated with the consumption of maize (corn). Initially, it was felt that fungal contamination had possibly made the maize toxic, and later, the blame shifted to the possibility of infection spread by insects. Goldberger doubted the infection theory since there were no records of doctors or nurses catching the disease from their patients. He and his team actually ate skin scrapings and excreta from pellagra patients to test his hypothesis. He found that supplementing the diets with eggs and milk resulted in fewer cases of the disease, and yeast supplements were effective in curing the condition. His group was actively working to fractionate yeast and identify its active factor at the time of his death in 1929. Only in 1935 was it identified as nicotinic acid (also renamed 'niacin'), an already familiar chemical.

Niacin exists in two forms—niacin (nicotinic acid) and niacinamide (nicotinamide). Both forms perform the functions attributed to niacin (but in megadose therapy, they differ in action). The two coenzyme forms of niacin are **nicotinamide adenine dinucleotide (NAD)** and **nicotinamide adenine dinucleotide phosphate (NADP)**.

The essential amino acid tryptophan is converted to niacin in the body. In well-nourished individuals, 60 mg of tryptophan is taken as equivalent to 1 mg niacin.

Functions

1. NAD and NADP are active participants in **oxidation-reduction reactions**. They function in at least 200 different reactions in cellular metabolic pathways, especially those used to **produce ATP**.
2. NAD participates in reactions, acting as an electron and hydrogen acceptor in **carbohydrate, proteins and fat catabolism**. NADH donates electrons and hydrogen to other acceptor molecules in the mitochondrial electron transport chain.
3. NADPH participates in synthesis pathways in the cell, for example, pathways for **fatty acid and steroid synthesis**. Cells that synthesise a lot of fatty acids, like the liver and female mammary gland, have high concentrations of NADPH.

4. NAD is also required for reactions involved in **DNA repair** and calcium mobilisation. It is involved in the oxidation of glucose to pentose in the pentose phosphate pathway.
5. **Alcohol metabolism** also requires niacin coenzymes.

Food Sources

Most protein foods are also good sources of niacin, for example, whole cereals, pulses, peanuts, meat, chicken, fish like tuna, mushrooms, wheat bran, etc. Eggs and milk lack niacin, but are rich in tryptophan. In fact, foods of animal origin are rich sources of tryptophan. While calculating the dietary intake of niacin, tryptophan contribution as niacin equivalents is added to that of preformed niacin.

> High-protein diets have also been found to cure and prevent pellagra. This is because the amino acid tryptophan is converted to niacin in the body. All animal proteins except gelatin have good amounts of tryptophan.

$$\text{Niacin equivalent (mg)} = \text{Niacin (mg)} + \frac{\text{Tryptophan (mg)}}{60}$$

Niacin is very heat stable and little is lost in cooking. Studies carried out on losses of niacin during Indian cooking indicate an average loss of 25 per cent.

Recommended Dietary Allowances

The ICMR (2010) Committee has recommended 6.6 mg of niacin equivalents/ 1,000 kcal as the adult RDA. Table 10.2 presents the recommendations for different age groups and according to different activity levels for adults.

Problem of Deficiency and Excess

The first official record of niacin deficiency was by Spanish physician Casal in 1735. He named it 'mal de la rosa' or the 'red sickness'. The typical redness appearing around the neck is hence referred to as **Casal's Necklace.** The deficiency symptoms of niacin are called **Pellagra** (in Italian, *pelle* means skin and *agra* means rough). Early symptoms of Pellagra include a reduced appetite, weight loss and weakness. The effects of Pellagra are known as the 4Ds—diarrhoea, dementia, dermatitis, and death. The dermatitis or rash is very typical, in that it is bilateral and worsens on exposure to the sun. In fact, it appears on skin exposed to sunlight, like the forearms, hands, face, and neck. Mental changes are also common. These include insomnia, apathy and progresses on to dementia (impairment of the intellectual function). Diarrhoea results from the inflammation of the intestinal mucosal surfaces.

In the USA, there were regions where corn was eaten as a primary component of the diet, and pellagra was very common. The quantity of niacin in corn is not low, but it is only marginally absorbed because it is tightly bound to protein. It is released by soaking corn in lime water (calcium hydroxide dissolved in water). This practice was common among traditional Latin Americans, who removed the skin of the corn in this manner in order to make dough easily. Unfortunately, this practice was not adopted by others who took on corn as their staple food, resulting in outbreaks of pellagra in poor communities who could not afford other protein-rich foods.

Deficiency is still seen in Southeast Asia and Africa. In south India, *jowar* (sorghum)-eating populations also suffer from pellagra. This is due to the excessive amount of amino acid leucine present in *jowar*. This imbalance between leucine and other related amino acids like isoleucine interferes with the conversion of tryptophan to nicotinic acid.

Toxicity

Megadoses of niacin (given in the form of nicotinic acid) have been shown to reverse the progression of atherosclerosis. Around 75–150 times the RDA, which is about 1.5–3g, can decrease LDL and triglycerides, and increase the HDL.

Side effects have, however, been seen at intake levels of 50 mg/day. These include flushing of the skin, itching ('niacin flush', which is a burning, tingling and itching sensation), nausea, liver damage, etc. An Upper Limit of 35 mg/day has been proposed by the US Food and Nutrition Board, and has been accepted by FAO/WHO (2004).

VITAMIN B_6

Vitamin B_6 is a family of three compounds—pyridoxal, pyridoxine and pyridoxamine. The generic name for vitamin B_6 is pyridoxine. All three are phosphorylated to the active co-enzyme forms. **Pyridoxal phosphate (PLP)** is the primary coenzyme.

Functions

It is required for the activity of over 100 different enzymes involved in carbohydrate, protein and fat metabolism.

1. It is required for the metabolism of amino acids, especially the **transamination** reactions. The PLP aids in the transfer of amino groups for the synthesis of non-essential amino acids. If these reactions did not take place, then all amino acids would be essential. The ability to add and remove amino groups makes PLP valuable in protein and urea metabolism as well.

> Although vitamin B_6 plays an important role in amino acid and protein metabolism, research does not support the claim that large doses of B_6 enhance muscle strength or physical endurance. Vitamin supplements can never compete with a nutritious balanced diet and physical training or exercise.

2. Vitamin B_6 is important for the **synthesis of heme**. PLP also aids in the binding of oxygen to haemoglobin. A microcytic hypochromic anaemia, resembling iron deficiency, can occur in B_6 deficiency.
3. It is also necessary for the **synthesis of white blood cells (WBCs),** and hence for **immunity.**
4. B_6 participates in **carbohydrate metabolism**, in the breakdown of glycogen, and the production of glucose from amino acids (**gluconeogenesis**).
5. It is required for the **synthesis of neurotransmitters** from amino acids, which allow the nerve cells to communicate, like serotonin, gamma-amino butyric acid (GABA), dopamine (DOPA), and norepinephrine.
6. It is required for the conversion of tryptophan to **niacin** and also for the **metabolism of homocysteine** to cysteine. Homocysteine is toxic to cells and has been linked to an increased risk of atherosclerosis.
7. It is also involved in the regulation of **gene expression**. Studies have also shown that the vitamin may help prevent cancer.

Food Sources

Meat, fish and poultry are good sources because B_6 is stored in the muscle tissue of animals. This is the more absorbable form of the vitamin. It is also present in nuts, pulses and whole grains, but may be lost if grains are refined. Other nutrient-dense sources include bananas, avocados, spinach, potatoes, and sunflower seeds.

Pyridoxine is the predominant form of the vitamin present in plant foods. In foods from animal sources, it is present majorly as pyridoxal and pyridoxal phosphate. Although the form present in plant foods is more stable to cooking losses than the form present in animal foods, glycosylated pyridoxine is less bio-available. B_6 is not stable under heat or alkaline conditions. Heat processing and other destructive processing techniques can decrease the B_6 content of food by 10–50 per cent, especially foods from animal sources.

Recommended Dietary Allowances

Adult men and women require 2 mg of B_6 in a day. In calculating requirements at present—since most Indian diets consist of foods mostly from plant sources—the cooking losses are taken as negligible, as pyridoxine is stable to heat. Athletes need extra because the use of glycogen as fuel increases in them. A high-protein diet usually supplies the extra B_6. Some drugs, such as the anti-tubercular drug isoniazid, increases B_6 needs by about five times the RDA. Also, too much B_6 decreases the effectiveness of this drug. Other drugs that decrease the amount of PLP in the blood include L-DOPA, used to treat Parkinson disease, and theophylline, used to treat asthma. Individuals on these medications may need supplements of vitamin B_6.

Homocysteine is an amino acid which is biosynthesised from methionine. It can be recycled into methionine or converted into cysteine with the aid of B-vitamins like riboflavin, folate, vitamins B_6- and B_{12}. Abnormally high levels of homocysteine in the serum are a medical condition, called hyperhomocysteinemia. This is considered a significant risk factor for the development of a wide range of diseases, including thrombosis, brain disorders and fractures.

Problem of Deficiency and Excess

A deficiency of B_6 alone is usually uncommon, and it generally occurs in association with a deficit in other B-vitamins. Pregnant women and women using oral contraceptives may be more at risk of a relative deficiency of this vitamin due to what is believed to be an effect of oestrogen on enzyme activity, for example, enzyme kynureninase (a PLP-dependent enzyme). There is also evidence of B_6 deficiency in the elderly. In addition, alcohol is found to contribute to the destruction and loss of the vitamin from the body. Deficiency can result in the following:

1. Impairment of protein synthesis and overall cell metabolism.
2. Microcytic hypochromic anaemia (smaller than normal-sized RBCs and pale in colour because of less concentration of haemoglobin).
3. Neurological disorders like depression, headaches, confusion, and convulsions.
4. Peripheral neuritis (inflammation of peripheral nerves, causing pain or loss of function).
5. Glossitis (inflammation of the tongue).
6. Seborrheic dermatitis.

Medicinal uses and Toxicity of B_6

Sometimes, pregnant women may be prescribed this vitamin in doses of 30–75 mg/day to reduce nausea. Carpal Tunnel Syndrome (nerve disorder of the wrist) is treated with 100–200 mg B_6 for three months, as it reduces the pain. However, 2–6g of B_6 per day for two or more months can lead to irreversible nerve damage. This is also seen in long-term use of more than 200 mg/day, for example, for PMS treatment or by body builders. **Premenstrual syndrome** or PMS is characterised by symptoms of depression, irritability, anxiety, headache, bloating, and mood swings, a few days before the menstrual period begins. Most menstruating women suffer from at least one symptom of PMS. However, people who consume such high levels of the vitamin experience symptoms like difficulty in walking, and hand and foot numbness, and the damage to ganglia (where the nerve fibres converge) is probably permanent. The Upper Level for adults is set at 100 mg/day (FAO/WHO 2004).

FOLATE

In the 1920s, scientists believed that folate deficiency and anaemia were the same condition. In 1931, Dr Lucy Wills identified folate as the nutrient needed to prevent anaemia during pregnancy. Dr Wills demonstrated that anaemia could be reversed with brewer's yeast. Folate was identified as the corrective substance in brewer's yeast in the late 1930s, and was first isolated in and extracted from spinach leaves by Mitchell and others in 1941. The name folate comes from the Latin word 'folium', meaning 'leaf'. This name was given to the vitamin, as green leafy vegetables are an excellent source.

Folic acid, also known as folacin or folate, is made up of a pteridine group, para amino benzoic acid (PABA), and the amino acid glutamic acid. If one molecule of glutamate is present, it is known as folate monoglutamate, and if three or more glutamate molecules are present, it is called folate polyglutamate. Polyglutamates must be broken down to monoglutamate form in the digestion process by the conjugate enzyme present in the cells lining the small intestine. About 75 per cent of the monoglutamate form is absorbed. Half of the body folate is stored in the liver, most of it in the polyglutamate form. Folate is excreted from the body through bile and urine.

Functions

Folate is very important for rapidly dividing cells. If folate is deficient, both the DNA and the methylation cycles (in which a methyl group is added to a substance) will reduce.

1. The coenzyme form of folate is Tetrahydrofolic acid (THFA). It participates in metabolic reactions by **accepting and donating single carbon groups,** for example, methylene (–CH_2-) groups, which are needed for:
   - synthesis of nucleic acids and DNA
   - metabolism of various amino acids and their derivatives
   - cell division
   - maturation of RBCs and other cells
2. **Formation of neurotransmitters** in the brain. Supplementation with folate can improve the depressed state in some cases of mental illness.
3. Folate supplements have been shown to **decrease the homocysteine levels** in blood, and thus prevent heart disease. Homocysteine is an intermediate product formed when methionine breaks down to cysteine. This is toxic to cells, including those lining blood vessels. The further metabolism of homocysteine requires folate.
4. Folate can also help in maintaining normal blood pressure and in reducing the risk of developing cancer.

Food Sources

Good sources include liver, legumes, and spinach and other green leafy vegetables. These foods have the largest quantity and the most bio-available folate. Other nutrient-dense sources are orange and orange juice, wheat germ, broccoli, cabbage, cauliflower, etc. An Indian meal has a density of approximately 50 μg of folate/ 1,000 kcal.

Food processing and preparation can destroy a significant amount (50–90 per cent) of folate. The average Indian cooking loss is taken as 33 per cent. It is susceptible to destruction by heat, oxidation and UV light. Vegetables should be cooked in minimum water and time, or eaten raw. Vitamin C in foods helps protect folate from oxidative destruction.

Recommended Dietary Allowances

It is assumed that about 33 per cent of folate is lost in the Indian style of cooking, and only about 50 per cent of the folate present in the diets is absorbed. Thus, for the purpose of calculating RDA, it is assumed that only one-third of the folate present in foods is bio-available. The RDA ranges from 25 μg for infants to 200 μg for adults and adolescents (16–17 years old). It is 500 μg for pregnant women and 300 μg for lactating women. In view of its low bio-availability, pregnant women are usually prescribed supplements to prevent neural tube defects in the foetus. It may also be necessary to fortify foods with this vitamin for the benefit of other age groups susceptible to anaemia.

Problem of Deficiency and Excess

A low intake, inadequate absorption, increased requirement, compromised utilisation, or increased excretion can all lead to folic acid deficiency. **Megaloblastic (macrocytic) anaemia** is seen in folate deficiency as folate is needed for DNA synthesis and RBC maturation. The precursor cells in the bone marrow cannot divide normally to become mature RBCs because they cannot form new DNA. Cells still grow in size and produce haemoglobin. Cells thus formed are large, immature megaloblasts. Unlike normal mature RBCs, megaloblasts retain the nucleus. With fewer normal-sized RBCs present in blood, the oxygen carrying capacity is reduced. This results in anaemia, with symptoms of weakness and tiredness. Large immature cells also appear along the entire length of the gastrointestinal tract during chronic folate deficiency. This leads to a decrease in the absorptive capacity of the tract and persistent diarrhoea. WBC synthesis is also disrupted by folate deficiency, and hence immunity may be lowered. Other clinical signs and symptoms seen are:

> As bio-availability of dietary folate and folic acid present as a fortificant varies, a dietary folate equivalent (DFE unit) is calculated, which reflects the difference in absorption.
>
> DFE (μg) = natural food folate (μg) + 1.7 × synthetic folic acid (μg)

- inflammation of the tongue and mouth
- abnormal pigmentation of the skin
- diarrhoea
- poor growth
- depression and mental confusion
- problems in nerve function
- elevated blood homocysteine

Maternal deficiency of folic acid leads to **Neural tube defects** in the foetus. The neural tube closes within the first 28 days of pregnancy. Folate deficiency can lead to a defect in the formation of the neural tube. About 75 per cent of the defects can be avoided by adequate folate status before conception. One of the defects seen is **Spina bifida,** in which the spinal cord or spinal fluid bulges through the back. The baby can suffer from a number of problems as a result, viz., paralysis, incontinence, hydrocephalus (fluid retention in the brain), and learning disabilities. There can also be Anencephaly (absence of brain), in which case the baby dies shortly after birth.

Toxicity

Individuals with epilepsy and on certain medications can have resumption of seizures if large supplements of folate are given. Doses of 1–10 mg can result in symptoms like hives (allergic skin reaction), respiratory distress, redness of skin, and itching. Consuming excessive amounts of folate can also mask a Vitamin B_{12} deficiency. This is because high doses of folic acid will correct the megaloblastic anaemia, but not the neuropathy associated with vitamin B_{12} deficiency. The US National Academy of Sciences has suggested an Upper Level of 1,000 μg.

VITAMIN B_{12} (COBALAMIN)

Vitamin B_{12} is also known as cobalamin. It is the only vitamin that has a mineral (cobalt) in its structure. The cyanocobalamin form of the vitamin forms two active coenzymes—**methyl cobalamin and 5-deoxyadenosyl cobalamin**. It is liberated from the food because of the action of gastric juice. The free B_{12} binds to an intrinsic factor, which is vital for its absorption. After absorption, it passes into the blood stream and moves to the liver, bone marrow and blood cells.

The discovery of vitamin B_{12}, its role in metabolism, and the effects and treatment of its deficiency occurred in phases over more than 100 years. The cure for pernicious anaemia, a usually fatal disease, was discovered quite by accident. George Whipple had been doing experiments in which he induced anaemia in dogs and then fed them various foods to observe which diets allowed them fastest recovery. In the process, he discovered that ingesting large amounts of liver seemed to most rapidly cure the anaemia. Thus, he hypothesised that liver ingestion might treat pernicious anaemia in 1920. After a series of careful clinical studies, George Richards Minot and William Murphy were able to partly isolate the substance in liver which cured pernicious anaemia in humans. Minot and

Murphy reported these experiments in 1926. After the successful intervention studies, the next advance was made by Castle, who discovered that a gastric component, which he called intrinsic factor, was missing in pernicious anaemia.

Functions

Vitamin B_{12} participates in a variety of reactions, especially methylation reactions (process of addition of a methyl group $-CH_3$), which are important for DNA and RNA regulation, myelin regulation, and the synthesis of many biochemical compounds.

> Vegetarian diets lack Vitamin $B_{12,}$ unless milk and milk products are included in the diet.

1. In **folate metabolism,** it is needed for the transfer of methyl groups. Lack of B_{12} will cause a secondary folate shortage, as THFA is trapped in the methyl-bound form. Hence, DNA and protein synthesis is affected, and it results in megaloblastic anaemia.
2. Its coenzyme form is required for the conversion of the amino acid homocysteine to methionine.
3. It plays a role in **maintaining the myelin sheath** that insulates nerve fibres. B_{12} deficiency hence results in a patchy destruction of the myelin sheath, especially in areas surrounding the nerves in the spinal cord.
4. B_{12} coenzyme is required for the enzyme methylmalonyl mutase, which helps in the **metabolism of fatty acids** with an odd number of carbon molecules. Fatty acids naturally present in the body and food have an even number of carbon atoms. It helps these fatty acids to be oxidised in the citric acid cycle to release energy.

Food Sources

All vitamin B_{12} compounds are synthesised exclusively by bacteria, fungi and algae. Animal foods are the only reliable source of the vitamin, as plants do not contain $B_{12,}$ except for minor contamination of vegetable products by bacteria and soil-containing microbes. The fermentation process may also contribute a small amount of B_{12} to the diet, as fermented foods mainly contain compounds similar to $B_{12,}$ but which do not function as B_{12}. Dietary sources include meat, poultry, seafood, eggs, organ meats—especially liver, kidney, heart—beef, ham, milk and milk products. About 15–70 per cent of dietary vitamin B_{12} is absorbed. Enterohepatic circulation is important in conserving B_{12} found in bile. The microorganisms living in our large intestine also produce vitamin $B_{12,}$ but it is not clear how much of this can be actually absorbed or used by our bodies. It is a relatively stable vitamin. While microwave cooking minimises the loss of most B vitamins, in the case of vitamin $B_{12,}$ it actually inactivates the vitamin.

Recommended Dietary Allowances

The ICMR (2010) has recommended 1 µg of vitamin B_{12} for men and women, 1.2 µg for pregnant women, and 1.5 µg for lactating women. For the rest of the age groups, the requirements range from 0.2 to 1.0 µg. Indians meet their requirement mainly from milk and milk products, and other foods of animal origin. The vitamin can be stored in the liver, and it would take years of eating a poor diet to develop a deficiency. Vegans (vegetarians who do not consume even milk) are at a greater risk of deficiency.

No adverse effects have been observed with excess vitamin B_{12} intake from food or from supplements, so there is no Upper Level for this vitamin.

Problem of Deficiency and Excess

It will take 20 years of consuming a diet free of B_{12} for a person to exhibit symptoms like nerve destruction. However, it takes only two to three years if the person is unable to absorb the vitamin. The elderly are especially susceptible to developing a deficiency, due to impaired absorption. **Pernicious** (which means 'leading to death') **anaemia** is a type of anaemia that results from an inability to absorb sufficient B_{12} (because of a lack of an intrinsic factor, which is produced by the parietal cells of the stomach). It is associated with nerve degeneration that can result in eventual paralysis and death.

Megaloblasts (macrocytes) are seen in the blood—like in folate deficiency—as there is abnormal haemopoiesis (formation of blood cells). This is primarily because a deficiency of B_{12} will result in impaired folate metabolism and a secondary folate deficiency. The difference between anaemia of folic acid and B_{12} deficiency lies in the fact that the nerve degeneration present is eventually fatal in B_{12} deficiency, but not in folic acid deficiency. This can only be treated by B_{12} injections, as supplements (unless given in high doses) would not be absorbed without the intrinsic factor. Other symptoms of B_{12} deficiency include:

- Weakness
- Painful red tongue (glossitis)
- Weight loss
- Anorexia
- Indigestion
- Diarrhoea
- Paresthesia in the extremities (abnormal spontaneous sensation, such as of burning, tingling, prickling, and numbness)
- Walking difficulties and loss of balance
- Mild dementia, disorientation
- Mental slowness
- Memory loss and loss of concentration

VITAMIN C

This vitamin was discovered by Dr James Lind, who observed that two oranges and one lemon a day could cure scurvy in British sailors. In fact, scurvy among sailors on long sea voyages in the fifteenth and sixteenth centuries was cured by adding a few fruits and vegetables to the sailors' diet. Most animals are capable of synthesising vitamin C from glucose. Humans, other primates like gorillas, guinea pigs, fruit bats, and a few birds and fish are unable to synthesise the vitamin, and hence need it in their daily diet. Vitamin C exists in a reduced form (ascorbic acid) and an oxidised form (dehydroascorbic acid), which are interchangeable. Dehydroascorbic acid is metabolised to oxalic acid and other compounds.

> Epidemiological studies indicate that diets with high vitamin C content have been associated with a lower risk of cancer, coronary heart disease and cataract development. However, supplementation with vitamin C has not shown consistent evidence. This means that the benefits of the vitamin are best derived when fresh fruits and vegetables are consumed, rather than pills. Other protective substances present along with the vitamin in foods may also be enhancing the protective effect.

Functions

Vitamin C acts as an electron donor (reducing agent or antioxidant), and most of the functions are because it acts as a non-specific reducing agent.

1. **Collagen synthesis.** Vitamin C acts as an electron donor for enzymes which participate in collagen hydroxylation. Collagen is the major protein of the material that holds together the various structures of the body. It is a fibrous protein, which is a major component of connective tissue. Collagen fibres are critical to the maintenance of bone and blood vessels, and are essential in wound healing.
2. **Antioxidant activity.** It is the water-soluble antioxidant of the cell. It works with vitamin E as a pair of free radical scavengers. It reactivates oxidised vitamin E, so that it can be used again. It also protects folate. Anaemia

has been seen as a common feature of vitamin C deficiency. Studies have shown that in humans suffering from scurvy, the excretion of oxidised folate derivatives increases. The antioxidant property of vitamin C is believed to stabilise folate in food and plasma. It is also effective in preventing certain cancers (oesophageal, oral and stomach), heart disease and cataracts in the eye.

3. **Iron absorption.** It increases the absorption of non-heme iron (primarily from plant foods) from the intestinal tract by forming a chelate (a particular way in which a molecule binds a metal ion). It also converts ferric ions to ferrous ions, which are more soluble in the slightly alkaline environment of the small intestine. Vitamin C also counters the action of certain food components that inhibit iron absorption.
4. **Synthesis of vital substances. Carnitine** is a transport compound that moves fatty acids from the cytoplasm into the mitochondria for energy production (this is important in the muscle tissue). The **Catecholamines** norepinephrine and epinephrine are synthesised with the action of a copper-containing enzyme and vitamin C. Synthesis of the amino acid **tyrosine**, hormone **thyroxin**, conversion of tryptophan to **serotonin**, and amidation of **peptide hormones** also requires vitamin C. Other hydroxylation reactions in the synthesis of **bile acids, DNA,** and **steroid hormones** also require vitamin C.
5. **Immune function.** Vitamin C is vital for the function of the immune system, especially the lymphocytes. Vitamin C is also used by the chemical-detoxifying mechanism in cells. So when an individual is suffering from an infection or consuming drugs, the need for vitamin C goes up. Vitamin C in supplement form is, however, not recommended either to prevent or cure infections, because of the very limited beneficial effects seen in research studies. Research findings supporting the use of supplements for curing common cold (where at least 1 gram of vitamin C is required daily) are controversial, as most show a decrease in the duration of cold by barely a day. Vitamin C deactivates histamine, which is a substance produced by the immune system in response to an antigen. Elevated blood histamine levels lead to symptoms of nasal congestion (runny, stuffy nose).

Food Sources

Rich sources of vitamin C include citrus fruits—lemon, lime, orange, grapefruit, sweet lime or *mausambi*, etc., *amla*, cherry, kiwi fruit, mango, papaya, strawberry, watermelon, honeydew melon, tomato, green peppers, cauliflower, potato, broccoli, lettuce, and spinach and other green vegetables. Five servings of fruits and vegetables per day would take care of the daily needs of a person. Some part of these should be eaten in the raw form, as the vitamin is easily destroyed during processing and cooking. It is very unstable when in contact with heat, light, iron, copper, or oxygen. Exposure to low pH enhances its stability, while a high pH will destroy it. Cooking reduces ascorbic acid content by more than 60–75 per cent.

> It is important to eat the vitamin C rich food along with the iron rich food in the same meal in order to increase absorption. Indian diets contain about 7 mg of iron per 1,000 kcal. Vitamin C should be at least 20 mg/1,000 kcal to facilitate iron absorption (2:1 molar ratio of vitamin C: iron).

Recommended Dietary Allowances

The calculation of the requirement of vitamin C assumes 50 per cent loss of the vitamin on cooking and storing foods. An RDA of 40 mg has been set for the adult. However, to get the antioxidant and other health benefits, 60 mg or more of vitamin C may need to be consumed. In pregnancy, the requirement increases to 60 mg, while in lactation, due to secretion in breast milk, the requirement increases to 80 mg. Cigarette smokers should consume at least 100 mg/day to overcome the rapid destruction of the vitamin in the lung due to an increase in oxidative stress. Women using oral contraceptives may also require additional vitamin C. Burns and trauma patients would benefit from vitamin C supplements as it helps in increasing collagen synthesis, which is important for their recovery.

As the source of vitamin C is fresh fruits and vegetables, the WHO goal for prevention of chronic disease is at least five servings of fruits and vegetables per day. It is recommended that some of these be eaten raw to meet the vitamin C requirement.

Problem of Deficiency and Excess

Deficiency is common in smokers, poor people, and others who do not consume fresh fruits and vegetables, and infants fed on boiled milk alone. **Scurvy** results from a deficiency of vitamin C. The deficiency prevents the normal synthesis of collagen, which causes significant changes in connective tissues throughout the body. The first signs appear within 20–40 days on a vitamin C-free diet. Three important manifestations of scurvy include gingival (gum) changes, pain in the extremities and haemorrhagic manifestations. These are followed by oedema, ulcerations and ultimately death. Symptoms seen are:

- Swollen bleeding gums
- Fatigue
- Pinpoint haemorrhages or petechiae around the hair follicles on the back of the arms and legs. Follicular hyperkeratosis may also be seen.
- Bleeding in joints, which is a classic sign of connective tissue failure.
- Impaired wound healing and opening of previously healed wounds
- Bone pain, fractures arising from a failure of osteoid (organic part of the bone) formation
- Diarrhoea
- Psychological problems in advanced scurvy, including depression

In **infantile scurvy,** the changes are mainly at the sites of most active bone growth. The infant experiences extreme pain on movement and so may avoid movement, giving the impression of paralysis. The pain is mainly because of swelling and haemorrhages.

Toxicity

The efficiency of the absorption of the vitamin decreases at higher intake levels. A side-effect of excessive vitamin C is diarrhoea. This is because unabsorbed vitamin C in the small intestine attracts water by its osmotic effect from the blood. Regularly consuming more than 1 g/day can cause stomach inflammation, diarrhoea and oxalate kidney stones, in people with a history of such stones. Oxalic acid is a major breakdown product when vitamin C intakes are moderate, that is, around 100 mg/day. Megadoses of vitamin C have not really shown to prevent or greatly reduce the susceptibility, severity, or duration of a cold. The Upper Level for vitamin C is 2 g/day, based on adverse gastrointestinal effects.

LESS-KNOWN VITAMINS

PANTOTHENIC ACID

Pantothenic acid is considered a water-soluble B vitamin. Its name originates from a Greek word '*Pantothen*', which means 'everywhere', indicating that small quantities of this vitamin are present in nearly all foods.

Functions

Pantothenic acid is a component of Coenzyme A (CoA). It is involved in energy metabolism, especially fatty acid metabolism. It participates in several reactions of the synthesis of lipids, neurotransmitters, steroid hormones, and haemoglobin.

Food Sources and Recommended Intakes

Common sources include milk, meat and vegetables, peanuts, egg yolk, mushroom, potatoes, tomatoes, broccoli, yeast. Any sort of processing reduces the amount of pantothenic acid present in the food. FAO/WHO (2004) recommends an intake of 5 mg/day for both men and women.

Deficiency

> High doses of vitamin C can give false positive results in tests for blood in stool. People going in for such tests should ensure that they stop consuming supplements a few days before the test.

Symptoms of deficiency include irritability, anorexia, postural hypotension (low blood pressure in standing position), impaired muscle co-ordination, numbness and tingling of the hands and feet ('burning feet' syndrome), gastric distress and constipation. Deficiency is, however, unlikely, due to the presence of this vitamin in a wide variety of foods. Toxicity has also not been observed.

BIOTIN

Biotin is also considered a water-soluble B vitamin. It functions as a coenzyme in metabolic reactions.

Functions

Biotin functions as a coenzyme with carboxylases, that is, it takes part in carboxylation reactions (in which carbon dioxide is added to compounds). This role is critical in energy metabolism. The biotin coenzyme also participates in gluconeogenesis (synthesis of glucose from non-carbohydrate sources), fatty acid synthesis, and the breakdown of certain fatty acids and amino acids. Evidence is accumulating that biotin also plays an important role in regulating gene expression, and hence in cell biology and foetal development.

Food Sources and Recommended Intakes

Biotin is present in a variety of foods, and foods like egg, liver, green leafy vegetables, and nuts are especially considered rich in this vitamin. Some biotin is also synthesised by bacteria in our gastrointestinal tract, although most of it may not really get absorbed. In any case, biotin is needed in very small amounts. The recommended intake of biotin for adults is 30 μg/day (FAO/WHO 2004).

Deficiency

Raw egg white has a protein called avidin, which binds the biotin. Consuming raw eggs for a prolonged period of time may predispose individuals to a deficiency. Cooking destroys avidin and makes biotin more available. People with malabsorption syndrome or those on parenteral nutrition may also develop a deficiency. Clinical signs of deficiency include dermatitis (redness and soreness of skin), conjunctivitis, alopecia (baldness, loss of hair), lethargy, depression, hallucinations, paresthesia (prickling or tingling sensation) of extremities in adults, and hypotonia (decreases the tone of muscles).

Toxicity

Toxicity is not a problem, as there is limited absorption of biotin.

CHOLINE

Choline was discovered by Adolph Strecker in 1864, and chemically synthesised in 1866. In 1998, choline was classified as an essential nutrient by the Food and Nutrition Board of the Institute of Medicine (USA). It can be synthesised in the body from the amino acid methionine, but not in quantities to meet the requirements. It is also sometimes referred to as a 'vitamin-like substance', which means that it is not universally recognised as a vitamin, although it is considered an essential nutrient.

Functions

Choline has several important metabolic functions. It, however, does not function like a coenzyme.

1. As phosphatidylcholine (lecithin), it is an important **structural element of cell membranes.**
2. It is also a component of sphingomyelin, which is essential for the **myelin sheath of nerves**. Choline requirements are therefore high during pregnancy and infancy, when **brain and nervous tissue development** happens at a very fast pace.
3. Choline is a precursor of the **neurotransmitter** acetylcholine, which is vital for muscle control, learning, memory, and attention. It is one of the supplements recommended in Alzheimer's disease.
4. Other functions are attributed to its ability to **donate methyl groups**. Choline may prevent neural tube defects, lower C-reactive protein (an indicator of inflammation in the body), and hence offer protection against heart disease.

Food Sources and Recommended Intakes

Most animal foods like eggs, chicken, meat, liver, and milk are rich in choline. Whole grains, nuts, fruits and vegetables also contribute to intake, but data on choline levels in food are lacking. Lecithin added to foods during processing may also contribute to intake.

The ICMR (2010) does not give any recommendations. The Food and Nutrition Board of the USA recommends an Adequate Intake of 550 mg/day for adult men and 425 mg/day for adult women.

Deficiency

The most common signs of choline deficiencies are fatty liver and haemorrhagic kidney necrosis.

Toxicity

The Upper Level for adults has been set as 3.5 g/day, as very high doses of choline have been associated with a fishy body odour (arising from a breakdown of metabolic product), vomiting, sweating, salivation, low blood pressure, and gastrointestinal symptoms.

Table 10.3: Summary of Functions, Rich Sources, Symptoms of Deficiency, and Excess of Water-soluble Vitamins

Vitamin	*Coenzyme Form*	*Functions*	*Rich Sources*	*Deficiency*
Thiamine	TPP (Thiamine Pyrophosphate)	Decarboxylation reactions in energy and amino acid metabolism, DNA and RNA synthesis, nerve function	Whole cereal grains, cereal products, wheat germ, sunflower seeds, yeast and legumes, pork, peanuts, mushrooms, liver, eggs, green beans, green peas, watermelon, etc.	Beriberi (wet and dry), Wernicke Korsakoff syndrome
Riboflavin	Flavin mononucleotide (FMN) and Flavin adenine dinucleotide (FAD)	Oxidation-reduction reactions in energy production from carbohydrates and fats, vitamin and mineral metabolism, antioxidant role of enzymes like glutathione reductase	Milk and milk products like curd, cottage cheese, cheese, etc., eggs, meat, liver, legumes, nuts, mushroom, spinach and other green leafy vegetables, broccoli and asparagus, etc.	Ariboflavinosis, glossitis, cheilosis, angular stomatitis, nasolabial dyssebacia, seborrheic dermatitis

Table 10.3 contd

Table 10.3 contd

Vitamin	*Coenzyme Form*	*Functions*	*Rich Sources*	*Deficiency*
Niacin	Nicotinamide adenine dinucleotide (NAD) and Nicotinamide adenine dinucleotide phosphate (NADP)	Oxidation-reduction reactions in energy production, carbohydrate, fat and protein catabolism, fatty acid and steroid synthesis, DNA repair	Most protein foods are also good sources of niacin, for example, whole cereals, pulses, peanuts, meat, chicken, fish like tuna, mushrooms, wheat bran, etc. Eggs and milk are rich in tryptophan, which can form niacin in the body	Pellagra-dermatitis, diarrhoea, dementia, and death (4Ds)
Pyridoxine	Pyridoxal phosphate (PLP)	Transamination reactions in synthesis of amino acids, synthesis of heme, WBCs and neurotransmitters, carbohydrate metabolism, metabolism of homocysteine, regulation of gene expression	Meat, fish, poultry, nuts, pulses and whole grains, bananas, avocados, spinach, potatoes and sunflower seeds, etc.	Anemia, glossitis, neurological disorders, peripheral neuritis
Folic Acid	Tetrahydrofolic acid (THFA)	Synthesis of nucleic acids and DNA, metabolism of various amino acids and their derivatives, cell division, maturation of RBCs and other cells, formation of neurotransmitters, metabolism of homocysteine	Liver, legumes, spinach and other green leafy vegetables, orange and orange juice, wheat germ, broccoli, cabbage, cauliflower, etc.	Megaloblastic anaemia, problems in nerve function, elevated homocysteine, neural tube defects, spina bifida
Vitamin B_{12}	Methyl cobalamin and 5- deoxyadenosyl cobalamin	Methylation reactions, folate metabolism, homocysteine metabolism, maintaining myelin sheath, metabolism of fatty acids.	Meat, poultry, seafood, eggs, organ meats especially liver, kidney, heart, beef, ham, milk and milk products	Pernicious anemia, megaloblastic anemia, glossitis, paresthesia, walking difficulties, mild dementia, nerve damage
Pantothenic acid	Coenzyme A (CoA)	Energy, especially fatty acid metabolism	Milk, meat and vegetables, peanuts, egg yolk, mushroom, broccoli, yeast, etc.	Irritability, anorexia, postural hypotension, impaired muscle co-ordination, numbness and tingling of hands and feet, gastric distress and constipation
Biotin	–	Carboxylation reactions in energy metabolism, fatty acid synthesis, breakdown of fatty acids, amino acids, gluconeogenesis, gene expression	Egg, liver, green leafy vegetables, nuts, and a wide range of other foods	Dermatitis, conjunctivitis, alopecia, lethargy, depression, hallucinations, paresthesia, hypotonia

Table 10.3 contd

Table 10.3 contd

Vitamin	Coenzyme Form	Functions	Rich Sources	Deficiency
Vitamin C	–	Collagen synthesis, antioxidant activity, iron absorption, synthesis of vital cell compounds, immune function	Citrus fruits—lemon, lime, orange, grapefruit, sweet lime or *mausambi*, etc.—*amla,* cherry, kiwi fruit, mango, papaya, strawberry, watermelon, honeydew melon, tomato, green peppers, cauliflower, potato, broccoli, lettuce, spinach and other green vegetables, etc.	Scurvy, swollen bleeding gums, pinpoint haemorrhages or petechiae, impaired wound healing, bone pain
Choline	–	Structural element of cells, of myelin sheath of nerves, neurotransmitter synthesis, can donate methyl groups	Eggs, chicken, meat, milk, whole grains, nuts, fruits and vegetables, etc.	Fatty liver and haemorrhagic kidney necrosis

SUMMARY

- Water soluble vitamins include the B vitamins (Thiamine, Riboflavin, Niacin, Pyridoxine, Folate, vitamin B_{12}) and vitamin C.
- Most B vitamins act as coenzymes and participate in energy, protein and fat metabolism. However, they have many other important functions to perform, related to immunity, bone health, nerve function, gene expression, antioxidant defence function, blood clotting and formation.
- Typically, 50–90 per cent of the B vitamins in the diet are absorbed. Most of these vitamins are easily destroyed during cooking, due to heat and alkalinity. They are all subject to leaching into the cooking water. Retention is best in foods prepared by steaming, stir frying, microwaving, and simmering in minimal moisture.
- Functions, rich sources, and deficiency of each of the vitamins is summarised in Table 10.3.
- Pantothenic acid, biotin and choline are nutrients whose role is slowly being understood and appreciated.

KEY WORDS

Anorexia: Loss of appetite

Ataxia: The loss of full control of bodily movements.

Carboxylation reaction: A chemical reaction in which a carboxylic acid group is introduced in a substrate. The opposite reaction is decarboxylation.

Cheilosis: A disorder of the lips marked by scaling and fissures (cracks) at the corners of the mouth.

Coenzyme: A substance that works with an enzyme to initiate or aid the function of the enzyme.

Dementia: Impairment of intellectual function, insanity

Glossitis: Inflammation of the tongue

Megaloblasts: Red blood cells which are large, immature and retain their nuclei

Methylation reaction: Process of addition of a methyl group

Microcytic hypochromic cells: Red blood cells smaller in size (microcytes) and having less colour due to less haemoglobin

Paresthesia: Abnormal spontaneous sensation such as of burning, tingling, prickling and numbness.

Peripheral neuritis: Inflammation of peripheral nerves, causing pain or loss of function.

Petechiae: Pinpoint haemorrhages around the hair follicles on the back of arms and legs.

Scrotal dermatitis: Itching, redness and skin lesions on the scrotum

Seborrheic dermatitis: A common inflammatory disease of the skin, characterised by scaly lesions, usually on the scalp, hairline and face.

Secondary deficiency: Here, it is a state of deficiency which results from a cause other than the lack of the vitamin in the diet. For example, B_{12} deficiency impairs folate metabolism, resulting in a secondary deficiency of folate, even when folate is present in adequate amounts in the diet.

Stomatitis: A general term for an inflamed and sore mouth

Transamination reactions: Reactions in which there is a transfer of amino groups

EXERCISES

1. Which vitamins are important for nerve function and nerve health?
2. Differentiate between dry and wet beriberi.
3. Describe the signs and symptoms of riboflavin deficiency.
4. What are the functions of the following vitamins:
   a. Vitamin C
   b. Niacin
   c. Folic acid
   d. Pyridoxine
5. How is the anaemia of folic acid and B_{12} deficiency different from iron deficiency anaemia?
6. How does B_{12} deficiency lead to a secondary folate deficiency?
7. Why do gums swell up and joints bleed during vitamin C deficiency?
8. Describe the symptoms of niacin deficiency. Why was it common in maize and sorghum eating populations?

REFERENCES

Byrd-Bredbenner C., G. Moe, D. Beshgetoor, and J. Berning, *Wardlaw's Perspectives in Nutrition*, 9e, New York: McGraw-Hill International Edition, 2013.

Food and Nutrition Board, *Dietary reference intakes for thiamine, riboflavin, niacin, vitamin B_6, folate, vitamin B_{12}, pantothenic acid, biotin and choline*, Washington DC: National Academy Press, 1998.

ICMR, 'Nutrient Requirements and Recommended Dietary Allowances for Indians', A report of the Expert Group of the Indian Council of Medical Research, 2010.

Lakshmaiah, N. and A. V. Lakshmi, 'Water Soluble Vitamins', in M. S. Bamji, K. Krishnaswamy and G. N. V. Brahmam (eds), *Textbook of Human Nutrition*, 3e, Oxford and IBH Publ Co., 2009.

Rolfes, S. R., K. Pinna and E. Whitney, *Understanding Normal and Clinical Nutrition*, 8e, Wadsworth Cengage Learning, 2009.

WHO/FAO, 'Vitamin and Mineral Requirements in Human Nutrition', Joint FAO/WHO Expert Consultation on Human Vitamin and Mineral Requirements, Bangkok, Thailand, 1998 (2e, 2004).

ONLINE SOURCES

Discovery of vitamins:

- Christiaan Eijkman, 'Beriberi and Vitamin B1', *Nobelprize.org*. Nobel Media AB 2013. Available at http://www.nobelprize.org/educational/medicine/vitamin_b1/eijkman.html (accessed 27 February 2014).

Discovery of a cure for beriberi:

http://www.nobelprize.org/educational/medicine/vitamin_b1/eijkman.html

Learn more about neural tube defects:

www.sbaa.org

11

DIGESTION AND ABSORPTION OF NUTRIENTS

HIGHLIGHTS

- Overview of the human digestive system
- Processes involved in the digestion and absorption of macronutrients in humans
- Processes involved in the absorption and utilisation of vitamins and minerals
- Enzymes and transporters involved in digestion and the absorption of nutrients

Food is one of the fundamental requirements of human beings. It provides the energy and nutrients needed for the normal functioning of the body. The nutrients are present in a complex matrix in foods. The human body cells cannot absorb the nutrients as such, and the ingested food needs to be processed and converted into components that can be utilised by the body. This process of breaking down of complex food molecules into simple usable forms that can be absorbed into the bloodstream and dispersed throughout the body is called **digestion**. Food remnants that are not absorbed after digestion are excreted out of the body as faeces.

The three major bio-macromolecules in food that serve as nutrients are carbohydrates, proteins and fats. In addition, vitamins, minerals and water are also required by the body. Vitamins and inorganic mineral elements are generally required in small amounts for a variety of biochemical functions. The water that we drink prevents dehydration of the body, and is also necessary for human metabolism. The digestive process involves the breakdown of dietary carbohydrates, mostly consisting of polysaccharides to monosacchrides, dietary proteins to amino acids, dipeptides or tripeptides, and dietary fats, largely consisting of fatty acids esterified to glycerol (**triacyglycerols**) to fatty acids and glycerol. The entire digestive process in humans occurs in the **gastrointestinal tract (GIT)**, also referred to as the **digestive tract**, the **alimentary canal** or the **gut**.

Let us learn a little more about the human digestive system.

THE HUMAN DIGESTIVE SYSTEM

The GI, which is continuous, starts from the mouth, goes through the oesophagus and leads to the stomach, small intestine and large intestine. It ends in the rectum, from where the undigested wastes exit through the anus. The entire tract is associated with accessory organs and glands that aid in digestion. These include the teeth, tongue, salivary glands, liver, and pancreas (Figure 11.1).

The process of digestion begins in the mouth. Here, the teeth and tongue work in combination to facilitate chewing (**mastication**) of ingested food particles and mixing it with the saliva. The saliva contains antibacterial compounds, electrolytes (Na^+,K^+,Cl^-,HCO_3^-), and digestive enzymes **salivary α-amylase** (secreted by the salivary glands) and **lingual lipase** (secreted by glands present on the tongue). The chemical process of digestion is started with the hydrolytic action of the digestive enzymes. Together, the teeth, tongue and saliva aid in the wetting and homogenising of food, ultimately propelling it into the oesophagus. The oesophagus is a muscular tube extending from the throat to the stomach. Through a series of muscular contractions (**peristalsis**), the oesophagus delivers food to the stomach.

> The type of food ingested dictates the rate at which it is digested and emptied by the stomach. Food rich in carbohydrates leaves the stomach in a few hours. Protein-rich food leaves more slowly, and emptying is the slowest after a meal rich in fats.

The stomach is a strong, muscular, sac-like organ that acts as a temporary food-holding station for four to five hours. The glands within the stomach secrete **gastric juice**, which is primarily a mixture of hydrochloric acid and several digestive enzymes (**pepsin and lipase**). The hydrochloric acid in gastric juice kills harmful bacteria, provides the necessary pH for enzymatic action, and stimulates the flow of bile. In the stomach, food mixes thoroughly with the gastric juice through the churning movements of its muscular wall, resulting in the formation of a semi-fluid mixture called **chyme,** and the process of breaking down of food continues. To prevent any damage to the stomach itself, its surface is lined with **mucosal cells** that secrete a protective slimy substance called **mucus**. The chyme is transported from the stomach to the next stop, the **small intestine**.

The small intestine is a coiled tube comprising three segments: **duodenum**, **jejunum** and **ileum**. As the chyme enters the duodenum from the stomach, the duodenal lining stimulates the release of bile from the **gall bladder** (storage organ for bile) and pancreatic juice from the **pancreas**. Bile aids in the emulsification of fats, that is, the breakdown of fats into micellar solution, and also activates lipases. The pancreatic juice contains several digestive enzymes that further break the food particles in chyme. Peristalsis also occurs in this organ, helping in the movement of chyme and its mixing with the digestive secretions. It is in the small intestine that the bulk of the nutrients are digested and absorbed. The duodenum and jejunum are mainly responsible for the breakdown of food particles, whereas in the ileum, it is mainly the absorption of nutrients that takes place, into either the lymph or the bloodstream, for dispersal to other parts of the body. The leftover material is 'waste', and enters the **large intestine**.

The large intestine, also called **colon,** has the principal function of storage and fermentation of indigestible material. It consists of four parts: the ascending colon, the transverse colon, the descending colon, and the sigmoid colon. Here, any remaining water left in the food waste is absorbed back, and the remaining waste is further compressed for excretion from the body.

The innermost layer of cells lining the lumen of the alimentary canal is called **mucosa,** and the cells are referred to as mucosal cells. The mucosal cells in the small intestine are called **enterocytes**. The mucosal cell layer forms irregular folds (**rugae**) in the stomach, and small finger-like folding called **villi** in the small intestine. A single villus is a finger-like projection containing a network of capillaries and a lymphatic vessel called **lacteal**. The free edges of the epithelial cells lining villi produce numerous microscopic projections known as **microvilli**. The microvilli make up the **brush border membrane**. The main aim of such modifications is to tremendously increase the surface area for absorption. The mucosal epithelium has **goblet cells** that secrete mucus, which is responsible for lubrication. The secretions of brush border cells and the goblet cells of the mucosa together constitute the intestinal juice.

ABSORPTION OF NUTRIENTS

The intestinal epithelial cells are majorly involved in the absorption of nutrients, electrolytes and vitamins. These cells are said to be polarised, that is, they have two distinct membrane sides or domains, which have different morphological appearance, membrane composition, and complement of enzymes and transporters. The **apical** or **brush border** membrane facing the lumen is extensively folded into **microvilli,** whereas the other side or the **basolateral membrane** is in contact with blood capillaries and lymph vessels. The brush border membrane is specialised for the terminal digestion of nutrients using a set of digestive enzymes present on its surface, and the absorption of nutrients through transporters or channels for monosaccharides, amino acids, peptides, fatty acids, cholesterol, and electrolytes. After absorption through the brush border membrane, the nutrient molecules pass through cytosol of enterocytes and exit through the basolateral membrane into the blood or lymph. The basolateral membrane possesses transporters necessary for the exit of absorbed nutrients. In this manner, the digested food becomes available to all the cells of the body.

The absorption of nutrients is carried out by two possible mechanisms:

1. **Diffusion**: In this process, the nutrient molecule moves from a region of high concentration to a region of low concentration (**concentration gradient**) without an input of metabolic energy. Here, the molecule in aqueous solution on one side of the membrane crosses the cell membrane and goes into the aqueous solution on the opposite side. The rate of diffusion is directly proportional to the concentration gradient of the molecule across the membrane. Monosaccharides, amino acids, fatty acids, and glycerol diffuse slowly along their concentration gradients into enterocytes from the intestinal lumen. Unlike **simple diffusion, carrier-mediated or facilitated diffusion** is also seen across a biological membrane. This type of diffusion is dependent on specific membrane protein transporters.
2. **Active transport:** This type of transport requires an input of metabolic energy, and is faster than simple diffusion. The energy required for the transport of a molecule across the membrane is sometimes derived from the coupled hydrolysis of ATP (adenosine triphosphate). Monosaccharides, amino acids, fatty acids, and glycerol may be actively transported into the enterocytes through transporters. Disaccharides, di- and tripeptides are also actively transported.

Let us learn about the mechanisms of digestion and the absorption of major nutrients. Let us first look at the major digestive enzymes to have an overview.

DIGESTION OF CARBOHYDRATES

Dietary carbohydrates generally make 50–60 per cent of the total daily caloric intake of humans, and consist of mono-, di- and polysaccharides. The major carbohydrates in the diet include sucrose and lactose (disaccharides) and starch (polysaccharide). The disaccharides require the activity of the intestinal brush border enzymes of the small intestine for hydrolysis into monosaccharides, whereas the hydrolysis of polysaccharides is dependent on both pancreatic amylase and the intestinal brush border enzymes for digestion. Monosaccharides such as glucose, galactose and fructose are directly absorbed across the intestinal epithelial cells.

Starch, a major nutrient, is a plant polysaccharide which forms 50–60 per cent of the total carbohydrates consumed. Starch is composed of the straight chain glucose polymer **amylose** (with α-1,4-glycosidic linkages) and the branched glucose polymer **amylopectin** (with α-1,6-glycosidic linkages). Glycogen is the storage polysaccharide in animals, and has a more branched structure than starch.

The hydrolysis of starch and glycogen is catalysed by salivary and pancreatic α-amylases, which are endosaccharidases present in saliva and pancreatic juice, respectively. These two α-amylases are specific for internal α-1,4 glycosidic bonds, and do not act on α-1,6 glycosidic bonds or α-1,4 glycosidic bonds next to the branch points or at the ends. The collective action of α-amylases result in the formation of dextrins, and subsequently a mixture of glucose, maltose, isomaltose (disaccharide same as maltose, but with α-[1→6] linkage instead of α-[1→4] linkage between glucose units), trisaccharides (like maltotrioses), oligosaccharides, and α-limit dextrins (oligosaccharides with branch points) is obtained (Figure 11.1). The outer portion of the brush border, that is, the membrane of the microvilli of intestinal epithelial cells, contains several disaccharidases, which further hydrolyse the end products of pancreatic α-amylase digestion (Table 11.1).

Table 11.1: Principal Digestive Enzymes

Enzyme	*Substrate*	*Enzymatic Action or Products*
In mouth		
Salivary-α-amylase	Starch	Cleaves internal (α1→4) glycosidic linkages to form α-limit dextrins, maltotriose and maltose
Lingual lipase	Triacylglycerols	Fatty acids and 1,2-diacylglycerols
In Stomach		

Table 11.1 contd

Table 11.1 contd

Enzyme	*Substrate*	*Enzymatic Action or Products*
Pepsin	Proteins, polypeptides	Hydrolyzes peptide bonds on the amino-terminal side of the aromatic amino acids
Gastric lipase	Triacylglycerols	Fatty acids and glycerol
In Small Intestine		
Trypsin	Proteins, polypeptides	Peptide bond cleavage on the carboxyl side of basic amino acids
Chymotrypsin	Proteins, polypeptides	Peptide bond cleavage on the carboxyl side of aromatic amino acids
Elastase	Elastin, other proteins	Peptide bond cleavage on the carboxyl side of aliphatic amino acids
Pancreatic lipase	Triacylglycerols	Fatty acids and monoacylglycerols
Bile-salt acid lipase	Cholesteryl esters	Cholesterol
Pancreatic α–amylase	Starch	Cleaves internal (α1→4) glycosidic linkages to form α-limit dextrins, maltotriose and maltose
Phospholipase A_2	Glycerophospholipids	Free fatty acids, lysophospholipids
Aminopeptidase	Polypeptides	Hydrolyzes successive amino terminal residues from peptides
Carboxypeptidase	Polypeptides	Hydrolyzes successive carboxyl terminal residues from peptides
Endopeptidase	Polypeptides	Hydrolyzes amino acid residues in mid-portion of the peptide
Dipeptidase	Dipeptides	Two amino acids
Maltase	Maltose, maltotriose, α-dextrins	Glucose
Lactase	Lactose	Galactose and glucose
Sucrase	Sucrose	Fructose and glucose
Inside Intestinal Mucosal Cells		
Peptidases	Dipeptides, tripeptides, tetrapeptides	Amino acids

Source: Adapted from Ganong 2005.

Figure 11.1: Digested End Products of Carbohydrates in the Lumen of Small Intestine

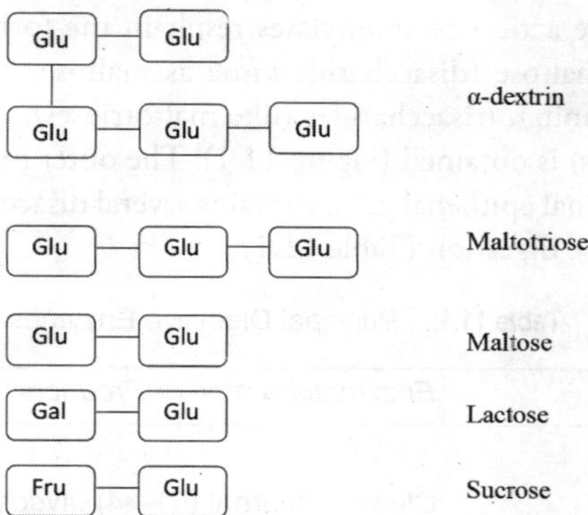

Note: Each rounded rectangle represents a hexose molecule.
Glu = glucose; Fru = fructose; Gal = galactose.
Source: Adapted from Ganong 2005.

Maltase, sucrase-isomaltase (a bifunctional enzyme hydrolysing both sucrose and isomaltose), sucrase, and lactase are disaccharidases that cleave one monosaccharide at a time from the oligosaccharides, or hydrolyse the disaccharides into monsaccharides. A special disaccharidase enzyme, trehalase, is present, which acts on trehalose, a disaccharide consisting of glucose units linked by α-(1$\rightarrow$1) linkage, which occurs in young mushrooms. The combined action of α-amylases and brush border membrane enzymes generates monosaccharides, which ultimately get absorbed (Figure 11.2).

Figure 11.2: Steps Involved in Carbohydrate Digestion with Important Enzymes to Yield Hexoses as Final Products

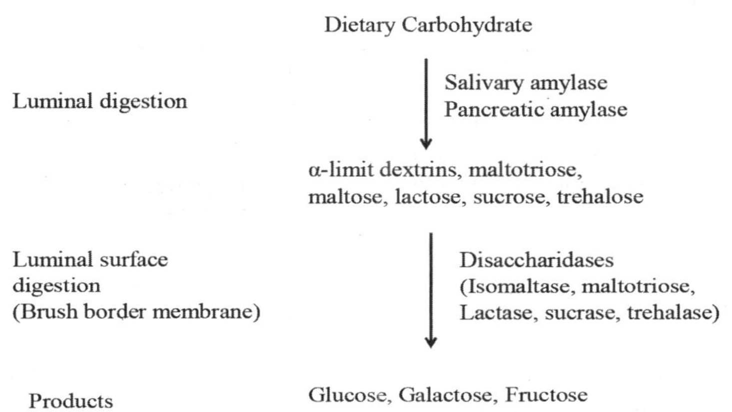

ABSORPTION OF MONOSACCHARIDES

Glucose, galactose and fructose, produced from the digestion of complex carbohydrates, are absorbed through two monosaccharide transporters present in the small intestine.

> The transport of glucose depends on the concentration of Na^+ in the intestinal lumen. A high Na^+ concentration on the mucosal surface of the cell facilitates, while a low concentration inhibits, sugar transport into the epithelial cells. This is because glucose and Na^+ have the same cotransporter, the SGLT1, Na^+-glucose cotransporter.

A sodium glucose transporter (**SGLT1**) mediates the active uptake of glucose and galactose into cells. The SGLT1 transporter is coupled to the Na^+-K^+ pump, and this allows glucose and galactose to be transported against their concentration gradients (Figure 11.3).

Figure 11.3: Glucose, Fructose and Galactose Transport across the Intestinal Epithelium

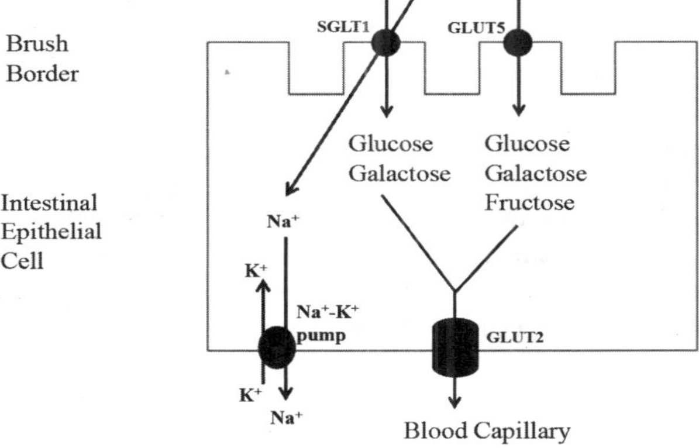

A sodium-independent glucose transporter (**GLUT5**) mediates the transport of glucose, galactose and fructose along their concentration gradient. Fructose and sugar alcohols are only absorbed down their concentration gradient, and an increased dietary intake of any of these results in their accumulation in the intestinal lumen, leading to bacterial fermentation. Bacterial fermentation results in the formation of gas and diarrhoea, thus causing discomfort.

The absorbed sugars in the enterocytes easily exit into the bloodstream through the **GLUT2** transporter.

LACTOSE INTOLERANCE

> The undigested lactose is fermented by bacteria in the colon, producing hydrogen gas, a portion of which is absorbed into the blood and exhaled in the breath. To diagnose lactose maldigestion, a breath hydrogen test is performed to estimate hydrogen levels in the breath.

Lactose intolerance is defined as the inability or decreased ability to digest lactose, a sugar found in milk and its products. This is the result of a deficiency of the **lactase** enzyme, and is a common condition usually experienced after the age of six, with increased incidence in adulthood and old age. The deficiency has been attributed to a genetic defect, a physiological decline of lactase with age, or due to injuries to the small intestine. The deficiency manifests itself as an inability to tolerate milk, with symptoms of bloating, gas, abdominal pain, and diarrhoea.

Even though the body's ability to produce lactase cannot be changed, the symptoms of lactose intolerance can be effectively managed with certain dietary changes. The introduction of small amounts of milk and milk products, or taking them with meals help people to adapt better, with fewer symptoms. Such individuals can tolerate yogurt, where lactose gets hydrolysed during the fermentation process of making yogurt. The intake of lactose-free milk, lactose-reduced products, or the use of commercially available lactase enzyme tablets can also improve the symptoms of people with lactose intolerance.

DIGESTION OF PROTEINS

The digestion of proteins is brought about by a plethora of proteolytic enzymes, each specific for peptide bonds between different amino acids (Figure 11.4). **Endopeptidases** attack internal bonds throughout the entire protein molecule to yield a number of peptide fragments. Pepsin and proteases (trypsin, chymotrypsin and elastase) present in the gastric and pancreatic juices, respectively, cleave the polypeptides into oligopeptides and amino acids. A special set of enzymes called **exopeptidases** remove one amino acid at a time from either the carboxyl end (carboxypeptidases) or the amino end (aminopeptidases). Endopeptidases act first, and this results in the breakdown of the protein molecule into smaller fragments, which can then be efficiently acted upon by exopeptidases. Dipeptidases present in the brush border of intestinal mucosal cells act on dipeptides that are not hydrolysed by exopeptidases.

> The powerful protein-splitting enzymes of pancreatic juice are secreted as inactive zymogens, so as to prevent any disruption and digestion of pancreatic tissues.

All the pancreatic proteases are secreted as inactive **zymogens,** where the active site of the enzyme is concealed by a small peptide chain, which is removed for activation by hydrolysis (Table 11.2). Pepsinogen is activated to pepsin by the action of gastric juice, and through autocatalysis by the activated pepsin in the stomach. The zymogen trypsinogen is cleaved by enteropeptidase to form the active trypsin. Trypsin then further catalyses the activation of other zymogens, for instance chymotrypsinogen to chymotrypsin, proelastase to elastase, procarboxypeptidase to carboxypeptidase, and proaminopeptidase to aminopeptidase.

Figure 11.4: Steps Involved in Protein Digestion to Yield Amino Acids and Small Peptides

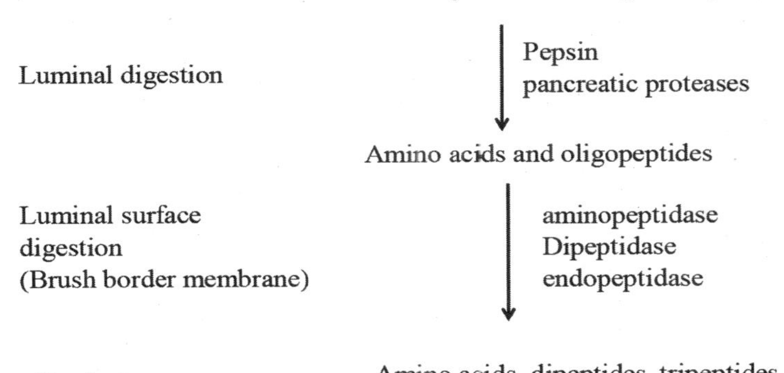

Table 11.2: Principal Brush-Border Membrane Enzymes of the Small Intestine

Carbohydrate (Substrate)	*Brush-Border Membrane Enzymes*	*Monosaccharide (Products)*
Amylopectin	Amylase and Isomaltase	Glucose
Amylose	Amylase	Glucose
Sucrose	Sucrase	Glucose and fructose
Lactose	Lactase	Glucose and galactose
Maltose	Maltase	Glucose
Isomaltose, α-limit dextrin	Isomaltase	Glucose
Trehalose	Trehalase	Glucose

Table 11.3: Peptidases Involved in Protein Digestion

Proenzyme	*Activator*	*Active Enzyme*	*Action*	*Products*
Pepsinogen A	HCl (gastric juice) and autoactivation by pepsin	Pepsin	Endopeptidase	Large peptide fragments and free amino acids
Trypsinogen	Trypsin	Enteropeptidase, Trypsin	Endopeptidase	Oligopeptides (2–6 amino acids)
Chymotrypsinogen	Trypsin	Chymotrypsin	Endopeptidase	Oligopeptides (2–6 amino acids)
Proelastase	Trypsin	Elastase	Endopeptidase	Oligopeptides (2–6 amino acids)
Procarboxypeptidase A	Trypsin	Carboxypeptidase A	Exopeptidase	Free amino acids
Procarboxypeptidase B	Trypsin	Carboxypeptidase B	Exopeptidase	Free amino acids
Aminopeptidase	-	-	Exopeptidase	Free amino acids

Source: Goodman 2010.

Absorption of Free Amino Acids and Small Peptides

The combined action of endopeptidases and exopeptidases results in a mixture of free amino acids and di- and tripeptides, which get absorbed across the intestinal mucosal cells through various specific amino acid or peptide transport systems (Figure 11.5). Depending on the nature of side chains of amino acids, there are specific transporters for different amino

Figure 11.5: Mechanism of Absorption of Amino Acids, Dipeptides and Tripeptides across Intestinal Epithelium

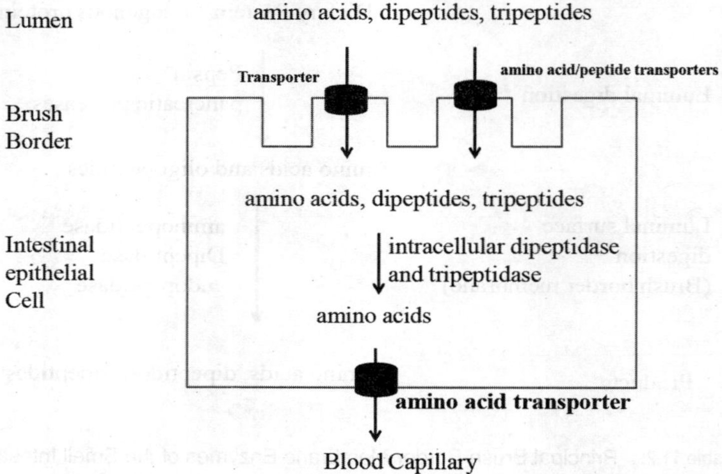

acids. Dipeptides and tripeptides that enter the brush border of the intestinal mucosal cells are further hydrolysed to free amino acids by the action of intracellular peptidases. The free amino acids generated exit into the hepatic portal vein through amino acid transporters. Comparatively large peptides are absorbed directly, either through mucosal epithelial cells (transcellular) or through tight junctions between the epithelial cells (paracellular). Some such large peptides evoke an antibody response in the body, and this is the reason for allergic reactions to certain food items.

DIGESTION OF LIPIDS

More than 90 per cent of the daily lipid diet of an adult human primarily consists of triacylglycerols. Phospholipids, cholesterol, cholesteryl esters, and free fatty acids comprise the rest of the lipids in the diet. Lipids are poorly soluble in water, and this poses a problem for both digestion and absorption. This is circumvented by the solubilisation of lipids by detergents (bile acids) to form very small droplets called **micelles** before absorption.

The initiation of lipid digestion starts in the mouth by the **lingual lipase.** The enzyme continues its action in the stomach along with **gastric lipase**, cleaving the *sn*-3 ester bond to form 1,2-diacylglycerols and free fatty acids. These products combine with bile salts to form emulsion droplets (Figure 11.6). Another major enzyme for the hydrolysis of triacylglycerol is **pancreatic lipase,** which is secreted into the small intestine in its active form. Pancreatic lipase also requires an additional pancreatic protein, **colipase,** for its activity. Pancreatic lipase hydrolyses the fatty acids present at 1 and 3 positions in triacylglycerol to produce free fatty acids and **2-monoacylglycerol** (Figure 11.7).

Figure 11.6: Steps Involved in Lipid Digestion

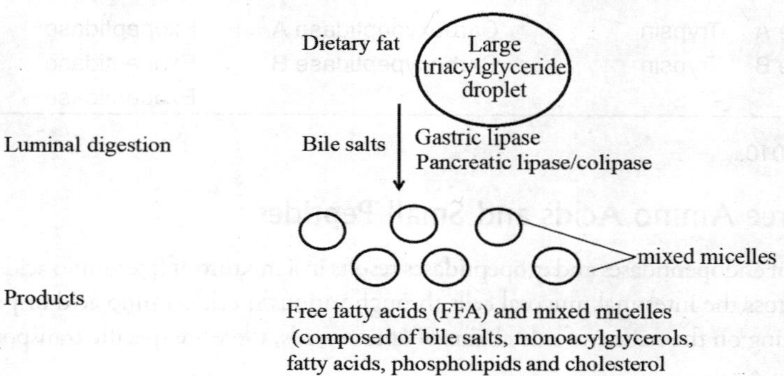

Figure 11.7: Lipase Action on Triacylglycerol

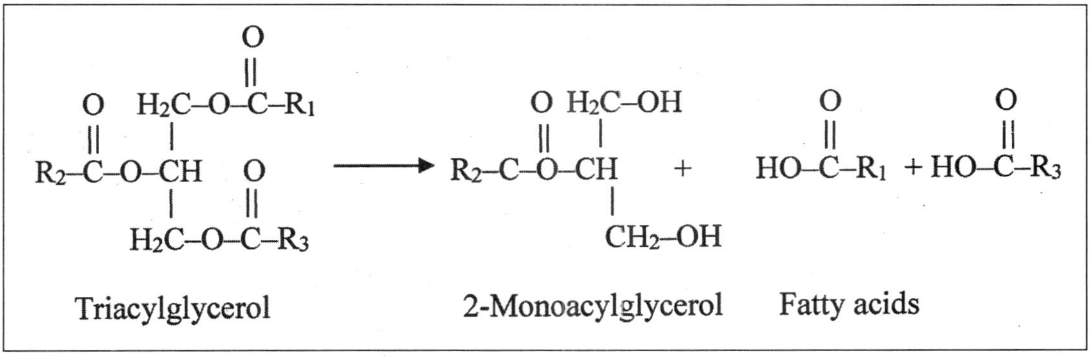

$$\underset{\text{Triacylglycerol}}{\begin{array}{l} \quad\quad\quad\; H_2C{-}O{-}\overset{O}{\overset{\|}{C}}{-}R_1 \\ \quad\quad\quad\;\; | \\ R_2{-}\overset{O}{\overset{\|}{C}}{-}O{-}CH \\ \quad\quad\quad\;\; | \\ \quad\quad\quad\; H_2C{-}O{-}\overset{O}{\overset{\|}{C}}{-}R_3 \end{array}} \longrightarrow \underset{\text{2-Monoacylglycerol}}{\begin{array}{l} \quad\quad\quad\; H_2C{-}OH \\ \quad\quad\quad\;\; | \\ R_2{-}\overset{O}{\overset{\|}{C}}{-}O{-}CH \\ \quad\quad\quad\;\; | \\ \quad\quad\quad\; CH_2{-}OH \end{array}} + \underset{\text{Fatty acids}}{HO{-}\overset{O}{\overset{\|}{C}}{-}R_1 + HO{-}\overset{O}{\overset{\|}{C}}{-}R_3}$$

Note: R is the hydrocarbon chain.

Another pancreatic lipase that gets activated by bile salts is **bile-salt activated lipase**, which catalyses the hydrolysis of cholesteryl esters, esters of fat-soluble vitamins and phospholipids, as well as triglycerides. Most of the dietary cholesterol is in the form of cholesteryl esters, and **cholesteryl ester hydrolase** present in pancreas also hydrolyses these esters in the intestinal lumen.

> Short-chain fatty acids (SCFAs) are produced physiologically in the colon and then absorbed from it. They are formed from the action of colonic bacteria on complex carbohydrates, resistant starches, and other components of dietary fibre, that is, the material that escapes digestion in the upper GIT and enters colon.

The digested products of lipids then combine with bile salts to form micellar solution or a microemulsion. As micelles are soluble, they act as major vehicles for ferrying the digested products of lipids through the aqueous environment of the intestinal lumen to the mucosal cells for absorption. The bile salts are transported back to the liver through the portal vein. The liver then re-secretes them into the intestinal lumen in the form of bile juice. This is known as **enterohepatic circulation.**

Absorption of Lipids

Inside the intestinal epithelial cells, the 2-monoacylglycerols get reacylated through the monoacylglycerol pathway to form triacylglycerols. Glycerol formed in the intestinal lumen is absorbed into the portal vein. However, glycerol formed in the intestinal epithelial cells is also used for synthesising triacylglycerols through the phosphatidic acid pathway.

Short and medium chain-length fatty acids ($\leq$ 10 carbon atoms) pass into the portal vein. Long-chain fatty acids and their monoacylglycerols are converted into triacylglycerols, which, together with cholesteryl esters, phospholipids and apolipoproteins, form globules called **chylomicrons** (Figure 11.8). Chylomicrons are exocytosed (movement of molecules out of the cell through plasma membrane) into intestinal lymph vessels, from where they subsequently enter the bloodstream via the thoracic duct (Figure 11.9).

Absorption of Phospholipids

The normal dietary intake of phospholipids (PL) is 2–8 grams per day, which represents 1–10 per cent of the total daily fat intake. The most common PL in food is phosphatidylcholine (PC) or lecithin, while other PLs, such as phosphatidylethanolamine (PE), phosphatidylserine (PS) and phosphatidylinositol (PI), are present in much smaller amounts. Dietary PC is almost completely absorbed (>90 per cent) by the human intestine. PL digestion starts in the small intestine, as lingual and gastric lipases cannot hydrolyse PC. The chemical breakdown of PLs is primarily dependent on the pancreatic phospholipase A2 (PLA_2). PLA_2 is secreted as a zymogen and gets activated by trypsin cleavage, and it also requires the presence of bile salts to show its activity. It interacts with PLs to yield free fatty acid and lysoPC (lysolecithin). Both components are taken up by the mucosal cell and resecreted and transported within chylomicrons as newly-formed PL or triglyceride.

Figure 11.8: Chylomicron Carrying Triglycerides

Triglycerides

Embedded apolipoproteins

Phospholipid

Source: OpenStax College. Lipid Metabolism, Connexions Website. http://cnx.org/content/m46462/1.3/

Figure 11.9: Lipid Absorption, Reconstitution of Triacylglycerols, and Formation of Chylomicrons

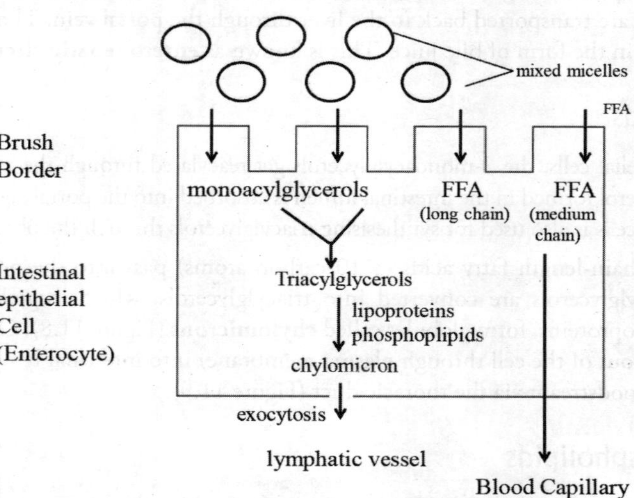

Absorption of Cholesterol

Intestinal absorption of cholesterol is important due to its clinical relevance. Of the total cholesterol passing through the small intestine, only half is absorbed, and the rest is eliminated in the faeces. The absorption of cholesterol readily occurs from the small intestine with the help of bile salts and pancreatic juice. Almost all the absorbed cholesterol gets incorporated into chylomicrons, which then enter the lymphatic system. Some non-absorbable plant sterols, like those present in soybeans, reduce the absorption of cholesterol, probably by competing with cholesterol for esterification with fatty acids.

It is time to learn about the digestion and utilisation of vitamins and minerals.

DIGESTION AND ABSORPTION OF VITAMINS AND MINERALS

Digestion of food results in the release of vitamins and minerals that must be absorbed and utilised. Various factors influence the absorption of vitamins and minerals. The fat-soluble vitamins are released from their association with protein by the acidic gastric juice or by proteolysis. Fat-soluble vitamins associate with other lipid digested products into micelles, which ferry them to intestinal epithelial cells for uptake by simple diffusion or via transporters. Once inside, they combine with lipids, forming chylomicrons, which are later transported out into lymph via exocytosis. The water-soluble vitamins and most mineral salts are absorbed in the small intestine either by active transport or by carrier-mediated diffusion.

Absorption of Vitamin A

> The HCl present in the stomach helps in the release of minerals and vitamins bound to dietary proteins by causing the unfolding of protein molecules. Low HCl can prevent the release of minerals from food component or vitamin supplements.

Vitamin A is essential for many intrinsic processes, especially in eye vision. The active form of vitamin A is **retinol**, which is rarely found in foods. However, dietary precursors of retinol are present in the human diet, which can be cleaved to yield retinol in the body. The precursors of retinol are actually fatty acid retinyl esters commonly found in foods of animal origin, like egg yolks, liver, fish, whole milk, and butter. Plants, however, contain carotenoids (most commonly beta-carotene), which can be converted to retinol inside the human body.

The principal site of vitamin A absorption from the diet is the intestine. The vitamin A esters present in food are hydrolysed to fatty acids and the free vitamin. The free vitamin is then incorporated into micelles within the intestinal lumen, and absorbed across the brush border into the enterocytes. Inside the enterocyte, the precursors of vitamin A are converted to active forms of vitamin A, packaged into chylomicrons and transported throughout the body through the lymphatic system.

Absorption of Folate

Folate is required by the human body for numerous metabolic functions like biosynthesis of RNA and DNA and DNA repair, which are essential for maintaining the integrity of human cells. Dietary folates exist as polyglutamates, the most common being **folate polyglutamate,** which is largely available in spinach, beans and liver. The absorption of folate requires deconjugation, that is, the removal of glutamate residues. Deconjugation is carried out by folate conjugase, an exopeptidase present in brush border which catalyses stepwise hydrolysis of glutamate residues of the polyglutamate chain. Subsequently, folate is transported into the intestinal mucosal cells via a transporter for absorption.

Absorption of Cobalamine (vitamin B_{12})

Cobalamine or vitamin $B_{12,}$ like others, is also released from the ingested protein in the stomach. The now-free vitamin B_{12} is transported and absorbed with the help of two vitamin B_{12} binding proteins, **haptocorrin** and **intrinsic factor,** present in the stomach. The deficiency of intrinsic factor or the absence of gastric acid causes pernicious anaemia. Consequently, vitamin B_{12} absorption is markedly reduced, and vitamin B_{12} deficiency develops.

Absorption of Calcium

The principal factor affecting calcium transport and absorption in the intestine is vitamin D. There are primarily three hormones intricately involved in maintaining calcium metabolism in the body. The first is a steroid hormone, **1,25-dihydrocholecalciferol,** formed from vitamin D. Its main action is to enhance calcium absorption from

Lead is quite pernicious to iron metabolism. Lead is taken up by iron absorption machinery and blocks iron through competitive inhibition. Also, lead interferes with iron-dependent heme biosynthesis. Thus, in children lead not only produces anaemia, but can also cause impaired development.

the small intestine. The second is **parathyroid hormone (PTH),** released by the parathyroid gland. This hormone induces the synthesis of **calcitriol**, the biologically active form of vitamin D, whenever the blood serum calcium concentration becomes low. The principal role of calcitriol is to maintain the blood calcium level. Calcitriol accomplishes this in three ways: it increases the absorption of dietary calcium in the small intestine, it increases the mobilisation of calcium from bone into blood, and it increases the reabsorption of calcium by the kidneys. The third hormone is **calcitonin**, primarily secreted by the thyroid gland. Its main function is to decrease calcium loss from the bones whenever the blood calcium concentration is high. All three hormones work together as a team to maintain the calcium level in the body fluids.

In addition, vitamin D induces the formation of **calbindins** (calcium binding proteins) and stimulates the synthesis of epithelial calcium channels and the plasma membrane calcium pumps. All this enhances the transport and absorption of calcium.

The absorption of calcium is reduced in the presence of high concentrations of fatty acids in the intestinal lumen, which form insoluble calcium salts. Oxalate present in certain foods like green leafy vegetables reduces calcium absorption by precipitating intestinal calcium as insoluble calcium oxalate. Phytic acid (inositol hexaphosphate) found in whole grain cereals forms insoluble calcium salts (phytia) in the intestine, thus preventing calcium absorption in the intestine.

Absorption of Iron

Absorption of iron is a tightly regulated process in the human body. This is particularly important as excess iron, once absorbed in the body, cannot be eliminated easily. Consequently, controlling the rate of intestinal iron absorption can regulate the body iron stores. The absorption is enhanced in iron-deficient individuals, whereas absorption is reduced in individuals with an iron overload.

There are two forms of dietary iron: **heme** and **non-heme**. In animal food, like red meat, fish and poultry, the iron is often attached to proteins called hemoproteins, and this form of iron is referred to as heme iron. In plant foods such as vegetables, grains, lentils, beans, and iron-fortified breakfast cereals, iron is not attached to heme proteins and is classified as non-heme iron. Heme iron is highly bioavailable as it gets readily absorbed, while non-heme iron is relatively poorly absorbed.

Dietary iron, which is mostly in the ferric state (Fe^{3+}), enters the stomach via the oesophagus. Gastric acid enhances the solubility of ferric iron and helps it to form complexes with solubilising agents such as ascorbic acid and other substances that aid in its reduction to the ferrous state (Fe^{2+}). The importance of this step is indicated by the fact that iron in ferrous form can be easily transferred into enterocytes. In addition, a brush border enzyme of the enterocyte, named **ferric reductase,** converts the ferric iron into ferrous iron. Thus, all the ferrous iron formed in the intestinal lumen is transported into enterocytes through an iron transporter (**DMT1**).

Inside enterocytes, the ferrous ion is stored bound to the protein apoferritin to form **ferritin**. When the ferritin in the cell gets saturated with iron, no more iron can enter the cells. Iron leaves the ferritin of the mucosal cell and enters the blood by getting associated with the iron transport protein in plasma, **transferrin**. The moment transferrin is saturated with iron, any more iron left in the intestinal mucosal cells cannot be used, and gets lost. This is why only about 3–8 per cent of the amount of ingested iron is normally absorbed by the body.

Heme iron is absorbed by a completely different mechanism than non-heme iron. Heme is transported into the enterocyte by a separate heme transporter (**HT**), where the **heme oxygenase** enzyme releases Fe^{2+} from the heme, making it readily available for binding to ferritin.

Various dietary factors affect the availability of iron for absorption. However, dietary factors appear to play a more significant role in non-heme iron absorption from plant foods than they do in heme iron absorption from animal foods. Ferric ions tend to form salt complexes with anions easily, and these are not readily absorbed. Ascorbic acid and citrate enhance the iron uptake by acting as solubilising agents and helping in the reduction of the insoluble ferric iron. Conversely, the absorption of iron gets inhibited by phytic acid, oxalates and tannins. Phytic acid is prominent in whole grain wheat and some other cereals, oxalates are found in green leafy vegetables, while tannins are found in tea. These compounds chelate iron, thereby preventing its uptake by the absorption machinery.

Absorption of Zinc

About 10–35 per cent of dietary zinc is absorbed from the digested food. The dietary zinc is exported into the intestinal cell through a zinc transporter present in the brush border membrane. The presence of dietary zinc induces the synthesis of a zinc-binding protein called **metallothionein**. Once bound, the complex containing zinc enters the blood circulation. Various factors, like the high intake of phytate and the presence of copper and iron (as they compete for absorption), decrease the absorption of zinc.

SUMMARY

- The process of conversion of complex food molecules into simple absorbable forms is called digestion, and is carried out by the gastrointestinal system in humans.
- The three major bio-macromolecules in food that serve as nutrients are carbohydrates (polysaccharides), proteins and fats (mainly triacylglycerols).
- The dietary carbohydrates, triacyglcerols and proteins are first hydrolysed to liberate their constituent monosaccharides, fatty acids and amino acids, respectively, before their absorption and utilisation.
- Vitamins and minerals, although required in small amounts, also need to be released from the complex food matrix before they can be absorbed or utilised.
- The process of digestion is carried out by soluble digestive enzymes secreted by the salivary glands, stomach and pancreas.
- The stomach stores food and mixes it thoroughly with the acidic gastric juice through churning movements, thus making digestion efficient and effective.
- The end products of digestion pass through the intestinal mucosa into the blood or lymph by the process of absorption.
- Absorption takes place by diffusion or active transport mechanisms, mostly in the small intestine.
- Pancreas is necessary for digestion as it releases a number of enzymes in the form of pancreatic juice.
- Liver plays an important role by secreting bile salts for efficient digestion and absorption of lipids.

KEY TERMS

Absorption: Here, uptake of end products of digestion through the wall of the intestine.

Amylase: A digestive enzyme produced largely by the salivary glands and pancreas, which converts starch and glycogen to simple sugars.

Bile: Liver secretion consisting of bile pigments, bile salts, cholesterol, and phospholipids required for the emulsification and digestion of dietary lipid.

Brush border: A dense microvilli covering formed by the plasma membrane present on the apical surface of intestinal mucosal cells.

Chylomicron: A lipoprotein particle consisting of triacylglycerols, phospholipids, cholesterol esters, fat-soluble vitamins, and proteins found in blood and lymph during the digestion of fat.

Chyme: It is a semi-fluid acidic mixture of ingested food and digestive secretions entering the small intestine from the stomach during digestion.

Digestion: The process of breakdown of complex food molecules into simple usable forms that can be absorbed into the bloodstream and dispersed throughout the body.

Enterocyte: The predominant cell lining the small intestinal mucosa.

Exocytosis: The movement of molecules out of the cell through the plasma membrane.

Heme iron: It is the iron occurring in the heme complex within haemoglobin and myoglobin, usually found in meat, poultry and fish.

Peptidase: An enzyme that hydrolyses the breakdown of peptides into its component amino acids.

Zymogen: Catalytically inactive protein precursor that becomes an active enzyme on limited proteolytic cleavage. It is also known as proenzyme.

EXERCISES

1. Discuss the digestion and absorption of carbohydrates.
2. Outline the processes occurring during the digestion of fats.
3. Describe how dietary fat is absorbed from the intestine into the bloodstream.
4. Describe the conversion of dietary protein into amino acids and small peptides in the intestine.
5. Discuss the role of vitamin D and hormones in the absorption of calcium.
6. Explain briefly how heme and non-heme iron are absorbed in the small intestine.

REFERENCES

Devlin, T. M., *Textbook of Biochemistry with Clinical Correlations*, USA: John Wiley and Sons Inc., 2011.

Ganong, W. F., *Review of Medical Physiology*, McGraw-Hill, 2005.

Goodman, B. E., 'Insights into Digestion and Absorption of Major Nutrients in Humans', *Adv Physiol Educ.* 34, 2010.

Heaney, R. P., 'Dairy Intake, Dietary Adequacy, and Lactose Intolerance', *Adv. Nutr.* 4, 2013, pp. 151–56.

Hoffbrand, A. V., 'Folate absorption', *J Clin Path.* 24, Suppl. (Roy. Coll. Path.) (5), 1971, pp. 66–76.

Holmes, R., 'Carbohydrate Digestion and Absorption', *J Clin Path.*24, Suppl. (Roy. Coll. Path.) (5), 1971, pp. 10–13.

ICMR,'Iron absorption and its implications on strategies to control iron deficiency anaemia', *ICMR Bulletin* 30(2), 2000.

Krebs, N. F., 'Overview of zinc absorption and excretion in the human gastrointestinal tract', *J. Nutr.* 130, 2000, pp. 1374S–1377S.

Milman, N., 'Intestinal Absorption of Folic Acid- New Physiologic and Molecular Aspects', *Indian J Med Res.* 136, 2012, pp. 725–28.

Murray, R. K., D. K. Granner, P. A. Mayes, and V. W. Rodwell, *Harper's Illustrated Biochemistry*, McGraw-Hill, 2008.

Wasserman, R. H., 'Vitamin D and the dual processes of intestinal calcium absorption', *J Nutr.* 134, 2004, pp. 3137–39.

West, E. S., W. R. Todd, H. S. Mason, and J. T. U. Bruggen, *Textbook of Biochmistry*, Macmillan Publishing Co. Inc., 1974.

12

METHODS OF COOKING

HIGHLIGHTS

- Objectives of cooking
- Methods of cooking
- Classification based on method of cooking
- Advantages and disadvantages of different methods of cooking
- Prevention of nutrient losses

OBJECTIVES OF COOKING

Cooking is perceived as both child's play and joy for adults.
Cooking done with care is an act of love.
Craig Claiborne

Food is one of the basic necessities of life. Although some food is eaten in the raw form, we mostly eat food in the cooked form. Have you thought about why it is necessary to cook food before we eat it? When we cook food, it enhances digestibility by breaking down complex nutrients into simpler forms, releases the necessary nutrients by freeing them from binding/inhibitory substances (like trypsin inhibitors in pulses and avidin in raw egg, which binds the vitamin biotin), destroys microbes (which are killed by heat), and gives the food an appealing colour, makes the texture either softer or crisper, enhances taste as the flavouring compounds are released, and hence generally improves palatability. Removal of moisture also concentrates nutrients and reduces the bulk in some foods, and hence more of these foods can be consumed at a time—for example, green leafy vegetables. Cooking involves combining different foods and ingredients to make a variety of dishes, different in texture and flavour. This makes food attractive and encourages us to eat.

However, cooking has its limitations. Heat-sensitive vitamins, like most B vitamins and vitamin C, are destroyed during cooking. Certain amino acids may also become unavailable as a result of chemical reactions during cooking.

METHODS OF COOKING FOOD

In order to cook food, we apply heat to it. Heat changes the complex chemical composition of raw food and converts it into a simpler form that can be utilised by the body. Let us now learn the various methods of applying heat using different mediums.

Heat is transferred to food through conduction, convection and radiation.

Conduction: In the culinary arts, conduction is a method of heat transfer where a piece of food is heated through direct contact with a hotter object like a hot pan. Conduction also occurs when heat is transferred from a hotter part of the food item to a cooler part.

Convection is broadly the movement of molecules through any fluid state, including liquid and gas. When water starts bubbling, these bubbles of hot water start rising to the surface. The surface heat is transferred from the hot water at the bottom to the cooler water at the top. At the same time, the cooler, denser water at the top sinks to the bottom, where it is then heated.

Radiation is the transfer of energy through waves of electromagnetic energy that travel rapidly through space. Radiation does not require direct contact between the energy source and food. When the waves travelling through space strike matter and are absorbed, they cause molecules in the matter to vibrate more rapidly, increasing the temperature. Two types of radiation are important in the kitchen—infrared and microwave.

CLASSIFICATION OF METHODS OF COOKING

Cooking methods can be classified on the basis of the medium used (Table 12.1).

Table 12.1: Classification of Methods of Cooking

Water Medium	*Oil Medium*	*Air Medium*	*Combination*
Boiling	Sauteing	Roasting	Braising
Simmering	Shallow frying	Grilling/Broiling	
Poaching	Deep frying	Toasting	
Stewing		Baking	
Blanching			
Steaming direct/indirect			
Pressure cooking			

We will now discuss each method, giving examples from everyday cookery.

Moist Heat Methods (Water Medium)

When water is used to transmit heat to the food to enable the cooking process, it is called moist cooking.

Boiling: Food is boiled by taking a pan of water and cooking food by immersing it in water and boiling it at 100°C, maintaining this temperature till the food is cooked. In boiling, you will see bubbles at the surface of the water, which break rapidly. The water is usually discarded or used in gravies. Water boils due to conduction and convection. Foods that are cooked using boiling are potato, rice, pasta, stock, and syrup.

Boiling is a simple method of cooking used on a daily basis, for example, making rice. Special utensils or equipment are not required for boiling, and you do not need to pay constant attention to the food during the process.

As the water used for boiling is usually discarded, the nutrients that leach out are lost. The loss can be minimised if the vegetables are boiled with their skin, or cut into big pieces. The nutrients lost in the water can be conserved if the water is used as stock for soups, or for making gravies. Boiling usually leads to a loss in colour and flavour as well, because both these leach out into the water. If the food is boiled for a long time or too vigorously, its texture also tends to get soft and mushy. Cooking food by boiling usually takes time, and hence considerable amounts of fuel is consumed.

Other methods conserve more nutrients, especially when the liquid in which the food is cooked is also used up.

Simmering: The food is immersed in liquid and cooked in a closed pan at a temperature below the boiling point (98°C). This is done to gently cook the food so that the cell tissues do not break due to friction. It is useful for food that takes long to cook, for example stock, soup, *kheer*, and meat. This method is especially used for fish curries so that the fish does not disintegrate while cooking. However, the method has its disadvantages. Due to the long cooking time, heat-sensitive nutrients are lost. A lot of fuel is also used.

Poaching: The method involves cooking in a small amount of liquid at a temperature of 80–85°C. This method is usually used for cooking eggs. Water is taken in a pan and kept simmering. The egg is broken and placed in a saucer, and slowly immersed into the water from the side. The egg is allowed to cook in the simmering water. Salt is added for taste, and acid, like vinegar, helps in coagulation and maintaining the shape of the cooked egg. In some cases, a ring mould is also kept in the simmering water into which the content of the egg is put, so as to retain the shape. Delicate foods like fish and fruit are also sometimes poached. It is a quick, as well as a fat-free method of cooking. However, poached foods tend to be very bland in taste. Water-soluble nutrients may also leach out into the water.

Stewing: It is a gentle method of cooking in a pan with a lid, into which the food is immersed in a small amount of liquid that covers the food partially. The liquid is allowed to boil and is maintained at 98°C. The steam inside the pan also cooks the food. This method of cooking is used for vegetables, meat and legumes, in the preparation of curries and stews. As the liquid used for cooking is not discarded, the nutrients, colour and flavour that leach out into the liquid are conserved, and the dishes are usually very flavourful. Some foods may take a long time to cook, and this may result in losses of heat-sensitive vitamins. Besides being time consuming, cooking by this method may also use up a lot of fuel.

Blanching: Immersing food in hot water for a few seconds and then cooling it under cold water is called blanching. It is usually done for foods that have to be frozen, for example peas, vegetables and fruits. This process inactivates the enzymes present naturally in foods and prevents the deterioration of food during freezing. It helps in preserving the natural colour of some vegetables. Tomatoes and almonds are usually blanched to remove the skin before use. Blanching also helps to reduce the microbial load of foods.

Steaming: Here, the food is cooked by steam. Steam is generated by boiling water, so that the food is completely surrounded by steam. Different kinds of steamers are used.

Wet steaming: The food comes into direct contact with steam and gets cooked, for example, *idlis*, when an *idli* maker or pressure cooker with moulds is used. This method can be used for steamed puddings, and snacks like *momos, dhokla*, etc.

Dry steaming: In this method, steam is used to provide heat to the container in which the food is cooked, without it coming into contact with the food. The steam is generated in a double boiler, which has two chambers. The one below contains water, which is heated to produce steam. The steam then heats the upper chamber and helps to cook the food placed in it slowly by supplying a moderate heat, for example, egg custard, milk. This helps in preventing the egg from curdling due to high heat, and prevents the scorching or burning of milk.

Steaming has the advantage of cooking faster than boiling, and also helps to conserve several nutrients. The colour and flavour of foods is also better retained by steaming as there is no leaching.

Figure 12.1: Different Methods of Steaming

Source: http://commons.wikimedia.org/wiki/File:Thi%C3%A8r%C3%A9_millet_couscous_1._sealing_steamer_with_millet_flour_paste.jpg

http://commons.wikimedia.org/wiki/File:Steamers.jpg

http://upload.wikimedia.org/wikipedia/commons/thumb/7/7a/Can-in-can_steaming.svg/220px-Can-in-can_steaming.svg.png

Waterless steaming: Here, steam is generated from within the food, which has some liquid mixture within it, for example cake. Food wrapped in banana leaves or aluminum foil is also cooked by this method.

Steamed vegetables retain their crisp texture, whereas foods like *idlis* and *dhoklas* acquire a soft, fluffy texture. Constant attention does not have to be paid to the food being steamed, and there is less chance of food being overcooked or burnt.

Pressure cooking: Usually, food is cooked at the boiling temperature of water. This takes time when we have to cook tough or hard foods like meat and pulses. So to shorten the cooking time, a pressure cooker is used; the principle here is to raise the boiling temperature of water by applying pressure. The temperature usually is about 120° C. Pressure cookers are typically made of aluminium or stainless steel. Aluminium pressure cookers may be stamped, polished, or anodised. Higher-quality stainless steel pressure cookers are made with heavy, three-layer, or copper-clad bottoms (heat spreader) for uniform heating, because stainless steel has a lower thermal conductivity. Some pressure cookers. have a non-stick interior

> Once the pressure is generated, food should be cooked on a low flame and the time noted from the first whistle. If the pressure cooker is releasing pressure frequently, there are chances of the food burning due to the quick evaporation of water as steam.

Figure 12.2: Parts of a Pressure Cooker

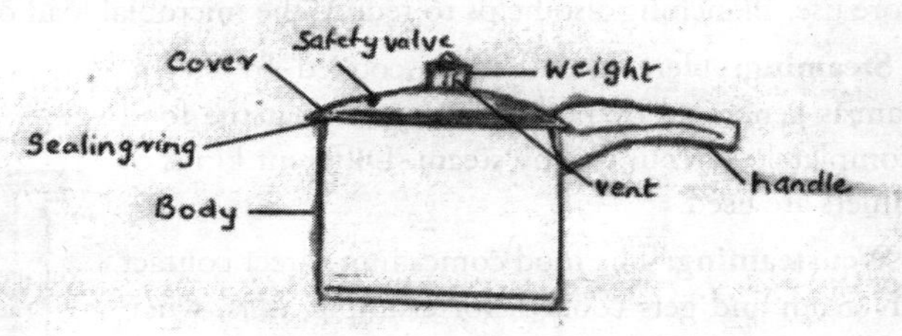

Pressure cookers have a lid with a nozzle and a safety valve. The lid is air-tight, and the water in the pan generates steam on heating. A weight is kept on the nozzle to build pressure and elevate the boiling point. Most pressure cookers have a working pressure setting of 1 standard atmosphere or 15 psi (pound force per square inch; this is a common unit of measurement for pressure). At this pressure, water boils at 121 °C (250 °F). When the pressure builds up to more than 15 psi, the weight lifts to let off steam, creating a whistling sound. The time taken for cooking is noted after the first whistle. Meat, legumes and potatoes are usually cooked in pressure cookers.

Among the moist methods used, pressure cooking has the advantage of cooking food in a shorter time, cooking it thoroughly, and also conserving nutrients and fuel. Although this method of cooking does not require constant attention and the chances of burning or scorching are less, care should be taken to not overcook the food. Precautions need to be taken while using a pressure cooker, otherwise accidents can happen. The safety valve and the vent pipe should be checked before each use. One should make sure that there are no food particles blocking the vent pipe. All the steam should subside before opening the lid of the cooker. The process can be hastened by keeping the pressure cooker under running water.

Fat as a Medium of Cooking

Sautéing: Just enough oil is used to cover the bottom of the pan and to coat the food lightly when foods like vegetables are tossed in it, and stirred with the help of a spatula. The pan may then be covered with a lid and the food allowed to cook in its own steam. The cooked food is slightly brown and moist in appearance. Several of the dry vegetable preparations in Indian cooking are prepared by this method.

> ***You get oily and soggy products if:***
> - the temperature of the oil is not hot enough;
> - if the same oil is repeatedly used for frying;
> - if the frying pan is overloaded, which brings down the temperature of the oil.

Frying: In this method, the medium of cooking is oil. The temperature at which food is cooked varies from 180–220° C. Cooking is faster, as food is exposed to a higher temperature.

In **shallow frying,** oil submerges only half of the product, and when browned, has to be turned over in order to brown the other half, for example, in *tikki* and *parantha.* Heat is transferred to the food by conduction from the heated pan it is in contact with, as well as from convection currents. Constant attention has to be paid to the product being fried, otherwise it can get scorched or burnt.

In **deep fat** frying, the food is immersed in hot oil to be cooked by convection currents. Generally, the oil has a smoking point, which indicates that the oil is hot. The products so cooked have a more uniform golden-brown colour, crisp texture and better flavour, compared to the products made by shallow fat frying. Although the amount of oil can be better controlled in shallow fat frying, if deep fat frying is done at the right temperature, the amount of fat absorbed by the food is very little as compared to the amount absorbed during shallow fat frying. To check when the oil has reached the correct temperature for frying, a small ball of the batter to be fried is dropped in the centre of the oil. If the ball rises quickly to the top, the oil is ready; if, on the other hand, it sinks to the bottom and takes a while to rise to the top, you will need to heat the oil a little more before frying. Foods cooked by deep fat frying include *samosas*, *bondas*, *pakoras*, French fries, chips, *mathri, kachori,* etc.

Overheating and heating the oil for a long time will decompose the oil. When oil begins to smoke, its chemical breakdown begins, and acrolein and free fatty acids are formed from glycerol. If oil is allowed to smoke further, then the acrolein formed causes irritation to the eye and the nostrils. This thermal breakdown is called pyrolysis. Oils are processed to make it solid by partial or total hydrogenation. Partial hydrogenation of vegetable oils has been the major source of dietary *trans* fatty acids. If oil is used for prolonged frying, it produces toxic aldehydes and other breakdown products that are harmful to health, and can even lead to cancer.

Recommended good practices for frying:

- Use minimal oil for sautéing.
- Use non-stick frying pans (Teflon coated) to minimise the oil used.
- Use oil with a high smoking point for frying to delay decomposition.
- Use only sufficient oil to immerse the product while frying.
- Do not continuously heat for more than four hours.
- Never mix the used oil with fresh oil.
- Avoid reusing the oil for deep fat frying.
- Oil that has once been used for frying can be used in cooking for sautéing, etc., provided it has not changed colour and has no suspended particles in it.
- Do not store heated oil for a long period. Remove any food particles that might have been left behind after frying, as these hasten the spoilage of oil.

Try to use oil rich in MUFA for daily cooking. Fat-soluble vitamins in vegetables are more bio-available when sautéed in a small amount of fat. For deep fat frying, groundnut oil, rice bran oil, and rapeseed oil are generally recommended. Avoid hydrogenated fats like *vanaspati* for deep frying, as these have trans fatty acids that are very harmful to health.

Braising: The word 'braising', which comes from the French word 'braiser', is a combination cooking method using both moist and dry heat; typically, the food is first seared at a high temperature, and then finished in a covered pot with a variable amount of liquid, resulting in a particular flavour. This method is used for cooking meat (both dry and gravy preparations). Typically, while making mutton curry, a combination of methods is used. Meat is sautéed in a little fat/oil so that it browns, and the protein coagulates. This helps in retaining the moisture /juice within the food. It is then stewed in water to soften it. Such a method of cooking helps to retain the flavour of the food. While making vermicelli *kheer,* the vermicelli is first roasted, and then cooked in simmering milk.

Dry Heat Methods (Air Medium)

Grilling/ Broiling: In this method, the food is placed above, below, or in between a hot surface, such as burning wood, charcoal, or heating elements. Food is cooked by radiation. The food is generally brown and dry. Constant attention is required to prevent charring. This is the method used in barbecues. Other foods cooked by this method include sweet potato, *papad,* corn on the cob, brinjal, etc. Broiling differs from roasting and baking, in that the food is turned during the process so as to cook one side at a time. Temperatures are higher for broiling than they are for roasting. Rotisseries are available to provide uniform heating. Toasting refers to keeping bread slices between two heated elements or under a grill, so as to brown them.

Pan roasting is when food is placed on a hot surface and roasted by the heat of the pan, for example, when roasting groundnuts or semolina. This is done either to improve the flavour of the food, or to reduce the moisture content. Roasting the cumin or coriander seeds first also makes it easier to grind or powder them. Constant attention is required in this method of cooking, as food can easily get burnt.

Baking: This is usually done in an oven, which has heating elements both on the top and the bottom. The medium of cooking is hot air. The food, placed in the centre, is cooked by radiation, as well as by the steam generated in the food. It is usually brown and crisp from the outside, and soft and moist inside, for example, a cake. Ovens can heat at temperatures of 120–250° C. Ovens usually have a thermostat to control the temperature, along with a timer. These ovens are operated by electricity or gas. Cakes, biscuits, puddings, breads, pizzas, etc., are all prepared by baking.

Other than the conventional oven method mentioned above, the microwave oven is now widely used for cooking and reheating food.

Microwave Oven

The microwave oven, like the conventional oven, is run by electricity, but has a different structure and principle of cooking.

Structure of unit: The microwave is a box-like structure with a glass door and a panel of switches with instructions. The magnetron element, wave guide and stirrer may be on one side or on the top. Inside the oven is a turn table, which rotates when food is placed on it and operated.

Figure 12.3: Structure of Microwave Oven (with Magnetron)

Source: https://commons.wikimedia.org/wiki/File:Microwave_oven.jpg
https://commons.wikimedia.org/wiki/File:Magnetron_(side).jpg?uselang=en-gb

Principle of cooking: Electromagnetic waves are produced from the power source magnetron in the microwave oven, and are absorbed by the food. It does not need a medium for the transfer of heat. Microwaves are absorbed, transmitted or reflected. Heat is generated inside food, rather than transferred.

The energy of the electromagnetic radiation excites the water molecule in food, which bears a positive charge in one position and a negative charge in the other. When the electric field of microwaves interacts with the water, it vibrates rapidly and produces heat. This brings about uniform heating; also, heating is faster than by conduction.

Food with water gets heated most efficiently. It is least efficient for heating fatty foods. While reheating cooked foods, it is advisable to place a bowl of water along with foods that are low in moisture.

Containers to be used: Preferably glass, ceramic, chinaware, or paper dishes. Only microwave-proof plastics should be used. If fissures appear in containers, they should not be put to further use. Do not use brown paper bags, stainless steel, or other metal containers.

Precautions while using a microwave:

- Be careful when you heat a liquid as it can splash.
- Do not try to deep fat fry in a microwave, as the oil can catch fire.

- When foods with little moisture are heated, they can dry out or even catch fire.
- Cover the food with covers with vents, or poke air vents in the covering to allow steam to escape.
- Do not wrap food in paper towels or cloth with synthetic fibres, as these can ignite.
- Handle finished food carefully because the outside may seem cool, while the inside is most likely hot.
- Keeping any metal, such as a spoon, can cause sparks and damage the oven, Avoid using aluminum foil as covering/wrapping material.
- Make holes with a fork in foods like potatoes, sweat potato, etc., before roasting in a microwave, otherwise these can burst because of a built-up pressure of steam. You cannot cook an egg in its shell in a microwave, as it will explode.
- Never switch on an empty microwave as it can damage the interior elements.

Many people forget—or do not know—that cooking some foods in a microwave can cause potentially serious results. A raw egg, still in its shell, will explode if cooked in a microwave. Uncovered sauces or soups will splash all over the oven when the heated centre expands and comes in contact with the cooler outside. Cheese is also notorious for having a volatile response, potentially causing serious burns. Liquids can also splash and cause burns, especially if containers are overfull. One should wait for 30 seconds before opening the door of the oven. Microwave oven is a source of radiation. So when in use, stay away from it. Some studies (albeit controversial) show that microwaved meats can lead to the formation of d-nitrosodiethanolamine, a chemical that has been linked to certain cancers.

Benefits of microwave cooking

- **Nutrient retention** is better due to little or no water added, covered cooking and shorter heating time.
- **Flavour enhancement.** As microwaved food is cooked in its own juices, its flavour is locked in. Cooking does not need the addition of fat or salt to facilitate the cooking process. Thus, this way of cooking is ideal for low fat and low salt preparations.
- **Real meals in less time.** Using a microwave is fast and easy. It also helps to cook nutritious meals, rather than a quick meal. Frozen food can be thawed in a few minutes.
- **Uniform cooking.** Food gets cooked uniformly. Reheating is also thorough as the temperatures of the core of foods, especially foods with fillings, can reach optimum levels required to kill germs. However, very thick pieces of food may not get cooked very well from the inside.

OTHER FUELS USED FOR COOKING

While cooking food, the main objective is to bring about a desirable change in food by the application of heat. For this, we use several resources such as wood, coal, LPG, and electricity. Most of these are not renewable, and hence the need to look for alternate sources of heating. Renewable forms of energy, like solar energy or biogas, may be used. We also need to look at the designs of cooking utensils, to see which have greater heat-retaining efficiency.

Solar cooker: This is an equipment that harnesses the rays of the sun to produce heat. The structure of the solar cooker is designed to absorb the heat and transmit it to the container kept within. It is like a box with a mirror on the inside of the lid. This is kept at an angle to trap maximum sun rays, so that they fall on the container placed in the box. The box and the containers are painted black to absorb and retain heat. A glass cover protects the food from dust and other contaminants.

There are many types of solar cookers available in the market, for both indoor and outdoor cooking. Some conserve the solar energy in batteries, and use them as fuel. Solar energy is also used for dehydrating food as a form of preservation.

Figure 12.4: Solar Cooker

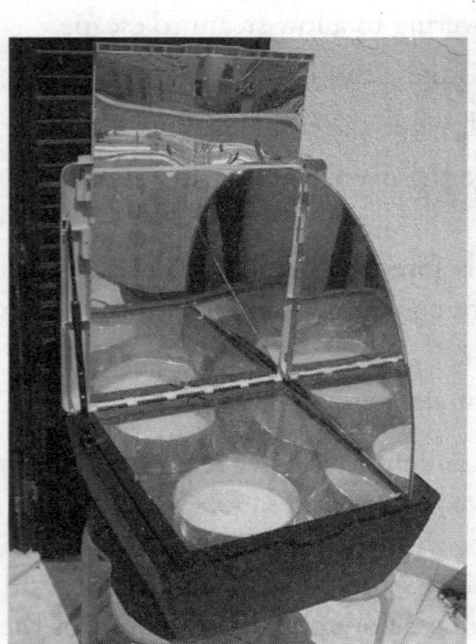

Source: http://en.wikipedia.org/wiki/Solar_cooker#/media/File:Solar_oven_Portugal_2007.jpg http://commons.wikimedia.org/wiki/File:ALSOL.jpg.

COOKING DIFFERENT FOODS

Not all foods can be cooked without water. For example, dehydrated foods such as rice, pastas, and dried beans and pulses have to be cooked using water. Fresh vegetables usually have enough natural moisture to cook without adding water, but vegetables which lack sufficient moisture require small amounts of water for cooking, for example potatoes, brussels sprouts, etc. Meats can be cooked in their own natural juices, or with added water.

Points to Keep in Mind

- The size of the utensil depends upon the amount of food to be cooked. Ideally, the utensil should be two-thirds full for the best results.
- The base sizes of the utensils available are usually equal to the most commonly used stove plate sizes. A stove plate of the same size as, or smaller than, the utensil base can be used, as the base distributes the heat evenly.
- Cover the utensil in which food is being cooked. Lifting the lid causes steam to escape, and food may burn. Additional oxygen may also enter the unit, resulting in unnecessary loss of heat and increased cooking time. If you have lifted the lid, put two or three tablespoons of water into the unit to replace the lost moisture. Keeping steam inside the unit also reduces the loss of nutritional value.
- Cooking time should be measured from the moment you have reached the desirable temperature.

The objective of cooking should not just be to prepare a tasty dish. Retaining the nutrients present in the food should also be on one's mind. After all, we eat food to nourish our bodies. It is very easy to prevent losses of nutrients while cooking. Box 12.1 presents some simple household tips.

Box 12.1: Simple Tips to Reduce Nutrient Losses during Cooking

- If rice and *dal* have to be soaked in water, wash them well first and then soak in water. Do not throw away the soaking water. Instead, use it for cooking.
- Do not throw away the water used to cook rice.
- Cook whole pulses in a pressure cooker to reduce cooking time. Soaking also reduces cooking time.
- Do not use soda to hasten the cooking of pulses, as it destroys the nutrients, especially B vitamins.
- Wash vegetables and fruits well before peeling and cutting—and not after cutting, as the nutrients will then be washed away.
- Do not leave cut vegetables in water, as the nutrients get leached out.
- Boil vegetables with the skin on them as this prevents nutrient loss.
- Cook vegetables/meat on high heat for a short time, as it gives better a colour and texture and also seals in the juices.
- Cook green leafy vegetables in an open pan for the initial five minutes as this helps to retain their bright green colour.
- Fruits and vegetables should be cut only just before consumption/cooking. Leaving cut surfaces exposed for long leads to a loss of nutrients.
- Cut the vegetables into large pieces. The smaller the pieces, greater is the total surface area of the food exposed, and the greater is the loss of nutrients due to leaching and oxidation.
- Conserve energy using cookware that conserve heat and hence use less fuel.

SUMMARY

- In this chapter, we have discussed various methods of cooking, and have also learnt about the ways to conserve colour, texture, flavour, nutrients, and save energy and time.
- Food is cooked to make it more digestible and tasty. Cooking kills microbes and makes the food safer. Cooking also improves the availability of nutrients in foods.
- Methods of cooking can be classified as moist and dry.
- Moist heat methods include boiling, simmering, poaching, steaming, and pressure cooking.
- Methods which use oil as a medium of heat transfer include sautéing, and shallow and deep fat frying.
- Dry heat methods include grilling, roasting and baking.
- Most foods are, however, cooked by a combination of methods.
- Microwave cooking is the fastest, and results in the least loss of nutrients.
- Solar cooking involves using a renewable source of energy.
- Reducing cooking time, cooking in a covered utensil, and using a minimum amount of liquid are steps which minimise nutrient losses during cooking.
- Leaching losses can be minimised by using the soaking and cooking water, cutting food into big pieces, and washing before cutting.

KEY WORDS

Broiling: The same as grilling. The term is used when the heat comes from above. It is a dry heat method of cooking where the food gets heated by radiation.

Magnetron: A component of the microwave oven, which generates microwaves. These help to cook food in the microwave oven.

Microwaves: Electromagnetic radiation of short wavelength.

Poaching: The process of gently simmering food in liquid, generally milk, stock or water.

Searing: The process of heating the surface of foods like meats to very high temperatures, resulting in browning.

EXERCISES

1. List the method of cooking involved in preparing:
   Cutlet
   Kofta curry
   Chicken curry
   Rice kheer.
2. What is the principle of the microwave oven? Suggest three dishes that can be cooked in a microwave.
3. List two foods cooked traditionally in leaves, bamboo, and iron vessels.
4. List three foods that are blanched before use.
5. What is the coating used in a non-stick pan?
6. What is the difference between the following methods of cooking:
   a) Boiling and steaming
   b) Shallow and deep fat frying
   c) Baking and grilling
7. List ways by which losses of nutrients can be minimised during pre-preparation and cooking.

ACTIVITY

Cook *rice kheer* in a solar cooker and evaluate the product for appearance, texture and flavour. Note the time it takes to cook.

REFERENCES

Application of Solar Energy-Domestic, Industrial and Commercial, Ministry of Non-conventional Energy Sources, www.mncs.nic.in.

Microwave cooking—Nutrition Family Health Guide, Harvard Health Publication, http://www.health.harvard.edu/fhg/updates/Microwave-cooking-and-nutrition.shtml.

Raina et al., *Basic Food Preparation—A Complete Manual*, 4e, Hyderabad: Orient BlackSwan, 2010.

Srilakshmi, B., *Food Science*, 5e, New Delhi: New Age International Publishers, 2010.

ONLINE SOURCE

http: // en.wikipedia.org/wiki/Craig_claiborne Quotations

13

Enhancing the Nutritional Quality of the Diet

HIGHLIGHTS

- Introduction
- Genetic Modification and Hybridisation
- Dietary Diversification
- Sprouting
- Fermentation
- Fortification / Nutrification
- Novel Foods / New Foods

INTRODUCTION

The recent technological developments have been a blessing, as they have brought about a revolution in many fields. We are all aware that post the Green Revolution, food production in India has increased substantially. Effort is being made to minimise post-harvest losses of food grains and perishable food items with innovative conservation technology. Scientific breeding techniques have improved quality, as well as increased the quantity of food. Today, one is able to develop a totally new generation of foods by a selective breeding process. The food preparation and consumption patterns of humans have altered radically over a period of time. Today, the use of 'ready to eat' (RTE), instant and synthetic foods have become common practice. The ready acceptance of these foods by consumers is accompanied by an increase in the research and development of newer and better processes in their formulation.

Fortification and the use of non-conventional foods like red palm oil or spirulina may be appropriate approaches to tackle the problem of hidden hunger (where a person gets enough to eat to satisfy her/his hunger, but the quality of the diet is so poor that the body does not receive sufficient amounts of vitamins and minerals, and hence the body is literally hungry for these micronutrients without consciously realising it). With limited economic resources and an increasing population, it is important to get maximum food value out of every bit of food that one can buy. At the household level, too, the improvement in nutritional quality can be achieved by the process of **Biological Ennoblement**—the enhancement in nutritive content that occurs following sprouting and fermentation procedures. Let us see how each of these measures can help us to enhance the nutritional quality of our diet.

GENETIC MODIFICATION AND HYBRIDISATION

The last century saw the rediscovery of Mendel's law of inheritance and birth of the science of genetics. This provided new instruments for tailoring plants to the needs of people. While the selective breeding of plants through the process of hybridisation is an old agricultural practice carried out by farmers since early historical times, it has recently been improved by the application of biotechnology. **Genetic engineering** of food *is the science that involves deliberate modification of the genetic material of plants or animals*. Plant breeding supplies the methodology for improving crop plants. It has been likened to the process of building; in fact, it is more like replacing the coloured marble pieces in an existing mosaic with pieces of another colour, ultimately changing the pattern substantially. In general, plant characters can only be changed one at a time, and therefore, the intent characters are to be prioritised.

Genetic engineering is described as the science whereby the characteristics of an organism are deliberately modified by the manipulation of the genetic material, especially DNA, and the transformation of certain genes to create new variations of life.

The second requirement is that the character under improvement should be readily identifiable by the breeder. In the 1950s and 1960s, it was a slow process of hybridisation. Today, it is relatively faster with genetic engineering. Genetic engineering of food is the science that involves the deliberate modification of the genetic material of plants or animals. By manipulating the DNA in different ways and transferring from one organism to another by the recombinant DNA technique, it has been possible to introduce traits of any organism to a plant, bacteria, virus, or animal. As a result, many food plants have been genetically modified for various purposes. There are several foods consumed today that are either genetically modified (GM) whole foods, or contain ingredients derived from gene modification technology.

Food crops produced or modified by genetic engineering techniques are called 'Genetically Modified Foods (GM foods)'. About 60 different GM foods are being marketed worldwide. GM versions of soyabean, canola, corn, potato, sugar beet, and cotton have been approved for sale. In India, GM food crops are under field trials only.

Benefits of GM Foods

Benefits of the GM foods include increased year-round food availability, improved nutritional quality, and an extended shelf life, which will benefit consumers, farmers and the environment. The newly developed tomato genotypes SEZ – 7 (open pollinated) and hybrid ARTH – 3 at Hissar (Haryana) have a longer shelf life, and the fruit is more firm and pulpy. Both varieties have a good nutritional profile, viz., the amount of ascorbic acid, lycopene and β Carotene, when analysed, was 31.33 and 2.82, 3.12 and 4.03, and 5.90 and 6.78 mg / 100g of raw tomatoes, respectively. Delayed ripening of some fruits and vegetables has led to superior flavour, colour, texture, longer shelf life, and better transporting and handling properties. Recently, sweet-tasting, firmer, seedless peppers and tomatoes have been produced.

In 1899, John Hopkins was the first scientist to observe the variability of protein and other chemical constituents of cereal grains. Development of varieties with better yield and stability of performance through built-in resistance to diseases and pests was the major goal of plant breeding research in the 1960s. Globally, either through the incorporation of dwarfing genes—as in wheat and rice—or through the exploitation of hybrid vigour (improved function of any biological quality in the hybrid)—as in maize, sorghum and pearl millet—major advances were made in increasing the yield potential of these crops. Breeding for quality in India has until recently implied mainly breeding for market and consumer preferences; for instance, in the case of wheat, the major stress was on colour, size, and lustre and vitreousness (a characteristic for good *chapati* rolling) of the grain. Gradually, there was a shift in GM research towards altering the protein and oil content of cereal grains. The initial work was confined to maize, where it was possible to increase the protein quantity from about 10–25 per cent. Unfortunately, the improvement in protein content resulted in a depreciation in protein quality. Later, in 1964, a significant breakthrough was made in the USA, where high lysine genes Opaque 2 and Floury 2 were identified in the maize. This discovery pointed towards the possibility of changing the nutritional quality of foods by genetic engineering. Currently, the thrust of genetic modifications are in the following:

- *To increase crop yield and reduce crop loss* by making plants tolerant to pests, weeds, insects, salinity, pH, temperature, frost, drought, and weather. Insect-resistant fruits such as apples, virus-resistant cantaloupes and cucumbers, and herbicide-tolerant corn, tomatoes, potatoes, and soyabeans have all been produced. Bt Brinjal is the first Genetically Modified food crop in India that had reached the approval stage for commercialisation, before the process was halted. Bt Brinjal had been developed by inserting a gene from a soil bacterium called Bacillus thuringiensis to make it more pest-resistant, and thus increase the yield of the crop.

- *To improve organoleptic quality* like colour, taste, texture, etc. Here, sorghum provides a good example. Sorghum has a sub-coat, the testa, which has a high polyphenol content; often, the grains are brown in colour and a direct relationship exists between the intensity of colour and polyphenol content. These pigments are bitter in taste and adversely affect digestibility. Now, a sorghum that has better digestibility is possible. The bright yellow colour of maize is another example, where, along with other carotenoid pigments, beta-carotene, a source of vitamin A is present in higher amounts.
- *To improve the nutritional profile of foods.* Genetic modification of oilseeds resulted in products yielding high oleic acid (18:1), high linolenic acid (18:3), increased lauric acid (12:0), and larger yields of many oilseeds such as canola (with high lauric acid content) and soyabean (with high oleic acid). Other GM foods with nutritional enhancement include rice with β-Carotene and iron, and potato with high protein. With the help of tissue culture, the IARI has developed a variety of mustard, BI0-902, named 'PUSA Jai Kisan', which has a high oil content.

Golden rice: A transgenic variety of rice with genes for the synthesis of beta carotene, taken from daffodil (Narcissus pseudonarcissus) and inserted into the genome of a temperate strain of rice using Agrobacterium tumefasciens as the vector, to effect the gene. This rice will be a good source of provitamin A.

- *To eliminate or minimise naturally occurring inhibitors and toxic factors,* such as Lathyrus sativus with low BOAA content.

The ICAR has identified the β-gene that can increase the β-carotene content of genetically engineered horticultural crops such as papaya, mango, tomatoes, and carrots. Shakti, Ratna and Protima were the first three composites released, incorporating Opaque – 2 and Floury – 2 mutant genes. These composites have about 10–12 per cent protein and approximately 69 per cent more lysine than the other maize varieties. The prospects of protein quantity and quality improvement in wheat and rice are encouraging. Semi-dwarf varieties like Kalyansona, Sonalika, Sharbati Sanora, and Lerma Roja have about 10–16 per cent protein, with 2.5–3.0 per cent lysine. These varieties also have good baking and *chapati*-making properties.

Today, not only are agricultural technologists able to alter the specific characteristic of food crops, but by genetic manipulation, they are also able to develop totally new food crops. One such man-made crop is 'triticale', produced from a cross between wheat and rye, first marketed in 1970. Triticale has 14.8 per cent protein and is also rich in lysine (3.5 per cent).

The GM Food Controversy

While the benefits are attractive, there are concerns that the genetic modification achieved through transgenic techniques may result in harm. Some of the specific fears expressed include an alteration in the nutritional quality of foods, potential toxicity, possible antibiotic resistance from GM crops, and potential allergenicity and carcinogenicity from consuming GM foods. Additionally, some more general concerns include environmental pollution, unintentional gene transfer to wild plants, possible creation of new viruses and toxins, limited access to seeds due to patenting of GM food plants, threat to crop genetic diversity, religious, cultural and ethical concerns, as well as a fear of the unknown.

The consumption of products from Bt (Bacillus thuringiensis) insect-resistant plants raised some controversy regarding the possible long-term effects of Bt on health. The introduction of novel proteins into foods, such as GM soyabean variety expressing methionine from Brazil nut and GM corn variety to produce Bt endotoxin Cry9C, may elicit potentially harmful immunological responses, including allergic hypersensitivity.

The Way Forward

Although genetic modification of food is important and beneficial, it should be adopted under conditions that avoid potential risks. Safety and nutritional assessment of these foods are of particular importance, especially for developing countries like India. The introduction of GM foods into the food chain needs to be regulated and well-controlled at various stages by both governmental and international regulatory systems. Time and effort must be devoted to field testing before the release of any new genetically engineered food. The GM process is subject to a three-tier regulatory system—in the laboratory, under contained conditions, and open-field experimentation. Safety assessment of GM foods are in general carried out on a case-by-case basis, taking into account modification features and comparison of the properties of the new food with that of its traditional counterparts. Labelling of GM foods will benefit both consumers and manufacturers.

> Today, there is an intense social debate concerning the risk associated with the production of GM foods. Two poles of opinion exist: on the one hand, the production companies interested in marketing their products, and on the other, lobbies—mainly environmentalist groups—who view GM foods as a risk to both health and the environment.

The revolution in biotechnology will help in addressing the pressing problems of food, health, nutrition, and water scarcity in coming years. In the twenty-first century, we will have to produce more and better foods. This will only be possible through the wise application of molecular genetic technology. The examples cited earlier are sufficient to indicate the pace of progress of genetic research, and the vast panorama of exciting possibilities it has opened up for scientists.

> In the future, biotechnology might help in getting cereal grains with high fibre, n-3 fatty acids and β-Carotene. Meat with reduced saturated fats or eggs with decreased cholesterol may also be possible. Currently, such nutrient modification in animal foods can only be done to a limited extent by altering the feed of the animals.

DIETARY DIVERSIFICATION

Foods provide several essential macro and micronutrients. Malnutrition, particularly micronutrient deficiency, usually occurs when diets lack variety. Diets and a food-based approach play an essential role in preventing micronutrient malnutrition by increasing the availability and consumption of micronutrient-rich foods. Regularly eating a variety of foods also promotes a healthy life, free from diseases. Thus, ***dietary diversity*** *is a measure of the number of individual foods or food groups consumed in a given period of time.* It can reflect household access to a variety of foods, and can also act as a proxy for individual nutrient adequacy. Measures of dietary diversity typically do not indicate the quality of food eaten.

Dietary diversification is a long-term strategy that is more sustainable. However, the benefit of such an approach, unlike direct nutrient supplementation, is not immediate. Food-based approaches are a preventive, cost-effective, and sustainable long-term strategy to combat malnutrition. There are several advantages of dietary diversification/modification:

> **Food-based approach** is defined by the FAO as 'a preventive and comprehensive strategy that use food, that is whole, refined, processed, fortified or a combination as a tool to overcome micronutrient deficiency'.

- It promotes year-round availability, access to and utilisation of foods, thereby promoting more intake and absorption of nutrients.
- Can be adapted to different cultural and dietary traditions.
- It is broad-based and aims to improve the overall quality of the diet of a population. It addresses the problem of multiple nutrient inadequacies simultaneously.
- The amount of nutrients consumed is within normal physiological levels, and hence the risk of toxicity gets minimised.

Table 13.1: Average Intake of Foodstuffs (g/CU/day) by Per Capita Income

Capita Income Rs./Month	*Cereals & Millets*	*Pulses & Legumes*	*Leafy Vegetables*	*Other Vegetables*	*Roots & Tubers*	*Nuts & Oilseeds*	*Fruits*	*Fish*	*Other Flesh Foods*	*Milk and Milk Products*	*Fats & Oils*	*Sugar& Jaggery*
< 30	531.3	35.9	14.7	38.4	19.9	11.4	31.8	0.0	18.0	78.4	16.4	24.5
90-150	485.9	26.7	19.8	37.0	40.1	4.0	21.8	3.9	2.2	45.1	9.4	15.2
600-900	410.6	28.2	15.4	64.6	51.3	31.7	29.6	28.4	6.9	136.3	14.3	27.4
≥1,500	369.7	35.8	13.6	73.8	73.0	61.6	38.7	45.0	9.6	263.0	20.2	32.5
States Pooled	449.5	28.6	14.8	46.7	43.5	16.2	24.0	15.0	4.2	85.5	11.6	21.0

Source: Adapted from NNMB – Report of Second Repeat Survey – Rural 1996–97.

- It links the cultivation of a variety of staple foods with a high vitamin and mineral content to nutrition education, and can thus encourage better consumer behaviour.

Dietary diversification as a strategy to improve the nutritional profile of a country can be implemented in the form of improved agricultural production, the development of vegetable plots, cultivation of a variety of foodstuffs, along with sound food choices and preparation procedures at the level of families, as well as nutritional advice and training for multiple stakeholders like agriculturists, policymakers, food technologists, and most importantly, the consumers.

Poor dietary diversity is a problem in low and middle-income countries, where the diets are frequently based on starchy / carbohydrate-rich staples such as rice, wheat, maize, and potatoes. Such diets often lack in pulses and animal foods (meat, fish, eggs, and dairy). Many contain only small amounts of fruits and vegetables. While cereals are an important source of energy in the diet, many of the important vitamins and minerals essential for healthy diets are found in abundance in fruits and vegetables, legumes and flesh foods. In addition, certain staple foods such as wheat, maize and millets may contain high levels of anti-nutrients such as phytates, which reduce the absorption of available micronutrients in the food source.

The very low consumption of fruits, vegetables, dairy products, and animal foods, and heavy dependency on cereals and millets in low-income groups in India, resulting in poor dietary diversity, is illustrated in Table 13.1.

The recent transition in a certain economic class of people towards increased consumption of processed refined food grains, oils and sugars has led to a reduced intake of micronutrients and a progressive loss of dietary diversity. The need for dietary diversification, as a food-based approach to improve the nutritional profile of our people, is important. Evidence suggests that dietary modification is the most cost-effective sustainable measure for improving the vitamin A and iron status of our people. Let us examine how.

Green leafy vegetables, as we are all aware, are good sources of micronutrients. In India, the existing vitamin A malnutrition reflects an inadequate intake of beta-carotene rich foods. Abundant sources of vitamin A exist in our country. Efforts to raise the vitamin A status must therefore be logically directed towards augmenting the intake of these relatively inexpensive provitamin A-rich foods. However, in practice, the contribution of such plants to alleviate micronutrient deficiency is greatly under-appreciated. Among the wide range of local green leafy vegetables, drumstick leaves and '*curry patta*' in particular provide a rich and inexpensive source of provitamin A, along with other micronutrients. Native to India, the tree grows abundantly in all tropical countries where vitamin A deficiency is a public health problem. Small amounts of less than 10g of fresh leaves can meet the daily requirement of vitamin A of a preschool child. Hence, advocating and implementing such dietary diversification can go a long way in improving the micronutrient status of population groups.

> Consumption of a judicious combination of pulses, cereals, and other plant foods can go a long way in improving the dietary quality of our people. Some of our traditional dishes, like *idli-sambhar*, *khichri*, or *rich-dal* and *chutney*, *chapati-dal*-vegetables, curd rice, *makki ki roti – sarson ka sag – jaggery*, are a few examples of nutritionally beneficial combinations of food.

Therefore, the objective of dietary diversification is to ensure that people get essential nutrients in sufficient quantities through their daily diet. The modification of behaviour, leading to a better selection or preparation of food to enhance the intake or bio-availability of nutrients, is the primary goal of this approach.

SPROUTING / GERMINATION

The process of sprouting of whole grains (cereals or pulses) is the simplest, most cost-effective, and culturally old method of improving nutritional quality. This technique, along with fermentation, is also called '**biological ennoblement**'. For centuries, Chinese people practised the sprouting of soyabean and green gram (*moong* beans) for their culinary use. Germination is a process that involves the soaking of whole pulses / cereals overnight. The water is drained, and the soaked grains tied in a loosely woven muslin cloth and hung. Water is sprinkled twice or thrice a day, depending on the weather conditions. In a day or two—depending on the atmospheric temperature and humidity level—germination takes place (Figure 13.1). Moisture and warmth are essential for sprouting. The method described is a household procedure. Today, sprouted foods are also available commercially, and sprouting is done under controlled conditions.

Figure 13.1: The Process of Germination

Step 1: Soaking in water | Step 2: Allowing to sprout in colander/ muslin cloth | Step 3: Germinated grain ready to eat

The changes during the process of germination involve the conversion of storage ingredients into simpler forms, which are utilised by the growing embryo. Thus, starch is converted into simple carbohydrates, namely sucrose, glucose and fructose, in the initial stages of germination, while later on, a greater amount of maltose is produced. During sprouting, dormant enzymes get activated and the digestibility of nutrients is improved.

The elaboration of an enzyme amylase resulting in a lower viscosity and thinning down of the starch slurry is extensively used in the formulation of infant foods, which are energy dense, both at home and at a commercial level.

The ratio of essential to non-essential amino acids changes, providing more of the essential amino-acids. Trypsin inhibitors are reduced due to the release of enzymes during germination. Similarly, tannins and phytate, which adversely affect bio-availability, are broken down by sprouting. The action of cytases and pectinases are activated and the cell wall is broken down, increasing the availability of nutrients. Fats are simplified to fatty acids. Sprouting releases the bound vitamins and minerals present in the seed. There is a manifold increase in water-soluble vitamins, like thiamine, riboflavin, niacin, folic acid, and vitamin C. So much is the net increase in vitamin C that Wittshire in 1918 succeeded in curing severe cases of scurvy by simply including germinated beans in the diet. Minerals like calcium, zinc and iron are released from the bound form. Figure 13.2 shows the effect of sprouting on the nutritive quality of cereals and pulses.

Figure 13.2: Effect of Sprouting and Fermentation on the Nutritive Quality of Moong Dal.

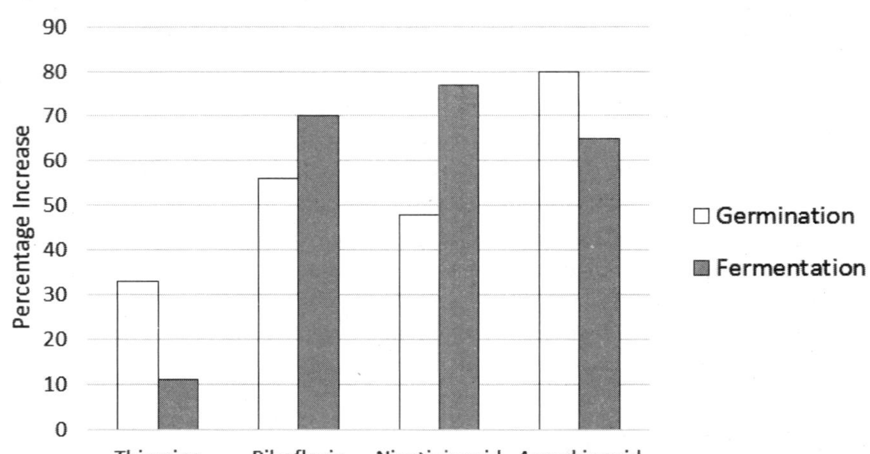

Note: For germination, pulse was soaked in water for 6 – 12 hours and allowed to sprout under warm moist condition for 24 hours.
For fermentation, batter prepared with coarsely ground grain, water and salt and allowed to ferment for 10 – 15 hours.
Source: Rajalakshmi 2013.

During sprouting, oligosaccharides get metabolised, and hence the germinated legumes do not produce gas or flatulence. These oligosaccharides would otherwise resist digestion in our small intestine, and instead be broken down in the large intestine by microbes, leading to the production of gas (flatulence) and discomfort. Germination also decreases the cooking time and mucus-inducing properties, and adds variety to the diet. The taste and texture of germinated pulses alter considerably, resulting in greater acceptability by the consumer.

> The simplest way to utilise sprouted pulses are to incorporate them into *chapati* dough, rice *pulao*, vegetable cutlets, infant foods, and *raita* (a curd preparation). Regular consumption of a serving of sprouts should be an integral part of our diet.

The process of sprouting should not be prolonged as too much root formation and metabolic weight loss of the grain may become a problem. An extended period of germination also reduces the nutrient content of the sprouts. The sprouts can be eaten raw or after cooking/steaming for a short time to minimise nutrient loss.

FERMENTATION

Fermentation is another simple process and a culturally old method of improving the quality of foods. The natural fermentation of food occurs when environmental conditions permit the interaction between a micro-organism and food substances. Bacterial and yeast fermentations are other methods common in India. Fermented *dosa* and *idli* mixtures, fermented whole wheat flour used for making *bhatura* or *naan*, and curd-making are good examples of fermentation by yeast and bacteria. The process of fermentation encourages the multiplication of specific micro-organisms and their metabolic activity in food. This is what happens during the preparation of curd from milk. We encourage the multiplication of the lactic acid bacteria in milk. If you observe curd under a powerful microscope, you will notice crawling bacteria. The significant point is that several of the end products of such food fermentation, especially the acid and alcohol produced, do not permit the growth of pathogenic micro-organisms that may find their way into food.

> Indigenous fermentation of green gram dal at 35°C for 18 hours reduces the anti-nutrients phytic acid and polyphenols by approximately 50 per cent, and hence it can be incorporated in infant food supplements.

Fermented foods are more nutritious than their unfermented counterparts (Table 13.2). The processing of pulses through fermentation increases their digestibility, palatability and texture. During the fermentation process, there is production of carbon dioxide and substances with an acidic taste (sour). There is also partial degradation of starch and proteins. Minerals are released from bound form with a decrease in the level of phytates. Additionally, toxic substances in pulses can be eliminated by fermentation. The micro-organisms synthesise several complex vitamins, such as riboflavin, vitamin B_{12} and vitamin C, and decrease the level of oligosaccharides and trypsin inhibitors. Just like sprouting, the fermentation process also has the advantage of reducing the cooking time, as it makes the raw food 'pre-digested' to an appreciable extent without any extra cost.

A large variety of fermented food products are used by people across the world. Some familiar ones are curd and buttermilk (made with the help of lactic acid bacteria); wines and vinegar (prepared with bacteria-producing acetic acid); beer, rum, whisky, brandy, and bread (made with yeast fermentation); cocoa, made by yeast along with acetic-acid producing bacteria; and soya sauce, prepared involving fungi, bacteria and yeast. The most common fermented Indian products are *idli, dosa, khaman, dhokla, bhatura, kulcha*, and *naan*.

FORTIFICATION / NUTRITIFICATION

Food fortification is an important food-based feasible strategy that may offer considerable public health benefits at an affordable cost. Today, almost all the food from farm to consumer are treated or processed in many ways. Several of the processes affect the nutritional quality. To compensate for such losses, foods are enriched with nutrients. On the other hand, some foods are fortified / nutrified by the governments of different countries in order to tackle specific nutritional problems. **Fortification,** as defined by the Codex Alimentarius, is:

the addition of one or more essential nutrients to a food whether or not it is normally contained in the food, for the purpose of preventing or correcting a demonstrated deficiency of one or more nutrients in the population or specific population groups.

The other common terms used interchangeably for the addition of nutrients to foods are 'restoration', 'enrichment' and 'nutrification'.

Restoration means the addition of essential nutrients to a food to make up for nutrients that are lost in spite of Good Manufacturing Practices (GMP) or during normal storage and handling procedures, in amounts that will result in nutrient levels originally present in the edible portion of food. In simple terms, it involves the 'restoration' of the levels of nutrients present before processing, storage or handling.

Food fortification has the advantage of not calling for a radical change in the dietary patterns of the population. It has been successfully used as a cost-effective tool to fight micronutrient deficiencies in many developed countries.

The success stories of the fortification of commonly consumed food products to fight 'hidden hunger' support the fact that it is an important public health measure. Food fortification is likely to prove most beneficial when one or more nutrients are in short supply in the community, but when the total amount of food available is not seriously inadequate. In other words, fortification improves the quality of the food without affecting the quantity.

It is essential to understand the purpose behind the addition of nutrients to a food. There are several situations when a nutrient is added:

Pellagra in the US was successfully combated through breads enriched with a combination of vitamin B complex and iron.

- *Fortification for the restoration of normal level.* When nutrient(s) are removed or destroyed in food processing or storage, the addition of nutrients may be undertaken to replace those removed or destroyed.
- *Fortification above the normal level.* Addition of nutrients to certain foods for special dietary uses, such as infant foods, or geriatric foods, or therapeutic foods such as weight management diets. In such cases, the nutrients may be added in quantities well above the natural level with the intention of supplying the total nutrient requirements in the minimum amount of food consumed.
- *Enrichment with a public health objective.* Where it is intended to meet a demonstrable need in the community, such as iodisation of salt to prevent IDD.
- *Enrichment of 'substitute' foods to the equivalent level.* For example, in simulated foods like margarine, which is a substitute for butter, vitamins A and D are added, or soya milk is enriched with nutrients comparable to natural milk.
- *Fortification to make the product complete in itself.* Such as 'ready to eat' foods, or sometimes to compensate the additional demands created by the metabolism of some food item in the body, for example, the addition of B vitamins to sugar-based energy drinks to take care of increased metabolic needs, and health drinks, which are complete in themselves as they have all vitamins and minerals added to them.
- *Addition of nutrients for non-nutritional purposes.* Such as the use of carotene or riboflavin as natural colouring agents, and vitamin E as an antioxidant in fats.

Food fortification is of value under two different sets of situations:

- It can be used to prevent or treat a nutritional deficiency disease in a population, subject to the nutritional disease having a sharply defined etiology.
- It can be used by affluent societies to provide insurance against the occurrence of a state of nutritional deficiency, especially where it is difficult to identify the people at risk.

Attempts have been made in India and other in countries to fortify water and foods to prevent nutrient deficiency. These include:

- Iodisation of salt to control Iodine Deficiency Disorders
- Double fortification of salt with iodine and iron

- Fortification of '*vanaspati*' (hydrogenated fat), refined oil and milk with vitamins A and D
- Fortification of wheat flour with iron
- Fluoridation of water to control dental caries (not in India)
- Fortification of sugar with vitamin A in Central American countries

The food industry has also responded by fortifying their products with different nutrients in an effort to make their products 'healthier options'. Thus, now bread, biscuits, beverages, ice candies, jams, and many other food products available in India are fortified with multiple nutrients.

Selection of the right food item to act as a **vehicle for fortification** plays a crucial role. Any contemplated programme of nutrification to be undertaken will depend on the following criteria:

- Should be consumed by a high proportion of the population in quantities that will make a significant contribution to the diet.
- Should be consumed in significant amounts by all socio-economic classes.
- Should have a low potential of being consumed in excess (so that it does not result in nutrient toxicity).
- Should not seriously interfere with the utilisation of the nutrients being added.
- The addition of nutrient(s) is not likely to create an imbalance of the essential nutrients present in the food.
- Fortification is technically feasible for the particular food, and the food is centrally processed or processed at only a few centres.
- The cost of fortification does not result in a significant change in the cost of the fortified food.

The **nutrient(s) being added (fortificants)** should have the following properties:

- Stable under normal conditions of handling, storage and use
- High bioavailability, that is, should be well-absorbed
- Addition of nutrients has no detrimental effect on flavour, taste, shelf-life, colour, texture, and on the cooking properties of food, so that there is no change in consumer acceptability.

Considering these aspects, several carriers for fortification have been identified and adopted in different countries. Table 13.2 lists the foods that can be used for fortification:

Table 13.2: Foods Fortified with Different Nutrients

Nutrients			
Vitamin A	*Iodine*	*Multiple nutrients*	*Iron*
Wheat flour	Corn flour	Wheat flour	Wheat flour
Rice	Bread	Rice	Rice
Sugar	Milk	Oil	Maize Meal
Salt	Salt	Curry powder	Sugar
Oil/ *Vanaspati*	Sugar		Salt
Butter			Fish sauce
Margarine			Curry powder
Milk			Infant formula
Tea			Biscuits
Curry powder			

Source: Adapted from Nestel 1993; Srilakshmi 2013; Wadhwa and Sharma 2003.

So far in India, salt is recognised as the most suitable vehicle for providing nutrients. It has all the properties of an ideal vehicle for nutrification.

Our country has a mandatory fortification policy for salt with iodine, and now a double-fortified salt with iodine and iron has been approved for public health use in safety net programmes. There is also a Gazette of India notification since 2011 on the fortification of whole wheat flour (*atta*) and refined wheat flour (*maida*) with 10 nutrients.

Why Salt Fortification ?

It is uniformly consumed in sufficient quantities by people, independent of economic strata.

The variability in consumption is within narrow limits.

Is produced in limited centres and is under the control of the government.

Conditions of storage, distribution and transportation do not alter its integrity.

Iodine Fortified Salt

Iodisation of salt is a time-tested, effective and cheap means of combating IDDs. Iodine is added in the form of potassium iodide or iodate. The level of iodine added as per the FSSA Act is not less than 30 parts per million (ppm) at the production point, and not less than 15 ppm of iodine at the consumer level.

Iron Fortified Salt

The National Institute of Nutrition (NIN) has developed a technology of fortifying salt with iron. Community trials have shown it to be effective in reducing iron deficiency anaemia. The level suggested is 1 mg of iron/g of salt from ferrous sulphate. In addition, there is a stabiliser and absorption promoter added to salt.

Double Fortified Salt (DFS)

Common salt is fortified with both iodine and iron. To maintain the stability of iodine in DFS (which is otherwise unstable in the presence of iron), a polyphosphate, sodium hexametaphosphate (SHMP), is included. The technology has been replicated and a series of community trials conducted by NIN have shown that iodine and iron provided through DFS is bio-available. Trials with DFS have shown a reduction in the incidence of anaemia and IDD in the community. Table 13.3 gives the composition of DFS. It would provide 1 mg of iron and 30 μcg of iodine/g of salt.

Table 13.3: Composition of Double Fortified Salt*

Ingredient	*Amount*
Common Salt (g)	1,000
Ferrous Sulphate (g)	5
Sodium Hexametaphosphate (g)	10
Potassium iodate (mg)	50

Note: * NIN formulation

Ultra Rice

This is the name given to the reconstituted vitamin A or iron fortified rice. Vitamin A-fortified rice is prepared by blending either vitamin A acetate or palmitate as fortificant in the rich flour, and extruding the paste to yield a concentrated rice product similar in appearance, density and taste to that of natural rice. The manufactured rice grains are then blended with unfortified rice in the ratio of 1:100 or 1:200 to provide an appropriate level of micronutrient. Generally, one kilogram of ultra-rice is fortified with 11.4 g of vitamin A palmitate.

'We all are aware of the crucial role of salt in the Nation's freedom struggle through *Dandi* March of Mahatma Gandhi. Now a spoon full of salt with iodine and iron would lead us to freedom from IDD and anaemia' (Wadhwa and Sharma 2003: 156).

Iron fortification of ultra-rice with a chelated, highly bio-available form of iron has also been tried. In comparison with vitamin A fortification, it is easier to nutrify rice with iron because of the inherent stability of the iron compound. However, so far the two nutrients cannot be added in the same rice because vitamin A gets oxidised by iron, leading to discoloration during storage.

Edible Oils

Use of fats and oils is an integral part of Indian cuisine. In India, fortification of fats and oils dates back to 1953, when it was made mandatory to fortify *vanaspati* (hydrogenated fat) with 250 IU of vitamin A and 25 IU of vitamin D/100g of fat. Since the production of hydrogenated fat was by medium to large oil industries, legislation regarding compulsory fortification was implementable.

Thus, although fortification seems to be an effective food-based strategy to combat the problem of hidden hunger in our people, so far, except for IDD control, it has not yielded as good a result as might be anticipated. Food fortification works well in countries that possess well-developed, efficiently monitored, and properly regulated nutraceutical and food processing sectors. Also, other possible factors such as political will, acceptability, availability, cost, and logistics might be contributing to its slow growth. As most of the food items commonly consumed are easily amenable to fortification, proper strategies can be adapted to ensure the easy reach of fortified foods among consumers. Strategies can be worked out to select appropriate dietary items specific to different geographic areas in the country, and then fortify and supply them to the people through the Public Distribution System Network.

NOVEL FOODS / NEW FOODS

Over the years, food preparation and consumption patterns have altered radically. Industrialisation and rapid urbanisation have resulted in a sociological change, thereby impacting the lifestyle of people. So much is the expansion of the food industry, that today we are in the midst of revolutionary developments that are making us rethink our views on food safety, regulation and nutrition. Globally, a whole series of new foods, ranging from nutraceuticals, low-cost nutritious food supplements, convenience precooked Ready to Eat (RTE) foods, health foods to space foods, are available in the market. We can now synthesise meat analogues and fat-free margarines, etc. The new nutrition technologies can be classified into five types, viz., nutraceuticals, formulated foods, texturised or engineered foods, the non-conventional sources of foods, and the synthetic foods. The basic criteria underlying the formulation and production of any new or novel food are the organoleptic properties and societal acceptability. In some cases, like foods being produced for welfare programmes, cost is another consideration.

Nutraceuticals

The word 'nutraceutical' is derived from 'nutrition' and 'pharmaceutical', and was first coined in 1989 by Dr Stephen L. DeFelice, Founder and Chairman of the Foundation for Innovation in Medicine (FIM). He defined **nutraceutical** as 'Food or parts of food, that provide medical or health benefits, including prevention of disease'. The term is applied to products that range from isolated nutrients, dietary supplements, herbal products, specific diets, and processed foods such as phytonutrients, vitamins, condiment extracts, soups and beverages, etc. Historically, the Indian, Egyptian, Chinese, and Sumerian are the few civilisations that have used food as medicine. Hippocrates, the father of Western medicine, said, 'Let food be thy medicine'. Given the global concern about chronic degenerative diseases, the modern nutraceutical market began to develop in Japan during the 1980s. In contrast to the natural herbs and spices used as folk medicine for centuries throughout Asia, the nutraceutical industry has grown alongside the expansion and exploration of modern technology.

Classification of Nutraceuticals

These are products derived from food sources that provide extra health benefits, in addition to basic nutritional value. Depending on the jurisdiction, products may claim to prevent chronic diseases, improve health, delay the ageing process, increase life expectancy, or support the structure or function of the body. Nutraceuticals can be placed into three groups: dietary supplements, functional foods and medicinal foods.

Dietary Supplements

These products contain nutrients derived from food products, and are concentrated in liquid or capsule form, to be taken orally. The dietary ingredients in these products may include vitamins, minerals, herbs or other botanicals, amino acids, and substances such as enzymes, organ tissues, glandular (freeze-dried glands or other tissues obtained from animals), and metabolites. They are mostly extracts or concentrates, and are available as tablets, capsules, soft gels, gel caps, liquids, and powders.

Phytonutrients from soya products, carrots, tomatoes, orange, spinach, berries, etc., are the most commonly used nutraceuticals for promoting health and preventing diseases.

Functional Foods

You have been introduced to the concept of functional foods in Chapter 1. Functional foods can be designed to allow consumers to eat enriched foods close to their natural state. Functional foods are usually enriched or fortified with nutrients.

New, emerging functional foods with a wide application in health and disease are listed in Table 13.4, along with their common usage.

Functional Food is a natural or processed food that contains known biologically-active compounds which, when consumed in defined amounts, provides a clinically proven and documented health benefit, and thus is important in the prevention, management and treatment of chronic diseases (Martirosyan 2011). Oats, bran, psyllium (*isabgol*), and fenugreek are a few commonly used examples of functional foods.

Table 13.4: Functional Foods, their Bioactive Components and Health Benefits

Foods	*Bioactive/Functional Component*	*Health Benefit*
Yoghurt, beverages and snacks fortified with prebiotics, whole grains and most vegetables and fruits	Oligofructose, inulin (Prebiotics), soluble fibre	Improvement of intestinal flora, lowering blood cholesterol, triglyceride and glucose levels.
Yoghurt, beverages and other dairy products	Live microbes (Probiotics)	Improvement of intestinal flora, immunological benefits and prevention of lifestyle disorders.
Fatty fish (salmon, tuna), fortified cereals, health drinks, flaxseed oil, walnuts	Omega – 3 fatty acids	Prevention of heart diseases
Green tea	Epigallocatechin gallate	Prevention of heart disease and cancer
Rice bran oil, wheat germ, wheat bran	Phytostanols and phytosterols	Reduction of LDL cholesterol
Soyabean and soya based foods	Isoflavones	Protects against heart disease, reduces menopausal symptoms and decreases risk of some cancers
Turmeric	Curcumin	Anti-inflammatory, antioxidant

Medicinal Foods

These are the preferred prescriptions of tomorrow. Modern technology has evolved vaccines that can be delivered to our bodies through foods like bananas and potatoes. The advantages are that it can eliminate the discomforts in administration, and the need for refrigeration in storage and transport (cold chain). However, these foods are to be administered only under medical supervision. A few examples of medicinal foods are:

- Milk from transgenic cow having high levels of lactoferrin (an iron-binding protein with antimicrobial properties) for the enhancement of immunity against mastitis (inflammation of the udder) in cows and diarrhoea in humans.

- Transgenic plants (for example, bananas and potatoes) for oral vaccination against infectious diseases like Hepatitis B.
- Health drinks with added medication.

Finally, what caused the rapid emergence of nutraceuticals?

- Consumers' dissatisfaction with the cost of drugs and conventional healthcare is making them turn to unproven and untested natural products for treatment and prevention.
- A phenomenal increase in chronic disease and poor therapeutic alternatives.
- Hurried impersonal exchanges with healthcare providers.
- Desire for personalised medicines.
- New focus on promotive and preventive health.
- Public perception that 'natural is good'.

Thus, nutraceuticals are the emerging alternative for wellness and disease prevention.

Low-cost Food Supplements

In the early 1960s, there was a wide gap between the food needs of the growing population and the agricultural produce. Simultaneously, there was also recognition that a large segment of our population, especially in the underdeveloped and developing world, suffers from malnutrition, particularly PEM. In order to improve the nutritional status and address the problem of PEM, low-cost, palatable, blended foods rich in energy and proteins, utilising oilseeds, were developed by the National Institute of Nutrition, Hyderabad, and the Central Food Technological Research Institute (CFTRI), Mysore. Later, several other national institutes and universities came forward to develop nutritious foods for our people.

> The National Dairy Development Board developed a soft *chikki* (brittle), whose major constituents were: groundnuts – 46 per cent, invert sugar – 28 per cent, puffed rice – 5 per cent, defatted soyaflour – 2 per cent, corn syrup – 1 per cent, palmolein – 4 per cent, and jaggery – 3 per cent. It is enriched with vitamins and minerals premixes. The *chikki* provides 447 kcals, 16.6g protein and 30 g fat / 100g.

Isolates from oilseeds constitute some of the most concentrated forms of food in nature. They contain a good amount of proteins, besides oil. The quality of proteins from oilseeds is very favourable for complementing cereal proteins. Unlike earlier days, when the oil cake residue left after the extraction of oil was mainly used for livestock feed or as manure, with the use of modern extraction technology, it is now feasible to get oil cake fit for human consumption. The protein isolates derived from the oil extraction process contain over 90 per cent protein. These protein isolates are being used in the formulation of several blended foods all over the world. INCAPARINA from central Mexico was the first weaning mixture formulated for feeding infants, to prevent or treat Protein Energy Malnutrition (PEM). Shortly afterwards, in the mid-1960s, '*Balahar*' was developed in India by CFTRI along similar lines. The basic principle behind these blended food supplements is a cereal: pulse /oilseed combination in the ratio of 1:3 or 1:4.

On an average, these blended foods contain about 20 per cent protein and 300 kcal / 100g. The ingredients used are normally locally available. They are primarily used by the respective countries for their government-operated supplementary feeding programmes. For example, Incaparina, which is a mixture of maize, cotton seed flour (or defatted soya flour), vitamin A, lysine and calcium, is used in Guatemala, Colombia and Mexico, and has on an average 27.5g% protein. Similarly, Protone, used in the United Kingdom, is made from maize, skim milk powder and yeast, and has 22.4g% protein. Corn Soya meal (CSM) formulated in the USA, was made from pre-cooked maize, defatted soyabean flour and skim milk powder 21g% protein. Wheat Soya Blend (WSB), also formulated in the US, was made from bulgar wheat flour and soya bean flour, and had 22 g% protein. Balahar in India was either made from fortified bulgar wheat, groundnut flour, or maize flour, or maize flour, gloundnut flour and soya flour, and had 21 g% protein. Milestone, also used in India, was made of vegetable milk from groundnut isolate, and had 4 g% protein

Amylase-rich germinated cereal flour (ARF) is another low-cost infant food. It is rich in alpha-amylase and helps to instantly liquefy or reduce the dietary bulk of the gruel made from cereal flour. Five grams of ARF is required per 250g of cereal: legume-blended flour. ARF can be prepared from whole *moong dal*. It is a good community-based technology, which can be used locally or by government infant-feeding programmes.

Processed and Convenience Foods

With the transition in food behaviour in the recent past, ready-to-eat, instant and simulated fabricated foods have flooded the markets. The ready acceptance of these foods by consumers is accompanied by an increase in the research and development of newer and better processes in their formulation. These are the prepared ready-to-cook, ready-to-eat, and ready-to-serve products, or those that may require little time for preparation. Thus, the foods conventionally produced in home kitchens are being transformed into market-oriented convenient products. Today, almost all cooked dishes are available in packets as ready-to-serve.

> Puff and serve *chapatis* are partially baked *chapatis*, and can be puffed just before consumption. The shelf life of partially baked chapatis is five to seven days.

Texturised Foods

Texturised or extruded foods are food products in which the ingredients are placed together and passed through a processing technology which gives us an entirely new product. They are designed and engineered. Extrusion cooking, being a high-temperature, short-time process, causes minimum loss of nutrients, while yielding a better product. In addition to processing advantages and good nutritional quality, texturised foods are also microbially safe. The process also destroys heat labile anti-nutritional factors and enzymes, which would otherwise have caused problems during storage and deteriorated product quality. A wide variety of texturised foods are available today, some of them expensive and some cheap, which can be used for nutrition-welfare programmes. Soya nuggets and granules are examples of the former category, and soya puffs (RTEs) of the latter.

> Extruded snacks, breakfast cereals, pet foods, cheese balls, flaked cereals, and puffed cereals are prepared using extrusion technology.

Pasta products are the most popular fabricated food. Pasta products can be defined as any 'shaped and dried dough prepared from semolina, the granular fraction of durum wheat flour mixed with water, milk or egg'. They are available in numerous shapes and sizes, which find versatile use in meals, as they can be served as main dish, salad and soups. Pastas take a short time to cook, are economical, nourishing dishes can be prepared using them, and they fit well with the food choices of today's generation.

Developments in the polymer-packing industry has enabled the introduction of Retort Processed Foods, also called 'Ready to Eat' foods. These are in the form of sachets that can be stored even at room temperature, and only need to be pre-warmed before consumption. Products such as *palak paneer, chana masala, shami kababs,* and fish curries are a few examples.

Energy bars are another type of food products, normally used in sports nutrition and weight management programmes as quick meals or energy supplements. They are normally prepared from oat, barley, wheat, corn, rice, and millets. Binding syrup not only provides sweetness, brown colour and flavour on cooking and baking, but also maintains an appropriate water activity. Fruit pastes from prunes, apples or strawberries give flavour, fibre, vitamins, and minerals. Energy bars provide protein, complex carbohydrates, sugar, fibre, friendly fats, vitamins, minerals, and even phytochemicals.

> Textured vegetable protein, meat analogues and meat extenders are prepared from soyabean. These products are close to meat in terms of their sensory properties, and have the potential of substituting meat.

Facsmile / Designer Foods

A range of imitation or engineered foods called Facsmile Foods or designer foods form another class of innovative new foods in the market. These foods are composed of a variety of natural and/or synthetic ingredients, which have been engineered and modified to simulate the appearance and taste of a particular food, for example non-dairy tea/ coffee creamers, dietetic beverages, and simulated fruit drink powders. Designer foods have the advantage of being available throughout the year, and have a good appearance and taste. In such foods, the desired nutritional quality can also be achieved. They often have a long shelf life and are easy to prepare.

Thus, the transition in the nature of food supply that one is experiencing now is welcome. From a health and nutrition point of view, the important criteria for the development of foods using modern technologies are that they should be safe to use, healthy and nutritionally rich. These foods should not create health hazards in our society. It is also clear that the next few decades will bring about a revolution in the food industry in the way food is grown, processed and distributed. Science and technology have given us the opportunity to drastically alter the nature of food supply. It is crucial for all of us to select food items that are appropriate for our health and fit into our lifestyle.

SUMMARY

- It is possible now with the use of appropriate technologies to stretch the food availability to its maximum, as well as optimise nutrient availability.
- Plant breeding supplies the methodology for improving crops. Biotechnology revolution will help in addressing the pressing problems of food, health and nutrition in the coming years. The introduction of GM crops—varieties bred for increased mineral and vitamin content, such as golden rice—would complement the existing nutrition approaches. However, safety concerns exist regarding their production. All foods produced using GM technology should be labelled.
- Dietary diversification to improve nutritional status is important. Dietary diversification promotes year-round availability, access to and utilisation of foods that promote the increased intake and absorption of nutrients.
- Sprouting and fermentation of foods, especially of pulses, are ways to get maximum nutritional value at no extra cost from some of our foods.
- Food fortification is considered the most efficient as well as the most cost-effective measure in eliminating micronutrient deficiencies. It has been successfully used as a tool to fight hidden hunger. The right food to be fortified, the right amount of nutrients, and the combination of nutrients in the most bioavailable form should be the criteria for successful fortification.
- A whole range of cost-effective nutritious and not-so-nutritious foods have been developed in recent years. The new foods / novel foods can be categorised as nutraceuticals, formulated foods, texturised or engineered foods, and synthetic or simulated ones. Besides nutrient content, the basic criteria in the formulation and production of such foods are the organoleptic properties and societal acceptability. The cost of these foods varies widely.

KEY WORDS

Biological ennoblement: Refers to the improvement in the nutritive value of foods, which may be produced by sprouting, fermentation, and similar biological processes.

Dietary supplements: These products contain nutrients derived from food products that are concentrated in liquid or capsule form, to be taken orally.

Facsmile Foods or designer foods: Are another class of innovative new foods in the market. These foods are composed of a variety of natural and/or synthetic ingredients, which have been engineered and modified to simulate the appearance and taste of a particular food.

Functional food: A natural or processed food that contains known biologically-active compounds which, when consumed in defined quantitative and qualitative amounts, provides a clinically proven and documented health benefit, and is thus important in the prevention, management and treatment of chronic diseases.

Hidden hunger: Does not refer to the overt and obvious hunger of individuals who are unable to afford enough to eat. It refers to the deficiencies of micronutrients.

Hybrid vigour: Increased vigour or general health, resistance to disease, and other superior qualities that are often manifested in hybrid organisms, especially plants and animals.

Medicinal foods: Are formulated to be consumed or administered under medical supervision. They are intended for the specific dietary management of a disease or condition for which there are distinctive nutritional requirements.

Nutraceuticals: Food or parts of food that provide medical or health benefits, including prevention of disease.

Texturised or extruded foods: Food products in which the ingredients are placed together and passed through a processing technology, which gives us an entirely new product. They are designed and engineered.

EXERCISES

1. What are genetically modified foods? Discuss the advantages and disadvantages of these foods.
2. Explain the effect of germination on pulses?
3. How is fermentation of food products beneficial?
4. Discuss the role of dietary diversification in combating nutritional problems.
5. What is food fortification? Explain giving examples.
6. Define nutraceuticals. How are they useful to us?
7. What are textured foods? Give examples
8. Name five convenience foods available in the market. Comment on their nutrient quality.
9. Comment on the philosophy of blended foods.

REFERENCES

Chandrashekhar, Usha, *Prepared and Convenience Foods, Food Science and Applications in Indian Cookery*, Phoenix Publishing House Pvt. Ltd, 2001.

Chitra, U., 'Genetically modified foods—Harmful or helpful?' *Research Reach, J. Home Science* 12(2), 2013, pp. 1–7.

Gupta, Aditi, A. Kawatra and S. Sehgal, 'Physical-chemical properties and nutritional evaluation of newly developed tomato genotypes', *African J. Food Science and Technology* 2(7), 2011, pp. 167–72.

Hardy, G., 'Nutraceuticals and functional foods—Introduction and meaning', *Nutrition* 16(7–8), 2000, pp. 688–689.

IGNOU, 'Public Nutrition', MFN—006, Unit 12: Strategies to Combat Public Nutrition Problems I, New Delhi: Indira Gandhi National Open University, 2006.

Martirosyan, D. M. (ed.), *Functional Foods and Chronic Diseases: Science and Practice*, Food Science Publisher, 2011.

National Nutrition Monitoring Bureau, 'Report of Second Repeat Survey—Rural (1996–97)', NNMB Technical Report No. 18, Hyderabad: National Institute of Nutrition Indian Council of Medical Research, 1999. Available at http://nnmbindia.org/NNMB-PDF%20FILES/Report_OF_2nd%20Repeat_Survey-96-97.pdf.

Nestel, P., *Food Fortification in Developing Countries*, New York: USAID/VITAL, 1993.

Rajalakshmi, R., *Applied Nutrition*, 4e, Oxford and IBH Publishing Pvt. Ltd, 2013.

Srilakshmi, B., *Food Science*, 5e, New Age International Publications, 2013.

Wadhwa, A. and S. Sharma, *Technologies to Improve the Quality of Foods: Nutrition in the Community*, Elite Publishing House, 2003.

Wikipedia—The free encyclopaedia: Nutraceuticals. Available at http://en.wikipedia.org/wiki/Nutraceutical (accessed 22 February 2014).

14

NUTRITIONAL LABELLING

HIGHLIGHTS

- Components of a label on a food product
- Importance of food labelling
- Global trends in labelling
- Health and nutrition claims on labels

INTRODUCTION

Throughout the world, major shifts in dietary patterns are resulting in changes in the nutritional status of people. These changes are termed 'Nutrition transition', and we are witnessing this transition or change because of a number of socio-demographic factors. Consumer attitude and food behaviour are changing. With the increase in the number of women gainfully employed outside the home, there is an increased income-in-hand for families. However, there is also less time for meal preparation. With trade liberalisation, transnational food corporations have entered the market, and with their aggressive marketing policies, have changed the perception of consumers. Now the diets are becoming Westernised, rich in fat, sugar, salt, and consisting of processed, ready-to-eat foods. Accompanying these changes in food consumption at a global and regional level are considerable health consequences, like a rise in the prevalence of obesity, cardiovascular diseases and diabetes.

However, today's consumer is health conscious and wants to know more about the food s/he eats. S/he wants to be able to select the healthier option out of the different types of ready-to-eat foods available off the shelf. To empower the consumer, food regulators have made it mandatory to display basic facts about what each food product contains on the outer label.

The Food Safety and Standards Authority of India (FSSAI) has defined '**Label**' as:

any tag, brand, mark, pictorial or other descriptive matter written, printed, stenciled, marked, embossed, graphic, perforated, stamped or impressed on or attached to container, cover, lid or crown of any food package and includes a product insert.

WHAT SHOULD A FOOD LABEL LOOK LIKE?

The Food Safety and Standards Act (2006), and Food Safety and Standards (Packaging and Labelling) Regulations, 2011, have laid down the requirements for the labelling of pre-packaged foods. It is mandatory that every package of food carry a label that bears all the information required under the Act. At the same time, it is also important that the label should not carry a false, misleading, or deceptive description or presentation of the pre-packaged food, and the labelling should not create a misleading impression regarding the character of food in any respect.

A Label Must Carry:

- Name of the food.
- List of ingredients in descending order of quantity present in the food.
- All food additives which have been used in the preparation of the product.
- Nutrition information.
- Name and complete address of manufacturer.
- Net content by weight or volume.
- Lot number/Batch identification, which helps to trace the food product in case there is a problem with a particular batch of food. There have been instances the world over, when a particular batch/lot of product has been accidentally contaminated. As soon as the problem was identified, the particular batch was immediately recalled from the market.
- Date of Manufacturing /Packing.
- Best Before Date, which is the date till which you can safely eat the product. Beyond this date, the manufacturer does not ensure the quality of the product.
- Logo, which indicates whether the product is vegetarian or not. This logo is a green dot if the product is vegetarian, and a brown dot if the product contains an ingredient that is non-vegetarian. The dot is enclosed in a box.
- Mandatory Declarations.

Regulations make it mandatory to declare certain facts on the label. These relate to the presence of certain food additives, like food colours, artificial sweeteners, flavouring compounds, edible oils and infant foods, etc. Given here are certain examples of these declarations.

(a) Declaration regarding **Food Colours**

CONTAINS PERMITTED NATURAL COLOUR(S)
OR
CONTAINS PERMITTED SYNTHETIC FOOD COLOUR(S)
OR
CONTAINS PERMITTED NATURAL AND SYNTHETIC FOOD COLOUR(S)

(b) Declaration regarding **shelf-life** can be in any of these forms:

'BEST BEFORE .... MONTH AND YEAR'
OR
'BEST BEFORE .... MONTHS FROM PACKAGING'
OR
'BEST BEFORE .... MONTHS FROM MANUFACTURE'

'BEST BEFORE ..... DATE/MONTH/YEAR'
OR
'BEST BEFORE .... DAYS FROM PACKAGING'
OR
'BEST BEFORE .... DAYS FROM MANUFACTURE'

(c) Declarations pertaining to **infant milk substitute and infant food** inform mothers that breast milk is the best for the baby, so that they are not misled in any way into believing that the infant food/formula being sold is better for their baby's health.

'MOTHER'S MILK IS BEST FOR YOUR BABY'

(d) Declarations pertaining to **edible oils and fats** mention the source or type of oil, for example, refined groundnut oil. If the oil is a blend, the label needs to declare the name of the oils that have been blended, and in what quantities. Other common declarations that you will see on the label of cooking oils is that the oil is not supposed to be sold loose, that is, without the package. Also present is a declaration by the manufacturer that the edible oil he is selling is free from argemone oil, which is a toxic oil often used as an adulterant.

> Refined (name of the Oil) Oil
> BLEND OF PALMOLEIN AND GROUNDNUT OIL
> Palmolein …. per cent
> Groundnut oil …. per cent
>
> NOT TO BE SOLD LOOSE
> FREE FROM ARGEMONE OIL

(e) Intake of **Monosodium Glutamate (MSG),** also popularly known as *ajinomoto,* may lead to symptoms like flushing of the face, numbness, tingling sensation, or headache. It was also referred to as the 'Chinese restaurant syndrome', as most people would get these symptoms after eating Chinese food. The safety of MSG in infants below the age of one has not been shown scientifically. Hence, foods containing MSG need to declare a warning:

> This package of (name of the food) contains added MONOSODIUM GLUTAMATE
>
> NOT RECOMMENDED FOR INFANTS BELOW -12 MONTHS

(f) **Artificial Sweeteners,** if added to foods, need to be declared separately. Along with the name of the sweetener needs to come the warning that the product is not recommended for children, as the safety of these sweeteners has not been tested in children. Phenylketonuria is a genetic condition in which the amino acid phenyalanine cannot be metabolised. People suffering from this disease should not consume the artificial sweetener aspartame, which contains this amino acid in its structure. Hence, products containing aspartame as a sweetener should also carry the declaration that Phenylketonurics should avoid that product.

> CONTAINS ARTIFICIAL SWEETENER AND FOR CALORIE CONSCIOUS
> Contains …. (name of artificial sweetener)
> Not recommended for children
> 'Not for Phenylketonurics'

(g) Declaration regarding whether the product is **vegetarian** or **non-vegetarian**. This is perhaps the most looked for symbol on packaged food in India, because of the religious sentiments attached. If any ingredient in a food has been taken from an animal source, the product has to be marked with a brown circle, indicating that it is non-vegetarian. For example, jelly made from gelatin (obtained from collagen present in the skin, bones and connective tissue of animals) is marked with a brown circle.

> 1. Every package of 'non vegetarian' food shall bear a declaration to this effect made by a symbol and shall consist of a brown colour filled circle.
>
> 
>
> 2. Where any article of food contains egg only as non-vegetarian ingredient, the manufacturer, or packer or seller may give declaration to this effect in addition to the said symbol.
> 3. Every package of vegetarian food shall bear a declaration to this effect by a symbol and shall consist of a green colour filled circle.

Nutritional Labelling *is the provision of information about the nutritional content of individual food products.* It is most commonly applied to pre-packaged food and beverage products, and comes in a variety of forms, like Nutrition claims, Health claims, Function claims, etc. When applied to dishes and other foods sold in restaurants and eateries, it is referred to as **menu labelling.**

As per the Food Safety and Standards (Packaging and Labelling) Regulations, 2011, **Nutritional information** *is the declaration of the nutritional composition of the food.* It provides an idea of the nutrition that can be derived from the food.

Nutritional information should always be stated in numerical terms. The nutrition information for a particular food article is declared per 100g or 100ml, or per serving of the food on the label. Figures 14.1 and 14.2 show what a typical nutrition label looks like, and how to read the label.

This declaration should compulsorily comprise of the following information:

- Energy value in kcal
- Protein, fat and carbohydrate, along with sugar quantity in grams
- Amount of any other nutrient for which a nutrition / health claim is made.
- The amount of vitamins and minerals in metric units.
- For nutrition declaration made per serving, the amount in one serving in grams or millilitre should be mentioned for reference beside the serving measure.
- When a claim is made on the amount or type of fatty acid, or the amount of cholesterol, the amount of saturated fatty acids, monounsaturated fatty acids, and polyunsaturated fatty acids in grams and cholesterol in milligrams should be declared. Along with this, the amount of trans fatty acids in grams should also be stated.

Figure 14.1: A Typical Nutrition Label

This pack contains 1 serving of 450 g		
NUTRITION INFORMATION		
	Per serving	**Per 100g**
Energy	760 kcal	170 kcal
Protein	36 g	8 g
Carbohydrates	59 g	13 g
Of which sugars	11 g	3 g
Fat	43 g	10 g
Of which saturates	18 g	4 g
Fibre	2 g	1 g
Sodium	1 g	Trace

It is also important that any pictorial device/graphic matter on the label should not be in conflict with the regulations. All declarations should be legible, conspicuous, plain, bold, and in contrast to the background colour. The height of the numeral is also specified according to the net quantity of the product. The **Principal Display Panel (PDP)** is that part of the container or package which is likely to be displayed or shown to the customer. Hence, all label information should be given on the PDP.

QUALITY MARKS ON LABEL

A mark or symbol which signifies that the product is of good quality reassures the consumer. In India, the **ISI** mark and **AGMARK** instil confidence in the consumer that some reliable authority is monitoring the quality of the food product. Although these quality marks are voluntary for most food products, the FSSA makes it mandatory for a few food items.

Figure 14.2: How to Read a Nutrition Label

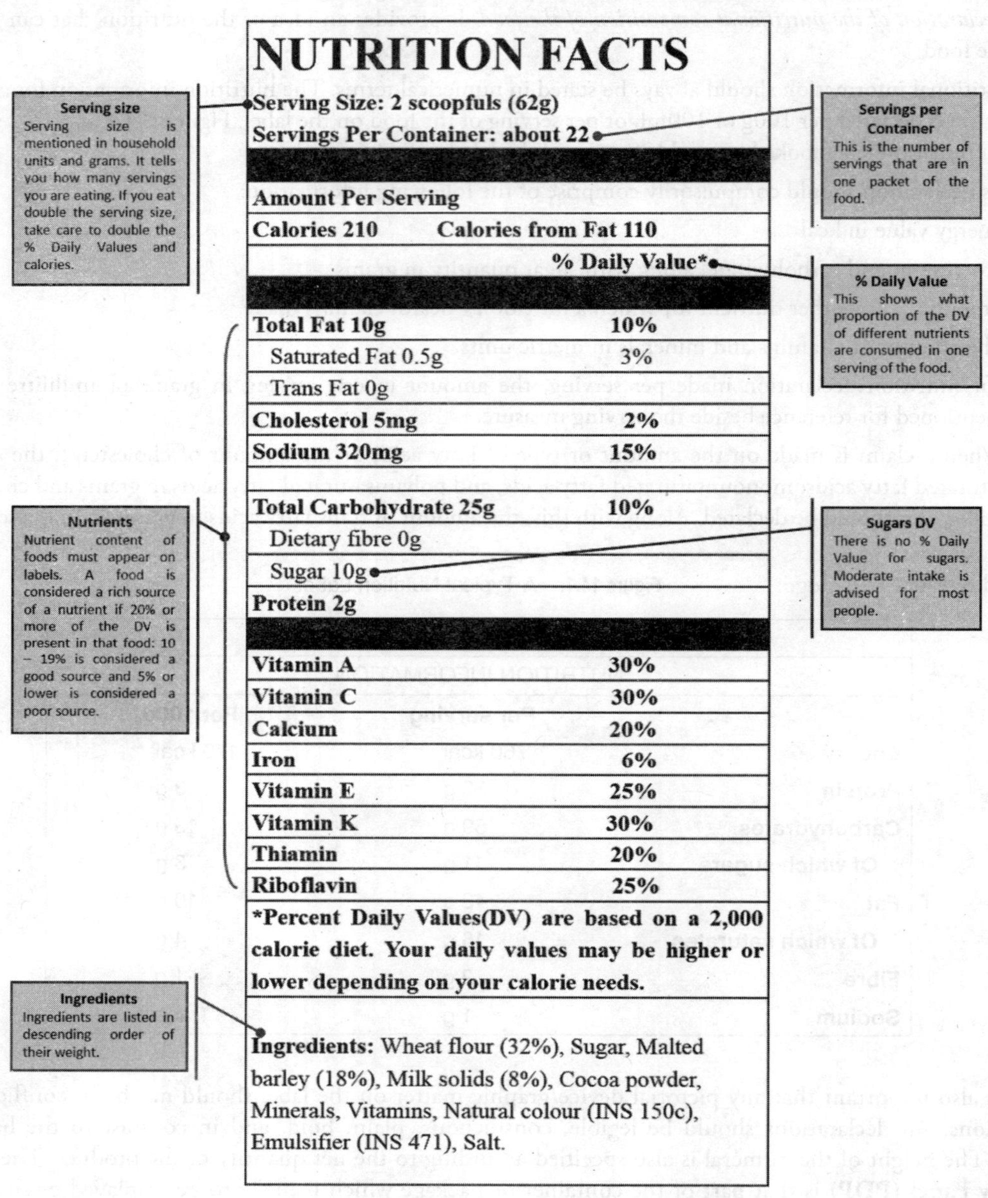

Source: Adapted from Wardlaw 2013 (http://www.fda.gov/Food/IngredientsPackagingLabelling/LabellingNutrition/ucm274593.htm).

The Indian Standards Institution (ISI), now called the Bureau of Indian Standards (BIS), is the national standards body of the country. The ISI certification mark scheme was launched in 1955–56 under the authority derived from the ISI (Certification Marks) Act, 1952. The ISI standards are for a wide range of products and include: specifications for different products, methods of testing the quality of products, codes of practice for different aspects of manufacturing and quality control, terminology and basic engineering aspects. With regard to food items, the ISI mark is granted to a food processing unit only if proper hygienic conditions are maintained, apart from the availability of testing facilities, etc., for checking the quality of production.

The ISI certification scheme is a voluntary scheme, that is, it is not compulsory for all food products to be ISI marked. However, the scheme assumes a mandatory nature when the ISI mark is made compulsory under certain other Acts and statutes. Food colours and milk powders, for instance, cannot be sold under the provisions of the FSS Act if they are not ISI marked.

Agricultural Produce (Grading and Marking) Act—AGMARK

Under the Agricultural Produce (Grading and Marking) Act, 1937, the earliest standards in terms of the grades used in measuring the quality of raw and semi-processed agricultural produce and certain notified food products were prescribed. An organisation willing to grade and pack produce in accordance with the provisions of this Act and the framed rules is authorised to use the AGMARK symbol, in addition to its own trade brands. From the point of view of the management of the quality control programme under AGMARK, grading and quality control has been made compulsory for exports, while it remains voluntary for the domestic market.

Commodities for which AGMARK specifications have been notified are foodgrains and allied products, fruits, vegetables, edible nuts, oilseeds, vegetable oils and fats, oilcakes, spices and condiments, essential oils, livestock products (including poultry), and other commodities like honey, tobacco, *jaggery*, etc. You must have seen this mark on packaged spice powders like turmeric or red chilli powder, or on wheat flour or honey packets. Figure 14.3 shows the three marks that you should look out for on your food packages—FSSAI, ISI and AGMARK. The Fruit Products Order (FPO) mark used earlier for all fruit and vegetable products has been replaced by the FSSAI logo.

Figure 14.3: Marks on Food Labels that Promise a Certain Quality

Source: https://www.google.co.in/search?q=FSSAI+label+images

IMPORTANCE OF LABELLING

Labels provide us with a lot of information. Imagine buying a packaged food product with no label on it. Even if the packaging is transparent, you would probably wonder who has manufactured the product; whether the product is freshly made or stale; what the product is made of (ingredients); whether it contains egg or any ingredient that you might be allergic to; and how much fat you would be consuming if you ate the whole packet?

> Nutrition labelling is important, and not only for people who want to check how many calories the food contains. Information on fat, saturated fat, trans fat, salt, and sugar included on the nutrition label also helps people to reduce their risk of heart disease, hypertension, diabetes, and cancer by choosing foods wisely.

The increase in the prevalence of obesity and associated chronic degenerative diseases has influenced policymakers and consumers alike to seek and spread nutrition information on healthy food choices. The provision of nutrition information on the label has been hailed as an important instrument in promoting healthier eating habits. Nutrition labels tell us about the nutritive value of a particular product. This information includes serving size, number of servings in the package, calories per serving, and the amount of the various nutrients contained in the product.

An **understanding of labels helps us** to:

- Choose a manufacturer or brand we trust
- Compare the prices of different brands selling the same food product
- Identify whether the product is vegetarian or not from the logo
- Check the freshness of the food product from the best before date or date of manufacture
- Look for ingredients which we would like/ not like in the food product. For example, we may want to see whether whole wheat flour is present in the bread we are selecting, as it will be more nutritious. Conversely, we may want to check if hydrogenated vegetable oil has been used in making the biscuits we are selecting, as these would contain harmful trans fatty acids.
- Check products for the presence of ingredients that we might be allergic to, like wheat, soya, peanuts, etc. Besides being mentioned in the list of ingredients, these are also separately declared on the label.
- Choose the foods/ brands that have no added preservatives or artificial colours, or have fewer additives in general. Diabetics and those wanting to avoid sugar may look for products which are sweetened with low or zero calorie artificial sweeteners.
- Choose the foods/brands which give us more of desirable nutrients like fibre, protein, vitamins, calcium, iron, iodine, etc.
- Reject foods/brands with high amounts of fat, saturated fats, cholesterol, trans fats, sodium, and sugar, which are harmful for health.
- Count calories and other nutrients contributed by packaged foods to our diet.
- Choose appropriate serving sizes of foods and beverages, which will help us to consume a variety of foods according to our requirement levels.

Nutrition information on food labels is thus an important tool to promote a balanced diet, thereby enhancing public health. This information assists consumers to better understand the nutritional value of food, and enables them to compare the nutritional values of similar food products and then make healthy food choices based on the relevant nutrition information. For those on special diets (for example, people suffering from diabetes or high blood lipid levels), nutrition information on food labels can be used to make suitable food choices.

GLOBAL TRENDS IN NUTRITION LABELLING

International food trade has existed for thousands of years; however, not too long ago food was mainly produced, sold and consumed locally. Over the last century, the amount of food traded internationally has grown exponentially, and a vast quantity and variety of food travels the globe today.

The Codex Alimentarius Commission is an intergovernmental body with over 170 members, within the framework of the Joint FAO/WHO Food Standards Programme established by the Food and Agriculture Organization (FAO) of the United Nations and the World Health Organization (WHO), with the purpose of protecting the health of consumers and ensuring fair practices in the food trade. The Commission also promotes the coordination of all food standards work undertaken by international governmental and non-governmental organisations.

Trans Fats

Look for the presence of 'hydrogenated' or 'partially hydrogenated' vegetable oil among the ingredients. If these are present, the food product is likely to contain trans fats. Trans fats are worse than saturated fat as these not only increase the levels of bad cholesterol, but also decrease the levels of good cholesterol in blood. This greatly increases the risk of cardiovascular diseases. Commonly consumed foods like bread, biscuits, frozen desserts, cakes, etc., are likely to contain trans fats.

Snapshot of Global Trends

At the national level, countries can be grouped into two broad categories based on their statutory regulations on nutrition labelling:

1. **Mandatory:** Those which make nutrition labelling mandatory even in the absence of a nutrition or health claim. These include **European Union (EU) member states, United States, Canada, Mexico, Argentina, Brazil, Chile, Colombia, Ecuador, Paraguay, Uruguay, Israel, India, Indonesia, China, Hong Kong, South Korea, Malaysia, Taiwan, Australia,** and **New Zealand**. They define which nutrients must be listed and on what basis (for example, per 100 g/per serving). They also allow voluntary initiatives to provide additional nutrition information.
2. **Voluntary:** Those which provide state-sponsored guidelines to be followed voluntarily. These include **Gulf Cooperation Council countries, Venezuela, Turkey, Singapore, Philippines, Thailand, Japan, Kenya, Mauritius, Nigeria,** and **South Africa**. They define which nutrients should be listed and on what basis; however, labelling is not mandatory unless a health or nutrition claim is made, or unless the food is for special dietary uses.

Mandatory Nutrition Labelling

In recent years, the global trend has been a move towards mandatory nutrition labelling, regardless of whether a health or nutrition claim is made. Reflecting this trend, the Codex guidelines were amended in 2012 to recommend that nutrition labelling be mandatory, even in the absence of health claims (Codex Alimentarius Commission 2012).

Many countries that had voluntary guidelines in place have now put in place mandatory nutrition labelling. For example, **China**, which previously had voluntary nutrition labelling, adopted a national standard for mandatory nutrition labelling, which took effect on 1 January 2013. In addition, the **EU** adopted in September 2011 a Regulation on Food Information to Consumers, which makes nutrition labelling mandatory as of 13 December 2016. In January 2013, the European Commission issued guidelines on the implementation of this regulation. The inconsistent presence of nutrition labelling on food and drink products fuelled the European debate, which led to this decision.

In many parts of the world, food companies, consumers and governments are re-examining the provision of nutrition information on food labels. It is important that the nutrition information provided be appropriate and understandable to the consumer, and that it impact food choices. Potentially, food labelling represents a valuable tool to help consumers make informed decisions about their diet and lifestyle. Food information organisations worldwide have been following consumer trends in the use of this information, as well as consumer attitudes vis-à-vis food, nutrition and health.

For truthful nutrition labelling, manufacturers must ensure accurate data on the composition of the nutrients contained in the food. Similarly, for nutrition and health claims, accurate data on the amounts of nutrients or food components are needed. For scientific substantiation of the claimed health effects, an accurate quantification of the amounts of these nutrients or components is essential. The regulatory agency should have well-equipped laboratories and well-trained personnel for surveillance and enforcement purposes.

FRONT OF PACK LABELLING SYSTEM

The need to address obesity and the rise in the prevalence of chronic diseases has prompted recommendations throughout the world for 'Front of pack' labelling. Putting the useful nutrition information or health claim on the front of the pack, which the consumer will first see, can be beneficial. When you go to a grocery shop or supermarket, observe the way the different food products are arranged. You will see that the front of the package is prominently displayed. The front of the package usually has little writing; instead, it has attractive pictures, the brand name, and possibly some claim with which the manufacturer wants to attract the consumer. For example, bargains like 'X g of extra food at the same price', 'Buy one get one free', and nutrition claims like 'Low fat', 'High fibre' are usually put on the front.

The front of the package is also usually made the most attractive, as that is what the consumer sees first. Hence, it makes sense to also place the important nutrition information on the front of the package, in the hope that the consumer will read it more carefully. Most consumers otherwise do not bother to read the fine print at the back, where most of the product and nutrition information currently is.

Studies in India have, shown that the consumer finds the information on the nutrition labels difficult to comprehend and use. For instance, if the label says that a particular biscuit has 2g of fibre per 100g of biscuit, one still does not know how much fibre one would get by eating four biscuits, or, for that matter, whether 2g is a good amount of fibre in 100g of biscuit. It is also difficult for a lay person to fathom how much of fat or added sugar in a product is too much. When the daily diet includes mainly fresh cooked meals and only few things which are packaged—like bread, biscuits, butter, cheese, and possibly some savoury snacks—it becomes difficult for a lay person to evaluate how much these contribute to the daily intake of calories or any other nutrient. So when deciding whether to buy a food product or not, most consumers are known to rely on brand name or taste, rather than nutritional content.

Studies from other countries have shown that although some consumers could understand some of the information on nutrition labelling, in general they reported finding nutrition labelling confusing, especially the use of some technical and numerical information. Consumers reported understanding the terms 'fat', 'calories/kilocalories', 'sugar', 'vitamins', and 'salt'. The concepts and terms reported as least well-understood were the relationship between calories and energy; sodium and salt; sugar and carbohydrate; and the terms cholesterol and fatty acids. Consumers had difficulty understanding the role that the different nutrients mentioned on labels played in their diet. They also had difficulty converting information from gram per 100 g to gram per serving; serving size information also proved difficult to interpret. In general, older consumers and people with lower levels of education or income were likely to have the most difficulty understanding the terms used on food labels.

> ***Allergens***
>
> Persons may be allergic to, or have serious reactions to, food allergens like milk, egg, soybean, peanuts, fish, wheat, tree nuts, etc. Always read the food label's ingredient list carefully to avoid the food allergens in question.

In order to help the consumer, several approaches have been experimented with. Instead of giving nutrient information only per 100 g/ml of the product, some labels give it per portion/serving size (that is, the amount of food that you are likely to eat at a time). The problem with this approach is that it is difficult to standardise how much of the food should constitute a single serving size. Serving size would vary with different age groups and sex of consumers. So if a consumer eats more or less than a serving as indicated on the label, s/he would need to do some calculations to figure out how much of the nutrients has been consumed.

Another approach is to give the nutrient values in terms of what per cent of the Recommended Dietary Intake is being met. To a lay person, this again does not make much sense, unless s/he understands the meaning of these recommendations. Also, since the recommendations are so different for different sexes and age groups, a single figure of 2,000 kcal is used for the calculations.

Nutrient profiling as an approach to communicate healthy food choices to consumers is now gaining momentum. It is a scientific method for assessing the nutritional quality of food and beverage items. It can be used by national authorities to promote public health dietary goals. An internationally recognised method for nutrient profiling could have a wide range of applications, but it is not known whether the criteria developed for one culture or cuisine, or for one purpose or setting, would be applicable to another.

To respond to this need, WHO (2011) started work on an evidence based framework and guiding principles that WHO Member States and Regions could adapt to develop and implement the nutrient profiling of foods for various uses. Such uses would include the marketing of foods to children, health and nutrition claims, product labelling logos or symbols, information and education, provision of food to public institutions, and the use of economic tools to orient food consumption. Nutrient profiling is also one mechanism that Member States can use in implementing the set of recommendations on the marketing of foods and non-alcoholic beverages to children, endorsed by the 63rd World Health Assembly. The main aim of the marketing recommendations was to guide efforts by Member States to design new policies or strengthen existing policies on food marketing communications to children, to reduce the impact that the marketing of foods high in saturated fatty acids, trans fatty acids, free sugars, or salt/sodium has on children.

Nutrient profile models fall into two groups, depending on what they are describing:

1. The nutrient levels in foods (for example, high fat; low fat; reduced fat; source of fibre; high in fat, sugars or salt/sodium; energy dense, nutrient poor); or
2. The effects of consuming the food on a person's health (for example, healthy, healthier option, less healthy).

Nutrient profiling is not a panacea; it cannot solve all problems in relation to food and health. One reason for this is that the nutrient composition of individual foods is not the only determinant of diets. Diets are also determined by the portion sizes of individual foods that consumers eat, the frequency of their consumption, the variety of different foods that make up the diets, and the combinations in which they are eaten. Also, nutrient profiling is concerned primarily with nutrients and with the energy content of foods, and it sometimes includes substances that are not nutrients, but may be considered alongside nutrients (for example, phytochemicals). It does not usually encompass other substances such as pathogens, contaminants and food additives. Nutrient profiling also does not embrace other concerns that people have about food (for example, ethical, religious and environmental concerns).

There has been a special emphasis in developed countries to use nutrient profiling for regulatory control for foods meant for children. Box 14.2 details the nutrient profiling adopted for foods meant for children in the USA. The Food Standards Agency, UK, has given guidelines for a Front of Pack Traffic Light Signpost Labelling. These are applicable only for certain popularly eaten foods, like burgers, pizzas, pies, pastries, breakfast cereals, and ready-to-eat meals, etc., which the Agency has identified based on consumer surveys.

According to the Agency's recommendations, the signpost labelling logo must incorporate each of the following four core elements:

- separate information on fat, saturated fat, sugars, and salt;
- red, amber or green colour coding to provide at a glance information on the level (that is, whether high, medium or low) of individual nutrients in the product;
- provision of additional information on the levels of nutrients present in a portion of the product;
- use of the nutritional criteria as set out in regulation to determine the colour banding.

Box 14.1: Guiding Stars

Nutrition scoring is an approach used by retailers in the United States. The approach was initiated by a supermarket retailer, Hannafords. Their 'Guiding Stars' scheme labels foods with either one star ('good' nutritional value), or two ('better'), or three ('best') (www.hannaford.com).

1 star is good

2 stars is better

3 stars is best

Source:

http://www.hannaford.com/content.jsp?pageName=GuidingStars&leftNavArea=

Box 14.2: Nutrient Profiling for Foods Meant for Children in the USA

Nutrients of concern identified for child health in the United States of America are saturated fatty acids, trans fatty acids, added sugars, and sodium. **Three levels of standards** have been proposed.

The **first level** includes foods that are exempt from marketing restrictions. These foods are considered to be part of a healthy diet; they may be marketed to children without meeting the other two standards:

- 100 per cent fruit and fruit juices in all forms
- 100 per cent vegetables and vegetable juices in all forms; must not exceed 140 mg of sodium per reference amount customarily consumed (RACC)
- 100 per cent non-fat and low-fat milk and yoghurt
- 100 per cent whole grains
- 100 per cent water.

The **second level** of the standard states that if foods are marketed to children, they must provide a meaningful contribution to a healthy diet. Two options are proposed for this standard:

- Foods must contain at least 50 per cent by weight of fruit; vegetable; whole grain; fat-free or low-fat milk or yoghurt; fish; extra lean meat or poultry; eggs; nuts and seeds; or beans; or any combination thereof.
- Food must contain a specific measurement per RACC; for example:
  - 0.5 cups fruit or fruit juice
  - 0.6 cups vegetables or vegetable juice
  - 0.75 oz. equivalent of 100 per cent whole grain
  - 0.75 cups milk or yoghurt; 1 oz. natural cheese; 1.5 oz. processed cheese
  - 1.4 oz. meat equivalent of fish or extra lean meat or poultry.

For the **third level** of standard, foods marketed to children must not contain more than the specified amounts of saturated fatty acids, trans fatty acids, sugars, and sodium:

- saturated fatty acids – 1 g or less per RACC, and not more than 15 per cent of calories
- trans fatty acids – 0 g per RACC (<0.5 g)
- sugars – no more than 13 g of added sugars per RACC
- sodium – no more than 200/240 mg per portion.

The standards for saturated fatty acids, trans fatty acids and sugars are based on healthy standards for children. Sodium is currently set at half the adult amount.

The green/amber (low/medium) boundaries are determined by the European Regulation (EC) No. 1924/2006 on Nutrition and Health Claims, which came into effect on 1 July 2007. The amber/red (medium/high) boundaries are based on existing advice from the Committee on the Medical Aspects of Food Policy (COMA) and the Scientific Advisory Committee on Nutrition (SACN) for fat, saturated fat, sugars, and salt, using 25 per cent of recommended intake levels per 100g and 30 per cent (40 per cent for salt) per portion.

The traffic light colour approach to nutritional signpost labelling requires criteria that define the green/amber (low/medium) and amber/red (medium/high) boundaries for the key nutrients, fat, saturated fat, sugars, and salt. The criteria for foods are set out in Table 14.1.

Table 14.1: Criteria for Traffic Light Approach for Labelling Food

	Green (Low)	*Amber (Medium)*	*Red (High)*	
Fat	≤ 3.0 g/100g	>3.0 to ≤ 20.0 g/100g	>20.0 g/100g	21.0g / portion
Saturates	≤ 1.5 g/100g	>1.5 to ≤ 5.0 g/100g	>5.0 g/100g	6.0g / portion
Sugars	≤ 5.0 g/100g	>5.0 to ≤ 12.5g/100g	>12.5g/100g	15.0g / portion
Salt	≤ 0.30 g/100g	>0.30 to ≤ 1.50g/100g	>1.50 g/100g	2.40g / portion

The colour code for sugars is determined in terms of both the total and added sugar components, as follows:

- **Green** if **total sugars** are less than, or equal to, **5g/100g**.
- **Amber** if **total sugars** exceed **5g/100g,** and **added sugars** are less than **12.5g/100g**.
- **Red** if **added sugars** are more than **12.5g/100g**.

In addition to the per 100g criteria, there are 'per portion' criteria for food. The 'per portion' criteria ensure that any food that contributes more than 30 per cent (40 per cent for salt) of an adult's recommended daily maximum intake for a particular nutrient is labelled red (high).

HEALTH AND NUTRITION CLAIMS

The Codex has given guidelines for making claims relating to the nutritional content of the food product (**Nutrition claim**), and the health benefits of a food (**Health claim**). However, it also states that these nutrition claims should be consistent with the national nutrition policy, and support that policy. Only nutrition claims that support the national nutrition policy should be allowed.

Nutrition claim *refers to any representation which states, suggests, or implies that a food has particular nutritional properties, including, but not limited to, the energy value and to the content of protein, fat and carbohydrates, as well as the content of vitamins and minerals.*

The following do not constitute nutrition claims:

1. The mention of substances in the list of ingredients;
2. The mention of nutrients as a mandatory part of nutrition labelling;
3. Quantitative or qualitative declaration of certain nutrients or ingredients on the label, if required by national legislation.

Nutrient content claim *is a nutrition claim that describes the level of a nutrient contained in a food* (examples: 'source of calcium'; 'high in fibre and low in fat').

Nutrient comparative claim *is a claim that compares the nutrient levels and/or energy value of two or more foods* (examples: 'reduced'; 'less than'; 'fewer'; 'increased'; 'more than').

Non-addition claim *means any claim that an ingredient has not been added to a food, either directly or indirectly.* The ingredient is one whose presence or addition is permitted in the food, and which consumers would normally expect to find in the food (example: a beverage claiming that it 'contains no fruit juice or fruit pulp').

Health claim *means any representation that states, suggests, or implies that a relationship exists between a food or a constituent of that food and health.* These claims should be consistent with the national health policy, including nutrition policy, and support such policies where applicable. Health claims should be supported by a sound and sufficient body of scientific evidence to substantiate the claim, provide truthful and non-misleading information to aid consumers in choosing healthy diets, and be supported by specific consumer education. The impact of health claims on consumers' eating behaviours and dietary patterns should be monitored, in general, by competent authorities in the country. In India, the FSSAI monitors both Nutrition and Health claims.

Nutrient function claim *is a nutrition claim that describes the physiological role of the nutrient in growth, development and normal functions of the body.*

> ***Example:***
>
> Nutrient A (naming a physiological role of nutrient A in the maintenance of health and promotion of normal growth and development). Food X is a source of/ high in nutrient A.

Table 14.2 provides the conditions for making nutrient claims, as outlined in the Codex document. The FSSAI is also working out a similar document for the Indian market.

Other function claims *concern specific beneficial effects of the consumption of foods or their constituents, in the context of the total diet on normal functions or biological activities of the body. Such claims relate to a positive contribution to health, or to the improvement of a function, or to modifying or preserving health.*

> ***Example:***
>
> Substance A (naming the effect of substance A on improving or modifying a physiological function or biological activity associated with health). Food Y contains x grams of substance A.

Reduction of disease risk claims *relate the consumption of a food or food constituent, in the context of the total diet, to the reduced risk of developing a disease or health-related condition.* Risk reduction means significantly altering a major risk factor(s) for a disease or health-related condition. Diseases have multiple risk factors, and altering one of these risk factors may or may not have a beneficial effect. The presentation of risk reduction claims must ensure, for example, by use of appropriate language and reference to other risk factors, that consumers do not interpret them as prevention claims.

> ***Examples:***
>
> 'A healthful diet low in nutrient or substance A may reduce the risk of disease D. Food X is low in nutrient or substance A.'
>
> 'A healthful diet rich in nutrient or substance A may reduce the risk of disease D. Food X is high in nutrient or substance A.

Nutrient function claims may be substantiated based on generally accepted authoritative statements by recognised expert scientific bodies, which have been verified and validated over time. Health claims should primarily be based on evidence provided by well-designed human intervention studies. Human observational and animal model studies may provide a supporting knowledge base for the relationship between the food or food constituent and the health effect, but cannot be considered sufficient *per se* to substantiate any type of health claim. When the claim is about a food or food constituent, the amount should not expose the consumer to health risks, and the known interactions among constituents should be considered. The expected level of consumption should not exceed relevant upper levels of intake for food constituents.

Nutrient Reference Values (NRV) is a parameter indicating a certain amount of energy or a nutrient in food. NRV is a unified standard for nutrition labelling. This parameter assumes that every person is taking 2,000 kcal of energy (about 8,400 kilojoules), and sets the amount of necessary intake for each nutrient. The daily intake of energy is different for everyone, depending on different occupations, ages, genders, and individual features. It varies from 2,000 kcal to 4,000 kcal. So this parameter is called Nutrient Reference Value only for the convenience of nutrition labelling. For food, the higher the NRV, the closer its nutrient content to the recommended daily intake.

Nutrition labelling can be an effective means of helping consumers to make healthy food choices, although existing evidence concerning the effect of health claims on diet and public health is insufficient. Regulations can play a crucial role in enhancing the potential of nutrition labelling and health claims to promote health. The effectiveness of nutrition labelling and health claims in improving national dietary patterns relies largely on a motivated and educated public, who can make healthy choices. This approach has limitations. If there is to be significant change, action on nutrition labels and health claims needs to be part of an integrated approach that tackles the increasing rates of diet-related, non-communicable diseases at a population level, as well as an individual level.

Table 14.2: Conditions for Nutrient Claims as Per Codex

Component	*Claim*	*Conditions* *Not More Than*
Energy	Low	40 kcal (170 kJ) per 100 g (solids) or 20 kcal (80 kJ) per 100 ml (liquids)
	Free	4 kcal per 100 ml (liquids)

Table 14.2 contd

Table 14.2 contd

Component	*Claim*	*Conditions* *Not More Than*
Fat	Low	3 g per 100 g (solids) 1.5 g per 100 ml (liquids)
	Free	0.5 g per 100 g (solids) or 100 ml (liquids)
Saturated Fat	Low	1.5 g per 100 g (solids) 0.75 g per 100 ml (liquids) and 10% of energy
	Free	0.1 g per 100 g (solids) 0.1 g per 100 ml (liquids)
Cholesterol	Low	0.02 g per 100 g (solids) 0.01 g per 100 ml (liquids)
	Free	0.005 g per 100 g (solids) 0.005 g per 100 ml (solids) and, for both claims, less than: 1.5 g saturated fat per 100 g (solids) 0.75 g saturated fat per 100 ml (liquids) and 10% of energy of saturated fat
Sugars	Free	0.5 g per 100 g (solids) 0.5 g per 100 ml (liquids)
Sodium	Low	0.12 g per 100 g
	Very Low	0.04 g per 100 g
	Free	0.005 g per 100 g
		NOT LESS THAN
Protein	Source	10% of NRV per 100 g (solids) 5% of NRV per 100 ml (liquids) or 5% of NRV per 100 kcal (12% of NRV per 1 MJ) or 10% of NRV per serving
	High	2 times the values for 'source'
Vitamins and Minerals	Source	15% of NRV per 100 g (solids) 7.5% of NRV per100 ml (liquids) or 5% of NRV per 100 kcal (12% of NRV per 1 MJ) or 15% of NRV per serving
	High	2 times the value for 'source'

SUMMARY

- Due to the emerging nutrition transition, there are major shifts in dietary patterns, resulting in changes in the nutritional status of people.
- With a rapid increase in the prevalence of chronic degenerative diseases, today's consumer has become health conscious, and wants to be able to select the healthier option out of the different types of ready-to-eat foods available off the shelf.
- To empower the consumer, food regulators have made it mandatory to display basic facts about what each food product contains on the outer label.

- The Food Safety and Standards Act (2006), and Food Safety and Standards (Packaging and Labelling) Regulations, 2011, have laid down the requirements for labelling of pre-packaged foods.
- It is mandatory that every package of food carry a label that bears all the information required under the Act. At the same time, it is also important that the label not be misleading.
- The Codex Alimentarius Commission works towards protecting the health of consumers and ensuring fair practices in the food trade.
- In many parts of the world, food companies, consumers, and governments are re-examining the provision of nutrition information on food labels.
- Nutrient profiling, as an approach to help communicate healthy food choices to consumers, is now gaining momentum. It is a scientific method for assessing the nutritional quality of food and beverage items.
- The need to address obesity and the increase in chronic diseases has prompted recommendations throughout the world for 'front of pack' labelling.
- The Food Standards Agency, UK, has given guidelines for a Front of Pack Traffic Light Signpost Labelling. Red, amber or green colour coding provides at a glance information on the level (that is, whether high, medium or low) of certain nutrients in the product.
- Codex has given guidelines for making claims relating to the nutritional content of the food product (Nutrition claim) and health benefits of a food (Health claim).
- Nutrition labelling can be an effective means of helping consumers to make healthy food choices. Regulations can play a crucial role in enhancing the potential of nutrition labelling and health claims to promote health.

KEY WORDS

Health claim: Any representation that states, suggests, or implies that a relationship exists between a food or a constituent of that food and health.

Label: Any tag, brand, mark, pictorial or other descriptive matter written, printed, stencilled, marked, embossed, graphic, perforated, stamped, or impressed on, or attached to, container, cover, lid, or crown of any food package, and includes a product insert.

Non-addition claim: Any claim that an ingredient has not been added to a food, either directly or indirectly.

Nutrition claim: Any representation which states, suggests, or implies that a food has particular nutritional properties, including, but not limited to, the energy value and to the content of protein, fat and carbohydrates, as well as the content of vitamins and minerals.

Nutrient comparative claim: A claim that compares the nutrient levels and/or energy value of two or more foods, for example, 'reduced'; 'less than'; 'fewer'; 'increased'; 'more than'.

Nutrient content claim: A nutrition claim that describes the level of a nutrient contained in a food, for example, 'source of calcium'; 'high in fibre and low in fat'.

Nutrient function claim: A nutrition claim that describes the physiological role of the nutrient in growth, development and normal functions of the body.

Nutrient profiling: A scientific method for assessing the nutritional quality of food and beverage items.

Nutrient Reference Values (NRV): Usually the levels of intake of essential nutrients considered adequate to meet the known nutritional needs of practically all healthy people for prevention of deficiency states. NRV is a unified standard for nutrition labelling. This parameter assumes that every person is taking 2,000 kcal of energy, and sets the amount of necessary intake for each nutrient.

Principal Display Panel: That part of the container or package likely to be displayed or shown to the customer; hence, all label information should be given on this.

EXERCISES

1. How are labels helpful for consumers?
2. Define 'label' and discuss the importance of nutritional labelling.
3. How can regulatory authorities help in implementing nutritional labelling?
4. Comment on global trends in nutritional labelling.
5. How is nutritional profiling helpful in developing healthy food choices among consumers?
6. What are nutrition and health claims? How are they useful for companies, consumers and regulatory authorities?

REFERENCES

Food Standards Agency, *Front of Pack Traffic Light Signpost Labelling*, UK: Technical Guidance, 2007.

Kant, A. K., 'Indexes of overall diet quality: A review', *J Am Diet Assoc* 96, 1996, pp. 785–91.

WHO/FAO, *Food Labelling*, 5e, Joint Food Standards Programme, Codex Alimentarius Commission, 2008.

WHO, 'Nutrient profiling', Report of a WHO/IASO technical meeting, London, 4–6 October 2010, Geneva: WHO, 2011.

European Food Information Council (EUFIC), *Global Update on Nutrition Labelling*, 2013.

Codex Guidelines on Nutrition and Health Claims (CAC/GL 23–1997).

ONLINE SOURCES

http://foodsafetyauthorityindia.blogspot.in/2011/12/nutrition-information-and-labelling.html

http://www.foodinsight.org.

http://www.eufic.org.

http://www.fao.org.

ftp://ftp.fao.org/docrep/fao

http://www.food.gov.uk/multimedia/pdfs/frontofpackguidance2.pdf

Figure 1: The Human Digestive System, Consist ng of the Alimentary Canal and Associated Glands

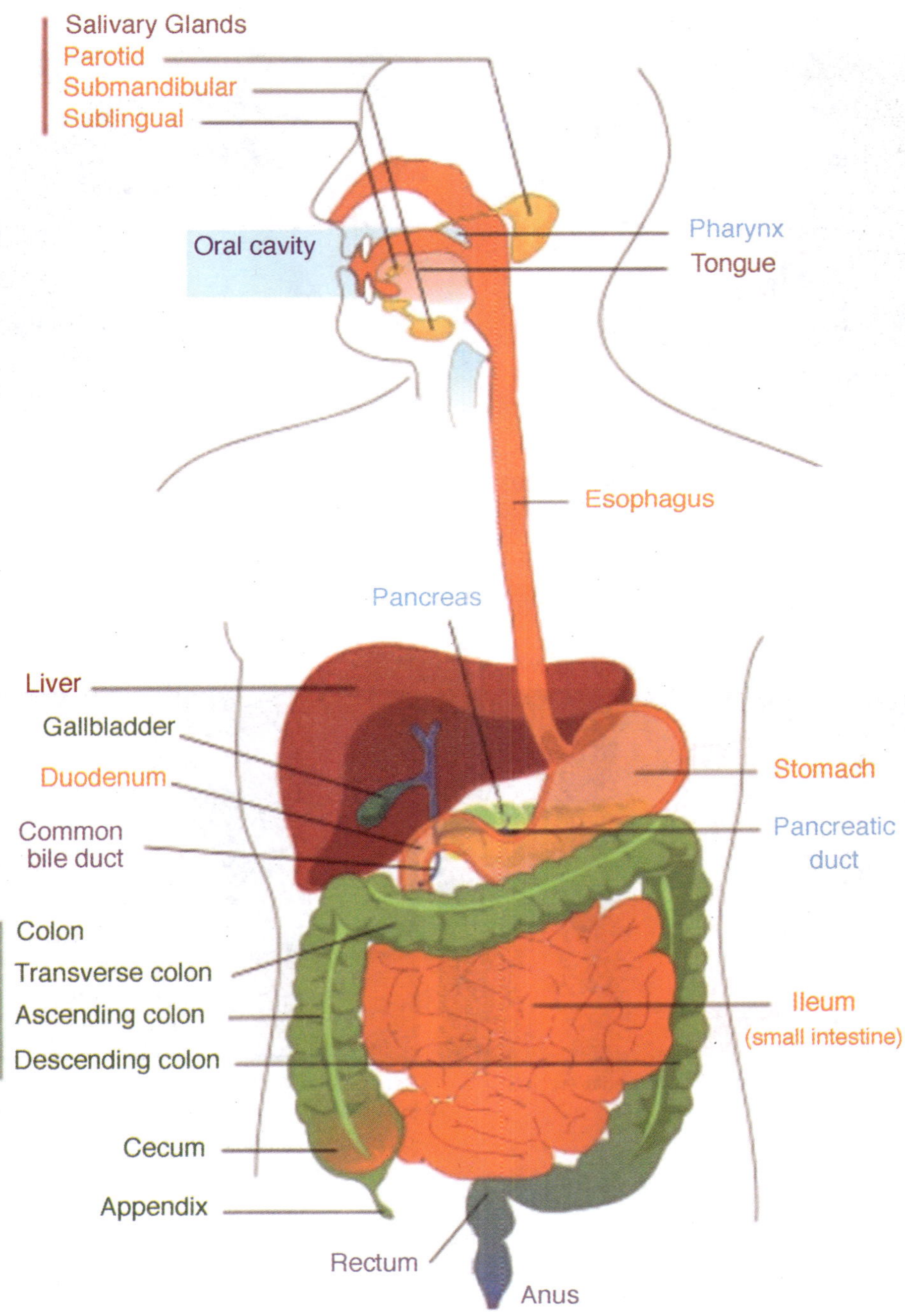

Source: http://commons.wikimedia.org/wiki/File: Digestive_System_diagram.png.

Figure 2: Clinical Signs of Vitamin A Deficiency

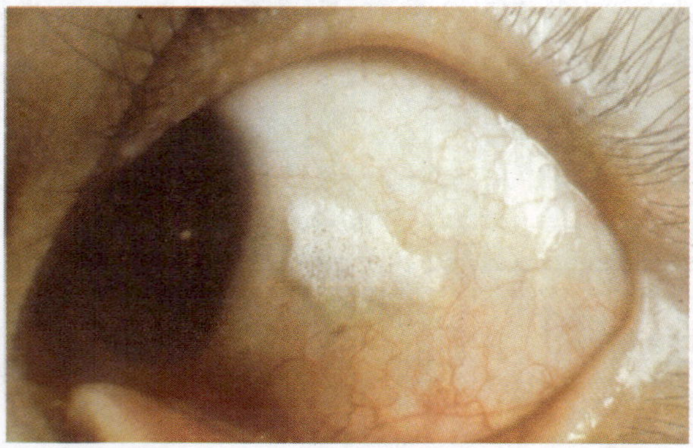

Bitot's Spot

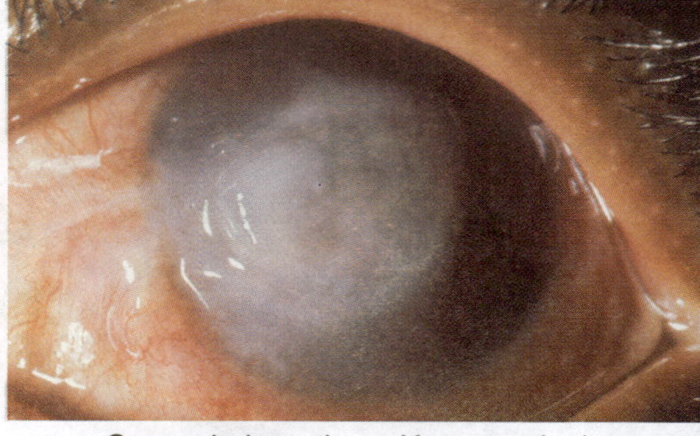

Corneal ulceration—Keratomalacia

Source: https://c2.staticflickr.com/6/5292/5444948403_dc3eaf084a_z.jpg
https://c1.staticflickr.com/9/8003/7602662428_e522d48bfe_z.jpg.

Figure 3: Signs of Fluoride Toxicity—Dental Fluorosis

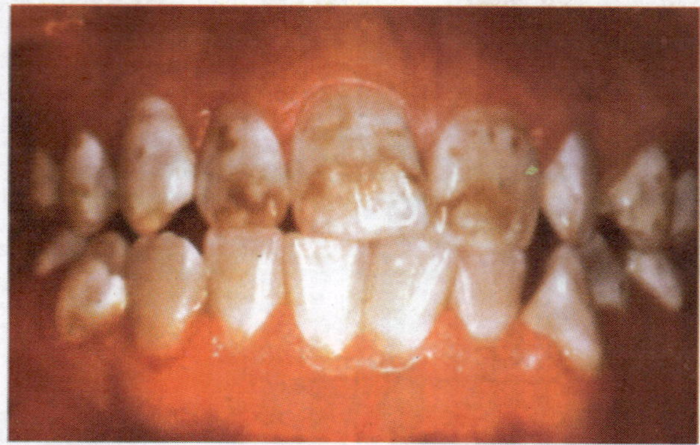

Source: http://upload.wikimedia.org/wikipedia/en/c/c5/Fluorosis_13.jpg

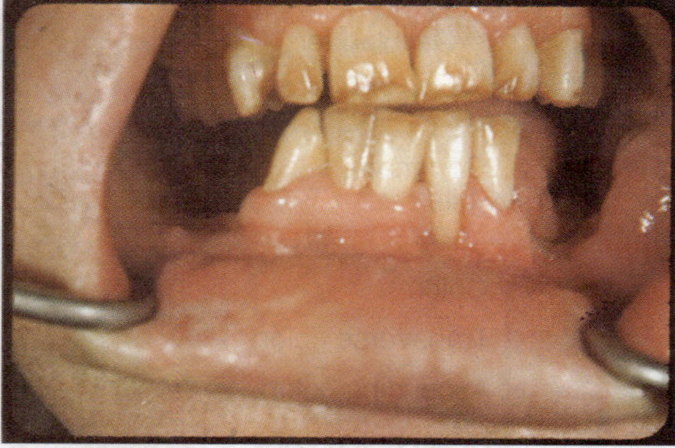

Source: http://upload.wikimedia.org/wikipedia/commons/thumb/a/ae/4724507933_07ac954c27_bFluorose.jpg/800px-4724507933_07ac954c27_bFluorose.jpg.

Figure 4: Beriberi

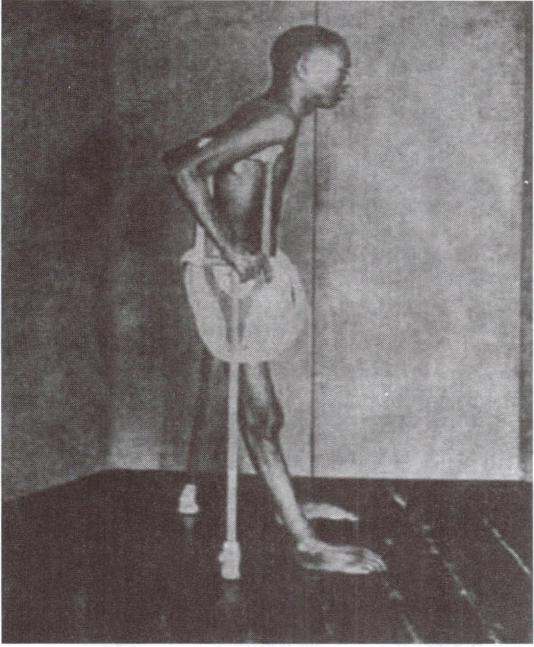

Source: http://upload.wikimedia.org/wikipedia/commons/7/72/Beriberi_USNLM.jpg.

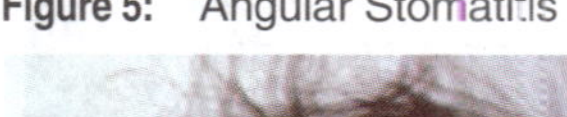

Figure 5: Angular Stomatitis

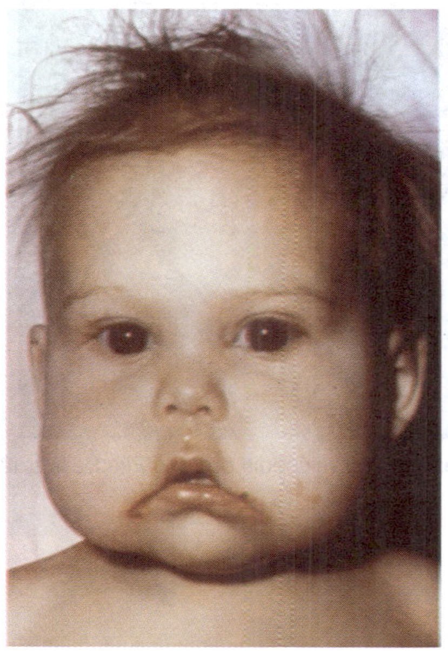

Source: http://upload.wikimedia.org/wikipedia/commons/4/4d/Kwashiorkor_6180.jpg?uselang=en-gb.

Figure 6: Spongy bleeding gums

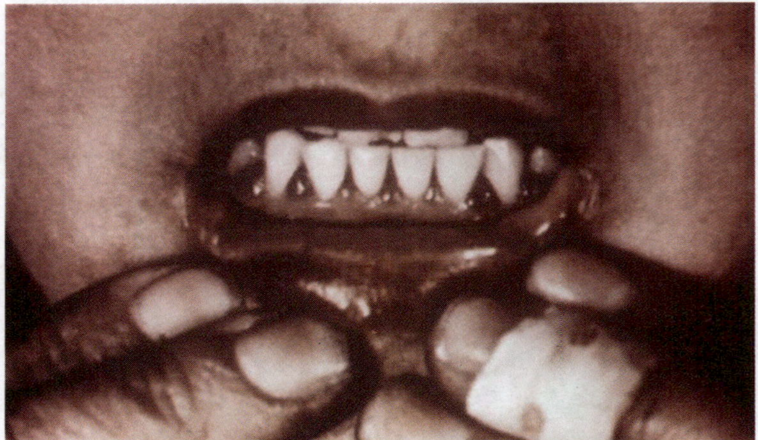

Source: http://upload.wikimedia.org/wikipedia/commons/8/88/Scorbutic_gums.jpg?uselang=en-gb

Figure 7: Pellagra

Source: http://en.wikipedia.org/wiki/File:Pellagra2.jpg.

Figure 8: Spina Bifida

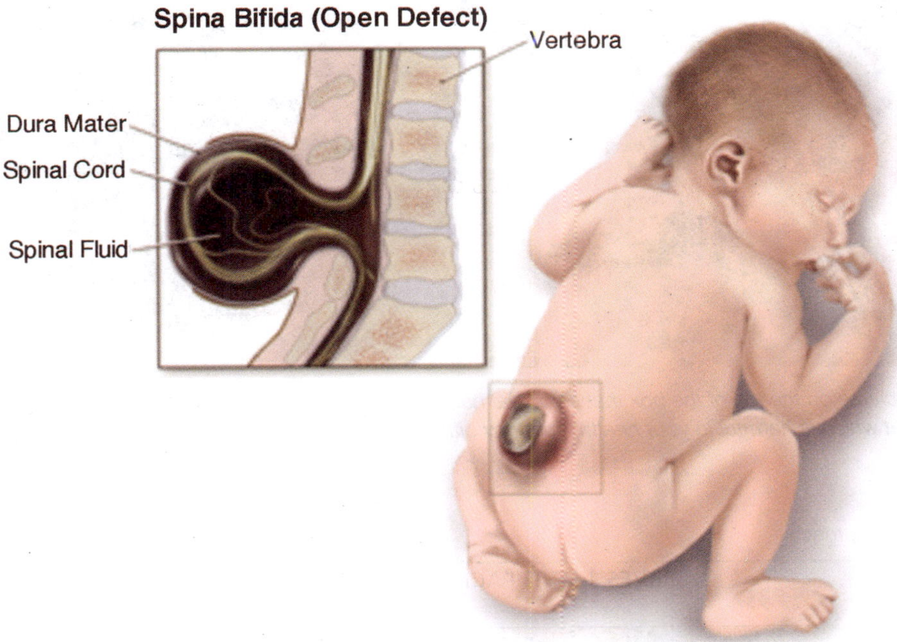

Source: http://upload.wikimedia.org/wikipedia/commons/6/6b/Spina_bifida-web.jpg.

Figure 9: Petechiae

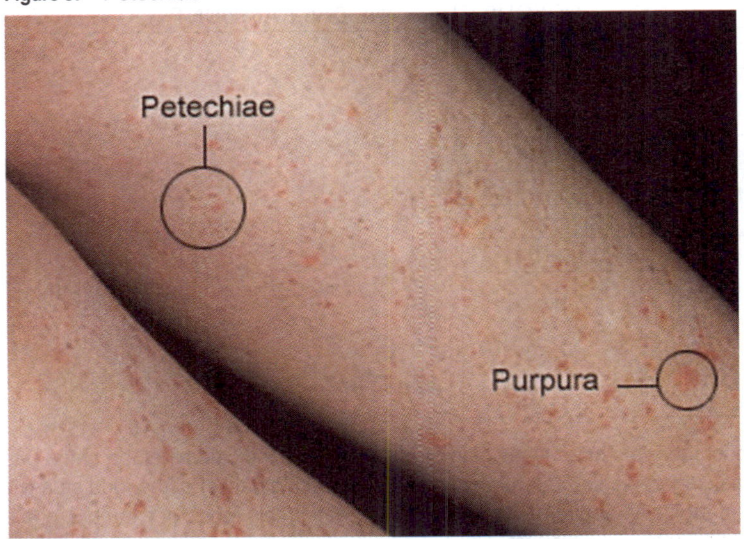

Source: http://pixshark.com/mild-petechiae-legs.htm.

Figure 10: Front of Pack Labeling

If your pizza boldly declares on the top of the box that if you eat half this pizza, you will be eating high amounts of fat, especially saturated fat which is harmful to your health, you may either eat less of the pizza or actually decide to avoid eating it!

Figure 11: Traffic Light Approach

A

SERVES 1- THIS PACK PROVIDES				
CALS 315 (16%)	**SUGAR 3.6g (4%)**	**FAT 12.6g (18%)**	**SAT FAT 8.1g (41%)**	**SALT 1.80g (30%)**
OF YOUR GUIDELINE DAILY AMOUNT				

B

	Per serving
FAT	7.7g
SATURATES	2.0g
SUGARS	42.2g
SALT	2.0g

High
Medium
Low

A- From this label, the consumer gets three types of information. First, it indicates that the entire packet is one serving and the amount of calories, sugar, fat, saturated fat, and salt one serving/packet of the food stuff will provide. Second, it tells us what percentage of the daily requirements will be met by eating this food, for example, one serving provides 41 per cent of the recommendation for saturated fat. Third, the label also indicates that total calories and sugar are within acceptable levels, fat and salt are in moderate amounts, but the amount of saturated fat is high.

B- This label gives in grams the amount of fat, saturated fat, salt, and sugar present in each serving of the food. The amount of sugar is high, salt is in moderate amounts, while fat and saturated fats are low.

SECTION II

LIFECYCLE NUTRITION

15

PRINCIPLES OF MEAL PLANNING

HIGHLIGHTS

- Concept of balanced diet
- Food groups
- Food Pyramid
- Food exchange list
- Steps in meal planning
- Factors affecting meal planning
- Factors influencing food choices

Most people may not have access to food composition tables, nor the knowledge or time to delve into the nutritional content of foods they normally consume. People need to be guided about balancing the intake of different nutrients in their diet and making healthy food choices. Food groups classify foods into categories, depending on their type, nutritional contribution and functions. These food groups can then be used to educate and counsel about planning diets which achieve nutrient intakes in accordance with Recommended Dietary Allowances (RDA). Understanding the factors that will determine the food choices of different family members is an important step in meal planning. However, keeping these factors in mind and then planning nutritionally adequate meals is the biggest challenge. Discussed here are guidelines to keep in mind while choosing foods and planning a balanced diet for oneself and for family members.

CONCEPT OF BALANCED DIET

You may often be advised to eat a 'balanced diet', but are not sure what it really means. The concept of a balanced diet stems from trying to balance the amount of different types of foods you eat everyday, so that you have a nutritionally adequate diet. Foods have been classified into different food groups to make this task easier. Choosing wisely from each food group is important in order to balance your diet. To do so, you need to understand why foods in a particular group are important for you. A balanced diet is one that includes foods from all food groups during the day. The quantities and proportions of these foods need to be such that they fulfil our daily requirements for all nutrients.

In addition, the nutrients should be in such amounts that a little bit can be stored in the body to take care of the days when food intake is insufficient. If, for any reason, you have not eaten well for a few days, it should not affect your health adversely. Besides meeting the physiological need for various nutrients and providing satiety, meals also need to be planned keeping economic, social, religious, and cultural factors in mind. Planning nutritionally balanced meals is an art, because you also need to take into account several factors that will make the meal tasty, visually appealing and acceptable to people.

Balanced diets usually provide 50–60 per cent energy from carbohydrates, 10–15 per cent energy from proteins, and 20–30 per cent energy from fats. In addition, the diet should also provide micronutrients and other protective substances like phytochemicals in sufficient quantities needed for maintaining optimum health.

BASIC FOOD GROUPS

Foods can be grouped into categories according to the type of food, or the nutrients that foods supply. The basic food group classification is based on the physiological role played by the foods of each group in our bodies. Thus, we have energy giving foods, body building foods, and protective or regulatory foods (Figure 15.1). In traditional Indian diets, you already see this in application, where the main meals have a cereal-pulse-vegetable combination (like *roti*/rice with *dal* and *sabji*), that is, a food from each of the three food groups.

Figure 15.1: Basic Three-Food Group Classification Based on Physiological Function

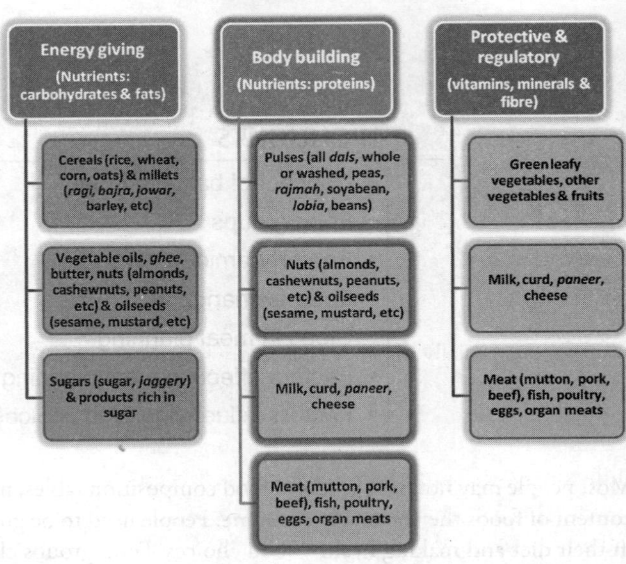

Foods like cereal grains, fats and oils, sugar, and products made from these, are 'energy-giving foods'. Carbohydrates and fats are the major nutrients supplying energy. Pulses, nuts, oilseeds, milk and milk products, meat, fish, poultry, and products made from these, constitute the 'body-building group'. The major nutrient that helps in body building is protein. Calcium, a mineral, helps to make bones strong. 'Protective foods', as the name suggests, are foods with nutrients that protect our body from diseases by strengthening our immunity. These are also known as regulatory foods, as the vitamins and minerals contained in them help the enzymes participating in various metabolic reactions to function efficiently.

The Indian Council of Medical Research (ICMR) classifies foods into five groups. Table 15.1 gives the different food groups and the nutrients they supply.

Table 15.1: The Five Food Group Classification

Food Group	*Main Nutrient Supplied*	*Other Nutrients Present*
Cereal Grains and Products	Energy, Protein	Invisible fat, B Vitamins (Thiamin, Riboflavin, Folic Acid), Iron, Calcium, Fibre
Pulses and Legumes	Protein, Energy	Invisible fat, B Vitamins (Thiamin, Riboflavin, Folic Acid), Iron, Calcium, Fibre
Milk and Meat Products	Protein	Fat, Riboflavin, Calcium, Vitamin B_{12}, Fat-soluble vitamins
Fruits and Vegetables	Vitamins (Carotenoids, Ascorbic acid, Folic acid, Riboflavin), Minerals (Calcium, Iron), Fibre	Invisible fats, trace minerals and vitamins
Fats and Sugars	Energy	Essential fatty acids

Source: Adapted from Nutritive Value of Indian Foods, ICMR.

Let us discuss these five food groups in detail, as well as how foods should be selected from each group.

1. **Cereal grains and their products.** This food group includes all cereals like rice, rice flakes, puffed rice or *murmura*, wheat, *dalia, sooji, atta, maida, ragi, bajra*, maize, corn flakes, jowar, barley, and foods made with these, like bread, rusk, biscuits, pasta, etc. Cereals are a good source of energy for us. They also provide us with valuable amounts of protein. The quality of protein, however, is not as good as that present in milk, eggs or meat. If the right combination of proteins is eaten—for instance, if cereals are eaten with pulses (*dals*), like *dal-chawal, roti-dal*, etc., or if cereals are eaten with milk or milk products, like with curd or *paneer*—a vegetarian can get very good quality protein, too. Cereals also provide us with other important nutrients like fibre, B vitamins, iron, and calcium. Fibre and B vitamins are generally present in the outer layer of cereals, called the bran layer. That is why it is important to have whole cereals like unpolished brown rice instead of polished white rice, whole wheat flour, that is, *atta* instead of refined flour or *maida,* and whole wheat bread instead of white bread made of refined flour.

2. **Pulses and legumes.** All *dals* come in this group, viz., *chana, moong, masoor, urad, arhar,* as well as *rajma, chana, lobia,* soyabean, peas, beans, and products made from them or their flour, like *besan,* nutri-nuggets and granules, etc. Pulses give us energy and are also a rich source of protein. The quality of the pulse protein can be improved by eating it in combination with cereals. In fact, one part *dal* with four or five parts of cereals provides very good quality protein. Pulses are also good sources of fibre and B vitamins, especially those eaten with the seed coat (whole pulses or *sabut/chilka dals*). Iron and calcium are also present in foods of this group.

3. **Milk and Meat products**. This food group primarily provides us with good quality protein, and hence is very important, especially during childhood when the body is growing rapidly. Adults also need protein to maintain the normal functioning of their bodies, and to look after the repair of worn-out body parts and tissues. Milk and milk products like curd, cheese, *khoa*, and *paneer*, and dishes made with these are also rich sources of calcium. Calcium is a mineral that is very important for bone health. In fact, milk and milk products are the best sources of calcium in the diet, as calcium from this source is most readily absorbed by the body.

Meat includes the flesh of animals like goat, sheep, pig and cow, chicken, egg, fish, shrimp, prawns, oysters, mussels, and other seafood, and meat products include bacon, ham, sausages, salami, etc. Besides being rich sources of protein, meats also contain iron in a readily absorbable form (heme iron). These foods are also a source of saturated fat and cholesterol. Hence, lean cuts of meat should be preferred. Fat in meat can easily be seen as a white layer interspersed between muscle tissues. These can usually be cut away or removed before consumption. In the case of chicken, the skin can be removed to reduce its fat content. Cheese, *paneer,* and curd made from full cream milk are also rich in saturated fat and cholesterol, and hence it is better to make these from low fat milk (toned, double toned, or skimmed milk).

4. **Fruits and Vegetables.** This is perhaps the most neglected food group, with most people eating very little of fruit and a limited variety of vegetables. Fruits and vegetables are full of important vitamins, minerals and also fibre, They help by improving our immunity and also regulating the metabolic reactions in our body. They also protect our bodies from a host of non-communicable diseases, like diabetes, heart disease, etc. Out of all the vegetables, green leafy vegetables like spinach, fenugreek (*methi),* amaranth (*cholai),* mustard (*sarson*), *bathua*, etc., are a storehouse of nutrients. Most types of vitamins and minerals are present in these vegetables. Tips to help you choose the right fruits and vegetables and derive maximum benefit are:

- Always include a variety in your diet. Do not keep eating the same vegetables every day. Vegetables equivalent to about 3–4 medium-sized cups (of volume approximately 200 ml) and a fruit everyday are considered healthy.
- Try to include as many natural colours while choosing. You have a choice of white, red, orange, yellow, green, and purple fruits and vegetables. Each colour pigment offers a different kind of protection to your body, so go ahead and add colour to your menu. Your goal should be to eat all colours in a week.
- Eating raw vegetables will ensure you get some vitamins like vitamin C, which gets destroyed during cooking. But be sure to wash any fruit or vegetable you eat with the peel thoroughly, to remove germs and chemicals/pesticides that stick to the surface. Eating the peel also ensures you get more fibre.
- Green leafy vegetable should be eaten at least 2–3 times a week.

5. **Fats and Sugars.** Fats and sugars provide us with energy. Fats, including cooking oil, butter, *ghee* (visible fats), and nuts like peanuts, almonds, cashew nuts, coconut, etc., and oilseeds like *til* and mustard (invisible fat) are a part of most Indian diets. Sugars include sugar, jaggery or *gur*, honey, and products made from these, like Indian sweets, candy, jam, sugar-sweetened beverages, etc. Eating too much of both fats and sugars is not desirable, as it may lead to weight gain and obesity. Obesity in turn increases the risk of other diseases, like diabetes, cardiovascular disorders, and certain cancers. Excessive intake of sugar sweetened foods is also linked to dental caries in children.

Visible or invisible fat can be of different types. Saturated fat is solid at room temperature, like *ghee,* butter, coconut oil, margarine, and *vanaspati* (hydrogenated fats). In fact, foods made from saturated fat will tend to become hard when refrigerated. Foods that naturally contain a lot of saturated fat (saturated fatty acids or SFAs) include red meats—the meat of goat, sheep, cow and pig—full cream milk, butter and cream. These foods are also rich in cholesterol. Other foods high in cholesterol are eggs (the yolk of the egg has cholesterol), organ meats like liver, kidney, brain, shrimp, prawns, etc. An excess of saturated fats and cholesterol are bad for our health, and increase the risk of heart disease and stroke. Hence, foods rich in these should be consumed in moderation, or only occasionally. Trans fats should be avoided totally because they not only increase bad cholesterol, but also decrease the amount of good cholesterol. Trans fats are naturally present in small amounts in meat and full cream milk. They are present in large quantities in hydrogenated fat.

Unsaturated fat is liquid at room temperature, like most vegetable oils. Unsaturated oils can be of two types—MUFA and PUFA-rich oils. MUFA refers to monounsaturated fatty acids and PUFA to polyunsaturated fatty acids. Both types of fatty acids are beneficial, as they help to reduce levels of bad cholesterol in the blood, and hence are protective against cardiovascular diseases. The other kind of fatty acid considered protective is the omega-3 fatty acids or alpha-linolenic fatty acids (ALA). These are present in fish and fish oils, mustard oil and soyabean oil, and in small quantities in cereals and pulses like wheat, *bajra*, black gram, *lobia, rajma* and soyabean, mustard seeds, fenugreek or *methi* seeds, and green leafy vegetables. Ideally, a healthy diet contains a combination of different kinds of fats. You can achieve this by using different kinds of oils for preparing different types of dishes.

Box 15.1: How the Food Group System Helps Us

Classifying foods into groups helps dieticians and healthcare professionals in a number of ways:

- **As a tool for nutritional assessment.** When dietary histories are taken, the data can be analysed to see whether there is any inadequacy/excess of nutrients because of under/over-consumption of foods from a particular food group. This is perhaps the first indication the professional gets that the individual or population group is at risk of developing a diet-related disease/condition. Such information can be used to assess the current nutritional status, as well as for monitoring and surveillance.
- **As a tool for nutrition education.** The concept of a balanced diet is best explained with the help of food groups. It is very difficult for the general community to understand and remember rich food sources of all macro and micronutrients that need to be consumed in a balanced diet. Hence, population guidelines are usually not in terms of specific foods but group of foods, which will, for instance, give us proteins.
- **Planning diets for normal healthy people.** The knowledge of food groups helps to balance the nutrients between meals and maintain a certain nutrient density.
- **In providing variety to the diet.** A variety of foods can be selected from a food group that supplies similar nutrients to make the diet more diversified and interesting during the week. This also ensures variety in taste, making meals more appealing.
- **Planning therapeutic diets.** Food groups assist in planning diets for patients suffering from particular diseases, and for counselling them. Foods from each food group that should be eaten and the ones that should be avoided can be more logically worked out if the foods are classified into groups. Compliance to such diets is also easier.
- **In the formulation of Nutrition Labels.** Food groups can be used to make nutrition information on food labels easier to understand for the common man. Too much technical information usually confuses the consumer.

Thus, to balance your diet, you need to include all food groups in your daily diet. The number of meals we have in a day depends on our lifestyle. It is, however, recommended to have smaller and more frequent meals, compared to two or three large meals in a day. Large meals are more difficult to digest, and also increase your tendency to put on weight (especially if you make dinner your heaviest meal of the day!). Actually, you should have a hearty breakfast to get you going for the day, followed by a good lunch, a snack with your evening tea, and a light dinner. Try to leave a gap of at least two hours between dinner and going to sleep at night.

FOOD PYRAMID

A food guide pyramid is a pyramid-shaped visual guide of food groups, divided into sections to show the recommended intake for each food group. It enables the individual to get the information about what s/he should eat and in how much quantity at a glance. Information related to quantity can be in terms of the number of servings of each food group in a day, or in relative terms like adequately, sparingly, moderately, and abundantly. Recommendations under the dietary guidelines of a country are used to formulate such pyramids. The most widely known food pyramid was introduced by the United States Department of Agriculture (USDA) in 1992, which consisted of four horizontal levels depicting four food groups. This was updated in 2005 and turned into a pyramid with vertical divisions representing food groups, and was referred to as the 'MyPyramid'.

Figure 15.2a: Visual Food Guides Promoted by USDA

Figure 15.2b

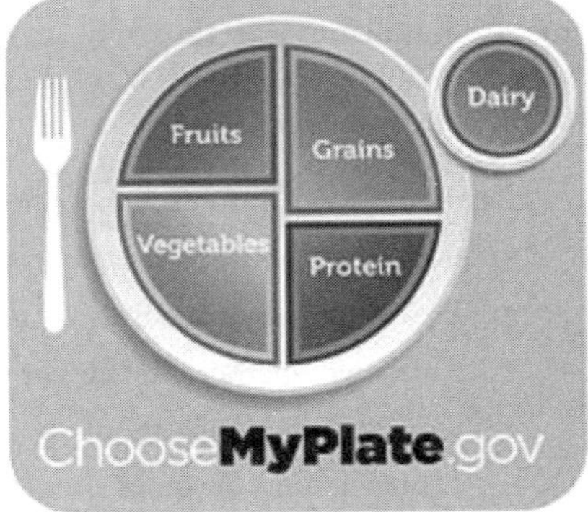

My Plate - United States

Source: USDA's Center for Nutrition Policy and Promotion; http://www.fns.usda.gov/

My Pyramid (Figure 15.2a) depicted six food groups in bands of differing widths, suggesting the proportional contribution of each food group to a healthy diet. Grains were shown in orange, vegetables in green, fruit in red, milk in blue, all in wide bands, indicating that the intake of these groups should be encouraged; oils in yellow comprised the slimmest band, and meat and beans in purple were also in a slim band, indicating that these foods had to be consumed in smaller quantities. The wide base was indicative of the liberal consumption of nutrient dense foods, while the narrow top represents restricted foods such as sugar, fat and salt-rich processed foods. The need for being physically active was represented by a person climbing steps on the pyramid.

In 2011, the pyramid concept was changed to a plate portioning out the different food groups. It was felt that the pyramid concept was poorly understood by the general public, and that a plate was more symbolic in indicating the serving size of each food group. The icon known as 'MyPlate' is shown in Figure 15.2b. MyPlate is part of a larger communications initiative based on the 2010 Dietary Guidelines for Americans to help consumers make better food choices. MyPlate illustrates the five food groups using a familiar mealtime visual, a place setting.

Many other countries and organisations have also published food pyramids. These have been presented in Chapter 16. Most of the pyramids are accompanied by advice to abstain from / limit alcohol intake, and to say no to smoking/use of tobacco. Most also talk about the importance of being physically active / exercising regularly. The common message across the board seems to be—eating a variety, eating in moderation, and balancing the food groups will promote good health.

The National Institute of Nutrition in India has also made a food pyramid, which was revised in 2010. The pyramid consists of four horizontal bands (Figure 15.3). As the base of the pyramid is the largest, cereals, which make up the largest proportion in an Indian diet, have been positioned here. This band also includes pulses and milk, which need to be consumed adequately in a healthy diet. The next band is for vegetables and fruits, which should be consumed liberally. As you go upwards, the bands become narrower, indicating that a lower amount of foods in these food groups should be consumed. So meat and meat products, and fats and oils should be consumed in moderation. The top-most level belongs to calorie-dense processed and ready-to-eat foods, with mostly high sugar and/or high fat, which need to be consumed sparingly. Advice to be physically active and exercise regularly is also included, along with icons for abstaining from alcohol and tobacco use.

Figure 15.3: Indian Food Pyramid

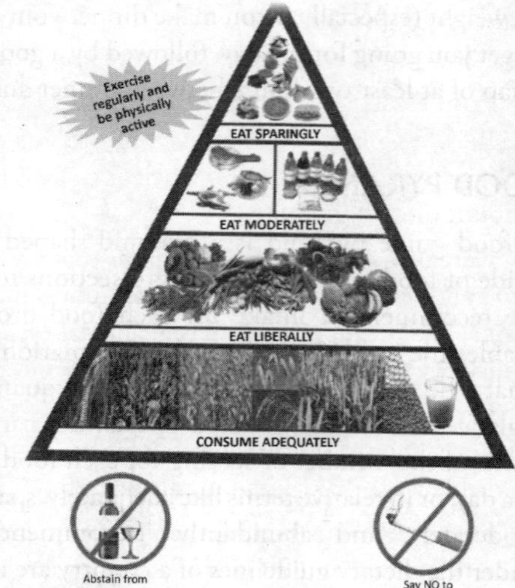

Source: Dietary Guidelines for Indians, NIN 2011.

USE OF FOOD EXCHANGES IN PLANNING A BALANCED DIET

A knowledge of food exchanges helps in nutritionally balancing meals. Let us learn how a food exchange list can be used for meal planning. Foods are organised into exchange groups, based on their carbohydrate, fat and protein content. Foods listed in any one exchange group can be used interchangeably. A specified weight of any food in one group can be substituted for another, and it will provide approximately the same nutritive value. Provided that the energy and protein requirements are fulfilled, all other nutrient requirements are likely to be met by a judicious selection of foods from the different exchanges. Special attention needs to be paid to selecting vitamin A and C-rich foods from the fruit and vegetable exchange. Similarly, a conscious effort needs to be made to include iron-rich foods.

Classifying foods into exchanges helps us to design balanced diets in the following ways:

- Choosing foods from each group helps to include all the nutrients we require in our meals.
- Providing variety in taste, as knowledge of food groups enables us to choose alternatives from the same group.
- Assessing whether our diets are nutritionally adequate.
- Counselling people about appropriate diet choices.
- Planning diets becomes simpler and quick.
- Improving flexibility in our planning.

The main features of the different exchanges are discussed here. The detailed exchange list used at Lady Irwin College, University of Delhi, and illustrated steps showing how to use the exchange list in planning a day's menu are given in Appendix 3.

Milk exchange provides 180 kcal (750 KJ) and 8 g protein per 250 ml (a medium glass) of toned/standardised milk. It includes all types of milk—full cream or buffalo's milk, toned or cow's milk, skim milk, milk powder, and products made from milk, like curd, *paneer,* cheese, etc. The amounts of each of these foods that would supply 8 g proteins have been worked out to exchange with one cup of milk.

Meat and Pulse exchange provides 7 g of protein. Meat (40g is one exchange of meat or egg) provides 80 kcal, lean meat, like chicken and fish (30g is one exchange), provides 35 kcal, while pulse (30 g is one exchange) provides 100 kcal per exchange. About 15 g of soyabean make one pulse exchange because of the high protein content.

Vegetables have been split into two categories—A and B—according to their carbohydrate content. Vegetables in the A category have only 3.5 g carbohydrate in one exchange of approximately 100 g. Vegetables in the B category have double the amount of carbohydrate, that is, 7 g.

Fruit exchange includes all fruits, and one exchange of approximately 100 g provides 10 g carbohydrate. A lower weight of the high-sugar fruits will provide the same amount of carbohydrate, for example, only 40 g of banana will give 10 g carbohydrate, whereas in a fruit of high water content like musk melon, 285 g will provide the same amount of carbohydrate.

Cereals include a group of foods that are rich in starch. It includes grains like wheat, rice and maize, millets like *bajra* and *jowar*, as well as roots and tubers like potatoes, sweet potatoes, etc., and products made chiefly from cereal grains, like bread, biscuits, pasta, and cakes. About 20 g of a cereal grain will provide 70 kcal and 15 g carbohydrate, while 30 g of bread or 65 g of potato would provide the same amount of energy and carbohydrate.

Fat exchange includes the visible fat like butter, ghee and cooking oil, and the invisible fat-rich nuts and oilseeds. One exchange of fat provides 5 g fat and approximately 45 kcal. This would be provided by about a teaspoon (5 g) of visible fat, or 8–13 g of a nut/oilseed.

Sugar exchange includes table sugar, jaggery, jam, and sugarcane or its juice. One exchange of 5 g supplies 5 g of carbohydrate and 20 kcal.

NEED FOR MEAL PLANNING

Giving due thought to planning meals not only makes it simpler to cook and serve meals which the whole family will relish, but also ensures that the nutritional needs of all family members will be adequately met. Planning helps if you want to spend within the budget. It also helps you to save time and energy. Once the menu has been planned for the day—or broadly, for a week—pre-preparation work required for cooking and serving the meals can be worked out in advance; for instance, the need to prepare a salad dressing in advance for the salad being served for dinner, or the need to sort, clean and boil spinach beforehand for the *palak paneer* planned for lunch. Soaking pulses and beans like *rajma, lobia* and soyabean the night before helps to cook them faster, and also saves time and fuel. In addition, a thought can be given to how vegetables that were not fully used in one meal can be used for the next meal, or how leftover boiled rice can be used to create another dish, like curd rice or tamarind rice. This helps to minimise wastage. If we do not plan the quantities of the different types of foods to be cooked, we end up cooking either too little or too much. While planning, you can give better thought to making the meals attractive by bringing in variety in taste, texture and colour.

Steps in Meal Planning

The first step in meal planning (Figure 15.4) is to consider the individual's age, sex and physical activity level, and see the Recommended Dietary Allowance (RDA) for the person. The RDA represents the level of the nutrient to be consumed daily to meet all the requirements of most individuals in a given population. In fact, the nutrient requirements of about 98 per cent of the population are covered. Once you know how much energy and protein needs to be given to an individual, a food plan is worked out, which details the number of exchanges from each food group that should be included in a day's diet to meet the energy and protein requirements.

Next, depending on the age group and lifestyle of the individual, the number and timing of meals are worked out. Usually, it is recommended that smaller and more frequent meals be consumed. A 4–5 meal pattern fits most work/school schedules. Besides the three main meals of breakfast, lunch and dinner, 1–3 small meals of snacks can be introduced between breakfast and lunch (mid-morning), and then between lunch and dinner (tea-time). A time gap of 2–4 hours can be given between the different meals.

The total number of exchanges of each food group is then distributed judiciously between the different meals. Each major meal should include foods from the three basic food groups—energy giving, body building and protective foods. This means cereal, along with pulse/milk/meat and vegetables/fruits. Even the smaller meals should be made nutrient-dense, as for most age and physiological groups, the reason for splitting the day's diet into so many meals is that they are not able to eat too much at a single meal. Healthy options of dishes for each meal have been discussed in subsequent chapters, along with diets for each age group. As a rule, individuals of all age groups should consume fried or very salty or sweet snacks only occasionally.

The last step is to plan the detailed menu for the day. Food selection from each group should be according to the likes and dislikes of the individual. Choose healthier options from each group, as discussed earlier and in Box 15.2. The meal should provide satiety (proteins, fats and fibre-rich meals provide greater satiety value) and variety in taste and flavour, colour and texture. Many other factors need to be kept in mind, which we will now discuss.

Figure 15.4: Steps in Menu Planning

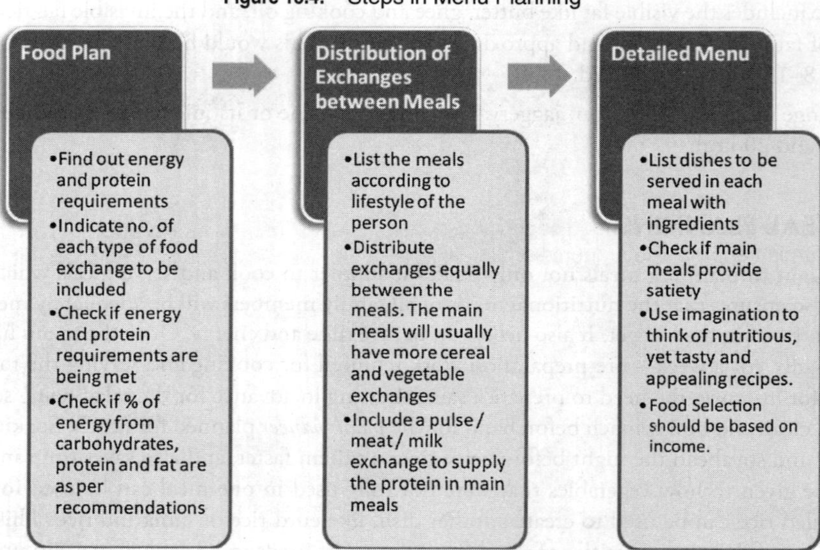

Box 15.2: Points to Remember While Planning Nutritionally Adequate Meals

- **Cereals** are a staple, which means that we include these in all our meals.
- To ensure good quality protein, combine cereals with **pulses, milk or milk products, meat or egg**. You can choose between a pulse, milk or meat product to provide sufficient protein in a meal. Overloading protein in a meal will actually have no extra benefit, as excess protein is broken down and excreted from the body!
- Always include **vegetables or fruits** in all your meals to add a dose of vitamins and minerals, because these actually help your body to utilise other nutrients better.
- Use **fats and sugars** to make your food more palatable, but be a miser while adding these to your dishes. Choose low fat foods like double toned or skim milk and its products, leaner cuts of meat, chicken without its skin, and fish. Walnuts, almonds and pistachios are healthier than cashewnuts. Also choose roasted nuts over fried and salted ones. Avoid foods rich in saturated fat, trans fat and cholesterol, as these increase the risk of heart disease.
- Eat a lot of **fibre** by including whole grain cereals and pulses in the daily menu, along with vegetables and fruits. So choose whole wheat flour (*atta*) bread and biscuits, rather than those made from *maida*. Soluble fibre in cereals, legumes, fruits, and vegetables also protects you from diabetes and heart disease by lowering your blood sugar and cholesterol.

Box 15.2 contd

Box 15.2 contd

- Use traditional **spices and condiments** liberally in preparing dishes. Ginger, garlic, *haldi,* red and green chilli, cloves, black pepper, etc., have many phytochemicals in them, which are beneficial to our health. Salt is the only seasoning that you have to add sparingly. Limit spices, especially chillies, for younger children
- To make sure you are getting all **vitamins and minerals** in your diet, eat a variety of foods, especially fruits and vegetables. You have to make a special effort to include foods rich in three nutrients—**vitamins A and C, and iron**. These nutrients are not present in sufficient quantities in many foods. Vitamin A can be obtained from green leafy vegetables, yellow and orange vegetables, and fruits like, carrot, pumpkin, papaya, mango, etc., and also from egg yolk, full cream milk and liver. Vitamin C is present in all fruits of the citrus family (like *mausmi*, orange, lemon, etc.), cabbage, capsicum, guava, strawberries, *amla*, sprouted pulses, etc.
- Iron is more readily absorbed from non-vegetarian foods like meat, egg and liver. Vegetarians should include an array of green leafy vegetables in their diet, like *methi, cholai, sarson ka saag, bathua dhania*, and *pudina.* Spinach also has some iron, but it is not a rich source. In addition, iron can be obtained from cereals like whole wheat, *bajra* and *ragi*, and from pulses, especially soyabean, *channa*, lentils. Among other vegetables and fruits that are rich in iron are lotus stem, watermelon, *seethaphal,* pineapple, apricot, beans, and green plantain. Most nuts are also rich in iron. We get most of the B group vitamins and other minerals in sufficient quantity from cereals, pulses, milk, and meat if we meet our daily calorie and protein requirement.
- In the end, the golden rule to good health and ideal nutritional status is **Moderation.** A nutritionally balanced diet will furnish appropriate amounts of all nutrients. It will avoid an excess of calories, fat, sugar, and salt, which are associated with an increased risk of diet-related diseases.

Factors Affecting Meal Planning

While planning meals, you need to keep several points in mind. The most important consideration, of course, is that the nutrient requirements of all members of the family have to be met. Meals have to be balanced in their nutritional content by including foods from all three basic food groups. Several factors must be considered before meal timings, the number of meals to be served, and the menu of different meals are decided. Generally, people like variety in colour, texture, taste, and flavour in their meals. Satiety is also an important factor in determining both the menu and the portion sizes. Let us discuss some of these factors in detail.

1. **Family Composition:** The first thing to be looked at is the composition of the family. What is the **age** of the different family members? Are there elderly people, children, pregnant women, and/or nursing mothers in the family? These groups would need special attention in planning. The menu decided upon should be suitable for all members. The elderly in the family generally prefer easily digestible, simple food that has been prepared traditionally. Children may, however, prefer a varied cuisine, and want to eat foods that are popular with their peer group. The person in charge of planning will have to balance each meal with dishes that all family members like. Nutrient needs also vary according to age. When the body is growing rapidly, as in infancy and adolescence, the requirement for all nutrients goes up drastically. Energy, protein, vitamin, and mineral needs increase steadily as the child reaches adulthood. After that, however, there is a gradual decline, particularly in energy needs, as the body ages. Part of the change in body needs is related to changes in body composition, as the individual moves from one stage of his lifecycle to the next.

   The requirement of nutrients also varies with **sex,** as the body size and composition of males and females is different, especially after the age of 10. Sometimes males and females may also have different food choices. It is important to keep the **number of family members** who will be consuming each meal in mind, in order to decide on the quantity of food to be cooked. If the food cooked is too little, family members may not be able to satisfy their hunger. On the other hand, too much food cooked at each meal will leave you with a lot of leftovers, leading to food wastage.

2. **Occupation and Lifestyle:** The occupation of different members of the family will determine their lifestyle, and how much **time** they have for meal preparation and consumption. It also majorly determines the timing and number of meals, and how elaborate the menu is for each meal. Working women, for instance, would not have the time to prepare elaborate meals, and would end up using more of convenience foods unless they have additional manpower in the form of domestic help to help with cooking. Some family members eat all their meals at home; work considerations may demand that some others eat at least one meal outside the home; while some others, like school and college-going children and office-goers, may carry a packed meal from home.
   Occupation also determines how much **income** comes into the house, and consequently how much money is available for purchasing food.
3. **Food Cost:** The greater the household income, the more the money available for purchasing food items. It has been observed that with an increase in income, there is an increase in the quantity and variety of food purchased by the family. Also, the quality of food selected is directly proportional to the income. For example, those with a limited family income will choose low-cost food groups like cereals to supply most of their caloric or nutrient requirements. They will use smaller quantities of the meat and milk group, and from the fruit-vegetable group, they will select the less expensive items. Less expensive meat cuts, seasonal vegetables, poor quality vegetables left over after market time, and cheap, locally grown fruits will probably be selected by those with a limited income. In contrast, when money is not a problem, the family selects a greater variety of food, selects good quality foods, exotic foods and processed foods, and tends to eat out more often. The cost of food is often equated with status. The rich will tend to select the more expensive foods, especially when entertaining.

Families can manage their budgets better by keeping a few points in mind. The first step is to make a budget according to the amount of money kept aside for food expenses. They then need to do a few exercises, like:

- Identifying shops and retail outlets that sell the food items at subsidised rates. Cereal grains like wheat and rice and edible oil are available from government fair price shops (ration shops) at very low rates. Besides this, there are *Kendriya bhandars* and other government-run outlets that will sell food products at very reasonable rates.
- Buying non-perishable foods in bulk sometimes helps to bring down prices, but one must be careful to never buy perishable food in bulk, as some of it will rot before you get a chance to eat it.
- Identifying the cheapest vegetables and fruits of the season. Buying seasonal foods is usually cheaper.
- Cooking just enough food that can be finished by the family members is important; otherwise, there are a lot of leftovers. Wastage of leftovers can be reduced by incorporating leftover foods in other recipes, for example, leftover rice can be turned into fried rice, lemon rice, or curd rice. Leftover dals can be used to make stuffed *parathas* or *rotis*.
- Maintaining kitchen gardens (even if vegetables can only be grown in pots) or keeping poultry (where space permits) provides a ready source of nutrient-rich foods at home.

4. **Climate or Weather Conditions:** The climate of a place determines the kinds of foods grown in and around that area. If the climate is generally cold and the place snow-laden for a good part of the year, the kind of foods that can be grown at home or in fields are very limited. The same problem applies to hot and dry climate areas. The availability of foods like fruits and vegetables is most affected by season. Seasonal foods are more easily available, of better nutritional quality, and cheaper. However, in big cities, because of the provision of cold storage facilities and food processing plants, fruits and vegetables may be available throughout the year. Canning and processing of fruits and vegetables reduces wastage from the spoilage of surplus crops, and at the same time, makes nutrient-dense foods available throughout the year. Frozen peas and other vegetables, tomato puree, canned mangoes, pineapples, cherries, and the pulp of different fruits and vegetables are now available off the shelf.

Besides availability, climate or weather conditions may also affect food choices. In cold weather, the consumption of hot beverages like tea and coffee, and high energy foods like nuts and oilseeds, in the form of roasted peanuts and jaggery brittles (*chikki, rewri, gazak*), go up. In summers, the consumption of cooling beverages like cold drinks, buttermilk, juices, ice lollies, ice creams, and foods with high water content, like watermelon, muskmelon, cucumber, etc., increases. Many traditional families believe very strongly in the concept of hot and cold foods, which alters their food selection depending on the weather and season.

5. **Availability of food:** The geographical location of the city/town or village where the family lives determines the availability of foods in a particular area. People living in remote areas, which are not well-connected to other towns, can select only those foods that are locally grown. However, with improved processing, preserving techniques, and with better infrastructure and transport facilities now available, a variety of foods are now available to the consumer all round the year, even in towns far away from the place where the food has been produced. But if the area has no big grocery stores or supermarkets, the variety of processed and convenience foods available will be less. The availability of food in a region can also be restricted because of calamities like floods, droughts and war.

6. **Socio-cultural factors, religion and family traditions:** Cultural influences on the choice of foods eaten by a family are very strong. Cooking styles, the ingredients used, and even recipes vary by region. Within a **region,** recipes for commonly eaten foods vary from family to family. Every family will have their own special seasoning for dishes. That is why the same dish will taste different when you eat it at your own home, and then at your friend's place. Coastal states use a lot of coconut in their cooking and also consume a lot of seafood. Traditionally, Bengalis use mustard oil in their cooking, people in Kerala like to use coconut oil, while unrefined groundnut oil is popular in Andhra Pradesh. Some families are very traditional about their way of cooking, while others have adapted their cooking and become more cosmopolitan, drawing cooking styles from various **cultural backgrounds**.

   Customs and beliefs concerning foods that should or should not be eaten have present in every group of people. These include religious beliefs, beliefs concerning the health properties of food, and the emotional responses to food. These beliefs are generally deep-rooted and difficult to change. **Religion** plays a significant role in food choices. Certain religions expect followers to shun particular foods. A lot of people do not consume non-vegetarian foods out of religious considerations. Others practice vegetarianism on particular days of the week. Cultural or religious **taboos** also demand that certain foods be avoided, these usually being specific to certain days of the week, or certain physiological states like pregnancy or lactation. There is no harm in following these restrictions as long as these do not affect our nutritional status or health.

   Special occasions, whether religious or otherwise, demand special menus. The special thing about celebrating festivals is the particular foods made especially for the occasion, for example, the special dishes of *Navratras* and *Janamashtami,* the *modak ladoos* of *Ganesh Chaturthi*, the special *Pongal* rice for the Tamil new year, *biryani* for Eid, and many more. Special foods are cooked on other celebratory occasions as well, for instance on weddings and birthdays. Even the simplest celebration is incomplete without food.

> **Food fads** usually refer to diets that do not follow common nutritional guidelines. A food fad may lead to undue reliance on, or avoidance of, a particular foodstuff. Fads are common in toddlers, adolescents, in people under stress, or those trying to lose weight. Fads usually spike in popularity at a particular point in time. They are like popular trends in foods. An example of a fad diet is that of eating only white-coloured foods for a week.

7. **Likes and dislikes:** This is perhaps the most important reason why you choose to eat a particular kind of food. Personal likes and dislikes generally govern the type of food that people select. Many factors determine an individual's or a family's food choices. Age, physiological status, lifestyle, culture, religion, economic status, and availability (as already discussed) will affect food choices. People also like meals that are both satiating and appetising. In addition, the following factors will also influence what families would like to eat:

- **Knowledge and attitudes towards foods.** Good health is a growing focus for some families. A good education helps family members to make full use of their opportunities and resources to improve their diets. For example, even low-income group families can improve the quality of their diets by sprouting pulses, and growing and consuming green leafy vegetables at home. Knowledge also helps them to overcome prejudices and wrong beliefs. However, it is simply not enough to have nutrition knowledge in order to make wise food choices. Attitudes also need to undergo a change before families can change their dietary habits.
- **Safety considerations.** Safety is one very important consideration when families make food choices. For instance, the belief that street food is unhygienic will make people prefer home-cooked meals. Most of us avoid uncooked foods like salads or milk-based products when we eat out, especially in summers. Fear of novel foods or fear of allergies can also make people reject a large variety of foods, especially seafood. People who are conscious of eating too many food additives will select fewer processed food items.
- **Nutrition information and misinformation:** Advertising can both help and hinder the process of making the right food choices. Mass media can be very powerful in influencing food choices. Nutrition information on food labels and the health claims made can become important influencers. Sometimes companies mislead consumers by making false or irrelevant claims; for instance, claiming that a particular brand of vegetable oil is 'cholesterol-free' may increase its sale. However, one must remember that all vegetable oils are actually free of cholesterol.

Early experiences with food shape later choices. Hence parents, and the family as a whole, have an immense responsibility in teaching their children how to make the correct food choices.

SUMMARY

- A balanced diet is one that includes foods from all food groups during the day. The quantities and proportions of these foods need to be such that they fulfil the daily requirements for all the nutrients we need. In addition, the nutrients should be in such amounts that a little bit can be stored in the body to take care of days when food intake is insufficient.
- Foods can be grouped into categories according to the type of food, or the nutrients that foods supply. The basic food group classification is based on the physiological role played by the foods of each group in our bodies, that is, energy giving foods, body building foods, and protective or regulatory foods.
- The Indian Council of Medical Research (ICMR) classifies foods into five groups—cereals, pulses, milk and meat, vegetables and fruits, and fats and sugars. Classifying foods into groups helps dieticians and healthcare professionals in several ways.
- A food guide pyramid is a pyramid-shaped visual guide of food groups, divided into sections to show the recommended intake for each food group.
- A knowledge of food exchanges helps in nutritionally balancing meals. Foods are organised into exchange groups based on their carbohydrate, fat and protein content. Foods listed in any one exchange group can be used interchangeably.
- Planning meals in advance helps to ensure that the nutritional needs of all members are being fulfilled. There is also a lot of saving on time for preparation, money spent and fuel used, and we also tend to waste food a lot less. Planned meals tend to be more attractive in terms of colour, flavour, taste, and texture.
- There are three basic steps in planning meals using the food exchange list. The first step is to make a food plan according to the RDA for energy and protein. The number of exchanges worked out for each food group are then distributed between meals, according to the lifestyle of the person. Detailed menus are finally worked out, taking care that besides trying to nutritionally balance meals, the likes and dislikes of the individual are kept in mind.

- Factors affecting this meal-planning exercise include family structure and composition, socio-cultural and religious factors, availability, economic status, climate, occupation and lifestyle, and likes and dislikes. It is also important that the meal provides satiety. Variety in colour, taste and texture also makes meals more appetising.
- Food choices are also influenced by the knowledge and attitude of families, considerations of safety, and information/misinformation provided by the food manufacturers and the media.
- Early experiences with food shape later choices. Hence, parents and the family as a whole have an immense responsibility in teaching their children how to make correct food choices.

KEY WORDS

Adequacy (dietary): Refers to providing all essential nutrients in amounts sufficient to maintain health.

Convenience food: A food, typically a complete meal, which has been pre-prepared commercially, and so requires minimum further preparation by the consumer.

Culture: The ideas, customs and social behaviour of people in a society.

Exchange list: A diet planning tool that organises foods by their proportion of carbohydrate, fat and protein. Foods on any single list can be used interchangeably.

Food fad: Diets that do not follow common nutritional guidelines.

Moderation (in diet): Eating enough, but not too much of a food.

Non-perishable foods: Foods that have a long shelf-life and do not spoil easily, for example, cereals and pulses.

Nutrient density: A measure of the nutrients a food provides relative to the energy it provides. The more the nutrients and the fewer the calories per unit weight of food, the more is its nutrient density.

Perishable foods: Those foods that have a very short shelf-life and spoil easily, like milk products, fruits and vegetables.

Satiety: The feeling of fullness after a meal.

EXERCISES

1. How does classifying foods into different groups help us?
2. How would you classify foods based on the physiological role they perform in our bodies?
3. Describe the ICMR five food group classification.
4. What is a food pyramid? Explain with the help of an example.
5. What is a food exchange list? How is it useful?
6. Why do we need to plan meals in advance?
7. Describe the steps involved in meal planning.
8. What are the factors affecting meal planning for families?
9. Explain how poor families can plan nutritionally balanced meals.
10. What are the various socio-cultural factors that affect the food choices of families?

ACTIVITIES

1. Conduct a market survey to find the cheapest pulse, cooking oil, seasonal fruit, and vegetable available. Compare the prices you noted down with what others in your class have found. Note the kinds of outlets that sell these foods at cheaper rates.
2. Make a list of foods that your family forbids pregnant women, nursing mothers and menstruating women from consuming. Find out the reason behind the food being considered taboo.

REFERENCES

Byrd-Bredbenner, C., G. Moe, D. Beshgetoor, and J. Berning, *Wardlaw's Perspectives in Nutrition*, 9e, McGraw-Hill International Edition, 2013.

Khanna, K., S. Gupta, S. J. Passi, R. Seth, R. Mahna, and S. Puri, *Textbook of Nutrition and Dietetics*, 2e, New Delhi: Elite Publishing House Pvt. Ltd, 2013.

ICMR, 'Nutrient Requirements and Recommended Dietary Allowances for Indians', A report of the Expert Group of the Indian Council of Medical Research, 2010.

NIN, *Dietary Guidelines for Indians—A Manual*, 2e, Hyderabad: National Institute of Nutrition, ICMR, 2011.

Rolfes, S. R., K. Pinna and E. Whitney, *Understanding Normal and Clinical Nutrition*, 8e, Wadsworth Cengage Learning, 2009.

Seth, V. and K. Singh, *Diet Planning Through the Life Cycle. Part I: Normal Nutrition—A Practical Manual*, 4e, Lady Irwin College, University of Delhi, New Delhi: Elite Publishing House Pvt. Ltd, 2005.

ONLINE SOURCES

http://www.fns.usda.gov/eatsmartplayhardhealthylifestyle/tools/mypyramidtracker.htm

http://www.choosemyplate.gov/images/MyPlateImages/JPG/myplate_green.jpg

16

FOOD-BASED DIETARY GUIDELINES

HIGHLIGHTS

- Relevance of food-based dietary guidelines
- Dietary guidelines for Indians
- Global scenario
- Overview of healthy food choices

INTRODUCTION

> **Dietary Guidelines** are recommendations for the population to promote healthy dietary practices, thereby improving the nutritional status.
>
> **Dietary Guidelines** are sets of advisory statements on diet for populations to promote overall nutritional well-being, which relates to all diet-related conditions (FAO/WHO 1995).

The development of a nation is largely dependent on the health, well-being and productivity of its people. Good nutrition is a prerequisite for a healthy and productive life. Dietary patterns and the adequacy of nutrients obtained from food are the key determinants of the nutritional status of an individual, as well as that of a population. It is advisable to obtain nutrients from food, rather than being dependent on nutrient supplements. In order to derive the maximum benefit of the various nutrient and non-nutrient (phytochemical) components of food, it is important to consume a well-balanced, nutritionally adequate diet. Therefore, it is essential to equip people with reliable and simple information to enable them to make judicious and informed food choices (as what we eat is food, and not the nutrients as such). In this direction, it is useful to formulate a set of advices to correct faulty dietary habits, and promote the healthy ones. This set of advices is known as Dietary Guidelines or Food Based Dietary Guidelines (FBDG). FBDG help in translating nutrient recommendations into specific dietary advice.

PURPOSE OF FOOD-BASED DIETARY GUIDELINES

Dietary guidelines translate scientific, nutrition-related knowledge into healthy food choices and eating patterns. These guidelines aim at transmitting knowledge about nutrition from the scientific desks of researchers to the tables of consumers. The ultimate goal is to improve nutritional status and bring about positive changes in food-related behaviour. On the one hand, these guidelines attempt to prevent dietary deficiencies, and on the other, they try to reduce the risk of disorders associated with dietary excess (chronic degenerative disorders). FBDG also address non-nutritional factors such as physical activity, safe food and water, and food preparation practices, which have a significant influence on health and nutritional status. They are usually meant for healthy populations. Moreover, they also serve as key tools for health/nutrition promotion, production of micronutrient-rich foods, and in formulating nutrition education policies for the general public.

In order to be effective, these guidelines must be comprehensible, science-based, holistic, and flexible, as well as sensitive to the dietary pattern, economic condition, cultural context, and lifestyle of the people for whom these are intended.

These guidelines are meant for the general public, and should therefore be stated in simple language so that they are easy to understand and practice in day-to-day life. Besides being based on the overall socio-economic situation of the country, these should be culturally acceptable to the people for whom it is envisioned. Moreover, these should also take into consideration the new research, developments and findings in nutrition science. When all these dynamics are considered while formulating guidelines, they become more holistic and practically applicable to almost all sections of society, irrespective of age, gender, education, occupation, income level, and activity pattern.

In India, a team of experienced nutrition scientists at the National Institute of Nutrition (NIN) has formulated dietary goals and guidelines to promote nutritionally adequate diets and healthy lifestyles, from the time of conception to old age.

Box 16.1: Dietary Goals

There are six dietary goals covering all stages of life, focusing on preventive and promotive nutrition. These are:

1. Maintenance of a state of positive health and optimal performance in populations at large by maintaining an ideal body weight.
2. Ensuring adequate nutritional status for pregnant women and lactating mothers.
3. Improvement of birth weights and promotion of the growth of infants, children and adolescents to achieve their full genetic potential.
4. Achievement of adequacy in all nutrients and prevention of deficiency diseases.
5. Prevention of chronic diet-related disorders.
6. Maintenance of the health of the elderly and increasing life expectancy.

Source: NIN 2011.

DIETARY GUIDELINES FOR INDIANS

In order to achieve these dietary goals, **15 food-based dietary guidelines** have been formulated. This section presents an overview of some of the recommendations given by NIN (2011). These guidelines are practical strategies to ensure the nutritional well-being of the population.

1. Eat a variety of foods to ensure a balanced diet.
2. Ensure the provision of extra food and healthcare to pregnant and lactating women.
3. Promote exclusive breastfeeding for six months, and encourage breastfeeding till two years or as long as one can.
4. Feed home-based semi-solid foods to the infant after six months.
5. Ensure adequate and appropriate diets for children and adolescents, both in health and sickness.
6. Eat plenty of vegetables and fruits.
7. Ensure a moderate use of edible oils and animal foods, and very little use of *ghee*/ butter/ *vanaspati*.
8. Avoid overeating to prevent becoming overweight and obese.

Box 16.2: Seven Steps for Developing Food-based Dietary Guidelines:

1. Identification of diet-health relationships
2. Identification of country specific diet-related problems
3. Identification of nutrients of public health importance
4. Identification of foods relevant for FBDG
5. Identification of food consumption patterns
6. Testing and optimising FBDG
7. Graphical representation of FBDG

Source: European Food Safety Authority (EFSA) 2007.

Table 16.1: The Quantitative Aspect of Dietary Guidelines: Balanced Diet for Indians

Food Groups	*g/portion*	*Number of Portions*																
		Adults						*Infants 6–12 months*	*Years*									
		Sedentary		*Moderate*		*Heavy*			*1–3*	*4–6*	*7–9*	*10–12*		*13–15*		*16–18*		
		Man	*Woman*	*Man*	*Woman*	*Man*	*Woman*					*Girls*	*Boys*	*Girls*	*Boys*	*Girls*	*Boys*	
Cereals and millets	**30**	12.5	9	15	11	20	16	0.5	2	4	6	8	10	11	14	11	15	
Pulses	**30**	2.5	2	3	2.5	4	3	0.25	1	1	2	2	2	2	2.5	2.5	3	
Milk and milk products	**100 ml**	3	3	3	3	3	3	4[a]	5	5	5	5	5	5	5	5	5	
Roots and tubers	**100**	2	2	2	2	2	2	0.5	0.5	1	1	1	1	1	1.5	2	2	
Green leafy vegetables	**100**	1	1	1	1	1	1	0.25	0.5	0.5	1	1	1	1	1	1	1	
Other vegetables	**100**	2	2	2	2	2	2	0.25	0.5	1	1	2	2	2	2	2	2	
Fruits	**100**	1	1	1	1	1	1	1	1	1	1	1	1	1	1	1	1	
Sugar	**5**	4	4	6	6	11	9	2	3	4	4	6	6	5	4	5	6	
Fat/oil (visible)	**5**	5	4	6	6	8	6	4	5	5	6	7	7	8	9	7	10	

Notes: Multiply grams per portion with the number of portions to calculate the day's requirement of different food groups for an individual.

[a] This is the quantity of top milk. Along with breast milk, 200 ml top milk is required.

Source: NIN 2011.

9. Exercise regularly and be physically active to maintain an ideal body weight.
10. Restrict salt intake to a minimum.
11. Ensure the use of safe and clean foods.
12. Adopt the right pre-cooking processes and appropriate cooking methods.
13. Drink plenty of water and take beverages in moderation.
14. Minimise the use of processed foods rich in salt, sugar and fats.
15. Include micronutrient-rich foods in the diets of elderly people to enable them to be fit and active.

The above guidelines are categorised and discussed below:

Guidelines to ensure nutritional adequacy and prevent deficiency diseases:

1. Eat a variety of foods to ensure a balanced diet.

A balanced diet should be quantitatively (amount-wise) and qualitatively (composition-wise) adequate for different age groups, genders, physiological states, and physical activity. A diet containing foods from various food groups in appropriate amounts ensures normal growth and development, and maintenance of body function and physical activity. The adverse consequences of an intake of food and nutrients below or above the body requirements are under-nutrition (deficiency diseases) or over-nutrition (diseases related to excess), respectively. Thus variety, adequacy and moderation are the tripods of a balanced diet (Figure 16.1).

Figure 16.1: Tripod of Balanced Diet

- Cereals and millets are consumed in large amounts, and they mainly contribute to complex carbohydrates.
- The food groups that primarily serve as the source of macronutrients (carbohydrate, fats and proteins) are cereals, millets, pulses, root vegetables, animal foods, nuts, oils, and sugar.
- A liberal intake of seasonal vegetables and fruits ensures an adequate supply of vitamins, minerals, fibre, and antioxidants.

2. Eat plenty of vegetables and fruits.

Fresh vegetables and fruits are the natural capsules of several vitamins, minerals, fibre, antioxidants, and phytochemicals. Their role in the prevention of various deficiency diseases and chronic disorders (cardiovascular diseases and cancer) makes them a vital part of our diet. They contain an abundant amount of minerals (like iron and calcium) and vitamins (like carotenoids, B-complex vitamins, vitamin C, and folic acid). From the large variety of vegetables and fruits, we can select the ones that provide high calories (like banana, potato, sweet potato, yam, colocasia), as well as those that provide low calories (like muskmelon, watermelon, bottlegourd, cucumber, spinach, etc.).

The Expert Committee of the Indian Council of Medical Research (NIN 2011) has recommended that every individual should consume at least 100g of fresh fruits and 300g of vegetables (Roots and Tubers—50g; Green Leafy Vegetables—50g; Other Vegetables—200g) daily. In order to derive the maximum benefit of vegetables and fruits, these should be consumed in raw form after thorough washing, as salads, whole fruits, fruit *chaat*, etc. Fresh and seasonal vegetables/fruits have a better taste and nutrient content. Moreover, consuming a variety of them in different colours not only enriches the diet with nutrients, but also adds colour to the meal.

Therefore, attempt should be made to make green, yellow, orange, red, and purple vegetables and fruits a part of our diet. One of the best ways to ensure fresh and economical vegetables is by growing them in the kitchen garden, if possible.

3. Drink plenty of water and take beverages in moderation.

Fluids, in the form of water and beverages, are required to relieve thirst and meet the fluid-electrolyte requirements of the body. A normal healthy person should drink at least eight glasses (2 litres) of water daily. However, one must ensure that the water and beverages available for consumption are safe and wholesome. Beverages can be nutritious or stimulating in nature.

- Milk is an excellent beverage, providing protein of high biological value as well as several other nutrients, like calcium, vitamin A, D, E, B_{12} and riboflavin. At least 250 ml of milk should be consumed in a day.
- Nutritious beverages like fruit juices, buttermilk, *lassi*, and coconut water should be preferred over synthetic carbonated soft drinks.
- Tea and coffee have a stimulating effect due to their caffeine content. The tannin present in them inhibits iron absorption. Therefore, tea/coffee consumption should be in moderation.
- Alcohol consumption should be avoided or taken in limited amounts due to its adverse effects on health and nutritional status.

Guidelines related to various stages of life:

4. Ensure the provision of extra food and healthcare to pregnant and lactating women.

Pregnancy and lactation are demanding periods, both physiologically and nutritionally. This is reflected in the increased requirements of most nutrients. In order to meet these nutritional demands, pregnant/lactating women should eat an adequate quantity of a variety of foods. Increased energy requirements can be fulfilled by eating more of whole grains, sprouted pulses and fermented foods, along with some oil and sugar. An adequate amount of animal foods (milk/meat/egg) ensures good quality protein. Moreover, diets containing plenty of seasonal vegetables and fresh fruits provide various vitamins, minerals and fibre. Pregnant/lactating women are, however, advised to take daily supplements of calcium, iron and folic acid.

5. Promote exclusive breastfeeding for six months, and encourage breastfeeding till two years or as long as one can.

Breast milk is a natural food, nutritionally tailor-made for the infant. It has several advantages, for both the infant and the mother. Breastfeeding should be started within an hour (or earliest possible) after delivery, and the colostrum should not be discarded. Colostrum is the yellowish, viscous milk secreted during the first three to four days after childbirth. It is rich in several nutrients and antibodies. Exclusive breastfeeding should be done up to six months; however, breastfeeding can be continued as long as possible (even up to two years), along with complementary foods. Exclusively breastfed infants do not need additional water. Feeding on demand helps in maintaining a good milk supply. A nutritionally adequate diet, relaxed atmosphere and adequate rest are essential for successful breastfeeding. Use of tobacco, alcohol and drugs should be avoided during pregnancy and lactation.

6. Feed home-based semi-solid foods to the infant after six months.

After six months of age, breast-milk alone is not adequate for infants, because of their progressively increasing requirements and the gradual decline in breast-milk secretion by the mother. Therefore, it is essential to introduce home-made complementary foods for infants after the completion of six months of age for the promotion of optimal growth. These can be liquid, semi-solid or solid preparations, depending on the age and acceptability of the child.

Low-cost, home-made complementary foods can be prepared using commonly used foods, such as cereals-pulse-nut-oil and sugar/jaggery combination. Such a combination will provide adequate calories, good quality protein, and other nutrients as well. By including fruits and well-cooked and mashed vegetables, the micronutrient and fibre content of the complementary foods can be enhanced. Consistency should be semi-solid, and small quantities should be fed at frequent intervals (three to four times a day). While preparing and feeding the complementary foods, hygienic practices must be carefully followed to prevent episodes of infection and diarrhoea.

7. Ensure adequate and appropriate diets for children and adolescents, both in health and sickness.

Childhood and adolescence are periods of continuous growth and development, and therefore it is essential to provide a nutritionally adequate and well-balanced diet. Young children should be given a variety of nutritious foods, as this is the stage when food habits form. Children and adolescents should consume plenty of milk and milk products in order to meet their high calcium requirement. Appropriate dietary and lifestyle practices should be promoted amongst them, with special emphasis on regular physical activity. This will ensure optimum body composition and reduce the risk of diet-related chronic diseases in later life.

8. Include micronutrient-rich foods in the diets of elderly people, to enable them to be fit and active.

Ageing is associated with decline in muscle mass, bone mass, digestion, metabolism, immune function, and physical activity. All these are the contributory factors for their reduced calorie requirements, while keeping the requirement of other nutrients high. Therefore, it is essential to provide them with nutrient-dense, rather than calorie-dense, foods. Low-fat protein foods, such as pulses, toned milk, lean meat, and egg-white, should be included to improve the quality of the diet. The Expert Committee of the NIN (2011) has recommended that the elderly need at least 200–300 ml of milk and milk products, and 400g of vegetables and fruits, daily. Oil intake should be less than 20g in a day, and vegetable oils should be preferred over animal fats (*ghee,* butter). Consumption of salty, spicy and fried foods should be avoided. A well-cooked, soft diet, consumed at frequent intervals, is better tolerated. Adequate consumption of water prevents dehydration and constipation. Thus, a combination of healthy food habits, along with a regular, comfortable level of physical activity, would enable the elderly to live an active healthy life.

Guidelines to maintain an ideal body weight and prevent chronic diet-related disorders:

9. Ensure a moderate use of edible oils and animal foods, and very little use of *ghee*/ butter/ *vanaspati*.

Fats and oils form the essential component of our diet, as they are rich sources of energy. Fats not only enhance the palatability of our diet, but also promote the absorption of fat-soluble vitamins (A, D, E, and K) and provide essential fatty acids (linoleic n-6 and alpha linolenic n-3). However, excessive intake of dietary fat increases the risk of obesity, heart diseases, strokes, and cancer. The total fat in the diet, including visible and invisible sources, should provide 20–30 per cent of the total calories. The diets of sedentary adults should contain about 25g of visible fat, whereas pregnant/lactating women should consume about 30g and children/adolescents should consume 30–50 g/day (NIN 2011). Cholesterol intake in a day should not exceed 200 mg. The dietary fat should contain SFA, PUFA and MUFA in almost same proportion (that is, 1:1:1), each providing about 8–10 per cent of the total energy intake.

Due to the high cholesterol content of egg, the consumption of three eggs/week is recommended. However, egg white is very low in cholesterol. Animal foods such as butter, *ghee*, cheese, meat, egg, and organ meats (liver, kidney, brain, etc.) should be consumed in limited quantities, as they have a high content of saturated fats and cholesterol. Low fat milk (toned/skimmed) should be preferred over whole milk. Fish, being a good source of preformed long chain n-3 PUFA, can be consumed more frequently (at least 100–200 g/ week), as compared to meat and poultry. Other foods rich in alpha-linolenic acid are legumes, green leafy vegetables, fenugreek, and mustard seeds. Preferably, a part of the visible and invisible fat from animal foods may be substituted by whole nuts and legumes. In order to get an appropriate proportion of the different classes of fatty acids, more than one type of vegetable oil should be consumed; for example, mustard oil may be consumed along with groundnut/sesame/rice bran. The use of hydrogenated fat and reheated fats/oils should be avoided, as the trans fatty acids present in them may increase the risk of heart disease.

10. Avoid overeating to prevent becoming overweight and obesity.

Maintaining a desirable/ideal body weight is a prerequisite for good health. Overweight and obesity are associated with several health-related disorders, as there is an increased risk of heart disease, hypertension, diabetes, hyperlipidemia, gallstones, osteoarthritis, and certain cancers. Undesirable weight gain is an outcome of an imbalance between energy intake and energy expenditure. One of the major contributory factors for this is overeating during infancy, childhood and adolescence, along with low physical activity. Therefore, in order to achieve energy balance (intake = expenditure) and attain a desirable body weight, it is essential to adjust the calorie intake along with regular physical activity.

However, extreme approaches towards weight reduction should be avoided. A gradual weight reduction (about half a kilogram per week) is considered safe and attainable. Weight-reducing diets should be low in fat and carbohydrate, rich in protein and all the nutrients, and provide not less than 1,000 kcal/day. The intake of sugar, salt, saturated fat, fatty foods, fried foods, refined foods, soft drinks, and alcohol should be restricted. However, foods providing complex carbohydrates, fibre, vitamins, and minerals can be consumed liberally, like whole grain cereals, whole pulses, fruits and vegetables. Low-fat, protein-rich foods should be included in the diet, such as low-fat milk, egg white, chicken, and low-fat fish. Small, frequent and regular meals are preferred over large, irregular meals.

11. Exercise regularly and be physically active to maintain an ideal body weight.

Regular physical activity not only helps to maintain a desirable body weight, but also reduces the risk of non-communicable chronic diseases and improves a sense of well-being. NIN (2011) has recommended at least 45 minutes of physical activity of moderate intensity for at least five days in a week to get various health benefits. However, for weight reduction, at least 60 minutes of moderate to vigorous-intensity physical activity is recommended. Individuals with health-related problems, pregnant women and the elderly should undertake an exercise programme in consultation with a physician.

Box 16.3: Categorisation of Physical Activities Based on Intensity

Moderate intensity:	*Vigorous intensity:*
Brisk walk (5–6 km/hr)	Jogging
Gardening	Running
Dancing (slow)	Dancing (fast)
Bicycling (about 16 km/hr)	Cycling (>16 km/hr)
Weight training	Swimming
Yogasanas	Aerobics
Pranayama	Competitive sports

Don't forget to 'warm-up' before exercise. Equally important is the 'cool-down' period after the exercise.

12. Restrict salt intake to a minimum.

Salt is an important component of our diet, and a major source of sodium as well. It is used as a vehicle for food fortification (iodine and iron). All foods contain sodium, and so even a moderate intake of salt can meet the sodium requirement. As a high intake of salt is associated with high blood pressure, salt intake should not be more than 6 g/day (ICMR 2010). Therefore, an attempt should be made to develop a taste for diets that are low in salt, as the taste for salt is an acquired one. The consumption of processed and preserved foods, such as *papads*, pickles, ketchup, sauces, etc., should be in moderation, due to their high sodium content. Fruits and vegetables should be consumed in good amounts regularly as they are rich in potassium, and thereby decrease blood pressure.

13. Minimise the use of processed foods rich in salt, sugar and fats.

Changes in lifestyle and urbanisation has resulted in an increased demand for processed, ready-to-eat and convenience foods. Traditional foods are being replaced by processed foods, which may not be nutritionally balanced as they are generally refined, lack fibre and micronutrients, and provide only empty calories. Over-indulgence in sugary foods may lead to obesity and elevated blood lipids. Therefore, traditional, home-made foods should be preferred over unhealthy processed foods. Moreover, most processed fruits and vegetables lose their nutritive value, and cannot be compared to the goodness of nutrient-rich fresh fruits and vegetables. It is advisable to read food labels while purchasing processed foods, to learn about the content of nutrients, their shelf-life, and the additives present in them.

Guidelines regarding food-related practices:

14. Ensure the use of safe and clean foods.

Contamination of food by microbes, adulterants, natural toxins, and chemical residues makes it unsafe for consumption. Therefore, food items should be purchased after careful examination and from reliable sources to ensure quality, freshness and wholesomeness. During storage, non-perishable dry foodgrains should be protected from moisture, and from damage by microbes, rodents and insects. Adequate personal hygiene measures must be observed while processing, handling and cooking the food. The place where food is cooked, stored and served, and the utensils used, must be kept clean to ensure food safety. Perishable as well as cooked foods should be stored at appropriate temperatures (refrigeration) to prevent spoilage. However, refrigerated cooked food should be heated prior to consumption. The levels of harmful pesticide residues in vegetables and fruits can be minimised by washing the foodstuffs thoroughly in running water, by peeling, or by cooking.

15. Adopt the right pre-cooking processes and appropriate cooking methods.

The nutrient content of the food that we finally consume is significantly influenced by several pre-cooking and cooking practices. It is important that foods be thoroughly washed before cooking to remove contaminants and extraneous matter. However, repeated washing of cereals and pulses results in the loss of certain water-soluble vitamins and minerals. Likewise, vegetables and fruits should be washed thoroughly prior to peeling and cutting. Vegetables should be cut into large pieces and the cut vegetables should not be soaked in water for long, so as to prevent the leaching loss of water-soluble vitamins and minerals. Methods such as fermentation (*used for making idli, dosa, dhokla*) and germination (sprouting) should be encouraged, as they improve the digestibility and availability of nutrients from food.

During cooking, the nutrients that are heat-labile and water soluble, like vitamin B-complex and C, are lost. However, such losses can be minimised by following appropriate cooking methods. The water used for cooking (for example, rice) should be just sufficient. The water left after boiling pulses or vegetables can be used in some other preparations, like soups, curries, kneading the dough, etc. Foods should be cooked covered rather than in an open vessel. Steaming/ pressure cooking should be preferred over deep frying/ roasting (high temperature cooking). Cooking oils should not be repeatedly reheated, to avoid the formation of peroxides and free radicals. The use of baking soda to hasten the cooking of pulses and enhance the colour of vegetables should be discouraged. Besides various cooking practices, there are various faulty food fads, taboos and beliefs that may have adverse effects on health and nutritional status. Such practices must be discouraged.

GLOBAL SCENARIO

Most countries of the world have developed their own national dietary guidelines to address their own specific health and nutritional concerns. The primary goal of these guidelines (which is common across countries) is to improve the health and nutritional status of a given community/ population. Therefore, the development of these food-based dietary guidelines takes into consideration the ecological setting, cultural factors and habitual dietary pattern of the people. Being designed for the general public, these guidelines translate nutrition recommendations in terms of what to eat and how much (food advice). Food-based dietary guidelines can be used as a basis for educational materials and media campaigns on nutrition (FAO/WHO 1996).

Box 16.4: Take-home Messages of USDA (2010) Dietary Guidelines for Americans

Balancing Calories

- Enjoy your food, but eat less.
- Avoid oversized portions.

Foods to Increase

- Make half your plate fruits and vegetables.
- Switch to fat-free or low-fat (1 per cent) milk.

Foods to Reduce

- Compare sodium in foods like soup, bread, and frozen meals, and choose the foods with lower numbers.
- Drink water instead of sugary drinks.

There is a remarkable similarity among the guidelines of various nations in terms of purpose, process of development, scientific base, practicality, use, and simplicity of language. These guidelines deliver comparable messages in different countries. They all strive for balance by giving recommendations in terms of variety, moderation, and adequacy of food and nutrients. The emphasis on the inclusion of plenty of vegetables, fruits and adequate fibre is evident in almost all the guidelines, while highlighting a moderate intake of fat, sugar, salt, and alcohol. However, there is great variation in several aspects among guidelines, such as the total number, food grouping, type and amount of fat, and weight maintenance recommendations. Only a few countries have included supplementary guidelines regarding food safety and physical activity.

Several countries have pictorial presentations of food guides to assist the implementation of dietary guidelines by the population. These visual illustrations vary widely in their shapes and recommendations. Some have a pyramid shape (India and Philippines), while others have a pagoda shape (China and Korea) or are circular (Australia, Germany and Sweden). While the food guide of Canada is in the shape of a rainbow, it is in the form of a food plate (complete with knife and fork) in the UK, Mexico and the US.

Box 16.5: Some Interesting Applications of Dietary Guidelines in Singapore

The dietary guidelines of Singapore are also being applied for food served by different food service establishments in schools, workplaces and hawker centres. A lot of people in Singapore eat out regularly and a need was felt to improve the nutritional quality of food served in these establishments. Food service providers were asked to include more whole-grains and vegetables in their dishes, while keeping the saturated fat, trans fat and salt low.

In addition the Health Promotion Board, Singapore (HPB) has promoted the Healthier Choice Symbol (HCS) to be used on packaged food products to help consumers make healthy food choices. Standards have been developed which the food product has to meet in order to use the symbol on the front of the pack. These standards draw upon the dietary guidelines.

Source: Lee 2011.

Box 16.6: Some Interesting Socio-cultural Aspects of Japanese Dietary Guidelines

Japanese dietary guidelines have interesting socio-cultural aspects. Not only do they specify what is healthy to eat, they also lay emphasis on how to eat. For instance the guidelines talk about eating meals with the family and communicating with the family while eating together. They also talk about respecting the Japanese food culture and applying it to the daily diet. They encourage people to participate in preparation of meals and acquiring the knowledge about foods and cooking methods.

Place importance on appropriate eating habits from an early stage of life.

Source: Nakamura 2011.

Table 16.2: Global Dietary Guidelines at a Glance

Dietary guideline	*India (2011)*	*Asia & the Pacific: China (2007), Japan (2005), Malaysia (2010), Singapore (2011), Thailand (2009)*	*Europe: France, United Kingdom (2006)*	*Canada (2011), United States of America (2010)*
Number of items	15	*China* - 10 *Japan* - 10 *Malaysia* - 14 *Singapore* - 3 categories *Thailand* - 9	*France* -9 *United Kingdom* - 9	*Canada* - 5 headings *United States of America* - 5 headings
Variety	Variety to ensure a balanced diet	*China* - Variety of foods *Japan* - # *Malaysia* - Variety within recommended intakes *Singapore* - Variety and balance *Thailand* - Variety of foods from each food group	*France* - # *United Kingdom* - #	*Canada* - Variety of foods from four food groups *United States of America* - #

Table 16.2 contd

Table 16.2 contd

Grains	Whole grain cereals and pulses	*China* - Appropriate amount of coarse grains *Japan* - Eat enough grains, such as rice and other cereals *Malaysia* - Prefer whole grains *Singapore* - Sufficient grains, especially whole grains *Thailand* - Adequate rice/ alternate carbohydrate	*France* - Starchy foods, depending upon appetite *United Kingdom* - Plenty of starchy foods, particularly whole grains	*Canada* - Emphasis on whole grains *United States of America* - Increase whole grain intake
Vegetables and Fruits	Eat plenty: at least 100g fresh fruits and 300g vegetables	*China* - Plenty of vegetables, fruits and tubers *Japan* - Plenty of vegetables and fruits everyday *Malaysia* - Eat plenty everyday (at least five servings) *Singapore* - Eat more fruits and vegetables everyday *Thailand* - Eat plenty	*France* - At least five per day *United Kingdom* - At least five portions	*Canada* - Have vegetables and fruits more often than juices. At least one dark green vegetable and one orange vegetable/fruit daily. *United States of America* - Increase intake
Milk	At least 250 ml/day	*China* - Consume milk, dairy products (or soyabean products) everyday *Japan* - Drink milk for calcium *Malaysia* - Adequately and daily *Singapore* - # *Thailand* - Consume daily	*France* - Three dairy products a day *United Kingdom* - Moderate, choose low-fat versions	*Canada* - Low fat milk and alternatives *United States of America* - Increase intake of low-fat milk and milk products
Meat	Consume moderate amounts; three eggs/ week	*China* - Appropriate amounts *Japan* - # *Malaysia* - Eat moderately *Singapore* - # *Thailand* – Consume regularly. Children: eggs daily Adults: 3–4 eggs/week	*France* - One to two times a day *United Kingdom* - Moderate	*Canada* - Lean meat, two servings of fish/day *United States of America* - Choose a variety of these that are lower in solid fat
Fat	-Limit total fat to 20–30% of energy. Cholesterol intake <200 mg. SFA, PUFA and MUFA in almost same proportion (that is,, 1:1:1), each providing about 8–10% of the total energy intake 3 eggs/ week	*China* - Use less cooking oil *Japan* - Avoid oily and fatty foods *Malaysia* - Limit total fat (20–30% of energy) Limit saturated fat (<10% of energy) *Singapore* - Less fat, especially saturated fat. *Thailand* - Moderate amounts (< 30% of energy) Limit saturated fat sources.	*France* - To limit *United Kingdom* - Eat less SFA not more than 11% of energy, PUFA – 6.5%, MUFA – 13%	*Canada* - 30–45 ml unsaturated fat per day. Limit saturated and trans fats. *United States of America* - Replace solid fats with oil, where possible, cholesterol less than 300 mg/day, less than 10% calories from saturated fats

Table 16.2 contd

Table 16.2 contd

Sugar	Minimise intake of sugary processed foods	*China* - # *Japan* - # *Malaysia* - Eat foods low in sugar *Singapore* - Choose food and beverages with less sugar *Thailand* - Avoid excessive intake	*France* - To limit *United Kingdom* - Eat less (non-milk extrinsic sugars not more than 11% of energy)	*Canada* - Limit foods high in sugar *United States of America* - Limit consumption of foods containing added sugar
Salt	Restrict intake to minimum Minimise intake of salty processed foods	*China* - Low salt *Japan* - Reduce the amount of salt intake to less than 10g per day *Malaysia* - Limit to 1 teaspoon/ day *Singapore* - Limit salt intake *Thailand* - Avoid excessive intake	*France* - To limit *United Kingdom* - Eat less (6 grams)	*Canada* - Limit foods high in salt *United States of America* - Reduce daily sodium intake to less than 2,300 mg.
Fluid	Plenty of water Beverages in moderation	*China* - Sufficient water everyday, rationally select beverages *Japan* - # *Malaysia* - Plenty (6–8 glasses daily) *Singapore* - # *Thailand* - #	*France* - At will *United Kingdom* -#	*Canada* - Prefer water over other beverages *United States of America* - #
Alcohol	Avoid/ limit	*China* - Limited amounts *Japan* - Avoid too much alcohol *Malaysia* - Avoid *Singapore* - Moderation *Thailand* - Avoid/reduce	*France* - # *United Kingdom* - #	*Canada* - # *United States of America* - If consumed, it should be in moderation—up to one drink per day for women and two drinks per day for men—and only by adults of legal drinking age.
Healthy weight	Avoid overeating to prevent overweight/ obesity Maintain ideal body weight	*China* - Don't overeat, maintain a healthy body weight *Japan* - Healthy body weight through balancing the energy intake with physical activity *Malaysia* - In healthy range *Singapore* - Healthy BMI *Thailand* - Maintain proper weight	*France* - # *United Kingdom* - #	*Canada* - Healthy body weight *United States of America* - Balancing calories to maintain weight
Physical activity	Exercise regularly Be physically active	*China* - Exercise everyday *Japan* - Acquire the habit of exercise *Malaysia* - Be active everyday *Singapore* - # *Thailand* - #	*France* - At least the equivalent of 30 minutes of brisk walking per day for adults (at least one hour for children and adolescents) *United Kingdom* - #	*Canada* - Adults at least 2½ hours of moderate to vigorous physical activity each week, and children and youth at least 60 minutes per day. *United States of America* - Increase physical activity

Table 16.2 contd

Table 16.2 contd

Specific guidelines for different life stages	All life stages covered: Pregnancy, lactation, infancy, childhood, adolescence, adulthood, and elderly	*China* - # *Japan* - # *Malaysia* - Lactation *Singapore* - Children, adolescents, adults, and older adults *Thailand* - #	*France* - # *United Kingdom* - Pregnant women, lactating women, children below five years	*Canada* - Children, women of childbearing age, people above 50 years. *United States of America* - Women capable of becoming pregnant, pregnant and lactating women, elderly
Food safety	Safe and clean foods	*China* - Fresh and sanitary foods *Japan* - # *Malaysia* - Safe and clean food and beverages *Singapore* - # *Thailand* - Clean and uncontaminated foods (with Thai FDA logo)	*France* - # *United Kingdom* - #	*Canada* - # *United States of America* - Follow food safety recommendations when preparing and eating foods to reduce the risk of food-borne illnesses.
Other	Right pre-cooking processes and appropriate cooking methods	*China* - # *Japan* - Communication at the table with family, emphasis on regular meals, using different methods of cooking. Check nutrition labels for choosing foods and selecting menus Reduce leftovers and waste through proper cooking and storage methods *Malaysia* - Nutrition labelling *Singapore* - *Thailand* -	*France* - # *United Kingdom* - #	*Canada* - # *United States of America* - #
Pictorial Food Guide Depictions	Pyramid	*China* - Pagoda *Japan* - Spinning Top *Malaysia* - Pyramid *Singapore* - Pyramid *Thailand* - Nutrition Flag	*France* - Staircase *United Kingdom* - Circle (Plate)	*Canada* - A rainbow *United States of America* - MyPlate, a plate icon

Source: of FBDG of different countries: Canada: www.hc-sc.gc.ca/fn-an/pubs/res-educat/res-educat-eng.php; China: Ge (2011); European countries: www.eufic.org; France: www.inpes.sante.fr, www.mangerbouger.fr/; India: NIN 2011; Japan: Nakamura 2011; Malaysia: Tee 2011; Singapore: Lee 2011; Thailand: Sirichakwal et al. 2011; UK: www.food.gov.uk; United States: www.cnpp.usda.gov.

SUMMARY

- Eat a variety of food from several food groups to get an adequate supply of nutrients.
- Whole grain cereals, millets and whole pulses should be consumed in adequate amounts.
- Eat plenty of seasonal vegetables and fruits.
- Regular consumption of animal foods, such as milk, egg, meat, and fish, provides good quality protein and several other nutrients.

- In order to limit the fat intake, adults and the elderly should select low-fat milk, lean meat, fish, and egg white.
- Vegetable oils should be preferred over animal fat.
- Hydrogenated fat should not be included in the diet.
- Intake of refined cereals and simple sugars should be replaced by complex carbohydrates.
- Ensure adequate intake of safe, potable water.
- During pregnancy/ lactation, adequate amounts of whole grains and animal foods, as well as plenty of vegetables and fruits, should be included in the diet.
- Children and adolescents should be given a variety of food to develop healthy food habits.
- Processed foods having a high content of calories, salt, sugar, and fats should be sparingly used.
- Attempt should be made to minimise the loss of nutrients before and during cooking.
- Be active. To attain a desirable body weight, dietary modification should be supplemented with adequate exercise.

KEY WORDS

Antioxidants: A group of substances that prevent the damage caused by the oxidation of fatty acids and proteins by free radicals.

Balanced diet: A diet containing all essential nutrients in adequate amounts and proper proportions that meet the requirements.

Body Mass Index: An index of the weight status of a person in relation to height. Weight(Kg)/(Height in metres).

Colostrum: Yellowish, viscous milk secreted during the first three to four days after childbirth. It confers various benefits on the infant.

Empty calories: Foods providing only energy without any other nutrient, such as alcohol and sugar.

Food-based Dietary Guidelines: Recommendations for the population to promote healthy dietary practices, thereby improving the nutritional status.

Free radicals: Highly reactive substances formed in the body, causing damage to cellular components by oxidation.

Invisible fats: The fat that is an integral component of foods (plant/animal) such as cereals, nuts, milk, and egg.

Monounsaturated fatty acids (MUFA): Unsaturated fatty acids having one double bond.

Nutrient-dense: Food and beverages providing fewer calories in a given amount and a relatively greater amount of vitamins, minerals, and other beneficial substances.

Polyunsaturated fatty acids (PUFA): Unsaturated fatty acids having two or more double bonds, for example, linoleic acid and linolenic acid.

Processed foods: Foods produced by converting raw foods into ready-to-use/eat foods or preserved foods.

Saturated fatty acids (SFA): These fatty acids do not have double bonds.

Trans-fatty acids: These are the harmful fatty acids mainly produced during the hydrogenation of oils.

Visible fats: Fats/oils that can be used as such, as in cooking.

Weaning foods: Foods given to infants during the transition from breastfeeding to normal diet.

EXERCISES

1. A 38-year-old overweight man wants to reduce weight. What kind of dietary and lifestyle modifications would help him in achieving weight reduction?
2. A nutrition education programme has been organised in an *anganwadi* for pregnant and lactating women. What dietary advice can be given to them for themselves and their infants?
3. Why should processed foods be consumed judiciously?
4. What advice would you give to the elderly in order for them to remain healthy and physically fit?
5. In what aspects are the dietary guidelines from different countries similar?
6. Discuss how the Japanese dietary guidelines lay a lot of emphasis on home food and eating environment.

REFERENCES

European Food Safety Authority (EFSA), 'Development of Food-based Dietary Guidelines', EFSA Scientific Colloquium No. 5, Summary Report, Parma, Italy: EFSA, 2007.

Food and Agricultural Organization/World Health Organization (FAO/WHO), *Food Based Dietary Guidelines*, Rome: Food and Agricultural Organization, World Health Organization, 1995.

_______, 'Preparation and Use of Food Based Dietary Guidelines', Report of a Joint FAO/WHO Expert Consultation, Nicosia, Cyprus, Geneva: World Health Organization, 1996. Available at www.fao.org/docrep/X0243E/x0243e00.htm.

_______, 'Preparation and Use of Food Based Dietary Guidelines', WHO Technical Report Series no. 880, Geneva: World Health Organization, 1998.

Available at http://www.who.int/nutrition/publications/nutrientrequirements/WHO_TRS_880.htm

Ge, K., 'The transition of Chinese dietary guidelines and food guide pagoda', *Asia Pac J ClinNutr* 20 (3), 2011, pp. 439–46.

Gibney, M. J. and B. Sandstrom, 'A framework for food-based dietary guidelines in the European Union', *Public Health Nutrition* 4, 2001, pp. 293–305.

NIN, Indian Coucil of Medical Research, *Dietary Guidelines for Indians—A Manual*, Hyderabad: National Institute of Nutrition, 2011.

Lee, B. L. C., 'Dietary Guidelines in Singapore', *Asia Pac J ClinNutr* 20 (3), 2011, pp. 472 –76.

National Coordinating Committee on Food and Nutrition, *Malaysian Dietary Guidelines*, Putrajaya: Ministry of Health Malaysia, 2010.

Nakamura, T., 'Nutritional policies and dietary guidelines in Japan', *Asia Pac J ClinNutr* 20 (3), 2011, pp. 452–54.

Radhika, M. S., in M. S. Bamji, K. Krishnaswamy and G. N. V. Brahmam (eds), *Textbook of Human Nutrition*, 3e, New Delhi: Oxford and IBH Publishing Co. Pvt. Ltd, 2009.

Sirichakwal, P. P., K. Sranacharoenpong and K. Tontisirin, 'Food based dietary guidelines (FBDGs) development and promotion in Thailand', *Asia Pac J ClinNutr* 20 (3), 2011, pp. 477–83.

Tee, E. S., 'Development and Promotion of Malaysian Dietary Guidelines', *Asia Pac J ClinNutr* 20 (3), 2011, pp. 455–61.

United States Department of Agriculture (USDA), 2010. Available at www.cnpp.usda.gov.

World Health Organisation European Region, *CINDI dietary guide*, Copenhagen: WHO, 2000. Available at http://www.euro.who.int/Document/E70041.pdf.

ONLINE SOURCES

www.cnpp.usda.gov/Publications/DietaryGuidelines/2010/PolicyDoc/PolicyDoc.pdf

www.eufic.org

www.fao.org/ag/humannutrition/nutritioneducation/49741.htm

www.fao.org/ag/humannutrition/nutritioneducation/fbdg.htm

www.food.gov.uk

www.hc-sc.gc.ca/fn-an/pubs/res-educat/res-educat-eng.php

www.inpes.sante.fr

www.mangerbouger.fr/

www.ninindia.org/DietaryguidelinesforIndians-Finaldraft.pdf

17

NUTRITION FOR ADULTS

HIGHLIGHTS

- Nutrient requirements for men and women
- Planning meals for adults
- Nutritional concerns
- Diet and lifestyle-related diseases and their prevention

Adulthood is that stage of life where physical growth and maturation is completed. A well-balanced, nutritious diet is needed at this stage of life for the maintenance of physical, mental and social well-being. Adequate nutrition and sufficient physical activity during adulthood will not only ensure good health, but will also prevent chronic degenerative diseases and disability in the years ahead.

PHYSIOLOGICAL CHANGES

The process of physical maturation, which usually entails attaining one's full height, gets completed by the end of adolescence. The cell growth and division necessary for the proper functioning of body organs continues during adult years. Physical abilities, bone mass and muscle strength peaks during 18–30 years of age. Thereafter, there is a decline in various physiological functions, which is termed ageing. Ageing is a normal biological process in human beings, which involves the gradual alteration of body structure, function, and tolerance to environmental stress. A person who is 60 years old may have a biological age of 45 years, depending on his health and fitness status. A well-balanced diet and physically active routine can reduce biological age and slow down the process of ageing.

Chronological age: Age of a person measured in years, months and days from the date the person was born.

Biological age: Biological age is determined by the physiology of a person, which includes aspects such as physical structure of his or her body, sensory awareness, motor skills, cognitive abilities, general mobility and functionality.

PSYCHOSOCIAL DEVELOPMENT

Cognitive development is completed by the end of adolescence, and as teenagers enter the early years of adulthood, they gain a sense of responsibility and move into adult roles. The increased ability in decision-making and independent functioning helps them to identify their career goals. They also have increased emotional stability. They tend to form new relationships with their parents, and gradually prepare themselves for marriage and family life.

NUTRIENT REQUIREMENTS FOR MEN AND WOMEN

Good nutrition plays a fundamental role in preserving overall wellness, maintaining a healthy weight, and in preventing diseases associated with ageing. The focus of nutrition has now shifted to maintaining a healthy and active lifestyle during adulthood, so as to prevent lifestyle-related disorders during old age.

The nutrient requirements of an individual are affected by age, gender, body weight, height, and level of physical activity. Nutrient intake is also dependent on various other factors, like food availability, accessibility and acceptability. Physiological and pathological conditions can also influence nutrient requirements.

The Recommended Dietary Allowance (RDA) is the amount of nutrient considered adequate to meet the needs of practically all healthy people. The Indian Council of Medical Research (ICMR) has used a scientific basis to obtain the RDA for all essential nutrients. As there is a lot of variability in requirements according to age, body size and physical activity level, the recommendations have been calculated based on a Reference man and woman (Box 17.1).

Box 17.1: Reference Indian Adult Man and Woman

Reference man is between 18–29 years of age, and weighs 60 kg with a height of 1.73m and a BMI of 20.3 kg/m^2, is free from disease and is physically fit for active work; on each working day, he is engaged in eight hours of occupation, which usually involves moderate activity; when not at work, he spends eight hours in bed, 4–6 hours in sitting and moving about, two hours in walking, and in active recreation or household duties.

Reference woman is between 18–29 years of age, non-pregnant, non-lactating (NPNL), and weighs 55 kg with a height of 1.61m and a BMI of 21.2 kg/m^2, is free from disease and physically fit for active work; on each working day, she is engaged in eight hours of occupation, which usually involves moderate activity; when not at work, she spends eight hours in bed, 4–6 hours in sitting and moving about, two hours in walking, and in active recreation or household duties.

Source: ICMR 2010.

The RDA of various important nutrients for adult man and woman are discussed below, and given in Table 17.1.

Table 17.1: Recommended Dietary Allowances (RDA) for Various Nutrients in Indian Adult Men and Women

Nutrient	*Men (Body Weight 60Kg)*			*Women (Body Weight 55Kg)*		
	Sedentary	*Moderate*	*Heavy*	*Sedentary*	*Moderate*	*Heavy*
Energy (kcal/d)	2,320	2,730	3,490	1,900	2,230	2,850
Protein (g/d)	60	60	60	55	55	55
Visible Fat (g/d)	25	30	40	20	25	30
Calcium (mg/d)	600	600	600	600	600	600
Iron (mg/d)	17	17	17	21	21	21
Zinc (mg/d)	12	12	12	10	10	10
Vitamin A (μg/d) Retinol/β-carotene	600/4,800	600/4,800	600/4,800	600/4,800	600/4,800	600/4,800
Thiamine (mg/d)	1.2	1.4	1.7	1.0	1.1	1.4
Riboflavin (mg/d)	1.4	1.6	2.1	1.1	1.3	1.7
Niacin Equivalent (mg/d)	13	18	21	12	14	16
Vitamin B_6(mg/d)	2.0	2.0	2.0	2.0	2.0	2.0
Ascorbic Acid (mg/d)	40	40	40	40	40	40
Dietary Folate (μg/d)	200	200	200	200	200	200
Vitamin B_{12} (mg/d)	1.0	1.0	1.0	1.0	1.0	1.0

Source: ICMR 2010.

Energy

Adults require enough energy to lead an active healthy life. Energy intake helps in maintaining body weight, temperature and metabolic activity. It is influenced by gender and level of physical activity. Energy can neither be created nor destroyed; it can only be transformed from one form to another. Body weight is stable when the energy consumed through food is equal to the energy expended in various activities. When energy balance is maintained over a prolonged period, an individual is considered as being in a steady state. This can include short periods of day-to-day imbalance between intake and expenditure. The energy is reserved in the body in the form of fat, which can take care of any imbalances between energy intake and expenditure.

The definition (ICMR 2010) of energy requirement is:

The level of energy intake from food that balances energy expenditure when the individual has a body size and composition and level of physical activity, consistent with long-term good health, also allowing for maintenance of economically essential and socially desirable activity.

The definition clearly states that

Total daily energy expenditure should = Daily average energy intake

Energy expenditure has three main components:

1. **Basal metabolic rate (BMR)**: This is the amount of energy expended daily by humans at rest. This energy is used for the functioning of the vital organs—the heart, lungs, nervous system, kidneys, liver, intestine, sex organs, muscles, and skin.
2. **Dietary induced thermogenesis (DIT):** The use of energy in digesting, absorbing, storing, and disposing of excretory products, as well as the body's response to stimuli such as cold, stimulants and drugs. This is also known as the Thermic effect of food (TEF), or specific dynamic action (SDA).
3. **Physical activity:** It includes the cost and quantum of activity as well as the type of activity, that is, occupational and non-occupational activity.

The component of energy expenditure related to thermogenesis is merged into measurements related to the cost of physical activity. Thus, energy expenditure is computed using only two components—BMR and physical activity. The factorial approach has been used to compute energy expenditure by an adult man and woman weighing 60 kg and 55 kg, respectively engaged in various levels of activity.

Sedentary activity: People who are engaged in occupations which do not involve much physical effort and they spend most part of their occupation sitting or standing, with little body displacement. These people generally use motorised vehicles for travelling longer distances and are not involved in any exercise or sports regularly, for example, business executive, housewife with domestic help, teacher, tailor, barber etc.

Moderate activity: People who are engaged in occupations which require more energy expenditure than people with sedentary activities. These people are regularly involved in moderate physical activities in their daily routine, for example, maid servant, fisherman, carpenter, agriculture labourer, rickshaw puller, electrician, driver, industrial worker etc.

Heavy activity: People who are engaged in occupations or activities for long hours involving vigorous activity or large energy expenditure, for example blacksmith, athletes, dancer, mineworker, woodcutter, stone cutter, mineworker, etc.

Daily energy expenditure of adults largely depends on the occupational activity, sleep and non-occupational activity of an individual. Factorial computation of energy expenditure at the three levels of activity, that is, sedentary, moderate and heavy by adult Indian population is given in Table 17.2 when each of the daily activities are carried out for eight hours. PAR values for various non-occupational activities are given in Table 17.3. The physical activity ratio (PAR) is the energy cost of an individual activity per minute to the cost of the basal metabolic rate per minute. PAR values for activities performed in a day (24 hours) can be aggregated to yield the physical activity level (PAL), which is the ratio of the energy expenditure for 24 hours and the BMR over 24 hours.

Total Daily Energy Expenditure= BMR x PAL, for example, the mean PAL of adult sedentary man is 1.53 and his BMR is 1515 kcal, then his energy expenditure is the product of PAL and BMR=2318 kcal≈ 2320 kcal. Therefore energy requirement of an adult sedentary man is 2320 Kcal (equal to energy expenditure). PAR value for occupational activity of heavy worker (3.8) is higher than sedentary (1.5) and moderate (2.3); therefore PAL value will also be higher (2.3). The energy expenditure by heavy worker would be higher than sedentary and moderate.

Table 17.2: PAR Values for Major Lifestyles and Energy Expenditure Based on Daily Activities

Main Daily Activities (Duration for each activity is taken as 8 hours)	*Sedentary*	*Moderate*	*Heavy*
Sleep	1.0	1.0	1.0
Occupational activity	1.5	2.3	3.8
Non-occupational activity	2.1	2.1	2.1
Mean (PAL value)	1.53	1.80	2.30
Men; body weight (60kg), BMR (1515kcal)	**2318**	**2727**	**3485**
Women; body weight (55 kg), BMR (1241 kcal)	**1899**	**2234**	**2854**

Source: Adapted from ICMR 2010.

In the case of energy requirements, no safe allowance is added as energy intake above the actual requirement is harmful, increasing the risk of obesity and other related diseases. BMR and energy requirement at the three levels of activity at different age groups and at different body weights are given in Table 17.4. Cereals, pulses, fats, and sugars are the energy giving food groups. Jaggery, nuts and oilseeds can be incorporated in the daily diet to meet the gaps in energy needs. However, saturated fats (butter, ghee and hydrogenated fats) and excessive sugars (energy drinks, carbonated beverages, sweets and desserts) should be consumed cautiously to prevent chronic degenerative disorders like obesity, diabetes, cardio-vascular diseases, and cancer.

Table 17.3: PAR Values for Various Non-occupational Activities

Daily Activities	*Duration (h)*	*PAR Value*
Personal care	1	2.3
Eating	1	1.5
Commuting to work by bus or by vehicle or by walk	1	2.0
General household or other activities	2	2.5
Walking at various speeds without load	1	3.2
Light leisure activity	2	1.4
Mean non-occupational activity	**8**	**2.1**

Source: Adapted from ICMR 2010.

Protein

Dietary protein in adults is necessary for the syntheses of new proteins to replace those being broken down. Most of the body nitrogen requirements are met by protein nitrogen, and therefore protein and nitrogen requirements are used interchangeably. ICMR (2010) has used two approaches for obtaining the protein requirements for Indian adult men and women—the factorial approach and nitrogen balance methods.

The factorial method of assessing the protein requirement of an individual is in terms of the obligatory loss of nitrogen through faeces, urine and skin. The directly observed obligatory nitrogen loss on a minimal protein diet in Indian adults has been shown to be 20 mg/kg/day and 37 mg/kg/day for faecal and urinary nitrogen excretion, respectively. The total obligatory nitrogen, after adding obligatory nitrogen loss through skin (11 mg/kg/day), would be 68 mg/kg/day. The efficiency of utilisation was assumed to be 50 per cent in the Indian population, and adding a safe level of intake (estimated average requirement + 1.96 SD) would work out to be 0.8 g/kg/day.

Data from various nitrogen balance studies have shown that the minimum dietary protein intake by an Indian adult to reach nitrogen equilibrium is 0.58 g/kg/day, and when allowance for sweat losses of 11 mg/kg/day is added, it works out to be 0.65 g protein/kg/day. The corresponding safe level intake works out to be 0.81 g protein/kg/day.

Data from both the factorial approach and nitrogen balance studies have shown that the safe level of protein requirement for Indian adults is 0.8 g protein/kg/day. The corresponding requirement on a mixed Indian diet (cereal-pulse-milk based diet) works out to be 1 g/kg/day. Thus, ICMR (2010) has recommended the intake of 60 g/day and 55 g/day for reference adult man and woman, respectively. Animal foods, such as milk and milk products, fowl, mutton, eggs, and fish, and plant foods such as pulses and legumes, are rich sources of protein. Animal foods are of high quality as they provide all essential amino acids, while plant sources lack one or the other essential amino acid. As Indians are primarily vegetarians, they should consume cereal-pulse combinations (rice-*dal*, *khichdi*, *idli-dosa-sambhar*, *chapati-dal*, *suji-besan cheela*) in their daily diet, as cereal and pulse have a supplementary effect on each other and provide better quality proteins. Other combinations, like cereal-milk, egg-cereal, meat-cereal, also enhance the protein quality of a mixed meal.

Table 17.4: Energy Requirement of Indian Men and Women at Different Ages and Body Weights

		18–30 years				30–60 years				> 60 years		
Sex	Body weight (kg)	BMR (kcal)	Sedentary	Moderate	Heavy	BMR (kcal)	Sedentary	Moderate	Heavy	BMR (kcal)	Sedentary	Moderate
Males	45	1298	1986	2336	2985	1324	2026	2383	3045	1039	1590	1870
	50	1370	2096	2466	3151	1358	2078	2444	3123	1103	1688	1985
	55	1443	2208	2597	3319	1433	2196	2579	3296	1167	1786	2101
	60	1515	2318	2727	3485	1487	2275	2671	3420	1231	1883	2216
	65	1588	2430	2858	3652	1542	2359	2736	3547	1295	1981	2331
	70	1660	2540	2988	3818	1596	2442	2873	3671	1359	2079	2446
	75	1773	2716	3191	4078	1651	2526	2971	3797	1423	2177	2565
Females	40	1031	1577	1856	2371	1120	1714	2016	2576	965	1477	1737
	45	1101	1685	1982	2532	1162	1778	2092	2673	1015	1553	1627
	50	1171	1792	2108	2693	1203	1841	2165	2767	1065	1630	1917
	55	1241	1899	2234	2854	1245	1905	2241	2864	1115	1706	2007
	60	1311	2006	2360	3015	1286	1966	2315	2958	1165	1782	2097
	65	1381	2113	2486	3176	1328	2032	2390	3054	1215	1860	2187
	70	1451	2220	2612	3337	1369	2095	2464	3149	1265	1936	2277

Source: ICMR 2010.

Dietary Fat

Dietary fat provides energy, and essential fatty acids serve as a vehicle for fat-soluble vitamins and facilitate their absorption. ICMR (2010) has recommended that the minimum total fat intake by Indian adults should be 15 per cent of the total energy intake, to ensure an adequate consumption of total energy, essential fatty acids and fat-soluble vitamins for most individuals. The maximum total fat intake should not exceed 30 per cent of the total energy so as to prevent chronic degenerative diseases. The total fat intake includes visible fat (vegetable oil, *ghee* and butter), invisible fat (fat is an integral part of each food item, like milk and its products, egg, meat and other flesh foods, cereals, pulses, nuts) and hidden fat (like in processed and ready-to-eat foods, for example, in cheese and mayonnaise).

> ***Blend of fats and oils Some of these combinations can be used to ensure the right proportion of essential fatty acids in the diet***
>
> Groundnut or sesame or rice bran + mustard or canola or soyabean
>
> Palmolein + mustard
>
> Safflower or sunflower + palmolein + mustard

A minimal intake of 12 g visible fat meets the essential fatty acid requirement. ICMR (2010) has recommended a higher level of visible fat intake (20g /day) to provide energy density and palatability to the diet. As fat requirements are based on energy requirements, the minimal intake of visible fats in Indian adults based on different levels of physical activity ranges from 20–40 g/day.

The ICMR (2010) also recommended the use of a correct combination or blend of two vegetable oils (groundnut, mustard, sunflower, rapeseed, safflower, soyabean, ricebran, and olive oil) to ensure the intake of good fatty acids (polyunsaturated, including n-3 and monounsaturated), limited intake of bad fatty acids (saturated), and eliminate industrially produced trans fat, with a focus on energy balance and physical activity.

Dietary Fibre

Dietary fibre is essential to maintain body weight and composition, lowering blood sugar levels, triglycerides and cholesterol. Dietary fibre refers to the remnants of the edible part of plants and carbohydrates that are resistant to digestion and absorption in the human small intestine, with complete or partial fermentation in the large intestine.

The requirements of fibre are assessed based mainly on normal large bowel function, reflected to provide enough bulk and substrates for fermentation. Thus, stool weight and gut transit time were taken as indicators of large bowel function. There have been no studies evaluating the dietary fibre requirements of Indians. Many Western studies have shown that a minimum intake of 20–35g of fibre is conducive for long-term good health. Taking into account the excessive use of refined grain products by urban Indians, ICMR (2010) has recommended a dietary fibre intake of 40 g/day to prevent chronic degenerative diseases. A part of an adult diet should have whole grain cereals and pulses, green leafy vegetables and fruits to gain the benefits of dietary fibre.

Calcium and Phosphorus

Calcium is the major element in the body, and most of it is present in the bone. Calcium is also required for many other functions in the body, like neuromuscular excitation, blood coagulation, membrane permeability, and others. Calcium in bone plays a role in maintaining blood level, even in a period of dietary calcium inadequacy. Calcium is required by the adult man to replace the calcium lost from the body through urine, stools, bile, and sweat. It is estimated that this loss in an adult man may be 700 mg/day.

Calcium requirement has been measured by long-term balance studies. The balance data from adults have indicated that intakes in the range of 500–600 mg/day are necessary for positive calcium balance. Studies on Indian adults have shown that they achieved zero retention of calcium at an intake of 334 mg; for retaining 40 mg/day of calcium to adjust for the insensitive losses, the calculated intake will be 480 mg/day. ICMR (2010) recommended a calcium intake of 600 mg/day for both adult men and women, after making allowances for the safe level. Milk and its products are rich sources of calcium. In populations where milk intake is low, plant sources like ragi, pulses like kidney beans, black beans and soyabean, green leafy vegetables, and oilseeds (gingelly seeds, mustard seeds) can be consumed to meet the calcium requirements of the body.

> Bones need plenty of calcium and vitamin D throughout childhood and adolescence to reach their peak strength and calcium content by about age 30. After that, bones slowly lose calcium, but people can help reduce these losses by getting the recommended amounts of calcium throughout adulthood and by having a healthy, active lifestyle that includes weight-bearing physical activity (such as walking and running). Exposure to sunlight ensures an adequate synthesis of vitamin D, which is essential for intestinal calcium absorption.

The functions and requirements of calcium and phosphorus are quite interlinked. The ICMR (2010) committee recommended that the calcium and phosphorous intake should be of the ratio of 1:1 in both adult men and women.

Iron

Dietary iron is required to replace the daily losses through sweat, urine and bile. Body iron loss and excretion in the adult man have been determined by turnover studies. The basal loss is proportional to the body size or surface area, and thus in a 60 kg man, it accounts for about 0.86 mg/day or be 14 µg/kg body weight/day.

In pre-menopausal women, besides the basal loss of 14 µg/kg body weight, iron is required to replace the blood lost in menstruation (16 µg/kg body weight). The requirement for an adult woman works out to be 14+16 =30 µg/kg or 1.65 mg/day.

> ***Universal Salt Iodisation***
>
> Adding iodine to salt is the simplest and most cost-effective technique for eliminating iodine deficiency disorders. In 2005, the Government of India reinstated a ban on the sale of non-iodised salt.
>
> Double Fortified Salt (DFS) contains 1,000 ppm iron and 35–40 ppm iodine. DFS provides the daily iodine requirement and one-third the requirement of iron. DFS is being used in all supplementary feeding national programmes of the country.

Iron absorption is inversely related to body iron stores. ICMR (2010) has recommended that absorption of iron from a cereal-pulse based diet in an adult man be 5 per cent, while it is 8 per cent for an adult woman. The RDA for iron, after multiplying with the bioavailability factor of 5 per cent and 8 per cent, works out to be 17 mg/d for adult men and 21 mg/day for adult women, respectively. Animal foods like chicken, mutton, organ meats, and fish are good sources of heme iron. Vegetarian diets should incorporate green leafy vegetables, whole cereals and millets, pulses, nuts, and jaggery in their daily diet to meet iron needs.

Bioavailability of iron from plant sources can be improved by limiting the intake of inhibitors of iron absorption, like phytate, certain tannins and phenols, which are present in whole cereals, pulses, fruits and vegetables, tea and coffee. Intake of vitamin C enhances iron absorption from the diet. Fermentation and germination of whole grains increase the vitamin C content and reduce phytate content, thus enhancing iron absorption. Intake of citrus fruits like, lemon, orange, sweet lime, and others like amla, guava and pineapple, and green leafy vegetables in the daily diet also increases the bioavailability of iron.

Zinc

Zinc is an integral component of many enzymes and is widely distributed in the body. Zinc deficiency could result in depressed immunity, anorexia, diarrhoea, altered skeletal system, and reproductive failure. Zinc requirements are obtained using chemical balance methods, or from turnover studies in adults. ICMR (2010) adopted zinc requirements of 12 mg for men and 10 mg for women (as given by the WHO Expert Committee). Flesh foods, liver, fish, and milk are very good sources of zinc. Whole cereals, pulses and nuts are also rich sources of zinc. However, the bioavailability of zinc from plant sources is very poor. Simple cooking processes, like soaking, fermentation and germination of whole grains, reduce phytate content and improve the bioavailability of zinc.

Iodine

Iodine is an essential micronutrient, needed for the synthesis of thyroid hormones, which control a number of metabolic activities. The normal daily dietary intake of iodine by an adult in an iodine-sufficient region is about 100–150 µg, which is readily absorbed from the gut. ICMR (2010) recommended a daily iodine intake of 150 µg/day for both adult men and women. The regular consumption of iodised salt is found to meet the iodine requirement in individuals.

Trace Mineral Elements

Based on clinical and experimental studies, ICMR (2010) has given the requirements of other trace elements, viz., copper (Cu), manganese (Mn), chromium (Cr), and selenium (Se), for Indian adults in terms of acceptable intake (Table 17.5). Seafoods, whole grains, legumes, and oils seeds like sesame, sunflower and nuts, as well as meat are rich sources of Cu, Mn and Cr.

Table 17.5: Acceptable Intake of Trace Elements for Indian Adults

Trace elements	Acceptable intake
Copper (mg/d)	1.7
Manganese (mg/d)	4.0
Chromium (μg/d)	50
Selenium (μg/d)	40

Water Soluble Vitamins

Thiamine

Thiamine stores in the body are small, and regular intake is necessary to maintain its metabolic functions. Thiamine, in the form of thiamine pyrophosphate, is involved in carbohydrate and lipid metabolism. Since the vitamin is needed for energy utilisation, its requirement is related to calorie intake. Several early studies showed that beriberi is seen among populations whose thiamine intake is less than 0.12 mg/1,000 kcal. However, intakes above 0.3 mg/1,000 kcal are consistent with good health. Depletion-repletion studies on Indian adults have indicated that 0.25–0.35 mg/1,000 kcal is the minimum requirement of thiamine. Thiamine, being water soluble and heat labile, is lost in considerable amounts during processing and cooking. ICMR (2010) recommended a dietary allowance of 0.5 mg/1,000 kcal after making allowances for cooking losses. Whole grain cereals, nuts, legumes, green leafy vegetables, organ meats, pork, liver, and egg are rich sources of thiamine.

Riboflavin

Riboflavin-derived coenzymes, FMN and FAD, are cofactors of numerous enzymes involved in oxidation-reduction reactions. Several of these enzymes are involved in the metabolism of energy and other vitamins like vitamin B_6, niacin and vitamin K. The data from depletion-repletion studies indicated that enzymes like erythrocyte glutathione reductase showed a linear increase with riboflavin intake, and reached maximum levels at intakes of nearly 0.5 mg /1,000 cal. After allowing for cooking losses, the ICMR (2010) committee recommended 0.6 mg/1,000 kcal. Inclusion of flesh foods, dairy products, whole grains, nuts and green leafy vegetables in the daily diet help in meeting riboflavin requirements.

Niacin

Niacin, in the form of nicotinic acid and niacinamide, is part of coenzymes connected with glycolysis, tissue respiration and synthesis of macromolecules. Dietary tryptophan can spare the requirements of niacin, as niacin is the metabolic end product of the essential amino acid tryptophan. In well-nourished individuals, 60 mg of tryptophan is taken as being equivalent to 1 mg niacin. Dietary intake of niacin is computed in terms of niacin equivalents, where

Niacin equivalents = niacin (mg) + (tryptophan [mg] / 60)

Niacin is present in good amounts in almost all cereals, except jowar and maize, in which niacin is present in bound form and thus is not freely available to the body. In some parts of India where jowar and maize are consumed as staple food and overall diet quality is poor, niacin deficiency is quite common. Although niacin is more stable than other water soluble B-complex vitamins, studies carried out in India have shown that nearly 25 per cent of niacin is lost during cooking.

Niacin requirements are estimated using both dietary surveys and load tests. Diet surveys from India show that the average intake of niacin is around 10 mg daily. Even in rice-eating populations, where intakes of niacin are lower, together with tryptophan, such diets provide about 6 mg niacin equivalents per 1,000 kcal. Pellagra which is a result of niacin deficiency, is rarely seen among this population. Load tests using nicotinic acid have shown that subjects consuming 6.5–7.2 mg of niacin equivalents per 1,000 kcal have a satisfactory niacin status. ICMR (2010) recommendations for niacin are 6.6 mg/ 1,000 kcal, which work out to be 16 mg and 14 mg niacin equivalents per day for adult men and women, respectively.

The requirements of B-complex vitamins—thiamine, riboflavin and niacin—are linked to energy intake. The requirements of these vitamins for adults engaged in various levels of physical activity are given in Table 17.1.

Vitamin B_6 - Pyridoxine

Vitamin B_6 is needed in the form of coenzymes for the various enzymes involved in important metabolic pathways, like gluconeogenesis, and the synthesis of neurotransmitters like dopamine, serotonine, etc. The enzyme is also involved in the immune system and nucleic acid metabolism. Vitamin B_6 includes three vitamins, viz., pyridoxine, pyridoxal and pyridoxamine, and their phosphorylated derivatives. Vitamin B_6 requirements are obtained using urinary pyridoxic acid levels, load tests, depletion-repletion studies, and the measurement of levels of plasma pyridoxal phosphate.

Pyridoxine requirement is linked to the protein content of the diet. Various studies have shown that a dietary vitamin B_6 ratio of 0.02 mg/g protein ensures normal biochemical status with regard to most parameters. However, bioavailability of this vitamin could be lower from vegetable sources, as compared to animal sources. Taking this into consideration, ICMR (2010) has recommended a daily intake of 2.0 mg/day of vitamin B_6 for both adult men and women.

Folic Acid

Folic acid is used in various forms in the body, and is majorly concerned with the synthesis of nucleic acid, along with vitamin B_{12}, methylation of DNA, and supply of methionine for the synthesis of various proteins. The major role of folic acid is to transfer single carbon in the synthesis of various metabolites in the body. Folic acid is present in fruits and green leafy vegetables. It is present in both free and conjugated form; however, the proportion of free and conjugated folate varies from food to food.

Folic acid requirements are assessed using dietary surveys, blood folate levels, load tests, and depletion-repletion studies. Initial studies have shown that an intake of 75 µg/ d folic acid may ensure adequate blood folate levels. It has been observed that one-third of the folic acid present in raw food is lost during the cooking of Indian diets, and only 45–50 per cent of folate is absorbed. Taking 75 µg/ d folic acid as the physiological requirement and making allowances for cooking losses and bioavailability, ICMR (2010) has recommended a daily intake of 200 µg/ d folic acid for Indian men and women.

Vitamin B_{12}

Vitamin B_{12} is a component of several coenzymes. It shares and complements the functions of folic acid. Vitamin B_{12} coenzymes, along with folic acid, are involved in one carbon metabolism and transfer of methyl groups essential for the synthesis of nucleic acids and proteins. Vitamin B_{12} is synthesised by microorganisms. It is abundantly present in animal sources like egg, meat, milk, liver, etc. This vitamin can be synthesised by the microflora of the large intestine, but its bioavailability is still questionable. Unhygienic practices and a polluted environment enable the growth of microorganisms in water and vegetable sources. It has long been speculated that the vegetarian population of our country actually meets their requirement of vitamin B_{12} through the intake of food and water contaminated with bacteria.

Vitamin B_{12} deficiency could lead to megaloblastic anaemia, which is quite prevalent in Indian adults, especially women. Vitamin B_{12} requirements are obtained from various approaches, namely dose-response, liver stores and radioisotopic turnover studies. Studies have shown that the amount of the absorbed vitamin is 0–1 µg/day. ICMR (2010) has recommended an intake of 1 µg/day of vitamin B_{12} for adults, after adjusting for cooking losses, uncertainties in absorption, and a small amount for storage.

Ascorbic Acid

The ascorbic acid requirement has been determined by depletion-repletion studies. A minimum daily intake of ascorbic acid to cure scurvy is as low as 6.5 mg. The minimum intake to saturate leucocytes after the depletion of adult volunteers was found to be between 10 and 20 mg.

The ascorbic acid requirements of Indian adults were determined based on the intakes necessary to maintain the vitamin in leukocytes at saturation level. After saturating the leukocytes with large doses of the vitamin, the concentrations of ascorbic acid in leukocytes could be maintained at saturation level for as long as 100 days on an intake of 20 mg. On the basis of these studies, ICMR (2010) has considered a daily intake of 20 mg of ascorbic acid sufficient to maintain a satisfactory level of ascorbic acid in leukocytes. Taking into account that about 50 per cent of ascorbic acid is lost in cooking, a dietary allowance of 40 mg per day is recommended. The committee also emphasised that habitual consumption of an adequate amount of ascorbic acid-rich foods, such as citrus and other fruits (orange, lemon, sweet lime, guava, amla, pineapple, etc.), green leafy vegetables, and pulse sprouts helps in the better absorption of iron, and thus could be used as a preventive strategy for iron-deficiency anaemia.

Fat-soluble Vitamins

Vitamin A

Vitamin A (Retinol) is essential for normal vision, for maintaining the integrity of epithelial tissues, and for various metabolic functions. Vitamin A can be stored in the liver. Vitamin A is present in either its preformed form, that is, retinol (in animal foods like milk and milk products, egg and flesh foods), or in the form of carotenoids (in green leafy vegetables, orange-yellow vegetables and fruits, like carrot, tomato, pumpkin, papaya). β- carotene and other carotenoids are converted into retinol in the body. Studies had shown that the rate of this conversion is 50 per cent physiologically, and that efficiency of absorption of β- carotenes in the human body is only one-third. The ICMR (2010) committee has recommended the conversion factor of 1: 8 for β- carotene into retinol.

Retinol equivalents = retinol + (β- carotene/ 8)

Vitamin A requirements were obtained using turnover studies and liver levels in a well-nourished population. It was proposed that for an adult man weighing 65 kg, the requirement would be 600 μg/day or 9.3 μg RE /kg body weight. At this intake, the liver stores and blood levels were maintained. Retinol and β carotene requirements for Indian men and women are given in Table 17.1.

Vitamin D

Vitamin D is now considered more a pro-hormone than a vitamin. It can be synthesised in the body in adequate amounts by simple exposure to bright sunlight for five minutes per day. Indian diets do not meet even 10 per cent of the vitamin D requirement. ICMR (2010) has recommended adequate sunlight exposure to meet vitamin D requirements. It also recommended 400 IU/day of vitamin D supplements in situations with minimal exposure to sunlight.

Vitamin E

Vitamin E (alpha tocopherol) has protective antioxidant properties. Studies have shown that Indians have satisfactory levels of blood alpha tocopherol (0.5 mg/kg/ml). Alpha tocopherol requirements are directly related to the levels of essential fatty acids. ICMR (2010) suggested the requirement of alpha tocopherol as 0.8 mg/g of dietary essential fatty acids, which works out to 8–10 mg tocopherol/day, depending upon the edible oil consumed.

Vitamin K

Vitamin K plays an important role in blood coagulation and in the chemical modification of bone matrix. Deficiency of vitamin K is not seen in Indians. However, ICMR (2010) has recommended an intake of 55 μg / day for adults.

PLANNING MEALS FOR ADULTS

A well-balanced diet, which contains all essential nutrients in adequate amounts, helps in maintaining good health and nutritional status in adults. ICMR (2011) has given dietary guidelines for Indians, which provide guidance to people in ensuring nutritional adequacy (Box 17.3). These guidelines help people to make correct dietary choices and follow the right nutritional behaviour.

Dietary Pattern and Food Selection

The following points should be considered while planning diets for adults:

1. **Balanced diet:** Meals for adults should be planned in such a manner that each meal of the day is nutritionally balanced, by selecting food items from different food groups. It is advisable to plan a four to five meals a day pattern to distribute a blend of nutrients throughout the day. A balanced diet should provide 50–60 per cent of the total calories from carbohydrates, preferably from complex carbohydrates like whole cereals, pulses, millets, and root vegetables; about 10–15 per cent from proteins; and 20–30 per cent from both visible and invisible fat. In addition, the inclusion of a variety of fruits and vegetables in the diet will provide adequate amounts of micronutrients, like iron, vitamin A, vitamin C, folic acid, and B-complex vitamins. These food groups are also rich sources of dietary fibre, antioxidants and phytochemicals, which provide positive health benefits. An adequate amount of calcium-rich foods like milk, meat, and other sources should be included to prevent osteoporosis in old age.
2. **Intake of fat, sugar and salt:** Data from various studies have shown that Indian adults are prone to various chronic degenerative diseases. The type and quantity of fat in the daily diet influences the level of cholesterol and triglycerides in the blood. Total fat (visible, invisible and hidden) intake should be restricted to 20–30 per cent of the total energy for adults, based on the level of physical activity. It is advisable to use a blend of fats, with the ratio of polyunsaturated fatty acids to saturated fatty acids of 0.8: 1.0. This could be ensured by the use of a blend of oils. A higher intake of trans fatty acids (*vanaspati* or other hydrogenated fats) may increase the risk of heart diseases; therefore, their intake should not exceed 1 per cent of the energy intake. The intake of food items like bakery products, ready-to-eat foods, and processed foods prepared using *vanaspati*, margarine or bakery fat should be minimised.

Box 17.2: Dietary Guidelines for Indian Adults

1. Eat a variety of foods to ensure a balanced diet
2. Eat plenty of vegetables and fruits
3. Ensure moderate use of edible oils and animal foods, and very little use of *ghee*/butter/vanaspati
4. Avoid overeating to prevent overweight and obesity
5. Exercise regularly and be physically active to maintain an ideal body weight
6. Restrict salt intake to a minimum
7. Ensure the use of safe and clean foods
8. Adopt the right pre-cooking processes and appropriate cooking methods
9. Drink plenty of water and take beverages in moderation
10. Minimise the use of processed foods rich in salt, sugar and fats.

Source: NIN 2011.

A high intake of salt (sodium chloride) is associated with high blood pressure and stomach cancer. All food items have sodium, but added salt during cooking is the major source of sodium. Preserved foods, such as pickles, sun-dried foods such as papads, sauces, and canned foods have a higher content of salt. The use of these food items should be limited to reduce excessive salt consumption. The intake of salt should not be more than 6 g /day (ICMR 2011).

Sugar is a rich source of energy. It provides empty calories and is present in enormous amounts in processed foods and drinks, like juices, aerated beverages, chocolates and toffees. Use of these food items should be limited to prevent diet-related chronic diseases.

3. **Socio-economic status:** The societies and cultures in which people live influence their food choices. Culturally and socially acceptable food items should be included in the diet. The cost of food affects food selection remarkably. Those people belonging to lower socio-economic groups can include more of cereals and pulses in their diets, and reduce the intake of more expensive items like meat and milk products. The protein quality of the diet can be improved by taking a cereal-pulse combination, as cereals lack an essential amino acid, lysine, and pulses lack another essential amino acid, methionine. If cereals and pulses are taken in combination, like *dal*-rice, *dosa*, *dal-chapati*, etc., they supplement each other and improve the protein quality of the diet. Locally available seasonal fruits and vegetables can be included in the diet, because they are not only cheaper, but are also nutritionally better. An individual belonging to an upper socio-economic group can eat a variety of food items, with a greater intake of milk, meat, fruits, and vegetables, and a reduced intake of cereals, pulses and fat.
4. **Level of physical activity:** The nutrient demands of an individual depend upon her/his occupation, for example, a mineworker needs more energy-dense foods as compared to an officer who is sedentary most of the day. The diet of the sedentary worker should include lower amount of cereals, fat and sugar to curtail energy needs, as compared to the heavy worker. The requirements of thiamine, riboflavin and niacin are higher for heavy workers as these are based on energy intake; however, the requirements of protein and other micronutrients are similar for both sedentary and heavy workers. Food selection is quite important to meet nutritional needs, for example, low calorie fruits and vegetables can be increased in the diet of sedentary workers to increase the content of vitamins, minerals, dietary fibre, and antioxidants.
5. **Gender:** Indian women have lower energy and protein requirements as compared to men. Adequate nutrition during this phase of life helps women to face the physiological stress during pregnancy and lactation. An adequate intake of green leafy vegetables, whole cereals, egg, and mutton to meet the high requirements of iron and calcium is recommended. This will also help to build up stores for pregnancy and lactation.

A combination of a variety of foodstuffs and judicious choices from different food groups can provide all the essential nutrients, and at the same time can prevent diet-related morbidity. A sample menu for a sedentary adult woman is given below:

SAMPLE DIET PLAN	
Age	25 years
Sex	female
Activity level	sedentary
Physiological state	non-pregnant non-lactating
Socio-economic status	middle-income group
Food habits	vegetarian
RDA (as per ICMR 2010)	
Energy	1,900 kcal/day
Protein	55 g/day
Iron	21 g/day
Menu Plan	
Meal	Menu (vegetarian)
Early morning	tea -1 cup + Rusk - 2
Breakfast	1 glass of milk
	methi dal parantha - 2
Mid-morning	Fruit *chat* – 1 bowl
Lunch	*chapati* – 1 medium
	Boiled rice - half plate
	chana dal – 1 bowl
	Vegetable preparation (any) - 1 bowl
	tomato *raita* - 1 bowl
Evening tea	coffee/tea - 1 cup
	Vegetable sandwiches - 2
Dinner	sour lentil soup - 1 bowl
	Chapati - 1 medium
	vegetable *pulao* - half plate
	palak paneer - 1 bowl
	salad - 1 bowl
	carrot *kheer* - 1 bowl

NUTRITIONAL CONCERNS

Currently, India is facing the double burden of malnutrition. Along with under-nutrition, which has plagued the country for decades, the burden of diet-related non-communicable diseases is rapidly increasing.

> ***Double burden of malnutrition***
>
> Data from the National Family Health Survey-3 (2005–06) had shown that 33 per cent of ever married adult women have BMI below normal (BMI <18.5 kg/ m^2), and nearly 15 per cent of adult women are overweight or obese (BMI> 25kg/ m^2). These data show that although the problem of under-nutrition is still a major issue, the problem of over-nutrition is emerging as a broader public health challenge in India.

Undernutrition

Under-nutrition in adults is due to a deficiency in energy and protein intake. Lack of food availability at affordable prices generally leads to under-nutrition among adults, especially women. Poverty and under-nutrition are interrelated. Under-nutrition in adults makes them less economically productive, and also more susceptible to infections. Under-nutrition in women is intergenerational. An undernourished woman will give birth to an undernourished child, who grows as an undernourished adolescent and undernourished woman, and the cycle continues. This intergenerational cycle can be broken down only by improving the nutritional status of women.

Anaemia

Anaemia is a major problem in India, especially in pregnant women. However, young adult women between the ages of 18–30, who are non-pregnant, are also vulnerable to anaemia. Although anaemia is less common among males, they too suffer from anaemia, considerably more than their counterparts in developed countries. Anaemia is due to the deficiency of iron, folic acid and vitamin B_{12}. Poor diet, lack of hygiene, social taboos, and poor economic status contribute to the overwhelming prevalence of anaemia. Anaemia can lead to reduced productivity, greater susceptibility to infections, and slow recovery from illnesses. Among women, poor nutrition can increase the risk of poor pregnancy outcomes, including obstructed labour, low birth weight babies, and postpartum haemorrhage. Anaemia can be reduced by increasing the consumption of iron-rich foods, like cereals, pulses, green leafy vegetables, and meat products. Regular consumption of vitamin C-rich foods, like orange, lemon and guava, can help in the better absorption of iron from the diet. The consumption of foods rich in phytates and tannins should be limited, as they inhibit the absorption of iron.

Iodine-deficiency Disorders

Iodine is an essential element in the synthesis of the thyroid hormone by the thyroid gland. Iodine deficiency could result in goitre in woman and cretinism in children, if an iodine-deficient adult woman enters into pregnancy. Deficiency of iodine could be due to environmental iodine deficiency, or because of the presence of goitrogens in the diet, like phenols, flavanoids, thiocyanates, etc. Deficiency of iodine could result in a series of disorders, termed 'iodine deficiency disorders (IDD)'. IDD can be prevented by fortification of iodine in food items like salt, sugar, etc. Consumption of iodised salt in the daily diet has shown benefits.

> An estimated 17.3 million people died from **cardiovascular diseases** in 2008, representing 30 per cent of all global deaths. Of these deaths, an estimated 7.3 million were due to coronary heart disease, and 6.2 million were due to stroke (WHO 2011).
>
> The Global Status on Non-Communicable Diseases Report (2011) has stated that there were more than 2.5 million deaths from CVD in India in 2008, two-thirds due to coronary artery disease and one-third due to stroke.
>
> A study conducted on young urban Indians had shown rapid escalation of cardiovascular risk factors, which include smoking, hypertension, dyslipidemias, diabetes, and stroke among 30–39 year olds (Gupta et al. 2009).

LIFESTYLE-RELATED DISORDERS

The consumption of convenient foods and processed foods like biscuits, salted snacks, prepared sweets, etc., has increased over the years. These food items have a higher content of sugar, salt and fat. The Indian population is moving away from traditional food items to food products consumed in Western countries, like bread, which is increasingly preferred over *chapati*. A decrease in the intake of coarse cereals, pulses, fruits, and vegetables, and an increase in the intake of meat products, fat, sugar, and salt, coupled with declining levels of physical activity due to rapid urbanisation, have resulted in escalating levels of non-communicable diseases, like obesity, metabolic syndrome, type 2 diabetes mellitus, and coronary heart disease in Indian adults.

Obesity

Overweight and obesity is defined as the accumulation of excessive fat in the body, which is hazardous to health and causes various diseases like diabetes and cardiovascular disorders. The WHO definition is:

- a BMI greater than or equal to 25 is overweight
- a BMI greater than or equal to 30 is obesity.

For Asian Indians, who are more susceptible to diabetes and cardiovascular diseases, it is proposed that lower cut-off values are used:

- a BMI greater than or equal to 23 is overweight
- a BMI greater than or equal to 25 is obesity.

Various studies have shown a high prevalence of abdominal obesity (excessive deposition of fat in the abdominal region) in South Asians. Abdominal obesity has been recognised as an important risk factor for diabetes, the metabolic syndrome and CVD. WHO cut-offs for abdominal obesity for South Asians are:

Waist Circumference ≥80 cm for Women and ≥90 cm for Men

Increased intake of foods high in fat and decreased physical activity due to urbanisation, changing modes of transportation, and sedentary occupational work are the major causes of obesity. Obesity can be reduced by limiting the intake of food items rich in fat and sugar, increasing the consumption of fruits and vegetables, and being physically active as part of one's daily routine.

Metabolic Syndrome

The constellation of dyslipidemia (high levels of serum triglycerides and low levels of high-density lipoprotein cholesterol), elevated blood pressure, impaired glucose tolerance, and central obesity is now identified as metabolic syndrome, also called syndrome X. Factors which increase the risk of metabolic syndrome include a higher body mass index, smoking, high carbohydrate intake, high saturated fat intake, alcohol consumption, and physical inactivity. Metabolic syndrome increases the risk of developing diabetes and cardiovascular disease.

> **Hypertension** is reported to be the fourth contributor to premature deaths in developed countries, and the seventh in developing countries. In India, hypertension is the leading NCD risk, and estimated to result in nearly 10 per cent of all deaths. The number of hypertensive individuals is expected to nearly double by 2025, from 118 million in 2000 to 213 million (WHO 2011).
>
> **Diabetes** is predicted to be globally the seventh leading cause of deaths by the year 2030 (WHO 2011).

Hypertension

Hypertension in adults aged 18 and older is defined as systolic blood pressure (SBP) of 140 mm Hg or greater, and/ or diastolic blood pressure (DBP) of 90 mm Hg or greater, or any level of blood pressure in patients taking anti-hypertensive medication. High intakes of salt, sugar and fat, physical inactivity, excessive alcohol intake, and smoking are the major risk factors for developing hypertension.

Cardiovascular Diseases

Cardiovascular diseases include all the diseases of heart and circulation, including coronary heart diseases, stroke, hypertension, and heart failure. Physical inactivity, an unhealthy diet, and excessive tobacco and alcohol use are the main causes of cardiovascular diseases. Cessation of tobacco use, reduced salt intake, consuming high fibre foods like fruits, vegetables and whole grains, increased duration and intensity of physical activity, and restricted use of alcohol can decrease the risk of cardiovascular diseases.

Diabetes

Diabetes is the condition in which the body is unable to utilise blood glucose, resulting in high blood glucose levels. Insulin is a hormone involved in metabolism and the utilisation of energy, mainly from glucose. Diabetes can be due to an absence of insulin (Type 1 diabetes) in the body, or occurs when the body does not make or use insulin well (Type 2 diabetes), as a result of which blood glucose levels are increased. Too much glucose in the blood could lead to serious problems. It could affect the eyes, feet and kidneys. In Type 2 diabetes, blood sugar levels can be maintained by limiting the amount of ingested glucose. Physical activity has also shown a positive effect in preventing diabetes. A large proportion of cases of diabetes and its complications can be prevented by maintaining a normal body weight, along with a healthy diet and regular physical activity.

Cancer is a leading cause of death worldwide, accounting for 7.6 million deaths (around 13 per cent of all deaths) in 2008. Lung, stomach, liver, colon, and breast cancer cause the most cancer deaths each year (WHO 2011).

Tobacco kills a third to half of all people who use it, on an average 15 years prematurely. Tobacco use causes one in 10 deaths among adults worldwide—more than five million people a year. By 2030, unless urgent action is taken, tobacco's annual death toll will rise to more than eight million (Mathers and Loncars 2006).

According to an article published in *Lancet Oncology*, nearly half of all cancers are cancers of the lung and oral cavity in men, and of the breast and cervix in women. Almost three of every five cancers in India are associated with tobacco or infectious disease. Tobacco use alone accounts for about 40 per cent of all cancers in India (Mallath et al. 2014).

Cancer

Cancer is the rapid creation of abnormal cells that grow beyond their usual boundaries, and which can then invade adjoining parts of the body and spread to other organs. More than 30 per cent of cancer deaths could be prevented by modifying or avoiding key risk factors such as tobacco use, overweight or obesity, alcohol use, and urban air pollution, and ensuring adequate fruit and vegetable intake and physical activity.

PREVENTION OF DIET-RELATED NON-COMMUNICABLE DISEASES

Diet-related non-communicable diseases, mainly cardiovascular diseases, cancers and diabetes, represent a threat to human health and development. These diseases are the world's biggest killers, causing an estimated 35 million deaths each year—60 per cent of all deaths globally—with 80 per cent in low and middle-income countries. These diseases are preventable. Up to 80 per cent of heart diseases, stroke, and Type 2 diabetes, and over a third of cancers could be prevented by eliminating shared risk factors, mainly unhealthy diets, physical inactivity, and the harmful use of alcohol and tobacco.

Physical Activity

Adults aged 18–64 should do at least 150 minutes of moderate-intensity aerobic physical activity throughout the week or do at least 75 minutes of vigorous-intensity aerobic physical activity throughout the week or an equivalent combination of moderate- and vigorous-intensity activity.

Guidelines for Diet and Physical Activity

- To achieve balance between energy intake and expenditure for maintaining healthy weight
- To limit energy intake from total fats
- To shift fat consumption from saturated fats to unsaturated fats and to eliminate consumption of trans fatty acids

- To increase intake of dietary fibre by increasing intake of fruits and vegetables, and legumes, whole grains and nuts in the daily diet
- To limit the intake of free sugars and salt (sodium)
- To ensure intake of iodized salt

Dietary Modifications

Diet is the most modifiable determinant of chronic degenerative diseases. Modifications in the diet can maintain appropriate body weight and composition and blood pressure, can regulate blood glucose levels, insulin, and blood lipid levels. Reduced consumption of saturated fats, trans fatty acids, sugars and processed foods, and increased consumption of foods with good fatty acids (PUFA and MUFA), low glycemic index and high fibre, along with healthy cooking practices like baking or steaming, can prevent or delay the onset of non-communicable diseases. Some easy tips for making these changes are given below:

- Prefer whole cereals, pulses and millets and their products over refined grains, as they are rich in complex carbohydrates with low glycemic index and high fibre content.
- Consumption of a variety of fruits and vegetables will not only make the plate colourful, but will also provide essential micronutrients (iron, folic acid, vitamin A, and calcium), antioxidants and dietary fibre.
- Choose low fat, protein rich foods, such as lean meat and fish over red meat to cut down the fat intake, saturated fat and cholesterol.
- Low fat dairy products can also be used to reduce the intake of total fat, saturated fat and cholesterol.
- Substitute a part of saturated fat (like *ghee*, butter, etc.) with foods rich in PUFA and MUFA, like whole nuts, legumes, fish, green leafy vegetables, mustard and fenugreek seeds.
- Minimise the consumption of ready-to-eat fast foods, bakery foods and processed foods prepared with hydrogenated fats (*vanaspati*).
- Develop a taste for foods that are low in salt. Restrict the intake of preserved and processed foods, such as *papads*, pickles, salted biscuits, chips, etc., as they have a higher content of salt and sugar. Fresh fruits should be preferred over canned fruits and juices.
- Cooking methods that require less fat, like steaming, baking and roasting, should be preferred over deep frying and sautéing, etc.
- Drink natural and fresh fruit juices (without removing the pulp and without adding extra sugar) instead of carbonated beverages. Carbonated beverages are rich in sugar and provide empty calories.

WHO has designed a Global Physical Activity Questionnaire to calculate a person's overall energy expenditure in the terms of MET (Metabolic Equivalents).

MET is the ratio of a person's working metabolic rate relative to the resting metabolic rate. One MET is defined as the energy cost of sitting quietly, and is equivalent to a calorie consumption of 1 kcal/kg/hour.

4 METs get assigned to the time spent in moderate activities and 8 METs to the time spent in vigorous activities.

WHO has recommended that physical activity for health per week should be an equivalent combination of moderate and vigorous intensity physical activity, achieving at least 600 MET-minutes.

Source: WHO 2010.

Exercise and Physical Activity

Energy expenditure through exercise and physical activity is an important part of the energy balance equation that determines body weight. Physical activity has a great influence on body composition—the amount of fat, muscle and bone tissue. An increase in energy expenditure with an increase in physical activity is the most likely factor to contribute to reducing the global epidemic of lifestyle-related disorders. Physical activity is essential to maintaining an ideal body weight by burning the excess calories, and is of vital significance for health and the prevention of non-communicable diseases.

Dietary guidelines for Indians, given by NIN (2011), recommended

- At least 45 minutes of physical activity of moderate intensity (brisk walking, dancing, bicycling) for at least five days a week.
- To reduce weight, exercise for at least 60 minutes, doing moderate to vigorous intensity physical activity, at least five days a week.

It is important to make physical activity and exercise a part of one's daily routine to decrease the risk of many adverse health conditions. Some easy tips to increase physical activity are given below:

- Exercising for 45 minutes at once is not necessary. It can be broken down into bouts of 15–20 minutes twice or thrice in a day, as suited to the daily routine.
- Make exercise enjoyable and fun by joining classes which help in increasing physical activity, like dance, yoga, any outdoor game, swimming, etc.
- At the workplace, physical activity can be increased by doing little things like walking in between meetings, taking the stairs instead of lifts/elevators, getting off the bus a stop earlier or parking the car a little far from the office and walking the rest of the way, and walking instead of driving to places that are within walking distance.
- Make exercise a social activity by involving family and friends for walking, jogging or swimming, etc. Exercise thus serves to improve not only physical, but also social and mental health.
- Keeping track of one's daily physical activity routine can help in maintaining and improving compliance, like using pedometers for step counting, etc.

Tobacco and Alcohol Use

Both tobacco and alcohol use have an effect on the cardiovascular health of people. Smoking is linked to a higher risk of nearly all forms of cardiovascular disease, including myocardial infarction, ischemic stroke and bleeding into the brain (that is, hemorrhagic stroke), congestive heart failure, and peripheral arterial disease. Smokers are at a higher risk of developing several types of cancers and chronic obstructive pulmonary diseases (lung problems). Alcohol provides 7 kcal/g, which is higher than the energy provided per gram by proteins or carbohydrates. Thus, excessive alcohol drinking could lead to obesity; also, alcohol interferes with the absorption and metabolism of nutrients, leading to nutritional deficiencies. Excessive alcohol drinking has adverse effects on health, which include high blood pressure, obesity, stroke, breast cancer, suicide, and accidents.

A nutritionally balanced diet and an active lifestyle are fundamental to maintaining good health during adulthood, as well as to preventing chronic degenerative disorders in later years. A diet rich in complex carbohydrates, an appropriate blend of fats and oils, liberal intake of seasonal fruits and vegetables, and restricted intake of processed foods, along with 30–45 minutes of moderate physical activity daily, lay the foundation for healthy living in the years ahead.

SUMMARY

- Good nutrition for adults is required to maintain a healthy and active lifestyle, and to prevent diseases.
- During adulthood, energy requirements are based on BMR and the level of physical activity. Energy requirements increase with an increase in the intensity and duration of physical activity, for both males and females.
- ICMR (2010) recommended 1 g/kg body weight/ day for meeting protein requirements.
- Fat requirements should be between 20–30 per cent of the total energy requirement, and should not exceed 35 per cent to avoid diet-related chronic degenerative diseases.
- Iron requirements for adult women are higher than men, owing to menstrual losses.
- At least 40 mg/day of vitamin C should be included in the diet for better absorption of iron.

- It is recommended that we consume at least 600 mg/day of calcium by including calcium-rich sources in the diet, to prevent osteoporosis.
- A balanced diet will not only provide all essential nutrients, but will also prevent diet-related non-communicable diseases in adults. Seasonal fruits and vegetables should be included in the diet to gain maximum nutritional benefits. Fruits and green leafy vegetables are rich sources of various nutrients, and also contain antioxidants, phytochemicals and dietary fibre.
- Cheaper and locally available foodstuffs should be included in the diet of individuals belonging to lower socio-economic groups.
- Individuals belonging to higher socio-economic groups are more prone to chronic degenerative diseases like hypertension, obesity, diabetes, and cardiovascular diseases. They should have a limited intake of fat, salt and sugar in their diet.
- Reduced intake of coarse cereals, fruits and vegetables, and excessive intake of unhealthy fats, including saturated fatty acids and trans fatty acids, dietary salt, and animal foods, could result in diet-related non-communicable diseases.
- Including exercise in your daily routine will boost both physical and mental health.

KEY WORDS

Bioavailability: Bioavailability of a given nutrient from a diet is the release of the nutrient from the food, its absorption in the intestine, and bio-response, which also has to be taken into account.

Balanced diet: Diet containing adequate amounts of all necessary nutrients required for healthy growth and activity.

Essential fatty acids: An unsaturated fatty acid that is essential to human health, but cannot be manufactured in the body.

Glycemic index (GI): The relative ability of carbohydrate-rich food to increase the level of glucose in the blood.

Physical activity: The state of being active or in energetic action or movement.

Recommended Dietary Allowance (RDA): The average daily dietary nutrient intake level sufficient to meet the nutrient requirement of nearly all (97–98 per cent) healthy individuals in a particular life stage and gender group.

Safe level of intake: The distribution of nutrient requirements in a population group is considered normal and the RDA corresponds to requirement, which covers most individuals (97.5 per cent) in a given population. This corresponds to mean ± 2SD.

EXERCISES

1. Discuss the requirements of the following nutrients in detail:
   a. Energy for a sedentary man
   b. Iron for an adult woman
   c. Calcium for an adult man
   d. Vitamin A for an adult woman
2. What are the common nutritional concerns for adults?
3. List the important dietary guidelines for adults.
4. What points will you consider while planning a diet for a 25-year-old male executive working in a multinational company?
5. Discuss the importance of physical activity or exercise in maintaining the nutritional status of adults.
6. What are the strategies to prevent diet-related non-communicable diseases in adults?

REFERENCES

FAO/WHO/UNICEF, 'Human energy requirements', Report of a Joint FAO/WHO/UNICEF Expert consultation, 2004.

Gupta, R., A. Misra, N. K. Vikram, D. Kondal, S. S. Gupta, A. Agrawal, and R. M. Pandey, 'Younger age of escalation of cardiovascular risk factors in Asian Indian subjects', *BMC Cardiovascular Disord.* 5, 2009, pp. 9–28.

Khanna, K. et al., 'Nutrition during adulthood', in *Textbook of Nutrition and Dietetics*, 2e, 2013, pp. 47–66.

ICMR, 'Nutrient requirements and recommended dietary allowances for Indians', A report of the expert group of the Indian Council of Medical Research, ICMR: Hyderabad, 2010.

Mallath, M. K., D. G. Taylor, R. A. Badwe, G. K. Rath, V. Shanta, C. S. Pramesh, et al., 'The growing burden of cancer in India: Epidemiology and social context', Lancet Oncology 15(6), 2014, pp. 205–12.

Mathers, C. D. and D. Loncar, 'Projections of global mortality and burden of disease from 2002 to 2030', *PLoS Medicine* 3(11), 2006, e442.

NFHS-3, National family Health Survey-3, Indian Institute of Population Sciences, 2005–06

NIN, *Dietary Guidelines for Indians—A manual*, Hyderabad: National Institute of Nutrition, ICMR, 2011.

Rao, B. S. N. and B. Sivakumar, 'Nutrient requirements and Recommended Dietary Allowances', in M. S. Bamji, K. Krishnaswamy and G. N. V. Brahmam (eds), *Textbook of Human Nutrition*, 3e, New Delhi: Oxford and IBH Publ Co. 2009, pp. 154–78.

WHO, *Global strategy on diet, physical activity and health*, Geneva: WHO, 2004.

———, 'World Health Organization Report on the Global Tobacco Epidemic', The MPOWER package, 2008.

———, *Global Recommendations on physical activity for health*, 2010. Available at http://www.who.int/dietphysicalactivity/pa/en/index.html.

———, *Global status report on noncommunicable diseases*, Geneva: World Health Organization, 2011. Available at http://www.who.int/dietphysicalactivity/strategy/eb11344/en/.

18

NUTRITION DURING PREGNANCY

HIGHLIGHTS

- Progressive anatomical, physiological and biochemical changes during pregnancy.
- Three stages of foetal development.
- Concept of critical period during development of the foetus.
- Factors affecting the outcome of pregnancy.
- Pre-conceptional maternal health status and its relation to foetal outcome.
- Nutrient needs during pregnancy.
- Common concerns and minor ailments during pregnancy and measures to treat them.
- Importance of antenatal checkups during pregnancy.

INTRODUCTION

Pregnancy is the most vulnerable phase of a woman's life. Although pregnancy is a normal physiological condition for the female body, it is stressful as all nutritional needs are increased in order to meet the needs of pregnancy. This phase also constitutes a special risk group. During pregnancy, a woman needs good nutrition in order to give birth to a healthy baby. Women who have poor nutritional status at the time of conception are at higher risk of disease and death; their health depends greatly on the availability of food, and they may be unable to cope with their increased nutrient needs during pregnancy in situations of food insecurity. Infections such as malaria, HIV and infestation with gastrointestinal parasites can further deteriorate the women's nutritional status. The problems affecting the health of the mother generally stem from multiple factors. However, they can be largely prevented with a greater knowledge about the predisposing risks and factors.

Women in India suffer from three major problems that affect their health during pregnancy. These are malnutrition, infections and unregulated fertility. The normal duration of pregnancy is 10 lunar months or 9 calendar months and 7 days, or 280 days or 40 weeks.

> Duration of pregnancy is 40 weeks, that is, 280 days.
>
> The objective of every pregnancy should be: 'Healthy baby born to a healthy mother'.

The outcome of pregnancy should be a healthy baby of an normal birth weight to a healthy mother. Healthy development of the foetus is associated with adequate nutrition; it can shape the baby's health throughout life.

Pregnancy is the most nutritionally demanding period of a woman's life. Optimal nutrition is necessary to support:

- Growth of the placenta
- An increase in blood volume
- An increase in cardiac output
- An increase in fluid levels

> Ideally, every woman should start with folic acid supplements under supervision, three months prior to conception.

- Hormonal changes
- Changes in breast tissue in preparation for breastfeeding
- Alterations in lung, kidney, urinary, and reproductive functions.

Optimal nutrition starts before conception—a good example is the B group vitamin, Folic Acid. Folic Acid is required for the normal development of the nervous system of the foetus, particularly the closure of the neural tube, which occurs during the first six weeks of pregnancy.

PHYSIOLOGICAL CHANGES IN PREGNANCY

During pregnancy, a woman's body undergoes progressive anatomical, physiological and biochemical changes. These changes involve all the organs of her body and help mainly in the adaptation of the mother to the increasing demands of her growing foetus. It is very important to understand these changes.

Hematological Changes

Blood volume starts increasing from the sixth week of pregnancy till 30–32 weeks of pregnancy. Blood volume increases by approximately 40–50 per cent above the non-pregnant state. This hypervolemia (too much fluid in the blood) has important functions to play:

a) Helps in meeting the increased physiological demands during pregnancy, especially of the enlarging uterus.
b) Helps the mother to cope with the adverse effects of blood loss during pregnancy.

Plasma volume increases by nearly 50 per cent above the non-pregnant state. Red blood cell mass increases by 20 to 30 per cent in pregnancy. This unequal increase in the rise of plasma and red blood cells concentrations produces a state of **Heamodilution.** In Heamodilution, there is a fall in the hemoglobin level; hence, at term there can be a fall of hemoglobin up to 2 g per cent from the non-pregnant state. The need for iron thus increases. Dietary iron may not meet this increased requirement, and hence pregnant women are prescribed iron supplements

> Heamodilution is physiologically a protective mechanism of the body during pregnancy.

Cardiovascular Changes

As the uterus enlarges due to the growth of the foetus, the diaphragm is pushed up, and hence the heart is pushed upwards and outwards. Cardiac output, which starts to increase from the fifth week of pregnancy, reaches its peak at about 30–34 weeks. The increase is approximately 40 to 50 per cent of the pre-pregnant stage. There is a great positional variation in cardiac output; it is the highest in the right or lateral position.

> As output is highest in the lateral position, a pregnant lady is always advised to rest in the lateral position, that is, on her side. It is beneficial to the baby.

The importance of the increased cardiac output is that it helps in meeting the additional oxygen requirement during pregnancy. There is an overall decrease in blood pressure by 5–10 mm Hg during pregnancy.

Respiratory System Changes

The total lung capacity is reduced by nearly 5 per cent as the diaphragm is pushed up by the enlarging uterus, especially in the later months of pregnancy. There is a state of hyperventilation (breathing becoming faster). The woman feels a shortness of breath. The acid-base balance is altered during pregnancy; there is a fall in the arterial carbon dioxide level from 38 to 32 mm of Hg, and a rise in the arterial oxygen level from 95 mm of Hg to 105 mm of Hg. This difference in partial pressures of the gases helps in transferring oxygen from the mother to the foetus, and in the transfer of carbon dioxide to the mother from the foetus. Pregnancy is a state of respiratory alkalosis (elevation of blood pH). The increased oxygen demand by the foetus, placenta and the maternal tissues increases the mother's oxygen consumption by nearly 20 to 40 per cent.

Urinary System Changes

The prominent changes seen in the urinary system are that the kidney and its structures, that is, the calyces, renal pelvis and attached ureters, all dilate or increase in size. The blood plasma flow to the kidneys is increased by 50 to 75 per cent by 16 weeks of pregnancy, and is maintained until 34 weeks. The Glomerular filtration rate (GFR) is the volume of fluid filtered from the Glomerular capillaries present in the nephron. A nephron is the functional unit of the kidney. The normal range of GFR is 100–130 ml/min; however, GFR is increased by 50 per cent throughout pregnancy. The renal tubules fail to reabsorb glucose, uric acid, amino acids; hence, sometimes in pregnancy the mother has renal glycosuria, which means a presence of glucose in urine. This should not be confused with diabetes mellitus or gestational diabetes, as this is a physiological condition.

Sometimes, due to a dilatation of the ureters and pressure over the urinary bladder, there can be stasis or collection of urine in the bladder and ureters at the brim. This can lead to repeated urinary tract infections in some women. There is also an increased frequency of micturition, which means that the mother has an urge to pass urine frequently, especially in the early and late weeks of pregnancy.

> Glycosuria, seen during pregnancy, should be evaluated properly to rule out Gestational Diabetes.
>
> Fluid and water intake should be good as it helps in preventing the urinary tract infections commonly seen during pregnancy.

Alimentary System Changes

The major changes seen are due to the high levels of progesterone during pregnancy. Starting from the mouth, the gums become spongy and may also bleed on touch; hence dental hygiene is of utmost importance to prevent infections and caries.

Muscle tone and motility of the gastrointestinal tract is decreased. The cardiac sphincter of the stomach relaxes under the influence of the progesterone hormone; this can lead to a regurgitation of gastric contents into the esophagus, causing heartburn. This diminished peristaltic movement of the gut has a dual effect—on the one hand, it enhances the absorption of the food materials, and on the other, it can lead to constipation.

In the liver cells, there is no histological change; however, the functions are decreased. The liver function tests are unaltered during pregnancy, except for a rise in the level of the enzyme alkaline phosphatase. Again, under the influence of a high level of progesterone, there is stasis of bile in the gall bladder. During pregnancy, the level of cholesterol rises. These two factors can lead to the formation of gall stones during pregnancy.

Metabolic Changes

In pregnancy, the basal metabolic rate increases by about 30 per cent. The amount of water retained at term is about 6.5 litres. Pregnancy is a state of hypervolemia, and there is an active retention of sodium, potassium and water.

Pregnancy is an anabolic state; there is a positive nitrogen balance throughout pregnancy.

There is a continuous supply of glucose to the foetus, even when the mother is fasting. This is due to an increase in the plasma insulin level. There is glycosuria (excretion of glucose in urine) in about 50 per cent of normal pregnant women due to increased filtration of glucose by the kidneys.

In pregnancy, around 3–4 kg of fat is stored in the abdominal wall of the mother. The hyperlipedimia (also known as hyperlipoproteinemia or abnormally elevated levels of any or all lipids or lipoproteins in the blood) of pregnancy is, however, not atherogenic (this term is loosely used to describe the factors that have the ability to promote the development of atherosclerosis, that is, the formation of a thick plaque in the coronary arteries, containing cholesterol and other lipids).

Iron Metabolism

Iron requirement during pregnancy is most significant in the last trimester. Approximately 1,000 mg of iron is required during pregnancy. Pregnancy is an iron deficient state, and the iron that is absorbed from diet and iron stores is inadequate to meet the increased demands during pregnancy. Dietary iron may not meet this increased requirement, and hence pregnant women are prescribed iron supplements. Iron supplementation increases the red cell mass by nearly 30 per cent.

Calcium Metabolism

There is an increased demand (around 80 per cent) of calcium, especially in the last trimester. Daily requirement in pregnancy and lactation is around 1 to 1.5 grams.

Weight Gain in Pregnancy

Ideally, the weight gain during pregnancy should depend on the mother's pre-pregnancy BMI. In a singleton pregnancy, a woman should gain around 11 kg of weight; the range is 11–16 kg. In the first trimester, there can be some weight loss, but in the second trimester till the last two to three weeks of pregnancy, weight gain should be constant. The major increase in weight is due to the uterus and its contents, breasts, and the increase in blood volume.

The approximate distribution of weight gain is under two major heads:

- Reproductive weight gain (6kg)
- Maternal weight gain (6kg)

Table 18.1: Major Components of Weight Gain

Component	*Weight (kg)*
Foetus	2.5–3.5
Placenta	0.5–0.6
Amniotic fluid	0.8
Uterus	0.9
Breasts	0.4
Accumulation of fat and protein	3.5
Increase in blood volume	1.3
Increase in extra-cellular fluid	1.2

Source: Cunningham et al. 2000.

A woman's pre-pregnancy BMI should determine her weight gain. In 2009, the Institute of Medicine (IOM) published the revised weight gain guidelines that are based on pre-pregnancy body mass index (BMI). These are standard guidelines and should be followed for most cases. However, these should be modified as per individual cases, and not be taken as a blanket rule for all.

Table 18.2: Weight Gain Recommendation for Pregnancy

Pre-pregnancy Weight Category	*Body Mass Index*	*Recommended Range of Total Weight (in Kg)*	*Recommended Range of Weight Gain in the Second and Third Trimesters Mean Range Kg/Wk*
Underweight	Less than 18.5	12.7 to 18.1	0.45 (0.45–0.59)
Normal weight	18.5 to 24.9	11.3 to 15.9	0.45 (0.36–0.45)
Overweight	25 to 29.9	6.8 to 11.3	0.36 (0.22–0.31)
Obese	30 and greater	5 to 9	0.22 (0.18–0.36)

Source: Modified from Institute of Medicine, US, 2009.

The mother's nutrition and her weight gain have a direct bearing on the newborn's weight. It is very important to keep a periodic weight record. Rapid weight gain or stationary or falling weight can be ominous signs, and need to be investigated further to detect the underlying cause.

STAGES OF FOETAL DEVELOPMENT

Prenatal development of the foetus happens in three periods.

Ovular period or period of implantation: This is the first two weeks after conception. In this period, the zygote gets embedded in the mother's uterine cavity.

Embryonic period: This period is from the third week to the eighth week of pregnancy. In this stage, the cells get differentiated into three layers—the endoderm, which gives rise to the digestive system, liver, pancreas; the mesoderm, which leads to the formation of the skeleton, muscles, heart, and blood vessels; and the ectoderm, which gives rise to the skin, nervous system, and sensory organs.

Foetal period: This period is from eight weeks to delivery. After eight weeks, the embryo is called a foetus. Foetal growth follows a pattern of hyperplasia, which is an increase in cell number; hyperplasia and hypertrophy, in which there is an increase in cell number and size; and finally, a stage of hypertrophy.

Major foetal growth happens in the last 20 weeks of pregnancy. By 20 weeks, the foetal body and the organs are fully formed, although they are much smaller in size.

During the prenatal development of the foetus, there are certain specific risk periods or critical periods, during which specific organs develop.

The first trimester of pregnancy is considered the **critical period of pregnancy**, as most of the organogenesis happens during this period. The preconception nutritional status of a woman plays a pivotal role in determining the pregnancy outcome. Nutritional deficiencies, drugs and medical disorders interfere with foetal development. These can result in foetal malformations and spontaneous abortions. Certain physiologic and genetic factors, for example race, sex of the baby, parental height and weight, and socioeconomic factors play an important role in determining foetal weight.

FACTORS AFFECTING THE OUTCOME OF PREGNANCY

It is of paramount importance to identify the risk factors that can lead to an adverse foetal and maternal outcome. Timely interventions can reduce low birth weight and improve the foetal outcome. There are many factors affecting the outcome of pregnancy. A number of social and environmental factors influence maternal and foetal outcome, for example, an interplay of the mother's age at the time of marriage and conception, the number of children she has, and the spacing between them, as well as the mother's level of education, economic status, and the customs and beliefs prevailing in her family.

The nature of maternal and child health problems are different in developed and developing countries. In India, the major health problems revolve around malnutrition, infection and unregulated fertility, leading to poor maternal health, perinatal mortality, and low birth weight babies. Let us discuss some of the factors.

1. **Age of the mother at the time of conception:** Both extremes of age affects the foetal outcome. In teenage pregnancies (15–19 years), teenagers are still growing themselves, and hence have greater caloric requirement. These women are generally anaemic, and have much greater chances of having a growth restricted baby, low birth weight baby, and higher infant mortality. Mothers over the age of 35 are at an increased risk of gestational diabetes, pregnancy-induced hypertension (PIH), preterm delivery, and still births. There is also an increased risk of congenital malformations and birth defects.
2. **Socio-economic status and spacing of pregnancy:** Women belonging to low socio-economic groups are at a greater risk of nutritional anaemia and poor maternal weight gain during pregnancy. Hence, there is an increased incidence of Low Birth Weight (LBW) babies, IUGR (Intra Uterine Growth Restriction) and PIH (Pregnancy-induced Hypertension) in mothers. There is also an increase in prenatal mortality, foetal

wastage, intra-uterine deaths, and still births. In women who belong to the upper socio-economic status, there is an increased incidence of gestational diabetes, big-size babies and operational deliveries.

If a woman has babies too close to one another, that is, within a time span of less than two years, there are increased chances of all nutritional deficiencies in the mother. The incidence of anaemia and calcium deficiency is greatly increased. The prevalence of LBW babies, abortions, and maternal and perinatal mortality increases. This increase is marked after the fourth pregnancy. A similar risk is posed if a woman has multiple pregnancy, that is, twins/triplets, etc. The incidence of multiple pregnancy has increased significantly, possibly due to the use of ovulation inducing drugs (which assist in dominant follicle formation during a menstrual cycle, and hence conception) and other assisted reproductive techniques (ART).

3. **Body Mass Index:** Both low BMI and high BMI have adverse pregnancy outcomes.
   a. Women with BMI <18.5 kg/m^2 and women of short stature (<145 cm) have an increased risk of low foetal birth weight and increased perinatal mortality. These babies are at a greater risk of getting non-communicable diseases, for example Type 2 Diabetes Mellitus, in adulthood.
   b. Women with high BMI (>25 kg/m^2), overweight and obese (> 30 kg/m^2) are at a risk of greater pregnancy complications, for example, PIH, Gestational diabetes, and increased chances of cesarean section. They also gain relatively more weight. The foetus born is generally larger in size; they also have a greater risk of obesity and Diabetes Mellitus type 2 later in life. There is also a greater risk of congenital malformations in babies born to obese mothers.
4. **Nutritional status of the mother during pregnancy:** A mother's nutritional status determines the healthy foetal outcome. Many factors are associated with deterioration in the nutritional status of women. These can be of varied types, like a reduction in the dietary intake below the normal intake, or an increase in physical activity as compared to the intake of food. Women who have a poor nutritional status at conception are at higher risk of maternal and foetal complications. A large number of women, especially in developing countries, have many micronutrient deficiencies due to various reasons.
   a. **Iron:** Very few women have sufficient iron stores and, along with other factors, are prone to developing Iron Deficiency Anaemia. Iron deficiency is linked with easy fatigability, increased susceptibility to infections, poor maternal health, and at times, low birth weight babies. These women are also at greater risk of maternal mortality, especially at the time of birth due to blood loss.
   b. **Iodine and Folic acid:** Deficiency of folic acid in the periconceptional period (three months before and after conception) is associated with a greater prevalence of spontaneous abortions, neural tube defects, growth restriction, and premature births. Deficiency of iodine can also lead to mental and physical retardation of the foetus. It can also lead to cretinism.
   c. **Calcium and Vitamin D:** These are essential for adequate bone and tooth development of the babies. Mothers deficient in calcium are at a greater risk of developing osteoporosis later in life. This is especially true in developing countries, where there is an added burden of repeated and too many pregnancies, along with inadequate supplementation—if at all—during pregnancy.

Vitamin D deficiency can cause rickets in the babies after birth; they have a poor growth pattern and inadequately calcified bones and teeth.

   d. **Others:** Severe **zinc** deficiency can lead to birth defects and growth restriction of the developing foetus. The mother might experience labour-related problems. Deficiency of **vitamin A** can lead to decreased weight gain in the foetus; it can also cause night blindness in the mother. The clinical signs suggestive of **Vitamin B Complex** deficiency, such as glossitis and angular stomatitis, are higher in pregnant women.

Maternal Infections at the Time of Pregnancy

Infections are an indirect cause of malnutrition. Maternal infections can have short-term and long-term effects on both the mother and the foetus. Short-term effects are foetal growth restriction, preterm labour, abortions, puerperal sepsis (a condition that affects the mother from an infection contracted during or following childbirth). Long-term effects are seen majorly in the children—the foetus generally has low immunity, and hence is susceptible to diarrhoea and respiratory infections, especially in the first year of life. Repeated infections make the child prone to protein energy malnutrition and other chronic infections, especially tuberculosis in our country.

> **Bacterial vaginosis (BV)** is a vaginal condition characterised by abnormal vaginal discharge.
>
> In this, there are fewer than usual lactobacilli, which are the usual vaginal bacteria.
>
> The main symptoms are a vaginal discharge that has a fishy odour, itching, and sometimes lower abdominal pain.
>
> BV can cause premature labour and delivery, and also infection of the uterus after delivery.
>
> Screening and treatment for BV during pregnancy should be done.

The most common maternal infections in our country are:

1. Urinary tract infection, which is reported in nearly 25 per cent of all pregnant women, and is mainly due to the changes taking place in the urinary system and retention of urine, because of the pressure on the bladder due to the enlarging uterus.
2. Chlamydial infection. Chlamydia is an intracellular pathogen, that is, a bacteria, which lives within human cells. It causes bacterial vaginosis and cervicitis, that is, inflammation of the cervix.
3. Pelvic inflammatory diseases.
4. TORCH group of infections, that is, toxoplasmosis, rubella, cytomegalovirus, and herpes simplex.
5. Malaria
6. Tuberculosis
7. Mothers who are HIV infected pose a risk of transmitting the infection to their babies transplacentally, that is, by vertical transmission.

Chronic Medical Diseases

Some chronic medical disorders play an important role in determining the pregnancy outcome. To mention a few:

Diabetes Mellitus: Pregnant women who have high blood sugar levels during the first trimester of pregnancy should be considered to have diabetes mellitus and not gestational diabetes. Their glycosylated haemoglobin should be checked to get their sugar levels of the past three months. These women are at greater risk of foetal malformations, especially neural tube defects, which increase by about 8–23 per cent, depending on the sugar level. The mother has an increased risk of abortions, infection during pregnancy, and associated PIH.

Chronic Hypertension: Hypertension may worsen the foetal and maternal prognosis. It may worsen the chances of preterm birth, IUGR, abortion, and perinatal mortality.

Hypothyroidism: There is an increase in thyroid disorders these days, especially hypothyroidism. Hypothyroidism can be a first-time diagnosis in pregnancy. Untreated hypothyroidism in early pregnancy can lead to abortion and foetal wastage. Hypothyroidism is also an important factor in deficient intellectual development in a child.

Miscellaneous Factors

A prospective mother should take special care and avoid all substances that can harm her developing foetus, especially during the first trimester.

a. **Alcohol:** In women who consume alcohol, there is an increased risk of foetal growth restriction, facial malformations, and mental retardation. There can be lifelong learning difficulties and short attention spans, that is, Attention Deficit Hyperactivity Disorder. Alcohol decreases the blood flow, and hence nutrients and oxygen supply to the developing foetus. In extreme cases, consumption of alcohol can lead to **Foetal Alcohol Syndrome,** which is characterised by fetal growth restriction, facial abnormalities, and central nervous system dysfunction.

b. **Smoking:** Smoking reduces blood flow to the growing foetus, and therefore decreases oxygen supply and nutrient supply. Smokers are at greater risk of spontaneous abortions and foetal growth restriction. They are also at greater risk of PIH.

c. **Caffeine:** High intake of caffeine increases the risk of spontaneous abortions and foetal growth restriction. There can be a decrease in the placental blood flow, and hence deficient absorption of certain nutrients such as calcium, iron and zinc.

d. **Drugs:** During pregnancy, drugs should only be taken under medical supervision. Any drug can cause problems during pregnancy by crossing the placental barrier and causing a decrease in the blood flow to the foetus, and hence the uptake of oxygen by the foetus.

Nutritional supplements should also be taken under supervision, for example, high doses of vitamin A can cause severe birth defects, and even abnormalities of the cardiovascular system and the nervous system.

e. **Domestic violence/abuse**: This should be carefully ruled out in women. Women belonging to the lower socio-economic strata of society are at greater risk. Sometimes family pressures create tremendous pressure on women, and hence on her developing foetus. The chances of PIH, growth restriction and LBW increase in these women.

Box 18.1: Factors Affecting the Outcome of Pregnancy

- Age of the mother at the time of conception
- Socio-economic status and spacing of pregnancy
- Body Mass Index
- Nutritional status of the mother during pregnancy
- Maternal infections at the time of pregnancy
- Chronic Medical Diseases
- Miscellaneous factors such as alcohol, smoking, drugs, caffeine etc.

Box 18.2: Antenatal Care (ANC)

Antenatal care (ANC) is the systemic supervision of women during pregnancy to monitor the progress of foetal growth, and to ascertain the well-being of the mother and the foetus.

The objectives are to:

- Recognise that 'every pregnancy is special, and every pregnant woman must receive special care'.
- To identify the complications that may occur in any pregnancy/childbirth, and be ready to deal with them if and when they happen.
- To ensure that ANC is used as an opportunity to detect and treat existing problems, if any, for example, essential hypertension.
- To prepare the woman and her family for the eventuality of an emergency.
- To make sure that the services to manage obstetric emergencies are available on time.

COMMON CONCERNS AND COMPLICATIONS DURING PREGNANCY

1. Exercise

Pregnancy is a normal physiological stage in a woman's life; it should not be treated as a period of confinement and total rest. A woman should continue with all her pre-pregnancy activities unless contraindicated by her doctor, for example, if she has a low lying placenta, she needs complete bed rest, etc. A woman should not excessively fatigue herself or risk injury to her foetus. It has been shown that women who exercised regularly had greater blood volumes during pregnancy; they also had shorter labours and fewer cesarean deliveries. However, women who were previously sedentary should not start with any new exercise regime during pregnancy. The safest for her would be walking, with regular periods of rest in between. However, in certain cases a pregnant woman is advised strict bed rest, for example, women with PIH, multiple fetuses, growth restricted baby, etc.

Box 18.3: Common Terms and Definitions

Small for Gestation Age (**SGA):** Birth weight less than 10th percentile for gestation age.

Appropriate for Gestation Age (**AGA):** Birth weight lies between the 10th and 90th percentiles for gestation age.

Large for Gestation Age (**LGA):** Infant's birth weight above the 90th percentile for gestation age.

Preterm baby: A baby born before 37 completed weeks of gestation.

Low birth weight baby (LBW) is defined as a baby with birth weight less than 2,500 g.

Very low birth weight (VLBW): Birth weight 1,500 grams or less.

Extremely low birth weight: Weight 1,000 grams or less (WHO).

Intra Uterine Growth Restriction (IUGR): This is when the birth weight of the baby is below the 10th percentile of the average weight for that gestational age.

2. Employment and Rest

A pregnant woman should continue with her usual activities throughout pregnancy. Ideally, no work should be continued to a stage of excessive fatigue. She should have regular periods of rest during the day. Especially during the last six weeks of pregnancy, she should sleep for a minimum of 10 hours in day—eight hours at night and two hours in the afternoon.

3. Travel

During the first and late last trimester of pregnancy, a woman should avoid long journeys. Air travel is safe till 10 days before her expected date for delivery. Train journeys are safer than road travel. A woman should take a walk every two hours to prevent venous stasis of blood (slow blood flow in the veins, especially in the legs). Seat belts should be tied securely below the abdomen to avoid discomfort.

4. Personal Hygiene and Habits

A pregnant woman should have a bath regularly; she should wear comfortable clothes and avoid high-heeled footwear. She should avoid excessive consumption of caffeine and refrain from smoking and alcohol.

5. Bowel Habits and Constipation

In pregnancy, there are decreased bowel movements, which are due to the effect of the increased progesterone hormone. There is also the pressure of the pregnant uterus on the colon. Decreased physical activity can also contribute to constipation.

Regular bowel habits can be established if the woman takes a proper balanced diet, rich in fibre, with plenty of vegetables, fruits and fluids. A reasonable amount of physical exercise facilitates proper bowel movements. In some cases, mild laxatives and stool softeners are prescribed.

6. Nausea and Vomiting

This is the most common complaint during pregnancy; in fact, it is so common that it is taken as a symptom of a normal pregnancy. It normally begins after the first or second missed period, and lasts till about 14 weeks or, at the most, till 22 weeks of pregnancy. Nausea and vomiting is usually worse in the mornings, but in more than 80 per cent of women, it lasts throughout the day. Therefore, the term 'morning sickness' is a misnomer.

The underlying cause is most probably the high levels of hCG (human chorionic gonadotropin) and the high levels of oestrogen hormones.

Nausea can be reduced by the following measures:

- Eating small and frequent meals.
- Foods rich in fats and spices should be avoided.
- Taking a dry toast, rusk, or biscuit before getting out of bed sometimes helps.
- The woman should avoid the foods or factors which trigger nausea, such as the smell of certain foods.
- To avoid dehydration, fluid intake should be adequate.

- In some cases, medicines are required.

7. Backache

This is again a very common problem in pregnancy, with around half of pregnant women complaining of lower back ache. The exact cause is not known. The reasons can be physiological, due to the presence of the hormone relaxin, which causes the relaxation of pelvic joints. Other causes can be pre-pregnancy backache, obesity, faulty posture, and sometimes, urinary tract infections.

Simple measures that can help in decreasing the symptoms are:

- Women should squat and avoid bending forward while working.
- Proper footwear helps at times.
- Controlled weight gain during pregnancy.
- Sometimes, a hard bed and resting with the feet elevated helps.
- Regular intake of milk and calcium supplements helps in preventing pregnancy induced osteoporosis.
- Back massage and mild painkillers should be used with discretion, and only under medical supervision.

8. Heartburn and Acidity

This is also a common condition in pregnancy. It is basically due to regurgitation or reflux of gastric contents into the lower part of the oesophagus. The increasing size of the uterus compresses the stomach, and hence the contents are pushed into the oesophagus. Progesterone also causes the relaxation of the lower oesophageal sphincter.

Measures that can relieve the symptoms are:

- The woman should have small, frequent meals.
- The diet should be non-spicy and low in fats and oils.
- The woman should not lie down immediately in a supine (flat) position after eating.
- Sleeping in a semi-reclining position sometimes helps in relieving the symptoms.
- Liquid antacids are used at times to relieve the symptoms.

9. Ankle oedema

Ankle oedema in pregnancy can be due to physiological or pathological causes. Pathological causes, like severe anaemia and hypertensive disorders in pregnancy, commonly cause ankle oedema. These should be treated accordingly. Physiological causes require no treatment, and are relieved by rest and slight foot elevation. Sometimes, a high protein diet also helps in relieving physiological ankle oedema.

10. PICA and Ptyalism

PICA refers to the strange food cravings seen in pregnant women. These cravings can also be for non-food items, for example, refrigerator frost, clay, chalk and slate, etc. It is seen that sometimes, these women have an underlying iron deficiency. These cravings generally subside upon correction of iron deficiency.

Ptyalism or profuse salivation is seen in some pregnant women. It is due to the stimulation of the salivary glands upon consumption of starchy food. Sometimes, eating high protein, low fat food items helps in relieving the symptoms. But in most cases, the cause is unknown.

11. Pregnancy Induced Hypertension

This refers to the hypertension that develops as a direct result of the gravid state of the uterus. It includes:

- Gestational hypertension
- Pre-eclampsia
- Eclampsia

Pre-eclampsia is a multisystem disorder of unknown etiology, characterised by the development of hypertension to the extent of 140/90 mm of Hg or more, with proteinuria, after the 20th week of pregnancy in a previously normotensive and non-proteinuric woman.

The major signs and symptoms are:

- Swelling over the ankles and feet (pedal oedema)
- Headache
- Rapid weight gain—more than 2.5 kg a month or more than 0.5 kg per week is significant.

Box 18.4: Warning Symptoms Indicating Complications in Pregnancy

- Fever
- Persistent vomiting
- Abnormal vaginal discharge/itching
- Palpitations, easy fatigability
- Breathlessness at rest/on mild exertion
- Generalised swelling of the body, puffiness of the face
- Severe headache and blurring of vision
- Passing smaller amounts of urine and burning sensation during micturition
- Vaginal bleeding
- Decreased or absent foetal movement
- Leaking of watery fluid Per Vaginum

Some preventive and curative measures of use in pre-eclampsia are:

- Regular antenatal check-up.
- Calcium supplementation of about 2 g/day reduces the risk of gestational hypertension.
- Antioxidants like vitamin E and vitamin C, nutritional supplementation with magnesium, zinc and fish oil, and a low salt diet are generally advocated. However, these have a limited benefit.

Box 18.5: Important Facts

PNDT Act: This refers to preconception and pre-natal diagnostic techniques. It is the prohibition of the sex selection act, 1994, amended in February 2003. It is enforced to prohibit sex selection before or after conception, to prevent its misuse (which leads to female foeticide).

Umbilical Cord Blood Banking;

Here, the haemopoietic stem cells (HSC) from the umbilical cord blood are preserved. These can later be transplanted for treatment, in case the child or her/his siblings ever develop a metabolic, hematological, or neurological disease. It is commonly used for hematological malignancy (leukaemia) in children.

- A balanced diet rich in protein (about 100 g) can be useful in reducing the risk.
- The usual salt intake should be permitted, although extra sprinkling of salt on food should be avoided.

Eclampsia: Pre-eclampsia, when complicated with generalised seizures, is termed eclampsia.

12. Gestational Diabetes (GDM)

This is defined as carbohydrate intolerance. It is seen for the first time during pregnancy after the 20th week of gestation.

Common risk factors for GDM are:

- Positive family history of Diabetes Mellitus in parents and siblings
- History of previous still birth
- History of birth of an overweight baby > 4 kg in the previous pregnancy
- Unexplained perinatal loss
- The mother's age is over 30 years
- Obesity

Screening for GDM

Ideally, all pregnant women should be screened for gestational diabetes between 24 to 28 weeks of gestation. Women who are at high risk—women over the age of 25, obese, with a family history of diabetes, history of GDM in the previous pregnancy, or having Glycosuria (glucose in urine) in the present pregnancy—can be screened by 20 weeks.

A fasting plasma glucose level >126 mg/dl or a casual plasma glucose >200 mg/dl is enough to diagnose GDM. Sometimes, in high-risk cases with borderline hyperglycaemia (raised blood sugar levels), an OGTT, that is, oral glucose tolerance test, is done.

Prevention and management

a. Preconception counselling.
b. Proper and regular antenatal care, and careful supervision of pregnancy.
c. Dietary modification—energy intake should be around 30 kcal/kg for a normal weight woman, 24 kcal/kg for an overweight woman, and 12 kcal/kg for morbidly obese women.
d. The diet should contain 50 per cent carbohydrates, 20 per cent of proteins, and around 25 to 30 per cent of fat. Fat can also be curtailed, depending on the BMI.
e. The diet should be fibre-rich.
f. Usually a three-meal regimen, with breakfast comprising 25 per cent of the total calorie intake, lunch 30 per cent, dinner 30 per cent, and several low-calorie snacks are quite suitable for most patients.
g. Regular exercise, like walking and aerobics, should be encouraged to keep the blood glucose levels in check.

Frequent blood sugar estimation is required.

NUTRIENT NEEDS DURING PREGNANCY

The nutrient needs of a pregnant woman should be such as to provide the extra calories and the specific nutrients required for the growth of the foetus.

The diet should be tailor-made according to the mother's preconception BMI, her age, and other associating factors (for example, PIH, gestational diabetes, chronic hypertension, etc.).

Recommended daily allowances should be taken as only guides to the needs of the mother, as the actual nutrient requirements vary widely and are specific to each woman and her circumstances. Some nutrients, especially self-prescribed, can be toxic, for example, Iron, Zinc, Selenium, Vitamin A, Pyridoxine, and Vitamin D. Hence, self-prescription should be avoided. Routine multivitamin supplementation is not recommended, except in cases where the mother is at greater nutritional risk, for example, multiple gestation and vegan dietary habits.

Nutrient needs increase during pregnancy mainly because of two reasons:

- To meet the nutritional demands of pregnancy.
- To meet the increased demands of the developing foetus.

There is an increased nutrient requirement due to the development of maternal organs such as the uterus, placenta and breast tissues. It is also imperative to build the body stores for utilisation at the time of labour and lactation. In addition, nutrients are needed to meet the requirements of the growing foetus.

Almost all nutrient demands, that is, macro and micronutrients, increase during pregnancy.

In the **First Trimester,** greater qualitative improvement, rather than a quantitative increase, is required in the diet. There is no quantitative increase in the recommended intake as there is no significant increase in the size of the foetus at this time. Also, during this trimester the woman's body is adjusting to the hormonal and physiological changes of pregnancy.

Table 18.3: Recommended Dietary Allowances (RDA) for Energy, Protein, Fat, and Minerals for Pregnant Indian Woman

Group	*Category*	*Body weight (Kg)*	*Energy (kcal/d)*	*Protein (g)*	*Visible fat (g/d)*	*Calcium (mg/d)*	*Iron (mg/d)*	*Zinc (mg/d)*	*Magnesium (mg/d)*
Women	Sedentary work	55	1,900	55	20	600	21	10	310
	Moderate work		2,230		25				
	Heavy work		2,850		30				
	Pregnant		+ 350	78	30	1,200	35	12	

Source: Nutrient Requirements and Recommended Dietary Allowances for Indians, ICMR 2010.

There is an increased energy and nutrient requirement mainly in the second and third trimesters of pregnancy. During the last two trimesters, the demands of the following nutrients increase—Energy, Protein, Fat, Calcium, Iron, and Vitamin B complex (especially thiamine, riboflavin, folic acid, and vitamin B_{12}).

Energy: The demand for energy increases during pregnancy because of:

- Foetal growth
- Increase in maternal organs and body size
- Deposition of fat, which would later be used during lactation
- Growth of the placenta
- There is a gradual increase in the BMR during pregnancy. BMR increases by 15 per cent in a singleton pregnancy. In the first and second trimesters of pregnancy, the BMR may increase by 5 per cent, while in the third trimester, it increases by 12–15 per cent.

The total weight gain during pregnancy may range from 10 to 14 kg (average 12 kg).

The energy demands for pregnant women are the same as those of non-pregnant women in the first trimester. During the second and third trimesters, the demand increases by 350 kcal per day (ICMR 2010). Additional energy requirements of Indian women during pregnancy are computed on the basis of reference, that is, Indian women who have weight gain in the range of 10–14 kg. Even if the weight gain during pregnancy is within desirable limits, the range of acceptable energy intake varies widely, given the individual differences in the energy output of BMR.

Proteins: There is an additional protein requirement in pregnancy to:

- Support the synthesis of maternal and foetal tissues
- Increase the maternal blood volume, and subsequently increase plasma proteins
- Form amniotic fluid
- Build stores for labour and lactation

The normal protein requirement of an adult woman is 1 g/kg body weight /day, that is, 55 kg x 1 = 55g/day. There is a maximal increase in protein demands in the third trimester.

Table 18.4: Additional Protein (High Biological Value) Requirements in Pregnancy

S.no	*Trimester*	*10 kg Weight Gain*	*12 kg Weight Gain*
1.	Ist	0.5 gm/day	0.6 gm/day
2.	IInd	6.9 gm/day	8.1 gm/day
3.	IIIrd	22.7 gm/day	27 gm/day

Source: ICMR 2010.

The ICMR (2010) recommends an additional protein intake of 23 gm/day, that is, 55+ 23 = 78 gm/day during pregnancy. For each additional foetus (twins and so on), another 25 gm/day of protein is necessary (Institute of Medicine 2002).

If the extra protein requirements are not met during pregnancy, it may lead to serious consequences, such as:

- Increased rise of abortions
- Intra Uterine Growth Restriction (IUGR)
- Decrease in the number of brain tissues
- Weak immunity of the offspring

Rich sources of protein of high biological value, such as milk, meat, fish, poultry, soyabean, etc., should be included in the diet of the pregnant woman. The Pulse : Cereal ratio should be at least 1:5 in a pregnant woman's diet. Limited intake of protein and energy usually occur together, so the right ratio of Pulse : Cereal or Protein : Carbohydrate is important to spare proteins for tissue building.

Carbohydrates: According to the Institute of Medicine (2002), 135–175 g/day carbohydrates are recommended to provide enough calories in the diet to prevent ketosis and to maintain appropriate blood glucose levels during the pregnancy period. Out of the total calories, 35 per cent should be provided by carbohydrates. In Indian dietaries, this is usually higher, with between 50–65 per cent of energy typically coming from carbohydrates. The choice of carbohydrates should be judicious, so as to include more of complex carbohydrates and less of simple ones.

Fibres: The Institute of Medicine (2002) has recommended 28 g/day of fibre intake during pregnancy. The common complaints of constipation during pregnancy can be easily managed with an intake of whole grains, green leafy vegetables, seasonal vegetables, and fresh and dried fruits on a daily basis.

Fats: The ICMR (2010) has recommended an intake of 30g of visible fat during pregnancy per day. The calories provided by the total amount of fat (visible and invisible) should be 20–30 per cent of the total energy.

DHA: DHA, that is, docosahexanoic acid, plays a very important role in vision as well as in cognitive function. During pregnancy, 200–300 mg of DHA/day is recommended for optimal foetal development.

Table 18.5: Recommended Dietary Allowances (RDA) for Water Soluble and Fat Soluble Vitamins for Pregnant Indian Women

Group	*Category*	*Body Weight (Kg)*	*Vitamin A (µg/d)*		*Thiamine (mg/d)*	*Riboflavin (mg/d)*	*Niacin Equivalent (mg/d)*	*Pyridoxine (mg/d)*	*Ascorbic acid (mg/d)*	*Dietary Folate (µg/d)*	*Vitamin B_{12} (µg/d)*
			Retinol	β–Carotene							
Women	Sedentary work	55	600	4,800	1.0	1.1	12	2.0	40	200	1.0
	Moderate work				1.1	1.3	14				
	Heavy work				1.4	1.7	16				
	Pregnant		800	6,400	+ 0.2	+ 0.3	+ 2	2.5	60	500	1.2

Source: Nutrient Requirements and Recommended Dietary Allowances for Indians, ICMR 2010.

The amount of recommended omega-6 PUFA (linoleic acid) and omega-3 PUFA (alpha linolenic acid) are 13 g/day and 1.4 g/day, respectively. Rich sources of linoleic acid are corn oil, cotton seed oil, safflower oil, and soyabean oil. Alpha linolenic acid is mainly present in fish oils, but is also found in green leafy vegetables, flax seeds, rape seed oil, soyabean, and walnuts.

Vitamins: All vitamins are required for optimal outcome of pregnancy. In some women, these specific vitamins are provided through the diet. In some other women, however, supplementation is needed. Most vitamins can easily be obtained from a well-balanced diet, but for vitamins like folic acid, supplements need to be taken.

Water-soluble Vitamins

B–Complex Vitamins

Thiamine: As per ICMR (2010), 0.5mg of thiamine is required per 1,000 kcal for a normal adult woman. During pregnancy, an additional 0.2 mg/day is required.

Riboflavin: As per ICMR (2010), the requirement of riboflavin increases by 0.3 mg/day during pregnancy. For a non-pregnant woman, 0.6 mg/day is required per 1,000 calories intake. The demand for riboflavin increases due to an increase in body size and the growth of the foetus. A lack of riboflavin has been linked to cartilage malformation and skeletal malformation in the foetus, and increased risk of pre-eclampsia in the pregnant woman.

Niacin: The ICMR (2010) recommendation is an additional 2 mg/day during pregnancy. Usually 6.6 mg niacin/day is required per 1,000 kcal/day.

Vitamin B_6 or Pyridoxine: It functions as a cofactor in amino acid metabolism. ICMR (2010) has suggested an intake of 2.5 mg/day during pregnancy. Women who use oral contraceptive pills before conception are usually found to have low tissue levels of B_6, but there is no satisfactory theory explaining whether it has some impact on the foetus. However, it reduces the amount of vitamin B_6 in breast milk during lactation.

Folic Acid: There is an increase in the requirement of folic acid due to the following reasons:

- Maternal erythropoiesis
- DNA synthesis
- Foetal and placental growth.

The ICMR (2010) has recommended an additional requirement of 300 µg/day during pregnancy. Maternal folate deficiency is majorly associated with an increased incidence of congenital malformations, including cleft lip and palate and Neural Tube Defects (NTD). Women who smoke, consume alcohol in moderate amounts or are heavy drinkers, and consume recreational drugs are at great risk of marginal folate status, as are those who have malabsorbtion syndromes.

Vitamin B_{12} (Cobalamin): This is needed for enzyme reaction and for the production of methionine. Vitamin B_{12} is exclusively found in foods from animal sources, such as all meats, milk and milk products. Therefore, vegan women are at greater risk of vitamin B_{12} deficiency. Vitamin B_{12} deficiency during pregnancy may lead to impaired cognitive motor development.

The normal requirement for an Indian adult woman for Vitamin B_{12} is 1 microgram, and during pregnancy, the need remains almost the same. During pregnancy, the capacity to absorb Cobalamin increases in the maternal body and a large amount transfers to the growing foetus, and hence foetal blood contains double the amount of vitamin B_{12} than maternal blood. Vegetarian pregnant women who avoid milk may require supplements during pregnancy. The foetal demand for vitamin B_{12} is 0.3 µg /day.

Vitamin C (Ascorbic acid): This is required for collagen synthesis and the development of vascular systems. It also functions as an antioxidant and is essential for iron absorption. A normal Indian adult woman requires 40 mg/day of vitamin C, and during pregnancy, an additional 10 mg/day is required (ICMR 2010) to fulfill the extra demands of the growing foetus, especially in the third trimester. Vitamin C is heat labile and reduces up to 50 per cent during cooking, which is why the RDA for vitamin C is 60 mg/day. During pregnancy, the ascorbic acid content of foetal blood is triple that of maternal blood. To meet the vitamin C requirement, the daily consumption of vitamin C-rich foods (amla, guava, oranges, lemon, sweet lime, etc.) should be encouraged. A deficiency of Vitamin C may lead to the premature rupturing of the foetal membrane and a high risk of neonatal mortality.

Fat–soluble Vitamins

Vitamin A: The ICMR (2010), on the basis of studies carried out by the NIN (National Institute of Nutrition) on pregnant women, has suggested 800 RE of vitamin A/day during pregnancy. Low maternal levels of vitamin A during pregnancy may lead to a reduced kidney size in newborns. Infants with birth prematurity have low levels of vitamin A and poor learning functions. Vitamin A supplementation is not recommended during pregnancy because of its teratogenic nature; the demand can be met by the daily consumption of vitamin A-rich foods such as liver, egg yolk, butter, dark green leafy vegetables, and yellow and orange vegetables.

Vitamin D: Concentration of vitamin D and its metabolites remains the same in foetal blood as in maternal blood during pregnancy. Vitamin D promotes immunity, and is also important for brain development. Vitamin D may also have a role to play in autism and multiple sclerosis. Low levels of vitamin D during pregnancy may lead to hypocalcemia in neonates, which may further lead to inadequate foetal bone formation and mineralisation, convulsions, and hypoplasia of the tooth enamel. Women who use a lot of sunscreen and also have a poor dietary intake of vitamin D are at greater risk of developing deficiency. An excess concentration of vitamin D also leads to complications, such as hypercalcemia, atherosceloris, and calcium deposits in many vital organs in infants.

Vitamin E: The requirement of vitamin E increases during pregnancy. Its deficiency during pregnancy may lead to miscarriage, preterm birth, and stillborn babies. A very small amount of vitamin E crosses the placenta, and hence infants have decreased concentration, which may persist up to the age of six.

Vitamin K: It is important for bone health as well as for blood coagulation, and hence plays a vital role in pregnancy. Vitamin K is very important to prevent neonatal hemorrhage.

Minerals

Calcium: Hormonal factors influence calcium metabolism in pregnancy to a great extent. These changes affect the promotion of progressive calcium retention to meet the increasing demands of foetal bones for mineralisation. The ICMR has suggested 600 mg/day of calcium for an adult woman. During pregnancy, the demand is 1,200 mg/day. Approximately 30 g of calcium accumulates during pregnancy, out of which 25 g accumulates in the foetal skeleton. Increase in calcium intake during pregnancy is essential for the mother, and important for the calcification of foetal bones and teething. It also restores calcium stores in the body; this calcium is required during lactation. To prevent hypocalcemia, adequate amounts of vitamin D should also be taken. Women should also avoid repeated pregnancies.

Iron: During pregnancy, there is a marked increase in blood supply, which influences the increased demand for iron. The requirement of iron increases because of:

- Expanding maternal tissue organs
- Increase in erythrocyte count
- Foetal growth
- Blood loss during labour
- Placental iron
- Need to build up iron stores in foetal liver

According to ICMR (2010), the daily iron requirement for a normal Indian adult woman is 14 mg/kg body weight/day. An additional 760 mg iron is required during pregnancy to support weight gain. The RDA of iron increases from 21 mg to 35 mg /day during the gestation period. Foods rich in vitamin C enhance the absorption of iron. Low iron consumption may lead to poor haemoglobin production, followed by the compromised delivery of oxygen to the reproductive organs and growing foetus.

Iodine: The ICMR (2010) recommendation for iodine during pregnancy is 250 µg /day. Deficiency of iodine during the gestation period may lead to spontaneous abortion, stillbirth, psychomotor defects, high perinatal mortality, congenital anomalies, and cretinism. It has been found that adequate iodine content in the blood during gestation is associated with a high IQ level in the child. To ensure optimal iodine during pregnancy, the expectant mother should consume iodised salt.

Zinc: Zinc deficiency during the gestation period leads to serious complications, such as congenital malformations in the newborn, abnormal brain development in the foetus, abnormal behaviour in the newborn, IUGR, decreased birth weight, and increased chances of premature birth. Rich sources of zinc are red meats, seafood, and all unrefined grains.

Sodium: The requirement of sodium during pregnancy is similar to that of a normal Indian adult woman. Sodium restriction and the use of diuretic drugs are not recommended for oedema, which sometimes happens during pregnancy. The blood volume increases during pregnancy, which simultaneously increases the glomerular filtration rate of sodium. If the blood sodium level decreases, either because of decreased consumption or increased excretion, the kidney starts producing rennin, which helps in sodium retention and in maintaining the sodium level of the body. Consumption of iodised salt should be encouraged during pregnancy, as well as during the lifecycle.

Magnesium: A full-term foetus contains about 1 g of magnesium during the gestation period. Magnesium supplementation during pregnancy reduces the chances of IUGR.

Phosphorus: Phosphorus is available in a great variety of food sources, and hence its deficiency is uncommon if a person eats a normal balanced diet. Low phosphorus content is found in women with recurrent vomiting, which leads to starvation. Phosphorus is vital in energy metabolism, and hypophosphatemia (low levels of phosphorus in the blood) can be life-threatening.

Copper: During pregnancy, copper is usually needed in marginal amounts; however, its deficiency can lead to altered embryo development.

DIET AND FEEDING PATTERN

Guidelines for Eating during Pregnancy

The principles of meal planning for pregnant women are similar to those for non-pregnant women. The diet of a pregnant woman should be balanced. It should contain the energy giving, body building, and protective and regulatory nutrients in the right proportions.

In the early months of pregnancy, many women complain of nausea and vomiting, commonly known as morning sickness. It should be managed, as discussed earlier.

The feeding pattern during the second and third trimesters of pregnancy should comprise a five to six meal pattern. This pattern should include the three major meals, that is, breakfast, lunch and dinner, along with healthy nutritious snacks two to three times a day in between.

To meet the increased protein requirements, high biological value protein sources, such as milk, milk products, meat, poultry, fish, and soybean, along with pulses and groundnuts, are good options.

To fulfil the extra calcium demands, milk is a good choice for expectant mothers. Milk and milk products, such as buttermilk, curd, *paneer,* yoghurt and flavoured yoghurts can be included to meet the calcium requirements. Other food sources containing calcium are spinach, and other green leafy vegetables, soyabean, tofu, *til* seeds, and almonds.

The diet of an expectant mother should include plenty of fluids, which should include at least eight to 10 glasses of water. Healthy beverages should also form a part of the fluid intake. She should also include vegetable soups, coconut water, milk shakes, green tea, etc., in her diet.

The increased iron demands during pregnancy can be met by the consumption of whole grain cereals, pulses, mustard greens, eggs, organ meats, raw banana, and dates regularly in the diet.

As stated earlier, to prevent or relieve constipation, the diet should include foods that are fibre-rich, such as whole grains and their products, pulses with husk, and raw fruits and vegetables.

To summarise, the diet during pregnancy should be planned as per the ICMR guidelines, but should be individualised as per the demands, choices, and nutrient requirements and needs of the individual woman.

She should follow a five-food group pattern by including three servings of milk and milk products; around two servings of meat, fish, poultry, or eggs, one serving of dark green vegetables, orange and yellow fruits and vegetables; two servings of pulses, mutually supplemented with cereal to improve the quality of protein; one to two servings of raw vegetables or fruits, especially citrus fruits (orange, mausami, etc.), and two servings of other vegetables.

Cereals and fats should be according to the calories advised or recommended.

These amounts make a base for a nutritionally adequate diet.

Daily Food Plan during Pregnancy

An individual food plan should be developed for each expectant mother to meet her specific nutritional demands.

The food plan should be based on the regular and basic food items available in the Indian market for Indian women, and should be designed to fulfil the increased nutrient demands of pregnancy.

The food plan should be based on the woman's ethnic background, her beliefs, economic status, food choices, and her lifestyle.

Special attention should be given to women at risk of developing complications during pregnancy, for example women who are undernourished, overnourished, anaemic, suffering from PIH, gestational diabetes, or with IUGR babies, etc.

Emphasis should be laid on designing a diet that fulfils specific nutrient deficiencies, as well as remains within the personal taste and budget of the woman for whom the diet is being planned.

During prenatal and antenatal dietary counselling sessions, the woman should be encouraged to avoid alcohol, caffeine, tobacco, and drugs. Expectant mothers should be educated about the direct impact of her nutritional status and her diet on the development of the baby.

Pregnant women must avoid fasting and skipping of meals, especially breakfast.

SAMPLE DIET PLAN

Age	24 years	Physiological state	pregnant, third trimester
Sex	female	Socio-economic status	middle-income group
Activity level	moderate	Food habits	vegetarian

RDA (as per ICMR 2010)

Energy day	2250 + 350 = 2580 kcal	Iron	35 mg
Protein	55 + 23 = 78 g	Thiamine	1.3 mg

Menu Plan

Meal	Menu (vegetarian)
Early morning	Tea 1 cup + Rusk 2
Breakfast	Milk – 1 glass
	Spinach *besan cheela* - 2
	Apple - 1 medium
Mid-morning	Soup – 1 bowl
	Vegetable *poha/upma* – 1 quarter plate
Lunch	*Dal* – 1 bowl
	Vegetable preparation (any) – 1 bowl
	Cucumber raita - 1 bowl
	Steamed rice -1/2 plate
	Chapati – 2
Evening tea	Fruit milk shake – 1glass
	Vegetable sandwiches – 2

Dinner	*Matar paneer* curry – 1 bowl Seasonal Vegetable – 1 bowl Salad - small helping	Steamed rice– 1 half plate *Chapati* –2 Dessert (*kheer* or custard) – 1 bowl

She should also have a glass of milk (preferably toned or double toned) at night before sleeping. Beverages like *nimbu pani* and coconut water can be had in between meals.

SUMMARY

- Pregnancy is the most vulnerable phase in a woman's life.
- During pregnancy, a woman needs good nutritional status to give birth to a healthy baby.
- Women who have a poor nutritional status at conception are at higher risk of disease and death.
- Women in India suffer from three major problems affecting their health during pregnancy—malnutrition, infections and unregulated fertility.
- The normal duration of pregnancy is 10 lunar months or nine calendar months and 7 days, or 280 days or 40 weeks.
- During pregnancy, a woman's body undergoes progressive anatomical, physiological and biochemical change. These are:
- Pregnancy is a state of haemodilution; there is a fall in the haemoglobin concentration up to 2g per cent at term from the non-pregnant state, and hence the need for iron increases.
- Cardiac output starts to increase to approximately 40–50 per cent of the pre-pregnant stage. It is the highest in the right or lateral position; it helps in meeting the additional oxygen requirement during pregnancy.
- Muscle tone and motility of the gastrointestinal tract is decreased. The cardiac sphincter of the stomach relaxes under the influence of the progesterone hormone; this can lead to the regurgitation of the gastric contents into the oesophagus, causing heartburn.
- In pregnancy, the basal metabolic rate increases by about 30 per cent.
- Iron requirement during pregnancy is the most significant in the last trimester. Approximately 1,000 mg of iron is required during pregnancy.
- There is an increased demand for calcium, especially in the last trimester, at around 80 per cent. Ideally, weight gain during pregnancy should depend on the mother's pre-pregnancy BMI.
- In a singleton pregnancy, a woman should gain around 11 kg of weight; the range is 11–16 kg.
- Prenatal development of the foetus takes place in three periods: ovular period, embryonic period and foetal period.
- The first trimester of pregnancy is considered a critical period, as most of the organogenesis happens at this time.
- A number of social and environmental factors influence the maternal and foetal outcome.
- Both extremes of age affect the foetal outcome.
- Women belonging to a low socio-economic status have a greater chance of contracting nutritional anaemia and poor maternal weight gain during pregnancy.
- Spacing in between pregnancies, the number of pregnancies, and multiple pregnancies increase the rate of LBW babies, abortions, and an increased incidence of maternal and perinatal mortality.

- Both low BMI and high BMI have adverse pregnancy outcomes.
- Women who have a poor nutritional status at conception are at higher risk for maternal and foetal complications.
- A large number of women, especially in developing countries, have many micronutrient deficiencies, due to various reasons.
- Iron deficiency is linked with easy fatigability, increased susceptibility to infections, poor maternal health, and at times, low birth weight babies.
- Deficiency of folic acid in the periconceptional period (three months before and after conception) is associated with a greater prevalence of spontaneous abortions, neural tube defects, growth restriction, and premature births.
- Mothers deficient in calcium are at a greater risk of developing osteoporosis later in life.
- Infections are an indirect cause of malnutrition. Maternal infections can have short-term and long-term effects on both the mother and the foetus.
- Some chronic medical disorders, like diabetes mellitus and chronic hypertension, have a poor foetal outcome.
- A mother-to-be should take special care and avoid all substances that can harm her developing foetus, especially during the first trimester, for example, alcohol consumption, smoking, excess intake of caffeine, etc.

- Some minor ailments are commonly encountered in pregnancy, for example, nausea and vomiting, constipation, backache, heartburn and acidity. These can generally be rectified by simple dietary and physical measures, and generally do not require active medical management.
- The nutrient needs of a pregnant woman should be such as to provide the extra calories and the specific nutrients required for the growth of the foetus.
- The energy demands of pregnant females are the same as non-pregnant females in the first trimester. During the second and third trimesters, the demand increases by 350 kcal per day (ICMR 2010).
- The ICMR (2010) recommends an additional protein intake of 23 gm/day, that is, 55 + 23 = 78 g/day during pregnancy.
- 135–175 g/day of carbohydrates are recommended to provide enough calories in the diet
- All vitamins are required for optimal outcomes of pregnancy.
- Maternal folate deficiency is majorly associated with an increased incidence of congenital malformations, including cleft lip and palate and NTDs.
- The feeding pattern during the second and third trimesters should comprise of a five to six meal pattern.

KEY WORDS

Hemodilution: A fall in the red blood cell and haemoglobin concentration of the blood due to increased blood volume.

Glycosuria: The presence of glucose in the urine.

PICA: The strange food cravings seen in pregnant women. These cravings can also be for non-food items, for example, refrigerator frost, clay, chalk and slate, etc.

Pregnancy Induced Hypertension: The hypertension that develops as a direct result of pregnancy.

Pre-eclampsia: A multisystem disorder of unknown etiology, characterised by the development of hypertension to the extent of 140/90 mm of Hg or more, with proteinuria, after the 20th week of pregnancy in a previously normotensive and non-proteinuric woman.

Proteinuria: The presence of protein, usually albumin, in the urine.

Ptyalism: Excessive production of saliva.

Teratogenic: Refers to any substance that causes malformations or abnormal development in the embryo or foetus.

Vegan: The dietary practice of avoiding all foods from animal sources, including milk.

EXERCISES

1. What physiological changes take place in a woman's body during pregnancy?
2. How do these changes help the woman to cope with the stress of pregnancy and childbirth?
3. Enlist four minerals that play an important role in pregnancy (for both the mother and the growing foetus), and also explain their role.
4. 'Nutrient needs increase during pregnancy.' Explain this statement.
5. Explain the impact of maternal nutrition on the outcome of pregnancy.
6. What are the complications commonly encountered during pregnancy? How can they be managed?
7. Give the complete RDA as suggested by the ICMR for energy, protein, calcium and iron for a pregnant woman.
8. Describe in brief the stages of foetal development. What is the critical period during the time of foetal development?

REFERENCES

Byrd-Bredbenner C., G. Moe, D. Beshgetoor, and J. Berning, *Wardlaw's Perspectives in Nutrition*, 9e, McGraw-Hill International Edition, 2013.

Cunningham, G. F., et al., *William's Obstetrics*, 21e, McGraw Hill, 2001.

ICMR, 'Nutrient requirements and recommended dietary allowances for Indians', A report of the Expert Group of the Indian Council of Medical Research, ICMR, 2010, pp. 43–44.

Khanna, K., et al., *Nutrition during pregnancy and lactation: Textbook of nutrition and dietetics*, 2e, 2013.

Konar, H., D.C Dutta. *Textbook of Obstetrics*, 4th rev. edn, New Central Book Agency, 2001.

Mahan, K. L., et al., *Nutrition in Pregnancy and Lactation, Krause's Food and Nutrition Care Process*, 13e, 2011.

Srilakshmi, B., *Nutritional and food Requirement of Expectant Mother*, Dietetics, 6e, Newage International, 2011.

19

NUTRITION DURING LACTATION

HIGHLIGHTS

- The physiological process
- Improving lactation performance
- Care of the lactating mother
- Common concerns during lactation
- Nutrient needs
- Food supplementation programmes

Although pregnancy ends with the birth of a new life, it heralds an absolutely new phase, in both the life of the mother and the infant. A newborn baby is completely dependent on the mother, not only for its everyday requirements, but even for its nutritional needs. Scientifically, it has been proven beyond doubt that for the first six months of life after birth, mother's milk is the only food that should be given to the baby. Even though exclusive breastfeeding continues only till the first six months of life, breastfeeding along with complimentary feeding should continue up to two years of life. Therefore, one can easily say that lactation is an extension of pregnancy as far as an infant's dependence on the mother is concerned.

The baby should be placed at the breast for feeding soon after birth. During the first two to three days after birth, a small amount of **colostrum**—yellowish thick milk—is secreted. However, this is enough for the baby. It is very rich in proteins and protective antibodies. It is almost like an oral vaccine to protect the baby against various infections. Mature milk starts from the third or fourth day, and the quantity of milk increases gradually. In about a week's time, lactation is well-established in most women, and there is a rapid increase in the amount of milk secreted. The colour of milk also changes to white. In first time mothers, though, it may sometimes take two to three weeks for lactation to establish itself.

In order to support breastfeeding, the mother's body undergoes a number of physiological changes. Lactation is a period of many physiological and hormonal changes, which place great demands on maternal tissues as the mother supports a fully developed and rapidly growing infant. The effects of any nutritional inadequacies during this period can adversely affect the total quantity of milk produced, although the quality of milk (protein, carbohydrate and calcium) might be maintained at the cost of maternal tissues. Even then, the levels of water-soluble vitamins in mother's milk are compromised when the mother is grossly under-nourished.

Lactation, therefore, is an important period when adequate nutrition will ensure the good health of both mother and child. In addition, there is growing recognition that lactation may have profound effects on the maternal nutritional status, and some effect on the maternal return of fertility after delivery. The advent of the next pregnancy, or contraceptive measures used to avoid this, may have an effect on lactation and maternal nutritional status.

THE PHYSIOLOGICAL PROCESS

Milk production and storage in breasts takes place in differentiated alveolar units, often called *lobules*, in the breast. In humans, the small ducts coalesce into 15–25 main ducts that drain sections of the gland. The main ducts dilate into small sinuses as they near the areolus, where they open directly in the nipple.

Puberty is the time when breast development starts, and develops a system of ducts, lobes and alveoli. Breast enlargement takes place in response to oestrogen secretion. In addition, there is ovarian maturation, follicular stimulation, growth and pigmentation of the areola and nipples. Further mammary development takes place when ovulation becomes established (12–18 months after the first menstrual cycle), as the characteristic lobular structure of the breasts develops under the influence of oestrogen and progesterone hormones. Breasts undergo continuous changes in response to hormonal stimuli during each menstruation cycle. Yet this system remains fairly inactive until a woman becomes pregnant.

During pregnancy, the production of large quantities of oestrogen by the placenta stimulates a proliferative stage of mammary gland activity. This brings about a rapid development of the glands in the breasts, resulting in the growth and branching of the duct system. Large quantities of progesterone stimulate the development of the alveoli, that is, it changes the glandular cells into secreting cells. Although high concentrations of oestrogen and progesterone result in mammary gland development during pregnancy, their high concentration by itself has an inhibitory influence on actual milk secretion. However, these two hormones return to their basal levels with the sudden expulsion of the placenta from the uterus at the time of delivery. Thus, the production of lactogenic hormones by the adenophysis of the pituitary gland begins post partum, which in turn brings about the production and secretion of milk. Figure 19.1 depicts the physiology of lactation.

To produce milk, four secretory processes are synchronised in the alveolar cell of the mature, functional mammary gland: (*i*) exocytosis, (*ii*) fat synthesis and secretion, (*iii*) secretion of ions and water, and (*iv*) transcytosis of immunoglubulins and other substances from the interstitial space.

Milk is synthesised continuously into the alveolar lumen, where it is stored until milk removal from the breast is initiated. The amount of milk produced is regulated by prolactin and local factors. When the infant sucks the breast, nerve impulses through the central nervous system are passed to the hypothalamus. This in turn stimulates the anterior pituitary, leading to the secretion of prolactin. Prolactin stimulates the alveoli in the breasts, resulting in milk production. This entire process of milk production is known as ***Prolactin Reflex.*** But the effect of prolactin is modified greatly by local factors that depend on milk removal from the breast. As long as the breasts are emptied of milk, the adenophysis continues to produce the lactogenic hormone. It could be considered that the consumption of one meal by the infant is itself a stimulus for the production of the next meal.

Removal of milk from the breast is accomplished by a process called *milk ejection*, brought about by a neuroendocrine reflex. As a result of sucking by the baby, nerve impulses pass to the brain (hypothalamus), which ends with the secretion of oxytocin from the posterior pituitary gland. Oxytocin mediates the milk let-down reflex by stimulating the contraction of the myoepithelial cells that surround the alveoli and ducts. This is known as ***Let-down reflex,*** and results in the squeezing out of milk and propelling it down towards the nipples. The let-down reflex is highly sensitive to emotional and psychological disturbances, as well as physical contact between the mother and an infant. Besides its role in breastfeeding, oxytocin is also responsible for uterus contraction, which helps to deliver the placenta and stops bleeding after delivery. Therefore, breastfeeding should start soon after delivery.

The composition of milk also changes during the course of a nursing session. The initial fore milk (milk at the front of the breast) is high in various nutrients, but low in fat content. As the infant continues to feed itself, due to ***draught reflex*** (the reflex that moves the hind milk towards the nipple), milk is released from the hind-most milk producing glands of the breast. This milk is known as hind milk, and is higher in fat content than the fore milk.

As long as adenophysis produces lactogenic hormones, it usually cannot produce sufficient follicle stimulating hormone (FSH) and luteinising hormones (LH), which bring about ovulation by the ovaries. This is the reason for lactation amenorrhea and natural contraception during lactation.

IMPROVING LACTATION PERFORMANCE

1. Physical Contact between Mother and Child: An infant's suckling, which elicits both prolactin and let down reflex, is considered essential to successful lactation. Physical contact between the mother and child, and suckling by an infant, give rise to a neuro-endocrine response in the mother's body, resulting in both the production and release of milk from the mother's breasts. Once the let down reflex is established, the sound of the infant's cry, or the mother's emotions, or even thoughts of the child may be an initiator of this reflex. Continuous emptying of the breasts is also important for the continuous production of milk.

In order to promote proximity between mother and child, the WHO and UNICEF launched The Baby-friendly Hospital Initiative (BFHI) in 1991, following the Innocenti Declaration of 1990. The initiative is a global effort to implement practices that protect, promote and support breastfeeding (see Box 19.1 for details).

2. Psychological Support: Feelings of fatigue, pain, emotional upset, anxiety, fear, and tension may inhibit the reflex. Therefore, lactation is not only a physiological mechanism, but is also subject to influence by a number of factors related to both the mother and her environment. These psychological and social factors may be responsible for certain circumstances and situations that may promote or prevent the mother from adequately nursing her child. By relaxing and eating well, the nursing mother increases her chances of successful breastfeeding.

Figure 19.1: Physiology of Lactation

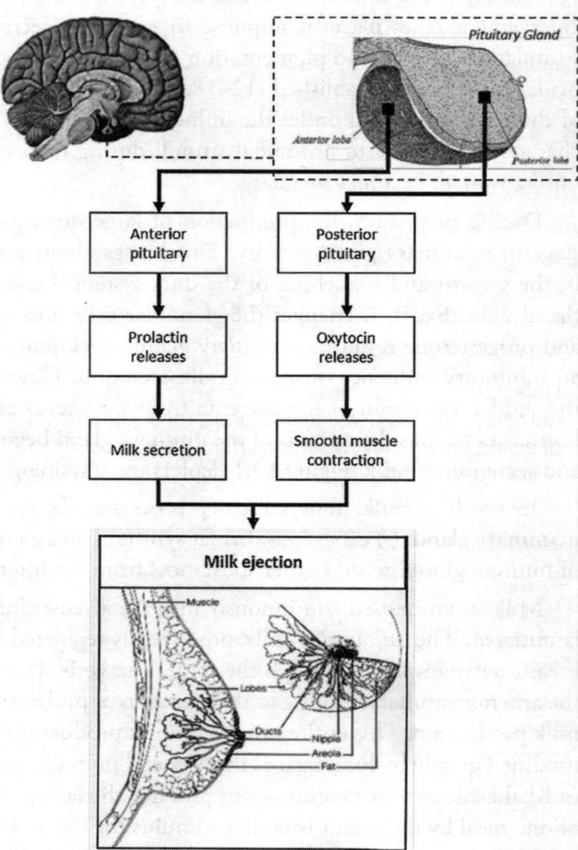

Source: Adapted from Austin Community College website http://www.austincc.edu
Images taken from http://commons.wikimedia.org.

Box 19.1: Baby Friendly Hospital Initiative (BFHI)

BFHI is a joint World Health Organization (WHO) and United Nations Children's Fund (UNICEF) project. The aim of BFHI is to create a healthcare environment where breastfeeding is the norm. It strives to promote practices associated with the health and well-being of all babies and their mothers. Under BFHI, healthcare facilities are assessed and accredited on the basis of the global standard of 10 steps to successful breastfeeding. A 'baby friendly' facility is one where the mother's informed choice of feeding is encouraged, respected and supported. All efforts are made in such facilities to initiate contact and breastfeeding within half-an-hour of birth. Mothers are supported with proper counselling and training for successful breastfeeding.

Source: Baby-friendly hospital initiative: revised, updated and expanded for integrated care. Section 1, Background and implementation. Produced by the World Health Organization, UNICEF and Wellstart International.

3. Good nutrition: This plays a key role in the adequate quantity and quality of milk production. Studies carried out at the National Institute of Nutrition have shown that among a low-income group population, there was no increase in dietary intake during lactation. Although undernourished mothers also produce between 500 ml to 800 ml milk/day, this is usually at the cost of their own nutritional status. As the quantity of milk becomes less, the total amount of nutrients available to a child also becomes inadequate. Although the quality of milk is maintained (particularly with regard to macro-nutrients) in a poorly nourished mother, this is done at the cost of the mother's own body stores. However, in severely malnourished mothers, vitamins, particularly vitamin A and fat content, are known to reduce significantly. Therefore, the importance of a well-balanced, nutritious diet cannot be over-emphasised during lactation.

4. Galactogogues: These are dietary or medicinal compounds thought to increase milk output. In all traditions, several herbs and foods are thought to increase milk output, although there is no scientific evidence attesting to their efficacy. As long as they do not interfere with a normal balanced diet, there is no need to restrict their use. In fact, they may provide some much needed psychological comfort to the lactating mother (see Box 19.2 for details).

Box 19.2: Galactogogues

Galactogogues are substances believed to assist either in initiation or maintenance, and/or augmentation of maternal milk production. Many medicines, foods, or herbs have been used as galactogogues. Although the mechanism(s) of action are unknown for many medicines, most exert their effects through antagonism of dopamine receptors. This is known to result in increased prolactin production. Medications are always recommended after evaluation of and counselling on modifiable factors.

Herbal/natural galactogogues

Throughout world history, certain herbs or foods have been used to enhance milk supply. The mechanisms of action for most of these substances have not been evaluated scientifically. However, traditional use suggests that most are safe, and that some are even effective. Herbs commonly mentioned as galactogogues include fenugreek, fennel seeds, goat's rue, milk thistle, anise, basil, blessed thistle, marshmallow, and others.

Many food products using some of these herbs are prepared specially for lactating mothers, such as *panjiri, laddoos*, etc.

Studies also show that there are several factors affecting breastfeeding initiation. First, infant feeding decisions seem to be made prior to, or irrespective of, contact with health professionals. It has been shown that the chances of initiating and continuing breastfeeding were significantly higher if:

- Women were exposed to a medium level of breastfeeding information via the media during the antenatal period;
- They strongly agreed that breastfeeding would have benefits for them and their baby;
- Their family preferred that they exclusively breastfeed, and if they had friends who also breastfed;
- Health professionals' opinions about breastfeeding also had an impact—if the clinician supported exclusive breastfeeding, the woman was more likely to initiate breastfeeding.

> Successful lactation requires adequate nutrition and rest, in addition to a warm encouraging environment provided by family and friends.

Thus, the mother's willingness to feed her baby is extremely important for the successful initiation and continuation of breastfeeding. In addition, her confidence, a relaxed frame of mind, and positive family support affects the let down reflex, which releases the milk to the baby. On the other hand, negative emotions such as lack of confidence, worry and anxiety can negatively influence her lactation performance.

Research studies suggest that health promotion campaigns have been influential in their ability to educate women about the benefits of breastfeeding. Generally, certain variables, such as three or more antenatal visits, breastfeeding advice received during antenatal and postnatal visits, delivery interval of 24 months or more, and birth weight of 2,500 grams or more, are considered to be positively associated with breastfeeding. Researchers also suggest that women's breastfeeding decisions can be influenced by a focus on increasing the antenatal knowledge of women on the benefits of breastfeeding; education practices that impact the woman's immediate family members; and efforts to improve the clinician's knowledge of, and subsequently their opinions on, breastfeeding.

CARE OF THE LACTATING MOTHER

The life of a new mother is extremely hectic. Giving birth to an infant is a stressful and exhausting experience. Yet she is to resume her duty as a nursing mother within an hour of delivery (as the infant should be put to breast within an hour of delivery), and also start looking after her baby. In addition, for first-time mothers, anxiety about how to look after their baby may add to their stress levels. Therefore, the traditional practice of putting new mothers under the care of an elderly lady is extremely helpful. This helps the mother not only physically, but is also essential for her psychological comfort.

For the first few days after delivery, all that the mother can do is feed herself and her baby. Gradually, as she starts gaining strength, she becomes involved in looking after her baby. Good nutrition and proper rest is extremely important for successful lactation and the mother's own recovery. New mothers benefit from napping when an infant naps.

Once the post-partum bleeding stops and the mother gains some strength, physical activity just before feeding and fresh air improve her overall well-being. During lactation, many women want to restore some kind of fitness and exercise regimen, and this is perfectly normal and compatible with breast-feeding. Physically active lactating women, who follow a healthy diet schedule without restricting the overall calorie intake, are able to carry out normal breastfeeding. In fact, most women may lose up to 4 kg body weight during the first six months of breastfeeding, provided they do not take in energy in excess of the recommendations.

A lactating woman should not, however, indulge in intense physical activity just before feeding as it increases the lactic acid concentration of breast milk, which affects the milk's taste. Generally, it is advisable to feed the baby or express milk before exercise, as babies do not like the taste of lactic acid-rich milk.

Many medicinal drugs are contraindicated during lactation, as they may reduce breast milk volume or enter the breast milk. Therefore, like in pregnancy, all medicinal drugs should be taken only under strict medical supervision.

Although most mothers might be able to move out of their homes 40 days after delivery, during the first six-month period of exclusive breastfeeding, mothers who work outside should be assisted with adequate maternity/breastfeeding leave from their employers. They should be encouraged to continue exclusive breastfeeding for six months by expressing milk to feed the baby while they are at work. They may be encouraged to carry the baby to a workplace crèche, wherever such a facility exists. The concept of 'Hirkani's rooms' (a specially allocated room at the workplace, where working mothers can express milk and store it in a refrigerator during their work schedule) should be encouraged at workplaces. Every mother leaving the maternity facility should be taught how to manually express her breast milk.

Smoking and alcohol consumption interfere with breastfeeding. Cigarette smoking reduces the breast milk volume, and alcohol easily enters breast milk. Furthermore, even a small amount of alcohol, like a can of beer consumed by the lactating mother, may significantly reduce the amount of breast milk intake by an infant. Smoking also exposes the infant to the risks of passive smoking. Likewise, the use of illicit drugs has serious consequences for the physical and emotional well-being of both mother and baby. These drugs may pass into breast milk in heavy doses, and cause irritability, tremors and hallucinations in infants.

Box 19.3: Common Concerns and Complications during Lactation

Engorgement: The breasts need to be frequently emptied by breastfeeding or manual expression of milk.

Areolar engorgement: Can be treated with the manual expression or pumping of milk.

Sore nipple: Result due to improper latch-on. The mother should insert the areola and nipple into the infant's mouth and position the infant correctly.

Cracked nipple: Is caused due to incorrect positioning/latch or contact of the nipple with coarse fabric. The mother should begin the breastfeeding session on the less-affected side and try to correct the cause by proper positioning of baby / use of nursing bra.

Mastitis: This problem is more common in engorged breasts. Mastitis is the inflammation of the mammary gland, typically because of a bacterial infection. If diagnosed with mastitis, the mother should continue to breastfeed while taking antibiotics. Frequent emptying of the breast is essential for relief and recovery.

Nipple confusion: So-called nipple confusion is really flow confusion. The infant becomes accustomed to receiving milk from a bottle, with immediate flow of milk upon sucking. The mother should express a little milk and feed the hungry and often crying baby before attempting to breastfeed. It is also recommended that the infant be exclusively breastfed for the first six months. Feeding breast milk using a bottle leads to the baby rejecting the breast, as s/he has to work harder to suck from the breast.

Premature infants: Preterm infants lack the fat pads in the mouth that allow a good seal around the nipple and areola. They also have difficulties with suck, swallow and breath. Putting an infant to an emptied breast first, to learn to suckle without a lot of milk flowing into her/his mouth, may be necessary to prevent choking. Gradually, as the infant matures over days to weeks, s/he develops oral motor control and is able to suck normally.

Infants with neurological issues: Infants with neurological issues may require an approach similar to that of the preterm infant; however, these infants may not show oral motor improvement. Each case must be assessed to adapt the breastfeeding process to the skills of the infant and the mother.

Source: http://emedicine.medscape.com/article/979458-overview#aw2aab6b9

NUTRIENT NEEDS

The amount of nutrient secreted in milk forms the basis for nutritional requirements during lactation. Most Indian studies show that on an average, a well-nourished lactating mother secretes 850 ml milk per day, while a poorly nourished woman generally secretes 600 ml of milk daily. The average amount of nutrient secreted in milk depends upon the breast milk composition. After calculating the amount of nutrient secreted in milk and taking into consideration the efficacy of food nutrients into milk nutrients, the requirements for lactation are arrived at. The ICMR (2010) has given the RDA for lactation in two categories, that is, 0–6 months (period of exclusive breastfeeding) and 6–12 months (period of partial breastfeeding, along with complimentary feeding), as shown in Table 19.1.

Table 19.1: RDA for Various Nutrients during Lactation (ICMR 2010)

Nutrient	*0–6 Months*	*6–12 Months*
Energy (kcal/d)	+600	+520
Protein (g/d)	74	68
Visible fat (g/d)	30	30
Calcium (mg/d)	1,200	1,200
Iron (mg/d)	21	21
Zinc (mg/d)	12	12
Magnesium (mg/d)	310	310
Vitamin A (Retinol μg/d)	850	950
Vitamin A (Carotene μg/d)	7,600	7,600
Thiamin (mg/d)	+0.3	+0.2
Riboflavin (mg/d)	+0.4	+0.3
Niacin equivalent (mg/d)	+4	+3
Vitamin B_6 (mg/d)	2.5	2.5
Ascorbic acid (mg/d)	80	80
Dietary folate (μg/d)	300	300
Vitamin B_{12} (μg/d)	1.5	1.5

Energy

The energy cost of lactation is determined by the breast milk output and its energy content. There is no evidence of any additional demand for lactation, besides the energy content of milk secreted for breastfeeding. There is no change in TEE during the lactation period over that in the non-pregnant period. A study on the energy expenditure of the Indian lactating woman indicates a negative energy balance, which could be corrected by the fat deposited during pregnancy.

A daily additional energy requirement of a woman doing exclusive breastfeeding during the first six months of lactation would be 600 kcal, and for partial breastfeeding during 7–12 months, it would be 520 kcal.

Protein

The ICMR (2010) has computed protein requirements during lactation using a factorial approach. The RDA is given on the basis of secretion of 9.4 g/day of protein in milk during 0–6 months, and 6.6 g/day during 6–24 months. The efficacy of the conversion of dietary nitrogen into milk protein equivalent can be assumed to be 47 per cent on Indian diets, as in the case of adults. After adding the safe allowance, an additional 19 g/day of protein is recommended during 0–6 months, and 13 g/day during 6–12 months. Consumption of high quality protein, containing foods with a high PE ratio, is recommended during lactation for proper milk production.

Fat and Essential Fatty Acids

The ICMR (2010) has recommended 30g visible fat/day. The minimum level of total fat in the diet of women in the reproductive age should be 20 per cent of the total energy, while it should not exceed 30 per cent of the total energy. The fat in the diet also provides much needed energy density to meet the higher energy needs during lactation.

Iron

Iron requirement during lactation is the sum of the requirement of the mother and the amount of iron secreted in breast milk. The iron content of breast milk is around 0.78 mg/l. Assuming an average milk secretion of 650 ml/d, roughly 0.5mg of iron is secreted in milk each day. This translates to 9 µg/kg/d. In addition to the basal requirement (14 µg/kg/d), this amount needs to be replenished each day. Since most women experience lactational amenorrhea, there is no requirement for iron loss due to menstruation. ICMR (2010) has suggested that the total iron requirement be the same as that for a non-pregnant non-lactating adult female, that is, 30 µg/kg, even though the actual requirement is a little less. This is to compensate for iron losses during pregnancy. Hence, the RDA for a lactating mother is that same as that for an adult woman—21 mg/day.

Calcium

Additional calcium is required for milk secretion. Mother's milk contains 30–40 mg of calcium/ 100 ml. The total calcium secreted through milk is about 300 mg/day. Therefore, in lactation an additional intake of calcium is essential to enable the retention of 300 mg of extra calcium daily. Since the dietary calcium retention in lactating women is 60 per cent, ICMR (2010) has recommended 1,200 mg calcium per day for lactating mothers. This amount is sufficient to meet her own calcium needs, as well as the extra calcium required for milk production.

Vitamin A

Since milk is a rich source of vitamin A (retinol), a lactating mother needs an additional amount of this vitamin. The additional needs during lactation are calculated on the basis of vitamin A secreted in milk. The average Vitamin A secreted in mother's milk is 350 µg of retinol/day. Considering this additional amount, ICMR (2010) has recommended a level of 950 µg of retinol, or 7600 µg of B-carotene per day for lactating mothers.

Thiamin, Riboflavin and Niacin

Although the basis of RDA for these nutrients during lactation is the amount of nutrient secreted in milk, in addition to the adult requirement, in the absence of many research studies on Indian women, ICMR (2010) has recommended an RDA based on additional calorie requirement. Thus, additional thiamin (0.5 mg/1,000 kcals), riboflavin (0.6mg/1,000 kcals) and niacin (6.6 mg niacin equivalents /1,000 kcal) are required in proportion to the increase in energy requirement during the two phases of lactation (Table 19.1).

Pyridoxine

The ICMR (2010) has recommended the same requirements for a lactating mother as those for a pregnant woman, 2.5mg of pyridoxine/day in the absence of any specific studies.

Folic Acid

Since folic acid is secreted in breast milk and is also important for preventing anaemia, an additional 100 µg folate is suggested by ICMR (2010) during lactation.

Cynocobalamine (Vitamin B_{12})

In the absence of any specific data, ICMR (2010) retained the earlier RDA of 1.5 µg of vitamin B_{12} per day, as this would take care of the additional B_{12} secreted in milk.

Ascorbic Acid

The additional needs during lactation are calculated on the basis of the vitamin C secreted in milk. Assuming a daily milk secretion of 700 ml/day and an ascorbic acid content of 3 mg/dL by well-nourished women, an additional requirement during lactation of 20 mg vitamin C/day is required. After taking into consideration the cooking losses, ICMR (2010) has recommended a total of 80 mg of ascorbic acid/day.

DIETARY HABITS

As evident from the nutrient needs during lactation, a nursing mother requires additional energy, protein, fat, calcium, vitamin A, thiamin, riboflavin, niacin, vitamin B_6, ascorbic acid, folic acid, and vitamin B_{12}. This list includes practically all the nutrients for which RDA is given. Therefore, it implies that practically all food groups (energy giving, body building and protective foods) need to be increased in her diet. This is against the traditional practice of just focusing on high energy foods in the diet of the lactating woman. Also, since milk has a lot of moisture, adequate water and fluids are essential to make up the water loss. There are no food restrictions during lactation, except for strongly flavoured and spicy foods, smoking, and alcohol and drug abuse, as they may pass into breast milk. Also, any medications (if required) should be taken under strict medical supervision, as they may also pass into breast milk.

Hence, a normal, well-balanced diet at frequent meal intervals (five to six times a day), along with adequate fluids in the form of plain water, juices, buttermilk, milk, soups, and other beverages should take care of all her food and nutrient needs. (See Boxes 19.3 and 19.4 for a well-balanced diet during lactation.)

Traditionally, certain foods considered to increase milk production, known as galactogogues (see Box 19.2), are also given to the nursing mother. As long as they do not interfere with the principles of normal nutrition, there is no need to stop their intake. They might even give psychological comfort and much needed confidence to the nursing mother, which are known to improve lactational performance.

FOOD SUPPLEMENTATION PROGRAMMES

In 1975, the Government of India initiated a national programme, known as the Integrated Child Development Services (ICDS), as an integrated approach for the delivery of healthcare, as well as nutrition and education services, for deprived populations at the village level and in urban slums through *anganwadi* centres. The ICDS can therefore be considered to function as a primary healthcare programme for preschool children (under the age of six), pregnant women, and lactating mothers. As a part of this programme, all lactating women are provided daily food supplements providing 600 kcals and 18–20g protein for 300 days in a year. This is supposed to provide the extra energy and protein required during lactation. Under this scheme, women are provided supplementary nutrition, either in the form of Micronutrient Fortified Food and/or energy dense food as Take Home Ration (THR). Energy dense food provided as Take Home Ration is given once in 15 days, and is different for different states; it includes food such as *panjiri, sukhadi, sheera, upma, laddu,* etc. Otherwise cooked food (women 350 grams) such as *khichdi, namkin dalia, pullau, mitha dalia,* and/or snacks (75 grams for women) like *kala channa, lobiya,* and white *matar* are provided to lactating women.

In addition, IFA supplementation (100 mg elemental iron and 500 mcg of folic acid) every day for at least 100 days in the post-partum period is given to all lactating mothers.

Table 19.2: Suggested Amounts of Food per Day

Food Group	*Amounts (g)*	*Household Measures*
Milk and Milk Products	750ml	3 cups
Meat and/or Pulse	90	3 bowls
Vegetables	300	3 bowls
Fruits	200	2 fruit
Cereals	320	16 servings
Fat	30	6t
Sugar	30	6t
	Energy: 2,470 kcals	Protein: 79g

Box 19.4: Sample Menu

Meal	*Menu*	*Household Measures*
Early morning	Tea	1 cup
	Biscuit (fibre-rich)	4
Breakfast	Whole wheat bread	2 slices
	Omelette	1 egg
	Milk	1 cup
	Papaya	1 medium bowl
Mid-morning	*Poha /Upma*	1 quarter plate
	Buttermilk (*chach*)	1 glass
Lunch	*Chapati*	3 medium
	Mixed vegetable	1 bowl
	Moong dal	1 bowl
	Cucumber raita	1 small bowl
Tea time	Banana/Mango milk shake	1 glass
	Grilled vegetable sandwich	2 slices
Dinner	Chicken curry	1 bowl
	Rice	½ plate
	Chapati	1 medium
	Palak mushroom	1 small bowl
	Cucumber-tomato salad	8–10 pieces

SUMMARY

- Lactation is a period of many physiological and emotional changes in a woman's life.
- Nutrient needs for almost all nutrients are high, as she supports rapid growth in an infant.
- It is important to serve simple, easy to digest foods at regular intervals, and provide ample support and care to a nursing mother.
- Energy, protein and iron deficiency is common among Indian lactating mothers.
- The Government of India has launched various programmes to support lactating women.

KEY WORDS

Draught reflex: As the infant continues to feed itself, due to the reflex that moves the hind milk towards the nipple, milk is released from the hind most milk producing glands of the breast. This milk is known as hind milk, and is higher in fat content than the foremilk. This is known as draught reflex.

Let-down reflex: As a result of sucking by the baby, nerve impulses pass to the brain (hypothalamus), which ends with the secretion of oxytocin from the posterior pituitary gland. Oxytocin results in squeezing out the milk and propelling it down towards the nipples by stimulating the contraction of the myoepithelial cells surrounding the alveoli and ducts. This is known as Let-down reflex.

Prolactin reflex: When an infant sucks the breast, nerve impulses through the central nervous system are passed to the hypothalamus. This in turn stimulates the anterior pituitary, leading to the secretion of prolactin. Prolactin stimulates the alveoli in the breasts, resulting in milk production. This entire process of milk production is known as Prolactin Reflex.

EXERCISES

1. Describe the physiological process of lactation.
2. Discuss the basis of computing RDA for energy, protein, calcium, and iron as derived by ICMR 2010.
3. Explain the strategies that can be used to improve the lactation performance of a lactating mother.
4. What are the common problems faced by the lactating mother, and how can they be remedied?

REFERENCES

FAO/WHO/UNU, 'Human Energy Requirements', Report of a joint FAO/WHO/UNU Expert Consultation, Rome, 17–24 October, Rome, 2004.

———, 'Joint FAO/WHO/UNU Expert Consultation on Protein and Amino Acid requirements in Human Nutrition', WHO Technical Report Series No. 935, 2007.

Food and Nutrition Board, *National Guidelines on Infant and Young Child Feeding (IYCF)*, New Delhi: Ministry of Human Resource Development, Department of Women and Child Development (Food and Nutrition Board), Government of India, 2004.

ICMR, *Nutrient Requirements and Recommended Dietary Allowances for Indians*, Hyderabad: ICMR, 2010.

Indian Academy of Pediatrics, 'Infant and Young Child Feeding Guidelines: 2010', *Indian Pediatr* 47, 2010, pp. 995–1004.

Rolfes, S. R., L. K. DeBruyne and E. N. Whitney, *Breast Milk, Infant Formula, and Lactation in Lifespan Nutrition Conception through Life*, 2e, Texas: Wadsworth Publishing Company, 1998.

20

NUTRITION DURING INFANCY

HIGHLIGHTS

- Physical and physiological changes that occur during infancy
- Nutritional needs during infancy
- Benefits of colostrum and breast milk
- Importance of complementary feeding, and links with nutritional requirements
- Feeding under special conditions
- Common problems of infants and their dietary management

The first year of life is a time of phenomenal growth and development. To attain full potential, the infant requires an abundant supply of nutrients. The infant's high nutrient needs and developing maturity define the foods most appropriate at each stage in the first year. This phase is extremely significant from the nutritional point of view, as during this stage the vulnerability to various diseases increases. The most interesting, innovative and challenging phase in human feeding is meeting the nutritional needs of infants, both qualitatively and quantitatively. The parent or caretaker has to be imaginatively patient and interested, and must devote undivided time to feeding this age group. Nutrition during the first year is the focus of this chapter.

Infancy: The period of life from birth through the completion of one year of age.

GROWTH AND DEVELOPMENT DURING INFANCY

Growth

Infancy is the period of most rapid growth, when one considers the entire period from birth to adulthood. A healthy child doubles her/his birth weight (around 3.2 kg) by six months, and triples it by the time the infant is one year old. Table 20.1 gives the weight and length profile of human infants in their first year of life. The infant's length changes more slowly than weight, from about 49.5 cm at birth to about 75 cm by 12 months. There is an increase of about 25 cm from birth to one year of age (about 50 per cent). Each child grows according to her/his potential, and the individual growth trajectory. This tremendous growth reflects the differing growth pattern of all the internal organs.

An infant weighing less than 2.5 kg at birth is termed a low birth weight (LBW) baby.

Table 20.1: Weight and Length Profile of Infants

Age (months)	*Boys*		*Girls*	
	Weight (kg)	*Length (cm)*	*Weight (kg)*	*Length (cm)*
0	3.3	49.9	3.2	49.1
1	4.5	54.7	4.2	53.7
2	5.6	58.4	5.1	57.1
3	6.4	61.4	5.8	59.8
4	7.0	63.9	6.4	62.1
5	7.5	65.9	6.9	64.0
6	7.9	67.6	7.3	65.7
9	8.9	72.0	8.2	70.1
12	9.6	75.7	8.9	74.0

Source: WHO Child Growth Standards, 2007.

Growth and Development

Physical growth and development is accompanied by a number of physiological changes, such as mental development, changes in the gastro-intestinal tract, development of the excretory system, and changes in the body composition. Externally, one can note that at birth, infants can only cry and cannot roll over. At one year, infants can crawl, and are beginning to walk and talk. Similarly, at birth infants can only suck; at one year, they can hold a spoon and even feed themselves. Among the internal physiological changes, the development of the gastro-intestinal tract and kidneys are of particular relevance to nutrition. These internal changes enable the infant to ingest, digest, absorb, and metabolise increasingly complex foods.

Changes in the Gastro-intestinal Tract

A full-term baby has the ability to suck and swallow at birth. In the beginning, these processes are a bit inefficient, but within a few days, the infant is better able to coordinate sucking, swallowing, and even breathing. Until about four to five months of age, all solid objects entering the infant's mouth are pushed out by the action of the tongue. This is how the infant manages to drink milk from the mother's breast or a bottle—sucking the nipple in, drawing the milk out of it, swallowing the milk, and further pushing the nipple out by tongue movement (extrusion reflex). The extrusion reflex also prevents food from being swallowed by the infant up to five to six months of age. In normal infants, the extrusion reflex disappears by six months, after which the infant is able to push food back to her/his mouth for swallowing.

At this stage, spoon-feeding of soft solid food promotes proper swallowing movements. Food in the back of the mouth touches the soft palate of the roof of the mouth, which triggers the swallowing reflex.

The major role of the stomach is to physically and chemically prepare food for digestion. During infancy, the capacity of the stomach and the ability to digest various food components changes rapidly (Figure 20.1). Initially, the infant's stomach is much smaller, shaped differently, and functionally immature compared to older infants. From about 2 tablespoons (30 ml) at birth, the capacity of the stomach increases to 4 tablespoons (55 ml) at two weeks, amd then to 8 tablespoons (120 ml) at three months.

During the first few months of life, foods move more slowly, and are mixed less efficiently in the stomach than they are in later infancy. A full-term baby has the ability to digest simple proteins, carbohydrates and emulsified fats. In a newborn infant, salivary secretion and the production of starch splitting enzymes is not satisfactory. The usual yardstick to introduce starchy foods to infants is when the weight doubles, which in most populations is by five to six months.

Renal System

In early infancy, the renal system is immature—the glomerular filtration is somewhat lower, and therefore the excretion of a high concentration of solutes is more difficult. As the kidney matures, they can handle higher solute loads. Until then, foods with a renal solute load result in higher obligatory water loss and cause dehydration. However, by the end of one year the kidneys reach their functional capacity.

Mental Development

Brain growth and development essentially begins with conception. There is an increase in the brain size. A rapid increase in the number of brain cells occurs in the first five to six months after birth, after which it slows down.

Body Composition

The changes in physical growth are also accompanied by certain alterations in tissue component or lean body mass and adiposity. The total body water decreases from approximately 70 per cent at birth to 60 per cent by age one, while the adipose tissue and lean body mass show a simultaneous increase. At birth, a child has 12–15 per cent fat, and by the end of the first year, it increases to about 24 per cent. The infant synthesises lean tissue, and hence there is an increase in body nitrogen from 2 per cent at birth to 3 per cent at one year of age. Body muscles are also better developed by the age of one.

> The limited capacity of the infant's immature renal system during the first few months of life further justifies delaying the introduction of solid foods till six months of age.

Optimum nutrition during infancy is thus a pre-requisite for laying a sound foundation for good health in later years. The rapid growth and metabolism of the infant demands a large supply of all the nutrients in proportion to their body size. The next section emphasises the energy and nutrient needs during infancy.

ENERGY AND NUTRIENT NEEDS

To keep pace with the very high rate of growth during this period, an infant's requirements of all nutrients are extremely high on the basis of per unit body weight, as compared to an adult (Table 20.2).

As infants are small, they need smaller total amounts of nutrients than adults; however, when comparisons are based on per kg body weight basis, infants need over twice as much of most nutrients. The RDA (ICMR 2010) for Indian infants is given in Table 20.3.

Table 20.2: RDA of Selected Nutrients for a 6-Month-Old Infant and an Adult Sedentary Male on the Basis of Per Kg/Day

Nutrient	*6-month-old Infant*	*Adult Sedentary Male*
Energy (kcal/kg/day)	92	39
Protein (g/kg/day)	1.16	1.0
Calcium (mg/kg/day)	93.3	10.0
Iron (µg/kg/day)	46	28
Vitamin A (Retinol) (µg/kg/day)	65	10

Source: ICMR 2010.

Energy

Energy needs per unit body weight of humans peak during the first year of life because of high basal metabolic rate and growth. For the one-month-old infant, 50 per cent energy intake is used for basal metabolic rate, 25 per cent for activity, and 25 per cent for growth. There is a drop in the energy needs, from 92 kcal/kg body weight during the first six months to 80 kcal/kg body weight per day in the latter six months of infancy. These values continue to drop until they reach the stable figures of adulthood. Nevertheless, the absolute values for energy continue to increase during the same period because of continuous growth, leading to an increase in body weight. Thus, a 6-month-old infant requires 497 kcal / day, as compared to 672 kcal /day of energy at one year of age. The high energy requirements of infancy are necessary for a high normal rate of growth and increasing activity during this period.

Protein

As the body growth is rapid, it is accompanied by the building of large amounts of body tissues. It is therefore necessary to provide proteins of high quality to sustain this rapid building process. The ICMR (2010) has spelt out the safe intake of proteins per kg body weight per day as the sum of maintenance and growth requirements of infants. Just like energy, the protein needs of an infant are also higher, about 1.5 times, on a per kg body weight basis, as compared to an adult (see Table 20.2). The recommendations are 1.16 g / kg body weight during the first six months, going slightly up to 1.69 g / kg body weight in the last six months of infancy.

Dietary protein is required to replace the daily losses of amino acids. An adequate protein intake supplies all nine essential amino acids in adequate amounts for maintenance and growth. The absence of any one can stunt growth. Young infants in India obtain almost all protein from breast milk, or sometimes from artificial feeding on milk.

Thus, the RDA for protein for infants is the same as the amount of protein provided by the quantities of breast milk that ensure an adequate rate of growth.

Protein recommendations are designed for healthy, full-term infants. Infections, premature births, illness, and genetic disorders increase protein requirements. Excess protein is harmful, as its metabolic products need to be de-aminated, and this stresses the kidney and the liver.

Table 20.3: Recommended Dietary Allowances for Indian Infants

Nutrient	Age	
	*0–6 Months (5.4 kg)**	*6–12 Months (8.4 kg)**
Energy (kcal/kg/day)	92	80
Protein (g/kg/day)	1.16	1.69
Visible fat (g/day)	-	19
Calcium (mg/day)	500	500
Iron (mg/day)	46 µg/kg/ day	5
Retinol (µg/day)	350	350
Or, β-carotene (µg/day)	–	2,800
Thiamine (mg/day)	0.2	0.3
Riboflavin (mg/day)	0.3	0.4
Niacin (µg/kg/day)	710	650
Vitamin B_6 (mg/day)	0.1	0.4
Ascorbic acid (mg/day)	25	25
Dietary folate(µg/day)	25	25
Vitamin B_{12} (µg/day)	0.2	0.2

Note: * Figures in brackets give the body weight.

Source: Adapted from the Nutrient Requirements and Recommended Dietary Allowances for Indians (ICMR 2010).

100 ml of breast milk contains 1.1 g of protein, or 6 per cent of the total energy.

Carbohydrates

The main source of all energy for human beings is carbohydrates. Carbohydrates spare protein from being used for energy. The brain relies almost exclusively on carbohydrates for energy. Breast milk provides about 40 per cent energy from carbohydrates, mainly lactose.

Protein Efficiency Ratio (PER): A measure of protein quality assessed by determining how well a given protein supports weight gain in laboratory animals

Fat

The infant requires a high concentration of fat in order to meet the energy demands of this period of rapid growth. Fat supports the normal development of the central nervous system, and helps to maintain body temperature. An adequately breast-fed infant gets nearly 30g fat per day. This amount of fat will contribute to almost 50 per cent of the total energy consumption of a 6-month-old infant. Further, about 10 per cent and 1 per cent of the total fat in breast

Lactose makes up about 90 per cent of the total carbohydrates in breast milk

Human milk is superior to other milk, as its long chain n-6 and n-3 PUFA content are biologically more potent.

milk comprises linoleic and linolenic acid, respectively. These two fatty acids are members of the omega-3 fatty acids family, which cannot be synthesised by the body. Breast milk is a relatively rich source of cholesterol. The essential fatty acid requirement of infants, which is estimated to be around 6 energy %, is largely fulfilled by breast feeding.

Water

One of the most essential nutrients for the infant, as for anyone else, is water. The younger the infant, the greater the percentage of body weight as water. Water from the infant's body can be more easily lost as compared with water in an adult's body. This is because a major amount of the infant's body water is located in the interstitial (extracellular) and vascular spaces. During the first six months, breast milk provides sufficient water for a healthy infant to replace water losses from the body. Under normal conditions, no supplemental water should be given to the baby until the introduction of semi-solid foods. Once the infant is eating solid foods, s/he needs more water than what breast milk can supply.

Minerals

Human milk contains most of the macro and micro elements required for body growth, including those required for the building of strong bones and teeth. The notable exception is the iron content of milk. The infant's need for calcium and iron are comparatively higher than that of an adult.

Calcium and Phosphorus

Calcium RDA during infancy: 500 mg / day
Phosphorus RDA during infancy: 750 mg / day

During infancy, the calcium content of the body increases faster relative to body size than at any other time in the life span. The calcium present in human milk is highly bio-available, and can sustain the rapid growth of the infant. A Calcium : Phosphorus ratio of 1:1.5 is recommended during infancy. Excessive dietary phosphorus relative to calcium may contribute to calcium loss from the bones. Breast milk or cow's milk supplies these minerals in sufficient amounts, if an adequate quantity is taken daily. As the infant grows older, other sources, such as green leafy vegetables and cereals like *ragi* and some pulses, can be added to the diet to meet calcium needs.

Iron

During gestation, the foetus receives high priority when it comes to the available iron, often at the expense of the mother. In fact, iron stores of newborn infants show negligible differences between infants of iron-deficient, anaemic mothers, and infants of iron-sufficient mothers. A normal infant acquires adequate iron stores during the foetal life, which can meet the growth needs for the first four to six months. The recommended iron intake for Indian infants is based on the average intake of healthy infants fed on breast milk. The iron present in breast milk, although negligible, is highly bio-available. As the iron needs of infants increase, the infant's diet must be supplemented with rich sources of iron from the age of six months onwards.

Iron RDA (ICMR, 2010) during infancy:
(0–6 m) - 0.23 mg / day or 46 μg / kg / day
(6–12 m) - 0.73 mg / day or 87 μg / kg / day

Zinc

Adequate zinc intake results in an increase in linear growth and weight gain in stunted and underweight young children. Zinc needs for infants are not well-defined. Infants fed on breast milk have an adequate level of zinc. The zinc concentration of human milk declines as lactation progresses. Colostrum (the first secretions from the mammary gland after birth) contains high levels of zinc, which promotes normal growth.

Iodine

It is an essential micronutrient needed for the synthesis of the thyroid hormone, required for the optimal growth and development of humans. A wide spectrum of disorders, termed iodine deficiency disorders (IDD), are observed in the Indian population. Children born to iodine-deficient mothers suffer from cretinism, psycho-motor defects, impaired coordination, and mental retardation. The ICMR Committee on Recommended Dietary Allowances for Indians (2010) has suggested an intake of 90 µg / day of iodine for 7–12-month-old infants. For infants in 0–6 months age group, breast milk is adequate to meet the iodine needs.

Vitamins

In well-nourished mothers, breast milk furnishes sufficient amount of vitamins, the only exception being vitamin D and perhaps vitamin C. Hence, the breast milk content of various vitamins has been used as the basis for making recommendations. The recommended vitamin allowances for Indian infants are listed in Table 20.3.

Fat-soluble Vitamins

Vitamin A: In the absence of direct evidence, the recommended intakes of infants are computed on the basis of vitamin A intake through breast milk. The average retinol content of breast milk is 41 µg / 100 ml. Assuming a milk intake of 750 ml / day in well-nourished communities, the average intake of vitamin A for the infant will be 308 µg / day. On this basis, the Expert Committee of ICMR (2010) has recommended a daily allowance of 350 µg retinol up to one year of age. The earliest clinical sign of vitamin A deficiency is impaired dark adaptation in the retina, which is difficult to detect in infants. As the deficiency progresses, failure to thrive, apathy, dry skin, and corneal changes appear. Incidence of vitamin A deficiency is high in Indian children, and serum vitamin A levels are generally low.

Vitamin A RDA during infancy (0–12 months):
350 µg retinol / day or 2800 µg β – carotene

Other fat-soluble Vitamins: The ICMR does not give recommendations for vitamins D, E and K for Indian infants. Since vitamin D can be synthesised in the body in adequate amounts through simple exposure to bright sunlight, the ICMR suggests sufficient sunlight exposure as a means of achieving vitamin D supply in the body. A good supply of enough vitamin D during pregnancy benefits the mother, and helps in the satisfactory development of the infant.

Water-soluble Vitamins

The requirements of B-vitamins—thiamine, riboflavin and niacin—are met through breast milk alone in healthy mothers, or from infant formulas. However, Indian mothers from low-income groups secrete only 15 µg thiamine/100 ml milk. With a milk output of 700 ml, the maximum secreted through milk would be 0.14 mg. The ICMR (2010) recommends 0.2 mg/day of thiamine for 0–6 months, and 0.3 mg/day for 6–12 months on the basis of additional calorie allowance.

The riboflavin status of infants of low-income group mothers has been observed to be better than that of their mothers, suggesting that the infants are protected against riboflavin deficiency. However, riboflavin inadequacy, as judged by EGR–AC (erythrocyte glutathione reductase activation test) values, was seen in infants between one to six months who received breast milk containing about 22 µg of riboflavin/100 ml. Here, too, assuming a milk output of 700 ml during the first six months of lactation, it would appear that riboflavin intake of 0.15 mg/day is adequate for the infants. The recommended allowances for Indian infants are 0.3 mg/day and 0.4 mg/day for 0–6 month and 6–12-month-old infants, respectively. These figures are based on the riboflavin calorie ratio of 0.6 mg/1,000 kcal.

In the absence of any information on special needs in infants for niacin, the ICMR committee of 2010 has suggested 710 µg / kg and 650 µg / kg of niacin equivalents for 0–6 month and 6–12 month-old-infants, respectively. The requirement is calculated on the basis of 6.6 mg of niacin/1,000 kcal.

The term B_6 includes three vitamins, pyridoxine, pyridoxal, pyridoxamine, and their phosphorylated derivatives. Deficiency of this vitamin in infants who consumed less than 0.1 mg of vitamin B_6 is associated with neurological symptoms and abdominal stress. The ICMR (2010) recommends 0.1 mg for infants between 0–6 months, and 0.4 mg for 6–12-month-old infants (Table 20.3). The vitamin B_6 content in the breast milk of Indian mothers is observed to be only 60–80 μg / litre.

Two of the B vitamins, folate and vitamin B_{12}, deserve special mention for their critical role in growth and development. Both vitamins perform an essential role in DNA synthesis, and thus support growth. Deficiency of folic acid and vitamin B_{12} leads to abnormal hemopoiesis and megaloblastic anaemia. The deficiency of these vitamins is rare in infants, because they are usually born with stores sufficient for the first year of life, and then receive additional amounts from the mother's milk. The RDA of dietary folate and vitamin B_{12} for Indian infants are 25 μg/day and 0.2 μg/day, respectively (Table 20.3).

Vitamin C

On the basis of the ascorbic acid ingested by breast-fed infants in well-nourished populations, the ICMR suggests 25 mg of ascorbic acid (Table 20.3) for infants. The vitamin C in breast milk is 3 mg/100 ml. Vitamin C deficiency is not observed in infants fed on mother's milk; however, in infants given cow's milk exclusively, signs of a deficiency of this vitamin are noticed. Symptoms of scurvy in infants include anorexia, diarrhoea, failure to gain weight, irritability, and increased susceptibility to infection. In severe deficiency, haemorrhages under the skin and a failure of spontaneous leg movement occur.

GROWTH MONITORING AND PROMOTION

Weighing the child regularly and plotting the weight on the mother and child card is an important tool to monitor the growth of the baby (see Annexure 5). Infants and young children should be weighed every month in the presence of their mothers, and their growth status should be explained to the mother / caretaker.

> Growth monitoring is a tool that helps to identify growth faltering at an early stage, and helps to institute corrective measures so that malnutrition can be prevented.

Besides identifying growth faltering and the growth trends of an infant, it also provides information on health monitoring, such as immunisation, record of infections, and on infant feeding.

FEEDING THE INFANT

Historical Overview of Infant Feeding

Prior to the eighteenth century, breast milk was the only source of nourishment for a newborn infant; satisfactory substitutes were non-existent. The *Charaka Samhita*, a treatise of Indian medicine, talks about the virtues of mother's milk, and has equated it with the nectar of life. In olden days, if the mother was unable to feed the baby, she hired a wet nurse (*dai ma*) to do the needful. Deplorable sanitary conditions, as well as prevailing traditional beliefs, precluded even the thought of using cow's milk to feed her infant.

Around the mid-1700s, women began to adopt the practice of feeding infants a mixture of bread soaked in water or rice cooked in milk once the first tooth had erupted. By the late 1700s, cow's milk was considered an option in the event of the unavailability of mother's milk. At that time, there were limited feeding vessels available. Different cultures devised their own feeding vessels, such as cow's horns, a round brass vessel with a long pouch, a simple cup and spoon prepared from coconut shell, or a cotton swab, etc. By the end of the nineteenth century, the usefulness of glass bottles and the need for cleanliness were recognised.

Formula feeding came into existence as the 'modern', efficient and practical way to feed an infant at the turn of the twentieth century. Formula feeding became a healthy alternative for infants of women who were unable to breastfeed, or had died during childbirth. It may be noted that formula feeding coincided with the shift from home-based childbirth to hospital births, and the associated practice of separating mothers from infants after delivery. Other twentieth-century technological developments also influenced the shift from breast milk to formula. One of the notable developments was to create an infant formula that was similar to human milk.

The sound practice of breastfeeding suffered a setback because of the aggressive media campaign by multinational companies producing baby milk powder and infant foods. The WHO, in the late 1970s, recognised the seriousness of the declining trend in breastfeeding, and introduced an International Code for Protection and Promotion of Breast Feeding in 1981.

Infant Feeding in Today's Context

Proper feeding of infants is necessary to ensure normal growth and development. Infant feeding is much like the infant—constantly changing and dynamic. Infant feeding practices during the first year of life, comprising both breastfeeding and complementary feeding, play a major role in determining the nutritional status of the child. Poor feeding practices in early infancy and early childhood, resulting in malnutrition, contribute to impaired cognitive and social development, poor school performance, and reduced productivity in later life. Optimal infant feeding practices—especially early initiation and exclusive breastfeeding for the first six months of life—help provide young children with the best possible start in life.

Breastfeeding

Nutritional superiority of breast milk: Breast milk has an ideal combination of nutrients, designed by nature to promote the growth and development of infants. Hence, it is the most natural and perfect food for the baby.

> Breastfeeding is an unequalled way of providing ideal food for the health, growth and development of infants; it is also an integral part of the reproductive process with important implications for the health of mothers. As a global public health recommendation, infants should be exclusively breast fed for the first six months of life. Thereafter, to meet their evolving nutritional requirements, infants should receive nutritionally adequate and safe complementary foods while breastfeeding continues up to two years of age or beyond (WHO 2002).

According to the National Infant and Young Child Feeding guidelines (2010), breastfeeding should be promoted to mothers and other caregivers as the gold standard feeding option for babies. The process should be initiated as soon as possible after birth. Colostrum, which is a rich source of nutrients and anti-infective factors, must be fed to the infants and not be discarded. No pre-lacteal fluids—such as honey, glucose solution, or water—should be given to the newborn.

Why should there be an early initiation of breastfeeding?

1. The newborn is very active and alert during the first hour of life, and then goes to sleep. Hence, if the baby is kept with the mother and an effort made to breastfeed, the infant learns sucking very fast. This early suckling by the infant starts the process of milk formation in the mother, and promotes the secretion of breast milk. The production and secretion of milk occurs by stimulating the prolactin and oxytocin reflex. In the case of operative birth, the mother may need motivation and support to initiate breastfeeding within the first hour.
2. It helps in better mother-child bonding and the development of the baby. Skin-to-skin contact between the mother and the newborn helps to provide warmth to the newborn—also called 'Kangaroo Mother Care'.

> Breastfeeding is a learnt behaviour that is most successful in a supportive environment.

3. It ensures the intake of colostrum by the newborn. Colostrum is the first breast milk; it is thicker and yellowish than the later milk, and is secreted only in small amounts in the first few days.
4. It reduces the chances of post-partum haemorrhage in the mother.

Nutritional Quality of Human Milk

The exceptional quality of human milk has been recognised for a long time. Mother's milk is designed for easy digestion and assimilation. Protein in mother's milk comes in a more soluble form, which is easily digested and absorbed by the delicate body system of the baby. Similarly, fat and calcium in human milk are easily absorbable. The milk sugar lactose in mother's milk provides energy. Lactose also facilitates calcium absorption. A part of lactose is converted into lactic acid in the intestine, which destroys the harmful bacteria present there. The amount of vitamins such as thiamine, vitamin A and vitamin C present in mother's milk depends on the maternal diet. Hence, its nutritional quality can be improved by improving the nutritional quality of the mother's diet. The proportion of energy yielding nutrients differs from those recommended for an adult. Figure 20.2 depicts the energy yielding nutrients in human milk and in recommended adult diets.

During the first 10–15 days of lactation, the concentration of proteins, fat-soluble vitamins, minerals, and immunoglobulins decrease, while energy, lactose, fat, and water-soluble vitamins increase. These changing trends reflect the changes in infant needs.

Figure 20.1: Percentage of Energy Yielding Nutrients in an Infant and an Adult Diet

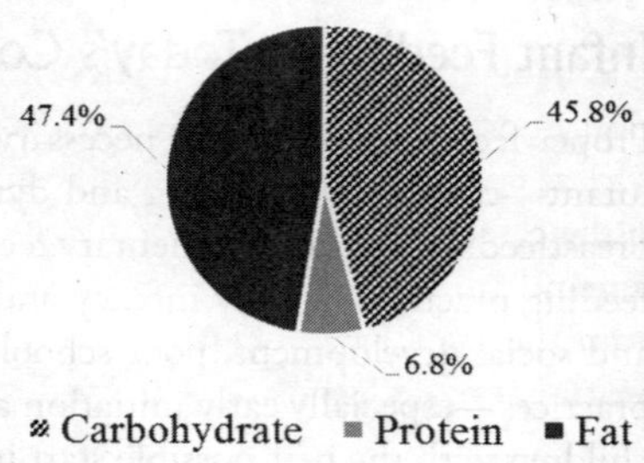

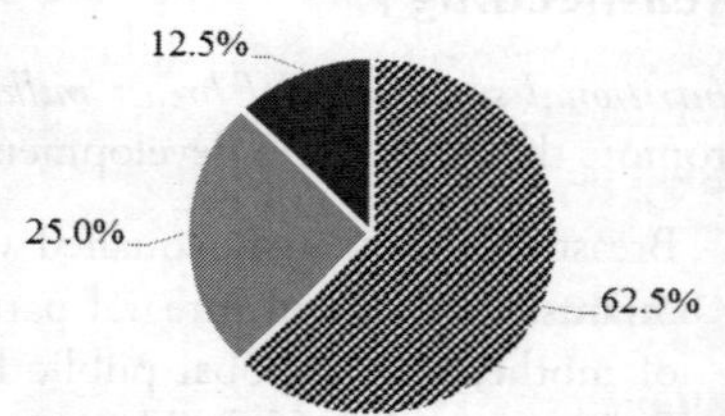

Note: Adult values taken from midpoints of ranges recommended for sedentary adults, that is, 10–15% protein and 20–30% fat calories, and carbohydrates 55–70% by ICMR (2010).

Source: Infant diet based on human milk composition values (Gopalan et al. 1989).

Bifidus Factors

Microbial growth factors, referred to as bifidus factors, are present in both colostrum and breast milk. The bifidus factor favours the growth of the 'friendly' bacteria *Lactobacillus bifidus* in the infant's intestinal tract, which inhibits the growth of potentially harmful bacteria. In this way, the infant is protected from gastric infections.

Why colostrum:

As described earlier, the milk secreted for a few days after childbirth is called 'colostrum'. It is yellowish in colour and sticky. It has a high protein and vitamin A content, and confers immunity against certain infections during the first few months. It has less fat and carbohydrate (lactose) than mature milk.

Advantages of breast milk:

- Breast milk is the best natural food for babies
- Breast milk is always clean
- Breast milk protects the baby from infections
- Breast milk is available 24 hours a day and requires no special preparation
- It establishes mother-infant contact and promotes mother-child bonding
- Breast milk is nature's gift to the infant and does not need to be purchased

It has been observed that the growth performance of exclusively breastfed infants is satisfactory up to six months of age.

Colostrum is basically the first immunisation the child receives from the mother.

- It prolongs the birth interval through the delayed return of menstruation (lactational amenorrhoea)
- Breastfeeding helps in the retracting of the uterus
- Breast milk helps a mother shed some of the extra weight gained during pregnancy
- Incidence of breast cancer is lower in mothers who breastfeed their children
- Breastfeeding is associated with better cognitive development, possibly due to the high content of docosahexaenoic acid (DHA), which plays an important role in brain development.

Process of Breastfeeding

The baby should be fed 'on cues'. Early feeding cues include sucking movements and sucking sounds, hand to mouth movements, rapid eye movements, soft cooing or sighing sounds, lip smacking and restlessness, etc. Crying is a late cue and may interfere with successful feeding. Periodic feeding is practised in certain situations, for instance, in the case of small infants who are likely to become hypoglycemic unless fed regularly, or an infant who 'does not demand' milk in the initial few days. Every mother, particularly the first timers, should receive breastfeeding support from the doctors, nursing staff, or community health workers with respect to the correct position, latching and treatment of problems such as breast engorgement, nipple fissures and delayed 'coming in' of milk.

During the first six months, exclusive breastfeeding should be practised. Breastfeeding is nearly universal in India among the rural and urban poor, but is less common among the middle and upper classes. The poor groups continue breastfeeding for longer durations than economically advantaged or working mothers. Exclusive breastfeeding is a good practice, as it prevents infections.

Since drugs (antibiotics, caffeine, hormones, and alcohol) get secreted into breast milk and could prove harmful to the breast-fed infant, caution should be exercised by the lactating mother.

Complementary Feeding

Complementary feeding is extremely essential from six months of age, while continuing breastfeeding 'ad libitum'. This is necessary to meet the increasing needs of the growing baby. Appropriately thick, homogenous foods made from locally available food supplies should be introduced. During this period, breastfeeding should be actively supported. Besides nutritional considerations, the other factors that influence the introduction of solid foods in an infant's diet at this point in time are:

- *Physical preparedness and willingness to participate in the feeding process.* By the time the baby is six months old, s/he is able to exercise head and neck control, and can sit up with support. Also, the extrusion reflex—thrusting the tongue forward and pushing food out—disappears by this time. In addition, as the infant grows, more specific skills, like learning to grab and putting objects into the mouth, are also acquired, which makes the introduction of solid foods easier. Invariably, the first teeth also erupt at this stage.
- *Physiological readiness.* The capability to digest starchy carbohydrates develops gradually as the infant ages. A very young infant, say two to three months old, will not be in a position to digest starchy foods. Similarly, the infant's kidney function is fairly restricted, which makes the excretion of waste products produced from high amounts of dietary protein or minerals difficult.
- *Reduced risk of allergies to proteins.* In early infancy, the infant's intestinal tract is unable to break down proteins into peptides. Hence, the absorption of proteins from 'top milk' or egg could predispose the infant to future allergies. With age, the intestinal tract develops, and thus the infant's gut is ready to utilise proteins.

To address the issue of a small stomach size, which can accommodate only a limited quantity of food at a time, each meal must be made energy dense by adding sugar/*jaggery* and fats like *ghee*/butter/oil. Additionally, the complementary food must be thick in consistency.

Low energy density of complementary foods given to infants and low frequency of feeding results in inadequate calorie intake, and thus malnutrition.

Another way of improving the density of food is by the process of malting. Malting reduces the viscosity of the foods, and thus the child can eat more at a time. Malting is germinating whole grain cereal or pulse, drying it after germination, and then powdering it. Cereal-pulse food mixes prepared after malting the cereal or pulse will provide more energy to the child.

The flours of germinated cereals that are rich in enzyme alpha-amylase are called Amylase-Rich Flour (ARF). Even small amounts of ARF added to an infant's food will liquefy and reduce the bulk of the cereal-based diets. Mothers can add ARF to foods prepared at home.

The consistency of foods should be appropriate to the developmental readiness of the child in munching, chewing and swallowing. Foods that can pose a choking hazard should be avoided. Introduce granular foods, and do not use mixers/grinders to make food semi-solid/pasty. Table 20.4 illustrates the type of food, texture, frequency, and average amounts that can be given to infants.

Table 20.4: Amount of Food to Offer at Different Ages

Age (months)	*Texture/ Consistency*	*Frequency*(per day)*	*Quantity*
6–8	Thick porridge, well mashed foods	2-3 meals	Start with 2–3 tablespoonfuls
9–11	Finely chopped or mashed foods, and foods that the baby can pick up	3–4 meals	½ bowl
12–23	Family foods, chopped or mashed if necessary	3–4 meals	¾ to one bowl

* In addition the infant should be breastfed. If baby is not breastfed, give in addition 1 – 2 cups of milk per day and 1 – 2 extra meals per day. Depending on appetite, 1-2 snacks can be offered to 9-23 months old children in addition to the meals.

1 bowl = 250 ml

Source: Adapted from Indian Academy of Pediatrics (2010) Indian Pediatrics. 47: 995–1004

Dos and Don'ts of Complementary Feeding

The amounts of food included in Table 20.4 are recommended when the energy density of the meals is about 0.8 to 1.0 kcal/g. If the energy density of the meal is about 0.6 kcal/g, it is recommended that the energy density be increased by adding special foods, or that the amount of food per meal be increased.

- Food supplements must be introduced in small quantities and one at a time. As the infant grows accustomed to foods other than milk, the quantity and variety can be subsequently increased.
- Parents must identify the staple homemade food comprising a cereal-pulse mixture with locally available products.
- Feed supplements 5–6 times a day.
- The food should be a 'balanced food' incorporating different food groups/components in different combinations.
- Give an extra dash of fat in one or two food items. Do not use excessive fat, salt or sugar.
- Iron-fortified foods, iodised salt, and vitamin A-enriched foods are to be encouraged.
- Avoid junk and commercial foods. Avoid giving readymade processed food from the market, such as canned food/juices, aerated drinks, chocolates, health drinks, ice creams, etc.
- Follow hygienic practices for food safety during the entire process of complementary feeding, viz., preparation, storage and feeding.

- Practice responsive feeding. Young children should be encouraged to take food by praising both them and their food. Self-feeding should be encouraged, despite spillage. Force-feeding, threatening and punishment interfere with the development of proper feeding behaviour.
- It is best to avoid pacifiers and bottle feeding. Research has, time and again, proved these to be harmful to the infant's health.
- Do not leave the baby's food standing for long hours. Micro-organisms may grow, which can make the child ill.

The infant masters the art of swallowing over time, so be patient. Spitting does not mean that s/he does not like the food. Rather, it indicates that the infant has yet to achieve the full coordination required for swallowing.

Artificial Milk Feeding

Although no milk can be a real substitute for mother's milk, sometimes there is a need to look for alternative milk to feed the infant. For children less than six months of age, alternatives to breastfeeding include:

- Expressed, heat-treated breast milk.
- Unmodified animal milk
- Commercial infant formula milk

(a) *Animal milks*: A variety of animal milks—from cows, buffaloes and goats—are available for feeding infants. In cities, packed pasteurised milk is the most widely available. This milk has a standardised fat and solid content, and is provided at an economical cost through various milk schemes. The nutrient composition of each milk is different (Table 20.5).

Cow's milk is the closest substitute for human milk in terms of composition. The fat content of buffalo milk can be reduced by separating the cream from the milk after boiling and cooling. In practice, it is not advisable to dilute the milk with water to make it suitable for infant feeding. Infants receiving such milk feeds need additional water supplementation, as opposed to exclusively breastfed infants, who do not require any water.

Table 20.5: Nutrient Comparison of Human Milk with Other Milks (Per 100 g)

Nutrient	*Human Milk*	*Cow's Milk*	*Buffalo's Milk*	*Toned Milk*
Water (g)	88	87.5	81	-
Energy (kcal)	65	67	117	58
Protein (g)	1.1	3.2	4.3	3.2
Carbohydrate (g)	7.4	4.4	5	4.7
Fat (g)	3.4	4.1	6.5	3.0
Calcium (mg)	28	120	210	118
Phosphorus (mg)	11	90	130	–
Iron (mg)	–	0.2	0.2	–
Vitamin A (μg)	41	53	48	–
Thiamine (mg)	0.02	0.05	0.04	–
Riboflavin (mg)	0.02	0.19	0.10	–
Caseinogen : Lactalbumin (ratio)	1.2	3.1	–	–
Vitamin C (mg)	3	2	1	–

Source: Gopalan et al. 1989.

The infant can be given any milk available in the family. It is increasingly being accepted that the mode of feeding should not be a bottle, but a cup and spoon. Many traditional infant feeding tools are used across India, which are convenient and easy to clean. Research has, time and again, proved the hazards of bottle feeding. Hence, bottle feeding should be discouraged at all levels.

(b) *Commercial standard infant formula*: National and international standards have been established for the nutrient content of infant formulas. The composition and instructions on how to use infant formulas are displayed on the label of the container. Labelling regulations now specify how the nutrient content and preparation must be listed on the labels. In May 1981, the World Health Assembly adopted an International Code of Marketing of breast milk substitutes. The Government of India also accepted this code for implementation in our country.

Under this code, an 'infant formula' means a breast milk substitute formulated industrially in accordance with applicable ISI standards, to satisfy the normal nutritional requirements between 4–6 months of age, and adapted to their physiological characteristics. The commercial infant formulas are based on alterations in cow's milk, so as to bring it as close as possible in composition to human milk. It is a non-fat cow's milk base, to which are added vegetable oils, lactose, vitamins, and minerals. Some formulas also use whey proteins. The preparation of the formula must be according to the proportions indicated, as well as follow strict hygienic measures.

Feeding in Difficult Circumstances

a. *Malnourished infants*: Infants who are malnourished are mostly found in environments where improving the quality and quantity of food is especially problematic. To prevent recurrence and to overcome the effects of chronic malnutrition, these children require extra care, both during the early rehabilitation phase and over the long term. Continued breastfeeding and, when necessary, re-lactation are important preventive steps, since malnutrition often has its origin in inadequate or disrupted breastfeeding.

   Safe and nutritionally adequate complementary food is advised, but at times may be difficult to obtain. Dietary supplements may be required for such children.

b. *Infant feeding in maternal illness*: Painful and / or infective breast conditions like breast abscess and mastitis, and psychiatric illness, which pose dangers to the child's life, may need a temporary cessation of breastfeeding. Treatment of the primary condition should be initiated, and breastfeeding resumed as soon as possible.

   Chronic infections like tuberculosis and leprosy, or medical conditions like hypothyroidism, require treatment of the primary condition, and do not warrant any discontinuation of breastfeeding.

   Breastfeeding is contraindicated if the mother is on certain drugs, like antineoplastic agents, immunosuppressants and atropine, etc.

c. *Pre-term and low birth weight infants*: Infants born before 37 weeks of gestation, low birth weight (LBW) or very low birth weight (less than 1.5 kg at birth), require special care in feeding, depending upon the extent of their prematurity. The relatively larger ones can suckle fairly well at the breast, and therefore should be breastfed. However, in very LBWs, alternative methods of feeding can be used, based on the neuro-developmental status. The alternatives include feeding the expressed mother's milk though intra-gastric tube, or with a cup and spoon. There is evidence showing that a pre-term mother's milk is well-suited to meet the needs for such an infant. Both the nutrient

> Pre-term milk contains higher concentrations of protein, and is lower in volume than term milk.

> **LBW:** A birth weight of less than 2.5 kg
>
> **Very LBW:** A birth weight of less than 1.5 kg
>
> **Pre-term infant:** An infant born prior to the 37th week of gestation, also called **premature infant**
>
> **Small for gestational age (SGA) babies:** Those who are smaller in size than the normal for the gestational age, most commonly defined as a weight below the 10th percentile for the gestational age.

concentration and milk volume differ from the term mother's milk to meet the specific needs of the pre-term infant. A pre-term baby should be fed every two hours, both day and night.

Breast milk is particularly important for pre-term infants and babies with low birth weight. The LBWs are at increased risk of infection, long-term ill health, and even death if breast milk is not available. Special formulas having higher concentrations of protein, minerals and vitamins can be given.

d. *Gastro-Esophageal Reflux Disease (GERD)*: Mild GERD is also treated conservatively through thickening the complementary foods, frequent small feeds, and upright positioning for 30 minutes after feeds.

e. *Lactose intolerance*: Primary lactose intolerance is congenital, and may require long-term lactose restriction. Secondary lactose intolerance is usually transient and resolves after the underlying gastro-intestinal tract (GIT) condition has remitted. Soya formulas are recommended for infants with lactose intolerance.

   Some infants with milk allergies are also allergic to soya protein. An infant with multiple food allergies or chronic diarrhoea may require hydrolysate formula. In a hydrolysate formula, casein is hydrolysed to amino acids and small peptides to permit easy absorption.

f. *Inborn errors of metabolism:* These warrant the restriction of specific offending agents and certain dietary modifications, for example, in galactosemia, dietary lactose and galactose should be avoided. This is probably the only contraindication to breastfeeding.

g. *Feeding in maternal HIV:* Current WHO recommendations advocate that all mothers known to be HIV-infected should be provided with anti-retroviral therapy or anti-retroviral (ARV) prophylaxis to reduce mother to child transmission, and in particular, to reduce post-natal transmission through breastfeeding. The national guidelines (2010) suggest that mothers who are known to be HIV negative or whose HIV status is unknown, or infants of HIV-positive mothers known to be HIV-infected, should exclusively breastfeed their babies for the first six months of life, and then introduce complementary foods while continuing breastfeeding for 12 months or beyond.

   Infants whose mothers are on anti-retroviral therapy or prophylaxis should receive Nevirapine (an anti-retroviral drug) daily, from birth until one week, after all exposure to breast milk has ended.

If a HIV-positive mother chooses not to breastfeed in spite of receiving ARV prophylaxis, etc., an alternative feeding described earlier is advocated. Risk factors during breastfeeding, which increase transmission, include breast pathology like sore nipples or even subclinical mastitis, which are curable problems. All HIV-positive mothers should receive extensive counselling on all aspects of infant nutrition and feeding.

Infantile colic is defined as episodes of crying for more than three hours a day for more than three days a week for three weeks in an otherwise healthy young infant. Along with high-pitched crying, the associated symptoms may include legs pulled up to the stomach, a flushed face and clenched hands. The cause is relatively difficult to diagnose, but the infant may be colicky if s/he is unable to digest food well, and there is production of excessive flatulence and hence abdominal pain. Infants fed formula milk, those weaned early, or fed sugary beverages are known to suffer from colic more frequently than exclusively breastfed babies.

Mothers of breastfed infants are advised to eat hypoallergenic diets, avoiding foods like wheat, egg, nuts, etc. The diet of the infant is otherwise scrutinised to identify what could possibly be causing an allergy or indigestion by a process of elimination of suspected foods. The problem needs to be examined by suitable laboratory investigations if it does not resolve, or if other symptoms appear, like vomiting, change in stool, or poor weight gain.

NUTRITION-RELATED HEALTH PROBLEMS

Diarrhoea

Diarrhoea refers to the passage of frequent loose, watery stools. It is also characterised by abdominal pain, cramping, and sometimes fever and vomiting. Such bowel movements indicate that the chyme has moved too quickly through the intestines for fluid absorption to take place, or that water has been drawn from the cells lining the intestinal tract and added to food residue. In both situations, the outcome is the same—extensive fluid and electrolyte losses. In cases of untreated diarrhoea, or if the duration of diarrhoeal episodes is long, an infant can quickly become dehydrated. The smaller and younger the child, the more life-threatening the condition. Nearly every child suffers from diarrhoea at one time or another.

Worldwide, nearly 500 million children are affected annually, and it is the leading cause of morbidity and mortality in children under five. In India, a large proportion of children suffer from malnutrition and acute diarrhoea, seriously threatening their nutritional status. With repeated episodes of diarrhoea falling close together, infants have little time to recover between bouts. A majority of cases occur due to pathogenic organisms, which include viruses, bacteria and parasites. The exclusively breastfed infants are well-protected against episodes of diarrhoea, but the incidence rises as the infant reaches the age of 6–11 months, and thereafter. During this period, foods other than breast milk are introduced in the diet of the baby. Additionally, the infant also starts exploring the environment on her/his own. The chances of picking up an infection from contaminated food or through direct contact with unhygienic/faecal matter are very high at this stage.

Well-nourished children with acute diarrhoeas can usually endure the uncomfortable symptoms without medical aid. Their nutrient reserves protect them from the detrimental effects of diarrhoea. Caregivers can support the infants during such episodes of diarrhoea by eliminating food irritants from the diet, offering clear fluids, and encouraging rest. Fruit juices aggravate diarrhoea, and therefore should be avoided. Foods with soluble fibre, such as rice gruel, oats and banana may help reduce diarrhoea.

For the malnourished child, frequent episodes of diarrhoea lead to further worsening of the nutritional status, which in turn makes them even more vulnerable to infections. Also, the means for nutritional restoration between the intervening periods of infection are hardly available to the majority of the poor, underprivileged children in our country. Thus, they continue to be in the grip of a vicious cycle of infection–malnutrition–infection (Figure 20.2).

Figure 20.2: Vicious Cycle of Malnutrition and Diarrhoea

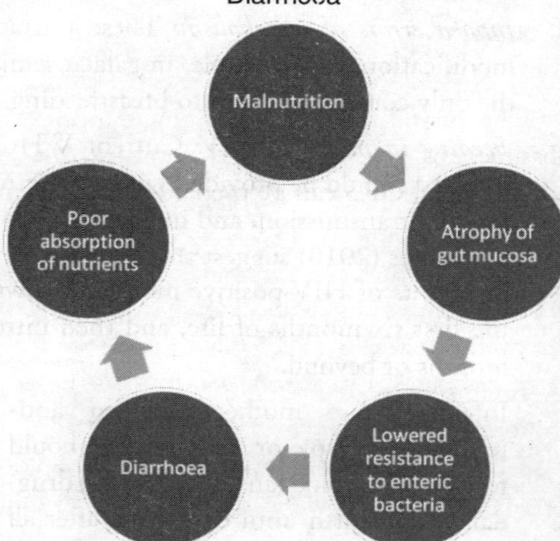

Source: Adapted from O. P. Ghai.

To Feed or Not To Feed

As in any other illness, diarrhoea can reduce the appetite of the child considerably, resulting in the baby's refusal to eat properly. In addition, the mother often withholds food during diarrhoea, fearing that the disease may become more severe. The notion of restricting food during diarrhoea does not merit medical approval. In such cases, mothers should be educated to feed the infant properly. The dietary considerations include:

1. Mothers to continue breastfeeding, especially if the infant is breastfed, or alternatively, give diluted top milk feeds.
2. Give well mashed, non-spicy foods that are easy to digest, such as well-cooked rice and *dal* preparations, thick blended soups, eggs and fish, etc.
3. Foods rich in potassium, such as mashed bananas, potatoes and carrots are advisable.
4. An infant should be fed as much as s/he wants, and at least five to seven times a day.
5. As soon as the diarrhoea begins, give the infant more fluids than usual, for example rice water *(kanjee),* coconut water, buttermilk, *dal* soup, fresh lime water, or any other fluid available at home and acceptable to the child.

6. Give oral rehydration salt solution (ORS) to the child. This helps in the prevention and control of dehydration, resulting from fluid and electrolyte losses in the stools during diarrhoea.

What is ORS?

ORS is a solution prepared from sugar and salt dissolved in water. The WHO recommended that oral rehydration salt (ORS) packets be freely available at primary health centres, sub-centres, or at pharmacies. The contents of the packets are to be dissolved in 1 litre of drinking water. The solution must be made fresh daily, and used within 24 hours.

Composition of ORS (WHO/UNICEF Formula)*

Sodium chloride	2.6 g
Trisodium citrate, dehydrate	2.9 g
Potassium chloride	1.5 g
Glucose	13.5 g
Potable Water	1000 ml (1 litre)

The infant should be fed the solution as frequently as possible, and after every loose stool. If the WHO packets are not available, ORS can be prepared at home, in the following manner:

Take one litre of clean water, add a three-finger pinch (5 g) of common salt and a four-finger scoop (20 g) of sugar, and mix well (Figure 20.3).

Infants with diarrhoea usually tolerate breast milk well, and breastfeeding can alternate with ORS.

Figure 20.3: Preparation of Oral Rehydration Mixture

Three – finger pinch of common salt

Four – finger scoop of sugar

Salt and sugar should be added in one litre of water

Pre-term Infants

As described earlier, the terms pre-term and premature refer to a shortened gestation period, as a result of which there is incomplete foetal development or immaturity of many body systems. These infants have an inadequately mineralised skeleton and poorly developed body tissues. The rate of weight gain in the foetus is greater during the last trimester of gestation than at any other time in the life span. Therefore, a pre-term infant is mostly an LBW baby as well. With premature birth, the infant is deprived of the nutritional support of the placenta during the period of maximum growth. As age advances and there is catch up or rapid weight gain, there are high chances of obesity and diabetes at later periods in life. Indian data shows that this contributes to three times a higher risk of Coronary Heart Disease during adulthood.

> The ORS provides an optimal glucose concentration, which favours rapid intestinal absorption of water and sodium. As a result, it effectively reverses dehydration, but may not correct diarrhoea.

> Colas, juices and sports drinks are not appropriate for Oral Rehydration Therapy.

In view of this, pre-term infants need proper care and nutrition for them to remain on their optimal course of growth. Measures would include keeping the babies warm, feeding colostrum, breastfeeding exclusively for the first six months, and providing iron supplements, as these infants have poor iron stores at birth.

Undernutrition

Under-nutrition is a major problem in India. It is caused by an overall less than adequate intake of nutrients, most of which are related to the gross energy intake. Hence, it is also called chronic energy deficiency, or failure to thrive

(FTT). According to NFHS–3 (2005–06), the prevalence of underweight children under the age of three is 40 per cent. It is the major underlying cause for about 50 per cent of the under-5 mortality in India each year. The consequence of prolonged energy deficit is a reduced body size. This, later in adult life, results in the reduction in body size, which in turn has been associated with poor work capacity.

The contributing factors of under-nutrition among these infants are household food insecurity and unequal intra-household food distribution, delayed introduction of quality, complementary food and inadequate quantity, and poor preventive and curative health services. The family of an FTT infant lives with financial instability in overcrowded or substandard housing, and often with emotional discord. Mothers of undernourished children are less affectionate and less verbal with infants. Undernourished infants are also less intelligent than normal healthy babies. The treatment of FTT usually includes medical, nutritional and social interventions.

Overnutrition / Obesity

Rapid growth during early infancy results in subsequent obesity. Growth studies show that weight gain in breastfed infants is slower than in formula-fed ones. There is also evidence that the growth rate during infancy can influence subsequent weight gain and BMI. This has led to the hypothesis that breastfeeding protects against obesity, while formula feeding may increase the risk. The chances of obesity are least if an infant is exclusively breastfed till six months of age. In infants between 6–12 months, excessive feeding of fat and sugar can lead to an upward shift of the growth curve. In the event of overshooting the normal growth curve, only visible fat and sugar intake needs to be controlled. An infant is never put on a reducing diet. Consistent moderation is the best strategy instead of a restricted diet, as fat is needed for the growth and development of the organs and the brain.

Obesity in infancy is the recently emerging nutritional problem in Indian society. Its far-reaching effects lend urgency to the need to find a remedy.

SUMMARY

- Infancy is a period of rapid growth and development. The foundation of future health is laid during the first year of life. Each child grows according to her/his potential, and individual progress is noted to record growth and development.
- Nutritional needs are the highest per unit of body weight in the first year of life, as compared to the subsequent years of growth up to adulthood. The high energy needs are due to high BMR, growth and activity. With body growth, the building of a large amount of tissues also takes place. It is therefore necessary to provide protein of good quality to sustain the building process.
- Exclusive breastfeeding is the best way to feed an infant in the first six months. Mothers need active encouragement and emotional support from caregivers.
- Breastfeeding provides development and learning opportunities to the infant, stimulating all five senses of the child, and fosters emotional security and affection.
- Realising the seriousness of the declining trend in breastfeeding, the WHO in 1981 introduced an International Code for Protection of Breastfeeding. The Indian government adopted it in 1983. The first National Guidelines on Infant and Young Child Feeding (IYCF) were formulated in 2004, and revised in 2010.
- The time of introduction of complementary foods is a vulnerable period for the infant. A wide variety of foods available in the family should be introduced to the infant to ensure nutritional adequacy. Strict hygiene should be maintained to avoid infections.
- Pre-term babies need special care during the first year of life. They are born with reduced nutritional stores and have limited nutrient absorption capacity and excretory functions. The goal for the management of premature or LBW babies is to provide optimal nutrition that corrects deficiencies, and promotes growth and development.

- There are certain pathological situations where a mother cannot breastfeed her infant. In such conditions, alternative feeding should be resorted to.
- HIV may be transmitted from mother to infant through breast milk. However, in certain situations, especially in countries like India, women may not have access to safe, hygienic and affordable replacement feeding options. Under such circumstances, every effort should be made to promote exclusive breastfeeding for up to six months in case of HIV-positive mothers. Thereafter, complementary feeding can be initiated. Discontinuation of breastfeeding at six months is suggested to reduce the transmission of HIV.
- During an episode of diarrhoea, the baby requires prompt correction of fluid and electrolyte loss, using ORS along with appropriate and adequate feeding.

KEY WORDS

Amylase-Rich Flour (ARF): The flours of germinated cereals, which are rich in enzyme alpha-amylase.

Colostrum: The milk secreted after childbirth for the first few days. It is yellowish in colour and sticky.

Complementary feeding: Food other than breast milk, given to the infant preferably after six months of age. It marks the transition from exclusive breastfeeding to family foods in the diet of an infant.

Gastro-Esophageal Reflux Disease (GERD): Refers to the disease in which the stomach contents/acid rise up the esophagus, causing a burning sensation.

Low birth weight: Birth weight less than 2.5 kg.

Oral rehydration salt solution (ORS): Helps in the prevention and control of dehydration, resulting from fluid and electrolyte losses in the stools during diarrhoea. It is made up of sugar and salts dissolved in water.

Premature: Born before 37 weeks of gestation.

Small for gestational age: Those babies who are smaller in size than normal for the gestational age, most commonly defined as a weight below the 10th percentile for the gestational age.

Very Low birth weight: Birth weight less than 1.5 kg.

EXERCISES

1. Define the term infancy. Describe the process of growth and development during infancy.
2. Give the RDAs of an infant aged three months and nine months.
3. Compare and contrast the nutritional needs of a child in the first year of life with those of an adult.
4. What is colostrum? Why is it important for a baby?
5. Compare the nutrient composition of human milk with that of cow's milk.
6. Breast milk is the best milk. Explain.
7. What is complementary feeding? Explain the factors that influence the initiation of solid foods.
8. Who is a pre-term infant? Discuss the nutritional management of a pre-term infant.
9. Discuss the nutritional management of an infant with diarrhoea.

10 Write short notes on under-nutrition and obesity in infancy.

REFERENCES

Byrd-Bredbenner, Carol, Gaile Moe, Denna Beshgetoor, and Jacqueline Berning, 'Nutrition Applications in Life Cycle', in *Wardlaw's Perspectives in Nutrition*, 9e, New York: McGraw-Hill International, 2013.

Ghai, O. P., *Understanding and Managing Acute Diarrhea in Infants and Young Children*, New Delhi: All India Institute of Medical Sciences.

Gopalan, C., B. V. Ramasastri and S. C. Balasubramanian, *Nutritive Value of Indian Foods*, Hyderabad: NIN, ICMR, 1989.

'IAP Infant and Young Child Feeding Guidelines', I. Y. C. F. Chapter, Indian Academy of Pediatrics, *Indian Pediatrics* 47, 2010, pp. 995-1004. Available at http://medind.nic.in/ibv/t10/i12/ibvt10i12p995.pdf.

ICMR, *Nutrient Requirements and Recommended Allowances for Indians*, Hyderabad: ICMR, 2010.

India: Situation Analysis for Transform Nutrition. Available at http://www.transformnutrition.org/files/2011/11/India_situation_analysis.pdf.

National Guidelines, on Infant and Young Child Feeding, New Delhi: Ministry of Women and Child Development, Food and Nutrition Board, GOI, 2006.

Narasinga Rao, B. S. Y. G. Deosthale and K. C. Pant, *Nutritive Value of Indian Foods*, rev. edn, Hyderabad: NIN, ICMR, 2004.

NIN, *Dietary Guidelines for Indians—A Manual*, 2e, Hyderabad: NIN, ICMR, 2011.

Reddy, V., *Infant Feeding and Obesity: Nutrition Foundation of India*. Available at http://nutritionfoundationofindia.res.in/.

Rodwell Williams, Sue, Bonnies Worthington Roberts, Eleanor D. Schlenker, Peggl Pipes, and Jane Mitchell Rees, *Nutrition Throughout the Life Cycle*, Moshy Year Book, 1992.

Rolfes, Rady, Sharon, Linda Kelly DeBruyne and Eleanor Noss Whitney, 'Breast Milk, Infant Formula and Lactation; in *Nutrition During Infancy in Life Span Nutrition, Conception Through Life*, 2e., West / Words Worth, 1998.

The HUNGAMA Survey Report—2011, Nandi Foundation, 2011. Available at http://hungamaforchange.org/HungamaBKDec11LR.pdf.

Wadhwa, Arvind and Sushma Sharma, *Nutrition in the Community—A Text Book*, Elite Publishing House Pvt. Ltd, 2013.

WHO, *Complementary Feeding: Family Foods for Breast Fed Children*, WHO / NHB / 001, Geneva: WHO, 2000.

21

NUTRITION FOR PRESCHOOLERS

HIGHLIGHTS

- Physical, cognitive, emotional, and social development during preschool years
- Nutrient needs among preschool children
- Developing healthy eating habits among preschoolers
- Importance of physical activity during preschool years
- Problem of Under-nutrition and Over-nutrition

The years between a child's first and fifth birthdays represent a period of rapid physical, social, intellectual, and emotional growth. Although the overall rate of physical growth is less than that during infancy, it is nonetheless an important phase of growth and development. Motor skills are fine-tuned during this period, and preschoolers are busy exploring the environment. During these years, children change from clumsy toddlers into lively explorers of their world.

GROWTH AND DEVELOPMENT

The term 'growth' denotes a net increase in the size or mass of tissues. The process starts from the time of conception and continues till adulthood. Growth continues at a rapid rate in preschool years, but is slower than growth during infancy. During the second year, the increase in height is about 12–15 cm and weight gain about 2.5 kg, as against almost 25 cm and about 6 kg in the first year. Between the ages of two to five, children, on an average, gain about 2 kg and about 7–10 cm per year (Table 21.1). Gains in height and weight occur in 'spurts'. Prior to a growth spurt, appetite and food intake increases, and the child puts on a little weight. During a spurt in growth, these energy stores are utilised to provide energy for an increase in height.

Table 21.1: Median Weights and Lengths of Children between 0–60 Months

	Boys		*Girls*	
Age in months	*Weight (kg)*	*Length (cm)*	*Weight (kg)*	*Length (cm)*
0	3.3	49.9	3.2	49.1
1	4.5	54.7	4.2	53.7
2	5.6	58.4	5.1	57.1
3	6.4	61.4	5.8	59.8
4	7.0	63.9	6.4	62.1
5	7.5	65.9	6.9	64.0
6	7.9	67.6	7.3	65.7

Table 21.1 contd

Table 21.1 contd

	Boys		Girls	
Age in months	*Weight (kg)*	*Length (cm)*	*Weight (kg)*	*Length (cm)*
7	8.3	69.2	7.6	67.3
8	8.6	70.6	7.9	68.7
9	8.9	72.0	8.2	70.1
10	9.2	73.3	8.5	71.5
11	9.4	74.5	8.7	72.8
12	9.6	75.7	8.9	74.0
18	10.9	82.3	10.2	80.7
24	12.2	87.8	11.5	86.4
30	13.3	91.9	12.7	90.7
36	14.3	96.1	13.9	95.1
42	15.5	99.9	15.0	99.0
48	16.3	103.3	16.1	102.7
54	17.3	106.7	17.2	106.2
60	18.3	110.0	18.2	109.4

Source: WHO Reference Values (MGRS 2006).

However, growth rates vary considerably for each individual child. This is thought to be associated with a variety of factors, including the parent's growth history. As long as the trend of the growth curve is maintained in the positive direction, there is no need to worry.

Body Composition

By the time the child reaches two years of age, much of the baby fat is lost, the muscles—especially in the back, buttocks and legs—are strengthened, and the leg bones lengthen. The increase in the length of bones and strengthening of muscles is obvious in the increase in height and strength of muscles. Bone mass as well as density continues to increase. As the child continues to grow, protein deposition continues, and other tissues, including connective tissues, teeth, body fat, skin, and the nervous system, also grow.

Physical and Motor Development

Preschoolers strive for independence and gain competence in various activities. They should be encouraged to participate in active play, as it provides an opportunity to develop gross motor coordination. By two years of age, most children can move up the stairs one at a time, draw simple strokes with a pencil, and kick a ball. By age five, they can tie their shoe laces, dress and undress themselves, write some lowercase and capital letters, and can pour milk. Since preschoolers cannot sit still for more than a few minutes, foods of appropriate texture and consistency should be chosen for them, which enhance the ease of eating. Finger foods, which the preschooler can easily hold and eat while playing or doing some other activity, are recommended.

Language

Preschool is an important time for language development. A 2-year-old can speak at least 50 words, and the child may know thousands of words by the time s/he is five years old. Preschoolers are able to carry on conversations and tell stories. A 2-year-old can begin to communicate with yes/no, or equivalent words about what they want/ do not want to eat. By three, a preschooler can verbally request for certain food items that they would like to eat. They start learning from peers and the media, and express their food preferences clearly from three to four years onwards.

Cognitive Development

Preschool years mark great improvements in the ability to think and reason. It is around this time that children learn their letters, counting and colours. They are usually inquisitive, asking 'Why' for everything. The kitchen provides an opportunity for experiments, crafts, and participation in food preparation. They are comfortable with the familiar, but are willing to try new challenges. Food fads are common at this time. Preschoolers may complain or whine about what is served; refuse certain foods, especially vegetables, pulses and meats; and push foods around the plate. This is known as 'picky eating'. But the good thing is that picky eating is temporary. Although variety may be limited while the fad persists, the preschooler is gradually expanding their food choices.

Emotional and Social Development

Between the ages of two and five, preschoolers gradually learn how to manage their feelings. This is the time when peers become increasingly important. Most preschool children like sharing food with friends and caregivers.

> Preschool years mark rapid physical, social, intellectual, and emotional growth. Preschoolers strive for independence and gain competence in various activities.

Each child grows and gains skills at her/his own pace. It is common for a child to be ahead in one area, such as language, but a little behind in another.

NUTRIENT NEEDS

Energy: Weight gain for growth, in addition to Total Energy Expenditure, forms the basis of energy requirement during preschool years. In the absence of any data on the energy expenditure of Indian children, ICMR (2010) has used the energy expenditure data computed by FAO/WHO/UNU (2004), based on body weight. Year-wise energy requirements for boys and girls who have attained the 95th percentile of weight for age and undertake moderate physical activity have been computed. However, RDA for this age group is given under two age categories: 1–3 years and 4–6 years (see Table 21.2). When feeding undernourished children, the actual weight should not be used for computing energy requirements.

Protein: Safe intake of proteins is the sum of maintenance and growth requirements. The ICMR (2010) has adopted FAO/WHO/UNU (2007) values of maintenance (0.66 g/kg/d) and growth (adjusted for efficacy of utilisation of 58 per cent.

However, since the traditional Indian diet is predominantly vegetarian, its protein quality is low. Taking the digestibility of protein at 85 per cent for traditional Indian diets, the PDCAAS (Protein Digestibility Corrected Amino Acid Score) is assumed at 77.4 for the 3–10 year age group while giving the RDA. The final RDA for protein is 16.7g/d for 1–3 years olds, and 20.1g/d for 4–6 year olds.

Fats: Fat requirement up to two years of age can be between 30–40 per cent of the total energy, and thereafter at 15–30 per cent of the total energy intake. This translates into visible fat intake of 27g/d for 1–3-year-old children and 25g/d for 4–6-year-old children.

Table 21.2: RDA for Various Nutrients for Preschool Children

Nutrient	*1–3-year-old Child*	*4–6-year-old Child*
Energy (kcal/d)	1,060	1,350
Protein (g/d)	16.7	20.1
Visible fat (g/d)	27	25
Calcium (mg/d)	600	600
Iron (mg/d)	09	13

Table 21.2 contd

Table 21.2 contd

Nutrient	*1–3-year-old Child*	*4–6-year-old Child*
Zinc (mg/d)	5	7
Magnesium (mg/d)	50	70
Vitamin A (Retinol µg/d)	400	400
Vitamin A (Carotene µg/d)	3,200	3,200
Thiamin (mg/d)	0.5	0.7
Riboflavin (mg/d)	0.6	0.8
Niacin equivalent (mg/d)	8	11
Vitamin B_6 (mg/d)	0.9	0.9
Ascorbic acid (mg/d)	40	40
Dietary folate (µg/d)	80	100
Vitamin B_{12} (µg/d)	0.2–1.0	0.2–1.0

Source: ICMR 2010.

Calcium: The requirements of children are calculated on the basis of the amount of calcium retained in the body during the period of growth. Calcium balance studies (short term), establishing an almost linear relationship between intake, excretion and retention, provide a strong basis for current requirements. Considering the retention of about 125mg for longitudinal bone growth and about 30 mg/d for sweat losses, the total retained calcium needed to meet the requirements of 3–9-year-old children is 200 mg/d. To obtain this level of retention, 600mg of dietary calcium intake is considered sufficient, assuming 33 per cent absorption.

Iron: During preschool years, iron requirements cover, in addition to basal losses, requirements for growth. Growth requirements refer to the requirements for the expansion of blood volume, lean muscle mass, and for building body iron stores. Table 21.3 summarises iron requirements for each of these components and the final RDA, assuming 5 per cent absorption from the diet.

Table 21.3: Iron Requirements during Preschool Years

Age	*Basal loss (mg/d)*	*Growth (mg/d)*	*Total (mg/d)*	*Absorption Assumed (%)*	*RDA for Iron (mg/d)*
1–3 years	0.181	0.270	0.451	5	9
4–6 years	0.253	0.380	0.633	5	13

Source: ICMR 2010.

Zinc: Since zinc requirements and the RDA based on balance and factorial data closely correspond to FAO/WHO recommendations, ICMR (2010) has adopted the figures recommended for different age and physiological groups along the lines of the FAO/WHO Expert Committee. In addition, since zinc supplementation has been found to reduce the duration and severity of diarrhoeal episodes, the routine use of zinc supplementation, at a dosage of 20 milligrams per day for children older than six months, or 10mg per day in those younger than six months, for 10–14 days, is generally recommended.

Vitamin A: For computing vitamin A requirements, data are interpolated from those of infants (50 µg/kg) and adults (9.3 µg/kg), taking into account growth rates at different ages. The interpolation results show that the vitamin A requirements of children range between 300–400µg retinol / day. While considering the RDA for preschool children, the ICMR (2010) reviewed studies showing that vitamin A deficiency is common at intakes below 100 µg/d, and that deficiency was rarely observed in children getting 300 µg/d. Field-level studies among 1–6-year-old children also indicate that no deficiency signs were observed at intakes ranging between 216–419 μg/day. Therefore, ICMR (2010) has recommended 400 μg/day of retinol equivalents, or 3,200 μg/day of β-carotene among preschool children.

Thiamin, Riboflavin and Niacin: In the absence of any reports on special needs during this age, the ICMR (2010) has recommended the RDA for thiamin (0.5 mg/1,000 kcals), riboflavin (0.6 mg/1,000 kcals) and niacin (6.6 mg niacin equivalents/1,000 kcals) on the basis of energy requirements.

Most of brain development is completed during infancy (70 per cent during pregnancy and 15 per cent during infancy). For the remaining 15 per cent brain growth during preschool years, an intake of EFA (Essential fatty acids) and DHA (Docosa Hexaenoic Acid) may have a positive influence on learning capability and academic performance.

Pyridoxine, Folic Acid and Cyanocobalamine: Since relevant data for the computation of RDA for these nutrients are not available, they have been arrived at by the interpolation of values for infants and children (see Table 21.2).

Box 21.1: Suggested Amounts of Food per Day

Food Group	*Age Group*			
	1–3 years		4–6 years	
	Amounts (g)	Household Measures	Amounts (g)	Household Measures
Milk and Milk Products	500ml	2 cups	500ml	2 cups
Meat and/or Pulse	30	1 bowl	30	1 bowl
Vegetables	200	2 bowls	300	3 bowls
Fruits	100	1 fruit	200	2 fruit
Cereals	60	3 servings	120	6 servings
Fat	25	5t	25	5t
Sugar	15	3t	15	3t
	Energy: 1,060 kcal	Protein: 16.7g	Energy: 1,350 Kcal	Protein: 20.1g

Box 21.2: Sample Menu

Meal	*Menu*	*Household Measures*
Early morning	Milk	1 cup
Breakfast	Egg/cheese sandwich	One
Mid-morning	Vegetable Poha	1 medium bowl
	Apple	1 medium size
Lunch	Vegetable *pulao*	1 bowl
	Cucumber *Raita*	1 small bowl
Tea time	Banana Milk shake	1 cup
	Baked *Paneer aloo tikki*	1 small *tikki*
Dinner	*Moong Dal* curry	½ bowl
	Lady finger vegetable	½ small bowl
	Chapati	One

Ascorbic Acid: The RDA for ascorbic acid is given keeping in mind the beneficial effects on the absorption of non-heme iron. However, in order to derive this benefit, iron and ascorbic acid would have to be consumed in the same meal (see Boxes 21.1 and 21.2 for a well-balanced diet during preschool years).

EATING HABITS

Figure 21.1: Active Feeding of Preschooler

Source: Neena and Akshit Kaul.

Preschoolers have two common preferences. First, they have a preference for routine in daily life. Most children need some structure and routine to their day. Generally, they prefer meals and snacks at regular times, as governed by the family's lifestyle.

Second, they have a preference for simplicity. Many children may like simply prepared, mild tasting foods that they can easily handle. They prefer foods they can manage, for example, cut-up vegetables they can eat with their fingers, and soups they can drink from a cup.

In the preschool years, children develop various associations with foods. For example, sweets may mean a reward for good behaviour. However, it is important to know that early impressions associated with the various uses of food affect food-related attitudes and practices throughout life. Food preferences can be influenced by parents and friends; television advertising may also influence the child to select certain foods over others.

A number of strategies can be adopted to encourage good eating habits among preschoolers:

- Establish routines where the children sit down with the whole family and eat and talk together during meal times. Avoid watching television during meal times.
- Meal times should not be made unpleasant by force-feeding picky eaters. This puts off children, and they develop a negative association with food and eating. Instead, 'active feeding' should be done by engaging the child in some activity while feeding her/him, thereby making it a fun experience (Figure 21.1).
- Keep a 'snack-box' handy, containing healthy snack foods such as pieces of fruit, vegetables, or small sandwiches.
- Do not give the child too large a serving. It is better to offer a second helping later. This helps children to learn not to waste food.
- Introduce new foods at the time when the child is really hungry. This increases the likelihood of its acceptance.
- If the child does not like particular foods, do not worry, as likes and dislikes change over time. Placing only small amounts of foods that the child dislikes on the child's plate at family meal timings increases its chances of being accepted. The child is encouraged to eat new foods when s/he observes the whole family enjoying them.
- Inculcating the habit of having breakfast before leaving for school is important, as research shows that children who eat breakfast in the mornings are able to concentrate better on their studies.
- In case the child does not like drinking milk, it can be given as milk shake (banana, mango, strawberry, etc.), or as custard, curd, yoghurt, *paneer, kheer*, or any milk-based food preparation.
- Food can be attractively served by using natural colours, or cut out in different shapes to make it interesting for children (see Figure 21.2).

Figure 21.2: Making Food More Attractive for Preschoolers

- Green leafy vegetables, and other vegetables that are generally not liked by children, can be incorporated in meals by disguising them, such as kneading them into dough to make *methi/bathua/palak parantha* or *poori*, or given as *lauki/* mint/ onion-tomato *raitas*, or as carrot *halwa*, pumpkin *kheer*, etc.
- One can also replace frying as a cooking method with baking or steaming.
- Extra sugar can be avoided by naturally sweetening desserts with fruits.

Preschoolers should be fed simple, easy to handle foods at regular intervals. Use of interesting colours and shapes enhances the appeal of food to preschoolers.

IMPORTANCE OF PHYSICAL ACTIVITY DURING PRESCHOOL YEARS

Active preschool children have:

- Lower chances of suffering from obesity and developing cardiovascular disease in later life;
- Improved Bone Density;
- A positive impact on psychosocial factors such as self-esteem; and
- Better motor skills acquisition during childhood.

The early years are an ideal window to promote physical activity, as physical activity levels during the early years of childhood are predictive of activity levels later in adulthood. Despite the evidence supporting the benefits of physical activity, there is a trend showing a decline in adequate physical activity. Studies show that parents' attitudes, behaviours, and parenting styles and practices have a profound influence on children's physical activity levels. Additionally, television viewing is associated with sedentary behaviour.

For healthy growth and development, toddlers (aged 1–2 years) and preschoolers (aged 3–4 years) should accumulate at least 180 minutes of physical activity at any intensity spread throughout the day, including

- A variety of activities in different environments
- Activities that develop movement skills
- Progression towards at least 60 minutes of energetic play by five years of age (Tremblay et al 2012).

An increase in daily physical activity provides greater benefits. Physical activity for preschoolers means moving about the home and exploring their environment, climbing stairs, brisk walking, running or dancing, and active play outside the home. As children grow older, different kinds of active play, such as hopping, jumping and skipping, replace activities like exploring their homes.

PROBLEM OF UNDERNUTRITION AND OVERNUTRITION

Indian preschool children continue to suffer from nutritional problems, such as protein energy malnutrition (PEM), anaemia and vitamin A deficiency. Figure 21.3 depicts levels of wasting, stunting and underweight among Indian preschool children. In addition, problems of overweight and obesity are also emerging as major public health problems.

Undernutrition

The diets and nutritional status of urban slum children in India is even worse than the rural average. The effects of intrauterine growth retardation are evident in the fact that low BMI for age and wasting (low weight for height) rates are the highest at birth. There is a further increase in stunting (Low height for Age) rates between the age of 9–23 months. This is accompanied by a steady decline in the wasting and low BMI rates. This improvement in weight status in relation to height should not be interpreted as an improvement in the nutritional status of children, as it is merely a reflection of poor linear growth.

Increase in the underweight (low weight for age) and stunting rates (low height for age) between 12–23 months is thought to be the result of inadequate energy intake when the children shift to a household diet. The reason for the poor diet among preschool-age children is that young children need to be fed five to six times a day to meet their food requirements from the habitual household diets with high calorie density. Frequent and adequate feeding is not done for these children due to a lack of awareness and knowledge regarding their food requirements, and the absence of a responsible adult caregiver. Therefore, the most common causes of malnutrition include faulty feeding practices, impaired utilisation of nutrients due to infections and parasites, inadequate food, and poor environmental conditions and lack of proper childcare practices.

Figure 21.3: Prevalence of Under-nutrition among Indian Preschool Children

Undernutrition in children under 5y

Source: NFHS-3, 2005–06.

Prevention of stunting in the first two years of life is important, as it is irreversible once it sets in. Stunting in the first two years is associated with low adult height, and in women, it is responsible for lower birth weight in their offspring—the trans-generational impact of childhood under-nutrition.

Malnutrition contributes to between 35–55 per cent of all childhood deaths. Although so far the focus of development programmes has been on the prevention of underweight or stunting, Severe and Moderate Acute Malnutrition, as characterised by low weight for height when compared to a standard reference population, small mid-upper arm circumference, or nutritional oedema, is also emerging as a challenge for public health programmes. **Severe Acute Malnutrition (SAM)** is defined by:

- Weight-for-length/height < –3SD (wasted) or
- Mid-upper arm circumference < 115 mm or
- Oedema of both feet (kwashiorkor with or without severe wasting).

On the other hand, **Moderate Acute Malnutrition (MAM)** is defined as weight for height between -3 and -2 Z scores of the WHO Child Growth Standards, or MUAC less than 12.5cm without oedema. The dietary management of children with moderate acute malnutrition is based on the optimal use of locally available foods to improve nutritional status, so as to prevent the development of severe acute malnutrition. On the other hand, children with SAM need standard WHO protocols for the treatment.

As part of the Indian government's efforts to prevent under-nutrition among preschool children, supplementary nutrition is provided to children from six months to six years of age in *anganwadi* centres of the ICDS programme. Under this programme, children are provided with 500 kcals and 12–15g protein per day for 300 days in a year. Since exclusive breastfeeding is recommended for children in the age group of 0–6 months, they are not part of any supplementary nutrition programme. Instead, lactating mothers are provided supplementary nutrition through the ICDS scheme.

For children in the age group of six months to three years, Take Home Ration is given in a form that is palatable to the child, such as *panjiri* or other foods. Children in the age group of 3–6 years are served a Hot Cooked Meal in AWCs. Since a child of this age group is not capable of consuming a meal containing 500 calories in one sitting, they are served more than one meal. A morning snack, in the form of milk/ banana/ egg/ seasonal fruits/ micronutrient fortified food, etc., is provided, in addition to the hot cooked meal around noon.

Growth Monitoring

The growth of a baby can be observed in many ways: increase in size, height and weight, clothes no longer fitting well, a string on the waist becoming tighter, etc. These are all signs of growth, but they cannot tell us if the child is growing well enough for her/his age. There are many ways of measuring the growth of a child.

The new WHO child growth standards represent a shift from describing how children grow, to prescribing how they should grow, to how they have a right to grow. They demonstrate for the first time ever that children born in different regions of the world and given an optimum start in life have the potential to grow and develop up to the same range of height and weight for age. The standards show that nutrition, environment and healthcare are stronger factors in determining growth and development than regional or ethnic background. The focus of these three factors are:

Optimal Nutrition

- Exclusive breastfeeding up to six months
- Appropriate complementary feeding

Optimal Environment

- No microbiological contamination
- No smoking

Optimal Health Care

- Immunisation (see Box 21.3 for the immunisation schedule)
- Paediatric routines

Box 21.3: Immunisation Schedule (Indian Medical Association)

Sl No.	*Age*	*Disease*	*Vaccination*	*Remarks*
1	AT BIRTH	HEPATITIS B	HEP B VACCINE -I	
2	AT BIRTH	POLIO	ORAL PV 0 DOSE	
3	BIRTH TO 6 WK	TUBERCULOSIS	BCG	
4	4–6 WEEKS	HEPATITIS B	HEP B VACCINE -II	
5	6 WEEKS	DIPHTHERIA PERTUSIS TETANUS POLIO	DPT-I OPV -I	
6	10 WK	DIPHTHERIA PERTUSIS TETANUS POLIO HEPATITIS B	DPT-II OPV-II HEP B VACCINE III*	*DELHI GOVT RECOMMENDATION
7	14 WEEKS	DIPHTHERIA PERTUSIS TETANUS POLIO	DPT-III OPV- III HEP B VACCINE IV*	*DELHI GOVT RECOMMENDATION
8	24 WEEKS	HEPATITIS B	HEP B VACCINE III*	*IAP RECOMMENDATION
9	9–12 MTHS	POLIO MEASLES	OPV-IV MEASLES	
10	15–18 MTHS	MUMPS MEASELES RUBELLA	MMR*	
11	18 MTHS	DIPHTHERIA PERTUSIS TETANUS POLIO	DPT–BOOSTER I OPV–V	*RECOMMENDED BY DELHI GOVT & IAP ONLY
12	24 MTHS	TYPHOID	TYPHOID*	*IAP RECOMMENDATION
13	4–5 YR	DIPHTHERIA PERTUSIS TETANUS POLIO	DPT BOOSTER–II OPV–VI	

Source: http://www.ima-india.org/page.php?page-ad=42.

The WHO growth standards (2006) state that BMI for age can used for the detection of under- and over-nutrition in preschool children. However, BMI for age has not been widely used as a method for the detection of under-nutrition in developing countries, perhaps because there had not been many studies demonstrating the association between low BMI and functional decompensation, such as increased risk of morbidity due to infections. Use of BMI for the assessment of current nutritional status in Indian children is essential in all settings where length / height measurements are possible, because: (*i*) early detection of current energy inadequacy leading to low BMI and interventions to correct it can prevent stunting; this is critical, because stunting cannot be reversed; (*ii*) the majority of Indian stunted children have an appropriate weight for their height and age (normal BMI/age); increased energy intake may make them prone to over-nutrition; and (*iii*) under-nutrition in early childhood, followed by a rapid increase in body mass index in early/ late childhood/ adolescence, may predispose the child to over-nutrition and non-communicable disease risk in early adult life.

The use of WHO 2006 standards for the assessment of underweight/stunting in Indian children clearly brings out the importance of low birth weight, very early introduction of breast milk substitutes, very late introduction of complementary feeds, poor young child feeding practices, high morbidity rates due to infections, and poor access to healthcare as the major factors associated with an increase in underweight/stunting rates in infants and young children. These data can be used for advocacy and awareness building for two critical interventions to improve the nutritional status of young children, namely nutrition education to ensure appropriate infant and child feeding practices, and health education to improve timely access to healthcare.

However, the most common measure of growth is weight gain. By weighing a child regularly, a change of even 100–200 g can be observed. This weight change is not visible by any other means of measuring growth. That is why children should be weighed regularly to see how much weight they have gained.

Weighing of the child at regular intervals, the plotting of that weight on a graph (called a growth chart) enabling one to see the changes in weight, and advising the mother based on this weight change is called '**Growth Monitoring**'. It must be done at regular intervals. For growth monitoring, it is the change in weight over a period of time that is most important, rather than the weight itself. It should be done more frequently, that is, once every month, up to the age of three, and at least once in three months thereafter.

Each time a child is weighed, the weight is recorded by marking a point on the chart. These points are joined by a line. This line is called a growth curve. If a child is growing and there is regular weight gain, the line will move in an upward direction. Thus, growth becomes visible to the worker and the mother when the weight is plotted on a growth chart. When growth falters, that is, when weight does not increase as expected, the line on the growth chart does not go upward, but stays flat. The line may even go in a downward direction, when a child loses weight.

Thus, monitoring the growth of a child every month shows periods of no growth or weight loss even before a child starts appearing thin. This acts as an early warning to take action to ensure that the child grows normally. Taking action on the first sign of growth faltering can easily restore health and proper growth.

MICRONUTRIENT DEFICIENCIES

Micronutrient deficiencies, such as vitamin A deficiency (VAD), iron deficiency anaemia (IDA), and iodine deficiency disorders (IDD), are the major nutritional problems observed among preschool children.

Vitamin A plays a vital role in maintaining eye health and vision, growth, immune function, and survival. **Vitamin A deficiency (VAD)** is associated with an increase in infections: respiratory infections, diarrhoea and measles, as well as childhood mortality. It is also the leading cause of paediatric blindness. There are 130 million estimated preschool children suffering from sub-clinical VAD (serum retinol <20μg/dl). VAD compromises the immune systems of children, increasing the risk of infections and childhood mortality. Its ocular manifestations include night blindness, cunjuctival xerosis, bitot's spot, corneal xerosis, keratomalacia, and total blindness.

To prevent VAD among children, the Government of India launched the National Prophylaxis Programme against Nutritional Blindness due to vitamin A deficiency in 1970. The programme covers children in the age group of nine months to 59 months. As part of the programme, a mega dose of vitamin A syrup is given to preschool children (first dose of 1,00,000 IU at nine months along with measles injection, and subsequently every six months 2,00,000IU).

Similarly, **IDD**, a group of disorders resulting mostly from an insufficient dietary supply of iodine, is also a major public health problem in most parts of India. Environmental destruction, leading to deforestation, melting of glaciers and frequent flooding, results in the leaching of iodine from the top crust of soil. As a result, crops grown on such soil are iodine deficient. Iodine deficiency is known to cause a spectrum of disorders, including goitre, cretinism, hypothyroidism, brain damage, mental retardation, psychomotor defects, and hearing and speech impairment. It can even cause abortion and still birth. IDD is thus a major public health problem, affecting brain development among preschool children. Information processing, fine motor skills, and problem solving are known to be poor among iodine-deficient school children. These children are also known to have a low IQ.

Therefore, in 1962, the Government of India launched the National Goitre Control Programme, which was renamed in 1992 as the National Iodine Deficiency Disease Control Programme (NIDDCP). As a part of this programme, the strategy of Universal Salt Iodisation has been adopted, and all the salt sold in the country is to have at least 15ppm iodine at the household level.

About 60–70 per cent of all children below the age of six suffer from various degrees of **anaemia**, which significantly contributes to childhood morbidity and mortality. The onset of anaemia in young children occurs generally after six months of age. Before this, the iron in breast milk is sufficient to meet the needs of a breastfed child. Iron from breast milk is also in a form that is more easily bio-available to the young child. Thereafter, the incidence of anaemia increases from 6–8 months, till the child is a year old. In India, diets for children in the age group of 6–23 months are predominantly plant-based, and provide insufficient amounts of micronutrients to meet the recommended nutrient intakes.

Many studies have found a correlation between iron-deficiency anaemia and poor cognitive and motor development, and behavioural problems. Longitudinal studies consistently indicate that children anaemic in infancy continue to have poorer cognition, school achievement, and more behaviour problems into middle childhood.

> Problems of both undernutrition and overnutrition co-exist in India. Protein Energy Malnutrition, Vitamin A deficiency, Iodine deficiency disorders, and iron deficiency anaemia are common among preschool children. Overweight and obesity are also emerging as public health problems among preschool children.

One ml of IFA syrup, containing 20mg of elemental iron and 100mcg of folic acid biweekly, provides 100 doses in a year. The syrup should be administered half an hour after food if the child has been breastfed (in LBW infants)/fed semi-solid/solid food. De-worming (Albendazole) tablets are also provided to children for biannual de-worming. Iron supplementation should be withheld in the case of acute illness (fever, acute diarrhoea, pneumonia etc.), Severe Acute Malnutrition (SAM), and in a known case of haemoglobinopathy/history of repeated blood transfusion. For all children aged between 6–60 months, it is proposed that a IFA supplement be administered under the direct supervision of an Accredited Social Health Activist (ASHA) on fixed days on a bi-weekly basis.

The benefits of a regular intake of IFA syrup have been observed in the physical and cognitive development of the child, for example, an improvement in well-being, attentiveness in studies and intelligence, etc. Although minor side effects associated with IFA administration, such as black discolouration of stools, are common, the benefits overweigh any side effects observed. Therefore, it is extremely important to ensure a regular intake of IFA supplement.

Overweight and Obesity

The incidence of chronic diseases is rising much more rapidly in developing countries than in developed ones. A marked increase in the prevalence of overweight and obesity has been observed in the past few decades, both in adults and in children in developing countries. Furthermore, overweight and obesity in preschool children is growing rapidly. Changes in lifestyle, urbanisation, malnutrition, use of high-calorie fast foods, and also decreased physical activity, due to watching excessive TV and playing sedentary games, are significant causes of childhood obesity. Childhood obesity is associated with serious health problems like increasing morbidity, and the premature development of obesity-related complications in the young adult, that is, increased risk of becoming an obese adult and developing related problems like diabetes and cardiovascular diseases. Hence, diagnosis and control, as well as prevention and treatment of obesity, should start early in life.

SUMMARY

- Preschool is a period of rapid growth and development, when the child acquires motor, emotional and social skills. It is also an important period of language and cognitive development.
- Nutrient needs for almost all nutrients remain high to support proper growth and development.
- Preschool is also a time to develop healthy food habits and form food choices.
- It is important to serve simple, easy to handle food in an interesting manner at regular intervals.
- Energy, protein and micro-nutrient deficiencies are common among Indian preschool children.
- Overweight and obesity are also emerging problems confronting Indian preschool children.

EXERCISES

1. Describe the development changes that take place in a preschool child.
2 Discuss the basis of computing RDA for energy, protein, vitamin A, and iron as derived by ICMR 2010.
3 Explain the strategies that can be used to inculcate healthy food habits and physical activities among preschool children.
4 What are the common problems of under and over-nutrition observed among preschool children?

REFERENCES

FAO/WHO/UNU, 'Human Energy Requirements', Report of a joint FAO/WHO/UNU Expert Consultation, Rome, 17–24 October, Rome 2004.

———, 'Joint FAO/WHO/UNU Expert Consultation on Protein and Amino Acid requirements in Human Nutrition', WHO Technical Report Series No. 935, 2007.

ICMR, *ICMR Nutrient Requirements and Recommended Dietary Allowances for Indians*, Hyderabad: NIN, ICMR, 2010.

NFHS-3, 2005–06, Available at http://www.rchiips.org/nfhs/pdf/India.pdf (accessed 7 October 2013).

Tremblay, M. S., A. G. LeBlanc, V. Carson, L. Choquette, S. C. Gorber, C. Dillman, M. Duggan, M. J. Gordon, A. Hicks, I. Janssen, M. E. Kho, A. E. Latimer-Cheung, C. LeBlanc, K. Murumets, A. D. Okely, J. J. Reilly, J. C. Spence, J. A. Stearns, and B. W. Timmons, 'Canadian Physical Activity Guidelines for the Early Years (aged 0–4 years)', *Appl. Physiol. Nutr. Metab.* 37, 2012, pp. 345–56.

WHO Multicentre Growth Reference Study Group (MGRS), *WHO Child Growth Standards. Length/ Height for Age, Weight for Age, Weight for Length and Body Mass Index for Age. Methods and development*, Geneva: WHO, 2006.

ONLINE SOURCES

For Iron deficiency anaemia control:

http://www.unicef.org/india/10._National_Iron_Plus_Initiative_Guidelines_for_Control_of_IDA.pdf (accessed 21 January 2014).

For interesting ideas on dishes to make for a preschooler, see

http://www.goodlifeeats.com/2012/02/5-ways-to-make-food-more-fun-for-kids.html

22

NUTRITION FOR SCHOOL-AGED CHILDREN

HIGHLIGHTS

- Growth and development during school age.
- Nutrient needs and Recommended Dietary Allowance for school-aged children.
- Food behaviour of school-aged children.
- Nutritional concerns of school-going children.

The period between 6–12 years is termed 'school-age'. It is a slow growth period in which occasional spurts of growth may occur. However, unlike infancy and adolescence, this phase is not very demanding. Often termed the 'lull before the storm', this phase prepares the body for rapid growth and development during adolescence. This chapter introduces you to the various aspects of growth and development, nutrient requirements, food behaviour, and nutritional concerns among school-aged children.

GROWTH AND DEVELOPMENT

Heredity and environment play a major role in the growth and development of a child. Growth in the early school years is slow and irregular, and body changes occur gradually. During this period, body types are established, and growth rates vary widely. Initially, girls are shorter and lighter as compared to boys but in late childhood, girls tend to be taller than boys of the same age. These changes become visible after the age of 10.

> This phase of childhood is known for slow yet steady growth, along with rapid motor and neuromuscular development. Motor skills, both in strength and coordination, improve, which is reflected in gradual improvements in different tasks.

The World Health Organization (WHO) has developed growth reference standards for school-aged children and adolescents in order to screen and monitor their nutritional status. The reference data includes Body Mass Index (BMI) for age and height-for-age for both boys and girls in the 5–19 year age group. A low BMI-for-age is the indicator for thinness, and high BMI-for-age shows the presence of overweight and obesity. Similarly, low height-for-age indicates stunting in school-aged children.

Changes in Height and Weight

Even though all school-aged children may grow at a different rate, the average gain in weight is about 1.5–3 kg per year. Variation in weight is more in comparison to height. The average increase in height is about 2–3 inches per year. The height of the children is determined by the height of the parents. The nutritional status of the child also influences growth and development. Height is reflective of long-term nutritional status, and weight is influenced by the short-term status. Recent episodes of ill health, for instance, will immediately result in a loss of weight. Such episodes will not affect height unless the disease is a chronic one, or the child has been eating less food for a long period of time.

The latter phase of childhood is marked by puberty, which begins earlier in girls (10–12 years) and later in boys (12–14 years). Puberty is the stage of sexual maturation and attainment of reproductive capacity. It is an overlapping period, as it starts in later school age and extends to early adolescence. With pubertal changes starting at a much earlier age in children, the WHO has defined the period of adolescence from 10–19 years.

Changes in Body Composition

Most children have a slimmer appearance during middle childhood than they did during preschool years, due to shifts in the accumulation and location of body fat. As a child's entire body size increases, the amount of body fat stays relatively stable, giving her/him a thinner look. Also, during this stage of life a child's legs are longer in proportion to her/his body than they were before. During the initial period of school age, boys and girls grow at the same pace; however, in late school age (11–12 years), girls are usually taller and heavier as compared to boys. There are changes in muscle mass, adipose tissue and skeletal structure. Girls accumulate more fat mass in their bodies, but boys tend to develop more of muscles.

Changes in Social and Psychological Behaviour

In contrast to the preschool age, where familial influence is higher, school-aged children are more influenced by their peer group. The members of the peer group are generally of the same sex. To become a part of a 'gang', children imitate their peer group in dressing style, behaviour and thoughts. At this age, children are generally over-burdened with increased academic demands. Children develop more concrete and logical thinking, and also become more independent due to the development of fine motor skills .

Health Behaviour in School-aged Children—A WHO Collaborative Cross-National Survey

The WHO regional office for Europe conducts this research every four years in 43 countries of Europe and North America. It collects data related to health complaints, diet, physical activity levels, and alcohol and tobacco use in 11–15-year-old boys and girls.

RECOMMENDED DIETARY ALLOWANCE (RDA)

Table 22.1 presents the RDA of various nutrients for school-aged children. The nutrient requirements are the same for boys and girls till the age of nine; however, from 10 years onwards, requirements vary because of the gender differences in growth rate and body composition.

Energy

The energy needs of healthy children are determined by basal metabolism, the rate of growth and energy expenditure on physical activity. The energy intake of children must be sufficient to ensure growth, and to spare protein from being used as a source of energy. However, excess weight gain should be avoided. Children between the ages of seven and nine need 1,690 kcal energy per day. Boys between 10–12 years need 2,190 kcal per day, while girls need 2,010 kcal per day, slightly less in comparison to boys. Excessive consumption of fast food leads to a high intake of energy from refined carbohydrates, fat and sugar, resulting in overweight and obesity in school-aged children.

Protein

Adequate dietary protein is essential during the growing years as protein deficiency at this stage will result in undernutrition and poor growth and development. The protein requirement—29.5 gm per day—is the same for both boys and girls in the 7–9 age group, while in the 10–12 age group, it is 39.9 gm and 40.4 gm per day for boys and girls, respectively. Proteins are available from animal as well as plant sources. Animal sources include egg, meat, fish, and milk, and plant sources include pulses, legumes and nuts. The quality of protein from animal sources is superior to that of plant protein, because it contains all the essential amino acids to support body building. The quality of protein

Table 22.1: RDA For School-aged Children

Group		*Children*	*Boys*	*Girls*
Category/ Age		7–9	10–12 years	10–12 years
Body weight (Kg)		25.1	34.3	35.0
Energy(kcal/d)		1690	2190	2010
Protein (g/d		29.5	39.9	40.4
Visible fat (g/d)		30	35	35
Calcium (g/d)		600	800	800
Iron (mg/d)		16	21	27
Zinc (mg/d)		8	9	9
Magnesium(mg/d)		100	120	160
Vitamin A	Retinol	600	600	600
(μg/d)	β-carotene	4800	4800	4800
Thiamine (mg/d)		0.8	1.1	1.0
Riboflavin (mg/d)		1.0	1.3	1.2
Niacin equivalent(mg/d)		13	15	13
Vitamin B_6 (mg/d)		1.6	1.6	1.6
Ascorbic acid(mg/d		40	40	40
Dietary Folate (μg/d)		120	140	140
Vitamin B_{12} (μg/d)		0.2–1	0.2–1	0.2–1

Source: ICMR 2010.

from plant sources can be enhanced by consuming cereal-pulse in combination, one plant protein supplementing the deficiency in the other (mutual supplementation). Cereals can also be combined with milk/meat and their products.

Fat

To meet the energy requirements, at least 25 per cent of the total calories should be provided as fat. To fulfill this requirement, the minimum level of visible fat in the diets of children should range between 25–35 grams per day (ICMR 2010). Importantly, excess consumption of fat in the form of junk foods should be avoided to prevent the risk of childhood obesity, which is on the rise. Consumption of *ghee*, butter, hydrogenated fat, coconut oil, full fat milk, and red meat products provides saturated fatty acids (SFA), which increases the risk of atherosclerosis. On the other hand, vegetable oils such as groundnut, ricebran and sesame are rich in monounsaturated fatty acids (MUFA), and sunflower, corn, mustard and soyabean are rich in polyunsaturated fatty acid (PUFA), which decrease the risk of cardio-vascular disease (CVD). To obtain the maximum benefit, different types of vegetable oils should be used.

Minerals

Calcium

Calcium is needed for the adequate mineralisation and maintenance of growing bones in children. The RDA of calcium for children between the ages of seven to nine is 600 mg per day, and it is 800 mg per day for both sexes in the 10–12 age group. Calcium has special significance for the 10–19 age group, since the requirement is at its maximum (with the exception of pregnancy and lactation) for the development of peak bone mass. Adequate intake of milk and its products, green leafy vegetables, nuts, oilseeds, and pulses will help meet the increased calcium requirements.

Iron

Iron is required for the expansion in blood volume and increase in lean body mass. The iron requirement for children in the seven to nine age group is 16mg per day. In the 10–12 age group, iron requirement is 27mg per day for girls and 21mg per day for boys. As is clearly visible, iron is the one nutrient that is required in larger amounts by girls in the 10–12 age group, as girls achieve menarche and menstrual blood loss increases the demands for iron. If these increased demands are not fulfilled, then the regular menstrual iron losses may lead to iron deficiency anaemia.

Menarche is the first menstrual bleeding. There has been a decline in the average age of menarche over the years. The etiology for early menarche is multifaceted. It is attributed mostly to improved nutrition (high calorie and protein intake), obesity, physical inactivity, exposure to endocrine disrupting chemicals, psychosocial factors and economic status.

Zinc

Adequate intake of zinc has been found to reduce childhood illness, enhance physical growth, and decrease morbidity and mortality in children. It is also needed for adequate sexual development. A deficiency of zinc has been linked to delayed physical growth and delayed sexual development in children. It also leads to impaired immune responses and increased susceptibility to infections such as diarrhoea and pneumonia in school-aged children. The RDA for zinc is 8mg per day for children in the seven to nine age group, and 9 mg per day for both boys and girls in the 10–12 age group.

Magnesium

Important for maintaining electrical potential in nerves and muscle membranes, magnesium deficiency can lead to neuromuscular dysfunction. The recommended intake is 100mg per day for 7–9-year-olds, and 120mg per day for boys in the 10–12 age group. The requirement of magnesium is higher for girls in the 10–12 age group (160mg per day), as compared to boys.

Fat-soluble Vitamins

Vitamin A

Vitamin A is essential for normal vision, for maintaining the integrity of epithelial tissue, and for a wide variety of metabolic functions. It is available in food in two forms—as preformed vitamin A (retinol) and provitamin A beta-carotene. Foods that provide retinol are animal sources such as milk, butter, egg, and fish, and beta-carotene is derived from plant sources such as leafy vegetables, and yellow and orange vegetables and fruits. The recommended intake of retinol is 600μg per day, or for β-carotene, it is 4, 800μg per day. This RDA remains constant for adolescents and adults. The deficiency of vitamin A is very common in preschool children, but is also prevalent in school-aged children.

Vitamin D

Vitamin D is a fat-soluble vitamin which can be synthesised in the skin on exposure to sunlight, so the ICMR has not given any RDA. However, vitamin D synthesis in the body is dependent on various factors like latitude, atmospheric pollution, clothing, skin colour, and duration and time of exposure to sunlight. The skin should be exposed to direct sunlight for 30 minutes to one hour every day for the synthesis of vitamin D, and proper absorption of calcium. This means that children should indulge in outdoor sports daily, for at least an hour, to get the adequate sun exposure. Vitamin D is very important for calcium absorption, and hence the health of bones.

Vitamins E and K

These two vitamins occur widely in vegetable oils (soyabean, corn, olive, and canola) and plant sources (green leafy vegetables such as spinach, turnip, broccoli, etc.), and hence dietary deficiencies are not normally encountered. Hence, the ICMR has not stated any RDA for these vitamins.

Water-soluble Vitamins

Vitamins B and C

Vitamin B includes thiamine, riboflavin, niacin, pyridoxine, folate, and vitamin B_{12}. B vitamins act primarily as coenzymes or as a part of coenzymes, and help catalyse various metabolic reactions in cells. All B vitamins function in energy-producing metabolic reactions, and some also participate in other aspects of cellular metabolism.

Vitamin C acts as an antioxidant, and is essential for the activity of many enzymes and for collagen synthesis. It is also important for immunity. Better immunity ensures that the child does not fall ill very often, and has uninterrupted growth.

Hence, a good diet which enhances the immune functions of the body is vital for good growth.

The current recommendations for these nutrients for school-aged children are given in Table 22.1.

Table 22.2: Balanced Diet for School-aged Children

Food Group	*g/ portion*	*Years*		
		7–9	*10–12*	
			Girls	*Boys*
Cereals and millets	30	6	8	10
Pulses	30	2	2	2
Milk (ml) and milk products	100	5	5	5
Roots and tubers	100	1	1	1
Green leafy vegetables	100	1	1	1
Other vegetables	100	1	2	2
Fruits	100	1	1	1
Sugar	5	4	6	6
Fat/ oil (visible)	5	6	7	7

Note: To calculate the day's requirement of the above food groups for children, multiply grams per portion with the number of portions. One portion of pulse may be exchanged with one portion (50g) of egg/meat/chicken/fish.

Source: Dietary Guidelines for Indians 2011.

FOOD BEHAVIOUR

The diet during childhood influences not only the immediate health of children, but may also impact their future health status. As the child's environment expands, a greater number of external factors influence the child's diet. Numerous influences determine food intake and the habits of school-going children. The habits, likes and dislikes established in the early years are carried throughout one's life. The food habits of school-aged children are more scheduled due to specific school timings. However, many external influences may affect the child's food choices.

In India, around 40–50 per cent of advertisements during children's programmes are for junk foods, which are high in fat, salt and sugar content.

Survey report: The Junk Food Generation, Consumers International Asia Pacific Office, 2000–01.

Home food environment: The dietary habits of parents and older siblings influence the food habits of school-aged children. Eating together with the family becomes less common because school-going children are more preoccupied with their school, homework, tuitions, and play. Due to the time constraints, meals generally include more convenience and fast foods.

Media: It is estimated that children are spending more time in front of a screen (television, computer and mobile), rather than in outdoor recreation. The ill-effects include decreased physical activity among children, as well as greater eye strain. Studies have shown that television advertising influences children's food preferences and purchasing requests, resulting in an inclusion of unhealthy foods which increase the risk of obesity, dental caries, deficiency of micronutrients, etc.

Society: Social events and parties often promote unhealthy eating habits. Popular snacks and beverages served at parties are generally high in sugar and fat.

> Research studies have shown that a strong association exists between television viewing and unhealthy eating habits among children. TV viewing increases the calorie intake, either by viewing food advertisements which lead to increased snack consumption, or by unhealthy snacking, which is very common while watching television. TV viewing also decreases energy expenditure because of the displacement of physical activity.

Peer pressure: Peer influences increase with age, and affect food attitudes and choices. This may result in refusal of / liking for a particular food, even if it was earlier liked/ disliked by the child.

School food environment: The food served in school canteens or school lunch programmes (the mid-day meal programme in India) also influences the food choices of children. The availability of junk foods in or around the school acts as an enticement, and children land up making poor food choices. Hence, it is very important to control the sale/service of unhealthy foods in the vicinity of schools. The mid-day meal programme, with a strengthened component of nutrition education, can work wonders in inculcating good food habits in children.

The Government of India launched the National Programme of Nutritional Support to Primary Education (commonly known as the Mid-Day Meal Scheme) in 1995, with the aim of increasing enrolment in schools and also improving the nutritional status of children in Classes I–V in government and government-aided schools. This scheme was revised in 2007 to include children in Classes VI-VIII as well. A cooked meal providing 300 kcal and 8–12 grams protein is given to all children studying in Classes I–V, while the Upper Primary meals provide 700 kcal and 20 grams of protein.

Healthy Eating Habits

Childhood provides an opportunity to establish healthy eating habits.

- The diet should be balanced, including foods from all food groups. This will not only provide all the nutrients, but will also add variety to the diet.
- The protein quality of the diet can be improved by consuming animal products like milk, meat, egg, etc. For vegetarians, cereal-pulse combinations can provide good quality protein.
- Including at least five servings of green leafy vegetables, other vegetables and fruits will fulfill the requirements of vitamins and minerals like β-carotene, calcium, iron, and dietary fibre.
- Breakfast, being the most important meal of the day, should not be neglected, as it affects school performance.

> ***Box 22.1: Healthy Tiffin Ideas***
>
> Hare bhare kabab (mixed vegetables with potato and soya/chana)
>
> Besan bathua cheela
>
> Palak poori
>
> Paneer kachori
>
> Cheese sandwich
>
> Dal tikki burger
>
> Vegetable pulao
>
> Poha / upma with vegetables
>
> Vegetable idli
>
> Vegetable uttapam

- Packed lunch / tiffin should have variety. Monotony in the week's menu should be avoided. Box 22.1 suggests some healthy tiffin ideas.
- Restricted intake of fast food and snacks will limit the intake of total fat, saturated fat and cholesterol, and prevent childhood obesity. The foods liked by children can be prepared at home using healthier options, like

low fat cheese for pizzas, whole wheat buns for burgers, adding a generous amount of vegetables in noodles, pizzas and burgers, etc.

- Limit the consumption of cold drinks because they are sources of 'empty calories'; substitute them with milk-based beverages and fruit juices (with pulp and no added sugar).
- While snacking, prefer home-cooked and healthy foods. Nothing like munching on fruits, raw carrot, fruit/vegetable/sprouts *chat.*

NUTRITIONAL CONCERNS

Iron Deficiency Anaemia (IDA) is a major public health problem in India. Anaemia is defined as the lack of an adequate amount of haemoglobin (Hb) in the blood. A low haemoglobin level affects the oxygen carrying capacity of the blood.

The risk factors for anaemia include increased requirements during the growing years, poor absorption of iron because of the presence of phytates and phenolic compounds in the diet, heavy menstrual losses, and parasite infection. Anaemia is prevalent in school-aged children because foods that are rich in iron, like green leafy vegetables, whole cereals and pulses, are disliked by children. Anaemia results in impaired cognitive performance, scholastic achievement and reduced mental alertness. It also results in increased morbidity from infectious diseases. The treatment includes providing iron supplementation and including iron sources in the diet, like egg, meat, liver, green leafy vegetables, nuts, etc. Including vitamin C in the diet enhances the absorption of non-heme iron.

Malnutrition refers to deficiencies, excesses, or imbalances in the intake of energy, protein, and/or other nutrients. Malnutrition includes both under-nutrition and over-nutrition. In children between the ages of 6–12, both forms of malnutrition are very common.

Under-nutrition: Throughout the world, most of the deaths of young children occur because of under-nutrition. The reasons can be food insecurity, poor appetite (Figure 22.1), a restricted diet, and acute or chronic illness. Under-nutrition affects cognitive development, and it also hinders the physical development of children, leading to short stature and low BMI. Malnutrition increases the risk of recurrent infections and also affects school performance.

Over-nutrition: Over-nutrition in school-aged children is commonly termed childhood obesity. The increasing prevalence of overweight children is a significant and alarming public health problem. Excess energy intake, low physical activity, a diet high in fat and refined carbohydrates, and low in fruits and vegetables, increase the risk of childhood obesity. An overweight child is likely to reach maturity at an earlier age, but at the expense of height. Most obese children become obese adults. In the long run, other health problems associated with obesity, such as cardiovascular disease, diabetes and hypertension, may develop. Overweight children are more likely to have academic difficulties and experience the psychological trauma associated with obesity. The only way to reduce weight is to increase physical activity and reduce the intake of fatty and sugary foods. Weight loss should be gradual. Consuming low-calorie and low-fat foods, including five servings of fruits and vegetables, and at least 60 minutes of moderate physical activity is needed daily in order to reduce the weight and maintain it later.

Figure 22.1: Children are often Fussy Eaters, which Results in Inadequate Intake of Nutritious Food

Photo courtesy: Naina Mathur

Box 22.2: Sample menu

Age	12 years
Sex	male
Socio-economic status	middle-income group
Food habits	ovo-vegetarian
RDA (as per ICMR 2010)	
Energy:	2190 kcal/d
Protein:	39.9 gms/d
Important nutrient:	calcium: 800mg/d

Meal	***Menu***
Breakfast	*Dalia* porridge – 1 bowl Boiled egg – 1
Packed Lunch	*Besan bathua cheela* – 2 medium-sized Orange –1
Lunch	*Chapati* –1 medium Rice – ½ plate *Rajmah* curry – 1 bowl *Gobhi aloo* vegetable – 1/2 bowl Sweet curd – 1 medium bowl
Evening tea	Milk – 1 glass Vegetable Cheese grilled sandwich - 2
Dinner	*Chapati* – 2–3 medium Soyabean potato curry - 1 bowl Salad – 8–10 pieces Fruit custard – 1 bowl

SUMMARY

- Children in the age group of 6–12 years are termed school-aged children.
- Growth and development in this phase is slow but steady.
- The average increase in height is two to three inches per year, and gain in weight is 1.5–3 kg.
- The focus of children shifts from parents to the peer group. Children also become more independent.
- The requirement for various nutrients remains the same for children in the seven to nine age group.
- Puberty starts in later school age and extends up to early adolescence. This is the stage of sexual maturation. Menarche increases the demand for iron in girls.
- In the 10–12 age group, requirements vary because of the differences in the growth rate in boys and girls. Girls have their pubertal growth spurt earlier than boys.
- Important nutrients are calcium, iron and zinc, because of their role in bone development, cognitive development and sexual maturation, respectively.
- Adequate energy intake from a judicious selection of cereals, sugar, and fats and oils will prevent underweight and obesity in children.
- Five servings of vegetables and fruits per day is a must to meet the requirements for vitamins and minerals.
- Food behaviour is generally influenced by the media and peer group. Consumption of fast foods, processed foods, snacks, and convenience foods is common in this age group.
- Breakfast should not be neglected, and the packed lunch should be nutritious.
- Involvement in some outdoor sport will not only help in the synthesis of vitamin D, but will also help children to maintain their weight and develop their muscular and skeletal tissues.
- Along with obesity and underweight, the other important nutritional concern in this age group is iron deficiency anaemia.

KEY WORDS

Coenzymes: Compounds that enable specific enzymes to function.

Malnutrition: Refers to the deficiencies, excesses, or imbalances in the intake of energy, protein, and/or other nutrients.

Mono unsaturated fatty acids (MUFA): These are fatty acids which have one double bond in the chain.

Over-nutrition: (Here) refers to a chronic condition where the intake of food is in excess of dietary energy requirements, resulting in overweight and/or obesity.

Peer Pressure: Influence from the members of one's peer group. (here, friends and schoolmates).

Poly unsaturated fatty acids (PUFA): Fatty acids having two or more double bonds in the chain.

Stunting: Stunting is defined as height-for-age z-score (HAZ) of <-2 standard deviation (SD). Short for age.

Under-nutrition: The result of food intake that is continuously insufficient to meet the dietary energy requirements, poor absorption, and/or poor biological utilisation of nutrients consumed. This usually results in loss of body weight.

EXERCISES

1. Define the following terms:
   (a) Iron Deficiency Anaemia
   (b) Childhood obesity
2. Describe growth and development in school-aged children.
3. List the dietary considerations that must be kept in mind while planning the diet for school-aged children.
4. Describe the food behaviour of school-aged children, and discuss how it affects their nutritional status.

REFERENCES

Arnold, Fred, Sulabha Parasuraman, P. Arokiasamy, and Monica Kothari, *Nutrition in India*. National Family and Health Survey (NFHS-3), India, 2005–06, Mumbai: International Institute for Population Sciences; Calverton, Maryland: ICF Macro, 2009.

Bamji, Mahtab S., Kamala Krishnaswamy and G. N. V Brahmam (eds), *Textbook of Human Nutrition*, 3e. New Delhi: Oxford and IBH, 2009.

Harris, Jennifer L. and John A. Bargh, 'The Relationship between Television Viewing and Unhealthy Eating: Implications for Children and Media Interventions', Available at http://www.ncbi.nlm.nih.gov/pmc/articles/PMC2829711/ (accessed 4 January 2014).

Indian Council of Medical Research (ICMR), 'Nutrient Requirement and Recommended Dietary Allowances for Indians. A Report of the Expert Group of the Indian Council of Medical Research 2010', Hyderabad: National Institute of Nutrition, 2010.

International Institute for Population Sciences (IIPS) and Macro International, *National Family and Health Survey (NFHS-3), 2005–06, India: Key Findings*, Mumbai: IIPS, 2007.

Joshi, Shubhangini A., *Nutrition and Dietetics: With Indian Case Studies*, 3e, New Delhi: Tata McGraw Hill, 2010.

Khanna, Kumud, Sharda Gupta, Santosh Jain Passi, Rama Seth, Ranjana Mahana, and Seema Puri, *Textbook of Nutrition and Dietetics*, 2e, India: Elite Publishing House, 2013.

Mahan, K., S. Escott-Stump and J. Raymond, *Krause's Food and Nutrition Care Process*, 13e, Saunders Elsevier, 2011.

National Institute of Nutrition, *Dietary Guidelines for Indians—A Manual*, 2e, Hyderabad: NIN, 2011.

Sachan, B., M. Z. Idris, S. Jain, R. Kumari, and A. Singh, 'Age at menarche and menstrual problems among school-going adolescent girls of a North Indian district', *J Basic Clin Reprod Sci* 1, 2012, pp. 56–59.

'The Junk Food Generation A multi-country survey of the influence of television advertisement on children', Available at http://epsl.asu.edu/ceru/Articles/CERU-0407-227-OWI.pdf (accessed 4 January 2014).

Wadhwa, Arvind and Sushma Sharma, *Nutrition in the Community*, India: Elite Publishing House, 2003.

Wardlaw, Gordon M., Jeffery S. Hampl and Robert A. DiSilvestro, *Perspectives in Nutrition*, 6e, New York: McGraw Hill, 2004.

Williams, Sue Rodwell, *Basic Nutrition and Diet Therapy*, 11e, India: Harcourt, 2001.

ONLINE SOURCES

http://sexualityandu.ca/uploads/files/CTR_EarlyMenarche_FEB2013-ENG.pdf on 18 January 2014

http://www.hbsc.org/ (accessed 4 January 2014)

23

NUTRITION DURING ADOLESCENCE

HIGHLIGHTS

- Growth and development in adolescence
- Nutrient needs of the adolescent
- Food behaviour and body image
- Diet and feeding pattern
- Nutritional concerns of the adolescent

The term 'adolescence' is derived from the Latin word *adolescere*, meaning 'to grow' or 'to mature'. Falling between the 13–18 age group, this period marks the transformation of a child into an adult. This stage is associated with marked physical growth, reproductive maturation, and cognitive transformations. Adolescence is further classified into early adolescence (12–14 years), middle adolescence (14–17 years) and late adolescence (17–20 years). As in infancy, growth and development is on full swing during this phase. The onset of puberty is earlier in girls, as compared to boys. A growth spurt occurs in the age group of 10–13 in girls, and 12–15 in boys. The rapid growth spurt in this phase increases the demand for nutrients, making it critical for adolescents to include nutritious foods in their diet. Under-nutrition at this stage will delay the adolescent growth spurt, whereas over-nutrition, in the form of an excess intake of carbohydrates and fats, can lead to obesity. Let us learn more about growth and development during adolescence.

GROWTH AND DEVELOPMENT DURING ADOLESCENCE

Adolescence is the period of rapid growth and development, and brings about manifold changes in physical parameters such as height, weight and body composition, which increase the requirement of nutrients. This period is also characterised by sexual maturity, changes in psycho-social behaviour, and eating habits.

Physical Changes

Boys and girls grow at different rates and follow different patterns. While girls attain 95 per cent of their adult height by menarche, growing only two to three inches in late adolescence, boys continue to gain height up to around 19–20 years. Initially, the growth spurt in girls is faster in comparison to boys, but in middle adolescence, boys leave girls behind in terms of physical development. While girls deposit more fat, growth in boys is greater in terms of skeletal development, increase in lean body mass, and muscle development. Body fat levels decrease among males during adolescence, dropping to an average of 12 per cent by the end of puberty. The average lean body mass of teen females decreases, while the average body fat levels increase up to 30 per cent by the end of adolescence.

Fat deposition in girls generally occurs in the abdominal area, hips and breasts, so as to prepare their bodies for future childbearing. As already discussed in Chapter 22, the World Health Organization (WHO) has developed a growth reference for school-aged children and adolescents, for screening and monitoring their nutritional status. On the basis of the Body Mass Index (BMI), adolescents are classified as underweight, normal weight and overweight. The height-for-age of boys and girls curves are also available, which can be used to check if the child's height is increasing satisfactorily.

Sexual Changes

Sexual development begins in the pre-teen years and continues into adulthood. The gonadotropin releasing hormone is produced by the hypothalamus in the brain. This hormone in turn stimulates the pituitary gland to produce the Luteinising Hormone (LH) and Follicle Stimulating Hormone (FSH). In girls between the ages of 10–14 years, the pituitary gland produces FSH and LH, which stimulates the ovaries to produce sex hormones (oestrogen and progesterone). These hormones are responsible for initiating the bodily changes that happen during puberty. The changes include breast development, widening of the hips and thighs, growth of pubic and axillary hair, production of eggs by the ovaries, and the onset of menstruation.

In boys, too, between the ages of about 12 and 15, the pituitary gland produces LH and FSH, which together stimulate the production of the male sex hormone. The testes start producing testosterone, which begins the development of secondary sexual characteristics, like deepening of the voice, facial and body hair growth, development of the genitals, and sperm production. Medical professionals today are concerned about children attaining puberty too early. This condition is referred to as precocious puberty. Besides pathological conditions which may increase the secretion of sex hormones, obesity, sedentary lifestyle, junk food, and environmental toxins have been blamed for the early development of secondary sexual characteristics.

Psychosocial Changes

The biological changes that occur in adolescence significantly impact social and psychological development. The sudden and rapid physical changes that adolescents go through make them self-conscious, sensitive, and worried about their own body changes. During adolescence, it is normal for young people to establish their own identity. The influence of the peer group—which can be either positive or negative—is at its maximum during this age. Since acceptance by a peer group is important, adolescents want to imitate their friends in behaviour, dressing style and diet. This increased similarity among peers provides them with a sense of security.

Dietary Changes

As the teenage growth spurt begins, the appetite of adolescents improves. Unlike school-aged children, they make their own food choices. Unfortunately, they tend to choose foods that are higher in saturated fat, trans fat, sugar and sodium. The intake of protective foods like fruits, vegetables and milk is low. An unbalanced diet, snacking, fast food consumption, eating away from home, and skipping meals (especially breakfast) are the common diet-related problems encountered amongst most adolescents. The older adolescent may start consuming alcohol because of peer pressure. Teenaged females are more concerned about weight gain, which leads to frequent dieting, excessive calorie restriction, and eating disorders like Anorexia Nervosa (AN) and Bulimia Nervosa (BN).

Precocious Puberty is when a child's body begins changing into that of an adult (puberty) too soon, that is, before the age of eight in girls and before the age of nine in boys. Scientists have proposed a number of potential explanations for the rising rates of early puberty, for instance, certain conditions such as infections, hormone disorders, tumors, brain abnormalities or injuries, but the one that deserves special attention is environmental chemicals, particularly oestrogen-mimicking chemicals, present in cosmetics, food additives, plastics, pesticides, etc.

RECOMMENDED DIETARY ALLOWANCE (RDA) DURING ADOLESCENCE

As mentioned earlier, adolescents experience dramatic physical growth and development during puberty, which increases their requirements of energy, protein, vitamins, and minerals. They are at greater nutritional risk because in this age group, the demand for nutrients is high, but since they make their own food choices, they end up consuming foods that are high in carbohydrate, fat and sugar, and low in nutrients like calcium and iron, thereby leading to calcium deficiency and iron deficiency anaemia. This section discusses the nutrient requirements during adolescence.

Energy

The energy requirements are different for boys and girls because of the differences in growth rate, body composition and physical activity level. On the one hand, increased consumption of calorie-dense fast foods, snacks and processed foods, and on the other, decreased physical activity makes the adolescent prone to obesity. Thus, maintaining a balance between energy intake and expenditure is important to prevent obesity.

Underweight, which is also a form of malnutrition, is also very common in adolescent girls. Besides inadequate intake due to poverty, it may result from excessive concern regarding weight, which leads to the skipping of meals or eating very little, leading to an energy deficit. Table 23.1 gives the recommended dietary allowance of energy for adolescents. Boys in the age group of 16–17 require maximum energy intake, which is 3,020 kcal/d, followed by 2,750 kcal/d among 13–15-year-old boys. Girls in the age group of 13–15 and 16–17 years require 2,330 kcal and 2,440 kcal per day, respectively.

Protein

To support growth, protein requirement is higher in the adolescent period. This protein requirement includes both the maintenance requirement and its deposition in the body. Inadequate protein intake at this age will lead to a reduction in linear growth, lean body mass and delayed sexual maturation. Protein requirements for 16–17-year-old boys (61.5 g/d) and girls (55.5 g/d) are slightly more than the requirements for adult males and females. Boys and girls in the 13–15 age group require 54.5 g/d and 51.9 g/d of protein, respectively. In order to improve the quality of protein, one should include milk, meat and their products in the diet. Also, consuming meals in cereal-pulse, cereal-meat and cereal-milk combinations enhances the protein quality of a staple cereal diet.

Fat

The RDA for visible fat intake is higher for boys in the 13–15 and 16–17 age groups, 45 grams and 50 grams, respectively, in comparison to girls in the same age group (40g for 13–15-year-old girls and 35g for 16–17-year-old girls). Fat intake depends on the total calorie intake. In a balanced diet, 25–30 per cent calories should be provided by fats, 55–60 per cent from carbohydrates, and 12–15 per cent from proteins. Fats, oils and nuts are ideal for increasing the energy density of a meal, and reducing the bulk. As boys need more calories, their fat intake is also greater in comparison to girls. Decreasing the amount of saturated fat and cholesterol and including foods containing the healthier monounsaturated and polyunsaturated fats is advisable to reduce the risk of cardiovascular disease in adulthood.

Fat-soluble Vitamins

Vitamin A: Vitamin A play a crucial role in vision, reproduction, growth, and differentiation. It is also needed for proper bone growth and immune functioning. The RDA of vitamin A remains the same for both boys and girls from 13–17 years, that is, 600 μg/d retinol or 4,800 μg/d of β-carotene. Adolescents should consume plenty of fruits and vegetables so as to improve the intake of vitamin A. Consumption of greens, yellow/orange fruits and vegetables, and animal products such as fish, liver, eggs, and milk will provide the required amount of vitamin A.

Vitamin D: As vitamin D helps in the absorption and metabolism of calcium, sufficient sunlight exposure is advised. Dietary sources like egg, fish and fortified foods are few, but can also contribute to vitamin D intake. Adolescents should be involved in some outdoor physical activity, during the day as it will not only help them to obtain sufficient vitamin D, but will also control or maintain their weight and encourage the development of muscular tissue.

Vitamins E and K: Vitamin E is an antioxidant vitamin and is readily available from vegetable oils, meat, eggs, and cereals. The amount that should be consumed is related to the intake of essential fatty acids. Vitamin K on the other hand, is needed for the proper clotting of blood. Food sources include green leafy vegetables, fish, liver, meat, and eggs. It can also be synthesised in the intestine by the bacteria. Both vitamins E and K are readily available in Indian diets, and so the ICMR has not given their RDAs.

Water-soluble Vitamins

Vitamin Bs and C: Vitamin B includes a wide range of vitamins—thiamine, riboflavin, niacin, vitamin B_6, folate, vitamin B_{12}. These B vitamins are needed for energy metabolism, and vitamin C acts as an antioxidant. With the increase in the RDA for energy with age, the requirements for thiamine, riboflavin, niacin, and folate increase, while the requirements for pyridoxine, vitamin B_{12} and vitamin C remain the same throughout adolescence (Table 23.1).

Minerals

Calcium: Calcium is needed to attain skeletal growth, body size, and increase in bone mineral density. Adolescents in the age group of 13–17 should consume 800mg of calcium. The requirement is highest in this age group, with the exception of pregnancy and lactation. Milk and its products are the richest sources of calcium, but adolescents generally tend to reduce their intake of milk as a beverage as they grow up. If they fail to meet the calcium requirements at this stage when the bones are developing their peak mass, it increases the risk of developing osteoporosis at a later age. Adequate calcium is needed to develop peak bone mass in the pre-adolescent and adolescent stages, so as to prevent osteoporotic fractures at a later stage.

> ***Peak Bone Mass (PBM)***
>
> Peak bone mass is defined as the maximum strength and size of the bones. A high peak bone mass reduces the risk of osteoporotic fractures later in life. Puberty and adolescence is the best time to develop strong bones, since almost 90 per cent of peak bone mass is acquired by age 18 in girls and age 20 in boys, and it continues till the age of 30. After that, bone remodelling occurs, and so one loses more bone mass as compared to gaining. To develop peak bone mass, adequate amounts of calcium and vitamin D should be included in the diet. Along with a healthy diet, regular physical activity is needed to develop peak bone mass.

Iron: Iron deficiency anaemia is the most common public health problem in adolescent girls. Adolescent girls are at increased risk of anaemia due to, rapid growth and development and menstruation, which increases the demand for iron. The requirement of iron in the age group of 13–15 is 32 mg/d for boys, and 27 mg/d for girls, respectively. There is a decrease in the RDA for iron for the 16–17-year-old adolescent; it is 28 mg/d for boys and 26 mg/d for girls.

In the diet, iron is available in two forms—heme iron and non-heme iron. Heme iron is found in animal sources such as meat, fish and poultry and is highly bio-available, while non-heme iron, found in plant sources such as vegetables, fruits and grains, is not readily absorbed. Since non-heme iron has low bio-availability, diets should include certain foods which enhance iron absorption. These include heme iron sources or vitamin C.

Zinc: This mineral is vital for protein formation and gene expression. Zinc is important for growth and sexual maturation in the adolescent. Zinc deficiency can adversely affect normal growth and delay sexual maturation. Zinc deficiency also lowers immunity, making adolescents more prone to infections. The recommended intake of zinc is 11 mg/d for 13–15-year-old adolescents, and 12 mg/d for 16–17-year-old adolescents, respectively. Zinc is present in flesh foods, fish, milk, pulses, and nuts.

FOOD BEHAVIOUR AND BODY IMAGE

The food behaviour of adolescents includes skipping meals, particularly breakfast, snacking and fast food consumption. Other eating behaviours that are generally common among adolescents are eating away from home, low intake of fruits and vegetables, as well as milk and milk products. Poor food choices can have a profound impact on their growth and development. Lifestyle, food behaviour, and psychological factors influence the health status of adolescents, and increase the risk of under-nutrition, obesity and micronutrient deficiencies.

Skipping Meals

The skipping of meals is a common practice in this age group, and this is more common in girls than in boys. Girls generally miss meals in an effort to lose/maintain weight. Generally, breakfast, which is the most important meal of the day, is not consumed. The reason could also be waking up late, and consequently getting late for school/college. As schools and colleges begin very early in the morning, many children do not feel like eating at that hour. The ill-effects of skipping breakfast are short attention span and lack of alertness in the classroom, which then negatively impacts the learning process.

Snacking and Fast Food Consumption

When adolescents skip meals, they tend to consume more snacks and fast foods. To satiate hunger sensations, they pick up foods readily available in their vicinity, like school/college canteens or fast food outlets in areas where they socialise. Fast foods tend to be energy-dense foods that are high in fat or sugar. They generally lack other important nutrients. Adolescents choose these foods for their taste and convenience. The affordable prices of snacks and fast foods also increase acceptability in this age group.

Body Image

Dissatisfaction with weight among adolescents is a common concern (Figure 23.1). Body image is a person's inner conception of her/his own physical appearance, and this may or may not match with objective reality. If adolescents are preoccupied with their weight, they follow strategies like dieting, skipping meals and fasting, and may develop eating disorders such as anorexia nervosa and bulimia nervosa. Such practices make adolescents prone to nutritional deficiencies and adversely affects their nutritional status.

> ***Interesting Fact***
>
> Breakfast skippers are at greater risk of obesity and weight gain. Teenagers who eat breakfast generally have a lower body mass index (BMI).

Table 23.1 RDA for Adolescents

Group		*Boys*	*Girls*	*Boys*	*Girls*
Category/ Age		13–15 years	13–15 years	16–17 years	16–17 years
Body weight (Kg)		47.6	46.6	55.4	52.1
Energy(kcal/d)		2750	2330	3020	2440
Protein (g/d		54.3	51.9	61.5	55.5
Visible fat (g/d)		45	40	50	35
Calcium (g/d)		800	800	800	800
Iron (mg/d)		32	27	28	26
Zinc (mg/d)		11	11	12	12
Magnesium(mg/d)		165	210	195	235
Vitamin	Retinol	600	600	600	600
A (μg/d)	β-carotene	4800	4800	4800	4800
Thiamine (mg/d)		1.4	1.2	1.5	1.0
Riboflavin (mg/d)		1.6	1.4	1.8	1.2
Niacin equivalent(mg/d)		16	14	17	14
Vitamin B_6 (mg/d)		2.0	2.0	2.0	2.0
Ascorbic acid(mg/d		40	40	40	40
Dietary Folate (μg/d)		150	150	200	200
Vitamin B_{12} (μg/d)		0.2-1	0.2-1	0.2-1	0.2-1

Source: ICMR 2010.

Figure 23.1: Body Image

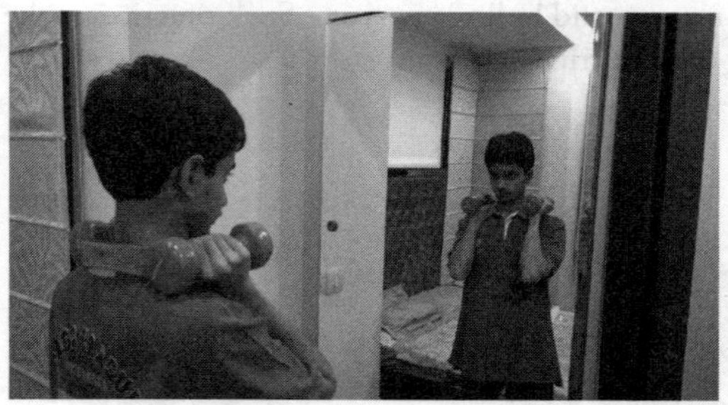

Photos courtesy: Naina Mathur and Kunal Mathur

DIET AND FEEDING PATTERN

A healthy diet throughout adolescence is important for adequate physical growth and cognitive performance. Parents and elders should play an active role in shaping the food behaviour of children. The home food environment needs to be appropriate for establishing healthy food behaviour. If elders in the family consume unhealthy foods themselves, or stock up on junk food and beverages at home, they will find it very difficult to teach their children about healthy food choices. The following are some tips for healthy eating:

- A nutritionally healthy diet should be consumed through a wise choice of foods from all the food groups (cereals, pulses, milk and meat products, fruits and vegetables, fats and sugar).
- The diet should have good quality protein, so meals should be consumed in cereal-pulse, cereal-milk and cereal-meat/egg combinations.
- Green leafy vegetables, other vegetables and fruits should be consumed in plenty. They not only provide vitamins and minerals like iron, calcium and β-carotene, but are also a source of dietary fibre.
- Milk and its products should be taken in adequate amounts, as this is the best time to make the bones strong.
- Fast foods and snacks can be made nutritious with slight modifications, for example, in burgers, *aloo tikki* can be substituted with *dal* or *paneer tikki*, and more vegetables can be added to noodles.
- Keep a check on the total fat consumption. Fried and bakery foods should be consumed in moderation, and not as a part of the daily diet.
- Excessive sugar and salt intake should be avoided.
- Avoid skipping meals, especially breakfast.
- Involve in at least 60 minutes of physical activity to develop healthy muscle tissues and bones.
- Abstain from smoking, chewing tobacco and drinking alcohol.

A sample menu plan (Box 23.1) and a balanced diet (Table 23.2) for adolescents has been drawn up. It gives the number of portions of the different food groups that must be consumed for the diet to provide an adequate amount of nutrients.

Table 23.2: Balanced Diet for Adolescents

Food Group	*g/ portion*	*Years*			
		13–15		*16–18*	
		Girls	*Boys*	*Girls*	*Boys*
Cereals and millets	30	11	14	11	15
Pulses	30	2	2.5	2.5	3
Milk (ml) and milk products	100	5	5	5	5
Roots and tubers	100	1	1.5	2	2
Green leafy vegetables	100	1	1	1	1
Other vegetables	100	2	2	2	2
Fruits	100	1	1	1	1
Sugar	5	5	4	5	6
Fat/ oil (visible)	5	8	9	7	10

Note: To calculate the day's requirement of the above-mentioned food groups for adolescents, multiply grams per portion with number of portions. One portion of pulse may be exchanged with one portion (50g) of egg/meat/chicken/fish.

Source: Dietary Guidelines for Indians, NIN 2011.

Box 23.1: Sample Menu Plan for a Day

Age	14 years
Sex	Female
Activity level	Sedentary
Socio-economic status	Middle-income group
Food habits	Vegetarian

RDA (as per ICMR 2010)

Energy: 2,330 kcal/d

Protein: 51.9 gms/d

Important nutrient: Iron: 27 mg/d

Sample Menu Plan

Meal	***Menu***
Breakfast	Milk – 1 glass
	Besan toast – 2
	Almonds – 6–8
Packed Lunch	*Parantha* – 2
	Paneer bhujia – 1 bowl
	Apple
Lunch	*Chapati* – 2
	Rice – ½ medium bowl
	Rajma curry – 1 bowl
	Aloo-Methi – 1 bowl
	Cucumber *raita* – 1 medium bowl
Evening tea	Milk shake – 1 glass
	Poha/upma – 1 bowl
	Peanut *chikki*
Dinner	*Chapati* – 2
	Rice – ½ medium bowl
	Dal – 1 bowl
	Cauliflower-potato *sabji* – 1 bowl
	Vermicelli *kheer* – 1 bowl

NUTRITIONAL CONCERNS

Anaemia: Iron Deficiency Anaemia (IDA) is a public health concern among adolescents. About half of the Indian adolescent population is anaemic. Menstruation in girls increases the demand for iron, and can lead to iron deficiency anaemia if the intake is not sufficient. Boys, on the other hand, are at risk for anaemia during their adolescent growth spurt. Risk factors for iron deficiency in teenagers are vegetarian eating styles (low intake of meat, fish and poultry), frequent dieting or restricted eating, altered absorption, and heavy menstrual periods. The consequences of anaemia are impaired cognitive function, decreased work capacity, and compromised immune functioning. Nutritional management includes the consumption of iron-rich foods like meat, fish and poultry, and green leafy vegetables and nuts. Foods rich in vitamin C (*amla*, orange, guava, lemon, etc.) should be taken in plenty along with the iron-rich food, because it enhances the absorption of non-heme iron.

Micronutrient deficiencies: Adolescents are prone to other micronutrient deficiencies, like those of vitamin A, iodine, calcium, and zinc. Although vitamin A deficiency is mainly a nutritional problem among young children, it is now being seen among adolescents as well. Vitamin A is needed for adequate bone growth and sexual maturation in puberty. A diet lacking in milk and milk products and in green leafy vegetables is the contributory factor for vitamin A deficiency.

Iodine deficiency: It affects neuromuscular and cognitive performance, retards physical development, lowers the IQ level, and affects school performance. Iodine Deficiency Disorder (IDD) can develop because of low levels of iodine in the diet, or because of the presence of goitrogens in the diet, which interfere with the normal utilisation of iodine. It is recommended that only iodised salt should be consumed.

Calcium deficiency: Calcium is needed for adequate skeletal development. The requirement of calcium is the maximum in the 10–17 age group, for the development of peak bone mass. Since the diet of adolescents may lack in milk and milk products and green leafy vegetables, a deficiency of calcium at this stage affects bone mineralisation, leading to a risk of osteoporotic fractures later in life.

Zinc deficiency: Zinc is needed for growth, fertility, and proper immune functioning. The inadequate intake of animal products and presence of phytates in cereals decreases the availability of zinc, leading to zinc deficiency. Zinc deficiency delays sexual maturation.

Obesity: In developing countries such as India, adolescent obesity is emerging as a major health problem, especially in urban populations (Figure 23.2). The reason is the increased consumption of calorie-dense foods and decreased physical activity. Obesity results from a positive energy balance, where the intake of energy (food) is greater than the expenditure. Obesity increases the risk of diabetes, heart disease, hypertension, and polycystic ovary syndrome (PCOS) in girls. It is a condition characterised by irregular or no menstrual periods, acne and excess hair growth. Obese adolescents often suffer discrimination by the peer group, and to compensate for that, they indulge in overeating, which further worsens their condition. The only way out is weight management through healthy eating and being physically active.

Figure 23.2: Etiology of Obesity

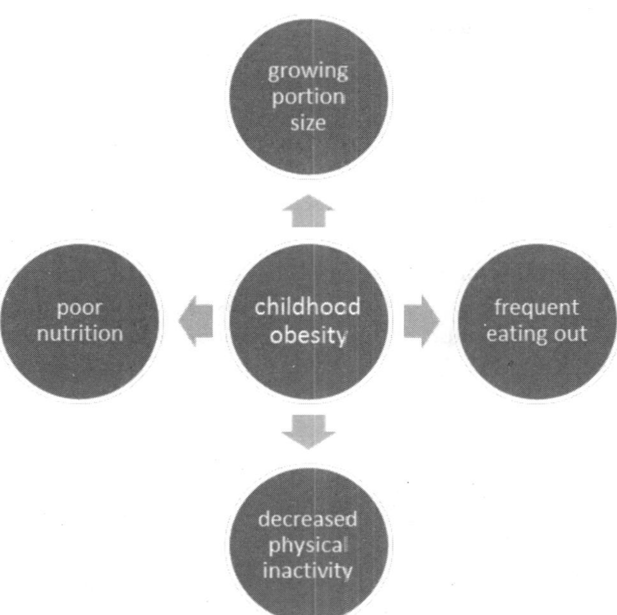

Eating Disorders

As mentioned earlier, excessive concern about weight amongst adolescents may lead to psychological illnesses like Anorexia Nervosa and Bulimia Nervosa (Figure 23.3). **Anorexia nervosa** is characterised by a failure to maintain adequate body weight, body image disturbance, and excessive dietary restriction, and it may be accompanied by periodic binge eating and purging (for example, self-induced vomiting, laxative use). The symptoms include muscle wasting, growth retardation, dry brittle hair, dry skin, and amenorrhea (absence of menses).

Bulimia Nervosa is characterised by recurrent binge eating (consuming large amounts of food while feeling out of control) accompanied by compensatory behaviours to prevent weight gain, and body image disturbances. Compensatory behaviours may be purging (self-induced vomiting, laxative, diuretic, or enema use) or non-purging (excessive exercise, fasting). Salivary gland enlargement, dental problems, heartburn, bloating, and irregular menstrual periods are some common problems associated with bulimia nervosa. Treatment is a long process and includes support from a psychologist, physician and dietician.

Figure 23.3: Common Eating Disorders

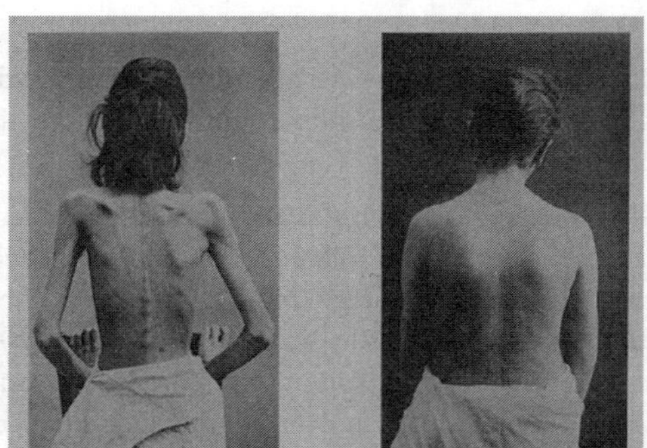

(a) Anorexia nervosa – before and after treatment

(b) Bulimia nervosa – vomiting after eating due to guilt

Source: http://commons.wikimedia.org.

Like Anorexia Nervosa and Bulimia Nervosa, **Bigorexia** is an obsessive compulsive disorder in males. It is also termed Muscle Dysmorphia. Phillips O'Sullivan and Pope introduced this term in 1997. Bigorexia or muscle dysmorphia is a disorder most commonly seen in males, wherein the individual is obsessed with his muscle size and has a constant desire to develop very large muscles. Persons afflicted with this disorder constantly obsess and worry about being underweight, despite having adequate muscle mass.

The individual spends an excessive amount of time working out in the gym and consuming a very high protein diet (full of eggs, meat and milk). The side effects of consuming a very high protein diet are damage to the kidneys and calcium loss from bones, leading to a risk of osteoporosis. Sometimes steroids or protein supplements are also consumed in order to build high muscle mass. Complications include muscle and bone injuries, and mental disturbances like anxiety and depression.

Teenage Pregnancy

Teenage pregnancy is pregnancy between puberty and the age of 19. In rural India, early childbearing is common, especially in states like Rajasthan, Haryana, Uttar Pradesh, Bihar, and Karnataka. Although by legislation the right age for marriage for both girls and boys is 18 years and 21 years, respectively, every year many girls get married and become

> ***An Alarming Fact***
>
> **Teenage pregnancy** is estimated at 16% in the 15–19 year age group.
>
> *Source:* NFHS 3 (2005–06).

pregnant or give birth to a child before turning 20 (teenage pregnancy). This is a result of early marriage, sexual violence and unprotected sex.

During adolescence, there is already an increased requirement for nutrients; over and above that, pregnancy further enhances the need for nutrients. Teen pregnancies carry extra health risks to both the mother and the baby. Often, teenagers do not receive timely prenatal care, and are at a higher risk for pregnancy-related high blood pressure and its complications. Risks for the baby include abortion, premature birth and a low birth weight.

SUMMARY

- Adolescence is a transition period between childhood and adulthood.
- It is a period of rapid growth and development.
- A diet adequate in the quantity and quality of nutrients is needed to support growth.
- Skipping meals, fast food consumption, snacking, and eating away from home are common among adolescents.
- Foods rich in iron should be included to prevent iron deficiency anaemia, and calcium should be consumed in plenty for the development of the skeletal system and peak bone mass.
- Obesity is a common problem in adolescents because of an excess consumption of calorie-dense foods and reduction in physical activity. Obese adolescents tend to become obese adults.
- Dieting should be discouraged, as it adversely affects growth and the nutritional status.
- Maintaining the energy balance is important. Limiting the intake of fat and sugar and engaging in regular physical activity will help.
- Excessive concern regarding one's weight makes the adolescent prone to eating disorders like anorexia nervosa and bulimia nervosa.
- Micronutrient deficiencies like those of iron, vitamin A, calcium, iodine, and zinc are also seen in the adolescent age group.
- Teenage pregnancy is a major contributor to maternal and child mortality, and it also leads to the vicious cycle of malnutrition.

KEY WORDS

Bone mineral density: The total mineral content of the bone, divided by the width of the bone.
Body Mass Index (BMI): Defined as body weight in kilograms divided by height in square metres.
Energy Balance: The state in which the intake of energy equals energy expenditure.
Menstruation: Normal vaginal bleeding that occurs as part of a woman's monthly cycle.
Osteoporosis: A condition of decreased bone mass, leading to porousness of bones.

EXERCISES

1. Define the following terms:
   (a) Energy balance
   (b) Anorexia nervosa
   (c) Bulimia nervosa
2. Describe growth and development in adolescents.
3. What are the common nutritional concerns for adolescents?
4. Describe the food behaviour of adolescents, and discuss how it affects their nutritional status.
5. Discuss any two nutrients that are of significance for the adolescent.

REFERENCES

Arnold, F., Sulabha Parasuraman, P. Arokiasamy, and Monica Kothari, *Nutrition in India*, National Family and Health Survey (NFHS-3), India, 2005–06, Mumbai: International Institute for Population Sciences; Calverton, Maryland: ICF Macro, 2009.

Bamji, Mahtab S., Kamala Krishnaswamy and G. N. V Brahmam (eds), *Textbook of Human Nutrition*, 3e, New Delhi: Oxford and IBH, 2009.

ICMR, 'Nutrient Requirement and Recommended Dietary Allowances for Indians', A Report of the Expert Group of the Indian Council of Medical Research, Hyderabad: National Institute of Nutrition, 2010.

International Institute for Population Sciences (IIPS) and Macro International, *National Family and Health Survey (NFHS-3), 2005–06, India: Key Findings*, Mumbai: IIPS, 2007.

Joshi, Shubhangini A., *Nutrition and Dietetics: With Indian Case Studies*, 3e, New Delhi: Tata McGraw Hill, 2010.

Khanna, K., S. Gupta, S. J. Passi, R. Seth, R. Mahana, and S. Puri, *Textbook of Nutrition and Dietetics*, 2e, India: Elite Publishing House, 2013.

Mahan K., S. Escott-Stump and J. Raymond, *Krause's Food and Nutrition Care Process*, 13e, Saunders Elsevier, 2011.

NIN, *Dietary Guidelines for Indians—A Manual*, 2e, Hyderabad: National Institute of Nutrition, 2011.

Wadhwa, A. and S. Sharma, *Nutrition in the Community*, India: Elite Publishing House, 2003.

Wardlaw, Gordon M., Jeffery S. Hampl and Robert A. DiSilvestro, *Perspectives in Nutrition*, 6e, New York: McGraw Hill, 2004.

Williams, S. R., *Basic Nutrition and Diet Therapy*, 11e, India: Harcourt, 2001.

World Health Organization (WHO), 'Nutrition in Adolescence: Issues and Challenges for the Health Sector', Discussion Paper on Adolescence, 2014. Available at http://whqlibdoc.who.int/publications/2005/9241593660_eng.pdf (accessed 3 January 2014).

24

NUTRITION FOR THE ELDERLY

HIGHLIGHTS

- The ageing process
- Changing nutrient needs
- Nutritional and health concerns and their management
- Nutrition and longevity

THE AGEING PROCESS

One of the fundamental and unavoidable facts of life is that our bodies change with age. Ageing is a gradual but inevitable phenomenon. It affects all species and is accompanied by a decrease in the individual's functional capacity and vitality. Ageing is a part of the lifecycle, which begins at conception and ends with death. Ageing is of multifactorial origin, and there is a programmed senescence of the cells in the body. Various degenerative mechanisms set in, which bring about physiological, psychological, immunological, biochemical, and morphological changes.

The ageing process is universal and the physical effects of old age are clearly noticeable. Yet, ageing is not a disease but a normal part of the lifecycle, which involves every dimension of an individual's life: physical, mental, social, and spiritual.

The exact timing of the onset of the ageing process cannot be ascertained, because the effect of age varies among different individuals. However, the chronological age is most often used by gerontologists to delineate the aged. In India, a cut-off age of 60 years is taken to classify people as 'old', and is used for census purposes. The elderly represent the fastest growing segment of populations throughout the world. In India, better health facilities and wider spread of medical care has raised the life expectancy. Longevity, accompanied by a decline in fertility, is leading to the rapid ageing of the Indian population. In India, the proportion of the elderly population (60 years and above) has steadily increased, from 6.8 per cent of the total population in 1991 to 7.4 per cent in 2001; and at present, the elderly constitute nearly 8.6 per cent of the total population.

The size of the elderly population has risen from 12.1 million in 1901 to about 77 million in 2001, and the number of the elderly is projected to rise to approximately 140 million by 2021 (Census 2011).Therefore, considering the present scenario, our health planners need to pay greater attention to the nutrition and health problems of the aged, so that healthy ageing is ensured for this fast growing segment of our population.

PHYSIOLOGICAL CHANGES ACCOMPANYING THE AGEING PROCESS

As we age, externally our hair greys and skin wrinkles, and internally, the function and efficiency of all tissues and organs decline. There is a change in the body composition and a progressive decline in water content and lean body mass.

> Various organs and systems of the body show a decline in function with ageing.

There is an average loss of 6.3 per cent lean body mass for each decade of age, which is compensated by an increase in body fat and a slight rise in body weight. By the time a person is 80 years of age, the muscle cells present in the body are reduced to 50 per cent. Muscle bulk and strength also diminish with ageing, although exercise regimens have been reported to deter the decline in lean body mass due to ageing. Conversely, chronic energy deficiency may accelerate the loss of lean body mass. Various organs and systems of the body show a decline in function, especially the gastrointestinal tract, sensory losses of vision, hearing, taste, smell, and also thirst. A decline in the efficiency of the liver, gall bladder, pancreas, kidney, and lungs, and a compromised immune system, may also be observed. Table 24.1 summarises the age-related physiological and pathological changes in the elderly.

Table 24.1: Age-related Changes in the Elderly

S. No.	*Function*	*Physiological and Pathological Changes*
1.	Oral	• Decline in taste acuity because of a decline in the number of taste buds. • Decline in the sense of smell, resulting in diminished appetite. • Loss of natural dentition due to tooth decay and gum disease. • Mastication difficulty due to loose painful teeth / ill-fitting dentures / edentulousness.
2.	Gastrointestinal tract	• Decreased secretion of stomach acid (hypochlorhydria) because of ageing or atrophic gastritis. • Decline in gastric, pancreatic and intestinal digestive enzymes, difficulty in digestion. • Decline in vitamin B_{12} absorption due to decreased secretion of intrinsic factor. • Distension and constipation. • Reduced stomach motility and peristaltic activity, along with slowing down in the movement of chyme through the intestine, decline in the liver's ability to metabolise drugs.
3.	Respiratory	• Decrease in lung capacity by 40–50%. • Decline in (BMR) by 8–12%.
4.	Senses	• Reduced sense of sight, hearing, odour, taste, and reflex actions.
5.	Nervous System	• Forgetfulness due to a reduction in nerve conduction velocity by 10–15%. • Less sleep.
6.	Cardiovascular	• Rigidity of blood vessels (atherosclerotic changes). • Narrowing of the lumen of vessels. • Decline in heart output. • Hypertension. • Disturbance in heart rhythm, decrease in the maximum heart rate, increased left ventricle muscle mass, and slowed ventricular relaxation.
7.	Genito Urinary	• Decline in the number of nephrons. • Reduced blood flow to kidneys. • Reduced filtration rate. • Water and electrolytes imbalance. • Urinary incontinence (inability to control the voiding of urine). • Renal function declines by about 30–50%.
8.	Skeletal	• Demineralisation of bones, leading to porous and fragile bones (osteoporosis), frequent fractures. • Stiffening of joints (flexibility reduces by 20–30%). • Reduction in bone mass by 25–30% in women, and 15–20% in men.

Despite these age-related changes, which are inevitable, one can still delay the onset of pathological problems with little care and caution, and enjoy healthy ageing. Healthy ageing can be achieved by giving due emphasis to the following lifestyle factors:

> Age-related physiological changes may not necessarily be accompanied by pathological problems.

1. Consuming a nutritionally adequate diet within one's resources, and avoiding excesses or nutritional inadequacies
2. Remaining physically active—activities could include walking, cycling, jogging, sports, gardening, household chores, and yoga.
3. Having positive social interactions within the family and the community, including religious discourses and workshops.
4. Medical care and health monitoring—periodic health check-ups are important with advancing age, as any alarming sign with respect to the lipid profile, blood sugar, blood pressure, haemoglobin, sudden weight gain or abnormal weight loss, could be indicative of chronic degenerative diseases, and can be checked before it becomes a fatal condition.

NUTRIENT NEEDS

There exists a wide variation in the ability of the elderly to ingest, absorb and utilise nutrients, which makes it difficult to generalise their nutritional requirements. However, due to decreased physical activity and lowered metabolism, the nutrient needs of the elderly are different from that of adults, particularly the energy requirements. The dietary guidelines for Indians, NIN (2011), suggests a reduced amount of calories, but adequate protein, carbohydrates, fat, vitamins, minerals, and dietary fibre. Also, an increase in the requirements for calcium, iron, zinc, vitamin A, and antioxidants to prevent age-related degenerative diseases for the elderly has been indicated.

> Energy requirements decrease with age because of a decline in physical activity and lowered metabolism.

The approximate percentage reduction in the total energy requirement recommended with advancing age is 20 per cent for those between 60–69 years of age, and 30 per cent for those between 70–79 years of age, and above. The ICMR recommendations for energy intake beyond the age of 30, based on body weight, BMR and activity pattern, is given in Table 24.2. Energy requirements decrease in old age because of a decline in the basal metabolic rate, due to a decrease in muscle mass and physical activity.

> Good nutritional status and a healthy lifestyle go a long way in ensuring healthy ageing.

The nutritional requirements for the elderly that are used presently have to rely on extrapolation from data collected on younger people. A growing body of scientific literature provides ample evidence that nutrient requirements are altered for ageing individuals, and that a need exists for redefining the recommended dietary allowances (RDAs).

Several clinical trials provide evidence of the changing nutrient requirements with age. The metabolic demand for vitamin B_6 to maintain glucose tolerance and normal cognitive function is higher in older adults. Vitamin B_6 and vitamin E supplementation has been shown to enhance the vigour of immune reactions, which slow down with age. The increase in the status of vitamins B_6, B_{12} and / or folate provides protection against elevations in homocysteine—an independent risk factor for cardiovascular disease, depression, and certain deficits of neuro-cognitive function. A good nutritional status of vitamin C, E and β-carotene (antioxidants) among the healthy elderly have shown a reduced risk of cancer, cataracts and heart disease.

Table 24.2: Energy Requirements of Indian Men and Women (60 Years and Above) According to Body Weights

Sex	*Body Weight Kg*	*Age 60 + years*		
			Activity	
		BMR kcal	*Sedentary Work kcal*	*Moderate Work kcal*
Males	45	1,039	1,590	1,870
	50	1,103	1,688	1,985
	55	1,167	1,786	2,101
	60	1,231	1,883	2,216
	65	1,295	1,981	2,331
	70	1,359	2,079	2,446
	75	1,423	2,177	2,565
Females	40	965	1,477	1,737
	45	1,015	1,553	1,627
	50	1,065	1,630	1,917
	55	1,115	1,706	2,007
	60	1,165	1,782	2,097
	65	1,215	1,860	2,187
	70	1,265	1,936	2,277

Note: PAR Values: Sedentary – 1.53; Moderate – 1.8; Heavy – 2.3.

Source: Nutrient Requirements and Recommended Dietary Allowances for Indians, ICMR 2010.

GUIDE TO HEALTHY EATING IN OLD AGE

The dietary guidelines given by the NIN (2011) recommend that since the elderly are physiologically less active, they need fewer calories to maintain their weight. The daily intake of oil should be restricted to 20 g, and the use of saturated fats like ghee, butter and *vanaspati* should be avoided. At least 200–300 ml of low fat milk and milk products, and 400 g of vegetables and fruits are recommended, which would provide fibre, micronutrients and antioxidants. Pulses and egg white are also important in the diet of the elderly. Small quantities of food need to be consumed at frequent intervals, and adequate water should be consumed to avoid dehydration, hyponatraemia (that is, decreased levels of sodium in the blood), and constipation. Figure 24.1 represents a food guide pyramid for the elderly. The food groups closer to the base of the pyramid need to be included in the diet, and as one moves towards the peak, the number of servings should be decreased.

The sensation of thirst is decreased in the elderly, and an effort may have to be made to drink adequate amounts of water.

Figure 24.1: Food Pyramid Guide for the Elderly

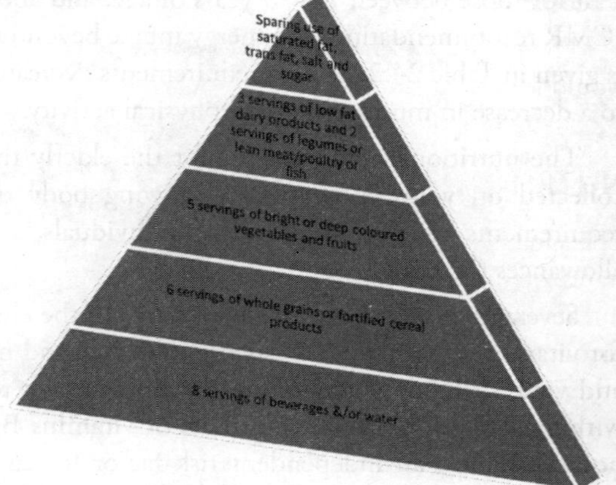

Source: Adapted from Modified Food Pyramid for older Adults, Tufts University, 2002

Foods that are nutrient-dense but low in sugar,oil and salt should be included in the menu of elderly people. Soft cooked vegetables, and adequate fluid and fibre in the from of soups help to relieve symptoms of constipation.

Box 24.1: A Day's Sample Menu for the Elderly

Early Morning	:	1 cup tea/coffee (with ¼ cup milk and 1 teaspoon sugar)
Breakfast	:	1 cup of low fat milk (with 1 teaspoon sugar)
		2 slices of bread/1 bowl porridge (*dalia*) / oatmeal / cornflakes, etc.
		25 g *paneer* /1 egg white
Mid-morning	:	Fruit *chaat* / sprouts *chaat*
		Lassi / juice/ fruits
Lunch	:	Salad / vegetable soup
		Chapati (whole wheat flour/combination of *besan* and whole wheat flour) 2–3 medium (20 gram each)
		Rice – 1 serving spoon
		Dal (with husk) – 1 bowl, or chicken / fish – 1 piece
		Vegetable preparation – 1 bowl
		Curd – 1 bowl
		Fruit – 1
		(use 1–2 teaspoon cooking oil)
Evening tea	:	1 cup tea/coffee (with ¼ cup milk and 1 teaspoon sugar)
		2–3 biscuits or *upma / poha* / sprouts – 1 small bowl)
Dinner	:	Same as Lunch
Bed Time	:	½ cup of low fat milk (with 1 teaspoon sugar)

Note: This menu provides approximately 1,600–1,700 kcal. The amount of different food items can be varied, depending upon the calorie requirement.

The sugar intake should be kept within 4 teaspoons / day (including the sugar in any dessert)

The elderly need more of vitamins and minerals to remain healthy and active, and therefore micronutrient-rich food should be included in the diets of elderly people to enable them to remain fit and active. Exercise has also been recommended for older adults to regulate body weight and decrease the risks of degenerative diseases. The exercise schedule, though, should be decided in consultation with a physician.

Therefore, one can delay the progression of physiological ageing by following judicious food choices, which would lead to a good nutritional status and ultimately good health and quality of life.

NUTRITIONAL AND HEALTH CONCERNS AND THEIR MANAGEMENT

> Both undernutrition and obesity pose serious threats to health of the elderly.

The elderly are typically a vulnerable group, as both the states of under-nutrition and over-nutrition pose serious threats to their health. The undernourished elderly may manifest chronic energy deficiency (CED), anaemia, and other micronutrient deficiencies like that of zinc, vitamin A and vitamin C.

Chronic under-nutrition increases the risk of morbidity, and can have serious health consequences like depressed immune function, increased risk of falls, fatigue, breathlessness, memory loss, and depression. The primary causes of under-nutrition among the elderly are decreased food intake, impaired absorption and poor utilisation of nutrients, along with the side effects of drugs, resulting in decreased appetite, increased urinary losses and drug nutrient interactions. Dysphagia and other physical problems may make eating difficult. Social causes may include living alone, inadequate income, and limitations in procuring and preparing food.

Obesity is also emerging as a cause of concern, especially among elderly women, as it predisposes them to reduced functional ability, cardiovascular diseases, arthritis, gout, and increased morbidity.

Osteoporosis is common among women in the post-menopausal phase of life, when there is a decrease in bone mass due to hormonal changes (oestrogen deficiency). As a result, the bones become lighter, porous and fragile, leading to frequent and spontaneous fractures and delayed healing. Negative calcium balance because of poor calcium intake, impaired intestinal absorption, reduced renal reabsorption, and decreased production of 1,25 dihydroxycholecalciferol (the active form of vitamin D) can aggravate bone demineralisation.

Osteoporosis is a metabolic accompaniment of advancing age, which leads to the thinning of bone, produces locomotor disabilities, and increases the risk of spinal compression fractures, and hip and wrist fractures. Chronic calcium and vitamin D deficiency can precipitate osteoporosis, especially in elderly women. Calcium and vitamin D supplementation in post-menopausal women helps to reduce the markers of bone turnover and slows the rate of bone loss, thereby benefiting women with low dietary calcium. Attaining an optimal accretion rate of bone mass during adolescence is important for optimum body size and skeletal maturity, and this attainment of peak bone densities is essential to prevent osteoporotic fractures in later life.

Nutritional Anaemias: Iron deficiency, folate deficiency and vitamin B_{12} deficiency anaemia are commonly observed in the elderly, and the causes could be nutritional, physiological or pathological. The physiological constraints of poor absorption and utilisation, along with low consumption of heme sources, green leafy vegetables, and fruits affect iron status. Also, the consumption of beverages like tea, which contain tannins, and phytates in cereal based diets inhibit the absorption of iron.

Diabetes: There is a progressive deterioration of glucose tolerance with age. Older adults have a greater susceptibility to non-insulin dependent diabetes mellitus (NIDDIM), and have the highest mortality from atherosclerotic complications related to NIDDM.

High blood sugar is also an important risk factor for cerebrovascular disease in elderly subjects. Weight management, dietary modification to maintain normal blood sugar level, and moderate exercise can help diabetic patients.

Cardiovascular Diseases: Cardiovascular diseases like atherosclerosis, acute myocardial infarction, angina pectoris, congestive cardiac failure, and hypertension are common among the elderly. Lifestyle modifications, by reducing salt intake, abstinence from alcohol and smoking/tobacco, maintenance of ideal body weight, and moderate physical activity can enhance HDL cholesterol, and reduce the tendency of the blood to form clots.

Arthritis: Arthritis is a disease that causes degeneration and roughening of the once smooth cartilage covering the bone joints, and formation of calcium deposits. These changes cause inflammation and pain in the joints. Osteoarthritis becomes more common with age, and is one of the leading causes of disability among the elderly. The only diet-related treatment that may offer some relief is to maintain an ideal body weight, as excess weight adds extra stress to the painful arthritic joints.

Constipation: Older adults may become constipated due to insufficient fluid intake, lack of physical activity and low intake of dietary fibre. It may also be caused by the effect of medications and delayed transit time in the gut. Consuming a fibre-rich diet, drinking plenty of fluids and exercising regularly help to prevent constipation.

Alzheimer Disease: Alzheimer disease is an irreversible and progressive deterioration of the brain, which causes patients to lose their memory, and their ability to reason and comprehend. It adversely affects the mental and physical health of older people. The causes of Alzheimer disease could be alterations in the protein production in the brain, strokes, obesity, diabetes, hypertension, altered blood lipoprotein composition, and high free radical levels.

An adequate intake of antioxidant nutrients, such as vitamins C and E, helps to protect the body from the damaging effects of free radicals. Adequate intakes of folate, vitamin B_6 and B_{12}, a diet rich in omega 3 and omega 6 foods and low in saturated and trans fatty acids, reduces the risk of Alzheimer disease. Regular physical activity is also known to improve the mental status in people afflicted with this disease.

WEIGHT STATUS AND CONSEQUENT MORBIDITY OR MORTALITY

The height, weight and BMI are good indicators for the risk of morbidity and mortality in young and middle-aged adults. Among the 50–65 year age group, overweight is an important public health problem in many countries. For those over the age of 65, the population data indicates that moderate overweight at older ages is associated with lower mortality. Among those older than 80 years, thinness and loss of lean body mass may be a more significant problem than overweight. Causes of death associated with low BMI are tuberculosis, obstructive lung disease, and cancer of the lung and stomach. Those related to high BMI are cerebrovascular disease, cardiovascular disease, diabetes, and colon cancer in men. Both overweight and thinness have detrimental effects and a risk of mortality; however, in the old, thinness carries a greater risk than overweight.

DIET AND FEEDING PATTERN FOR THE ELDERLY

The focus while planning diets for the elderly should be nutrient-based dietary guidelines, in order to reduce the burden of chronic disease afflicting this group. Foods that are nutrient-dense in vitamins and minerals but low in sugar, oil and salt should be included in the menu. It is important to consume easily digestible foods and small portion sizes. An effort should be made to incorporate at least eight glasses of water per day, as the thirst perception in the elderly may be diminished. Swallowing may be difficult because of decreased secretion of saliva, and therefore very dry meals should be avoided. A liberal intake of fruits and vegetables should be ensured for the provision of folate, antioxidant nutrients, vitamin C, and protective phytochemicals. Within the milk and milk product group (curd, *paneer*, cheese, etc.), emphasis should be on low fat dairy products for the provision of adequate amounts of protein, calcium and vitamin D, while at the same time avoiding the saturated fat and cholesterol of full fat milk. From the protein-rich group of pulses, poultry, fish, eggs, and nuts, individual choices can be made, based on availability, affordability, chewability, and ease of preparation.

> ***Health Benefits of Traditional Indian Food***
>
> Indian traditional herbs, spices and condiments have many health benefits which may help to delay chronic degenerative mechanisms.
>
> Certain bioactive compounds like phytochemicals, antioxidants, calcium, iron, and zinc modulate the ageing process.
>
> The elderly are custodians of tradition and have a lifetime of experience. They form the best resource for food and health beliefs.
>
> Some positive aspects of Indian cereal-based dietaries include vegetarianism, presence of fibre, and low dietary saturated fat.

Foods high in dietary fibre and adequate fluid intake should be stressed to relieve symptoms of constipation, and counter the decreased thirst sensation.

For the edentulous elderly, or those with artificial dentures and who have chewing difficulties, the following suggestions may be helpful:

- Chopping and grinding mechanically the foods that are hard to chew, or grating vegetables.
- Soft foods like *paneer*, eggs, soft cooked fish, finely minced meat or poultry can be used.
- Soft ripe fruits like banana, papaya, mango, cooked apples and pears, and fresh fruit juices with pulp can be given.
- Vegetable soups and soft cooked vegetables, chopped or mashed, can be incorporated.
- Cooked rice, *suji*, vermicelli, *poha*, and puddings can be given, although the elderly with diabetes would need sugar restriction; in such cases, artificial sweeteners may need to be used.
- Boiling/steaming can soften hard textured foods and give it a smoother consistency, ensuring the use of less fat, for example sprouts, *idli*, *dhokla*

NUTRITION AND LONGEVITY

Nutrition can play a major role in retarding the ageing process. All individuals show variations in the rate of ageing. Chronological age alone may not be useful in predicting the physical health status, as various other factors, like genetics, environment and lifestyle, impact the rate of ageing, and the consequent morbidity and mortality.

There are also certain bioactive compounds (both nutrients and non-nutrients) that play an important role in the physiological process modulating the ageing process. These include phytochemicals, antioxidants, calcium, iron, and zinc. Correction of nutrient deficiencies, especially of iron, zinc and vitamin C, has been found to overcome the sub-optimal immune competence in the elderly. Impaired immunity in the elderly is the major cause behind the proneness to infections and morbidity, especially to respiratory diseases. Phytochemicals, which are a variety of compounds produced by plants, help in slowing down the ageing process and reducing the risk of diseases, including heart disease, cancer, stroke, high blood pressure, cataracts, osteoporosis, and urinary tract infections.

Phytochemicals are related to plant pigments, and therefore yellow, orange, red, green, blue, and purple fruits or vegetables contain the most phytochemicals and nutrients.

Box 24.2: Man's Quest for Longevity

Finding an elixir of life to counteract the inevitability of the ageing process has been an obsession for many. History stands testimony to their relentless efforts to discover the magic potion that would bless them with immortality. Ponce de Leon, the sixteenth-century Spanish conqueror, actually scoured the wilderness in the present-day area of southern United States, searching for the 'fountain of youth'. Several scientists working in the quest of longevity, by way of serendipity, made many other significant discoveries. Plenty of literature is now available on this subject. Nutrition has been found to play a vital role in prolonging youth and vitality. The role of anti-oxidants like β-carotene, vitamins C and E, phytochemicals, and also the role of minerals like zinc, selenium, copper, and chromium as age-erasers have been extensively researched. Calorie restriction in animals has shown to delay the ageing process.

The Guinness World Records, the global authority on record-breaking achievements, announced **112-year-old** Salustiano Sanchez Blazquez from Grand Island, New York, as the world's **oldest living man** in July 2013. The greatest fully authenticated age to which any human has ever lived is 122 years, 164 days by Jeanne Louise Calment of France (www.guinnessworldrecords.in). Reports of extreme longevity have been documented from certain remote areas in the world—Hunzas from the Karakoram mountains, Abkhasians of the Caucasus, Vilcabambans of Ecuador, etc., where most residents live to be more than 100 years old. The physical process of ageing seems to be delayed in these people. A study of their lifestyles suggests common factors, like a fresh, clean mountainous environment, low calorie intake, life-long physical activity, and liberal intake of fresh fruits and vegetables, which could have contributed to their extreme longevity.

Source: Mathur 1996.

FACTORS AFFECTING LONGEVITY AND HEALTH

In developed nations, the average human lifespan is 80 to 85 years of age. While genetic predisposition influences longevity, other factors, such as diet, exercise and disease management, have a greater impact on the lifespan. Epidemiological studies reveal that factors like physical activity, diet, smoking, and alcohol influence cardiovascular health, and consequently life expectancy.

It is important to have a good quality of life, and not merely an extension of life. In order to achieve this, a healthy lifestyle needs to be adopted, which includes:

A balanced diet, which is antioxidant-rich, nutrient-dense, but not calorie-dense, comprising at least four to five servings of fruits and vegetables, six servings of whole grain cereals, two to four servings of low fat dairy products, and two servings of legumes and lean meat, which can help to retard cell damage responsible for the ageing process. At least six to eight glasses of water or clear fluids are also recommended to promote optimal organ function.

Regular **physical activity** can lower the risk of chronic degenerative disorders, like hypertension, diabetes and elevated cholesterol. Exercise enhances respiratory and cardiovascular functions, increases bone mass, and slows the decline in muscle strength. The digestion and bowel functions remain in good condition. Also, regular physical activity induces sound sleep and prevents depression.

Smoking causes adverse effects on health, and is associated with chronic degenerative diseases. However, cessation of smoking reduces the risk of heart disease, stroke, bronchitis, and certain cancers.

Alcohol. Limiting alcohol to one glass of wine per day has been shown to reduce the risk of liver diseases and certain cancers. But with advancing age, the adverse consequences of alcohol use become multifold. Older adults metabolise alcohol slowly, and even small amounts may react with the prescribed medications of the elderly. Alcohol aggravates hypertension and increases the risk of stroke in older adults.

The reduction of **anxiety and stress** helps to strengthen the immune system, and decreases the proneness to disease.

Social support and mental health. Social interaction and support prevent depression and reduce stress as individuals age. Regular mental activity, stimulation and life-long learning also lead to healthy mental functioning.

Therefore, lifestyle factors influence both the quality of life and life expectancy. A good quality of life during late adulthood can actually amount to a 'second adult lifetime', and can be called successful or healthy ageing.

HEALTH BENEFITS OF INDIAN TRADITIONAL CUISINE

The ancient Greek physician Hippocrates said, over 2,000 years ago, 'Let food be your medicine and medicine be your food'. Herbs, spices and condiments are an indispensable component of Indian traditional cuisine. Besides stimulating the appetite, they also promote digestion, and have general medicinal and curative properties. Table 24.3 enlists the health benefits of some commonly consumed condiments and spices.

Table 24.3: The Health Benefits of Common Condiments and Spices

Herbs/Spices /Condiments	*Characteristic Constituent*	*Health Benefits*
Carom Seed *(Ajwain)*	Thymol	Stimulant, anti-spasmodic, carminative, remedy for indigestion
Aniseed *(Saunf)*	Anethole	Mouth freshener, antiflatulent, mildly carminative
Asafoetida *(Hing)*	Odour components (for example, ferulic ester)	Anti-microbial, anti-flatulent, remedy for toothache and respiratory disorders.
Clove *(Laung)*	Eugenol	Carminative, anti-microbial assists in digestion, analgesic, relieves toothache, muscular cramps and headache.
Fenugreek seeds *(Methi)*	Saponins and alkaloids	Hypoglycemic and hypocholestrolemic
Garlic	Allicin	Anti-microbial, vasodilator, hypotensive, hypocholestrolemic, anti-carcinogenic
Ginger	Gingerol	Anti-microbial, expectorant, anti-carcinogenic. Beneficial in joint pain and prophylactic use in treating migraine headaches. Appetite stimulant, alleviates nausea.
Onion	Allylpropyl disulphide	Anti-microbial, hypocholestrolemic.
Turmeric *(Haldi)*	Curcumin, turmerones	Anti-microbial, disinfectant, anti-oxidant, anti-carcinogenic hypo cholestrolemic
Cumin *(Zeera)*	Cumino (an aldehyde)	Stimulant, diuretic, carminative
Cardamom *(Elaichi)*	Cineol, terpinyl acetate pinene, sabinene, limonene	Remedy for indigestion and genito-urinary disorders
Black Pepper *(Kali Mirch)*	Peperine	Household remedy for throat infections.

The elderly can definitely benefit from the hypoglycaemic, anti-carcinogen, hypocholestrolemic effects of common seeds like fenugreek and condiments like garlic, which have been clinically proven and tested.

SUMMARY

- The nutritional needs of the elderly are different from that of adults, particularly energy requirements, which decline due to lowered metabolism and decreased physical activity.
- Various organs and systems of the body show a decline in function and efficiency.
- The interrelationship between nutritional status, health, disease, and morbidity among the elderly has to be understood to promote a healthy lifestyle.
- The elderly may need special modifications in the texture and consistency of their diet because of dental problems, and appropriate menus considering the age-related physiological changes should be planned.
- The elderly are a vulnerable group, as both states of under and over-nutrition pose serious threats to their health.

KEY WORDS

Chronological age: A person's age stated in hours, days, weeks, months, or years and months since birth.

Constipation: A condition characterised by difficulty in passing stools.

Edentulous: Condition of being toothless to some degree.

Hypochlorhydria: A decreased secretion of hydrochloric acid in the stomach.

Osteoporosis: A progressive bone disease, characterised by a decrease in bone mass and density, which can lead to an increased risk of fracture.

Senescence: The organic process of growing older and displaying the effects of increased age.

Texture: Refers to structure, appearance, and consistency of foods or food items.

Quality of life: Refers to a general sense of happiness and satisfaction with one's life and environment.

EXERCISES

1. Whom would you designate as the 'elderly'?
2. What are the physiological changes that accompany the ageing process?
3. What are the factors that adversely affect the appetite of older persons?
4. Plan a one day's sample menu for an edentulous elderly.
5. What are the guidelines for planning a balanced diet for the elderly?
6. Why do energy requirements decrease with an increase in age?

REFERENCES

Census of India, 2011. Available at www.censusindia.net/results/resultsmain.html.

ICMR, 'Nutrient Requirements and Recommended Dietary Allowances for Indians', A Report of the Expert Group of the Indian Council of Medical Research, Hyderabad: ICMR, 2010.

Mathur, P., 'Nutrition and Longevity', *Nutrition* 30(4), 1996, pp. 3–14.

NIN, *Dietary Guidelines for Indians—A Manual*, Hyderabad: National Institute of Nutrition, ICMR, 2011.

World Health Organization, 'Physical status: The use and interpretation of anthropometry', Report of a WHO expert committee, Technical Report Series No. 854, Geneva: WHO, 1995.

ONLINE SOURCE

http://nutrition.tufts.edu

25

EXERCISE, SPORTS AND NUTRITION

HIGHLIGHTS

- Benefits of an active lifestyle
- Difference between physical activity, exercise, fitness, and sport
- Health-related and sport-related components of physical fitness
- Recommendations for physical activity and exercise
- The energy systems used in exercise and sport
- Dietary recommendations for various phases of competitive sport

INTRODUCTION

Physical activity, exercise or fitness is increasingly being emphasised for a good quality of life and long-term good health. An individual who is fit is capable of living life to its fullest extent. Lack of adequate physical exercise, however, may predispose an individual to long-term ill-health, and exacerbate the precipitation of chronic ailments based on genetic predisposition. Although the physical activity required by individuals at different stages in the lifecycle may differ, a moderate-intensity exercise regime of about 30–60 minutes has been reported to have a positive effect on several aspects of human health.

BENEFITS OF PHYSICAL ACTIVITY AND EXERCISE

The many benefits of exercise and physical activity are now well-documented. Regular physical activity has the ability to improve several physiological and biochemical parameters, reduce the risk of several major chronic diseases, as well as promote quality of life and a sense of well-being. The main advantages of regular physical activity include:

- Improved strength of bones, muscles and joints, and lowered risk of osteoporosis, thus improving abilities such as speed, power, flexibility, and agility
- Improved weight management
- Lower total blood cholesterol levels and higher good cholesterol (HDL) levels
- Lower risk of type 2 diabetes
- Lower risk of some cancers
- Lower blood pressure

> Physical activity, when performed regularly, contributes towards several physiological and biochemical parameters that lead towards a better quality of life.

- Reduced risk of a heart attack
- Better recovery from a heart attack
- A general feeling of well-being with more energy, a healthier and relaxed state of mind, and improved sleep.

DEFINITION OF PHYSICAL ACTIVITY, EXERCISE AND PHYSICAL FITNESS

'Physical activity', 'exercise' and 'physical fitness' are often used interchangeably, although each term has a different meaning.

Physical activity is defined as any bodily movement produced by skeletal muscles, which results in energy expenditure. The energy expenditure can be measured in kilocalories.

Physical activities in daily life may be categorised in a variety of ways. In India, physical activities have been commonly classified into light, moderate or heavy intensity activities by the Indian Council for Medical Research (ICMR). Light activities require a small amount of energy to be performed, only marginally greater than for sleep, for example, sitting, reading, standing, dressing, and walking slowly. Moderate activities require a reasonably high amount of energy to be performed, for example, walking briskly, jogging, cycling, etc. Heavy intensity activities require a very high level of energy to be performed, for example, sprint running, jumping, skipping, lifting weights, throwing, and swimming. Most sports, such as athletics, basketball, hockey, and football, require a series of heavy intensity activities.

Another simple categorisation of activities uses the time of occurrence of the activity, that is, at sleep, at work and at leisure; yet another divides them into wilful (activities you choose to do) or compulsory activities (activities you are assigned to do by an authority); or those performed weekly or on weekends; or they may be divided into occupational (related to your occupation or profession), sports, conditioning (training), household, or other activities. Various activities are performed by all individuals to sustain life; however, the amount and type of physical activity may vary from time to time and from person to person.

Exercise is a subset of physical activity that is planned, structured and repetitive, and has as a final or an intermediate objective the improvement or maintenance of physical fitness (Box 25.1).

Box 25.1: Important Elements of Physical Activity and Exercise

Physical activity

- Movement of the body using the skeletal muscle
- It causes energy to be expended
- Expenditure of energy is continuous and keeps varying during the activity
- It enhances a person's physical fitness

Source: Casperson et al. 1985

Exercise

All the aspects of physical activity

AND

- Series of repetitive bodily movements carefully planned for specific objectives
- It is adopted specifically with the aim of improved physical fitness

Physical fitness is a set of attributes that people have or achieve that are either health or skill-related. Being physically fit has been defined *as the ability to carry out daily tasks with vigour and alertness, without undue fatigue and with ample energy to enjoy leisure time pursuits and to meet unforeseen emergencies.*

COMPONENTS OF PHYSICAL FITNESS

Any bodily movement produced by skeletal muscles, which results in energy expenditure, is defined as **physical activity.**

Exercise is a subset of physical activity that is planned, structured and repetitive, and has as a final or an intermediate objective the improvement or maintenance of physical fitness.

A set of attributes that people have or achieve, which are either health or skill-related, is termed **physical fitness.**

Although components like vigour, alertness, fatigue, and enjoyment, mentioned in the definition of physical fitness, are difficult to measure, there are other attributes that comprise physical fitness and are important to public health as well as to sports ability. Hence, physical fitness may be classified into two types:

1. **Health-related fitness**
2. **Skill or sport-related fitness**

Both types of fitness consist of certain specific attributes that are measurable, and therefore easy to monitor. The attributes of the **health-related fitness** are:

1. **Cardio-respiratory endurance:** This component relates to the ability of the circulatory and respiratory system to supply fuel and oxygen during sustained physical activity, and to eliminate products produced due to fatigue, for example, lactic acid in muscle.
2. **Muscular endurance:** This component relates to the ability of muscle groups to exert external force for many repetitions or successive exertions.
3. **Muscular strength** relates to the amount of external force that a muscle can exert.
4. **Body composition:** This component relates to the relative amount of muscle, fat, bone, and other vital parts of the body.
5. **Flexibility** relates to the range of motion available at a joint.

The degree to which people have these attributes can be measured with specific tests. The most commonly used laboratory tests used to assess health-related physical fitness (Figure 25.1) are:

- Maximal oxygen uptake in the treadmill or bicycle ergospirometer systems for cardio-respiratory endurance;
- Hydrostatic weighing (the gold standard) for body composition;
- Cable tensiometer for muscle strength;
- Iso-kinetic dynamometer for dynamic muscle work (strength and endurance); and
- Flexometer for flexibility.

Figure 25.1: Some Equipment used to Assess Health-related Physical Fitness

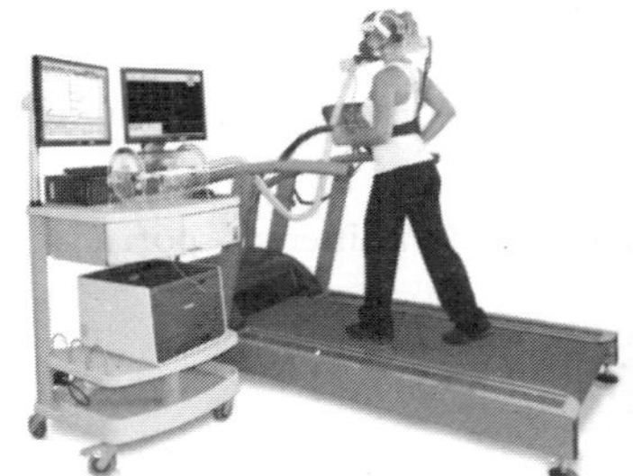

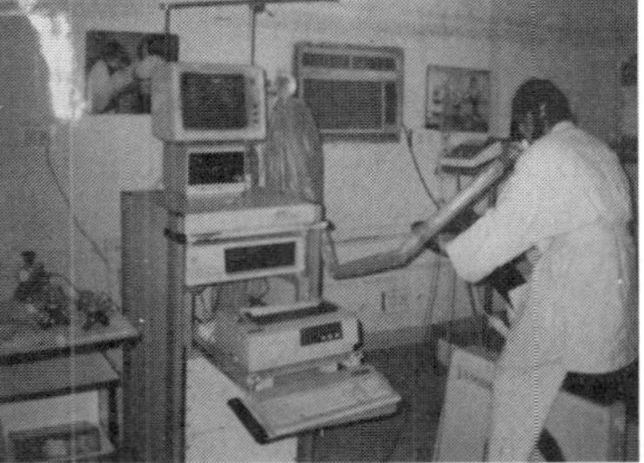

Treadmill and a bicycle ergometer for measuring cardio-respiratory endurance

Source: http://upload.wikimedia.org/wikipedia/commons/d/db/Ergospirometry_laboratory.jpg

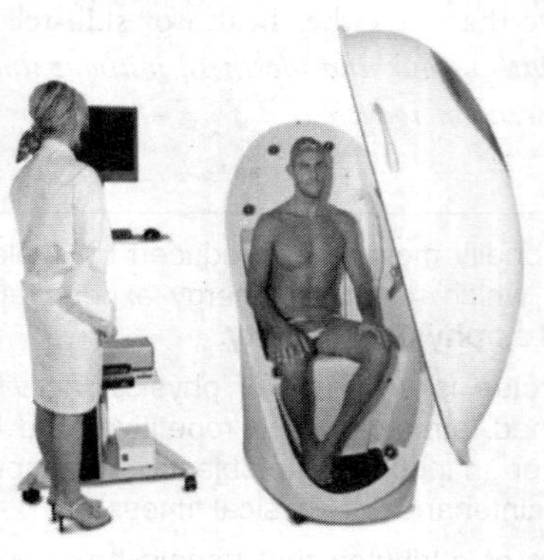

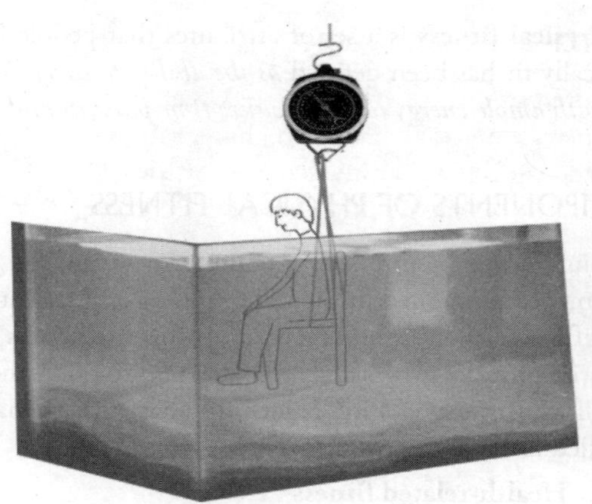

Air displacement plethysmography and under water weighing chamber for measuring body composition

Source: http://upload.wikimedia.org/wikipedia/commons/3/3d/Adult_body_composition_through_air_displacementplethysmography.jpg

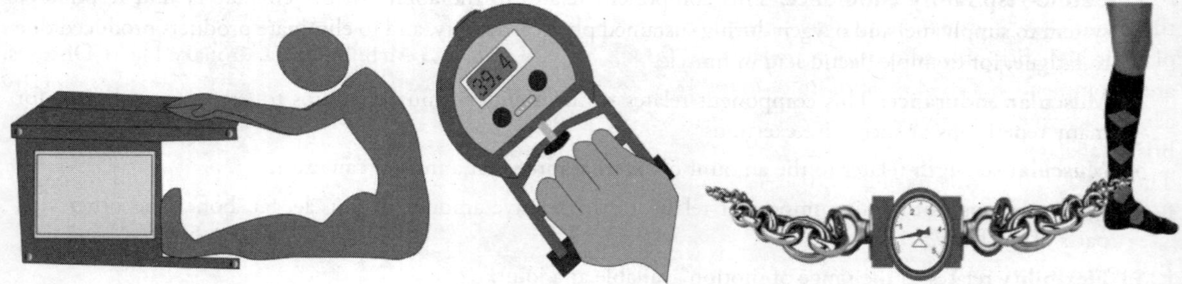

Flexometer for flexibilityHand grip dynamometer and Cabletensiometer for strength

Skill or sport-related fitness concerns athletes and related personnel who train towards maximal performance in a particular event or sport. The components of this type of fitness are:

1. **Agility:** Relates to the ability to rapidly change the position of the entire body in space with speed and accuracy.
2. **Balance:** Relates to the maintenance of equilibrium while stationary or moving.
3. **Coordination:** Relates to the ability to use the senses, such as sight and hearing, together with body parts in performing motor tasks smoothly and accurately.
4. **Speed:** Relates to the ability to perform a movement within a short period of time.
5. **Power:** Relates to the rate at which one can perform physical activity, or the ability to exert maximal force in as short a time as possible. Activities such as weight throwing or jumps require power.
6. **Reaction Time:** Relates to the time elapsed between the stimulus and the beginning of the reaction to it.

Various laboratory tests and sport-specific field tests using a variety of equipment are used to assess these skill-related components, and draw up fitness profiles for athletes involved in different sports.

PHYSICAL ACTIVITY AND EXERCISE THROUGH THE LIFESPAN

Maintaining an active lifestyle is important for all age groups, although exercise recommendations for different stages of life differ as per their needs.

Exercise for Children

Children in the age group of 5–11 years should accumulate 60 minutes of moderate (for example, bicycle riding and playground activities) to high intensity workouts (for example, running and swimming) every day. This should include vigorous intensity activities at least thrice a week, and activities that strengthen muscle and bones at least thrice a week. Higher durations of exercise give greater health benefits.

Exercise for Adolescents

Adolescents and youth in the age group of 12–17 years also need about 60 minutes or more of moderate (for example, bike riding, team games like basketball, football, or skating) to high intensity workouts (swimming or martial arts/fitness class) every day. This should include at least three days of high intensity and at least three days of moderate exercise or play.

Exercise for Adults

Adults in the age group of 18–64 years are globally recommended to gather at least 150 minutes of moderate to vigorous intensity workouts in a week, in bouts of 10 minutes or more. Regular exercise of 30 minutes at least five days in a week would also be beneficial. In addition, strengthening activities for the muscle and bones, using the major muscle groups on two days of the week for 30 minutes each day, are beneficial. Asian Indians, in view of their high risk of/predisposition towards developing Type 2 Diabetes Mellitus and Coronary Heart Diseases, are recommended a total of 60 minutes of exercise every day, including at least 30 minutes of moderate-intensity aerobic activity, for example, brisk walking, jogging, swimming, etc., and 15–30 minutes of work-related (such as a brisk walk to work) and muscle-strengthening exercises, like push ups, curls and neck/back strength exercises, etc. The ICMR (2010) also recommends at least 60 minutes of exercise such as walking at different speeds without load, in addition to other household and leisure physical activities, for about four hours.

Exercise during Pregnancy

Pregnant women benefit with regular activity of moderate intensity for 15–30 minutes every day. This includes walking, low-impact aerobics, pre-natal yoga, swimming, and slow static bicycling, in addition to other light physical activities performed in the household, such as cooking, dusting, sweeping, and washing utensils or clothes. Such activities should be taken up, especially by sedentary women, only under the recommendation of the gynaecologist or under proper supervision, and all necessary precautions to keep the impact low—such as warm-up and cooling down, starting slow, avoiding sudden jerks and jumps, avoiding breathlessness, taking adequate breaks, and adequate hydration—must be followed.

Exercise for Older Adults

Older adults in the age group of 65 years or more should exercise to improve their balance and limb mobility to avoid falls, especially if mobility is beginning to be a problem for them. If in good health, older adults should continue to work out like their younger adult counterparts, that is, they should gather at least 150 minutes of moderate to vigorous intensity workouts in a week in bouts of 10 minutes or more, or perform regular workouts of 30 minutes at least five days in a week. In addition, strengthening activities for the muscle and bones, using the major muscle groups on two days of the week for 30 minutes each day, are beneficial.

A total of 60 minutes of exercise every day, including at least 30 minutes of moderate-intensity aerobic activity, 15 minutes of work-related activity, and 15 minutes of muscle-strengthening exercises are recommended for Asian Indians by the 'Activity consensus group for physical activity guidelines for Asian Indians'.

ENERGY SYSTEMS IN EXERCISE

The human body needs a constant supply of energy for it to perform its many complex functions, including various physical activities and exercise. Energy demands increase with an increase in exercise, and the body must provide increased energy, or the exercise will cease.

Adenosine Tri Phosphate (ATP)—The Energy Currency of the Body

The body derives energy from the carbohydrates, fats and proteins ingested daily. The energy trapped within these nutrients is released when metabolic pathways within the cells break down the foods into their constituent parts—carbon dioxide and water. Some of the energy released during this conversion is conserved and used to make another high energy chemical, called **adenosine tri phosphate (ATP),** and the rest is lost as heat. ATP is the fuel used for all the energy requiring processes within the cells of the body, and is called the **energy currency** of the cell.

The energy produced from the breakdown of ATP provides the fuel that activates the processes of muscle contraction. The energy from ATP is transferred to the contractile filaments (myosin and actin) in the muscle, which attach to form **actomyosin**. Once activated, the myofibrils slide past each other and cause the muscle to contract.

Re-synthesis of ATP—The ATP-CP System

ATP is stored in the body in very limited amounts. Only about 3 ounces (85g approximately) of ATP can be stored in the body at one time, which amounts for energy that is sufficient only for less than a minute, or for several seconds of activity. To constantly provide energy for activity, ATP must be continuously re-synthesised.

Figure 25.2: Re-synthesis of ATP in the ATP–PC system

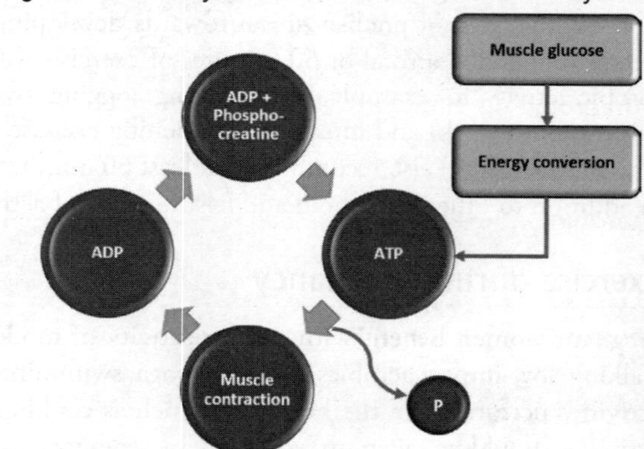

Source: Adapted from http://llewisbtecsport.blogspot.in/p/unit-one.html.

To release energy, ATP loses a phosphate bond and converts to **adenosine di phosphate (ADP).** This ADP combines with another high energy phosphate from **Creatine Phosphate (CP)** to re-synthesise ATP (Figure 25.2). Re-synthesis accounts for an energy release up to five times that from ATP alone, as the concentration of high energy phosphate bonds from CP is five times higher than the muscle ATP content. This is the fastest way in which ATP can be produced, and it takes place without the use of oxygen (anaerobically).

The ATP–CP system, although powerful, is time limited, due to the limited CP stores in the body. The energy released by this system will only support an all-out exercise effort of a few seconds, such as a weight lift, tennis serve, sprint run, long jump. If the all-out activity continues for over eight seconds, or if a moderate activity has to proceed for longer periods, the ATP–CP system alone will be insufficient. The body then relies upon the two other main systems to support continuous activity. These metabolic systems are:

1. **Anaerobic or lactic acid pathway:** The pathway used for supplying ATP beyond eight seconds of all-out exercise (continued exercise till exhaustion) is the lactic acid pathway, also called the anaerobic glycolysis or anaerobic pathway, as it functions without the presence of oxygen. The substrate for this pathway is glucose, which, after glycolysis, produces lactic acid and contributes ATP that can suffice for all-out effort lasting up to 60–120 seconds.

An athlete can continue to exercise even after the production of lactic acid if the intensity of activity comes down, as this helps in the conversion of lactic acid back to pyruvic acid in the presence of oxygen. If, however, the oxygen supply is insufficient to support this conversion, lactic acid accumulates in the exercising muscle, lowering the pH of that muscle and causing fatigue. Lactic acid can be removed from the muscle, transported into the bloodstream, eventually converted into energy in muscle, liver and brain; and especially stored in muscle and liver as glycogen. The rate and amount of this conversion and storage increases with physical training.

2. **Aerobic pathway:** If energy is to be produced constantly for more than 90–120 seconds, it requires the presence of oxygen (Table 25.1). This pathway takes place in the mitochondria (Kerb's cycle) and generates 36–38 ATPs per molecule of glucose. Apart from using glucose as a substrate, the aerobic pathway can also utilise fat and protein as substrates. This pathway continues to provide energy for exercise of moderate intensity, unless the availability of the substrate or oxygen gets limited. Conditioning (training with a regimen of exercise, diet and rest, etc., to enhance specific abilities such as endurance, speed and muscle strength) can greatly influence the use of substrate and the availability of oxygen for longer durations of activity.

Table 25.1: Contribution of Energy for Physical Activity by Various Systems

Energy System	*Time Span for Which it Contributes Energy*	*Activity For Which it is Useful*
ATP	Only a few seconds	ATP stores can fuel high intensity activity usually at the start of exercise, for example, starting a sprint
ATP-CP	Up to 8 seconds	ATP–CP fuels exercise to exhaustion, if the activity is of the highest intensity and finishes in 8 seconds
	or 15–20 seconds	ATP–CP fuels exercise at moderate intensity for more than 8 seconds up to 20 seconds
Anaerobic (Lactic acid pathway)	Up to 60–120 seconds	For the highest intensity exercise up to 60–120 seconds, anaerobic pathway is required
Aerobic pathway	Longer than 90–120 seconds	For exercise at moderate intensity, lasting more than 90 seconds, aerobic pathway is required

Source: Compiled from Mahan and Stump 2012.

The Energy Continuum

For exercise to be performed, no single energy pathway is sufficient to provide the energy needed. The interplay of various systems ensures its continuity. At the start of any activity, ATP and CP stores are utilised to provide energy. As exercise continues, the lactic acid system produces energy. If, at this stage, the exercise is at moderate intensity, the aerobic pathway becomes the dominant pathway, and the activity can continue for a long duration. However, if the activity is at high intensity, the lactic acid pathway is the dominant fuel supplier, and the activity has to stop or continue intermittently, for example, 200m swim and runs or high intensity runs in football, basketball and hockey, followed by low intensity jogs for recovery.

The energy system used is dependent on the availability of oxygen. Oxygen is available to the body only during low or moderate intensity exercise. The capacity for higher intensity aerobic exercise can be increased by training, up to a certain extent. However, at high intensities, the availability of oxygen decreases, and the lactic acid pathway is utilised. Hence, exercise at very high intensity cannot be prolonged for long durations. It either has to stop, or be continued intermittently.

DIETARY RECOMMENDATIONS FOR SPORTS

Athletes pursuing competitive sports may benefit from altering their diets in the following four phases:

1. The training phase

This phase accounts for most of the athletes' time and effort. Athletes take up various types of conditioning and training to continually gain performance in their specific sport. Appropriate dietary inputs help athletes take up maximal training loads, prevent nutritional deficiencies, aid daily recovery, and thereby ensure continuous performance gains.

2. Pre-competition phase

The phase after training and before the athletes take part in the competition is referred to as the pre-competition phase. During this period, athletes can benefit from alterations in diet, to maximise fuel and nutrient stores that are commensurate with continuous all-out exercise, sometimes lasting over several days. It also covers the pre-competition meal, before the athlete goes for the competitive event.

3. Competition phase or in-between events

This phase may last only a day (as in the case of marathons), or a few days, and is usually the period between the first competitive event and the last event in case of a series or championships.

4. Recovery phase

This phase is different from the day-to-day recovery from training. Athletes who have participated in a series of high-intensity competitions over a few days may need 7–10 days recovery after continuous and hard competition. This is the phase where an athlete initiates fuel and muscle regeneration with milder fitness exercise regimes and appropriate diets, to augment complete recovery before training can re-start.

Nutritional Considerations for Exercise and Sports

Energy

The most important component of successful sports training and performance is to ensure adequate calorie intake to support the energy being expended in training, and to support the maintenance of strength, endurance, muscle mass, and overall health. Energy requirements may vary, depending upon an athlete's weight, height, age, sex, and metabolic rate, and the type, frequency, intensity, and duration of the training and performance. Individuals who participate in an overall fitness programme, 30–40 minutes/day, thrice a week, generally need 25–35 kcals of energy/kg body weight/day. This amounts to 1,800–2,400 kcal/day, from a normal diet.

However, a 50 kg athlete engaging in more intense training of 2–3 hours/day, 5–6 times a week, or high volume training of 3–6 hours in one or more workouts each day, 5–6 days a week, may need an additional 600–1,200 kcals a day. This will amount to 50–80 kcal/kg/day, or a total of 2,500–4,000 kcal per day.

For elite athletes, such as the national or international-level athletes or heavier athletes, daily calorie needs can reach 150–200 kcal/kg body weight/day. This amounts to approximately 7,500–10,000 calories a day, depending on the volume and intensity of different training phases.

Estimating as well as meeting the calorie needs of athletes is challenging as energy expenditure changes very rapidly, between training sessions and during competition and recovery phases. Also, athletes need to balance daily routines, work, family responsibilities, sport-related travel and meal timings, quantum and quality effectively. Therefore, to meet the daily energy needs with adequate macronutrient distribution, athletes may need to add sports drinks and some industrialised or pre-packaged food, such as juices, cereals, and cereal or energy bars, along with fresh food. A flexible dietician, who takes into consideration individual athletic lifestyles, can effectively help athletes meet their energy and nutrient needs from daily diets. Athletes also need to be advised to weigh themselves regularly, and to monitor if they are consuming sufficient energy for each stage of their training and competition.

Macronutrients

For a general fitness programme, athletes can meet their macronutrient needs by consuming a normal diet of 45–55 per cent calories from carbohydrates (3–5 g/kg/day); 10–15 per cent from protein (0.8–1 g/kg/day); and 25–35 per cent from fat (0.5–1.5 g/kg/day). For moderate to high volumes of training, a minimum of 50 per cent, but ideally 60–70 per cent of total calories, should be met by carbohydrates. The remaining calories should be obtained from protein (10–15 per cent) and fat (20–30 per cent).

Carbohydrate

Carbohydrates are the main fuel for muscular work, and the only fuel for the brain. All fitness trainees need a minimum of 5–7 g/kg/day of carbohydrates for general training needs, and athletes training for endurance need 7–10 g/kg/day. High Glycemic Index foods, such as fruit juice, milk shakes, white bread sandwiches, etc., are useful for quick fuel recovery immediately after training sessions, and up to 24 hours after strenuous all-out exercises, such as during and after competitions.

Pre-exercise Carbohydrate Intake

Athletes need to train on an empty stomach, with sufficient stored fuel and fluids. Hence, this meal should be consumed at least 2–4 hours before training, and be high in carbohydrate content, that is, providing 55–60 per cent of energy. Fat delays stomach emptying (delays the emptying of food from the stomach to the intestines), and so should be limited to 25 per cent of the total energy if the meal is eaten 3.5–4 hours before training. If eaten closer to training sessions, fat should be less than 25 per cent of energy and carbohydrates higher than 60 per cent. Proteins should contribute 10–15 per cent of the total energy.

Pre-competition Meal

The high carbohydrate eating pattern is particularly important during **pre-competition meals**. This meal should be eaten 3–4 hours before an event, and should provide 200–350g of carbohydrates, or about 4g of carbohydrates/kg body weight. This allows sufficient time for digestion and absorption and addition to the fuel stores with complete emptying of the stomach. If the time lapse between eating and the competition is less, athletes should consume fewer carbohydrates, amounting to 1g carbohydrate/kg for each hour, for example, one hour before – 1g carbohydrate/ kg body weight, two hours before – 2g carbohydrate/kg, and so on. Easy to digest meals, such as potatoes (baked), bread, semolina, rice, or liquid meals are the best choices for a pre-competition meal.

Carbohydrate during Exercise (Training or Competition)

Up to one hour of exercise, no fuel except water is needed for replenishment. As exercise progresses beyond one hour, consuming fuel along with water enhances performance, acceptance of water, and a feeling of well-being during and after exercise. Carbohydrate intake can help delay fatigue, although it cannot prevent fatigue totally. The benefit of consuming carbohydrates during exercise depends on how quickly it can be emptied from the stomach. Research indicates that up to 6–8 per cent carbohydrate solution (6–8g carbohydrate in 100 ml of water), with minimum other additives except a pinch of salt, are most readily emptied by the stomach, absorbed and utilised quickly by the body, and are the most effective in delaying fatigue. The amount of such fluids required is 50–200ml (one cup), every 15–20 minutes of exercise. The form of carbohydrate consumed does not matter, and sports drinks, natural juices diluted to the right concentration, and even solids or gels, along with water, have the same effect, as long as the rate of carbohydrates is 26–30g every 30 minutes.

Carbohydrates after Exercise

Carbohydrates are required to generate glycogen fuel stores after exhaustive exercise, which takes up to 20 hours for complete regeneration. This is fastest if high amounts of carbohydrates (1–2 g/kg body weight/hour) are consumed immediately after exercise, frequently, that is, at 15–60 minute intervals, up to five hours after exercise. If eating carbohydrates is delayed by several hours after exercise, glycogen synthesis will be considerably slower and less. High Glycemic Index carbohydrates are better regenerators of glycogen, especially when consumed immediately after exercise (in the first few hours), than carbohydrates with a low Glycemic Index. This is most effective when 5–9g of protein is added with every 100g of carbohydrates, for example, sweetened milk shakes, jam and white bread sandwiches, pasta, baked potatoes, white rice, cornflakes, and gruels.

Protein

For individuals involved in general fitness programmes, the normal amount of protein (normal RDA, for example, 1 g/kg body weight for adults, or 1.06–1.18 g/kg for adolescents) will be sufficient. If 12–15 per cent of the total energy eaten is from proteins, this requirement of protein is met in fitness athletes of all age groups. However, for competitive or more intense sport, athletes need to consume 1.5–2 g/kg/day to maintain protein balance. Most athletes meet this requirement with 15 per cent protein energy intake, and a few who are involved in high intensity power sports, such as heavy weight categories in wrestling and weight lifting, may require about 20 per cent energy from protein sources, along with 25–30 per cent from fat and 50 per cent from carbohydrates. Consuming more protein than needed by the body will convert it into fat, and will not contribute to any increase in muscle mass.

Fat

Although the most readily available fuel for exercise and sport is carbohydrate, fats also contribute as fuel for exercise. It is also important for the maintenance of cellular membranes, skin, hormones, and the transport of fat-soluble vitamins. It is the major source of fuel for light to moderate intensity activities, such as brisk walking, jogging, cycling, etc. However, a total fat intake of more than 20–30 per cent is not required in most athletes. Athletes eating higher amounts of fat also use higher amounts of fatty acids as energy, while those eating high carbohydrates use more carbohydrate as fuel. However, high fat diets lower fat oxidation, while fasting for six hours before exercise optimises fat oxidation during an exercise session. For best performance results, therefore, carbohydrate intake is important.

The long-term use of high fat diets can have negative effects on health. Following a low fat diet protects against the risk of obesity, cardiovascular disorders, diabetes, and some cancers. Similarly, severe fat restriction (less than 15 per cent) may limit performance and affect health negatively, and is not advised. Hence, the consumption of fat should be maintained as 20–30 per cent of the total calories, on a long-term basis.

Vitamins and Minerals

Several micronutrients are important in exercise and sport, including folate, other B vitamins, calcium, and zinc. Less than one-third of the daily needs of thiamin, riboflavin, pyridoxine and vitamin C may lead to a decline in aerobic performance within a few weeks. In vegetarians, iron and B_{12} may also be of concern. Athletes involved in heavy training may need more of many nutrients, such as thiamin, riboflavin and pyridoxine, because they are important in energy production. Iron, vitamin D and calcium are of concern since the intakes of these may be low in athletes, especially children and adolescents. Further, the micronutrient intakes of athletes may be low due to training and work schedules, unplanned low nutrient snacks, infrequent nutrient-dense meals, and low calorie intakes due to concern with weight or appearance. Hence, frequent monitoring of vitamin and mineral status and supplementation (limited to 100 per cent RDA) when their diet is deficient, or they are clinically deficient, is safe for athletes.

Antioxidants—vitamin A, vitamin D, vitamin E, vitamin C, selenium, and phytonutrients—are important since they protect cell membranes from damage caused by free radicals. Physical exercise may increase oxygen uptake by 10–20 fold in the body, and a 100–200 fold increase in peripheral exercising skeletal muscle, which may increase free radical production. However, an increase in the antioxidant intake over and above the normal RDA has not been shown to provide additional benefits. Hence, athletes should consume a varied diet, rich in B vitamins, antioxidants, and minerals such as iron and calcium, and monitor themselves for dietary or clinical deficiencies regularly. However, athletes may sometimes take vitamin and mineral supplements even without dietary deficiencies for a long time. This does not benefit athletes in any manner; hence, regular supplementation for a long time should be avoided.

Fluids

Athletes lose fluid as sweat and insensible losses very rapidly, especially in hot and humid climates. This can cause a substantial decrease in performance in the very next bout of exercise, and pose a risk of heat injuries amongst athletes. Hence, athletes need to maintain their fluid balance, with fluid intakes matching or slightly exceeding their fluid loss on a daily basis. Each athlete has a unique pattern of fluid loss, and hence athletes should monitor their weight before and after training to be aware of their fluid losses. Athletes also have an altered thirst response, and need to lose 1.5–2 litres of water before they experience thirst. Hence, awareness of the amount of fluid they lose will help them to drink adequate amounts of fluids and avoid severe dehydration.

Before Exercise

Athletes need to start exercise in a hydrated state, or the negative effects of dehydration will start early during their exercise session. Hence, athletes should drink water or other fluids up to one hour before exercise (it takes about one hour for the kidneys to flush out excessive water), and ensure that their urine colour is pale or white before the start of the exercise session. The best fluids to consume before exercise are water or moderate concentration carbohydrate drinks, such as diluted fruit juices, lemonade, or sports drinks.

During Exercise

Fluid replacement beverages are most useful when they are emptied by the stomach at a fast rate, and quickly absorbed by the body to make up for lost sweat. Water is sufficient for exercises lasting up to one hour; however, for longer duration, a carbohydrate and electrolyte solution is better accepted by athletes, better absorbed, and more useful as a fuel and fluid replenisher. About 150–350ml of fluid for every 5–20 minutes of exercise, when started within the first half hour of exercise, is beneficial for the maintenance of hydration. Fluids cooler than the room temperature are emptied faster from the stomach. Similarly, carbohydrate solutions of 6–8 per cent, with small amounts of sodium and chloride (such as sports drinks), are emptied faster and better tolerated by athletes. However, individual needs must be recognised in order to drink exactly the amount that is lost by an athlete during exercise, or slightly more than that.

After Exercise

Athletes need to drink 25–50 per cent more fluids than the existing weight loss to ensure hydration, 4–6 hours after exercise. A little over 1 litre of fluid should be consumed for every kg loss of body weight. After exercise, an athlete may consume a variety of fluids that provide energy and other nutrients, in addition to water, for example, fruit juices, milk shakes, buttermilk, smoothies, soups, and gruels. Although sweat contains sodium, it is not recommended to consume high amounts of sodium in sports drinks, as sweat has very little sodium and loss of water may concentrate the sodium content in blood. Hence, small amounts of sodium, such as a pinch of salt per 200ml of fluid, in post-exercise drinks is sufficient, as the rest is met by the daily diet.

Ergogenic Aids

Any dietary substance that may improve the athletic performance or training adaptation of athletes is termed an ergogenic aid. Many athletes use such supplements in an attempt to improve athletic performance. The reasons for such supplementation may be health benefits, compensation for a poor diet, improved speed, agility and power, weight loss, muscle gain, immune system enhancement, and/or performance enhancement.

Amongst the supplements used are creatine, protein foods, or isolates such as whey protein, milk protein, soya protein, branched chain amino acids or individual amino acids, such as arginine, glutamine, vitamin and mineral supplements, antioxidant supplements, chokeberry (small black berries native to North America) juice as an antioxidant, bitter orange, coffee, green tea extract, oxygenated water, sodium bi-carbonate, sodium phosphate, ginseng, herbal tonics, and certain illegal supplements, such as hormones, etc.

Of all the legal supplements mentioned above, only creatine, sodium bi-carbonate and sodium phosphate have been reported as significantly beneficial for some athletes. Creatine phosphate is a natural animal product present in meats and is synthesised from amino acids in the body. When consumed as an isolate in small amounts of up to 2 g/day, it increases the ATP reservoir for exercise. Hence, athletes can perform more high intensity exercise. When used in combination with high intensity exercise, it improves strength and muscle mass. Also, no side effects have yet been reported. Sodium bi-carbonate acts as a buffer to convert lactic acid produced during anaerobic activity to pyruvic acid, which can be used again for exercise. However, it causes side effects such as stomach distress, bloating and diarrhoea, and if consumed in high amounts, even alkalosis. Sodium phosphate also acts as a buffer, and may improve aerobic performance and delay anaerobic energy production, but also causes severe stomach distress.

Box 25.2: Myths and Facts Regarding Diets for Sport

Myth 1. Athletes need large amounts of protein-rich foods in their diet

Fact: Athletes have sufficient raw material to build muscle mass and gain strength from a normal diet that provides sufficient energy and carbohydrates. Since muscle is made of protein, consuming excess protein will not build extra muscle, as exercise, and not protein, is the stimulus for muscle building. To gain lean mass and muscle strength, athletes need to strength train with appropriate exercises, and consume sufficient carbohydrates for fuel during these exercises from a normal, balanced diet.

Myth 2. Protein supplements over and above a normal diet are a must to build muscle

Fact: Athletes need 1.5–2 g/kg/day of total proteins for building muscle strength and gaining lean mass. Gaining muscle is a slow process, and an adequate normal balanced diet is sufficient to provide the substrate needed for this purpose. Hence, athletes do not need any protein supplement unless their diets are deficient in proteins.

Myth 3. Athletes should not eat or drink during exercise, as it leads to stomach cramps

Fact: Athletes need to replenish carbohydrates and fluids for exercises that last beyond one hour, to be able to maximise their performance. Hence, carbohydrate solutions with 6–8 per cent carbohydrates are needed to be consumed during exercise, in small amounts that can be tolerated by individual athletes. Some athletes can even tolerate solid or gel food along with water, to provide the carbohydrate and fluids required as replenishing fuel and fluids. Hence, athletes should start slow and try out what suits them, in order to avoid cramps, instead of avoiding fluids or carbohydrates totally.

Myth 4. The WHO ORS makes a good sports drink or re-hydrator during exercise

Fact: Athletes best tolerate up to 8 per cent carbohydrate solution and a pinch of salt in amounts of 150–350ml during exercise. Fluid and electrolyte losses in sweat are much less than those lost in diarrhoea and/or vomiting. Hence, the WHO ORS solution may be too concentrated a fluid for an exercising athlete, and may delay gastric emptying due to additional constituents, causing cramps.

Myth 5. Drinking immediately after exercise may give you throat infection or common cold

Fact: Fluids, carbohydrates and proteins are required immediately after exercise, and can best replete the fuel and fluid stores of an athlete when consumed within one hour of exercise. Such an intake is unrelated to catching a cold. Some athletes, especially untrained athletes, however, may have lower levels of immunity immediately after exercise, and need to keep themselves warm and ensure food safety immediately after exercise to avoid viral infections, etc., which are not related to fluid intake post-exercise.

Myth 6. All athletes need vitamin and mineral supplements

Fact: Only athletes who are clinically deficient in some nutrients, or are consuming diets that are nutrient-deficient, for example, a vegan diet, need to supplement for a short term, sometimes repeatedly. However, athletes consuming balanced diets with variety do not need supplements. Continuous supplementation is not beneficial in any way. Most of the excess nutrients are flushed out of the body in urine. It is expensive to consume supplements regularly, and may even lead to toxicity of certain nutrients.

SUMMARY

- Physical activity is important for long-term good health; therefore, it is planned and structured to bring in various benefits (known as exercise) that enable individuals to develop certain traits (known as physical fitness) concomitant with long-term good health. Hence, physical activity, exercise and fitness are three different terms, all associated with health and performance benefits.
- Health-related and skill-related physical fitness are important for human health and skill, or sports performance, respectively. They have different sets of parameters and equipments to quantify and assess them.
- All Indians, including children, adolescents, pregnant women and lactating mothers, adults, and the aged are recommended a minimum of about one hour of exercise, or planned physical activity, to help them maintain good health and lower the risk of degenerative disorders. For competitive sports, however, athletes need to train at a much higher intensity and duration, as per the needs of their specific sport.
- The main systems that provide energy during exercise are: the ATP-CP system, the lactic acid (anaerobic) system and the aerobic system. All three systems are involved in varying degrees for various activities for the exercise continuum.
- Athletes need to eat sufficient energy from balanced diets to provide for the fuel needs of exercise. While a fitness trainee may need almost as much as a sedentary person, athletes need substantially higher amounts of energy, depending on the intensity and duration of their workouts. Athletes should monitor their body weight regularly to ensure they are eating sufficiently for their training.
- A carbohydrate content of 50–60 per cent, protein content of 2–15 per cent or a maximum of 20 per cent, and fat intake of 20 per cent to a maximum of 30 per cent is needed to ensure sufficient fuel and muscle-building substrate for athletes.
- Fluids are important for athletes, and they need to consume adequate amounts of water or carbohydrate solutions before, during and after exercise to start exercise hydrated, remaine hydrated, and make up all fluid losses before the next session. This may improve athletic performance, delay fatigue, and lower the risk of heat injury in athletes. Certain ergogenic substances like creatine may be useful with no side effects, while others, like sodium bi-carbonate or phosphate, have side effects. Several supplements consumed by athletes as ergogenic aids offer no benefit, and are best avoided.

KEY WORDS

Agility: Relates to the ability to rapidly change the position of the entire body in space with speed and accuracy.

Balance: Relates to the maintenance of equilibrium while stationary or moving.

Body composition: Relates to the relative amount of muscle, fat, bone, and other vital parts of the body.

Cardio-Respiratory endurance: Relates to the ability of the circulatory and respiratory system to supply fuel and oxygen during sustained physical activity, and to eliminate products produced due to fatigue, for example, lactic acid in muscle.

Coordination: Relates to the ability to use the senses, such as sight and hearing, together with body parts in performing motor tasks smoothly and accurately.

Exercise: A subset of physical activity that is planned, structured and repetitive, and has as a final or an intermediate objective the improvement or maintenance of physical fitness.

Flexibility: Relates to the range of motion available at a joint.

Glycemic index: A figure representing the relative ability of a carbohydrate food to increase the level of glucose in the blood.

Muscular endurance: Relates to the ability of muscle groups to exert external force for many repetitions or successive exertions.

Muscular strength: Relates to the amount of external force that a muscle can exert.

Power: Relates to the rate at which one can perform a physical activity, or the ability to exert maximal force in as short a time as possible. Activities such as weight throwing or jumps require power.

Physical fitness: A set of attributes that people have or achieve that are either health or skill-related. Being physically fit has been defined as 'the ability to carry out daily tasks with vigour and alertness without undue fatigue and with ample energy to enjoy leisure-time pursuits and to meet unforeseen emergencies'.

Physical activity: Defined as any bodily movement produced by the skeletal muscles, which results in energy expenditure.

Reaction Time: Relates to the time elapsed between the stimulus and the beginning of the reaction to it.

Speed: Relates to the ability to perform a movement within a short period of time.

Skill or sport-related fitness: Concerns athletes and related personnel who train towards maximal performance in a particular event or sport.

EXERCISES

1. Define and differentiate between physical activity, exercise and physical fitness.
2. Differentiate between the health-related and sport-related components of fitness. How are they measured?
3. What are the main energy systems for exercise and sport? Explain how these contribute towards the maintenance of continued exercise.
4. What is the energy requirement and recommendations of various macronutrients for exercise and sport?
5. How would you alter carbohydrate intake before, during and after exercise?
6. How do you need to alter the intake of vitamins and minerals for sport?
7. What tips would you give a national-level athlete for his fluid maintenance?

REFERENCES

Casperson, C. J., K. E. Powell and G. M. Christenson, 'Physical activity, exercise, and physical fitness: Definitions and distinctions for health-related research', *Public Health Report* 100 (2), 1985, pp. 126–31.

Fink, H. H., A. E. Mikesky and L. A. Burgoon, *Practical Applications In Sports Nutrition*, 3e, Burlington, MA: Jones and Bartlett Learning, 2012.

ICMR, *Nutrient Requirements and Recommended Dietary Allowances For Indians*, A Report of the Expert Group of the Indian Council of Medical Research, ICMR, 2010.

Mahan, L. K., J. L. Raymond and S. E. Stump, Krause's Food and Nutrition Care Process, 13e, Missouri, Canada: Saunders Elsevier, 2012.

Misra, A., P. Nigam, A. P. Hills, D. S. Chadha, V. Sharma, K. K. Deepak, N. K. Vikram, S. Joshi, A. Chauhan, K. Khanna, R. Sharma, K. Mittal, S. J. Passi, V. Seth, S. Puri, R. Devi, A. P. Dubey, and S. Gupta, 'Physical activity consensus group. Consensus physical activity guidelines for Asian Indians', *Diabetes Technol Ther.* 14 (1), 2012, pp. 83–98.

'President's Council on Physical Fitness and Sports', *Physical Fitness Research Digest*, Series 1, no. 1, Washington D. C., 1971.

26

FEEDING CHILDREN WITH SPECIAL NEEDS

HIGHLIGHTS

- Conditions influencing feeding in children with special needs
- Development of the feeding process in children
- Common feeding disorders/issues
- Management of common feeding and diet-related problems
- Feeding implications in common disabilities/medical conditions
- Importance of the assessment of feeding issues and the child's nutritional status

The special child has the same rights and needs as any other child for safe, wholesome nutritious food and good health.

WHO DO WE CONSIDER A CHILD WITH SPECIAL NEEDS?

Children with special needs may broadly be defined as *those who may have a condition since birth or one that develops later, which can affect their normal growth and development.* This makes these children more prone to health and nutritional problems compared to other children, and hence to special healthcare needs. Many such children face feeding difficulties related to their condition, which can impact their nutritional status adversely. The nutrition issues faced by these children may be serious—such as the child who requires a special diet or feeding method—or moderate—for instance, a child who may need help through the developmental stages of feeding. In certain cases, the nutrition concerns may also be similar to those of other healthy children.

The underlying conditions resulting in special needs are often heterogeneous and of multiple etiology. Some commonly occurring conditions in children with special needs include medical disorders: congenital defects like cleft palate or those related to the Gastrointestinal (GI) Tract; genetic defects such as Inborn Errors of Metabolism (IBEM), heart or lung disease; disabilities like Down syndrome, cerebral palsy, autism, and physical or visual handicap; nutritional conditions like premature birth, growth failure/severe malnutrition, or nutritional deficits; behavioral disorders like food refusal and disruptive meal-time behaviour; or other miscellaneous disorders that can have a nutritional impact, including unsuitable environmental factors. Some of the common causes of a child having special feeding needs are summarised in Table 26.1.

Many feeding disorders improve with time, but it is useful to be aware of the strategies to improve feeding and nutrition in these children. This is of significance as many of these conditions associated with feeding disorders and problems are known to affect food intake, its digestion, absorption or utilisation, and the nutritional and health status.

Table 26.1: Common Conditions in Children with Special Needs that Influence Feeding

Nutritional	*Medical*	*Behavioural*	*Miscellaneous*
• Growth failure • Severe malnutrition • IUGR (Intra Uterine Growth Retardation) • Preterm and small for gestational age • Severe stomatitis, cheilosis, etc.	• Congenital malformations, especially of GI tract • GER (Gastro Esophageal Reflux) • Other GI tract disorders, like anorexia, nausea, constipation • Chewing difficulty or swallowing difficulty (dysphagia) • IBEM (Inborn errors of metabolism) • Neuro-developmental disorders • Other disabilities • Chronic childhood diseases, like heart, renal, respiratory	• Refusal to eat related to volume, texture, or type • Maladaptive behaviour • Disruptive meal-time behaviour	• Food allergy or intolerance • Inappropriate home environment

DEVELOPMENT OF FEEDING PROCESS IN CHILDREN

> A child's feeding development determines when solids should be introduced, the appropriate food texture, or how feeding is to be done.

The feeding process involves suckling, sucking, swallowing, and breathing, as also biting, chewing and self-feeding. Knowledge of the feeding skill development in children is helpful to effectively manage the feeding of children with special needs. Awareness of the child's developing oral-motor skills and hand and body control facilitates the use of appropriate food texture and feeding techniques.

It must, however, be clearly understood that all children develop at their own pace, especially some children with special needs. For example, these skills may develop more slowly in a child with a neuro-developmental disability, where a 3–4-year-old may only have reached the developmental stage of an 8–11-month-old infant, who is just learning to self-feed with a spoon.

Table 26.2 indicates the development of feeding skills in healthy infants and children, till they are able to eat adult foods on their own.

Although the processes of sucking, swallowing or chewing are considered routine, they require considerable coordination of the mouth, jaw and throat. A child who has trouble with this coordination may have problems with one or all of these skills. Such a child would need help and encouragement to learn how to suck, swallow and chew on her/his own.

The development of the feeding process thus involves oral-motor, gross motor, fine motor, and behavioural skills. **Oral motor skills** involve suckling, sucking, swallowing, chewing, biting, tongue elevation, and lateralisation. **Gross motor ability** includes posture, and all infants at birth are dependent, requiring support for stability of position. A stable feeding position develops by 6–8 months. In fact, feeding position is an important consideration for all children. For a child with special needs, it is as important as the careful planning for proper foods and textures. It is essential that the child has adequate support for the head, trunk and legs. In children with oral-motor problems, appropriate positioning is a pre-requisite for comfort and feeding safety.

Behavioural aspects of eating include positive behaviours like the acceptance of a wide variety of foods and textures, age-appropriate self-feeding, remaining seated while eating, eating at a reasonable pace, eating and drinking quietly, and chewing and swallowing properly. Negative behaviours include crying, refusing food, gagging on food being offered, and vomiting.

Children with special needs often take more time to eat than other children. They may have difficulty in self-feeding, resulting in a mess while feeding. Therefore, it is important that effort is made to develop the child's feeding/eating skills.

The term '**feeding disorder**' usually implies difficulty in consuming adequate or proper nutrition by mouth.

Many feeding disorders improve with time, but strategies to tackle the associated problems are important for caregivers. Efforts may involve making changes in the feeding routine, and in schedules like bowel habits and sleep routine. In some cases, specialised feeding by tube may be required, bypassing the oral route.

Table 26.2: Development of Feeding Skills in Healthy Infants and Young Children

Age (months)	*Oral-motor Development and Skills*	*Hand and Body Control*	*Type of Food and Feeding*
0–5	Rooting, suckle, suck, swallow, tongue thrust, and gag reflex	Head, neck and trunk control poor	Milk Swallow liquids, but push solids out of the mouth
4–5	Up and down munching, transfer food from front to back of tongue to swallow, decrease of tongue thrust, rooting, and gag reflex	Good head control, sits with support and grasps food/ objects in full hand (palmer grasp)	Soft pureed, semi- solid food Can swallow without choking
5–9	Control food position in the mouth, up and down munching	Begins to sit without support, follow food with eyes, and use index finger and thumb to pick up food/objects (Pincer grasp)	Ground, mashed foods Eat from a spoon easily, drink from a cup with some spill, begin self-feeding
9–12	Move food from side to side in mouth, start rotatory chewing, begin to curve lips round rim of cup, munching	Sits alone easily Better hand-to-mouth coordination, begins to put spoon in mouth, begins to hold cup	Ground, finely chopped, or small pieces of soft food, soft table foods Drink from a cup with less spill, self-feeding with help
12–24	Munching, rotatory chewing	Runs, holds cup, uses spoon	Normal cooked and raw foods

Source: Adapted from USDA/Food and Nutrition Service 1993.

FEEDING DISORDERS / ISSUES

Children with special needs usually face more challenges, and also pose more challenges for the person responsible for their feeding. An understanding of the feeding issues and disorders is thus required in these children. A child may be considered to have a feeding disorder if s/he refuses food and will not eat, has difficulty in chewing, difficulty in swallowing (dysphagia), eats too much (hyperphagia), has difficulty in self-feeding, or shows very definite food selectivity, amongst other conditions. Feeding disorders are reportedly quite common in children, with 25–35 per cent normal children having mild feeding disorders, and up to 80 per cent children with developmental disabilities having difficulty in feeding.

While children with feeding disorders constitute a heterogenous group, they may be broadly divided into three types:

- healthy children without a significant disease condition;
- those with digestive disorders; and
- those with special needs, especially chronic neurological disorders.

In some children, the feeding disorder may be temporary and resolve easily, or reduce with increasing age. In others, these problems may persist and require continued attention.

Feeding disorders may affect appetite and ingestion of food, that is, they may affect oral-motor reflexes. Thus, for ensuring proper growth and nutritional status of children with special needs, along with other treatment and rehabilitation measures, a nutritionally adequate balanced diet based on feeding development, with due consideration for texture, consistency, portion size, meal enjoyment, and feeding method must be given equal importance, so that poor nutrition does not become a barrier to the child's well-being and full potential for growth and development.

Meal times for children with special needs can be quite difficult and challenging, but their understanding can prevent feeding becoming a significant issue or problem. The major components affecting the child's feeding and ability to eat, especially the special child, are mostly sensory, oral-motor, behavioural, medical, and home environment issues.

Sensory-based feeding issues are a component of most feeding difficulties in children. Certain food textures, temperature and taste can be problematic for these children and cause frustration. Children usually tend to prefer and eat only foods they are familiar with.

Oral-motor-based feeding problems, involving oral, pharyngeal and oesophageal swallowing, are mostly linked to muscle tone and strength. Good gross motor coordination and movement in their body helps in the development of oral-motor skills. However, sensory issues must usually be tackled first before the oral-motor difficulties, as good sensory input has been found to result in good oral-motor output.

Behavioural and home environment-related issues that can affect feeding can be varied. Not eating or eating only a few things is a common way of getting the attention of parents or caregivers. Parents and caregivers play a vital role in determining how and what the child is fed, and problems may arise if they tend to feed their children in an inappropriate manner.

Medical issues can affect feeding, like in gastro-intestinal (GI disorders), heart or lung-related disorders, developmental disabilities, as also visual impairment, when the child simply cannot see what s/he is eating, or congenital defects. A frequently occurring medical-based feeding issue in infants and young children continues to be Gastro Esophageal Reflux (GER), resulting in the spitting out or vomiting of food, and the child refusing food. Medications can also affect feeding.

COMMON FEEDING AND DIET-RELATED PROBLEMS AND THEIR MANAGEMENT

Some of the common feeding and diet-related difficulties encountered in children with special needs include:

- Chewing difficulty
- Swallowing difficulty
- Gagging and choking
- Stress at meal times
- Prolonged feeding time
- Poor appetite or anorexia
- Very specific food preferences
- Constipation or diarrhoea
- Food fads and beliefs of parents/caregivers
- Underweight or overweight (due to hyperphagia and reduced physical activity)
- Food intolerance/allergy
- Behavioural problems
- Inborn Errors of Metabolism (IBEM)
- Cleft palate
- Other medical problems, like heart disease, renal and respiratory diseases, which place the child at special risk.

Dietary Recommendations to Manage these Problems

Feeding is based on age, development, and the special needs of the underlying condition. Several strategies and tips are available to handle the various feeding problems and difficulties faced by children with special needs. Many of the underlying conditions, although heterogeneous, may result in similar feeding problems. The management strategies, if well-understood and implemented, can help to maintain satisfactory nutritional status in these children, which in turn can result in a better quality of life as an outcome.

Chewing Difficulty

- Provide soft food combinations cooked well, mashed or blended.
- Some examples of foods of choice are *chapatis* soaked and mashed in *dal*, or vegetable gravy or curd. Other easy to chew foods include sliced/cubed cheese, cottage cheese, scrambled egg, baked fish, bananas, musk melon, cereal porridges, buttered noodles/rice, cooked soft and diced vegetables like carrots and potatoes.

To promote chewing:

- Introduce lumpy foods gradually to begin the chewing process, and slowly progress to ground texture.
- When a child is learning the skill of chewing, be sure to offer foods that are easy to chew.
- Leave some lumps in hot cereals when cooking them.
- Give the child foods to bite through, such as crackers and rusks, even if the child spits them out. This helps to develop jaw control for chewing.
- Give the child enough time between bites to become used to the texture change and chewing pattern.
- Encourage the child as the chewing develops.

Swallowing Difficulty

- Provide thick liquid to soft foods. Thin liquids are more difficult to handle and swallow, and there is a greater chance of their entering the airway passage.
- Preferred foods include foods and fluids of a smooth texture, pleasant tasting, sweet and cool foods, as these are easy to swallow.
- Dry, lumpy, slippery, and easily fragmented foods are best avoided, as they are difficult to swallow.
- Multi-textured foods consisting of thin liquid and solids together can also pose swallowing problems.
- Foods that do not dissolve, such as raw fruits and vegetables, are best avoided, as they are difficult to swallow.

A child's diet should include foods with a variety of textures, as far as possible, as this helps in the development of swallowing and chewing skills. With proper feeding and food selection, children with special needs can also advance to more textures in their food. To diversify the diet, begin slowly and in stages with a favourite food, and gradually alter this food. Also, there are many oral-motor exercises that can help strengthen the jaw, tongue and lips, which are mainly the domain of the paediatrician, occupational therapist or speech therapist. Coordination with them is thus important.

Gagging and Choking

Gagging and choking can occur due to food aversion, a new food, especially of unacceptable or inappropriate texture, swallowing difficulty, or faulty feeding technique or improper positioning of the child. Gagging may also be a behavioural response to get attention. Some ways to prevent or reduce gagging and choking are:

- Feed soft cooked foods.
- Cut foods into small or thin pieces that can easily be chewed.
- Remove skin and seeds from fruit.

- Avoid whole nuts and seeds, and give only if ground finely or chopped.
- Ensure proper feeding position of the child (Table 26.3).

Stress at Meal Times, Prolonged Feeding Time, Poor Appetite

Meals can be stressful for both the child with special needs and the caregivers, due to oro-motor related feeding difficulties, lack of self-feeding, longer time taken for meals compared to other children, and other related problems. However, there are ways to reduce meal-time stress and make it a relaxed and enjoyable process.

- Give small meals at a time, but increase the frequency.
- Have regular meal times, a fixed place for eating, and a meal time routine.
- Make sure that the child's posture is upright and suitable for eating.
- Avoid force feeding.
- Try and include some favourite foods of appropriate texture and consistency, but mainly from habitual family foods.
- Colourful meals and foods liked by the child can stimulate appetite.
- Accept some mess as part of the special child's feeding.
- Use special feeding equipment (Figure 26.1), if required, to facilitate self-feeding, and ensure proper feeding position.
- While attempts should be made to reduce prolonged meal times by making eating less stressful, the child should be given enough time to eat.

Table 26.3: Some General Recommendations for Positioning a Child

General Recommendations:
• The child's body and head should be upright in a sturdy, comfortable seat, with the head slightly forward with the chin tucked in.
• Arms should rest comfortably on the tray or table.
• Legs should be bent in a sitting position at an angle of about 90 degrees, with feet resting flat on a firm surface.
• Sometimes a special chair or seat belt is needed to provide the child support and a proper position.

Very Specific Food Preferences

- Some children with special needs exhibit extreme food selectivity, as observed in children with autism.
- Feed the child a variety of foods for nutritional adequacy and taste development, but introduce only one new food at a time, in small amounts, preferable mixed initially with an accepted food.
- Introduce new foods when the child is rested and hungry.
- Select nutrient-rich alternatives of the same texture or colour for unhealthy preferred foods, like cereal pulse-based crispies or banana chips, instead of potato chips.
- Changes made in texture, temperature, colour, or taste should be slight, but apparent, to diversify the diet.

Food Intolerance and Allergies

- In case of milk or lactose intolerance, curd, cheese or buttermilk may be given if tolerated, or soya milk.
- If wheat is not tolerated, as in ***celiac disease***, rice, *chapati*s, or *dosa*s or *cheelas* (Indian pancakes) made from maize, gram, *bajra*, or rice flour may be used.
- Wheat and wheat products, barley and rye must be eliminated from the diet in celiac disease.

- Any other foods producing allergy, like egg, peanuts, or soyabean, must be avoided.
- Food labels on commercial food products must be read for any allergenic food component.

Figure 26.1: Some Adaptive Feeding Equipment

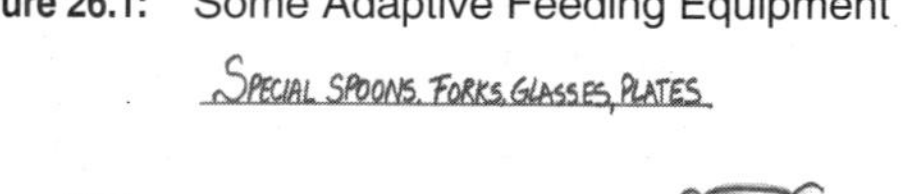

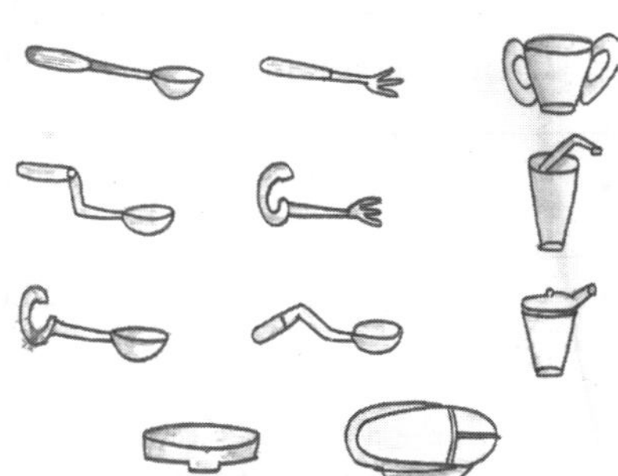

Constipation

This is common in children with various disabilities.

- Give fibre-rich foods like whole grain products, such as whole wheat flour (*atta*) and broken wheat (*dalia)*, whole pulses, sprouted pulses, and plenty of fruit and vegetables.
- Give the child plenty of water and other fluids. Give unstrained juices and soups.
- If the child resists drinking water, give small amounts, even a few teaspoonfuls, at frequent intervals.
- Fibre supplements like *'Isabgol'* or psyllium husk may be given to the child—½ to 1 teaspoon a day, based on the age and need of the child.

Underweight

Many children with special needs tend to be underweight and undernourished because of the underlying disorder (**Cystic fibrosis, IUGR, Prematurity**), the feeding difficulties, and inadequate intake of food and nutrients. Improving their weight and nutritional status constitutes an integral part of their management. For this, some recommendations are:

- Add nutrient-dense food products like milk powder, protein concentrates, butter or oil, and soya flour or nuts to foods given to the child to increase the protein and energy density of the diet.
- Use foods like nuts, dried fruit, cheese, cottage cheese or *paneer*, and tofu, which provide more nutrients in less bulk.
- Give the child small, less bulky but nutrient-dense meals more frequently, to facilitate an increased intake of food, energy and nutrients.
- Low birth weight and preterm babies may need special formula and tube feeding if unable to suckle and swallow.

Overweight

Reduced physical activity due to the underlying disorder (**various disabilities like physical handicap, spina bifida, Down Syndrome**) can result in the child gaining excess weight. In Down Syndrome, the child's appetite may also increase; this can also happen due to certain medications. To improve the weight status of the child, which will also help in better mobility:

- Reduce the intake of calorie-rich foods, while ensuring nutritional adequacy through good food selection.
- Foods of choice should include skim milk and its products, low-fat white meats, foods with less fat and sugar, steamed, roasted and baked foods rather than deep fried, vegetables and fruit (except those that are very sweet or starchy), and foods rich in fibre.
- Encourage whatever physical activity or exercise is feasible.

Behavioural Problems

Some common meal-time behaviour problems are refusal to try new foods, refusal to eat some particular foods, eating the same food day in and day out, and unacceptable and disruptive behaviour at meal times. Sometimes, behavioural feeding issues can be fairly similar to sensory-motor feeding issues. It is important to identify and tackle both aspects of feeding.

Suggestions for reducing behavioural problems include:

Introduce one new food at a time, in case of refusal to try new foods. All children tend to accept new foods more readily when they are hungry, and not tired or forced to eat.

- Respect and heed a child's food preferences to the extent possible.
- Do not punish, force, or bribe a child to eat, as this attention may worsen food refusal.
- Set a good example by ensuring an intake of a variety of foods by siblings and caregivers.
- Try and introduce variety in colour, texture and shapes in the meal, to the extent possible, to make meals attractive and appetising.
- Ignore negative and undesirable behaviour.
- Give attention and positive reinforcement to desirable behaviour.

CARE FOR SOME COMMON DISABILITIES AND OTHER MEDICAL PROBLEMS

In these cases, specific dietary and nutritional interventions may be needed, based on the associated feeding disorder or disorders, some of which have already been discussed. In addition, medical intervention with inputs from paediatricians, and occupational, physical and speech therapists are mostly required.

Cerebral Palsy (CP)

This is a group of disorders caused by damage to the central nervous system early in life. The symptoms relate to posture, muscle tone, and motor coordination problems, and may result in difficulties with sucking, chewing and swallowing, the bite reflex, and self-feeding.

Feeding Implications:

Special feeding equipment (Figure 26.1), specific feeding positioning (Table 26.3) and modifications in food texture may be needed.

Down Syndrome (DS)

This is a genetic disability that causes mental retardation and slower growth with developmental delays, including in oral-motor and self-feeding skills. Such children often tend to be overweight.

Feeding Implications:

Some modifications in food texture and help with the development of self-feeding skills are needed, along with weight control in some cases.

Congenital Heart Disease

A birth defect of the heart, congenital heart disease mostly results in delayed growth and development. Fluid tends to be retained in the body as the disease advances. Feeding tends to tire the child, and the medications used may cause loss of appetite, nausea, or constipation.

Feeding Implications:

A high-calorie diet, more frequent feeding and possible fluid restrictions may be needed.

Type 1 Diabetes Mellitus

Diabetes is a metabolic disorder in which the body cannot utilise the sugar glucose. Most children need daily injections of insulin, the hormone that helps the body to utilise glucose.

Feeding Implications:

Restriction of simple sugars and concentrated sweets is recommended in a child with diabetes mellitus to control the child's blood sugar level. Consistency and regularity in the timing of meals and snacks are important. The meals, snacks and insulin are adjusted based on the child's activity level, growth and general health.

Inborn Errors of Metabolism (IBEM)

These are relatively rare inherited disorders that affect the body's ability to use a protein, amino acid, fat, or a specific carbohydrate, caused by enzymatic or metabolic defects, some examples being ***Phenylketonuria (PKU)*** and ***galactosemia***. If left untreated, the nutrient or its metabolites accumulate in the blood, and can impair brain development and result in mental retardation and other severe life-threatening problems.

Feeding Implications:

Specific nutrients or their metabolites that are not broken down and accumulate in the body need to be excluded from or restricted in the diet. For example, in children with ***galactosemia,*** a diet that avoids all milk and milk products is needed, as galactose is a component of the milk sugar lactose. Infants need special formulae, or soy milk may be used. In PKU, the amino acid phenylalanine needs restriction. Children with PKU must be on a low-protein diet, with nutritional supplements to ensure normal growth, and special phenylalanine-free milk formulae.

Some Other Medical Problems

Conditions like ***cleft palate*** or ***cleft lip,*** where there is congenital incomplete closure or cut in the lip or palate, may adversely affect the child's nutrition and weight by making drinking and eating difficult. Specially designed nipples in the feeding bottles or special cups may have to be used for feeding, till the defect is surgically corrected.

In cases of ***kidney disorders*** and some ***respiratory disorders***, meeting age-appropriate energy needs and modifications in the electrolyte and mineral content (for example, sodium, potassium, calcium, etc.) are required.

If a child has ***visual impairment***, s/he should be prepared for the feeding. The spoon with the food or the food itself should be touched to the lower lip first, so that the child gets a little taste of the food.

In addition, children with other ***physical handicaps*** may need specially designed feeding equipment, like special cups, spoons, plates, and glasses. Children who cannot take in food orally may need *special feeding methods.*

OTHER GENERAL MANAGEMENT STRATEGIES

Modified diets and meal-time routines may be needed for some children. Also, along with dietary modifications, other measures like rehabilitative exercises for improving chewing, swallowing and muscle strength are important. Meal-time environment is another important factor in feeding the special child. Every attempt should be made to make the child comfortable, and ensure a pleasant, cheerful and positive environment. Emotional upheavals at meal times can interfere with chewing and swallowing. Loud, distracting noises are also better avoided during meals. Attention should be paid to a child's non-verbal cues regarding hunger, satiety, or food choices, besides the verbal cues, especially for the child who is unable to speak. While attempting to reduce prolonged meal times, the child should be given enough time to eat.

Some other helpful suggestions for improving the food, and hence the nutrient intake of children with special needs is to encourage the child to eat with other children, as peer influence can be beneficial. A consistent routine at and for meal times helps the child know what to expect, which may improve various aspects of feeding.

While feeding the child, attention must be paid to the sense of smell and sight, food appearance, portion size, and temperature. These attributes of food are equally important for the child with special needs, as it is for the normal child.

ASSESSMENT OF FEEDING ISSUES AND THE CHILD'S NUTRITIONAL STATUS

For the management of feeding problems, a pre-requisite is assessment of the feeding issues in the child with special needs, as well as their nutritional status. Nutritional deficiencies in children with developmental disabilities and special healthcare needs, due to feeding problems, have been commonly reported. Nutritional assessment in children with special needs is essentially similar to other children, involving aspects like anthropometric measurements to indicate growth and body composition, clinical signs of nutritional deficiencies, the blood levels of nutrients (if available), dietary intake, medications, if any, and family background. The child's nutritional status helps to determine her/his nutrient and fluid needs, and the need for nutritional supplements.

> It must, however, be understood that normal RDAs (Recommended Dietary Allowances) are not always applicable to children with special needs, due to differences in their growth rate and activity pattern. The normal nutritional requirements act as a guideline, but each child needs individual assessment to determine her/his needs.

For the child with special needs, additional information on feeding issues is needed, such as:

- The textures usually eaten by the child, like pureed, mashed, chopped, soft, or normal.
- Self-feeding ability or requirement of assistance in feeding, and the type of assistance.
- Use of normal or specialised eating equipment.
- The time taken for eating a meal.
- The child's appetite, and if the child normally finishes a meal or not.
- Any specific food selectivity.
- Food intolerance or food allergies, if any.
- Need for a modified or special diet, in terms of quality or quantity of nutrients, based on the child's medical condition.
- Special seating, if required.
- Presence of associated medical problems, such as diarrhoea, constipation, choking/gagging, dysphagia, inability to communicate food or water need, refusing to eat new foods, etc.
- Medications, can suppress appetite (anorexia), cause nausea, GI irritation, diarrhoea, constipation, and reduced nutrient absorption and/or utilisation.

After the initial assessment, regular follow-up assessment is important for monitoring progress, and managing the feeding disorders and food intake of the child. Appropriate feeding of children with special needs goes a long way in not only improving their nutrition and health status, but also aiding their social and emotional growth, sensory development, and that of self-feeding and independence, or sense of autonomy.

SUMMARY

- Children with special needs may be defined as those children who have a condition since birth or one that develops later, which affects their growth and development. This makes these children more prone to health and nutritional problems compared to other children, and hence to special healthcare needs.
- The underlying conditions may be heterogenous in nature, but many such children face feeding difficulties and disorders related to their condition.
- Some commonly occurring conditions in children with special needs include medical disorders: congenital defects like cleft palate or those related to the Gastrointestinal (GI) Tract; genetic defects like Inborn Errors of Metabolism, heart or lung disease; disabilities like Down Syndrome, cerebral palsy, autism, and physical or visual handicap; nutritional conditions like premature birth, growth failure/severe malnutrition, or nutritional deficits; and behavioural disorders like food refusal and disruptive meal-time behaviour.

- A feeding disorder is said to exist when there is difficulty in consuming adequate or proper nutrition by mouth, including difficulty in self-feeding.
- Feeding disorders thus mostly interfere with the adequate and appropriate intake of food and nutrients, which in turn can impact the nutritional status of the child with special needs adversely.
- Feeding disorders and difficulties may be sensory, oral-motor, or gross motor related, or behavioural in nature, and include the inability to self-feed.
- An understanding of the feeding process and the feeding disorders common in these children is essential to manage them and facilitate satisfactory food intake and nutritional status.
- Based on the underlying disorder and its impact on feeding and nutritional status, modifications may need to be made in aspects such as food texture and consistency, choice of foods, portion size, feeding position, feeding routine, feeding technique, and feeding equipment. In some cases, nutritional supplements may be required.
- Along with food modification, in many children coordination with the paediatrician, occupational therapist, speech therapist, and physical therapist is essential for the medical interventions required, and the improvement of feeding skills.
- Individualised feeding and nutritional assessment in children with special needs to identify the interventions needed, with follow-up, is recommended.

KEY WORDS

Anorexia: Loss of appetite

Autism: Autism or ASD (Autism Spectrum Disorder) are both general terms for a group of complex disorders of brain development, characterised by varying degrees of difficulties in social interaction, verbal and non-verbal communication, attention problems, and repetitive behaviours. Autism can also be associated with difficulties in motor coordination, gastrointestinal disturbances and feeding selectivity.

Cerebral Palsy (CP): A group of disorders caused by damage to the central nervous system early in life, with symptoms related to posture, muscle tone and motor coordination problems, which may result in difficulties with sucking, chewing and swallowing, the bite reflex, and self-feeding.

Children with special needs: May be defined as those who may have a condition since birth or one that develops later, which can affect their normal growth and development and makes them more prone to health and nutritional problems compared to other children, and hence to special healthcare needs.

Cleft lip/palate: A congenital defect in which there is incomplete closure or development resulting in a cut in the lip or palate, which makes feeding difficult.

Congenital Heart Disease: A birth defect of the heart that mostly results in delayed growth and development, easy fatigue, and possible fluid retention in the body. Medications used may cause loss of appetite, nausea, or constipation.

Constipation: Infrequent and difficult passage of stools, which tend to be dry and hard in nature.

Down Syndrome (DS): A genetic disability that causes mental retardation, slower growth with developmental delays, including oral-motor and self-feeding skills. Such children often tend to be overweight.

Dysphagia: Difficulty in swallowing due to abnormal swallowing reflex.

Feeding disorder: A term usually applied when there is difficulty or refusal in consuming adequate or proper nutrition by mouth.

GER: Gastro Esophageal Reflux or regurgitation, which results in a child's spitting out, vomiting, and hence refusing food.

Gross motor skills: These refer to the skills involved in the movement of the body and posture.

Hyperphagia: Excess hunger, or eating too much.

IBEM: Inborn Errors of Metabolism, or genetic metabolic defects in the infant, which, if left untreated, can result in impaired physical and mental growth and development, and other serious life-threatening consequences.

Nutritional Status: The state of health, as determined by not only the intake, but also the utilisation of nutrients by the body.

Oral-motor skills: These refer to skill in suckling, sucking, swallowing, chewing, biting, and tongue movements.

Special feeding methods: Feeding methods other than via the oral route, such as a feeding tube inserted into the GI tract or via the intravenous route.

Type 1 Diabetes Mellitus: A metabolic disorder in which the body cannot utilise the sugar glucose due to a deficiency of insulin, the hormone that helps the body to utilise glucose.

EXERCISES

1. Define the following:
   - a child with special needs
   - feeding disorders
   - oro-motor skills
2. Why is the feeding of children with special needs different from that of other children?
3. Enlist two to four conditions each, associated with feeding difficulties that are: a) nutritional, b) disability-related, c) behavioural, and d) medical in origin.
4. Why is it important to understand the feeding process development in children to handle feeding disorders in children?
5. Outline briefly the feeding recommendations for children with: a) dysphagia, b) meal-time stress and prolonged feeding time, c) specific food selectivity, and d) constipation.
6. Why is the individual assessment of feeding and nutrition status important in the management of feeding in children with special needs?

REFERENCES

Ekvall, S. W. and V. K. Ekvall, *Pediatric Nutrition in Chronic Diseases and Developmental Disorders*, 2e, New York: Oxford University Press Inc., 2005.

Koletzko, B., P. Cooper, M. Makridesm, C. Garza, R. Uauy, and W. Wang, *Pediatric Nutrition in Practice*, Basel: Karger, 2008.

Mahan, L. K., S. Escott-Stump and J. L. Raymond, *Krause's Food and the Nutrition Care Process*, 13e, St. Louis: Elsevier, 2011.

Project Chance, *A Guide to feeding young children with special needs*, Arizona: Department of Health Services, Offices of Nutrition Services, 1995.

Seth, V., S. Kashyap and S. Sharma, *Nutrition Issues in Children with Disabilities*, Germany: Lambert Academic Publishing, 2011.

USDA/Food and Nutrition Service, *Infant Nutrition and Feeding*, 1993. Available at www.clas.uluc.edu/fulltext/cl102220/cl102220.html (accessed 31 July 2013).

27

NUTRITION AND INFECTION

HIGHLIGHTS

- Host defence mechanisms
- Interaction between nutrition, infection and immunity
- Impact of malnutrition on immunity and occurrence of infection
- Effect of infection on nutritional status
- Biological and Operational Implications

The prevalence of nutritional deficiencies continues to be high worldwide. Historic accounts of famine and disease have highlighted the relationship between starvation and reduced resistance to infection. This was followed by systematic studies which showed the relation between specific nutrient deficiencies and impaired immune responses. There are multiple host defence mechanisms involved in protecting our body. The action of some is localised, while others have a more systemic effect. Let us learn more about the different mechanisms in our body which protect us from diseases, and also how nutrition is important in optimally maintaining these defences.

HOST DEFENCE MECHANISMS

A number of factors may determine whether a person exposed to a particular pathogenic (disease-causing) organism will develop the disease or not. The most important of these factors are the virulence (disease-causing ability) of the agent and the resistance offered by the host. If the host's resistance is low, then even the least virulent strain of a germ will lead to symptoms of the disease. In an alternate case scenario, a virulent organism like the measles virus may cause the disease in even a well-nourished individual, who generally has a fairly good resistance.

The immuno-competence of the host is her/his ability to produce a normal immune response after exposure to an antigen, which can be a toxin or any other foreign substance. The body has a number of defence mechanisms against disease-causing germs, as well as other foreign substances which may harm the body. The **first line of defence** of the body is to prevent the entry of these pathogens or foreign substances into the body. This function is usually performed by the physical barriers—skin, mucous membranes and mucous, which line all our tracts like the respiratory tract, genito-urinary tract and gastro-intestinal tract. In addition, hair and hair-like projections or cilia help in the removal of substances that may inadvertently gain entry into some of these tracts.

Innate immunity occurs naturally as a result of a person's genetic constitution or physiology, and does not arise from a previous infection or vaccination. It is also referred to as the second line of defence, or the non-specific immune system. It does not confer long-lasting or protective immunity to the host. **Acquired immunity** is the immunity produced by exposure to antigens, which stimulates the production of antibodies. This type of immunity can be active or passive, and is more long lasting, in some cases life-long.

Active immunity results from the development of antibodies in response to an antigen, like when the body is exposed to an infectious disease (naturally acquired active immunity) or vaccination (artificially acquired active immunity). **Passive immunity** results from the transmission of readymade antibodies, like the ones transferred from the mother to the foetus through the placenta (naturally acquired passive immunity), or by the injection of antiserum (artificially acquired passive immunity). Antisera are prepared by injecting an antigen into the body of another human being or animal. The other human or animal then produces antibodies to fight the antigen. These are isolated from the blood and injected into others to provide them immunity.

There are several **non-specific factors which offer resistance** to foreign substances, like the Complement system, Phagocytes, Lysozymes, Iron-binding proteins like transferrin and lactoferrin, and Interferon, to name a few. These are not specific to a particular type of antigen; they protect the body through different mechanisms. So, for instance, the **phagocytes** engulf the foreign substance and destroy it. **Lysozyme** is an enzyme occurring naturally in breast milk, human tears, saliva, and other body fluids, capable of destroying the cell walls of certain bacteria and thereby acting as a mild antiseptic. The **complement system** is a part of the immune system that helps or complements the ability of antibodies and phagocytic cells to clear pathogens from an organism. The complement system consists of a number of small proteins found in the blood, in general synthesised by the liver, and normally circulating as inactive precursors (pro-proteins).

> ***Did you know?***
>
> Fever lowers the concentration of iron in serum and favours resistance to infection. Almost all bacteria depend on iron to live and multiply. Limiting the microorganisms' access to iron can reduce their virulence, thereby potentially reducing the severity of infection.

Interferons are proteins made and released by host cells in response to the presence of pathogens, such as viruses, bacteria, parasites, or tumor cells. Usually a virus-infected cell will release interferons, causing nearby cells to put up their anti-viral defences. Iron-binding proteins control the level of free iron in biological fluids like the blood (for example, transferrin) and breast milk (for example, lactoferrin). Iron is important for microbes to multiply. Thus, by restricting the availability of an essential nutrient, the infection can be controlled.

Specific immunological responses of the body are the main defence against specific infectious agents. These responses are mainly a result of the action of **immunoglobulins** or antibodies. What makes their action specific is the presence of antigen-recognising receptors on the surface of leucocytes. On the basis of function and cell surface markers, the lymphocytes are classified as thymus-dependent T lymphocytes, and bone marrow or Bursa-dependent B lymphocytes. The former confer **Cell-mediated immunity,** while the latter confer **Humoral immunity**. Both are types of **Acquired Immunity**. Both T and B cells are formed initially in the bone marrow, but T cells migrate to the thymus for maturation (Figure 27.1), while B cells mature within the bone marrow.

Cell-mediated immunity is considered more vital for survival. The T-cells do not secrete antibodies, but are responsible for the recognition of the antigen. They initiate a chain of reactions by secreting lymphokines, which stimulate the macrophages. The activated macrophages perform a much more efficient phagocytic function. It is the main defence against viruses, fungi, parasites, and some bacteria. T lymphocytes are classified into two major groups, depending on the type of protein molecules called CD antigens (cluster of differentiation). So, lymphocytes containing CD4 and CD8 antigens are typically called T4 and T8 lymphocytes, respectively. The B-cells, on the other hand, manufacture specific antibodies after the macrophages present them with antigens. Humoral immunity is the body's major defence against many bacteria and bacterial toxins.

The thymus is located just above and slightly over the heart, and produces a vital component of the immune system, called T-cells, which fight infections and regulate the immune response.

Figure 27.1: The Thymus

Source: http://commons.wikimedia.org/wiki/File:Gray1178.png.

Phagocytosis is the process by which cells of the immune system, called phagocytes, engulf and digest micro-organisms. These cells are responsible for removing dead cells and microorganisms. Elimination of microbes by phagocytosis takes place in the following steps:

1. The phagocyte comes near the pathogen, for example a bacterium.
2. The phagocyte latches on to the bacterium and slowly surrounds it.
3. The phagocyte completely engulfs the bacterium and kills it.
4. The bacterium is then digested with the help of enzymes.

Figure 27.2: Diagrammatic Representation of Phagocytosis

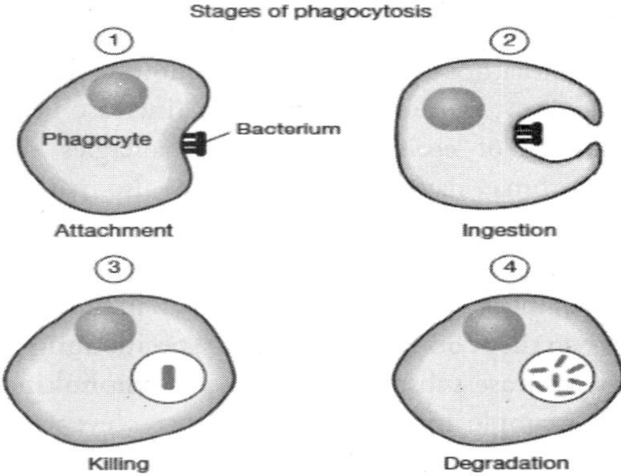

Source: http://immune-ash16.wikispaces.com/What+is+Phagocytosis%3F

> **Cell-Mediated Immunity** is the mechanism our body uses to reject transplanted organs and eliminate any abnormal cells that may form spontaneously in the body.

In the blood and lymph, the cells responsible for defending the body are called White Blood Cells (WBCs), also known as Leucocytes (or leukocytes). These are produced in the bone marrow from stem cells (Figure 27.3). Table 27.1 presents the distinguishing features of each type of leucocyte. Those that have granules in their cytoplasm are referred to as **Granulocytes,** while those that do not have granules are referred to as **Agranulocytes**. These granules are nothing but tiny sacs containing enzymes that can digest the microorganisms. The granules, when stained, exhibit different colours, and that becomes one of the distinguishing features for the WBCs when examined under the microscope.

Table 27.1: Distinguishing Features of Different Types of Leucocytes

Leucocyte	*Nucleus*	*Granules in Cytoplasm (Colour of Stain)*	*Function*	*Fraction of Total Leucocytes in Blood*
Neutrophil	Multi-lobed (polymorphonuclear)	Present (purple in colour)	Active against bacteria and fungi; phagocytic action	40–60%
Basophil	Bi- or tri-lobed (polymorphonuclear)	Present (blue in colour)	Primarily deal with allergic and antigen response, inflammatory response	< 1%
Eosinophil	Bi-lobed (polymorphonuclear)	Present (red in colour)	Primarily deal with parasitic infections	1–4%
Monocyte	Kidney shaped (mononuclear)	Absent	Like neutrophils, these too have phagocytic action	3–8%
Lymphocyte	Eccentric (mononuclear)	Absent	Help to produce cellular immunity by stimulating monocytes and macrophages	20–40%

Source: Crowley 2010 and MedlinePlus.

Neutrophils are active in phagocytosing bacteria and are present in large amount in the pus of wounds. **Eosinophils** are also the predominant inflammatory cells in allergic reactions. The most important causes of eosinophilia (increase in the number of eosinophils) include allergies such as asthma, hay fever, hives, and also parasitic infections. **Basophils** release histamine, which causes vasodilation. **Lymphocytes** are present much more in the lymph, rather than in the blood. When they come in contact with specific antigens, they release substances known as **Lymphokines,** for example Interleukins. **Monocytes** eventually leave the bloodstream and become tissue **macrophages**, which remove dead cell debris as well as attack microorganisms.

Figure 27.3: Types of Leucocytes or White Blood Cells

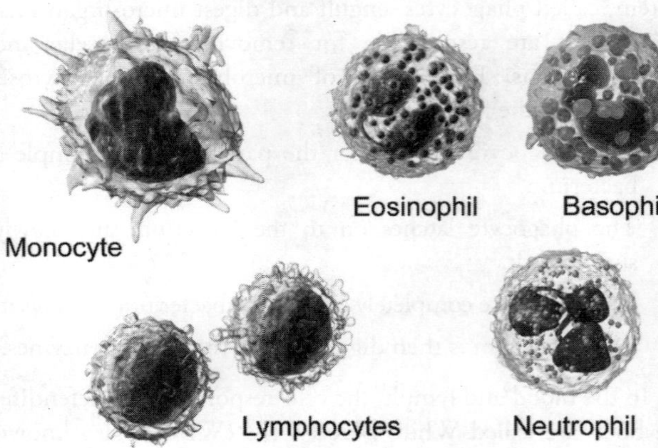

Source: Blausen.com staff. 'Blausen gallery 2014',. Wikiversity Journal of Medicine, DOI:10.15347/wjm/2014.010. ISSN 20018762.

Box 27.1: Some Terms You Should be Familiar With

Cytokines are hormone-like soluble proteins produced by different cell types. These act as a chemical messenger or communicator system of the immune system. There are different types of cytokines:

Interferons are broad-spectrum antiviral agents manufactured by various cells in the body. They act by interfering with the multiplication of viruses within the cells.

Interleukins are produced by leucocytes like B cells, T cells, monocytes, and macrophages. These send regulatory signals between the cells of the immune system.

Lymphokines are produced by lymphocytes.

Monokines are produced by monocytes.

Tumor necrosis factors can destroy foreign or abnormal cells.

Acute phase reactant proteins are a unique series of proteins produced in the early phase of an infection. Infection of an acute nature stimulates the liver to produce and release these as part of the host's defence against the infection.

Antibodies are globulins produced by plasma cells, and are usually called **Immunoglobulins** to emphasise their role in immunity. There are five main classes of immunoglobulins—IgG, IgM, IgA, IgD, and IgE—with sub-classes within them. Each class represents a different functional group. These antibodies circulate in the body and act by neutralising the microbe or its toxin. The microbe hence becomes susceptible to attack by polymorphonuclear leucocytes and monocytes. Antibodies are very specific in their action.

Hypersensitivity is an increased responsiveness of the body to an antigen. It is usually manifested by an intense inflammatory reaction at the site of contact with a foreign substance.

Autoimmune diseases result from tissue damage caused by our own immune system. Destructive lymphocytes and antibodies are produced, which are directed against our own cells and tissues as they perceive the proteins present in them as antigens. Such antibodies are called **auto-antibodies** (auto =self).

Natural killer cells (NK cells) are lymphocytes capable of destroying foreign or abnormal cells, although they have not had any prior antigenic contact with the cells. Their main target is virus-infected cells and cancer cells.

Reticuloendothelial system or the mononuclear phagocyte system is responsible for the phagocytosis of damaged or old cells, cellular debris, foreign substances, and pathogens, removing them from circulation. It plays a major role in the non-specific immune response of the body. This is found in large concentration in the spleen, liver, lymph nodes, and other tissues.

INTERACTION BETWEEN NUTRITION, INFECTION AND IMMUNITY

For the first time in 1968, the WHO monograph on 'Interactions of Nutrition and Infection' suggested that the biological effects of malnutrition and infection combined were greater than the two of them added separately. It presented research evidence for the adverse effect of infections on nutritional status, and the decreased immunity level of malnourished individuals, which made them susceptible to infections. Some of the earlier studies were on children suffering from protein-energy malnutrition (PEM). Malnutrition and infection were seen to interact, each aggravating the other. Figure 27.4 uses a Venn diagram to depict how the nutritional status of a person, her/his immunity level, and the frequency and duration of any infectious diseases s/he suffers from, are not independent of each other. Abnormality in one field affects the other two as well. Hence, a nutritional deficiency impairs immune-competence, and makes the individual more susceptible to infection. Similarly, an illness may adversely affect the nutritional status of the individual, precipitating a state of malnutrition and further depressing immune responses.

Infections have been known to precipitate the deficiency of vitamin A, thiamine and niacin in vulnerable individuals. Antimicrobial systems in the body are affected by malnutrition. There is a depressing effect of a number of nutrient deficiencies on antibody formation and leukocyte function. The prevalence and severity of many infections have been increased by specific nutritional deficiencies, a phenomenon described as **synergism**. At the same time, deficiency of certain nutrients is known to adversely affect the replication of certain infectious agents, a phenomenon described as **antagonism.** Worm infestations, and even poliomyelitis in malnourished animals, show an antagonistic response, with the number of worms being less and lesions being smaller in infected malnourished animals as compared with normally nourished infected controls. Murray and Murray (1977) have summarised the historic and epidemiologic information pertaining to World War II prisoners of concentration camps. They found that starvation suppressed infection and re-feeding activated it. Well-fed prisoners in English jails suffered a higher morbidity and mortality, which were perhaps infection-related.

Synergism is, however, more common, and seen in the case of most infectious diseases, which adversely affect the nutritional status of the affected individual. It is equally common to see malnourished individuals being more susceptible to infections. In the first half of the twentieth century, large segments of the population in several countries around the world suffered from malnutrition. Studies from that time indicate how tuberculosis was more malignant, and resulted in high mortality. With improvement in diets, and consequently in nutritional status, the morbidity promptly reduced, an effect that was not seen after merely improving hygiene and sanitation in these areas. The simultaneous presence of malnutrition and infection has much more serious consequences than either one present independently.

Figure 27.4: Relationship between Nutritional Status, Immuno-competence, and Frequency and Severity of Infection

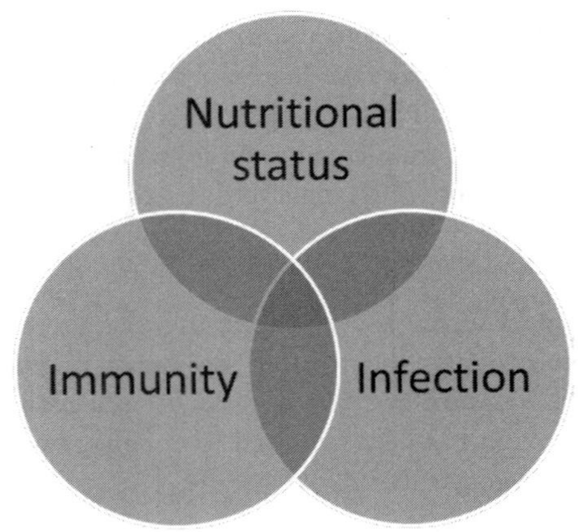

IMPACT OF MALNUTRITION ON IMMUNITY AND OCCURRENCE OF INFECTION

Undernutrition and Specific Nutrient Deficiencies

Several experimental studies on animals, as well as studies on human subjects, have strengthened the evidence for the damaging effect of nutritional deficiencies on immunity. Nutrients have an important role to play in providing the body with resistance to fight infections. The role of some nutrients for which research evidence is strong are presented here.

Protein deficiency has adverse effects on immunity, as most immune mechanisms are dependent on cell replication or the production of active protein compounds. Children suffering from protein energy malnutrition (PEM) have impaired antibody formation, decreased serum immunoglobulins, decreased functioning of the thymus and production of splenic lymphocytes, as well as impairment of physical barriers and secretory substances such as lysozymes and mucus. The Narangwal studies in India are widely quoted, which show the inability of poorly nourished children to resist disease. Such children also tend to show a poor response to routine immunisation. The effect on immune function varies with the type of immunoglobulin, the presence and nature of concurrent infection, and the nature and severity of the nutritional deficiency. **Specific amino acid** deficiency can also result in impaired immunity. The role of arginine and glutamine on different immune system cells has been extensively studied. Dietary supplementation with arginine enhances immunocompetence in human adults by increasing the production of T-lymphocytes. Arginine-derived nitric oxide also plays a major role in inflammation and immunity. Glutamine is utilised rapidly by the cells of the immune system, to support the production of lymphocytes and the secretion of cytokines. It also helps to maintain the structural integrity of the intestinal wall.

Vitamin A deficiency has been shown to be associated with increased susceptibility to infection. Vitamin A-deficient experimental animals have decreased spleen and thymus sizes, and lower response of the immune system cells like lymphocytes to stimulation by mitogens. Viral infections also tend to be more severe in vitamin A-deficient animals.

Vitamin A is responsible for maintaining the health and integrity of the epidermal and mucosal cells that line our skin and all the tracts of our body (gastrointestinal, genito-urinary and respiratory). These are the first line of defence of our bodies. However, high intakes of vitamin A produce mixed effects, by enhancing some immune functions while suppressing some others.

Can Vitamin C Prevent or Treat Colds?

Overall, experts have found little to no benefit from vitamin C for preventing or treating common cold. Large doses of supplements (>1g/day) are hence not recommended. Excess vitamin C is metabolised to oxalic acid, which, along with calcium, can precipitate as oxalate stones in the kidney. Excess of the vitamin may also cause diarrhoea. It is better to get your vitamin C from fresh fruits and raw vegetables.

β-carotene also helps to improve immune function by increasing the human natural killer cells and T helper cell numbers. Mortality rates are higher in children with a history of vitamin A deficiency. Improving the vitamin A status of young children has been shown to reduce mortality rates for deaths attributed to measles, diarrhoea and malaria. Vitamin A supplementation is recommended for children who develop measles, as it decreases the severity, and hence, mortality. Two massive doses of vitamin A to be given at a gap of 24 hours, are recommended for all children diagnosed with measles. The first massive dose of vitamin A in India's National Prophylaxis Programme against Nutritional Blindness due to vitamin A deficiency is given along with the measles vaccine at nine months.

Vitamin D serves as a hormone that regulates the immune system as well as lymphocyte differentiation. In animal experiments, the reduced resistance of vitamin-deficient animals was restored by adding vitamin D to the diet. **Vitamin E** deficiency results in a reduced killing power of lymphocytes and leukocytes. Vitamin E supplementation has been reported to enhance both humoral and cell-mediated immunity, and also improve the efficacy of phagocytosis.

B vitamins, like pyridoxine, pantothenic acid, folic acid, vitamin B_{12}, and choline, have also been shown to affect immunity. Deficiency of these vitamins leads to a reduced immunologic response. Pyridoxine deficiency has been associated with reduced cell-mediated immunity, while a pantothenate-deficient diet is associated with reduced response to tetanus toxoid. Folic acid and vitamin B_{12} are important for cell replication, and a deficiency of these vitamins adversely affects antibody formation. In folic acid deficiency anaemia, cell-mediated immunity is depressed. Choline, folic acid and vitamin B_{12} deficiency has been linked to thymic atrophy.

Although several studies have shown impaired phagocytic function and decreased killing power, and reduced antibody response along with loss of epithelial tissue integrity, the evidence is not conclusive for **vitamin C** deficiency leading to alterations in either cell-mediated or humoral immunity. In fact, the several claims of the beneficial effects of massive doses of vitamin C in the prevention of infection, or in reducing its severity and duration, are controversial.

There is a lot of data available from community-based studies that associate **iron** deficiency with increased morbidity from infectious diseases. In fact, some studies have shown that when iron-deficient populations are supplemented with iron, their immunity improves and they have less frequent episodes of infections. Iron deficiency adversely affects leucocyte function and cell-mediated immunity. It has also been associated with increased prevalence of respiratory infection, diarrhoea and malaria.

However, iron is required for a wide variety of biochemical reactions by not only our bodies, but also the disease-causing microbes. Hence, iron needs to be withheld from the microbes during an infectious episode. Transferrin, the transport form of iron, found in our blood and body fluids, is the natural mechanism for withholding iron from infectious agents. Ferritin, the storage form of iron, and lactoferrin, present in human milk, are also protective in a similar way. This also means that when an iron-deficient person is suffering from an infection, s/he should not be supplemented with large doses of iron. This may result in worsening the infection as the infectious agent uses the iron for its multiplication faster than our body's immune system responds. Small doses of up to 100 mg/day for adults are well-tolerated, and help the person to recover faster.

Zinc is a trace mineral that is important for the development and maintenance of the immune system, affecting both lymphocyte and phagocyte cell functions. The effect of zinc deficiency on immune function has been demonstrated in experimental studies, but not very clearly in population-based studies. Zinc supplementation during diarrhoeal episodes has also been shown to decrease the severity and number of episodes of diarrhoea. It is now given along with Oral rehydration solution (ORS) as a standard practice for managing diarrhoea, as it has been shown to reduce stool output and significantly decrease the need for hospitalisation. It also decreases the duration of cough, sore throat and nasal congestion. However, excessive zinc intakes can also suppress the immune system.

Other mineral deficiencies also affect the immune system. **Copper** deficiency in experimental animals has been shown to affect a number of immune responses. In children with Menkes syndrome (a congenital disease resulting in copper deficiency), there is an increased risk of bacterial infections, diarrhoea and bronchopneumonia. Similarly, **magnesium** and **selenium** deficiency has also been linked to a decrease in several immune responses. There is limited evidence on cell-mediated immunity being impaired by **iodine** deficiency.

Overnutrition

The incidence, and possibly the severity, of infectious illness in obese individuals are higher compared with their normal weight counterparts. Lower respiratory tract infections have been reported to be higher in obese infants. Several laboratory-based studies have shown that obese animals develop a more severe infection than normally fed or slightly under-fed animals. Studies on experimental animals have also shown increased morbidity and mortality from certain viral and bacterial infections in over-fed obese animals. Over-nutrition seems to have a depressing effect on the reticuloendothelial system, and its capacity to produce protective immunoglobulins. Dogs are usually used for these experiments as they tend to over-feed, and upon restriction of their physical activity, become obese like humans. Also, some of the viruses and bacteria that cause severe infection in dogs are similar to the ones that cause diseases in humans.

Excessive intakes of most vitamins and minerals by means of high dose supplements have also shown no extra protective effect. In specific cases, like high dose supplementation with vitamin A, zinc or iron, there has been a suppression of the immune system or more rapid proliferation of the infectious agent. Hence, for most nutrients, moderation in intake is desirable for optimal immunity.

EFFECT OF INFECTION ON NUTRITIONAL STATUS

After studying about the effect that nutritional deficiencies can have on immunity, there is a need to examine how infection, per se, can affect the nutritional status. The Institute of Nutrition of Central America and Panama (INCAP) studies on protein energy malnutrition during the time period 1949–59 indicate that most cases of Kwashiorkor were precipitated in young children by an episode of either diarrhoea or some other infectious disease. There are several ways in which infections can affect the nutritional status. These have been summarised below:

1. **Anorexia** (or loss of appetite). When a person falls ill, this is perhaps the first symptom to appear. The affected individual tends to eat less, and if this continues for some time, it can adversely affect the nutritional status. Several factors may lead to a decrease in appetite, like gastrointestinal discomfort (mouth ulcers, nausea, vomiting, abdominal pain), decreased levels of zinc or interleukins in the blood, or mental depression related to the illness. Certain medications may also affect the appetite of the patient.
2. **Socio-cultural practices.** Often, when a person is sick, the response of the caregiver is to restrict her/his food intake. It is a common practice across cultures to withdraw foods during sickness, for example, milk is usually not given to young children suffering from diarrhoea. Moreover, the food and beverages offered to the sick child are likely to be of low-calorie density. This results in the child not receiving adequate nourishment, and hence slipping into a state of malnutrition. In infants being breast-fed, it is recommended that breastfeeding should continue when the child has diarrhoea.
3. **Decreased intestinal absorption.** It is a known fact that during certain ailments like diarrhoea, the absorption of nutrients is severely affected because of intestinal hurry. Malabsorption may also be seen in other ailments like fever and respiratory infections, which affect vitamin A absorption, for instance.
4. **Catabolic losses.** Catabolism refers to metabolic processes which lead to a breakdown of substances. During an infectious ailment, there is loss of protein from the body due to protein breakdown. This process, if not halted in time, would lead to a state of malnutrition. Amino acids are diverted from their function of tissue synthesis and repair to gluconeogenesis (formation of glucose from non-carbohydrate sources).
5. **Anabolic losses.** Anabolism refers to the metabolic processes which lead to the synthesis of substances. During infection, amino acids are diverted from their normal functions for the synthesis of immunoglobulins, lymphokines, C-reactive protein, and other proteins like liver enzymes.
6. **Fever.** Fever increases the basal metabolic rate by 13 per cent for every 1°C rise in temperature. This uses up a lot of energy, and if the patient has anorexia, then s/he tends to lose weight as s/he slips into a negative energy balance (where the intake of energy is less than the expenditure). Additionally, nitrogen and amino acids may be lost in sweat.
7. **Intestinal losses.** When the intestinal mucosal cells responsible for the absorption of nutrients are damaged by parasites, bacteria or viruses, they are unable to absorb nutrients effectively. There are excessive losses of protein in the faeces, especially with E.coli and rotavirus diarrhoea. Faecal fat losses have also been reported in infections. In the case of worm (like hookworm) infestations, there is blood loss from the intestine, resulting in iron deficiency. This problem has been recognised, and all anaemia prevention programmes now have a component that involves the de-worming of the population.

There is impaired utilisation of nutrients during infection. **Energy** requirements usually increase during infections, primarily due to an increase in the basal metabolic rate.

Proteins are lost from the body as a result of infections, at a rate of 0.6 g/kg body weight/day on an average. This loss is substantial, considering the fact that the average estimated protein requirement is 0.66 g/kg body weight/day. Higher losses have been observed in other severe infections, for instance typhoid fever and dysentery.

Levels of plasma **lipids** like triacyglycerols, fatty acids and ketone bodies are also affected in infections. Changes are dependent on age, degree of fever, and on the severity and duration of infection. Fat may also be mobilised from fat depots of the body in response to under-feeding.

Carbohydrate metabolism is also altered during infection. There is a depletion of glycogen stores in the liver. There is increased gluconeogenesis in acute infection, even if the carbohydrate intake is sufficient. If the infection affects the liver—as it does in hepatitis—there may be hypoglycaemia. The concentration of hormones regulating carbohydrate metabolism, like insulin and glucagon, changes during infections.

Vitamin A concentration in the serum declines in acute infections. Deficiency signs like xerophthalmia (abnormal dryness of the conjunctiva and cornea of the eye, with inflammation) and keratomalacia (softening and ulceration of the cornea) are precipitated as a result of infection in people already marginally deficient. This effect is particularly severe with measles and chicken pox, but is also seen in acute respiratory infections, gastroenteritis (inflammation of the stomach and intestines), rheumatoid arthritis, and infectious hepatitis.

Ascorbic acid concentrations in the plasma decrease, and excretion in urine is seen to increase with infection. The classic nutritional deficiency diseases of **B vitamins,** beriberi and pellagra were known to precipitate in vulnerable individuals by a variety of infections. Serum **Iron** is also known to decrease as a consequence of infection. The reticuloendothelial system (part of the immune system) sequesters the iron. Lactoferrin, with a high iron-binding capacity, is released by phagocytes to deprive the infectious agent of iron for its replication, and hence to inhibit the spread of infection. This is because iron is an important nutrient that the infectious agent needs to survive. Infections also decrease both serum **copper and zinc.** Patients of acute diarrhoea have been shown to go into a negative balance of these minerals.

Infection also adversely affects the growth of children. Usually, after an episode of illness, there is reduction in the weight of the child. Catch-up growth may occur during the recovery period, provided adequate nourishment is provided to the child. In low-income group children who do not have access to good nutrition, the catch-up growth is hampered, and the child becomes underweight or stunted. This is especially true in cases where the child falls prey to infections frequently. Recurrent attacks of diarrhoea have been shown to cause stunting and poor growth in children. They are also known to precipitate clinical signs of vitamin A deficiency. Measles also precipitates severe kwashiorkor and keratomalacia in a child with a marginal nutritional status. Malaria, worm infections and amoebiasis have all been linked to poor growth in children. Blood loss and the destruction of red blood cells contribute to anaemia in some of these infections. De-worming has been shown to improve weight gain and growth.

Box 27.2: The Special Case of HIV/AIDS

Human immunodeficiency virus infection and acquired immune deficiency syndrome (HIV/AIDS) is a disease of the human immune system, caused by infection with the human immunodeficiency virus (HIV). The infection interferes with the immune system of the body, making the person much more susceptible to common infections like tuberculosis, as well as opportunistic infections and tumors that do not usually affect people with healthy immune systems. The virus impairs the immunity, and a poor nutritional status increases the susceptibility to disease progression. The nutritional requirements of an AIDS patient also increase. If appropriate diet therapy is not provided, the nutritional status of the patient rapidly declines, weight loss and wasting being the classic symptoms. The level of micronutrients in serum also tends to decline in this disease, further impacting immunity. Hence, for the nutritional management of patients living with AIDS, it is recommended to increase their energy and protein intake. Micronutrient supplementation is also recommended, as it has been associated with the increased survival of patients. Supplementation is usually at RDA levels.

BIOLOGICAL AND OPERATIONAL IMPLICATIONS

The information presented on the effect of the nutritional status on immunity and the effect of infections on the nutritional status of the individual gives us important leads on using this information to improve the health and well-being of our population in general, as well as in clinical practice while dealing with infectious diseases.

The morbidity and mortality associated with infections is much greater in undernourished individuals. Hence, correction of the nutritional status is vital to decrease the severity or seriousness of infections, and to ensure better survival. Undernourished people also tend to pick up more opportunistic secondary infections, especially after an illness or surgery, as a result of stress/trauma and semi-starvation (because of the inability to eat well during the illness episode or the post-surgery period). Appropriate parenteral (intravenous feeding) or enteral (feeding using tubes inserted through the nose, stomach or intestine) nutritional care becomes vital during hospitalisation when the patient is unable to take in food through the normal oral route.

Infections during pregnancy also affect foetal and post-natal growth. In addition to the several ways that infection can adversely affect the nutritional status of an individual, detailed earlier, the foetus can also be affected by diminished blood flow to the uterus, as a result of the infection. Sometimes, the infection spreads to the placenta and the foetus. The infection may also alter the structure and function of the placenta, thus interfering with intrauterine growth. The immunity of infants born prematurely or small-for-gestational age is compromised. The thymus gland has been found to be involuted (shrunken) in babies born to undernourished mothers. Nutritional deprivation and prenatal infections have an additive effect, and give the baby a serious handicap in life. The intergenerational effects of malnutrition, infection and immune-competence are hence a major worry. Maternal nutrition and timely healthcare for pregnant women is vital to protect the next generation.

As infections and malnutrition lead to impaired growth and development in children and decrease the work productivity of adults, it is vital to check the progress of both. Public health programmes hence need to look at both issues together, and not separately. We have been distributing food and nutrient supplements to children for years together as a part of the national programmes in India, yet malnutrition rates have not come down significantly. On the other hand, immunisation programmes have not met with the success that they should have because of the poor nutritional status of the recipients. The reason may well be that enough efforts have not gone into improving environmental hygiene and sanitation levels, alongside the efforts to improve nutritional status.

Both cell-mediated and humoral immune functions decline gradually with advancing age. With age, there is also an increase in the development of autoimmune disorders and cancer. Nutrition may play a big role in slowing down age-related changes in the immune system, and improve longevity and survival in the elderly. Scientists working on longevity (extending the human lifespan) are looking at the role played by several nutrients and phytochemicals. Research relating to cancer, and how nutrients can prevent cells from turning malignant, is also a priority area.

Allergies have also been linked to malnutrition and an impaired functioning of the immune system. Food antibodies have been detected in the serum of undernourished children in a number of studies. Usually, these are antibodies against dietary proteins. Malnutrition causes atrophy of the pancreas and intestinal mucosal membranes, hence reducing the enzyme supply. Impaired digestion leads to a greater presence of potentially antigenic protein molecules, which are absorbed intact through the thin mucosa. Impaired local immunity in malnourished individuals permits the passage of antigens more freely. Hence, food allergies may be greater in undernourished people.

Since under-nutrition impairs immune responses, the efficacy of vaccinations given to children as protection against deadly infectious diseases may be reduced by nutritional deficiencies. It may be better to plan vaccination campaigns in a season or time when the children's nutritional state is the best. It is important for the attending physician/healthcare worker to make sure that the child/adult approaching a health centre or medical facility is not suffering from malnutrition, or from any other infection at the time of vaccination.

Although synergism is the relationship of greater clinical and public health significance, antagonism is of practical significance when supplementary feeding is done for malnourished individuals with an underlying infection. Thus, giving iron in high doses to a sick child also suffering from kwashiorkor may actually increase the severity of infection. A relapse of malaria has also been seen in certain cases in Somalia, where starving refugees were being re-fed rapidly. Hence, it is important to keep both relationships in mind when dealing with the concomitant presence of infection and malnutrition. Table 27.2 lists the points we need to keep in mind while strategising about the programmes needed to reduce the burden of malnutrition and infection in the community.

Table 27.2: Operational Implications and Strategies to Prevent Malnutrition and Infection

Preventing Malnutrition	*Preventing Infection*
1. *Providing Food and Nutrition Security* • Providing employment opportunities to alleviate poverty • Improving the production of food, especially micronutrient-rich fruits and vegetables • Improving distribution to ensure easy accessibility • Nutrition education about healthy food choices • Food supplementation for vulnerable groups	1. *Immunisation* • Ensuring universal and complete immunisation against infectious diseases • Taking care that the child is not sick or malnourished at the time of immunisation • Improving access to medical facilities to ensure timely treatment
2. *Growth Monitoring and Nutritional Surveillance* • Timely detection of growth faltering • Appropriate intervention to correct faltering • Monitoring the micronutrient status of vulnerable groups like children, pregnant women and the elderly	2. *Hygiene and Sanitation* • Preventing overcrowding and unplanned construction • Improving the ventilation of homes and workplaces • Constructing a sewerage and covered drainage system • Control of vectors like mosquitoes, flies, etc., by appropriate measures • Educating about personal hygiene • Safe disposal of faecal and other waste
3. *Diet during Sickness* • Identification and correction of faulty feeding practices like withholding food during sickness, and stopping breastfeeding in diarrhoea • Educating about the modifications required in the diet during illness episodes, for example, soft, easily digestible foods • Awareness about how nutrient needs get altered, for example, energy and protein requirements increase due to an increase in BMR and tissue catabolism • Need for special attention to diet during convalescence and catch-up growth	3. *Medical Facilities* • Easy access to good quality, low cost medical treatment • Timely treatment of infections • Complete treatment of an ailment to prevent relapses • Knowing about drug-nutrient interactions, like the tuberculosis drug isoniazid increasing the requirement of vitamin B_6 • Preventive health check-ups, especially for vulnerable groups • Protection against secondary infections
4. *Nutrition Intervention Programmes* • Giving zinc supplements along with ORS therapy during diarrhoeal episodes (10–20mg of zinc per day for 10–14 days). • De-worming before giving iron tablets and as a routine • Vitamin A prophylactic dose along with measles vaccine, or during an episode of measles • Tackling commonly prevalent infections in a community before initiating a nutrient or food supplementation programme for maximum benefits	4. *Potable drinking water* • Ensuring a supply of clean drinking water for all, as unclean water is the major source of communicable diseases • Educating about appropriate storage and handling practices • Household water purification techniques, which are low-cost
5. *Maternal and Infant nutrition* • Dietary care of the pregnant and nursing mother • Appropriate infant and young child feeding practices	5. *Maternal and Infant Health* • Ante natal check-ups • Appropriate medical care during and after childbirth • Timely medical attention to illness during pregnancy and infancy

SUMMARY

- The body has a number of defence mechanisms against disease-causing germs, as well as other foreign substances which may harm the body.
- The first line of defence of the body consists of skin, mucous membranes, and mucous and hair/cilia, which prevent the entry of these pathogens or foreign substances into the body.
- There are several non-specific factors that offer resistance to foreign substances, like the Complement system, Phagocytes, Lysozymes, Iron-binding proteins like transferrin and lactoferrin, and Interferon, etc.
- Specific immunological responses of the body (as a result of the action of immunoglobulins or antibodies) are the main defence against specific infectious agents.
- On the basis of function and cell surface markers, the lymphocytes are classified as thymus-dependent T lymphocytes and bone marrow or Bursa-dependent B lymphocytes. The former confer cell-mediated immunity, while the latter confer humoral immunity.
- In the blood and lymph, the cells responsible for defending the body are called White Blood Cells (WBCs), also known as Leucocytes/leukocytes. The different types of WBCs are neutrophils, eosinophils, basophils, lymphocytes, and monocytes. Monocytes eventually leave the bloodstream and become tissue macrophages, which remove dead cell debris as well as attacking microorganisms.
- Malnutrition and infection aggravate each other. Nutritional deficiency impairs immuno-competence and makes the individual more susceptible to infection. Similarly, an illness may adversely affect the nutritional status of the individual, precipitating a state of malnutrition and further depressing immune responses.
- Protein and amino acid deficiency has adverse effects on most immune mechanisms.
- Most vitamin and mineral deficiencies also impair the immune responses of the body.
- High doses of some nutrients, however, may actually lead to a suppressed immune response or aggravation of the infection.
- The incidence, and possibly the severity, of infectious illness in obese individuals are higher, compared with those in lean counterparts.
- Anorexia, faulty feeding habits, decreased intestinal absorption, increased catabolic losses, increased intestinal losses, and increased nutrient requirements during infections, coupled with a poor diet, may adversely affect the nutritional status.
- Infections may precipitate frank forms of nutritional deficiency, like Kwashiorkor, keratomalacia, anaemia, etc.
- The biological implications of the correlation between nutrition, immunity and infection need to be understood to operationally plan better programmes targeted at improving the health and nutritional status of the community.

KEY WORDS

Active immunity: Immunity developed as a result of infection or by specific immunisation, and usually associated with the presence of antibodies or cells having specific action on a microorganism or its toxin.

Acute infection: An infectious disease with a rapid onset and/or a short course.

Atrophy (here of body tissue or an organ): To waste away, especially as a result of the degeneration of cells.

Antiserum: Blood serum that contains specific antibodies against an infective organism or poisonous substance. Antiserums are produced in animals (for example, horse, sheep, ox, rabbit) and humans in response to infection, intoxication, or vaccination, and may be used in another individual to confer immunity to a specific disease or to treat the bites or stings of venomous animals.

Gastroenteritis: Inflammation of the stomach and intestines, typically resulting from bacterial toxins or viral infection, and causing vomiting and diarrhoea.

Host: Here, refers to the person infected with the disease-causing organism.

Morbidity: A diseased state or condition

Mortality: Death.

Mitogen: A substance that induces mitosis (or cell division) and cell transformation, especially lymphocyte transformation.

Passive immunity: When antibodies produced in one body (human or animal) are transferred to another to induce protection against disease.

Phagocytosis (phago means 'to eat' in Greek): The process by which a cell engulfs particles such as bacteria, other microorganisms, aged red blood cells, foreign matter, etc. The principal phagocytes include the neutrophils and monocytes (types of white blood cells).

Reticuloendothelial System: Also called the mononuclear phagocyte system (MPS) or Macrophage System, it is a part of the immune system that consists of the phagocytic cells located in reticular connective tissue. The cells are primarily monocytes and macrophages, and they accumulate in lymph nodes and the spleen.

Sequester: To set apart, withdraw or seclude.

Susceptible: Likely to be harmed by a particular thing (here, infectious agents), vulnerable to, defenceless against.

EXERCISES

1. Differentiate between the following terms:
   a. Innate and acquired immunity
   b. Active and passive immunity
2. What is the effect of protein deficiency on the immune system of the body?
3. 'The simultaneous presence of malnutrition and infection has much more serious consequences than either one present independently.' Justify the statement giving appropriate examples.
4. What are the operational implications of this relationship between nutrition and infection?
5. Explain, giving examples, the effect of micronutrient deficiencies on the immune status of individuals.
6. Discuss the effect of infection on the nutritional status of an individual.

REFERENCES

Chandra, R. K. and P. M. Newberne, *Nutrition, Immunity, and Infection—Mechanisms of Interactions*, Plenum Press: New York, 1977.

Crowley, L. V., 'Immunity, Hypersensitivity, Allergy, and Autoimmune Diseases', in *An Introduction to Human Disease—Pathology and Pathophysiology Correlations*, 8e, USA: Jones and Bartlett, 2010, pp. 69–78.

Hemalatha, R., 'Nutrition and Infection', in M. S. Bamji, K. Krishnaswamy and G. N. V. Brahmam (eds), *Textbook of Human Nutrition*, 3e, New Delhi: Oxford and IBH Publ Co.,2009, pp. 220–32.

MedlinePlus, US National Library of Medicine, National Institute of Health, http://www.nlm.nih.gov/medlineplus/ency/article/003657.htm (accessed 19 November 2014).

Murray, M. J. and A. B. Murray, 'Starvation suppression and refeeding activation of infection, an ecological necessity?' *Lancet* 1, 1977, p. 123.

Scrimshaw, N. S. and J. P. SanGiovanni, 'Synergism of nutrition, infection and immunity: An overview', *Am J Clin Nutr* 66, 1997, pp. 464S–77S.

Scrimshaw, N. S., C. E. Taylor and A. J. E. Gordon, 'Interactions of Nutrition and Infection', WHO monograph series no. 57, Geneva: World Health Organization, 1968.

Tomkins, A. and F. Watson, 'Malnutrition and Infection—A Review', United Nations ACC/SCN State of the Art Series, Nutrition Policy Discussion Paper No. 5, UK: The Lavenham Press Ltd., 1989.

Appendix 1

RECOMMENDED DIETARY ALLOWANCES (RDA)

Table 1: Recommended Dietary Allowances for Energy, Protein, Fat and Minerals for Indians, 2010

Group	*Category/Age*	*Body Weight (kg)*	*Net Energy (kcal/d)*	*Protein (g/d)*	*Visible Fat (g/d)*	*Calcium (mg/d)*	*Iron (mg/d)*	*Zinc (mg/d)*	*Magnesium (mg/d)*
Men	Sedentary work	60	2,320	60.0	25	600	17	12	340
	Moderate work		2,730		30				
	Heavy work		3,490		40				
Women	Sedentary work	55	1,900	55.0	20	600	21	10	310
	Moderate work		2,230		25				
	Heavy work		2.850		30				
	Pregnant		+350	78	30	1,200	35	12	
	Lactating 0–6 m		+600	74	30		21		
	6–12 m		+520	68	30				
Infants	0–6 months	5.4	92 kcal/kg/d	1.16 kcal/kg/d	--	500	46 µg/kg/d	--	30
	6–12 months	8.4	80 kcal/kg/d	1.69 kcal/kg/d	19		5		45
Children	1–3 years	12.9	1,060	16.7	27	600	9	5	50
	4–6 years	18.0	1,350	20.1	25		13	7	70
	7–9 years	25.1	1,690	29.5	30		16	8	100
Boys	10–12 years	34.3	2.190	39.9	35	800	21	9	120
Girls	10–12 years	35.0	2,010	40.4	35		27	9	160
Boys	13–15 years	47.6	2,750	54.3	45		32	11	165
Girls	13–15 years	46.6	2,330	51.9	40		27	11	210
Boys	16–17 years	55.4	3,020	61.5	50		28	12	195
Girls	16–17 years	52.1	2,440	55.5	35		26	12	235

Source: Nutrient Requirements and Recommended Dietary Allowances for Indians, ICMR 2010.

Table 2: Recommended Dietary Allowances for Water-soluble and Fat-soluble Vitamins for Indians, 2010

Group	*Category/Age*	*Body Weight (kg)*	*Vitamin A (μg/d)*		*Thiamine (mg/d)*	*Riboflavin (mg/d)*	*Niacin equivalent (mg/d)*	*Vitamin B6(mg/d)*	*Ascorbic Acid (mg/d)*	*Dietary Folate (μg/d)*	*Vitamin B^{12} (μg/d)*
			Retinol	*β-carotene*							
	Sedentary work				1.2	1.4	16				
Men	Moderate work	60	600	4,800	1.4	1.6	18	2.0	40	200	1.0
	Heavy work				1.7	2.1	21				
	Sedentary work				1.0	1.1	12				
	Moderate work		600	4,800	1.1	1.3	14	2.0	40	200	1.0
Women	Heavy work	55			1.4	1.7	16				
	Pregnant		800	6,400	+0.2	+0.3	+2		60	500	1.2
	Lactating 0–6 m		950	7,600	+0.3	+0.4	+4	2.5	80	300	1.5
	6–12 m				+0.2	+0.3	+3				
Infants	0–6 months	5.4	350	--	0.2	0.3	710 μg/kg	0.1	25	25	0.2
	6–12 months	8.4		2,800	0.3	0.4	650 μg/kg	0.4			
	1–3 years	12.9	400	3,200	0.5	0.6	8	0.9		80	
Children	4–6 years	18.0			0.7	0.8	11		40	100	0.2–1.0
	7–9 years	25.1	600	4,800	0.8	1.0	13	1.6		120	
Boys	10–12 years	34.3			1.1	1.3	15	1.6		140	
Girls	10–12 years	35.0			1.0	1.2	13				
Boys	13–15 years	47.6	600	4,800	1.4	1.6	16		40	150	0.2–1.0
Girls	13–15 years	46.6			1.2	1.4	14	2.0			
Boys	16–17 years	55.4			1.5	1.8	17			200	
Girls	16–17 years	52.1			1.0	1.2	14				

Source: Nutrient Requirements and Recommended Dietary Allowances for Indians, ICMR 2010.

Appendix 2

FOOD EXCHANGE LISTS

Table 1: Comprehensive Food Exchange List

S. No.	*Exchange*	*Approximate Amount of Raw Food (g)*	*Measure of Raw Food*	*Energy (kcal)*	*Protein (g)*	*Carbohydrate (g)*	*Fat (g)*
1.	(i) Milk (toned, standardised)	250	1 cup	150	8	11	7.5
	(ii) Skin milk, liquid	320	1 ¼ cup	93	8	15	Neg
	Meat						
2. a.	(i) Mutton, egg	40	2 pieces or 1 egg	80	7	Neg	6
	(ii) Chicken, lean fish	30	2 pieces	35	7	Neg	0.5
b.	Pulses and Legumes	30	3 tbsp	100	7	17	Neg
3. a.	Vegetable A	100	½ cup	20	1	3.5	Neg
b.	Vegetable B	100–150	½ cup	40	2	7	Neg
4.	Fruit	80–100	1 portion	45	Neg	10	Neg
5.	Cereal/Starch	20 / variable	3 tbsp	70	2	15	Neg
6.	Fat	5	1 tsp	45	Neg	Neg	5
7.	Sugar	5	1 tsp	20	Neg	5	Neg

Note: Neg – Negligible amounts.

Table 2: Detailed Food Exchange Lists

1. MILK EXCHANGE
8 g protein, 11 g carbohydrate, 7.5 g fat, 150 kcal

S. No.	*Foodstuff*	*Amount (g)*	*Protein (g)*	*Carbohydrate (g)*	*Fat (g)*	*Energy (kcal)*
1.	Buffalo Milk	185	8	9.3	12.0	216
2.	*Channa* (Paneer), Buffalo	60	8	4.7	13.8	175
3.	*Channa* (Paneer), Cow	44	8	0.5	9.2	117
4.	Cheese	33	8	2.1	8.3	115
5.	Cow Milk	250	8	11.0	10.3	168
6.	Curds	258	8	7.7	10.3	155
7.	# Double toned milk (1.5% fat)	250	8	11	3.75	114
8.	# Full cream milk (6% fat)	250	8	12	15	215
9.	*Khoa*, Buffalo	55	8	11.3	17.2	231
10.	*Khoa*, Cow	40	8	10.3	10.4	165
11.	** *Khoa* skim buffalo	36	8	9.3	0.6	72

Table 2 contd

Table 2 contd

S. No.	Foodstuff	Amount (g)	Protein (g)	Carbohydrate (g)	Fat (g)	Energy (kcal)
12.	** Skim milk, liquid	320	8	14.7	Neg	93
13.	** Skim milk powder	21	8	10.7	Neg	75
14.	# Toned milk (3% fat)	250	8	11	7.5	150
15.	Whole milk powder	31	8	11.8	8	154

Notes: ** Add 1.5 fat exchanges because these forms of milk contain no fat.
Take the nutritive value of cow's milk for all other nutrients but for fat, energy and vitamin A, reduce the values proportionate to the fat content of the particular type of milk.
Other important nutrients provided are retinol, calcium and riboflavin.

Table 2a: Meat Exchange

(i) Mutton, egg: 7 g protein, 6 g fat, negligible carbohydrate, 80 kcal

S. No.	Foodstuff	Weight (g)	Protein (g)	Fat (g)	Energy (kcal)
1.	Crab	63	7	6.1	106
2.	Egg	53	7	7.0	81
3.	Egg yolk	39	7	11.3	138
4.	Hilsa	32	7	6.2	87
5.	Mutton, muscle	38	7	5.1	73
6.	*Channa*, buffalo	52	7	12.0	162
7.	*Channa*, cow	38	7	7.9	101
8.	Cheese	29	7	7.3	101

(ii) Chicken, lean fish: 7 g protein, 0.5 gm fat, negligible carbohydrate, 35 kcal

S. No.	Foodstuff	Weight (g)	Protein (g)	Fat (g)	Energy (Kcal)
1.	Fowl	27	7	0.2	29
2.	Goat meat	32	7	1.2	38
3.	Goat liver	35	7	1.1	38
4.	Sheep liver	35	7	2.6	53
5.	Katla	35	7	0.8	39
6.	Pomfret	41	7	0.5	33
7.	Prawn	37	7	0.4	32
8.	Sardines	32	7	0.6	34
9.	Rohu	42	7	0.6	41
10.	Singhara	34	7	1.0	53
11.	Egg white	58	7	Neg	26
12.	Protinex	12.5	7	Neg	28

Note: Other important nutrients provided are thiamine, niacin, iron (heme iron from flesh foods) and retinol.

Table 2b: Pulse and Legume Exchange

7 g protein, negligible fat, 17 g carbohydrate, 100 kcals

S. No.	*Foodstuff*	*Weight (g)*	*Protein (g)*	*Fat (g)*	*Carbohydrate (g)*	*Energy (kcal)*
1.	Bengal gram whole	41	7	2.2	25	148
2.	Bengal gram dal	34	7	1.8	20	125
3.	Bean, dry	35	7	0.4	20	105
4.	Black gram dal	29	7	0.4	17	101
5.	Cheese	29	7	7.3	1.8	101
6.	Cow pea	29	7	0.3	16	94
7.	Green gram dal	28	7	0.3	17	101
8.	Green gram whole	29	7	0.4	16	97
9.	Lentil	29	7	0.2	16	96
10.	Red gram dal	31	7	0.5	18	104
11.	*Rajma*	30	7	0.5	18	105
12.	Soyabean	16	7	3.2	3.4	70
13.	*Channa* (paneer), buffalo	52	7	12.0	4.1	162
14.	*Channa* (paneer), cow	38	7	7.9	0.5	101
15.	Nutrinuggets	14	7	0.1	4.2	48

- **GERMINATION**

		Dry weight (g)	*Weight after sprouting (g)*	*Thiamine (mg)*	*Riboflavin (mg)*	*Niacin (mg)*	*Vitamin C (mg)*
(i)	Green gram whole	100 30g (1 exchange)	300 90	0.63 0.19	0.42 .13	3.1 0.9	80 24
(ii)	Bengal gram whole	100 30g (1 exchange)	300 90	.35 .11	0.23 0.07	4.18 1.25	60 18

- **FERMENTATION**

		Dry weight (g) 30 g (1 exchange)	*Weight after Fermentation (g)*	*Thiamine (mg)*	*Riboflavin (mg)*	*Niacin (mg)*	*Vitamin C (mg)*
(i)	Bengal gram whole	100 30 g (1 exchange)	400 120	0.35 0.11	0.24 0.07	4.41 1.32	- -

Notes:
- Values for all other nutrients can be taken for the equivalent dry weight from the nutritive value book.
- Other important nutrients provided are B group vitamins, non-heme iron, dietary fibre (whole pulses).

Table 3a: Vegetable A Exchange

3.5g carbohydrate, 1g protein and negligible fat, and 20 kcal

S. No.	Foodstuff	Weight (g)	Carbohydrate (g)	Protein (g)	Energy (kcal)
1.	# * *Bathua* leaves	121	3.5	4.5	36
2.	Bitter gourd	83	3.5	1.4	21
3.	# Bottle gourd	140	3.5	0.3	17
4.	Brinjal	88	3.5	1.2	21
5.	# Giant chillies (Capsicum)	82	3.5	1.1	20
6.	# Cauliflower	88	3.5	2.3	27
7.	# * Coriander leaves	56	3.5	1.9	25
8.	Cucumber	140	3.5	0.6	18
9.	# Drumstick	96	3.5	2.4	25
10.	Ghosala, *Ghia tori*	121	3.5	1.5	22
11.	# Knolkhol	92	3.5	1.0	20
12.	Lettuce	140	3.5	2.9	29
13.	# * Mint leaves	60	3.5	2.9	29
14.	Mushroom	82	3.5	1.2	24
15.	# * Mustard leaves	109	3.5	4.4	35
16.	# Parwar	159	3.5	3.2	32
17.	# * Radish leaves	146	3.5	5.5	41
18.	Radish white	103	3.5	0.7	18
19.	Ridge Gourd, *torai*	103	3.5	0.5	18
20.	Snake Gourd, *chichinda*	106	3.5	0.5	18
21.	# * Spinach	121	3.5	2.4	31
22.	Tinda	103	3.5	1.4	22
23.	# Tomato ripe	97	3.5	.9	20
24.	# Broccoli	77	3.5	1.8	21

Notes: # Vitamin C rich foods

* Carotene rich foods

Other important nutrients provided are carotenes, vitamin C, folic acid, calcium, non heme iron, and dietary fibre.

Table 3b: Vegetable B Exchange

7 g carbohydrate, 2 g protein, negligible fat, 40 kcals

S. No.	Foodstuff	Weight (g)	Carbohydrate (g)	Protein (g)	Energy (kcal)
1.	# * Amaranth, tender	115	7	4.6	52
2.	Beetroot	80	7	1.4	34
3.	# Beans, scarlet runner, *sem*	23	7	1.7	36
4.	Broad beans, *bakla*	97	7	4.4	47
5.	# Cabbage	152	7	2.7	41
6.	* Carrot	66	7	0.6	32
7.	Cauliflower greens	92	7	5.4	61
8.	# * Colocasia leaves	103	7	4.0	58

Table 3b contd

Table 3b contd

S. No.	*Foodstuff*	*Weight (g)*	*Carbohydrate (g)*	*Protein (g)*	*Energy (kcal)*
9.	* Curry leaves	37	7	2.3	40
10.	# * Drumstick leaves	56	7	3.8	52
11.	# * Fenugreek leaves	117	7	5.1	57
12.	# French beans	156	7	2.6	41
13.	Jackfruit tender	75	7	2.0	39
14.	Ladies finger	109	7	2.0	38
15.	Maize, tender	28	7	1.3	35
16.	Onion	56	7	1.0	33
17.	Peas	44	7	3.2	41
18.	Pumpkin, *kaddu*	152	7	2.1	38
19.	# Turnip	113	7	0.6	33

Notes: # Vitamin C rich foods.
* Carotene rich foods.

Other important nutrients provided are carotenes, vitamin C, folic acid, calcium, non-heme iron, and dietary fibre.

Table 4: Fruit Exchange

10g carbohydrate, negligible protein and fat, 45 kcal

S. No.	*Foodstuff*	*Weight (g)*	*Carbohydrate (g)*	*Energy (kcal)*
1.	# *Amla*	74	10	42
2.	* Apricot	86	10	46
3.	Apple	75	10	44
4.	Banana	40	10	42
5.	Cherries, red	72	10	46
6.	Dates, fresh	30	10	43
7.	Dates, dry	13	10	41
8.	# Grapefruit	143	10	46
9.	Grapes, green	61	10	41
10.	Grapes, blue	76	10	44
11.	# Guava	80	10	45
12.	# Lemon sweet (*nimbu*)	92	10	54
13.	# Lichi	73	10	44
14.	# Lime sweet *(Malta)*	128	10	46
15.	# Lime sweet *(Mausami)*	107	10	46
16.	* Loquat	104	10	44
17.	* Mango, ripe	59	10	44
18.	* Melon, musk *(Kharbooja)*	286	10	49
19.	# * Orange	92	10	44
20.	# * Papaya	139	10	44

Table 4 contd

Table 4 contd

S. No.	*Foodstuff*	*Weight (g)*	*Carbohydrate (g)*	*Energy (kcal)*
21.	Pear	84	10	44
22.	Peach	95	10	48
23.	# Pineapple	93	10	43
24.	Plums	90	10	47
25.	Pomegranate	69	10	44
26.	# * Raspberry	86	10	48
27.	Raisins	13	10	41
28.	Sapota	47	10	46
29.	# Strawberry	102	10	45
30.	Melon, water	303	10	49

Notes: # Vitamin C rich foods.

* Carotene rich foods.

Other important nutrients provided are carotenes, vitamin C and dietary fibre.

Table 5: Cereal/Starch Exchange

15g carbohydrate, 2g protein, negligible fat, 70 kcals

S. No.	*Foodstuff*	*Weight (g)*	*Carbohydrate (g)*	*Protein (g)*	*Energy (kcal)*
1.	*Bajra*	22	15	2.6	79
2.	Barley	22	15	2.5	72
3.	Biscuit, salty	28	15	1.8	150
4.	Biscuit, sweet	21	15	1.3	96
5.	Bread, brown	31	15	2.7	76
6.	Bread, white	29	15	2.3	69
7.	Cake, plain	31	15	1.0	88
8.	Cake, sponge	25	15	1.5	67
9.	Cornflakes	18	15	1.4	72
10.	*Jowar*	21	15	2.1	73
11.	Maize, dry	23	15	2.5	79
12.	Maize, tender	61	15	2.9	76
13.	Oatmeal	24	15	3.3	90
14.	Pasta - Noodle, Macaroni, Spaghetti, etc.	20	15	2.3	70
15.	Ragi	21	15	1.5	69
16.	Rice	19	15	1.3	66
17.	Rice flakes	20	15	1.3	65
18.	Rice puffed	20	15	2.1	66

Table 5 contd

Table 5 contd

S. No.	Foodstuff	Weight (g)	Carbohydrate (g)	Protein (g)	Energy (kcal)
19.	Sago	17	15	Neg	60
20.	Semolina	20	15	2.1	70
21.	Vermicelli	19	15	1.7	67
22.	Wheat, flour	22	15	2.7	75
23.	Wheat, flour (refined)	21	15	2.3	73
24.	Colocasia	71	15	2.1	69
25.	Lotus stem (dry)	29	15	1.7	63
26.	Lotus stem (fresh)	75	15	1.7	63
27.	Potato	66	15	1.0	64
28.	Potato sweet	53	15	0.6	64
29.	Yam	58	15	0.8	64

Notes: For convenience, when only one or two servings of plain cake or biscuits are consumed in a day, instead of calculating for all ingredients, use 20–25g cake/biscuits as 1 cereal exchange and take it as equivalent to nutritive value of 20g refined wheat flour for calculations.

Other important nutrients provided are B group vitamins, non-heme iron and dietary fibre (whole cereals).

Table 6: Fat Exchange

5g fat, negligible carbohydrate and protein, 45 kcal

S. No.	Foodstuff	Weight (g)	Protein (g)	Fat (g)	Energy (kcal)
1.	Almonds	8	1.7	5	53
2.	Bacon	10	3.5	5	60
3.	Butter	6	0	5	45
4.	Cashewnuts	11	2.3	5	66
5.	Coconut, dry	8	0.3	5	53
6.	Coconut, fresh	12	0.5	5	53
7.	Cooking oil	5	0	5	45
8.	Cream 40%	15	Neg	5	45
9.	Cream, light 20%	25	Neg	5	45
10.	Ghee	5	0	5	45
11.	Gingelly seeds	12	2.2	5	58
12.	Groundnuts, roasted	13	3.4	5	74
13.	Hydrogenated oil	5	0	5	45
14.	Mayonnaise	6	Neg	5	45
15.	Walnuts	8	1.3	5	55

Table 7: Sugar Exchange

5g carbohydrate, 20 kcal

S. No.	*Foodstuff*	*Weight (g)*	*Carbohydrate (g)*	*Energy (kcal)*
1.	Honey	6	5	19
2.	Jaggery, cane	5	5	19
3.	Jam	6	5	19
4.	Sugar, cane	5	5	20
5.	Sugarcane juice	55	5	21

REFERENCES

Food Exchange List, University of Delhi; Department of Food and Nutrition, Lady Irwin College, 2005.

Gopalan, C., B. V. Ramasastri, S. C. Balasubramanian, B. S. Narasinga Rao, Y. S. Deosthale, and K. C. Pant, *The Nutritive Value of Indian Foods*, Hyderabad: NIN. ICMR, 1999.

Rajalakshmi, R., *Applied Nutrition*, 3e, New Delhi: Oxford and IBH Publishing Co. Pvt. Ltd., 1984.

Turner, Dorothy, *Handbook of Diet Therapy*, Chicago: The University of Chicago Press, 1959.

Appendix 3

MEAL PLANNING MADE SIMPLE

Meal planning can be a very simple exercise with the help of a food exchange list.

Here is a step by step explanation of how to use the food exchange list in order to plan meals for an individual.

Say, for example, you need to plan a day's diet for a 17-year-old girl belonging to the middle-income group. The first step is to look up the RDA for energy and protein for this individual from the ICMR RDA tables (given in Appendix 1). Thus, from the tables:

RDA for Energy = 2,440 kcal, Protein = 55.5g.

Among micronutrients, all are important, especially calcium and iron, and so while planning the menu, we must take care to include a variety of foods from each food group or exchange. A variety ensures that different nutrients and protective phytochemicals are included in the day's diet. Special care needs to be taken to include calcium and iron-rich foods in the menu.

Diet planning, as already described in Chapter 15, involves 3 steps.

Step 1: Formulate a food plan based on the RDA for energy and protein

Table 1: Food Plan - Deciding the Number of Exchanges for Food Groups

Food Exchange	*No. of Exchanges*	*Amount (g)*	*Energy (kcal)*	*Protein (g)*	*Carbohydrates (g)*	*Fat (g)*
Milk	2	500	300			
Meat	1	40	80			
Pulse	2	60	200			
Vegetable A	2	200	40			
Vegetable B	3	300	120			
Fruit	1	100	45			
Cereal						
Fat	8	40	360			
Sugar	5	25	100			
Total			**1,245**			

First, assign the number of exchanges to each food group except cereals, as shown above. We assume she is a non-vegetarian. For a vegetarian, we would simply replace one meat exchange for a pulse exchange. Calculate only the energy for all exchanges, except cereals. To calculate the number of cereal exchanges,

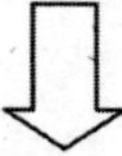

Add the amount of energy contributed by these groups. This works out to 1,245 kcal.

Subtract from the total energy you need to plan for (that is, the RDA for energy).

that is, 2,440 – 1,245 kcal = 1,195 kcal. This is the amount of energy that cereals need to provide.

Now divide the energy to be supplied by the cereal exchange by 70 (that is, the amount of energy provided by one cereal exchange). This will give the number of cereal exchanges.

that is, 1,195 ÷ 70 = 16.8 or 17

Now fill this number in the food plan and calculate the total energy. The total energy should be within the range of RDA +/- 50 kcal.

Table 2: Food Plan - Calculation of Macronutrients

Food Exchange	*No. of Exchanges*	*Amount (g)*	*Energy (kcal)*	*Protein (g)*	*Carbohydrates (g)*	*Fat (g)*
Milk	2	500	300	16	22	15
Meat	1	40	80	7	-	6
Pulse	2	60	200	14	34	-
Vegetable A	2	200	40	2	7	-
Vegetable B	3	300	120	6	21	-
Fruit	1	100	45	-	10	-
Cereal	**17**	**340**	**1,190**	**34**	**255**	**-**
Fat	8	40	360	-	-	40
Sugar	5	25	100	-	25	-
Total			**2,435**	**79**	**374**	**61**

The per cent calories contributed by carbohydrates, proteins and fats can be calculated as follows:

Total carbohydrates eaten in a day (according to food plan) = 374 g. One gram carbohydrate yields 4 kcal, which means that total calories coming from carbohydrates = 374 x 4 = 1,496 kcal.

Per cent energy contributed by carbohydrates = 1,496 x 100/ 2,435 = 61 %.

Total protein eaten in a day (according to food plan) = 79g. One gram protein yields 4 kcal, which means that total calories coming from proteins = 79 x 4 = 316 kcal.

Per cent energy contributed by proteins = 316 x 100/ 2,435 = 12.9 %.

Total fat eaten in a day (according to food plan) = 61g. One gram fat yields 9 kcal, which means that total calories coming from fat = 61 x 9 = 549 kcal.

Per cent energy contributed by fat = 549 x 100/ 2,435 = 22.5 %.

Total energy from fat should be kept at less than 30 per cent, which means that the number of fat exchanges can be increased and the number of cereals can be reduced.

Step 2: Distribute these exchanges among the different meals for the day

The number and timing of meals are usually dependent on the lifestyle of the person concerned. Small, frequent meals are usually preferred. Assuming that this person is away at school or college till the afternoon, returning home by 2–3 PM, we can plan for a five-meal pattern. If she spends longer hours at college, then the lunch would also be packed.

Table 3: Distribution of Exchanges between the Meals

Food Exchange	*Breakfast*	*Packed Tiffin*	*Lunch*	*Evening Tea*	*Dinner*	*Total*
Milk	1	-	-	1	-	2
Meat	-	1	-	-	-	1
Pulse	-	-	1	-	1	2
Vegetable A	½	-	½	½	½	2
Vegetable B	-	½	1	½	1	3
Fruit	1	-	-	-	-	1
Cereal	3	3	4	3	4	17
Fat	1	1	2	2	2	8
Sugar	1	-	-	2	2	5

The reason for splitting the day's meals is to distribute the calories that need to be consumed. It also means that the other foods should be split between the different meals in order to make them all balanced. Some points to remember while distributing:

1. Make sure that all meals have good quality protein (this is important, as the adolescent is growing and needs proteins all through the day). All meals should have either a milk/milk/ pulse exchange in them.
2. Cereals, being the staple, should be present in all the meals.
3. Protective foods, that is, fruits and/or vegetables, should also be there in all the meals.
4. The total number of exchanges column should be the same as what you planned in the food plan.

Step 3: Plan the menu for each meal

The most common mistake that students make is planning the menu first, and then working backwards to calculate the food plan. The food plan should always be made before, as this does not change from day to day. Distribution may change a little, but the menu must change every day, otherwise it leads to boredom.

To plan the menu, the detailed food exchange list is used to introduce variety in the diet. For planning a feasible and practical menu, one must keep all the factors for menu planning in mind (discussed in Chapter 15). It is important to keep in mind how much time is available for the preparation and consumption of these meals. Make sure the menu matches with the exchanges you have allotted for each meal. Menu options for the different meals are described here. Breakfast has been worked out in detail.

Table 4: Number of Food Exchanges for Breakfast

Food Exchange	*Breakfast*
Milk	1
Meat	–
Pulse	–
Vegetable A	½
Vegetable B	–
Fruit	1
Cereal	3
Fat	1
Sugar	1

Breakfast

For a school or college-going student who has to leave home early in the morning, this meal is best kept simple (single dish) but filling. Now, for breakfast, we have the following exchanges available with us:

Different options for breakfast can be as follows:

Table 5: Different Menu Options for Breakfast

Option	*Menu*	*Ingredients*	*Exchange Group*	*No. of Exchanges*	*Approximate Amount (g)*
A	Mango Shake	Milk	Milk	1	250
		Mango	Fruit	1	60
		Sugar	Sugar	1	5
	Grilled sandwich	Whole wheat bread	Cereal	2	60
		Potato	Cereal	1	65
		Butter	Fat	1	5
		Tomato	Vegetable A	¼	25
		Capsicum	Vegetable A	¼	20
B	Cornflakes/Oats/ Wheat porridge	Cornflakes/oats/ *dalia*	Cereal	1	20
		Milk	Milk	½	125
		Apple	Fruit	½	35
		Banana	Fruit	½	20
		Sugar	Sugar	1	5
	Pizza toast	Whole wheat bread/ pizza base	Cereal	2	60
		Cheese	Milk	½	15
		Tomato	Vegetable A	¼	25
		Capsicum	Vegetable A	¼	20
		Butter	Fat	1	5
C	Mango smoothie	Mango	Fruit	1	65
		Curd	Milk	½	130
		Sugar	Sugar	1	5
	Paneer parantha	Whole wheat flour	Cereal	3	60
		Paneer	Milk	½	22
		Oil	Fat	1	5
	Mint-coriander *chutney*	Mint	Vegetable A	¼	15
		Coriander	Vegetable B	¼	15

Remember that the 'Approximate amount in grams' column is filled from the detailed food exchange list. Similarly, several other options can be planned. For the other meals, menu suggestions are as follows:

Mid-morning packed tiffin

Option A: Chicken/egg sandwich with vegetables

Option B: *Parantha* with egg *bhurji*

Option C: Cutlets with egg/minced chicken or meat. Meat could occasionally be replaced with *paneer*, which is also listed in the meat exchange because of a similar protein content.

Lunch/Dinner

Lunch and dinner menus can be similar, in that there is a cereal preparation, a *dal* preparation and a vegetable preparation. During dinner, the sugar exchange can be used to make a sweet dish along with a cereal exchange, like *halwa*/*chikki*/*laddoo*. Since the cereal exchanges are four and the girl may not want to eat four rotis, part of the cereal exchange could be used as potato in a vegetable preparation. This way, some vegetables could be put aside and given raw as a salad.

Option A: *Chapati*/rice with *dal* and a vegetable preparation of choice and salad.

Option B: Vegetable *pulao* with pulse incorporated as sprouts/*kala chana*/ soya nuggets

This option is very convenient to use as packed lunch.

Option C: Vegetable noodles with pulse incorporated as sprouts/soya nuggets/*paneer* (note that *paneer* is also listed in pulse exchange because of a similar protein content).

Tea-time snack

Option A: Milk with sugar/health drink mix like Bournvita/Horlicks, etc., along with pasta preparation.

Option B: Sweet *lassi* with *poha*

Option C: Cold coffee with vegetable cutlets/vegetable sandwiches

You can think of many more options, and work out the details as given for 'Breakfast'.

To help you decide on the portion sizes that need to be planned for in each meal, the following tables have been prepared after being standardised in the laboratory of Lady Irwin College. The portion sizes for a meal mentioned are suitable for adults; however, the same are also applicable for school-going children and adolescents. For preschoolers, you would need to approximately halve the portion size.

Household measures

1 bowl = 250 ml

1 medium *katorie* = 200 ml

1 glass = 250 ml

Table 6: Raw Ingredients and Cooked Portions of Some Commonly Consumed Indian Foods

S. No.	*Dish*	*Cooked amount (Household Measure)*	*Ingredients*	*No. of Exchanges*	*Amount in Grams*
1.	Cracked wheat/ semolina porridge (*dalia/suji*)	1 bowl	Cracked wheat/semolina	1	20
			Milk	¾–1	190–250 ml
			Sugar	1–2	5–10
2.	*Poha/suji upma*	1 quarter plate	Rice flakes/semolina	2	40
			Vegetables (your choice)	½	50 (approx)
			Peanuts	½	5
			Oil	1	5
3.	*Cheela (besan-suji)*	2–3 (depending on diameter)	*Besan* (gramflour)	1	35
			Suji (semolina)	1	20
			Green leafy vegetable (optional)	¼	25–30
			Oil	1–2	5–10

Table 4 contd

Table 4 contd

S. No.	*Dish*	*Cooked amount (Household Measure)*	*Ingredients*	*No. of Exchanges*	*Amount in Grams*
4.	*Roti*	3 (5–5 ½ inch diameter)	Whole wheat flour (*atta*)	3	60
5.	*Parantha* (plain)	2 medium (7 inch diameter approx)	Whole wheat flour	3	60
			Oil/*ghee*	1–2	5–10
6.	*Parantha* (stuffed)	2 medium	Whole wheat flour	3	60
			Vegetable (for stuffing)	1–2	50 (approx)
			Oil/*ghee*	1–2	5–10
7.	*Poori*	3 (4–4 ½ inch diameter)	Whole wheat flour	3	60
			Oil	3	15
8.	Boiled rice	1 full plate	Rice	4	80
9.	Pulao	1 full plate	Rice	3	60
			Vegetables	½–1	50–60
			Oil	1	5
10.	Vegetable curry	1 medium *katorie*	Vegetable	½–1	50–100 (approx)
			Onion	¼	15
			Tomato	¼	25
			Oil	1	5
11.	Vegetable (dry preparation)	½–1 medium *katorie*	Vegetable	1–1 ½	100–150 (approx)
			Oil	1	5
12.	Pulse preparation (*dal*)	1 medium *katorie* (medium consistency)	Pulse (*dal*)	1	30
			Oil	½–1	3–5
	For *baghar/tadka* in the *dal* can add Onion		Tomato	1/8	10–15
			1/8	10	
13.	*Raita*	1 medium *katorie*	Curd	½	125
			Vegetable	¼–½	25–50
14.	*Kheer*	1 medium *katorie*	Milk	1	250
			Cereal or Vegetable	½	10 or 50
			Sugar	1–2	5–10
15.	Fruit Custard (made with custard powder)	1 medium *katorie*	Milk	½	125
			Fruit	½	50 (approx)
			Sugar	1	5

Note:
- Half exchange of whole pulse (15 g) becomes about 45g on sprouting
- For salad, you can use ½–1 exchange of vegetables/fruits

Appendix 4

THE WHO MULTICENTRE GROWTH REFERENCE STUDY (MGRS)

The WHO Multicentre Growth Reference Study (MGRS) was undertaken between 1997 and 2003 to generate new growth curves for assessing the growth and development of infants and young children around the world. The need was felt for new growth standards as the National Center for Health Statistics (NCHS) data, generated in the late 1970s, did not adequately represent early childhood growth. Most of the concerns centred on the infant charts, and were largely associated with characteristics of the Fels data used to generate them. The Fels data came from a single longitudinal study of mainly formulafed, white, middle-class infants from a limited geographic area of south-western Ohio, collected between1929–75.

In addition to not being from a nationally representative sample, the Fels observations were made at birth and 1 month, at 3-month intervals from 3–12 months, and at 6-month intervals from 12–36 months. These intervals were considered inadequate to properly identify growth patterns during periods of rapid change. Moreover, the size and growth patterns of Fels infants were believed not to adequately represent the current growth patterns of combined breast and formula-fed infants in the population. Also, the statistical methods used at the time the NCHS/WHO growth curves were constructed were too limited to correctly model the pattern and variability of growth.

The need was felt by the 47th World Health Assembly, in May 1994, to revise the reference data so as to obtain the growth of breastfed infants. Also, as the NCHS data was collected only from the United States of America, it was decided to include other countries across the world in generating data for the new growth curves. The 1977 charts were revised in part when more recent and comprehensive national data on body measurements in US children were available from the NHANES surveys, to generate the Centres for Disease Control and Prevention (CDC) growth curves in 2000. However, by then the MGRS had been undertaken.

The MGRS collected primary growth data and related information from approximately 8,440 healthy breastfed infants and young children from widely different ethnic backgrounds and cultural settings in six countries of the world (Brazil, Ghana, India, Norway, Oman, and the USA). It combined a longitudinal follow-up from birth to 24 months, and a cross-sectional survey of children aged 18–71 months. The MGRS is unique, in that it purposively selected privileged healthy children living under conditions likely to favour the achievement of their full genetic growth potential. Even the mothers of the children selected practised fundamental health-promoting activities, like breastfeeding and not smoking. Thus, the study was designed to produce a standard, and not just reference data. Although standards and references both serve as a basis for comparison, each has a different interpretation. A standard defines how children should grow. Any deviations from the pattern it describes are evidence of abnormal growth. A reference, on the other hand, does not provide as sound a basis for such value judgements. In practice, however, references are often mistakenly used as standards.

The new WHO growth curves provided a single international standard that represented the best description of physiological growth for all children from birth to five years of age, and established the breastfed infant as the normative model for growth and development. Breastfeeding is the recommended standard for infant feeding. The WHO charts reflect growth patterns among children who were predominantly breastfed for at least four months, and were still breastfeeding at 12 months. Thus, the new standards adopted a fundamentally prescriptive approach designed to describe how all children should grow, rather than merely describing how children grew at a specified time and place.

The WHO standards are based on a high-quality study designed explicitly for creating growth charts. The WHO standards were constructed using longitudinal length and weight data, measured at frequent intervals. For the CDC growth charts, weight data were not available between birth and 3 months of age, and the sample sizes were small for sex and age groups during the first six months of age. Another key characteristic of the new WHO standards is that they include windows of achievement for six gross motor developmental milestones.

FOR CHILDREN OLDER THAN FIVE YEARS

To construct growth curves for school-aged children and adolescents in 2007, a reconstruction of the 1977 NCHS/WHO reference was undertaken by WHO. It used the original NCHS data set, supplemented with data from the WHO child growth standards sample for under-fives. To develop this reference, the same statistical methodology was used as in the construction of the WHO standards.

Data from the 1977 National Center for Health Statistics (NCHS)/WHO growth reference (1–24 years) were merged with data from the under-fives growth standards' cross-sectional sample (18–71 months) to smooth the transition between the two samples. State-of-the-art statistical methods used to construct the WHO Child Growth Standards (0–5 years), that is, the Box-Cox power exponential (BCPE) method with appropriate diagnostic tools for the selection of best models, were applied to this combined sample.

REFERENCE

The WHO Growth Charts can be accessed from the website: http://www.who.int/childgrowth/standards/en/.

Appendix 5

MOTHER AND CHILD PROTECTION CARD

The Mother and Child Protection Card was introduced by the Ministry of Women and Child Development and the Ministry of Health and Family Welfare in 2010, with the objective of educating mothers and family members about the positive practices aimed at achieving good health of the pregnant mother, the newborn, infant, and young child. It also provides information about the various types of nutrition and health-related services for the mother and child, like immunisation, health check-ups and referrals. The aim of the card is to empower families to make decisions for the improved health and nutritional status and development of young children on a continual basis. The MCP card acts as a nutrition education tool, to be used by the Auxiliary Nurse Midwife (ANM), Anganwadi worker (AWW), Accredited Social Health Activist (ASHA), and other community health workers.

The card is issued to the pregnant mother once she is registered by the health worker. The ANM, or any other health worker, fills the information on the cover page as well as the other details before giving it to the families. Families are advised to bring the card along when they visit the AWC, sub-centre, primary health centre, private doctor, and a hospital. Families are advised to keep the card in a safe place, to prevent it from wear and tear. The various sections of the card are explained, using support material, before the card is given to the families.

The card is divided into various sections:

1. Antenatal care
2. Postnatal care
3. Newborn care
4. Infant and young child feeding practices
5. Growth charts for boys and girls

Antenatal care: The ANM or any other health worker records all the events related to the antental period, like weight gain, blood pressure, haemoglobin levels, TT immunisation, and any obstetric complications in each visit of the pregnant mother. The card also pictorially depicts care and feeding during pregnancy, and the danger signs and steps for ensuring institutional delivery or safe home delivery.

Postnatal care: The date, place and type of delivery, complications, gender, weight, exclusive breastfeeding details, and post-partum status of the mother and neonate are recorded at the time of delivery on the MCP card by the health worker.

Newborn care: The card provides information about taking care of the newborn, the danger signs and immunisation details as per the Universal Immunisation Programme (UIP) schedule. The immunisation details are also recorded by the ANM or health worker on the card.

Infant and young child feeding practices: The card provides detailed information about the feeding of the infant and young child. The card lays emphasis on exclusive breastfeeding till six months, the initiation of complementary feeding at six months, appropriate and adequate complementary feeding along with breastfeeding, use of iodised salt, and the importance of playing and communicating with the young child. It also provides information on feeding and care during illness, especially during diarrhoea, acute respiratory infection and fever.

Growth charts for boys and girls: The MCP card also has separate growth charts for boys (blue chart) and girls (pink chart) to monitor their growth from birth to three years. Weight is a linear measurement, and it increases rapidly during the first two years of the life span. Moreover, a change in weight status (gain or deficit) is easily understood, as compared to other anthropometric measurements, and therefore weight-for-age WHO growth charts are used for growth monitoring in India (see Appendix 5).

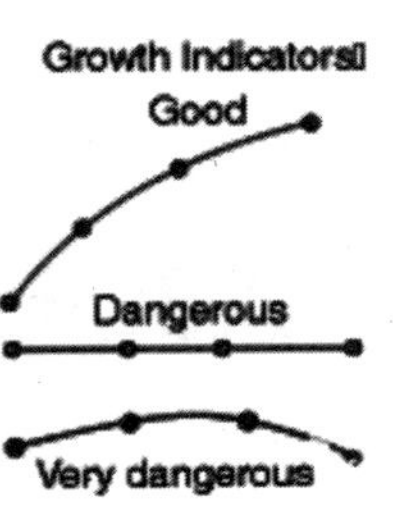

The *anganwadi* worker weighs the child and records her/his weight for age on the growth chart every month, and the weight for each month is joined by a line. The direction of the line indicates whether the child is growing or not, and makes it visible to the family.

– An **upward growth curve**, showing adequate weight gain for the age of the child, indicates that the child is growing and is healthy.

– A **flat growth curve** indicates that the child has not gained weight, and requires attention by the AWW and the mother.

– A **downward growth curve** indicates loss of weight, and requires immediate attention by the AWW and the family.

The nutritional status of children is colour-coded in the growth charts, where the green portion stands for normal nutritional status, yellow for moderately underweight (between -2SD and -3SD), and orange for severely undernourished (below -3SD). This will help the mother to know the current and past nutritional status, and she can visually see the growth of her child. The child is said to be growing normally if the colour remains unchanged in subsequent readings. The deviation from growth occurs when the child's growth curve changes colour in subsequent readings, which is a matter of concern when it changes from green to yellow or from yellow to orange. The AWW or the health worker should immediately take action, and provide appropriate and adequate nutrition and health advice to retain the nutritional status of the child subsequently.

The MCP card is an effort to link maternal and child health with the Integrated Child Development Scheme of the Ministry of Women and Child Development, and the National Health Mission of the Ministry of Health and Family Welfare. The MCP card helps in the timely identification, referral and management of complications during pregnancy, childbirth, and the postnatal period. The card also serves as a tool for providing complete immunisation to infants and children, promoting early and exclusive breastfeeding, appropriate complementary feeding, and monitoring their growth.

Samples of Mother Child Protection cards are available at:

https://lh5.googleusercontent.com/-M6zvaSVDUXs/TZRWAbq_gcI/AAAAAAAAAyM/o77cP79SkPs/w1423-h1322/Mother%2Band%2BChild%2BProtection%2BCard1.jpg

https://plus.google.com/photos/101701208237657197330/albums/5590183062645129153/5590187519039823026?pid=5590187519039823026&oid=101701208237657197330

ABOUT THE EDITORS AND CONTRIBUTORS

THE EDITORS

Ravinder Chadha is Associate Professor, Department of Food and Nutrition, Lady Irwin College, University of Delhi. Her research interests are in the fields of public health nutrition, nutritional assessment—diet and anthropometric assessment, nutrition education—behaviour change communication, nutrition counselling, nutrition programme development and evaluation, capacity enhancement of programme functionaries for infant and young child feeding care, overweight among children and adults, metabolic syndrome and other risk factors of cardio-metabolic disease among adults, and nutrition-related concerns among children with special needs.

Pulkit Mathur is Assistant Professor, Department of Food and Nutrition, Lady Irwin College, University of Delhi. Her research interests are in the fields of different aspects of food safety, like the risk analysis of different food hazards—adulterants, contaminants and food additives, microbiological quality of food and use of the HACCP approach to ensure food safety in small-scale food industries/catering establishments. She is also interested in nutrient profiling, metabolic syndrome, body composition and its relationship to disease, and human nutritional requirements. She has several national and international publications to her credit.

THE CONTRIBUTORS

Neena Bhatia is Associate Professor, Department of Food and Nutrition, Lady Irwin College, University of Delhi. Her research interests are in the fields of public nutrition, diet counselling and epidemiological research, development of computer software for nutrition counselling, micronutrient profile of vulnerable groups, and the development, implementation, and evaluation of public health and nutrition programmes.

Shavika Gupta is Assistant Professor (ad hoc), Department of Food and Nutrition, Lady Irwin College, University of Delhi. Her research was on the relationship of morbidity and nutritional status as assessed using various anthropometric indicators among infants and young children. She has been associated with various projects related to public health nutrition, which have included the evaluation of various national programmes, the dual burden of malnutrition in India, and micronutrient deficiencies.

Suman Kumari is Assistant Professor (ad hoc), Department of Food and Nutrition, Lady Irwin College, University of Delhi. Her research interests include food and nutrition policies, food safety, food standards on labelling and claims, pesticides and antibiotic residues, chemical risk analysis in food chain, and capacity building of the Food Safety and Standards Act, 2006, for Food Business Operators, consumers and other stakeholders.

Priti Rishi Lal is Assistant Professor, Department of Food and Nutrition, Lady Irwin College, University of Delhi. She has several publications to her credit in both national and international journals. Her research interests are in the field of clinical nutrition, sports nutrition, and spiritual tools in behaviour change communication.

Prachi Mishra is Assistant Professor, Department of Food and Nutrition, Lady Irwin College, University of Delhi. She teaches basic and lifecycle nutrition and therapeutic nutrition. Her research interest lies in the field of clinical nutrition.

Shailly Nigam is Assistant Professor (ad hoc), Department of Food and Nutrition, Lady Irwin College, University of Delhi. Her research interests lie in the field of immunology, cell biology and molecular biology. She has worked extensively in fluorescence and confocal microscopic techniques.

Pooja Raizada is Assistant Professor, Department of Food and Nutrition, Lady Irwin College, University of Delhi. Her research interests lie in the field of physiology and food microbiology, and adolescent health and hygiene.

Manisha Sabharwal is Assistant Professor, Department of Food and Nutrition, Lady Irwin College, University of Delhi. Her research interests lie in the field of geriatric nutrition, nutritional epidemiology of the elderly, determinants of functional ability and dependence in the elderly, development of resource material for nutrition programmes of the elderly, capacity building of community-level health workers for newborn care and infant feeding, and nutrition and health communication.

Veenu Seth is Nutrition Consultant and Former Associate Professor, Department of Food and Nutrition, Lady Irwin College, University of Delhi. She is an Executive member of the Indian Dietetic Association, Delhi Chapter, as well as an RD Board member. She is also Clinical Director, Health Promotion for Special Olympics and Nutrition Associate, CDDMASS.

Sushma Sharma is Nutrition Consultant and Former Reader, Department of Food and Nutrition, Lady Irwin College, University of Delhi. She has executed several research projects and has several publications in national and international journals. She is the recipient of the Lifetime Achievement Award for training students in Nutrition and Dietetics.

Meenal Shrivastav is Assistant Professor (ad hoc), Department of Food and Nutrition, Lady Irwin College, University of Delhi. She has developed nutrition education modules for adolescents. She has also been associated in the community as a resource person for several workshops and training programmes conducted by non-government organisations like PRADAN and SPOWAC.

Anupa Siddhu is Head, Department of Home Science, and Director, Lady Irwin College, University of Delhi. Her research interests lie in the field of body composition and energy requirements, anthropometric growth assessment, age-related changes in work capacity, sport nutrition, lipid intakes and requirements, clinical nutrition, prevention of low birth weight, stunting, obesity, diabetes, and heart diseases. She has several publications in national and international journals.

Salila Thomas is Associate Professor, Department of Food and Nutrition, Lady Irwin College, University of Delhi. Her research interests lie in the field of food science, nutrition and capacity building, evolving innovative methods to address the nutritional needs of children and adolescents, and facilitating food service providers through awareness and capacity building. She has monitored and provided technical support to programmes like ICDS and the Midday meal scheme.